DATE DUE FOR RETURN

	21. JUN 1991	- 2 NOV 1998
13. MAR 87.	26. JUN 1992	23 NOV 1998
05. OCT 87.	26. JUN 1992	11 DEC 1998
21. OCT 87.		
18. 01. '83	18 JUN 1993	19 MAR 1999
18. 01. '83	30 SEP - 93 (JKH)	3 MAY 2002
22. JAN '88	30 - Sep - 94 (EOD)	
24. JUN 1988		27 SEP 2002
28.02.89	16 JUN 1995	
22. JUN 1990	17 NOV 1995	1 9 MAR 2008
	21 JAN 1998 SEP 2009	
21. JUN 1991	23 JUL 1998 - 2 OCT 1998	

RAMAN SPECTRA OF MOLECULES AND CRYSTALS

M. M. SUSHCHINSKII

RAMAN SPECTRA OF
MOLECULES AND CRYSTALS

 ISRAEL PROGRAM FOR SCIENTIFIC TRANSLATIONS

NEW YORK · JERUSALEM · LONDON · 1972

© 1972 by
Israel Program for Scientific Translations Ltd.

Distributed by

KETER INC., NEW YORK
KETER PUBLISHING HOUSE, JERUSALEM
KETER PUBLISHERS LTD., LONDON

ISBN 0 7065 11034
IPST Cat. No. 2310

This book is a translation from Russian of
SPEKTRY KOMBINATSIONNOGO RASSEYANIYA MOLEKUL I KRISTALLOV
Izdatel'stvo "Nauka"
Moskva 1969

PREFACE

Raman scattering was discovered nearly 45 years ago, in 1928. During this period, Raman spectroscopy has advanced to take its place among other, older methods of investigating the structure and composition of matter, and its importance is still increasing. It received a particularly large impetus in the recent years, with further development of experimental techniques and the introduction of lasers as excitation sources. With the advent of the new methods, one is no longer restricted to the Raman spectra of transparent objects: disperse system and absorbing objects can also be investigated by Raman spectroscopy. Very small samples are now required in order to obtain the spectrum, and the range of objects that can now be tackled by the methods of Raman spectroscopy has increased appreciably.

The rapid progress in the practical applications has been accompanied by marked advances in the theoretical interpretation of Raman scattering as a physical phenomenon. The discovery of a new nonlinear optics effect—stimulated Raman scattering—has aroused considerable interest. This discovery has focused the attention of the scientific community on a number of topics linked with the nature of Raman scattering and its position among related phenomena. The expanding range of applications and the new discoveries in Raman scattering are attracting ever increasing circles of physicists and chemists to Raman spectroscopy. Yet Placzek's book, with its conciseness of presentation and style which make for fairly difficult reading, seems to be the only one among the extensive literature on this subject which provides a sufficiently detailed and systematic treatment of the general problems related to Raman scattering. Other books in this field deal with measurement techniques or cover a fairly limited range of topics associated with the chemical applications of Raman spectroscopy. A number of books devoted to computations of the vibrational spectra of molecules also deal with Raman scattering, but here the phenomenon is delegated to a position of secondary importance.

Our aim was to fill the existing gap in the literature on Raman scattering by providing a systematic presentation of the basic topics which are necessary for a thorough understanding of the physics of this phenomenon and its relation to other optical effects. We also tried to highlight the various possible applications of Raman spectroscopy to studies of the structure of matter. This category includes data on chemical structure, geometrical configuration, and numerous geometrical, dynamical, and electro-optical parameters of molecules. Separate chapters are devoted to the Raman spectra of crystals and stimulated Raman scattering.

The book is intended for a wide audience of spectroscopists without previous background in Raman spectroscopy. All the topics are therefore discussed in considerable detail, with appropriate examples and illustrations. Whenever necessary, the required mathematical background is provided, although quite concisely. Molecular vibrations are computed only to the extent that they are needed for the analysis of the particular problems.

Measurement techniques are described in few cases only, in connection with relatively unfamiliar or new techniques. The numerical and experimental data are mainly intended as an illustration of the basic theory and are far from providing a complete coverage of the literature.

In conclusion, I would like to extend my thanks to V. S. Gorelik for his assistance in the preparation of Secs 18–21, to T. I. Kuznetsov, V. A. Zubov, L. A. Shelepin, and I. K. Shuvalov for valuable discussions of certain parts of the book, and to V. P. Sochel'nikov for his help in the preparation of the manuscript.

Thanks are also due to Ya. S. Bobovich and Kh. E. Sterin who read the manuscript and offered a number of valuable observations.

M. M. Sushchinskii

TABLE OF CONTENTS

CHAPTER I

General Theory of Raman Scattering

1. INTRODUCTION

Raman scattering (or combination scattering) is one of the processes resulting from
the interaction of radiation with matter. A characteristic feature of Raman scattering
is the change in the frequency of the scattered light: the frequency of the scattered
radiation is different from the frequency of the primary (exciting) radiation. As
distinct from luminescence, where the frequency of the re-emitted radiation is also
changed, in Raman scattering the system is not excited for any measurable (not
even very small) length of time to a higher energy level. All excitations in scattering
processes are purely virtual states (see §4).

Raman scattering was discovered simultaneously by G.S. Landsberg and L.I.
Mandelstam in the USSR in their study of light scattering in crystals [1] and by
C.V. Raman and K.S. Krishnan in liquids [2]. Long before these discoveries, Lommel
[3] developed the mathematical theory of light scattering by an anharmonic oscillator. According to Lommel, the scattered radiation should contain shifted ("combination") frequencies, equal to the sum and the difference of the incident radiation
frequency and the oscillator eigenfrequency. In 1923, Smekal [4] analyzed the
quantum transitions in atoms excited by photons of frequency v and showed that
the scattered radiation should contain the frequencies $v \pm \Delta E/h$, where ΔE is the
energy difference between the corresponding states and h is Planck's constant.
These theoretical predictions, however, had no relation to the actual discovery of
Raman scattering. Mandelstam and Landsberg looked for frequency shifts in scat-

tered radiation as a result of the modulation of the incident light by the eigenfrequencies of the crystal. Raman was guided in his studies by the optical analog of Compton scattering.

During the 40 years which have elapsed since the discovery of the Raman effect, over 8000 publications on the subject became available. The Raman spectroscopy developed into a prominent branch of molecular spectroscopy, and its methods are widely used (alongside with infrared spectroscopy) in the study of material composition and structure and in molecular spectral analysis. Study of the Raman effect itself, however, has followed a number of independent trends.

No complete theory of Raman scattering can be built without extensive use of quantum concepts. Some basic conclusions, however, can be derived from classical physical treatment also.

The fundamental physical principles used in the classical theory of Raman scattering can be formulated as follows.

1. The light is scattered as a result of forced oscillations of the molecular dipole moment induced by the electromagnetic field of the incident light wave.

2. The light in the visible and the near ultraviolet is mainly scattered by the electron hull of the molecule; the atomic nuclei, which are the backbone of the molecule, are displaced insignificantly.

3. Raman scattering is attributable to the coupling between the movement of electrons in the molecule and the movement of the nuclei, viz., the configuration of the nuclei determines the intramolecular field that the electrons see. The deformability of the electron cloud in the electric field of the light wave depends on the nuclear configuration at any given time. As the nuclei oscillate about their respective equilibrium positions (and also during other periodic motions, e.g., molecular rotation), the deformability of the electron cloud varies with the oscillation frequency of the nuclei. On the other hand, deformation of the electron cloud may induce vibration of the molecular nuclei. Thus a complex interaction is observed between the atomic core and the electron hull.

From this classical point of view, Raman scattering is associated with the modulation of the induced dipole moment by the molecular skeletal vibrations.

Consider a light wave $E = E_0 \cos(\omega t)$ incident on the molecule. The dipole moment P induced in the molecule by this light wave is

$$P(t) = \alpha E, \qquad (1.1)$$

where α is the polarizability of the molecule. In the classical theory, polarizability is a phenomenological quantity. Suppose that the molecular polarizability α depends on the distance between the atomic nuclei at any given time. Let q_i be the vibrational coordinate which describes the particular vibration mode of the molecule, so that we may write $\alpha = \alpha(q_i)$. Assuming that q_i is small, we can expand α in a power series in q_i around the equilibrium value of this coordinate $q_i = 0$:

$$\alpha(q_i) = \alpha_0 + \left(\frac{\partial \alpha}{\partial q_i}\right)_0 q_i + \cdots \tag{1.2}$$

Taking $q_i = q_{i0} \cos(\omega_i t + \delta_i)$, we write

$$P(t) = \left[\alpha_0 + \left(\frac{\partial \alpha}{\partial q_i}\right)_0 q_{i0} \cos(\omega_i t + \delta_i)\right] E_0 \cos \omega t = \alpha_0 E_0 \cos \omega t +$$

$$+ \frac{1}{2}\left(\frac{\partial \alpha}{\partial q_i}\right)_0 E_0 q_{i0} \cos\left[(\omega - \omega_i)t + \delta_i\right] + \frac{1}{2}\left(\frac{\partial \alpha}{\partial q_i}\right)_0 E_0 q_{i0} \cos\left[(\omega + \omega_i)t + \delta_i\right].$$

$$\tag{1.3}$$

We see from Eq. (1.3) that modulation of the induced dipole moment by the vibration frequencies of the atomic nuclei gives rise to sum and difference frequencies $\omega + \omega_i$ and $\omega - \omega_i$ in the spectrum of scattered radiation, i.e., here scattering involves a change in frequency. We have mentioned above that Landsberg and Mandelstam were actually led to the discovery of what they termed "combination scattering" by their analysis of the effects of modulation of incident light by the eigenfrequencies of the solid crystal.

The intensity of the Raman scattering lines, according to (1.3), is proportional to the square of the derivative of polarizability with respect to the vibrational coordinate. If higher terms in expansion (1.2) are taken into consideration, the intensities of overtones and combination frequencies can be similarly related to the squares of the higher derivatives

$$\left(\frac{\partial^2 \alpha}{\partial q_i^2}\right)_0^2, \quad \left(\frac{\partial^2 \alpha}{\partial q_i \partial q_k}\right)_0, \quad \text{etc.}$$

2. THE SCATTERING TENSOR

In general, the scattering system is characterized by a certain anisotropy, its properties differing in different directions. The ability of electrons to move away from their equilibrium positions under the action of the electromagnetic field in an anisotropic system depends on the orientation of the field relative to certain preferred axes in the scattering system. The induced dipole moment P in general does not point in the direction of the electric field vector E.

In this section we consider light scattering by individual free molecules (the case of a crystal is treated in Chapter III). Let X, Y, Z be the fixed axes, and x, y, z the own moving axes of the scattering molecule (Figure 1). This moving system is quite arbitrarily oriented in the fixed frame X, Y, Z. If E_k are the components of the vector

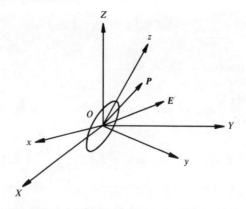

Figure 1

The fixed axes (X, Y, Z) and the moving axes (x, y, z) attached to the molecule.

E in the moving system x, y, z, the coordinates of the vector P in general form can be written as

$$P_i = \sum_k \beta_{ik} E_k \qquad (i, k = x, y, z). \qquad (2.1)$$

The set of parameters β_{ik}, which determine the properties of the scattered radiation, constitute the *scattering tensor*. The tensor β_{ik} is defined by the matrix of its components

$$\| \beta_{ik} \| = \left\|\begin{matrix} \beta_{11} & \beta_{12} & \beta_{13} \\ \beta_{21} & \beta_{22} & \beta_{23} \\ \beta_{31} & \beta_{32} & \beta_{33} \end{matrix}\right\|. \qquad (2.2)$$

The components of the scattering tensor in general are complex numbers without any special symmetry properties. The relation of the scattering tensor to the properties of the scattering molecule (in particular, its polarizability) is established by the methods of quantum mechanics. Here we will only consider some general properties of the scattered light.

The scattering tensor, like any other general tensor, can be written in the form

$$\beta_{ik} = S_{ik} + a_{ik}, \qquad (2.3)$$

where S_{ik} is a symmetric tensor $(S_{ki} = S_{ik})$ and a_{ik} is a skew-symmetric (or an anti-symmetric) tensor $(a_{ki} = -a_{ik}, a_{ii} = 0)$. Using the obvious identity

$$\beta_{ik} = \tfrac{1}{2}(\beta_{ik} + \beta_{ki}) + \tfrac{1}{2}(\beta_{ik} - \beta_{ki}),$$

and putting

$$S_{ik} = \tfrac{1}{2}(\beta_{ik} + \beta_{ki}), \quad a_{ik} = \tfrac{1}{2}(\beta_{ik} - \beta_{ki}), \tag{2.4}$$

we clearly get (2.3).

The scattering tensor can be simplified if the principal axes are chosen as the moving frame. When the tensor has any special symmetry properties, it assumes a diagonal form in the principal axes. In a quite general mathematical form, any symmetry property can be expressed by the relation [5]

$$BB^+ = B^+B. \tag{2.5}$$

Here B^+ is the transpose conjugate of the matrix B. Its components satisfy the equality

$$B_{ik}^+ = B_{ki}^*. \tag{2.6}$$

Condition (2.5) is clearly satisfied for matrices with the property

$$B_{ik} = B_{ki}^* \tag{2.7}$$

or

$$B^+ = B.$$

Matrices (and tensors) of this kind are called *Hermitian*. It follows from (2.7) that for Hermitian matrices the eigenvalues $B_{kk} = B_k$ are all real.

For symmetric matrices, condition (2.6) takes the form

$$B_{ik}^+ = B_{ik}^*,$$

i.e., $B^+ = B^*$. Putting $B = B_1 + iB_2$, where B_1 and B_2 are real symmetric matrices, we reduce condition (2.5) for symmetric matrices to the form

$$B_2B_1 = B_1B_2. \tag{2.8}$$

This requirement is evidently satisfied if the matrices B_1 and B_2 can be transformed to a diagonal form by the same transformation of coordinates. In this case $B_{kk} = B_{1kk} + iB_{2kk}$, i.e., the eigenvalues of symmetric matrices are complex.

We assume that condition (2.8) is satisfied for the symmetric part of the scattering tensor S_{ik}. This tensor is then diagonalized by transformation to the principal axes, and

$$\| B_{ik} \| = \begin{Vmatrix} \beta_1 & 0 & 0 \\ 0 & \beta_2 & 0 \\ 0 & 0 & \beta_3 \end{Vmatrix} + \begin{Vmatrix} 0 & a_{12} & a_{13} \\ -a_{12} & 0 & a_{23} \\ -a_{13} & -a_{23} & 0 \end{Vmatrix}. \tag{2.9}$$

The constants $\beta_{ii} = \beta_i$ and a_{ik} characterize the scattering properties of the molecule.

Let us calculate the scattered field — the field of the wave radiated by the induced dipole — at distances much greater than the diameter of the scattering system. According to the general theory of radiation of electromagnetic waves (see, e.g., [6]), the electric field E' and the magnetic field H' of the wave radiated by a system with a dipole moment P are

$$E' = \frac{1}{c^2 R} \left[[\ddot{P} n'] n' \right], \tag{2.10}$$

$$H' = \frac{1}{c^2 R} [\ddot{P} n']. \tag{2.11}$$

Here n' is the unit vector in the direction of scattering, R is the distance from the scattering system to the field point.

The radiation intensity dI in a solid angle $d\Omega$ is defined as the quantity of energy passing in unit time through a surface element $R^2 d\Omega$ of a sphere of radius R centered at the origin. The scattered intensity in the direction n' is [6]

$$dI = \frac{c}{4\pi} | H' |^2 R^2 d\Omega. \tag{2.12}$$

Inserting H' from (2.11), we get

$$dI = \frac{1}{4\pi c^3} | [\ddot{P} n'] |^2 d\Omega. \tag{2.13}$$

The dipole vibrates as a harmonic oscillator of frequency ω' (in general, $\omega' \neq \omega$):

$$P = P_0 e^{i\omega' t}. \tag{2.14}$$

In this case $\ddot{P} = -\omega'^2 P$, and thus

$$dI = \frac{\omega'^4}{4\pi c^3} | [P n'] |^2 d\Omega. \tag{2.15}$$

Eq. (2.15) is considerably simplified if the scattered light is observed in a special system of fixed axes. The axis Z is directed along n', the axis X lies in the plane of the vectors n' and E,† and the axis Y is perpendicular to this plane (Figure 2). If i, j, k are the unit vectors along these axes, we have

$$[P n'][P^* n'] = \begin{vmatrix} P_X & P_Y & P_Z \\ 0 & 0 & 1 \\ i & j & k \end{vmatrix} \begin{vmatrix} P_X^* & P_Y^* & P_Z^* \\ 0 & 0 & 1 \\ i & j & k \end{vmatrix} = P_X P_X^* + P_Y P_Y^*.$$

---

† It is assumed that the incident wave is linearly polarized. In this case the amplitude E_0 can be taken as a real number.

Thus

$$dI = \frac{\omega'^4}{4\pi c^3} (P_X P_X^* + P_Y P_Y^*) \, d\Omega, \tag{2.16}$$

i.e., the scattered intensity is a sum of two components $I_X \sim P_X P_X^*$ and $I_Y \sim P_Y P_Y^*$, each relating to a certain axis in the field coordinate system. The ratio of these components

$$\bar{\rho} = \frac{I_Y}{I_X} \tag{2.17}$$

is called the *depolarization* of the scattered light.

Let θ be the angle between the direction of scattering $\boldsymbol{n'}$ and the electric field vector $\boldsymbol{E}$ of the incident wave. Then

$$E_X = E \sin \theta, \; E_Y = 0, \; E_Z = E \cos \theta. \tag{2.18}$$

Eq. (2.16) is the scattered intensity contributed by a single molecule. In Raman scattering, at low incident intensities, each molecule is treated as a scattering center independent of the other molecules, so that the light scattered by different molecules is incoherent (the case of coherent scattering is considered in Chapter IV). The total scattering intensity in a given direction in this case is proportional to the number of molecules N, and Eq. (2.16) should be averaged over all the various orientations of the scattering molecules relative to the fixed axes.

To simplify the notation of the components, we will agree to assign the subscripts i, k to the moving axes ($i, k = x, y, z$) and l, m to the fixed axes ($l, m = X, Y, Z$). The cosines of the angles between the axes of the two systems will be designated n_{il}; the first subscript refers to the moving axes and the second to the fixed axes, e.g.,

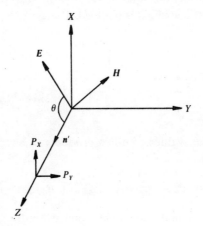

Figure 2

The coordinate axes for observations of scattered light.

$\cos(x, Y) = n_{12}$, $\cos(y, X) = n_{21}$, etc. The equations relating the components of the incident electric field E in the moving and the fixed axes are thus

$$E_k = \sum_m n_{km} E_m, \tag{2.19}$$

and correspondingly

$$P_l = \sum_i n_{il} P_i. \tag{2.20}$$

Inserting P_i from (2.1) and using (2.19), we find

$$P_l = \sum_i n_{il}\left[\sum_k \beta_{ik} E_k\right] = \sum_i n_{il}\left[\sum_k \beta_{ik}\left(\sum_m n_{km} E_m\right)\right] =$$

$$= \sum_{ikm} \beta_{ik} n_{il} n_{km} E_m = \sum_m E_m \sum_{ik} \beta_{ik} n_{il} n_{km}. \tag{2.21}$$

Using (2.21), we obtain the following expression for the products $P_1 P_1^*$ and $P_2 P_2^*$:

$$P_l P_l^* = \sum_{ikm} \sum_{i'k'm'} \beta_{ik} \beta_{i'k'}^* n_{il} n_{km} n_{i'l} n_{k'm'} E_m E_{m'}. \tag{2.22}$$

These expressions should be averaged over all the possible orientations of the molecule, i.e., over the various orientations of the moving axes relative to the fixed axes. Before we can proceed with calculations, we obviously have to find the mean values of the products of the direction cosines of the form $\overline{n_{il} n_{km} n_{i'l} n_{k'm'}}$. This can be done in the following way.

Let ϑ be the angle between the i-th axis of the moving system and the l-th axis of the fixed system of coordinates. We identify this angle with the polar angle in a spherical system of coordinates (r, ϑ, ϕ). Then

$$\overline{n_{il}^4} = \overline{\cos^4 \vartheta} = \frac{\displaystyle\int_0^{2\pi} \int_0^{\pi} \cos^4 \vartheta \sin \vartheta \, d\vartheta \, d\phi}{\displaystyle\int_0^{2\pi} \int_0^{\pi} \sin \vartheta \, d\vartheta \, d\phi} = \frac{1}{5}. \tag{2.23}$$

To find the mean values of other products of direction cosines, we will have to use the equalities

$$n_{il}^2 + n_{im}^2 + n_{ip}^2 = 1, \quad n_{il} n_{kl} + n_{im} n_{km} + n_{ip} n_{kp} = 0, \text{ etc.}$$

Squaring the first equality, averaging, and using the symmetry properties, we find

$$3\overline{n_{il}^4} + 6\overline{n_{il}^2 n_{im}^2} = 1.$$

Hence

$$\overline{n_{il}^2 n_{im}^2} = \frac{1}{15} \quad (l \neq m).$$

(2.24a)

Similarly

$$\overline{n_{il}^2 n_{kl}^2} = \frac{1}{15} \quad (i \neq k).$$

(2.24b)

Squaring the second identity, we similarly find

$$\overline{n_{il} n_{im} n_{kl} n_{km}} = -\frac{1}{30}.$$

(2.25)

Finally, taking the product

$$(n_{il}^2 + n_{im}^2 + n_{ip}^2)(n_{kl}^2 + n_{km}^2 + n_{kp}^2) = 1,$$

we obtain after averaging

$$3\overline{n_{il}^2 n_{kl}^2} + 6\overline{n_{il}^2 n_{km}^2} = 1, \quad \overline{n_{il}^2 n_{km}^2} = \frac{2}{15} \quad (i \neq k, l \neq m).$$

(2.26)

The other products of the direction cosines average out to zero.

Note that each subscript occurs twice in Eq. (2.25). Other equations contain squares of the direction cosines, i.e., each index again occurs an even number of times. Hence it follows that if any subscript enters an averaged product of direction cosines in (2.22) only once, the corresponding term vanishes.

Using this rule of even indicial combinations, we conclude that after averaging (2.22) will only contain terms with $m = m'$, i.e., we will end up with an expression of the form

$$\overline{P_l P_l^*} = \sum_{iki'k'm} \beta_{ik} \beta_{i'k'}^* \overline{n_{il} n_{km} n_{i'l} n_{k'm}} E_m^2.$$

(2.27)

With regard to the subscripts i, k, i', k', the following three possibilities should be considered: 1) $i = k, i' = k'$; 2) $i = i', k = k'$; 3) $i = k', k = i'$.

To further simplify Eq. (2.27) for these different subscript combinations, we decompose the scattering tensor into a symmetric and an antisymmetric component, in accordance with (2.3). Thus,

$$\beta_{ik} \beta_{i'k'}^* = (S_{ik} + a_{ik})(S_{i'k'}^* + a_{i'k'}^*).$$

(2.28)

Inserting (2.28) in (2.27), we split the resulting expression into a sum of four terms,

$$\overline{P_l P_l^*} = \overline{(P_l P_l^*)}_s + \overline{(P_l P_l^*)}_a + \overline{(P_l P_l^*)}_{sa} + \overline{(P_l P_l^*)}_{as},$$

(2.29)

where

$$\overline{(P_l P_l^*)}_s = \sum_{iki'k'm} S_{ik} S_{i'k'}^* \overline{n_{il} n_{km} n_{i'l} n_{k'm}} E_m^2, \tag{2.30a}$$

$$\overline{(P_l P_l^*)}_a = \sum_{iki'k'm} a_{ik} a_{i'k'}^* \overline{n_{il} n_{km} n_{i'l} n_{k'm}} E_m^2, \tag{2.30b}$$

$$\overline{(P_l P_l^*)}_{sa} = \sum_{iki'k'm} S_{ik} a_{i'k'}^* \overline{n_{il} n_{km} n_{i'l} n_{k'm}} E_m^2, \tag{2.30c}$$

$$\overline{(P_l P_l^*)}_{as} = \sum_{iki'k'm} a_{ik} S_{i'k'}^* \overline{n_{il} n_{km} n_{i'l} n_{k'm}} E_m^2. \tag{2.30d}$$

Decomposition (2.29) is valid in any system of coordinates. We choose the principal axes as the molecule's own moving system. In the principal axes the only nonzero components of the tensors S_{ik}, $S_{i'k'}^*$ are of the form S_{ii}, $S_{i'i'}^*$. In case 1, expression (2.30c) contains only the factors $S_{ii'} a_{i'i'}^*$ and expression (2.30d) the factors $a_{ii} S_{i'i'}^*$, which all vanish because the tensor a_{ik} is skew-symmetric. Thus, $\overline{(P_l P_l^*)}_{sa} = 0$, $\overline{(P_l P_l^*)}_{as} = 0$ and only two terms remain in (2.29):

$$\overline{(P_l P_l^*)} = \overline{(P_l P_l^*)}_s + \overline{(P_l P_l^*)}_a. \tag{2.31}$$

Hence it follows that the intensity of scattered light is made up of two independent components—the respective contributions of the symmetric and the antisymmetric part of the scattering tensor.

Using the notation of Eq. (2.9) and remembering that a_{ik} is skew-symmetric, we write (2.30a) and (2.30b) in the form

$$\overline{(P_l P_l^*)}_s = \sum_{ikm} \beta_i \beta_k^* \overline{n_{il} n_{im} n_{kl} n_{km}} E_m^2, \tag{2.32}$$

$$\overline{(P_l P_l^*)}_a = \sum_{ikm} a_{ik} a_{ik}^* (\overline{n_{il}^2 n_{km}^2} - \overline{n_{il} n_{km} n_{kl} n_{im}}) E_m^2. \tag{2.33}$$

Cases 2 and 3 of indicial combinations are allowed for in (2.33).

Seeing that $E_2 = 0$, we obtain

$$\overline{(P_1 P_1^*)}_s = \sum_i \beta_i \beta_i^* [\overline{n_{i1}^4} E_1^2 + \overline{n_{i1}^2 n_{i3}^2} E_3^2] + \sum_{i \neq k} (\beta_i \beta_k^* + \beta_k \beta_i^*)[\overline{n_{i1}^2 n_{k1}^2} E_1^2 + \overline{n_{i1} n_{i3} n_{k1} n_{k3}} E_3^2]$$

$$= \frac{E^2}{15} \left[(3 \sin^2\theta + \cos^2\theta)\left(\sum_i \beta_i \beta_i^*\right) + \left(\sin^2\theta - \frac{1}{2}\cos^2\theta\right) \times \right.$$

$$\times \left(\sum_{i \neq k} (\beta_i \beta_k^* + \beta_k \beta_i^*) \right) \Bigg] = \frac{E^2}{15} \Bigg[(1 + 2\sin^2\theta) \left(\sum_i \beta_i \beta_i^* \right) +$$

$$+ \frac{1}{2}(3\sin^2\theta - 1) \left(\sum_{i \neq k} (\beta_i \beta_k^* + \beta_k \beta_i^*) \right) \Bigg], \tag{2.34a}$$

$$\overline{(P_2 P_2^*)}_s = \sum_i \beta_i \beta_i^* [\overline{n_{i1}^2 n_{i2}^2} E_1^2 + \overline{n_{i2}^2 n_{i3}^2} E_3^2] +$$

$$+ \sum_{i \neq k} (\beta_i \beta_k^* + \beta_k \beta_i^*)[\overline{n_{i1} n_{i2} n_{k1} n_{k2}} E_1^2 + \overline{n_{i2} n_{i3} n_{k2} n_{k3}} E_3^2] =$$

$$= \frac{E^2}{15} \Bigg[\left(\sum_i \beta_i \beta_i^* \right) - \frac{1}{2} \left(\sum_{i \neq k} (\beta_i \beta_k^* + \beta_k \beta_i^*) \right) \Bigg], \tag{2.34b}$$

$$\overline{(P_1 P_1^*)}_a = \sum_{i \neq k} a_{ik} a_{ik}^* (\overline{n_{i1}^2 n_{k3}^2} - \overline{n_{i1} n_{k1} n_{i3} n_{k3}}) E_3^2 = \frac{1}{3} E^2 \cos^2\theta \left(\sum_{i < k} a_{ik} a_{ik}^* \right), \tag{2.34c}$$

$$\overline{(P_2 P_2^*)}_a = \sum_{i \neq k} a_{il} a_{ik}^* [\overline{n_{i2}^2 n_{k1}^2} E_1^2 + \overline{n_{i2}^2 n_{k3}^2} E_3^2 - \overline{n_{i1} n_{i2} n_{k1} n_{k2}} E_1^2 - \overline{n_{i2} n_{i3} n_{k2} n_{k3}} E_3^2] =$$

$$= \frac{1}{3} E^2 \left(\sum_{i < k} a_{ik} a_{ik}^* \right). \tag{2.34d}$$

Let

$$S_{ci} = \begin{Vmatrix} S_{c1} & 0 & 0 \\ 0 & S_{c2} & 0 \\ 0 & 0 & S_{c3} \end{Vmatrix}, \qquad S_{ai} = \begin{Vmatrix} S_{a1} & 0 & 0 \\ 0 & S_{a2} & 0 \\ 0 & 0 & S_{a3} \end{Vmatrix} \tag{2.35}$$

where

$$S_{c1} = S_{c2} = S_{c3} = \tfrac{1}{3}(\beta_1 + \beta_2 + \beta_3) = \tfrac{1}{3} b, \tag{2.36}$$

$$S_{a1} = \tfrac{1}{3}[(\beta_1 - \beta_2) + (\beta_1 - \beta_3)], \quad S_{a2} = \tfrac{1}{3}[(\beta_2 - \beta_3) + (\beta_2 - \beta_1)], \tag{2.37'}$$

$$S_{a3} = \tfrac{1}{3}[(\beta_3 - \beta_1) + (\beta_3 - \beta_2)]. \tag{2.37''}$$

Clearly, $S_{ci} + S_{ai} = S_{ii}$. Thus, using (2.3) and (2.9), we write the scattering tensor in the principal axes as a sum of two diagonal tensors and a skew-symmetric tensor:

$$\beta_{ik} = S_{ci} + S_{ai} + a_{ik}. \tag{2.38}$$

The sum of the diagonal terms, known as the trace or the spur, provides a fundamental characteristic of any tensor. This sum has the attractive property of invariance: in *any* coordinate system

$$\mathrm{Tr}\,(\beta_{ik}) = \sum_i \beta_{ii} = \sum_i \beta_i = b.$$

To simplify Eqs. (2.34a) and (2.34b), we use the traces of the tensors $S_{ci}S_{ci}^*$ and $S_{ai}S_{ai}^*$:

$$\beta_c = \mathrm{Tr}\,(S_{ci}S_{ci}^*) = \sum_i S_{ci}S_{ci}^* = \tfrac{1}{3}(\beta_1 + \beta_2 + \beta_3)(\beta_1^* + \beta_2^* + \beta_3^*) =$$

$$= \frac{1}{3}\left[\sum_i \beta_i\beta_i^* + \sum_{i \neq k}(\beta_i\beta_k^* + \beta_k\beta_i^*)\right], \tag{2.39}$$

$$\gamma^2 = \mathrm{Tr}\,(S_{ai}S_{ai}^*) = \sum_i S_{ai}S_{ai}^* =$$

$$= \tfrac{1}{9}\{[(\beta_1 - \beta_2) + (\beta_1 - \beta_3)][(\beta_1^* - \beta_2^*) + (\beta_1^* - \beta_3^*)] +$$

$$+ [(\beta_2 - \beta_3) + (\beta_2 - \beta_1)][(\beta_2^* - \beta_3^*) + (\beta_2^* - \beta_1^*)] +$$

$$+ [(\beta_3 - \beta_1) + (\beta_3 - \beta_2)][(\beta_3^* - \beta_1^*) + (\beta_3^* - \beta_2^*)]\} =$$

$$= \frac{1}{3}\left[2\sum_i \beta_i\beta_i^* - \sum_{i \neq k}(\beta_i\beta_k^* + \beta_k\beta_i^*)\right]. \tag{2.40}$$

The quantities $\tfrac{1}{3}(\beta_1 + \beta_2 + \beta_3)$ and γ^2 are known as the *mean polarizability* and the *anisotropy*, respectively. They are generally defined only for real β_i. In our treatment, these parameters remain meaningful for complex β_i also, since in what follows we will only use β_c and γ^2, which are always real.*

---

* For a tensor $(S_a)_{ik}$ without transformation to the principal axes, we have $(S_a)_{ik} = \beta_{ik} - (S_c)_{ii}$ when β_{ik} is a real symmetric tensor, and by (2.36) and (2.40),

$$\gamma^2 = \sum_i \sum_k [(S_a)_{ik}(S_a)_{ki}] = \sum_i (\beta_{ii} - \tfrac{1}{3}b)^2 + \sum_{i \neq k} \beta_{ik}^2 = \sum_{i,k} \beta_{ik}^2 - \tfrac{1}{3}b^2. \tag{2.40a}$$

The anisotropy γ^2 defined by (2.40) and (2.40a) is related to the g^2 often used by other authors by the equality

$$g^2 = \tfrac{3}{2}\gamma^2. \tag{2.40b}$$

By (2.39) and (2.40) we have

$$\sum_i \beta_i \beta_i^* = \beta_c + \gamma^2; \quad \sum_{i \neq k} (\beta_i \beta_k^* + \beta_k \beta_i^*) = 2\beta_c - \gamma^2 . \tag{2.41}$$

Inserting (2.41) in (2.34a) and (2.34b), we find

$$\overline{(P_1 P_1^*)}_s = \frac{E^2}{15} \left[5\beta_c \sin^2\theta + \frac{1}{2}\gamma^2(3 + \sin^2\theta) \right], \tag{2.42}$$

$$\overline{(P_2 P_2^*)}_s = \frac{E^2}{15} \left(\frac{3}{2}\gamma^2 \right). \tag{2.43}$$

The antisymmetric components of the scattered light according to (2.34c) and (2.34d) are proportional to

$$\beta_a = 2 \sum_{i < k} a_{ik} a_{ik}^* = \text{Tr}\,(a_{ik} a_{ik}^+) . \tag{2.44}$$

Here, β_a is the trace of the tensor $a_{ik} a_{ik}^+$, i.e., this is another invariant. In terms of this invariant, we have

$$\overline{(P_1 P_1^*)}_a = \frac{1}{6} E^2 \beta_a \cos^2\theta , \tag{2.45}$$

$$\overline{(P_2 P_2^*)}_a = \frac{1}{6} E^2 \beta_a . \tag{2.46}$$

Eqs. (2.42)–(2.46) show that the three components of the scattering tensor (2.38) give rise to three corresponding components in the scattered light, each associated with only one of the tensor components. The scattered light components in this representation are characterized by the invariant traces of the corresponding tensors, $S_{ci} S_{ci}^+$, $S_{ai} S_{ai}^+$, $a_{ik} a_{ik}^+$. The scattered radiation component associated with the tensor S_{ci} is known as *scalar* or *isotropic scattering*. The part of the scattered light associated with the anisotropy γ^2 and corresponding to the tensor S_{ai} will be referred to as *anisotropic scattering.**. Finally, the component associated with the tensor a_{ik} will be called here *antisymmetric scattering.***

Using Eqs. (2.42)–(2.46) and (2.16), (2.17), we can find the intensity and the de-

---

* Placzek [7] uses the term *quadrupole scattering*, while Landau and Lifshits [8] refer to *symmetric scattering*.

** See [8]. *Magnetic dipole scattering* is the term used in [7].

polarization of each component in Raman scattering of linearly polarized light:

$$dI(\beta_c) = \frac{E^2\omega'^4}{60\pi c^3} 5\beta_c \sin^2\theta d\Omega = \frac{I_0\omega'^4}{15c^3} \cdot 5\beta_c \sin^2\theta d\Omega, \tag{2.47}$$

$$dI(\gamma^2) = \frac{E^2\omega'^4}{60\pi c^3} \cdot \frac{1}{2}\gamma^2(6 + \sin^2\theta) d\Omega = \frac{I_0\omega'^4}{15c^3} \cdot \frac{1}{2}\gamma^2(6 + \sin^2\theta) d\Omega, \tag{2.48}$$

$$dI(\beta_a) = \frac{E^2\omega'^4}{24\pi c^3} \beta_a (1 + \cos^2\theta) d\Omega = \frac{I_0\omega'^4}{15c^3} \cdot \frac{5}{2} \beta_a (1 + \cos^2\theta) d\Omega, \tag{2.49}$$

$$\bar{\rho}_\theta(\beta_c) = 0, \tag{2.50}$$

$$\bar{\rho}_\theta(\gamma^2) = \frac{3}{3 + \sin^2\theta}, \tag{2.51}$$

$$\bar{\rho}_\theta(\beta_a) = \frac{1}{\cos^2\theta}. \tag{2.52}$$

Here $I_0 = E^2/4\pi$ is the intensity of the incident radiation.

Another useful parameter is the *effective scattering cross section*. This cross section is defined as the ratio of the energy scattered in a given direction in unit time to the incident energy flux density. The effective scattering cross section is expressed in area units, which explains the origin of the term.

From (2.47)—(2.49) we obtain for the effective cross section of Raman scattering

$$d\sigma = \frac{\omega'^4}{15c^4}\left[5\beta_c \sin^2\theta + \frac{1}{2}\gamma^2(6 + \sin^2\theta) + \frac{5}{2}\beta_a(1 + \cos^2\theta)\right] d\Omega. \tag{2.53}$$

Integration over $d\Omega = \sin\theta \, d\theta \, d\phi$ gives the total cross section for Raman scattering

$$\sigma = \frac{8\pi\omega'^4}{9c^4}(\beta_c + \gamma^2 + \beta_a). \tag{2.54}$$

Eq. (2.54) shows that the total cross sections of the three scattered components are proportional to the traces of the corresponding tensors, $\text{Tr}(S_{ci}S_{ci}^+)$, $\text{Tr}(S_{ai}S_{ai}^+)$, $\text{Tr}(a_{ik}a_{ik}^+)$, all taken with the same proportionality coefficient.

Alongside with the total intensity and the effective scattering cross section (2.53), one often considers the two scattered components polarized in the plane of the vectors E' and n' (the component $\overline{P_1 P_1^*}$) and at right angles to that plane (the component $\overline{P_2 P_2^*}$). From (2.42)–(2.46) we obtain (omitting the differentiation symbol wherever this does not cause confusion to simplify the notation)

$$I_1 = \frac{I_0 \omega'^4}{15 c^3} \left[5\beta_c \sin^2\theta + \frac{1}{2} \gamma^2 (3 + \sin^2\theta) + \frac{5}{2} \beta_a \cos^2\theta \right], \qquad (2.55)$$

$$I_2 = \frac{I_0 \omega'^4}{15 c^3} \left[\frac{3}{2} \gamma^2 + \frac{5}{2} \beta_a \right], \qquad (2.56)$$

$$I = I_1 + I_2 = \frac{I_0 \omega'^4}{15 c^3} \left[5\beta_c \sin^2\theta + \frac{1}{2} \gamma^2 (6 + \sin^2\theta) + \frac{5}{2} \beta_a (1 + \cos^2\theta) \right]. \qquad (2.57)$$

For the depolarization we have from (2.17)

$$\bar{\rho}(\theta) = \frac{I_2}{I_1} = \frac{3\gamma^2 + 5\beta_a}{10\beta_c \sin^2\theta + \gamma^2 (3 + \sin^2\theta) + 5\beta_a \cos^2\theta}. \qquad (2.58)$$

Consider an important particular case $\theta = \pi/2$ (the electric vector of the incident light E is perpendicular to the plane through the vectors n and n'). In this case

$$I\left(\frac{\pi}{2}\right) = \frac{I_0 \omega'^4}{15 c^3} \left[5\beta_c + \frac{7}{2} \gamma^2 + \frac{5}{2} \beta_a \right], \qquad (2.59)$$

$$\bar{\rho} = \bar{\rho}\left(\frac{\pi}{2}\right) = \frac{3\gamma^2 + 5\beta_a}{10\beta_c + 4\gamma^2} \qquad (2.60)$$

(the depolarization for $\theta = \pi/2$ is designated $\bar{\rho}$).

Using these particular values of intensity and depolarization, we can write the general expressions (2.57) and (2.58) in the highly attractive form

$$I(\theta) = I\left(\frac{\pi}{2}\right) \left[1 - \frac{1 - \bar{\rho}}{1 + \bar{\rho}} \cos^2\theta \right], \qquad (2.61)$$

$$\bar{\rho}(\theta) = \frac{\bar{\rho}}{1 - (1 - \bar{\rho}) \cos^2\theta}. \qquad (2.62)$$

These relations show that the angular dependence of the intensity and the depolarization of Raman scattering lines is determined by a single parameter, $\bar{\rho}$, which incorporates the three invariants of the scattering tensor, β_c, γ^2, and β_a. Therefore, analysis of the angular distribution of the intensity and the depolarization in θ does not give the separate values of the three invariants. If one of the invariants is known from theoretical considerations, measurement of $\bar{\rho}$ will give the ratio of the other two parameters; in principle, by measuring the intensity at $\theta = \pi/2$, we can find their absolute values. However, in general, when all the three invariants are unknown, measurements using linearly polarized incident radiation are insufficient for determining these parameters. Because of this, it is worth considering in some detail the method proposed by Placzek [7] for independent determination of all the three invariants of the scattering tensor, which uses both linearly polarized and circularly polarized exciting light.

Consider a light wave propagating along the Z axis. In case of circular polarization, the electric field rotates in a plane perpendicular to the direction of wave propagation, and its tip describes a circle, as shown in Figure 3. Depending on the sense of rotation of the electric vector, we distinguish between right-hand and left-hand circular polarization. When viewed against the direction of propagation, the electric vector in a right-polarized wave is seen to turn clockwise and that in a left-polarized wave turns counterclockwise. Right- and left-hand polarizations are henceforth identified by subscripts R and L.

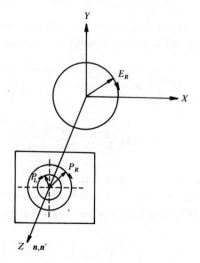

Figure 3

Scheme illustrating the definition of the reversal ratio.

When Raman scattering is excited by circularly polarized light, the scattered light in general will show two circularly polarized components: one with the same sense of polarization as the incident radiation and the other with the reverse sense of polarization. The intensity ratio of the reversed component to the primary component is known as the *reversal ratio*. For right-polarized incident radiation (Figure 3), the reversal ratio is

$$\mathcal{P} = \frac{I_L}{I_R}.\qquad(2.63)$$

The reversal ratio is a directly measurable quantity, so that it can be used, together with depolarization, as an experimental characteristic of the scattered radiation. Reversal measurements are generally carried out in the direction of incident radiation or in the opposite direction. The second approach is preferable, since the direct light from the excitation source does not hit the spectral instrument. A typical setup for these measurements is shown in Figure 4 [9]. The exciting radiation emitted by the mercury lamp Hg is collected by a lens L_1 inside the vessel R holding the test liquid. The light beam is successively passed through a cell with running water W, a filter F, a Glan–Thomson polarization prism N, and a quarter-wavelength plate G. The light thus reaches the scattering liquid after it has been circularly polarized. The back-scattered light is collected on the spectrograph slit Sp by a small mirror S and a lens L_2. The scattered light passes through the same quarter-wavelength plate G, so that if it is circularly polarized on leaving the vessel R, it becomes linearly polarized after emerging from the plate G. The scattered component which is circularly polarized in the same sense as the incident radiation is converted by the quarter-wavelength plate into linearly polarized light with polarization perpendicular to the plane of oscillation of the vector E of the incident light (after this light has passed through the polarization prism N). Indeed, the phase shifts acquired during the direct and the reverse passage through the quarter-wavelength plate add up, and the plane of oscillation is rotated through 90°. Conversely, the scattered component which is circularly polarized in the opposite sense is converted by the quarter-wavelength plate into linearly polarized light whose electric field vector oscillates in the same plane as the vector E of the incident radiation. A birefringent prism K mounted in front of the spectrograph slit splits these two linearly polarized components and two distinct images are formed on the slit. Thus, two spectra are photographed on the spectrograph plate. The intensity ratio of the corresponding line components in these spectra gives the reversal ratio.

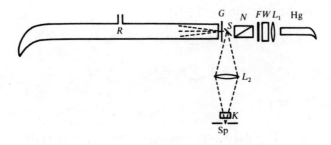

Figure 4

Experimental setup for measuring the reversal ratio.

Note that the reversal ratio for back-scattered light $\mathscr{P}(\pi)$ is the reciprocal of the reversal ratio $\mathscr{P}(0) = \mathscr{P}$ for forward scattering:

$$\mathscr{P}(\pi) = \frac{1}{\mathscr{P}}.$$

This is so because a vector seen turning clockwise when viewed at $0°$ angle is seen to turn counterclockwise when viewed from the opposite direction, and vice versa.

Let us now establish a relation of the reversal ratio to the scattering tensor invariants. We will only consider the case of forward scattering, i.e., when the scattered light propagates in the direction of the Z axis together with the incident radiation (Figure 3). We define "circular" coordinates in the X, Y plane:

$$R = X + iY, \quad L = X - iY. \tag{2.64}$$

The electric vector E of the incident wave and the induced dipole moment P are correspondingly decomposed into a "right" and "left" component:

$$E_R = E_X + iE_Y = E_1 + iE_2, \quad E_L = E_X - iE_Y = E_1 - iE_2, \tag{2.65}$$

$$P_R = P_1 + iP_2, \quad P_L = P_1 - iP_2. \tag{2.66}$$

If the incident wave is right-polarized, we have $E_L = 0$, so that

$$E_2 = -iE_1. \tag{2.67}$$

Also evidently $E_Z = E_3 = 0$.

To calculate the reversal ratio, we have to find the intensity ratio of the two oppositely polarized components of the scattered wave, I_L and I_R. These intensity components are proportional to the mean values of the products $\overline{P_L P_L^*}$, $\overline{P_R P_R^*}$, where the averaging is done over all the orientations of the scattering molecule relative to the fixed axes. The problem is thus reduced to the calculation of the mean products of the induced dipole moment components corresponding to left-hand and right-hand circular polarization.

Eq. (2.21) for the components of the induced dipole moment in fixed cartesian axes is written in the form (using (2.67))

$$P_1 = E_1 \sum_{i,k} \beta_{ik} n_{i1}(n_{k1} - in_{k2}),$$

$$P_2 = E_1 \sum_{i,k} \beta_{ik} n_{i2}(n_{k1} - in_{k2}). \tag{2.68}$$

Inserting in (2.66), we get

$$P_R = E_1 \sum_{i,k} \beta_{ik}[(n_{i1}n_{k1} + n_{i2}n_{k2}) + i(n_{i2}n_{k1} - n_{i1}n_{k2})],$$

$$P_L = E_1 \sum_{i,k} \beta_{ik}[(n_{i1}n_{k1} - n_{i2}n_{k2}) - i(n_{i2}n_{k1} + n_{i1}n_{k2})]. \tag{2.69}$$

Taking the products $\overline{P_R P_R^*}$ and $\overline{P_L P_L^*}$ as in the case of linear polarization, we find

$$\overline{P_R P_R^*} = \frac{2E_1^2}{15}(10\beta_c + \gamma^2 + 5\beta_a), \tag{2.70}$$

$$\overline{P_L P_L^*} = \frac{2E_1^2}{15} \cdot 6\gamma^2. \tag{2.71}$$

For the reversal ratio we thus get

$$\mathscr{P} = \frac{6\gamma^2}{10\beta_c + \gamma^2 + 5\beta_a}. \tag{2.72}$$

As we have noted above, independent measurements of the reversal ratio $\mathscr{P}$ and the depolarization $\bar{\rho}$ in principle give the relative value of the scattering tensor invariants. Indeed, if $\gamma^2 \neq 0$, we have from (2.72) and (2.60)

$$\frac{\beta_c}{\gamma^2} = \frac{1 - 2\bar{\rho} + (3/\mathscr{P})}{5(1 + \bar{\rho})} = \frac{1 - 2\bar{\rho} + 3\mathscr{P}(\pi)}{5(1 + \bar{\rho})}, \tag{2.73}$$

$$\frac{\beta_a}{\gamma^2} = \frac{3[\bar{\rho} - 1 + (2\bar{\rho}/\mathscr{P})]}{5(1 + \bar{\rho})} = \frac{3[\bar{\rho} - 1 + 2\bar{\rho}\mathscr{P}(\pi)]}{5(1 + \bar{\rho})}. \tag{2.74}$$

The general expression describing the reversal ratio as a function of the angle ϑ between the direction of the incident wave $\boldsymbol{n}$ and the direction of the scattered wave $\boldsymbol{n}'$ can also be found by the same method. The result has the form (see [7, 10])

$$\mathscr{P}(\vartheta) = \frac{1 - \dfrac{1 - \bar{\rho}}{2(1 + \bar{\rho})}\sin^2\vartheta - \dfrac{1 - \mathscr{P}}{1 + \mathscr{P}}\cos\vartheta}{1 - \dfrac{1 - \bar{\rho}}{2(1 + \bar{\rho})}\sin^2\vartheta + \dfrac{1 - \mathscr{P}}{1 + \mathscr{P}}\cos\vartheta}. \tag{2.75}$$

In conclusion, let us consider a curious particular case, when the scattered light only contains the anisotropic component, i.e., when $\beta_c = \beta_a = 0$, $\gamma^2 \neq 0$. It will become clear from the following that this case obtains for a number of Raman scattering lines. From (2.72) we then find $\mathscr{P} = 6$. This signifies that the sense of rotation of the scattered light is very strongly reversed—the intensity of the left-polarized component is 6 times the intensity of the right-polarized component (assuming right-polarized incident radiation).

3. ANGULAR DISTRIBUTION OF RAMAN SCATTERING

We have so far derived expressions for the intensity and the degree of depolarization of the Raman scattering lines produced by linearly polarized incident radiation.

If natural (unpolarized) light is used for excitation, the scattered intensity should be averaged over all the possible directions of the vector E in a plane perpendicular to n (i.e., the direction of propagation of the incident wave).

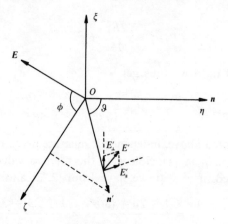

Figure 5

Excitation of Raman scattering by natural light.

Let ϑ and ϕ be the polar angle and the azimuth of n' (the direction of scattering) relative to n; the angle ϕ is reckoned from the plane through the vectors n and E (Figure 5). Then $\cos \theta = \sin \vartheta \cos \phi$ and for the scattered intensity in the direction n' we find from (2.47)–(2.49)

$$I(\beta_c) = \frac{I_0 \omega'^4}{3c^3} \beta_c (1 - \sin^2\vartheta \cos^2\phi), \qquad (3.1)$$

$$I(\gamma^2) = \frac{I_0 \omega'^4}{30c^3} \gamma^2 (7 - \sin^2\vartheta \cos^2\phi), \qquad (3.2)$$

$$I(\beta_a) = \frac{I_0 \omega'^4}{6c^3} \beta_a (1 + \sin^2\vartheta \cos^2\phi). \qquad (3.3)$$

Seeing that

$$\overline{\cos^2\phi} = \frac{1}{2\pi} \int_0^{2\pi} \cos^2\phi \, d\phi = \frac{1}{2}, \qquad (3.4)$$

we obtain after averaging over ϕ

$$I_n(\beta_c) = \frac{I_0 \omega'^4}{6c^3} \beta_c (1 + \cos^2\vartheta), \qquad (3.5)$$

$$I_n(\gamma^2) = \frac{I_0\omega'^4}{60c^3}\,\gamma^2(13 + \cos^2\vartheta)\,, \tag{3.6}$$

$$I_n(\beta_a) = \frac{I_0\omega'^4}{12c^3}\,\beta_a(2 + \sin^2\vartheta)\,. \tag{3.7}$$

The subscript n signifies that the intensity corresponds to natural incident light. Eqs. (3.5)–(3.7), originally derived by Placzek [7], express the dependence of the intensity of the three scattered components on the scattering angle ϑ. Figure 6 shows the corresponding polar diagrams: the radius-vector of each point on the curve is proportional to the scattered intensity at a given scattering angle ϑ.

Let us now find the depolarization of the scattered light. The electric vector E' of the scattered wave is decomposed into two perpendicular components, $E'_{\parallel}$ lying in the plane through n and n' (the scattering plane) and $E'_{\perp}$ at right angles to this plane (Figure 5). The component $E'_{\perp}$ and the corresponding intensity component

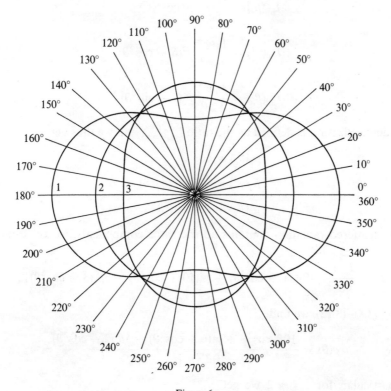

Figure 6

Angular distribution of the Raman scattering intensity in natural light:

1) scalar scattering,   2) anisotropic scattering,   3) antisymmetric scattering.

$I_{n\perp}$ clearly do not depend on the scattering angle ϑ. This intensity component therefore can be calculated for some particular value of ϑ, e.g., for $\vartheta = \pi/2$. For this ϑ, the plane $\xi On'$ contains the incident wave vector E, and $I_{n\perp}$ therefore can be calculated using Eqs. (2.42) and (2.45) averaged over all the values $\theta = \phi$. Simple manipulations give

$$I_{n\perp}(\beta_c) = \frac{I_0 \omega'^4}{6c^3} \beta_c,$$ (3.8)

$$I_{n\perp}(\gamma^2) = \frac{7 I_0 \omega'^4}{60c^3} \gamma^2,$$ (3.9)

$$I_{n\perp}(\beta_a) = \frac{I_0 \omega'^4}{12c^3} \beta_a.$$ (3.10)

Using these equations and Eqs. (3.5)–(3.7), which obviously give the sums $I_{n\perp} + I_{n\parallel}$, we find

$$I_{n\parallel}(\beta_c) = \frac{I_0 \omega'^4}{6c^3} \beta_c \cos^2\vartheta,$$ (3.11)

$$I_{n\parallel}(\gamma^2) = \frac{I_0 \omega'^4}{60c^3} \gamma^2 (6 + \cos^2\vartheta),$$ (3.12)

$$I_{n\parallel}(\beta_a) = \frac{I_0 \omega'^4}{12c^3} \beta_a (1 + \sin^2\vartheta).$$ (3.13)

The depolarization is defined as the ratio $I_{n\parallel}/I_{n\perp}$, and we thus get

$$\rho_\vartheta(\beta_c) = \cos^2\vartheta,$$ (3.14)

$$\rho_\vartheta(\gamma^2) = \tfrac{1}{7}(6 + \cos^2\vartheta),$$ (3.15)

$$\rho_\vartheta(\beta_a) = 1 + \sin^2\vartheta.$$ (3.16)

If the scattered radiation contains all the three components, we get from (3.5)–(3.7)

$$I_n = \frac{I_0 \omega'^4}{60c^3} \left[10\beta_c(1 + \cos^2\vartheta) + \gamma^2(13 + \cos^2\vartheta) + 5\beta_a(3 - \cos^2\vartheta) \right].$$ (3.17)

Using (3.8)–(3.13), we find

$$\rho(\vartheta) = \frac{10\beta_c \cos^2\vartheta + \gamma^2(6 + \cos^2\vartheta) + 5\beta_a(2 - \cos^2\vartheta)}{10\beta_c + 7\gamma^2 + 5\beta_a}.$$ (3.18)

In particular, for $\vartheta = \pi/2$ we get

$$I_n\left(\frac{\pi}{2}\right) = \frac{I_0 \omega'^4}{60c^3} (10\beta_c + 13\gamma^2 + 10\beta_a),$$ (3.19)

$$\rho = \rho\left(\frac{\pi}{2}\right) = \frac{6\gamma^2 + 10\beta_a}{10\beta_c + 7\gamma^2 + 5\beta_a}.$$ (3.20)

(In what follows, ρ will always designate the depolarization for $\vartheta = \pi/2$).

Comparison of (3.20) and (2.60) gives a general expression relating the depolarization in linearly polarized light to that in natural exciting radiation:

$$\rho = \frac{2\bar\rho}{1 + \bar\rho}.$$ (3.21)

Using (3.19) and (3.20), we can write the intensity and the depolarization as a function of the scattering angle for the case of natural incident light:

$$I_n(\vartheta) = \left[1 + \frac{1 - \rho}{1 + \rho}\cos^2\vartheta\right]I_n\left(\frac{\pi}{2}\right),$$ (3.22)

$$\rho(\vartheta) = 1 - (1 - \rho)\sin^2\vartheta.$$ (3.23)

The formulae expressing the angular dependence of the intensity and the depolarization of the Raman scattering lines with natural exciting radiation thus contain a single parameter, ρ. Natural and linearly polarized radiation are equivalent in this respect (see (2.61), (2.62)). Note that since ρ is related to $\bar\rho$ by Eq. (3.21), this is not an independent parameter and consequently it cannot be used in separate determination of the invariants β_c, γ^2 and β_a. It also follows that experimental measurements of the angular distribution of scattered radiation do not give the scattering tensor invariants. Nevertheless, these measurements are of considerable interest, since they provide a check on the general equations (3.22), (3.23) and thus confirm the validity of the underlying theory.

Experimental studies of the angular distribution of Raman scattering are few so far, although the first measurements were carried out back in 1930 [11]. The most detailed studies were carried out by Korotkov et al. [12, 13], who used the setup shown schematically in Figure 7. The light from the mercury lamp S immersed in a water-cooled cylindrical jacket M hit the cylindrical beaker K with the test liquid. The incident light was passed through a plate diaphragm D which reduced the beam divergence to no more than $1°$. The scattered light reached the spectrograph slit Sp. The aperture of the collimating objective was $8°20'$. The source L, the diaphragm D and the beaker K were fixed on a common support that could be turned only about the vertical axis coinciding with the axis of the cylinder K; the detector remained stationary throughout the measurements. The Raman scattering lines were detected photoelectrically.

The scattering volume defined by the collimator aperture varied as the apparatus was turning about the vertical axis. The corresponding correction was calculated graphically and then introduced into the measurement results. The measurements were carried out at scattering angles from 40 to $150°$.

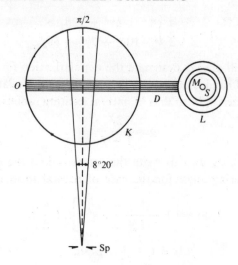

Figure 7

Experimental setup for measuring the angular distribution of Raman scattering.

A total of 16 Raman scattering lines in 6 liquids were measured (benzene, CCl_4, $CHCl_3$, CH_3OH, toluene, dichloroethane). The measurements were carried out with natural light, so that the results of intensity measurements were assumed to fit Eq. (3.22). The data are plotted in Figure 8. The angular distribution is clearly sensitive to the type of vibration which determines the depolarization of the Raman scattering line. Thus, an almost spherical distribution of scattered intensity is observed for the depolarized lines 217 cm^{-1}(CCl_4), 313 cm^{-1}(CCl_4), and 1176 cm^{-1} (benzene), whereas the highly polarized lines 459 cm^{-1}(CCl_4) and 992 cm^{-1}(C_6H_6) give a typical stretched distribution with a dip at $\vartheta = 90°$. These experimental data fit the theoretical results of Eq. (3.23) if suitable corrections are introduced for various

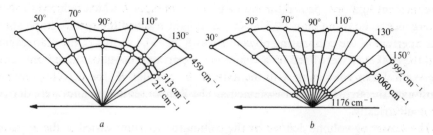

Figure 8

Angular distribution of Raman scattering for various lines:

a CCl_4,   *b* benzene

experimental errors (in particular, into the measured depolarization of the various lines). The most significant divergence between theory and experiment is the asymmetry of the angular distribution: the intensity of forward-scattered light is somewhat higher than the intensity of back-scattered light measured at the symmetrical angle. The asymmetry of the angular distribution observed in [13] reached up to 30% for the highly polarized lines. The depolarized lines showed no effect of this kind.

Sokolovskaya and Simova [14] studied the angular distribution of scattered intensity in a wide range of ϑ (from 20 to 160°). A definite asymmetry of the distribution was again noted, the average value of the I_n (20°)/I_n (160°) ratio reaching 1.8. The angular distribution of the depolarization, however, does not show any "forward–backward" asymmetry. The experimental findings in this respect are adequately fitted with the theoretical equation (3.23). Figure 9 plots the depolarization vs. the scattering angle from the data of Korotkov [15] for two highly polarized lines.

A recent report [16] describes measurements of the angular distribution of scattering using a gas-laser beam. The application of lasers as light sources operns new horizons for measurement of the angular distributions of the Raman scattering parameters because of the extremely small divergence angle of the laser beam. Several benzene lines were measured using a linearly polarized laser beam, so that the experimental results should be compared with the theory on the basis of Eqs. (2.47), (2.48), and (2.61). The measured angular distributions for the benzene

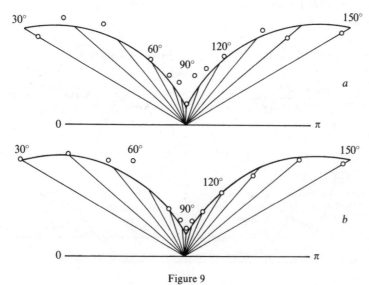

Figure 9

Depolarization vs. scattering angle:

a the CCl_4 459 cm^{-1} line ($\rho = 0.06$),   *b* the benzene 992 cm^{-1} line ($\rho = 0.08$).

lines 992 cm^{-1} and 1586–1606 cm^{-1} are shown in Figures 10 and 11. When the electric vector E is perpendicular to the scattering plane, the intensity is independent of the scattering angle (bottom curves). When E lies in the plane spanned by the inci-

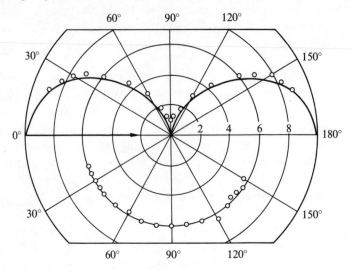

Figure 10

Angular distribution of the benzene 992 cm^{-1} line for Raman scattering excited by linearly polarized light.

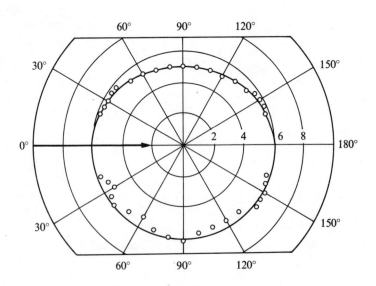

Figure 11

Angular distribution for the benzene lines 1586–1606 cm^{-1}.

dent and the scattered ray, the intensity of the 992 cm^{-1} line (highly polarized) is proportional to sin$^2 \theta$ (in accordance with (2.47)); the intensity of the depolarized 1586–1606 cm^{-1} lines is proportional to $1 + \frac{1}{6} \sin^2 \theta$ (in accordance with (2.48)).*

The angular distribution curves in [16] clearly do not show any "forward–backward" asymmetry. Further studies of the angular distribution of scattering are therefore most desirable, to provide sufficient information for comparison with the theory. Note that the observed departure of the angular distribution from the theoretical shape (in particular, the "forward–backward" asymmetry) may be associated with partical coherence of Raman scattering in liquids.

4. THE QUANTUM THEORY OF THE INTERACTION OF RADIATION WITH MATTER

We have shown that various important features of Raman scattering are adequately described in terms of classical concepts. However, a complete theory of Raman scattering must be developed on the basis of the quantum theory of radiation.

Consider a system of particles (for simplicity we will refer to them as molecules) immersed in a radiation field. In quantum theory, this system is described by a wave function $\Psi(t)$ which satisfies the wave equation

$$i\hbar \frac{\partial \Psi}{\partial t} = \hat{H}\Psi. \tag{4.1}$$

Here $\hat{H}$ is the system Hamiltonian, which is written as the sum of the molecule Hamiltonian, the electromagnetic field Hamiltonian $\hat{H}_s$, and the interaction Hamiltonian $\hat{H}_{int}$. These Hamiltonians are generally assumed to be Hermitian operators and their eigenvalues are therefore real. However, in order to allow for damping— a property of all real systems—we will have to forego this convenient assumption. The molecule Hamiltonian is thus taken as a sum of a Hermitian operator $\hat{H}_m$ and a non-Hermitian "damping operator" $\hat{H}_d$, which is assumed to be small compared to $\hat{H}_m$. Thus,

$$\hat{H} = \hat{H}_m + \hat{H}_s + \hat{H}_d + \hat{H}_{int}. \tag{4.2}$$

The behavior of atomic systems in radiation fields is generally determined using Dirac's time-dependent perturbation theory [17]. We will consider the damping-free molecule and the radiation field as the "unperturbed" system with the Hamiltonian

$$\hat{H}_0 = \hat{H}_m + \hat{H}_s, \tag{4.3}$$

---

* The angles marked in Figures 10 and 11 are the viewing angles $\theta - \pi/2$.

whereas $\hat{H}_d$ and $\hat{H}_{int}$ are regarded as the "perturbation" operators. The interaction operator is an explicit function of time. We assume that this operator can be written as a product of some function of time $\eta(t)$ and a position-dependent operator $\hat{H}'(x)$ which does not depend explicitly on time. The perturbation operator $\hat{H}'(x, t)$ is thus written in the form

$$\hat{H}'(x, t) = \hat{H}_d + \eta(t)\hat{H}'(x) . \tag{4.4}$$

(The coordinate x incorporates all the variables which determine the state of the system).

Let $\Psi_n(x, t)$ be the eigenfunction of the operator $\hat{H}_0$ which describes the unperturbed system in the state n (n incorporates all the quantum numbers of the molecule and the photons in the absence of any interaction). The energy of the system in state n is designated E_n. The function $\Psi_n(x, t)$ satisfies the unperturbed equation

$$i\hbar\frac{\partial\Psi_n(x, t)}{\partial t} = \hat{H}_0\Psi_n(x, t) . \tag{4.5}$$

Taking

$$\Psi_n(x, t) = \psi_n(x)e^{-iE_nt/\hbar} , \tag{4.6}$$

we obtain for the position-dependent function $\psi_n(x)$

$$\hat{H}_0\psi_n(x) = E_n\psi_n(x) . \tag{4.7}$$

The perturbation alters the state of the system. The solution of the fundamental equation (4.1) for the perturbed system can be written as a superposition of the eigenfunctions of the unperturbed system:

$$\Psi(x, t) = \sum_n b_n(t)\Psi_n(x, t) . \tag{4.8}$$

The superposition coefficients $b_n(t)$ are functions of time alone, being independent of position. Physically, $|b_n(t)|^2$ is the probability that at the time t the system occupies the unperturbed state n. The expansion coefficients in (4.8) can also be interpreted in a slightly different way. Suppose that initially ($t = 0$) the system was in state m. Then

$$b_m(0) = 1, \quad b_n(0) = 0 \quad (n \neq m) . \tag{4.9}$$

By the time t, the system may have jumped from state m to other states, and conditions (4.9) no longer apply. Then, $|b_n(t)|^2$ can be considered as the probability of transition of the system from state m to state n in time t.

Inserting (4.8) in Eq. (4.1) and using (4.5), we find

$$i\hbar\sum_n \dot{b}_n(t)\Psi_n(x, t) = \sum_n \hat{H}'(x, t)b_n(t)\Psi_n(x, t) . \tag{4.10}$$

Left-multiplying by $\Psi_m^*(x, t)$, we integrate the result over the entire space. Since the wave functions $\Psi_n(x, t)$ of the unperturbed system are orthogonal, we find

$$i\hbar \dot{b}_m(t) = \sum_n [\eta(t)H'_{nm} + (H_d)_{nm}] b_n(t) \exp [i(E_m - E_n)t/\hbar] . \tag{4.11}$$

Here H'_{nm} is the matrix element of the operator $\hat{H}'(x)$ for the transition of the system from state m to state n, defined by the integral

$$H'_{nm} = \int \psi_m^*(x)\hat{H}'(x)\psi_n(x)dx . \tag{4.12}$$

The matrix elements H'_{nm} are assumed Hermitian, i.e., $H'_{nm} = H'^*_{mn}$. In our particular case, $H'_{nn} = 0$, and it therefore follows from (4.11) that the diagonal elements of the operator $\hat{H}_d$ make the greatest contribution. In what follows we will only concentrate on the diagonal elements of the damping operator. These diagonal elements are assumed pure imaginary numbers, so that

$$(H_d)_{nn} = \int \psi_n^*(x)\hat{H}_d\psi_n(x)dx = -\tfrac{1}{2} i\Gamma_n \quad (\Gamma_n > 0) . \tag{4.13}$$

Thus, in order to determine the transition probabilities of the system from one state to another in the electromagnetic field, we have to solve a set of differential equations (4.11) with initial conditions (4.9). In general, this is a highly complicated problem. We will derive the solution for a particular case, when $\eta(t)$ can be regarded constant for $0 \leqslant t \leqslant \theta$:

$$\eta(t) = \eta.$$

We rewrite Eqs. (4.11) in the form

$$i\hbar \dot{b}_m(t)e^{-iE_mt/\hbar} = -\tfrac{1}{2} i\Gamma_m b_m(t)e^{-iE_mt/\hbar} + \eta \sum_n H'_{nm}b_n(t)e^{-iE_nt/\hbar} \tag{4.14}$$

and change over to new unknown functions:

$$B_n(t) = b_n(t)e^{-iE_nt/\hbar} . \tag{4.15}$$

Eqs. (4.14) thus take the form

$$i\hbar \dot{B}_m(t) = (E_m - \tfrac{1}{2} i\Gamma_m) B_m(t) + \eta \sum_n H'_{nm}B_n(t) . \tag{4.16}$$

Eqs. (4.16) are a set of linear homogeneous equations with constant coefficients, and they can be solved by any standard method (see, e.g., [18, 19]). Let

$$B_k(t) = c_k e^{\alpha t} \quad (k = 1, 2, \ldots, n) . \tag{4.17}$$

Inserting (4.17) in (4.16), we obtain a set of linear homogenous equations for the unknown constants c_k:

$$(E_m - \tfrac{1}{2} i\Gamma_m - \lambda) c_m + \eta \sum H'_{nm}c_n = 0 , \tag{4.18}$$

where we set

$$\lambda = i\hbar\alpha .$$

The system is solvable only if

$$\begin{vmatrix} E_1 - \frac{1}{2}i\Gamma_1 - \lambda & \eta H'_{21} & \cdots & \eta H'_{n1} \\ \eta H'_{12} & E_2 - \frac{1}{2}i\Gamma_2 - \lambda & \cdots & \eta H'_{n2} \\ \cdot\ \cdot\ \cdot & \cdot\ \cdot\ \cdot\ \cdot & \cdot\ \cdot\ \cdot & \cdot\ \cdot\ \cdot \\ \eta H'_{1n} & \eta H'_{2n} & \cdots & E_n - \frac{1}{2}i\Gamma_n - \lambda \end{vmatrix} = 0 . \qquad (4.19)$$

Let

$$E'_k = E_k - \tfrac{1}{2}i\Gamma_k . \qquad (4.20)$$

E'_k can be considered as complex energies. The corresponding states of the system (states with complex energy) are called *quasi-stationary states* (see [20], §132). Γ_k characterizes the width of the k-th level. By assumption, the widths of quasi-stationary levels are small compared to the energy gaps between these levels.

The roots of Eq. (4.19) are general complex numbers:

$$\lambda_k = \lambda_{0k} - \tfrac{1}{2}i\gamma_k . \qquad (4.21)$$

As a first stage, we assume that all the roots of Eq. (4.19) are different for $\eta \to 0$. We further assume* that the perturbation caused by the interaction of the system with the radiation field is small compared to the energy difference $|E'_j - E'_k|$. Then expanding the determinant in (4.19), we need only retain the lower powers of η. Up to second-order terms, we get

$$\lambda_j = E'_j + \eta^2 \sum_{k \neq j} \frac{H'_{kj}H'_{jk}}{E'_j - E'_k} \qquad (j = 1, 2, \ldots, n) . \qquad (4.22)$$

We insert one of the roots λ_j in (4.17). This gives the set of functions

$$B^j_1(t) = c^j_1 e^{-i\lambda_j t/\hbar} , \qquad B^j_2(t) = c^j_2 e^{-i\lambda_j t/\hbar} , \ldots \qquad (4.23)$$

---

* Some numerical estimates justifying this assumption will be given in §16. If this assumption is not applicable, the system should be approximately considered as degenerate (see below).

The constants $c_1^j, c_2^j, \ldots, c_n^j$ are obtained from Eqs. (4.18). One of these constants can be assigned an arbitrary value (we take in what follows $c_j^j = 1$). In calculating c_k^j, we again make use of the fact that the perturbation is small. Up to second-order terms in η, we find

$$c_k^j = \frac{\eta H'_{jk}}{E'_j - E'_k} - \frac{\eta^2}{(E'_j - E'_k)} \sum_{l \neq j} \frac{H'_{jl} H'_{lk}}{E'_l - E'_j} \qquad (j \neq k). \tag{4.24}$$

The root $\lambda = \lambda_j$ thus corresponds to the following particular solution of Eqs. (4.16):

$$B_1^i(t) = c_1^j e^{-i\lambda_j t/\hbar},$$

$$B_2^j(t) = c_2^j e^{-i\lambda_j t/\hbar},$$

$$\cdot \quad \cdot \quad \cdot \quad \cdot \quad \cdot \quad \cdot$$

$$B_j^j(t) = e^{-i\lambda_j t/\hbar}, \tag{4.25}$$

$$\cdot \quad \cdot \quad \cdot \quad \cdot \quad \cdot \quad \cdot$$

$$B_n^j(t) = c_n^j e^{-i\lambda_j t/\hbar}.$$

The general solution of Eqs. (4.16) can be written in the form

$$B_k(t) = \sum_j C_j B_k^j(t) \qquad (k = 1, 2, \ldots, n), \tag{4.26}$$

where C_j are constants.

Let us now consider the case when Eq. (4.19) has multiple roots, i.e., when say,

$$\lambda_1 = \lambda_2 = \ldots = \lambda_m.$$

Strictly speaking, the roots of Eq. (4.19) can be equal only for some special values of the perturbation. As we are not interested in any particular values of the perturbation, we will only consider the case of multiple roots for $\eta \to 0$, i.e., the case when

$$E'_1 = E'_2 = \ldots = E'_m.$$

The corresponding energy levels are said to be m-fold degenerate. Note that perturbation "relieves" the degeneracy, i.e., the roots are no longer multiple.

The form of the solution of Eqs. (4.16) depends on the rank r of the matrix formed by the coefficients of (4.18). In general, if λ_1 is a m-tuple root, the solution will contain terms of the form

$$e^{-i\lambda_1 t/\hbar}, te^{-i\lambda_1 t/\hbar}, \ldots, t^{m-1} e^{-i\lambda_1 t/\hbar}.$$

In our approximate treatment, we will only consider those solutions which reduce to solutions (4.26) (obtained assuming simple, i.e., different, roots) when the perturbation does not vanish. These solutions may not contain terms of the form $te^{-i\lambda_1 t/\hbar}$,

$\ldots, t^{m-1}e^{-i\lambda_1 t/\hbar}$. In accordance with the general theory of systems of linear differential equations (see [18]), solutions of this type are possible only if

$$r = n - m.$$

We will thus obtain solutions of the desired form if the system of linear algebraic equations (4.18) reduces to $r = n - m$ independent equations for $\lambda = \lambda_1$. We know from the theory of linear equations that in this case the general solution of Eqs. (4.18) contains m arbitrary constants: let these constants be

$$c_1^{(1)} = C_1, \quad c_2^{(1)} = C_2, \quad \ldots, \quad c_m^{(1)} = C_m.$$

The other r unknown constants $c_{m+1}^{(1)}, \ldots, c_n^{(1)}$ are obtained from the r independent equations in (4.18) for $\lambda = \lambda_1$. They are expressed by linear combinations of the arbitrary constants $C_1, \ldots, C_m$.

Setting successively for one of the constants $C_i = 1$, and taking for the other constants $C_j = 0$ $(j \neq i)$, we obtain m particular solutions corresponding to the m-tuple root λ_1:

$$B_1^{(1)}(t) = e^{-i\lambda_1 t/\hbar}, \quad B_2^{(1)}(t) = 0, \ldots, B_m^{(1)}(t) = 0,$$

$$B_{m+1}^{(1)}(t) = c_{m+1}^{(1)}e^{-i\lambda_1 t/\hbar}, \ldots, B_n^{(1)}(t) = c_n^{(1)}e^{-i\lambda_1 t/\hbar},$$

$$B_1^{(2)}(t) = 0, B_2^{(2)}(t) = e^{-i\lambda_1 t/\hbar}, \ldots, B_m^{(2)}(t) = 0,$$

$$B_{m+1}^{(2)}(t) = c_{m+1}^{(2)}e^{-i\lambda_1 t/\hbar}, \ldots, B_n^{(2)}(t) = c_n^{(2)}e^{-i\lambda_1 t/\hbar}, \tag{4.25a}$$

$$\cdots \cdots \cdots \cdots \cdots \cdots \cdots$$

$$B_1^{(m)}(t) = 0, B_2^{(m)}(t) = 0, \ldots, B_m^{(m)}(t) = e^{-i\lambda_1 t/\hbar},$$

$$B_{m+1}^{(m)}(t) = c_{m+1}^{(m)}e^{-i\lambda_1 t/\hbar}, \ldots, B_n^{(m)}(t) = c_n^{(m)}e^{-i\lambda_1 t/\hbar}.$$

Here to terms quadratic in η

$$c_p^{(j)} = \frac{\eta H'_{jp}}{E'_j - E'_p} - \frac{\eta^2}{E'_j - E'_p} \sum_{l \neq p} \frac{H'_{jl} H'_{lp}}{E'_l - E'_j} \tag{4.24a}$$

$$(j = 1, 2, \ldots, m; p = m + 1, \ldots, n).$$

For $j > m$, Eq. (4.24) remains valid.

The general solution again has the form (4.26), but now the particular solutions from (4.25) have been replaced by the corresponding solutions from (4.25a).

To return to the original unknown functions $b_k(t)$, we find from (4.15) and (4.26) (considering first the case of Eq. (4.19) with simple roots)

$$b_k(t) = B_k(t)e^{iE_k t/\hbar} = \sum_j C_j c_k^j e^{i(E_k - \lambda_j)t/\hbar}. \tag{4.27}$$

This solution should satisfy the initial conditions (4.9). Setting, say, $b_1(0) = 1$, $b_k(0) = 0$ $(k \neq 1)$, we obtain from (4.27) a set of n equations for the constants C_j. Again seeing that the perturbation is small and retaining only terms to the order of η^2, we obtain the approximate relations

$$C_1 = \frac{1}{\Delta}(1 - c_2^3 c_3^2 - c_2^4 c_4^2 - c_3^4 c_4^3 - \ldots) = (1 + c_1^2 c_2^1 + c_1^3 c_3^1 + c_1^4 c_4^1 + \ldots),$$

$$C_2 = \frac{1}{\Delta}(- c_2^1 + c_2^3 c_3^1 + c_2^4 c_4^1 + \ldots),$$ (4.28)

$$C_3 = \frac{1}{\Delta}(- c_3^1 + c_3^2 c_2^1 + c_3^4 c_4^1 + \ldots),$$

. . . .

where

$$\Delta = 1 - \sum_{j \neq k} c_k^j c_j^k$$ (4.29)

is the determinant of (4.27) for $t = 0$.

Thus, to terms of the order of η^2, we find for the general solution of Eqs. (4.11) satisfying the initial conditions (4.9)

$$b_1(t) = e^{i(E_1 - \lambda_1)t/\hbar} + c_1^2 c_2^1 (e^{i(E_1 - \lambda_1)t/\hbar} - e^{i(E_1 - \lambda_2)t/\hbar}) +$$

$$+ c_1^3 c_3^1 (e^{i(E_1 - \lambda_1)t/\hbar} - e^{i(E_1 - \lambda_3)t/\hbar}) + \ldots,$$ (4.28a)

$$b_2(t) = \frac{1}{\Delta}[c_2^1 (e^{i(E_2 - \lambda_1)t/\hbar} - e^{i(E_2 - \lambda_2)t/\hbar}) +$$

$$+ c_3^2 c_3^1 (e^{i(E_2 - \lambda_2)t/\hbar} - e^{i(E_2 - \lambda_3)t/\hbar}) + c_2^4 c_4^1 (e^{i(E_2 - \lambda_2)t/\hbar} - e^{i(E_2 - \lambda_4)t/\hbar})] + \ldots$$ (4.28b)

The expressions for the functions b_3, b_4, ... can be formed in a similar manner, and they are not given here in explicit form. The solution (4.28) obviously satisfies the initial conditions.

Inserting for the coefficients c_k^j their expressions from (4.24), we obtain the final expressions for the amplitudes of the transition probabilities:

$$b_1(t) = e^{i(E_1 - \lambda_1)t/\hbar} - \sum_{l>1} \frac{\eta^2 H'_{1l} H'_{1l}}{(E'_l - E'_1)^2} (e^{i(E_1 - \lambda_1)t/\hbar} - e^{i(E_1 - \lambda_1)t/\hbar}),$$ (4.29a)

$$b_k(t) = \frac{1}{\Delta}\left[\left(\frac{\eta H'_{1k}}{E'_1 - E'_k} + \frac{\eta^2}{(E'_1 - E'_k)} \sum_{l>1} \frac{H'_{1l} H'_{lk}}{E'_1 - E'_l}\right)(e^{i(E_k - \lambda_1)t/\hbar} - e^{i(E_k - \lambda_k)t/\hbar}) + \right.$$

$$\left. + \sum_{l>1} \frac{\eta^2 H_{1l} H'_{lk}}{(E'_1 - E'_l)(E'_l - E'_k)}(e^{i(E_k - \lambda_k)t/\hbar} - e^{i(E_k - \lambda_1)t/\hbar})\right],$$ (4.29b)

where $k = 2, 3, \ldots, n$.

If Eq. (4.19) has multiple roots, the particular solutions are of the form (4.25a). Acting along the same lines as before, we obtain the analogs of (4.29a), (4.29b). The most interesting case is that of a system with a degenerate initial state. Let m be the degeneracy of the initial level. Then (4.29a), (4.29b) are replaced with

$$b_1(t) = e^{i(E_1 - \lambda_1)t/\hbar} - \sum_{l>m} \frac{\eta^2 H'_{1l}H'_{l1}}{(E'_l - E'_1)^2} \left[e^{i(E_1 - \lambda_l)t/\hbar} - e^{i(E_1 - \lambda_1)t/\hbar} \right],$$ (4.29c)

$$b_k(t) = \frac{1}{\Delta} \sum_{l>m} \frac{\eta^2 H'_{1l}H'_{lk}}{(E'_1 - E'_l)(E'_l - E'_k)} \left[e^{i(E_k - \lambda_k)t/\hbar} - e^{i(E_k - \lambda_1)t/\hbar} \right]$$ (4.29d)

for $k \leq m$, and with

$$b_k(t) = \frac{1}{\Delta} \left[\frac{\eta H'_{1k}}{E'_1 - E'_k} + \frac{\eta^2}{E'_1 - E'_k} \sum_{l>m} \frac{H'_{1l}H'_{lk}}{E'_1 - E'_l} \left(e^{i(E_k - \lambda_1)t/\hbar} - e^{i(E_k - \lambda_k)t/\hbar} \right) + \right.$$

$$\left. + \sum_{l>m} \frac{\eta^2 H'_{1l}H'_{lk}}{(E'_1 - E'_l)(E'_l - E'_k)} \left(e^{i(E_k - \lambda_k)t/\hbar} - e^{i(E_k - \lambda_1)t/\hbar} \right) \right]$$ (4.29e)

for $k > m$.

Let us consider in more detail the factor which determines the time-dependence of the amplitudes $b_1(t)$, $b_k(t)$. In exponentials containing the differences $E_k - \lambda_l$ with $k \neq l$ we may approximately write (using (4.20))

$$E_k - \lambda_l \approx E_k - E'_l = E_k - E_l + \tfrac{1}{2} i\Gamma_l.$$ (4.30)

For $k = l$ we have from (4.22)

$$E_k - \lambda_k = \tfrac{1}{2} i\Gamma_k + \eta^2 \sum_{l \neq k} \frac{H'_{lk}H'_{kl}}{E'_l - E'_k} \approx \alpha_k + \tfrac{1}{2} i\beta_k,$$ (4.31)

where

$$\alpha_k = \eta^2 \sum_{l \neq k} \frac{H'_{lk}H'_{kl}(E_l - E_k)}{(E_l - E_k)^2 + \tfrac{1}{4}(\Gamma_l - \Gamma_k)^2},$$

  (4.32)

$$\beta_k = \eta^2 \sum_{l \neq k} \frac{H'_{lk}H'_{kl}(\Gamma_l - \Gamma_k)}{(E_l - E_k)^2 + \tfrac{1}{4}(\Gamma_l - \Gamma_k)^2} + \Gamma_k.$$

Thus the time dependence of the amplitudes $b_1(t)$, $b_k(t)$ is expressed by functions of the form

$$f_{kl}(t) = e^{i(E_k - \lambda_k)t/\hbar} - e^{i(E_k - \lambda_l)t/\hbar},$$

which contain products of oscillating and damped factors. Ignoring terms proportional to η^2, we find†

$$f_{kl}(t) = e^{-\frac{1}{2}\Gamma_k t/\hbar} - e^{-\frac{1}{2}\Gamma_l t/\hbar} e^{i(E_k - E_l)t/\hbar} . \tag{4.33}$$

Using the functions f_{kl}, we rewrite the fundamental expressions for the amplitudes $b_1(t)$, $b_k(t)$ in a more compact form:

$$b_1(t) = e^{i(E_1 - \lambda_1)t/\hbar} - \sum_{l>1} \frac{\eta^2 H'_{1l} H'_{1l}}{(E'_l - E'_1)^2} f_{1l}(t) , \tag{4.34a}$$

$$b_k(t) = -\frac{1}{\Delta} \frac{\eta H'_{1k}}{E'_1 - E'_k} f_{k1}(t) - \frac{\eta^2}{\Delta(E'_1 - E'_k)} \sum_{l>1} \frac{H'_{1l} H'_{lk}}{E'_1 - E'_l} f_{k1}(t) +$$

$$+ \frac{\eta^2}{\Delta} \sum_{l>1} \frac{H'_{1l} H'_{lk}}{(E'_1 - E'_l)(E'_l - E'_k)} f_{kl}(t) . \tag{4.34b}$$

In what follows the factor $1/\Delta \approx 1$ is omitted.

Eq. (4.34b) contains three terms: the first describes direct transitions of the system from the initial state to the k-th state, and the second and third terms correspond to transitions through intermediate states. Transitions of the first kind are associated with light absorption and emission. The second and the third term in Eq. (4.34b) will be shown in what follows to describe Raman scattering and resonance fluorescence, respectively. Thus,

$$b_k(t) = [b_k(t)]_a + [b_k(t)]_R + [b_k(t)]_f , \tag{4.35}$$

where

$$[b_k(t)]_a = \frac{\eta H'_{1k}}{E'_k - E'_1} f_{k1}(t) , \tag{4.36}$$

$$[b_k(t)]_R = \frac{\eta^2}{(E'_k - E'_1)} \sum_{l>1} \frac{H'_{1l} H'_{lk}}{E'_1 - E'_l} f_{k1}(t) , \tag{4.37}$$

$$[b_k(t)]_f = \eta^2 \sum_{l>1} \frac{H'_{1l} H'_{lk}}{(E'_1 - E'_l)(E'_l - E'_k)} f_{kl}(t) . \tag{4.38}$$

The time dependence of the transition probabilities is described by the functions

$$f_{kl} f_{kl}^* = e^{-\Gamma_k t/\hbar} + e^{-\Gamma_l t/\hbar} - 2e^{-\frac{1}{2}(\Gamma_k + \Gamma_l)t/\hbar} \cos \frac{(E_k - E_l)t}{\hbar} . \tag{4.39}$$

† This simplification is inapplicable to the first term in Eq. (4.29), where the corrections proportional to η^2 are of the same order of magnitude as the other terms of the equation.

The corresponding transition probabilities are given by

$$W_a = \eta^2 |H'_{1k}|^2 \frac{\left[e^{-\Gamma_k t/\hbar} + e^{-\Gamma_1 t/\hbar} - 2e^{-\frac{1}{2}(\Gamma_k + \Gamma_1)t/\hbar} \cos \frac{(E_k - E_1)t}{\hbar} \right]}{|E'_k - E'_1|^2}, \qquad (4.40)$$

$$W_R = \eta^4 \left| \sum_l \frac{H'_{1l}H'_{lk}}{E'_1 - E'_l} \right|^2 \times$$

$$\times \frac{\left[e^{-\Gamma_k t/\hbar} + e^{-\Gamma_1 t/\hbar} - 2e^{-\frac{1}{2}(\Gamma_k + \Gamma_1)t/\hbar} \cos \frac{(E_k - E_1)t}{\hbar} \right]}{|E'_k - E'_1|^2}, \qquad (4.41)$$

$$W_f = \eta^4 \left| \sum_l \frac{H'_{1l}H'_{lk}}{(E'_1 - E'_l)(E'_l - E'_k)} (e^{-\frac{1}{2}\Gamma_k t/\hbar} - e^{-\frac{1}{2}\Gamma_1 t/\hbar} e^{i(E_k - E_1)t/\hbar}) \right|^2. \qquad (4.42)$$

We will be mainly concerned with transitions of the following three kinds:

(a) The transition of the system from state 1 to state k through the intermediate state l (Figure 12a).

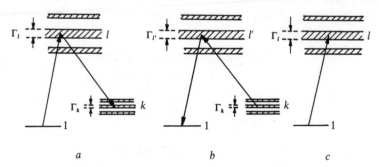

Figure 12

Transition diagrams:

a, b Raman scattering,   c absorption.

In state 1 (energy E_1), our system comprises a molecule in an electronic ground state of energy ε_1 plus a photon $\Phi_l = \hbar\omega_l$. In state l (energy E_l), the molecule has been excited to an electronic state of energy ε_l, and the photon Φ_l has been absorbed. In state k (energy E_k), the molecule has dropped again to the electronic ground state, but it occupies a new vibrational (or rotational) level with energy ε_k and a photon $\Phi_k = \hbar\omega_k$ has been emitted. The $1 \to l$ transition thus corresponds to absorption of the photon Φ_l, and the $l \to k$ transition to emission of the photon Φ_k. We thus have

$$E_k = \varepsilon_k + \Phi_k , \tag{4.43}$$

$$E_l = \varepsilon_l , \tag{4.44}$$

$$E_1 = \varepsilon_1 + \Phi_l , \tag{4.45}$$

$$\varepsilon_k - \varepsilon_1 = \Phi_i, \quad \varepsilon_l - \varepsilon_1 = \Phi_i^e , \tag{4.46}$$

where $\Phi_i = \hbar\omega_i$ is an infrared photon corresponding to the transition from the initial state to the k-th vibrational level, $\Phi_i^e = \hbar\omega_i^e$ is a photon corresponding to the transition from the initial state to the electronic l-th level.

(b) Transition from state 1 to state k (the same states as in case (a) above) through the intermediate state l' (Figure 12b). In state l' (energy $E_{l'}$) the molecule occupies the same excited electronic state with energy ε_l as in case (a), but there are two photons in the system, Φ_l and Φ_k. The $1 \rightarrow l'$ transition is accompanied by emission of the photon Φ_k and the $l' \rightarrow k$ transition by absorption of the photon Φ_l. Eq. (4.44) is now replaced by

$$E_{l'} = \varepsilon_l + \Phi_k + \Phi_l . \tag{4.47}$$

Eqs. (4.43), (4.45), and (4.46) are not affected.

(c) Transition from state 1 to state l with absorption of the photon Φ_l (Figure 12c). In state 1 (energy E_1) the molecule has energy ε_1 and the system also includes the photon Φ_l; in state l (energy E_l) the molecule is with energy ε_l and the photon Φ_l has been absorbed. We thus write

$$E_l = \varepsilon_l , \tag{4.48}$$

$$E_1 = \varepsilon_1 + \Phi_l . \tag{4.49}$$

Raman scattering in general may follow the scheme described under (a), as well as that under (b). The probability of Raman scattering with absorption of the photon Φ_l and emission of the photon Φ_k, involving transition through the l-th intermediate excited electronic state of the molecule, is therefore given by

$$W_R = |(b_a)_R + (b_b)_R|^2 . \tag{4.50}$$

From (4.43)–(4.47) we get

$$E_k - E_1 = \varepsilon_k + \Phi_k - \varepsilon_1 - \Phi_l = \Phi_k + \Phi_i - \Phi_l , \tag{4.51}$$

$$E_l - E_k = \varepsilon_l - \varepsilon_k - \Phi_k = \Phi_i^e - \Phi_i - \Phi_k , \tag{4.52}$$

$$E_l - E_1 = \varepsilon_l - \varepsilon_1 - \Phi_l = \Phi_i^e - \Phi_l , \tag{4.53}$$

$$E_{l'} - E_1 = \varepsilon_l + \Phi_k - \varepsilon_1 = \Phi_k + \Phi_i^e . \tag{4.54}$$

Let

$$\hbar x = \Phi_k + \Phi_i - \Phi_l, \quad \hbar y_l = \Phi_i^e - \Phi_l, \quad \hbar z = \Phi_i^e - \Phi_i - \Phi_k, \quad (4.55)$$

$$q_k = \frac{\Gamma_k}{2\hbar}. \quad (4.56)$$

Here*

$$E_k - E_1 = \hbar x, \quad E_k' - E_l' = \hbar[x + i(q_1 - q_k)], \quad (4.51')$$

$$E_l - E_k = \hbar z, \quad E_l' - E_k' = \hbar[z + i(q_k - q_l)], \quad (4.52')$$

$$E_l - E_1 = \hbar y_l, \quad E_l' - E_1' = \hbar[y_l + i(q_1 - q_l)], \quad (4.53')$$

$$E_{l'} - E_1 = \hbar(\omega_i^e + \omega_k), \quad E_{l'}' - E_1' = \hbar[\omega_i^e + \omega_k + i(q_1 - q_l)]. \quad (4.54')$$

For the transition probabilities we thus get

$$W_a = \frac{\eta^2 |H_{11}'|^2 [e^{-2q_l t} + e^{-2q_1 t} - 2e^{-(q_1 + q_l)t} \cos y_l t)]}{\hbar^2 [y_l^2 + (q_1 - q_l)^2]}, \quad (4.57)$$

$$W_R = \frac{\eta^4}{\hbar^4} \left| \sum_l \frac{H_{11}' H_{lk}'}{y_l + i(q_1 - q_l)} + \frac{H_{11'}' H_{l'k}'}{\omega_i^e + \omega_k + i(q_1 - q_l)} \right|^2 \times$$

$$\times \frac{[e^{-2q_k t} + e^{-2q_1 t} - 2e^{-(q_1 + q_k)t} \cos (xt)]}{[x^2 + (q_1 - q_k)^2]}, \quad (4.58)$$

$$W_f = \frac{\eta^4}{\hbar^4} \left| \sum_l \frac{H_{11}' H_{lk}'}{[y_l + i(q_1 - q_l)][z + i(q_k - q_l)]} (e^{-q_k t} - e^{-q_l t} e^{-izt}) \right|^2. \quad (4.59)$$

These expressions are valid for an incident photon of a definite energy Φ_l; moreover, the incident radiation propagates in a definite direction. If the exciting radiation is characterized by some spectral distribution of intensities $\rho(\omega_l - \omega_e)$ (with a maximum at $\omega_l = \omega_e$) and some angular distribution of intensities $\rho(\Omega)$, the transition probabilities should be integrated over these distributions. The distribution functions

---

* According to Eqs. (4.51')—(4.54'), the transition probabilities contain the differences of the widths of the coupled levels. This conclusion naturally cannot be extended to processes which involve statistical averaging over the frequencies and the widths of various atoms (molecules), when the general summation rule for the widths of the combination levels is applicable. The discussion of the general topic of spectral line widths falls outside the scope of this book. The particular expressions for the line widths are of no relevance in our analysis.

$\rho(\omega_l - \omega_e)$ and $\rho(\Omega)$ are normalized by the following conditions:

$$\int_{-\infty}^{\infty} \rho(\omega_l - \omega_e)\,d\omega_l = 1 , \qquad (4.60)$$

$$\int_{\Omega} \rho(\Omega)d\Omega = 1 \qquad (4.61)$$

Integration of Eqs. (4.57)–(4.59) is carried out using (4.55), where $\Phi_l = \hbar\omega_l$ is treated as the variable of integration and $\Phi_k = \hbar\omega_k$ as a parameter. This gives

$$W_a = \frac{\eta^2}{\hbar^2} \int_{\Omega} |H'_{1l}|^2 \rho(\Omega) \int_{-\infty}^{\infty} \frac{[e^{-2q_1 t} + e^{-2q_1 t} - 2e^{-(q_1 + q_l)t} \cos(y_l t)]}{y_l^2 + (q_l - q_1)^2} \times$$

$$\times \rho(y_l - a_l)\,d\Omega dy_l , \qquad (4.62)$$

$$W_R = \frac{\eta^4}{\hbar^4} \int_{\Omega} \int_{-\infty}^{\infty} \left| \sum_l \frac{H'_{1l}H'_{lk}}{y_l + i(q_1 - q_l)} + \frac{H'_{1l'}H'_{l'k}}{\omega_l^e + \omega_k + i(q_1 - q_l)} \right|^2 \times$$

$$\times \frac{[e^{-2q_k t} + e^{-2q_1 t} - 2e^{-(q_1 + q_k)t} \cos(x t)]}{x^2 + (q_k - q_1)^2} \rho(x - a)\rho(\Omega)\,dx\,d\Omega , \qquad (4.63)$$

$$W_f = \frac{\eta^4}{\hbar^4} \int_{\Omega} \int_{-\infty}^{\infty} \rho(\Omega) \left| \sum_l \frac{H'_{1l}H'_{lk}}{[y_l + i(q_1 - q_l)][z + i(q_k - q_l)]} (e^{-q_k t} - e^{-q_1 t} e^{-izt}) \right|^2 \times$$

$$\times \rho(y_l - a_l)\,dy_l d\Omega , \qquad (4.64)$$

$$a_l = \omega_l^e - \omega_e, \qquad a = \omega_k + \omega_i - \omega_e . \qquad (4.65)$$

We will consider the different kinds of transitions separately.

1. Light absorption and emission

The time dependence of the $1 \to l$ transition probabilities is expressed by the integral

$$F_l(t) = \int_{-\infty}^{\infty} \frac{e^{-2q_1 t} + e^{-2q_1 t} - 2e^{-(q_1 + q_l)t} \cos(y_l t)}{y_l^2 + (q_l - q_1)^2} \rho(y_l - a_l)dy_l . \qquad (4.66)$$

Let us first evaluate the integral in (4.66), assuming that the difference $q_l - q_1$ is small compared to the width of the exciting line q_e. The dispersion function in the integrand has a sharp peak at $y_l = 0$, so that we may factor out the value of ρ at $y_l = 0$, i.e.,

$$F_l(t) = 2\rho(a_l) \int_0^\infty \frac{e^{-2q_1 t} + e^{-2q_1 t} - 2e^{-(q_1 + q_1)t} \cos(y_l t)}{y_l^2 + (q_l - q_1)^2} \, dy_l. \qquad (4.67)$$

The integrals in (4.67) are evaluated without much difficulty. We have

$$\int_0^\infty \frac{dx}{x^2 + q^2} = \frac{\pi}{2q}, \qquad \int_0^\infty \frac{\cos xt \, dx}{x^2 + q^2} = \frac{\pi}{2q} e^{-qt}. \qquad (4.68)$$

Thus,

$$F_l(t) = \frac{\pi \rho(a_l)}{(q_l - q_1)} \left[e^{-2q_1 t} - e^{-2q_1 t} \right]. \qquad (4.69)$$

For small t, when

$$q_l t \ll 1, \qquad q_1 t \ll 1,$$

we have

$$F_l(t) = 2\pi \rho(a_l) t. \qquad (4.70)$$

The transition probabilities under these assumptions are directly proportional to time. A time dependence of this sort follows from a theory without damping, i.e., a theory which ignores the finite level widths (see, e.g., [20], §42).

Let us consider another important case, when $q_e \ll |q_l - q_1|$. The shape of the exciting line for small q_e is described with fair accuracy by the dispersion function:

$$\rho(v) = D_e(v) - \frac{q_e}{\pi} \frac{1}{v^2 + q_e^2}. \qquad (4.71)$$

$D_e(v)$ is normalized so that

$$\int_{-\infty}^\infty \rho(v) \, dv = 1.$$

Thus

$$F_l(t) = \frac{q_e}{\pi} \int_{-\infty}^\infty \frac{e^{-2q_1 t} + e^{-2q_1 t} - 2e^{-(q_1 + q_1)t} \cos y_l t}{[y_l^2 + (q_l - q_1)^2][(y_l - a_l)^2 + q_e^2]} \, dy_l. \qquad (4.72)$$

Changing over to a new variable $\xi = a_l - y_l$, we get

$$F_l(t) = \frac{q_e}{\pi} \int_{-\infty}^\infty \frac{e^{-2q_1 t} + e^{-2q_1 t} - 2e^{-(q_1 + q_1)t} \cos(a_l t) \cos(\xi t)}{(\xi^2 + q_e^2)[(\xi - a_l)^2 + (q_l - q_1)^2]} \, d\xi. \qquad (4.73)$$

Factoring out the value of the second factor in the denominator at $\xi = 0$, we end up with an integral of the same form as in (4.67). We thus have

$$F_l(t) = \frac{e^{-2q_1 t} + e^{-2q_l t} - 2e^{-(q_1 + q_l + q_e)t} \cos(a_l t)}{a_l^2 + (q_l - q_1)^2}. \qquad (4.74)$$

The function $F_l(t)$ is plotted in Figure 13. For small t,

$$F_l(t) = \frac{2q_e t}{a_l^2 + (q_l - q_1)^2}. \qquad (4.75)$$

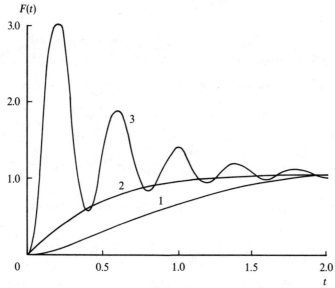

Figure 13

Transition probability as a function of time. The vertical axis gives the function $F(t) = F_l(t)[a_l^2 + (q_l - q_1)^2]$ for $q_l = 0$, $q_1 = 1$:

1) $a_l = \pi/4$, $q_e = 0.1$, 2) $a_l = \pi/4$, $q_e = 1$, 3) $a_l = 5\pi$, $q_e = 1$.

The transition probabilities in this case are

$$W_l = \frac{2\eta^2 q_e t}{\hbar^2 [a_l^2 + (q_l - q_1)^2]} \int_\Omega |H'_{1l}|^2 \rho(\Omega) d\Omega. \qquad (4.76)$$

It would be interesting to compare the above relations with Weisskopf's famous solution [21, 22]. For first-order processes (emission and absorption of light), we have according to Weisskopf*

$$|b_1(t)|^2 = e^{-\gamma t}, \qquad (4.77)$$

* Note that Weisskopf's functions, strictly speaking, are not a solution of Eqs. (4.11).

i.e., the probability of finding the system in the initial state decreases exponentially and $1/\gamma$ is the mean lifetime of the excited state. For small γt, when Weisskopf's theory is applicable, we have

$$|b_1(t)|^2 \approx 1 - \gamma t. \tag{4.78}$$

A similar solution is obtained from (4.34a), which can be written, using the notation from (4.32), (4.51)–(4.54'), in the form

$$b_1(t) = e^{(i\alpha - \beta)t} - \sum_{l>1} \frac{\eta^2 H'_{1l} H'_{l1}}{(E_l - E'_1)^2} (e^{-q_1 t} - e^{-q_l t} e^{-i y_l t}). \tag{4.79}$$

Here

$$\alpha = \frac{\eta^2}{\hbar^2} \sum_{l>1} \frac{H'_{1l} H'_{l1} y_l}{y_l^2 + (q_l - q_1)^2}, \qquad \beta = \frac{\eta^2}{\hbar^2} \sum_{l>1} \frac{H'_{1l} H'_{l1}(q_l - q_1)}{y_l^2 + (q_l - q_1)^2} + q_1. \tag{4.80}$$

In calculating $|b_1(t)|^2$, we use the Hermitian property of the matrix elements H'_{kl},

$$H'_{1l} = H'^*_{l1}, \qquad H'_{1l} H'_{l1} = |H'_{1l}|^2. \tag{4.81}$$

Calculations give

$$|b_1(t)|^2 = e^{-2\beta t} - \frac{2\eta^2}{\hbar^2} e^{-\beta t} \sum_{l>1} \frac{|H'_{1l}|^2}{[y_l^2 + (q_l - q_1)^2]^2} \{ e^{-q_1 t}(\cos \alpha t \, [y_l^2 - (q_l - q_1)^2] +$$

$$+ 2\sin(\alpha t)\, y_l(q_l - q_1)) - e^{-q_l t}(\cos(y_l t)[y_l^2 - (q_l - q_1)^2] + 2\sin(y_l t) y_l(q_l - q_1)) \}$$

$$+ \frac{\eta^4}{\hbar^4} \left| \sum_{l>1} \frac{|H'_{1l}|^2}{[y_l + i(q_1 - q_l)]^2} (e^{-q_1 t} - e^{-q_l t} e^{-i y_l t}) \right|^2. \tag{4.82}$$

Eq. (4.82) should be multiplied by $\rho(y_l - a_l) dy_l (l = 2, 3, \ldots, n)$ and integrated using the inequality $q_e \ll |q_l - q_1|$. Acting along the same lines as before, we obtain to terms of the order of η^2

$$|b_1(t)|^2 = e^{-2\beta t} - \frac{2\eta^2}{\hbar^2} e^{-\beta t} \sum_{l>1} \frac{|H'_{1l}|^2}{[a_l^2 + (q_l - q_1)^2]^2} \{ e^{-q_1 t} \cos \alpha t [a_l^2 - (q_l - q_1)^2] -$$

$$- e^{-(q_1 + q_e)t} (\cos a_l t [a_l^2 - (q_l - q_1)^2] + 2(q_l - q_1)[a_l \sin a_l t + q_e \cos a_l t]) \}. \tag{4.83}$$

For small t, we have

$$|b_1(t)|^2 = 1 - 2q_1 t - \frac{2\eta^2}{\hbar^2} \sum_{l>1} \frac{|H'_{1l}|^2}{a_l^2 + (q_l - q_1)^2} \left[1 + \frac{2(q_l - q_1)(2q_1 + q_e)}{a_l^2 + (q_l - q_1)^2} \right] q_e t. \tag{4.84}$$

We have thus obtained an expression analogous to (4.78), and

$$\gamma = 2q_1 + \frac{2\eta^2}{\hbar^2} \sum_{l>1} \frac{|H'_{1l}|^2}{a_l^2 + (q_l - q_1)^2} \left[1 + \frac{2(q_l - q_1)(2q_1 + q_e)}{a_l^2 + (q_l - q_1)^2} \right] q_e. \tag{4.85}$$

From (4.76), omitting the integration over $d\Omega$, we get

$$W_{\text{stim}} = \sum_l W_l = \frac{2\eta^2}{\hbar^2} \sum_{l>1} \frac{|H'_{1l}|^2}{a_l^2 + (q_l - q_1)^2} q_e t , \qquad (4.86)$$

where W_{stim} is the total transition probability of the system from the initial state to any final state in a radiation field (the probabilitiy of a forced, or stimulated, transition). Comparison of (4.85) and (4.86) gives (ignoring the last term in brackets in (4.85))

$$\gamma t = 2q_1 t + W_{\text{stim}} = W_{\text{spont}} + W_{\text{stim}} = W , \qquad (4.87)$$

where W_{spont} is the spontaneous transition probability. Thus, γ retains its original meaning of the total transition probability in unit time. If the initial level is infinitesimally narrow ($q_1 = 0$), the usual relation of the damping-free theory is observed for small t, i.e., $\sum_i |b_i|^2 = 1$.

For the transition probability to the l-th state we have in this case from (4.76) (inserting for a_l its expression from (4.65))

$$W_l = \frac{2\eta^2 |H'_{1l}|^2 q_e t}{\hbar^2 [(\omega_l^e - \omega_e)^2 + q_l^2]} , \qquad (4.88)$$

i.e., the usual expression of Weisskopf's theory.

Note that the basic results of Weisskopf's theory can be recovered in our treatment under certain simplifying particular assumptions.

We have so far considered the case of small t.* For large t, $t \to \infty$, the factors $\exp(- q_l t)$ lead to a rapid damping of the second and the third term in (4.66). For $q_1 = 0$, the first term is a "convolution" of the exciting line contour and the measured line contour. For the transition probabilities we thus get

$$W_l(\infty) = \frac{\eta^2}{\hbar^2} \int_\Omega |H'_{1l}|^2 \rho(\Omega) d\Omega \cdot I_l(a_l) , \qquad (4.89)$$

where

$$I_l(a_l) = \int_{-\infty}^{\infty} \frac{\rho(y_l - a_l)}{y_l^2 + q_l^2} dy_l . \qquad (4.90)$$

2. Raman scattering

Generally, Raman scattering is studied using a very narrow exciting line. We may therefore take $q_e \ll |q_l - q_1|$. In (4.63), $|\sum_l|^2$ can therefore be factored out from the

---

* The general theory of radiative processes with damping for $t \to \infty$ was developed by Heitler [23]. The application of this theory to Raman scattering was given in [24].

integrand for $x = a$ or $\omega_l = \omega_e$. The Raman scattering probability is thus given by

$$W_R = \frac{\eta^4}{\hbar^4} F_k(t) \int_\Omega \left| \sum_l \frac{H'_{1l}H'_{lk}}{a_l + i(q_1 - q_l)} + \frac{H'_{1l'}H'_{l'k}}{\omega_l^e + \omega_k + i(q_i - q_l)} \right|^2 \rho(\Omega)\, d\Omega . \quad (4.91)$$

Here

$$F_k(t) = \int_{-\infty}^{\infty} \frac{\left[e^{-2q_1 t} + e^{-2q_k t} - 2e^{-(q_1+q_k)t} \cos xt \right]}{x^2 + (q_k - q_1)^2} \rho(x - a)\, dx \quad (4.92)$$

differs from (4.66) only in the particular values of the parameters. Integrating for $q_e \ll |q_k - q_1|$ and assuming a dispersion profile for the exciting line, we obtain an expression analogous to (4.74):

$$F_k(t) = \frac{e^{-2q_1 t} + e^{-2q_k t} - 2e^{-(q_1 + q_k + q_e)t} \cos(at)}{a^2 + (q_k - q_1)^2}. \quad (4.93)$$

For large t, the last term with the rapidly oscillating factor can be ignored in the integral in (4.92). Then

$$F_k(\infty) = (e^{-2q_1 t} + e^{-2q_k t}) \int_{-\infty}^{\infty} \frac{\rho(x - a)\, dx}{x^2 + (q_k - q_1)^2}. \quad (4.94)$$

This integral is the convolution of the exciting line contour and the "true" contour of the Raman scattering line. The latter is described by a dispersion function with a halfwidth $2(q_k - q_1)$, which depends only on the properties of the initial and the final level of the particular transition.* The distribution $F_k(\infty)$ is peaked at $a = 0$ or, according to (4.65), at

$$\omega_k = \omega_e - \omega_i . \quad (4.95)$$

This selection rule for frequencies is characteristic of Raman scattering. The probability of Raman scattering for large t is

$$W_R = \frac{\eta^4}{\hbar^4} F_k(\infty) \int_\Omega \left| \sum_l \left(\frac{H'_{1l}H'_{lk}}{a_l + i(q_1 - q_l)} + \frac{H'_{1l'}H'_{l'k}}{\omega_l^e + \omega_k + i(q_1 - q_l)} \right) \right|^2 \rho(\Omega)\, d\Omega . \quad (4.96)$$

3. Resonance fluorescence

No more than one intermediate resonance level need be considered in the analysis of resonance fluorescence. The equation for the transition probability (4.64) then

* The case $q_1 = 0$ corresponds to Stokes scattering, and $q_k = 0$ to anti-Stokes scattering.

takes the form

$$W_f = \frac{\eta^4}{\hbar^4} F(z, t) \int_\Omega |H'_{1l}|^2 |H'_{lk}|^2 \rho(\Omega) d\Omega \int_{-\infty}^{\infty} \frac{\rho(y_l - a_l)}{y_l^2 + (q_l - q_1)^2} dy_l, \quad (4.97)$$

where

$$F(z, t) = \frac{e^{-q_k t} + e^{-2q_1 t} - 2e^{-(q_k + q_1)t} \cos zt}{z^2 + (q_l - q_k)^2}. \quad (4.98)$$

The function $F(z, t)$ is significantly different from the previously considered functions $F_l(t)$ and $F_k(t)$ in that, for small t, it shows a quadratic dependence on time (see Figure 13, curve 1). For large t,

$$W_f = \frac{\eta^4 (e^{-2q_k t} + e^{-2q_1 t})}{\hbar^4 [z^2 + (q_l - q_k)^2]} \int_{-\infty}^{\infty} \frac{\rho(y_l - a_l)}{y_l^2 + (q_l - q_1)^2} dy_l \int_\Omega |H'_{1l}|^2 |H'_{lk}|^2 \rho(\Omega) d\Omega. \quad (4.99)$$

The line emitted by resonance fluorescence thus has a dispersion contour with half-width $2(q_l - q_k)$ and a peak at $z = 0$ or

$$\omega_k = \omega_i^e - \omega_i. \quad (4.100)$$

The position of the maximum of this line is independent of the frequency of the exciting line. The selection rule (4.100) for frequencies is characteristic of resonance fluorescence and of the Shpol'skii effect. It is significant that neither the shape nor the width of the resonance fluorescence line depend on the properties of the exciting line. In particular, this line may be substantially narrower than the exciting line. Note that for independent absorption and emission processes, the fluorescence line shape, according to (4.90), is the convolution of the exciting line contour and the true emission line contour, i.e., it is invariably wider than the exciting line (see [23], §20).

The probability of resonance fluorescence also depends on the second factor in (4.99),

$$I_l(a_l) = \int_{-\infty}^{\infty} \frac{\rho(y_l - a_l)}{y_l^2 + (q_l - q_1)^2} dy_l. \quad (4.101)$$

$I_l(a_l)$ is the convolution of the exciting line contour and the absorption line contour with a maximum at $a_l = 0$ or $\omega_e = \omega_i^e$. The intensity of the resonance line of frequency ω_k depends on I_l and is thus determined by the difference $\omega_i^e - \omega_e$.

An important particular case of resonance fluorescence, when the system returns to the initial state after jumping to the intermediate state (a $1 \to 1$ transition), is described by the last term in (4.82). It should be remembered that the absorbed frequency ω_l and the emitted frequency ω_k are different. For the transition probability of this process we find

$$[W_f]_1 = \frac{\eta^4}{\hbar^4} \int_\Omega |H'_{1l}|^4 \rho(\Omega) d\Omega F(y_k, t), \tag{4.102}$$

where

$$F(y_k, t) = \frac{1}{y_k^2 + (q_l - q_1)^2} \int_{-\infty}^{\infty} \frac{e^{-2q_1 t} + e^{-2q_l t} - 2e^{-(q_1 + q_l)t} \cos y_l t}{y_l^2 + (q_l - q_1)^2} \rho(y_l - a_l) dy_l. \tag{4.103}$$

The emitted line has a maximum at $y_k = 0$ or $\omega_k = \omega_l^e$. In other respects, this case is identical to that considered above.

4. Mixed processes

The total probability of a transition from state 1 to state k is determined by $|b_k|^2$ and, according to (4.34b), it should contain three "mixed" terms, in addition to the terms describing absorption, Raman scattering, and resonance fluorescence. The probabilities of the corresponding "mixed" processes are

$$W_1 = (b_k)_R (b_k^*)_f + (b_k^*)_R (b_k)_f =$$

$$= \frac{\eta^4}{\hbar^4} \int_\Omega \int_{-\infty}^{\infty} \frac{|H'_{1l}|^2 |H'_{lk}|^2 \cdot F_1(x, y, z, t) \rho(x - a) \rho(\Omega)}{[y_l^2 + (q_l - q_1)^2][x^2 + (q_k - q_1)^2][z^2 + (q_l - q_k)^2]} dx \, d\Omega, \tag{4.104}$$

$$W_2 = (b_k)_a (b_k^*)_f + (b_k^*)_a (b_k)_f, \tag{4.105}$$

$$W_3 = (b_k)_a (b_k^*)_R + (b_k^*)_a (b_k)_R =$$

$$= \frac{2\eta^3}{\hbar^3} \int_\Omega \left[\sum_{l>1} \frac{(q_l - q_1)g_2 - a_l g_1}{a_l^2 + (q_l - q_1)^2} \right] F_k(t) \rho(\Omega) d\Omega. \tag{4.106}$$

Here g_1 is the real part, and g_2 is the imaginary part of the product of the matrix elements $H'_{1l} H'_{lk} H'_{k1}$, the function $F_k(t)$ is expressed by Eq. (4.92), and the function $F_1(x, y, z, t)$ for large t takes the form

$$F_1(x, y, z, t) = 2(q_k - q_1)(q_l - q_k)e^{-2q_k t}. \tag{4.107}$$

The process described by Eq. (4.105) will not be considered here in detail. The mixed process of Raman scattering with a simultaneous absorption of an infrared quantum, in accordance with Eq. (4.106), may lead under certain conditions to a substantial enhancement of Raman scattering. The probability W_1 of the mixed process involving Raman scattering and resonance fluorescence, according to (4.104) and (4.107), is proportional to

$$A = \frac{1}{z^2 + (q_l - q_k)^2} \int_{-\infty}^{\infty} \frac{\rho(x-a)dx}{[y_l^2 + (q_l - q_1)^2][x^2 + (q_l - q_k)^2]}. \quad (4.108)$$

The first factor in this relation describes resonance fluorescence, and the second factor represents Raman scattering. Both these processes are thus excited simultaneously.

5. THE INTENSITY OF RAMAN SCATTERING LINES

The expressions for the transition probabilities derived in the previous section can be applied, in principle, to determine the intensities of the spectral lines corresponding to these transitions. This requires the calculation of the matrix elements H'_{kl} defined by Eq. (4.12). The wave functions in (4.12) are the wave functions of the unperturbed system comprising the radiation field and the molecule. Since the Hamiltonian of the unperturbed system is the sum of the radiation field Hamiltonian and the molecule Hamiltonian, the wave functions ψ_k, ψ_l of the system can be written in the form of products

$$\psi_k = \psi_{km}\psi_{ks}, \qquad \psi_l = \psi_{lm}\psi_{ls}, \quad (5.1)$$

where the subscripts m and s identify the molecule and the radiation field, respectively.

The perturbation operator entering (4.12) can be derived from the standard expression for the Hamiltonian of a particle in the electromagnetic field. In the non-relativistic approximation, which is quite adequate for the entire range of topics under discussion, we have

$$H = \sum_{\sigma} \frac{1}{2\mu_\sigma} \left(p_\sigma - \frac{e_\sigma}{c} A \right)^2.$$

Here e_σ and μ_σ are the particle charge and mass, p_σ is the momentum, A is the vector potential of the radiation field at the point occupied by the particle; the summation extends over all the particles in the system. Dropping the constant term, we obtain the interaction operator

$$H' = \sum_{\sigma} \left\{ -\frac{e_\sigma}{c\mu_\sigma}(p_\sigma A) + \frac{e_\sigma^2}{2\mu_\sigma c^2} A^2 \right\}. \quad (5.2)$$

Inserting the expression for H' from (5.2) and for the wave functions from (5.1), we can find the matrix elements of the transitions from Eq. (4.12).* In practice, these

---

* Note that when the perturbation operator is used in the form (5.2), the small perturbation parameter η (see (4.4)) is included in the matrix elements.

calculations can be carried out only partially, since the wave functions ψ_m of complex molecules are not known. The solution of the problem is nevertheless of the greatest significance even in particular cases, since it gives the actual expressions for the matrix elements and sheds light on the entire question of line intensities.

The properties of the radiation field enter the perturbation operator (5.2) via the vector potential A, which is a function defined at any point in space and at any time. In the classical theory, the vector potential of the electromagnetic field should satisfy the wave equation

$$\nabla^2 A - \frac{1}{c^2} \ddot{A} = 0, \quad \text{div } A = 0. \tag{5.3}$$

To quantize the radiation field, we will first write the field equations in the "canonical" form.

Suppose that the entire radiation field is confined in some finite volume, say a cube L^3 whose side L is large compared to the characteristic dimensions of the system. Periodic boundary conditions are assumed, i.e., the potential A is a periodic function on the surface of the cube. The general solution of equation (5.3) is then written as a superposition of normal modes

$$A = \sum_\lambda [q_\lambda(t) A_\lambda(r) + q_\lambda^*(t) A_\lambda^*(r)], \tag{5.4}$$

where A_λ is a function of position only, and q_λ is a function of time only. The functions A_λ and q_λ are so chosen that Eq. (5.3) is satisfied. Inserting (5.4) in (5.3), we find

$$\nabla^2 A + \frac{\omega_\lambda^2}{c^2} A_\lambda = 0, \quad \text{div } A_\lambda = 0, \tag{5.5}$$

$$\ddot{q}_\lambda + \omega_\lambda^2 q_\lambda = 0, \tag{5.6}$$

A_λ remaining periodic on the surface of the cube.

A solution of Eqs. (5.5), (5.6) is a plane wave propagation in the direction of the vector κ_λ:

$$A_\lambda = e_\lambda \sqrt{4\pi c^2} e^{i(\kappa_\lambda r)}, \quad q_\lambda = |q_\lambda| e^{-i\omega_\lambda t}. \tag{5.7}$$

Here e_λ is a unit vector characterizing the wave polarization, $|\kappa_\lambda| = \omega_\lambda/c$. Different waves with different subscripts λ, μ, etc., are orthogonal, so that

$$\int_v A_\lambda A_\mu^* dv = 4\pi c^2 \delta_{\lambda\mu}, \tag{5.8}$$

where

$$\delta_{\lambda\mu} = \begin{cases} 1 & \text{for } \lambda = \mu, \\ 0 & \text{for } \lambda \neq \mu \end{cases} \tag{5.9}$$

(to simplify the mathematics, we took $L^3 = 1$).

Because of the periodic boundary conditions, the components of the vectors κ_λ may only take on a discrete set of values:

$$\kappa_{\lambda x} = \frac{2\pi}{L} n_{\lambda x}, \qquad \kappa_{\lambda y} = \frac{2\pi}{L} n_{\lambda y}, \qquad \kappa_{\lambda z} = \frac{2\pi}{L} n_{\lambda z}, \qquad (5.10)$$

where $n_{\lambda x}, n_{\lambda y}, n_{\lambda z}$ are positive or negative integers. Note that any wave with a given κ may have two independent (mutually perpendicular) polarizations.

Having described the radiation field as a superposition of plane waves, we can go one step further and introduce the "canonical" variables of Hamiltonian mechanics (see, e.g., [25], Ch. VII). By (5.4), the time variation of the plane wave is described by the functions $q_\lambda(t), q_\lambda^*(t)$ which satisfy Eq. (5.6). This is in fact the equation of a harmonic oscillator. Although q_λ, q_λ^* are not canonical ("normal") variables, a simple transformation,

$$Q_\lambda = q_\lambda + q_\lambda^*, \qquad P_\lambda = - i\omega_\lambda(q_\lambda - q_\lambda^*) = \dot{Q}_\lambda, \qquad (5.11)$$

gives the canonical variables of the field. Eq. (5.6) is now seen to follow directly from the Hamilton equations

$$\frac{\partial H_\lambda}{\partial Q_\lambda} = - \dot{P}_\lambda, \qquad \frac{\partial H_\lambda}{\partial P_\lambda} = \dot{Q}_\lambda \qquad (5.12)$$

with a Hamiltonian

$$H_\lambda = \tfrac{1}{2}(P_\lambda^2 + \omega_\lambda^2 Q_\lambda^2). \qquad (5.13)$$

The function (5.13) expressed in terms of the variables P_λ, Q_λ is the Hamiltonian of a harmonic oscillator. Each plane wave thus corresponds in the canonical representation to a certain harmonic oscillator. The entire field is described by the Hamiltonian

$$H_s = \sum H_\lambda, \qquad (5.14)$$

i.e., it can be treated as a system of independent oscillators. Let us now find the number dN of field oscillators in the cube L^3 with a given sense of polarization, with propagation vectors lying within a solid angle $d\Omega$, and with frequencies between ω and $\omega + d\omega$. It can be written in the form

$$dN = \rho(\omega)\, d\omega\, d\Omega\, L^3, \qquad (5.15)$$

where $\rho(\omega)$ is the density of states for the radiation field. On the other hand, dN can be interpreted as a volume element in the space of the variables $n_{\lambda x}, n_{\lambda y}, n_{\lambda z}$, i.e., it may be written in the form

$$dN = n^2\, dn\, d\Omega. \qquad (5.16)$$

By (5.10),

$$\kappa_\lambda^2 = \frac{\omega_\lambda^2}{c^2} = \left(\frac{2\pi}{L}\right)^2 (n_{\lambda x}^2 + n_{\lambda y}^2 + n_{\lambda z}^2) = \left(\frac{2\pi}{L}\right)^2 n^2 . \tag{5.17}$$

Using (5.17) and equating (5.15) and (5.16), we find

$$\rho(\omega)\, d\omega\, d\Omega\, L^3 = \frac{L^3}{(2\pi c)^3}\, \omega^2 d\omega d\Omega . \tag{5.18}$$

The number of field oscillators in unit volume is thus

$$\rho(\omega)\, d\omega\, d\Omega = \frac{\omega^2}{(2\pi c)^3}\, d\omega\, d\Omega . \tag{5.19}$$

Once the radiation field has been written in the canonical form, it can be quantized following the standard prescriptions of quantum mechanics. The canonical variables of each field oscillator are replaced with the corresponding operators. The result of this quantization procedure in application to a harmonic oscillator with the Hamiltonian (5.13) is standard knowledge. The energy eigenvalues of this oscillator are

$$E_\lambda = (n_\lambda + \tfrac{1}{2})\, \hbar\omega_\lambda , \tag{5.20}$$

where n_λ is an integer. The canonical variables Q_λ are replaced by a Hermitian matrix with the elements (see [23], §7)

$$Q_{n_\lambda, n_\lambda + 1} = Q_{n_\lambda + 1, n_\lambda}^* = \sqrt{\frac{\hbar(n_\lambda + 1)}{2\omega_\lambda}} ,$$

$$Q_{n_\lambda, n_\lambda'} = 0, \quad \text{if} \quad n_\lambda' \neq n_\lambda \pm 1 . \tag{5.21}$$

Thus, Q_λ has nonzero matrix elements only for transitions in which the quantum number n_λ increases or decreases by unity. The corresponding expressions for the amplitudes q_λ, q_λ^* from (5.11) are

$$q_{n_\lambda, n_\lambda + 1} = \sqrt{\frac{\hbar(n_\lambda + 1)}{2\omega_\lambda}} ,$$

$$q_{n_\lambda + 1, n_\lambda}^* = \sqrt{\frac{\hbar(n_\lambda + 1)}{2\omega_\lambda}} , \tag{5.22}$$

$$q_{n_\lambda + 1, n_\lambda} = q_{n_\lambda, n_\lambda + 1}^* = 0 .$$

The state of the radiation field is now described by the quantum numbers n_λ of all the field oscillators.*

Inserting (5.22) in (5.4) and using (5.7), we find

$$A_{n_\lambda, n_\lambda + 1} = \sum_\lambda \sqrt{\frac{2\pi c^2 \hbar (n_\lambda + 1)}{\omega_\lambda}} \, e_\lambda e^{i(\kappa_\lambda r)}, \tag{5.23}$$

$$A_{n_\lambda + 1, n_\lambda} = \sum_\lambda \sqrt{\frac{2\pi c^2 \hbar (n_\lambda + 1)}{\omega_\lambda}} \, e_\lambda e^{-i(\kappa_\lambda r)}. \tag{5.24}$$

The transition $n_\lambda + 1 \rightarrow n_\lambda$ corresponds to the absorption of a photon, and the transition $n_\lambda \rightarrow n_\lambda + 1$ to the emission of a photon. Using (5.23) and (5.24), we can find the matrix elements of the corresponding transitions by substituting $A_{n_\lambda, n_\lambda + 1}$ or $A_{n_\lambda + 1, n_\lambda}$ in the first term in Eq. (5.2). For each particle we then have

$$H'_{kn_\lambda, ln_\lambda + 1} = \int \psi^*_{lm} \psi^*_{ls} H' \psi_{km} \psi_{ks} dx =$$

$$= -\frac{e}{\mu} \sqrt{\frac{2\pi \hbar (n_\lambda + 1)}{\omega_\lambda}} \int \psi^*_{lm} (e_\lambda p) e^{i(\kappa_\lambda r)} \psi_{km} dx , \tag{5.25}$$

$$H'_{kn_\lambda + 1, ln_\lambda} = -\frac{e}{\mu} \sqrt{\frac{2\pi \hbar (n_\lambda + 1)}{\omega_\lambda}} \int \psi^*_{lm} (e_\lambda p) e^{-i(\kappa_\lambda r)} \psi_{km} dx .$$

In what follows, we omit the subscript of the wave function, always remembering that it refers to the molecule. It is moreover implied that the system has n_λ photons at $t = 0$. The absorption of a photon then corresponds to a transition $n_\lambda \rightarrow n_\lambda - 1$.

The expressions for absorption and emission take the form

$$H'_{kn_\lambda - 1, ln_\lambda} = -\frac{e}{\mu} \sqrt{\frac{2\pi \hbar n_\lambda}{\omega_\lambda}} \int \psi^*_l (e_\lambda p) e^{i(\kappa_\lambda r)} \psi_k dx , \tag{5.26}$$

$$H'_{kn_\lambda + 1, ln_\lambda} = -\frac{e}{\mu} \sqrt{\frac{2\pi \hbar (n_\lambda + 1)}{\omega_\lambda}} \int \psi^*_l (e_\lambda p) e^{-i(\kappa_\lambda r)} \psi_k dx . \tag{5.27}$$

---

* The representation in which the amplitudes are expressed by time-independent operators is known as the Schrödinger representation. In the Schrödinger representation, the time dependence of the physical processes is incorporated in the wave function. Since in the classical theory $\dot{Q}_\lambda = P_\lambda$, $\dot{P}_\lambda = -\omega_\lambda^2 Q_\lambda$, it follows from (5.11) that $\dot{q}_\lambda$, $\dot{q}_\lambda^*$ go over into the operators

$$\dot{q}_\lambda \rightarrow -i\omega_\lambda q_\lambda, \quad \dot{q}_\lambda^* \rightarrow i\omega_\lambda q_\lambda^* .$$

The second term in (5.2) is proportional to

$$A^2 = \sum_{\lambda\mu} [q_\lambda q_\mu (A_\lambda A_\mu) + q_\lambda q_\mu^* (A_\lambda A_\mu^*) + q_\lambda^* q_\mu (A_\lambda^* A_\mu) + q_\lambda^* q_\mu^* (A_\lambda^* A_\mu^*)] . \quad (5.28)$$

The corresponding matrix elements are not zero when two photons are absorbed or emitted or when one photon is emitted and one is absorbed. These matrix elements have the form

$$H'_{k,n_\lambda + 1, n_\mu - 1; l, n_\lambda, n_\mu} = \frac{e^2}{\mu} \frac{2\pi\hbar}{\sqrt{\omega_\lambda \omega_\mu}} \sqrt{(n_\lambda + 1)n_\mu} \, (e_\lambda e_\mu) \int \psi_l^* e^{i(\kappa_\mu - \kappa_\lambda)r} \psi_k dx , \quad (5.29)$$

$$H'_{k,n_\lambda + 1, n_\mu + 1; l, n_\lambda, n_\mu} = \frac{e^2}{\mu} \frac{2\pi\hbar}{\sqrt{\omega_\lambda \omega_\mu}} \sqrt{(n_\lambda + 1)(n_\mu + 1)} (e_\lambda e_\mu) \int \psi_l^* e^{-i(\kappa_\lambda + \kappa_\mu)r} \psi_k dx , \quad (5.30)$$

$$H'_{k,n_\lambda - 1, n_\mu - 1; l, n_\lambda, n_\mu} = \frac{e^2}{\mu} \frac{2\pi\hbar}{\sqrt{\omega_\lambda \omega_\mu}} \sqrt{n_\lambda n_\mu} (e_\lambda e_\mu) \int \psi_l^* e^{i(\kappa_\lambda + \kappa_\mu)r} \psi_k dx . \quad (5.31)$$

In the above expressions, the volume L^3 of the electromagnetic field was taken as unity. Otherwise, Eq. (5.4) would contain a factor $L^{-3/2}$. As a result, the matrix elements of one-photon processes will be proportional to $L^{-3/2}$ and the matrix elements of two-photon processes proportional to L^{-3}.

The expressions for the matrix elements can be simplified if we remember that the molecular dimensions are small compared to the wavelength.* Therefore, $e^{i(\kappa_\lambda r)}, e^{-i(\kappa_\lambda r)}$ can be factored out from the integrand, since they are nearly constant in the entire region where ψ_k, ψ_l do not vanish. Moreover, we may write

$$\frac{p}{\mu} = v, \qquad e_\lambda v = |v| \cos \theta . \quad (5.32)$$

From this definition, θ is the angle between the direction of polarization and the vector v. For matrix elements we have

$$\frac{1}{\mu} \int \psi_l^* (e_\lambda p) e^{i(\kappa_\lambda r)} \psi_k dx = \cos \theta e^{i(\kappa_\lambda r)} \int \psi_l^* |v| \psi_k dx . \quad (5.33)$$

Here $|v_{kl}|^2 = v_{xkl}^2 + v_{ykl}^2 + v_{zkl}^2$, and v_{xkl} is the matrix element for the x component of the velocity v, corresponding to the $l \rightarrow k$ transition. From the general rules of quantum theory (see footnote to p. 51),

$$v_{xkl} = \dot{x}_{kl} = - i\omega_\lambda x_{kl} . \quad (5.34)$$

---

* We shall not consider Rayleigh scattering and other processes where scales of the order of λ and greater are significant.

Thus,

$$\int \psi_i^* |v|^2 \psi_k dx = \omega_\lambda \int \psi_i^* |r| \psi_k dx . \tag{5.35}$$

Inserting (5.32)–(5.35) in (5.26), (5.27), we sum over all the charges of the system in accordance with Eq. (5.2) in order to obtain the total interaction operator. This summation introduces a new factor in the integrand in (5.35),

$$\sum e_\sigma r_\sigma = P , \tag{5.36}$$

which corresponds to the total electric dipole moment of the system. We thus obtain

$$H'_{kn_\lambda - 1, ln_\lambda} = - \sqrt{2\pi\hbar\omega_\lambda n_\lambda} \cos\theta e^{i(\kappa_\lambda r)} P_{kl} , \tag{5.37}$$

$$H'_{kn_\lambda + 1, ln_\lambda} = - \sqrt{2\pi\hbar\omega_\lambda(n_\lambda + 1)} \cos\theta e^{i(\kappa_\lambda r)} P_{kl} . \tag{5.38}$$

Here P_{kl} is the matrix element of the dipole moment:

$$P_{kl} = \int \psi_k^* |P| \psi_l dx . \tag{5.39}$$

Hence, for the squares of the matrix elements entering the expression of the probabilities

$$|H'_{kn_\lambda - 1, ln_\lambda}|^2 = 2\pi\hbar\omega_\lambda n_\lambda \cos^2\theta P_{kl}^2 = 2\pi\hbar\omega_\lambda n_\lambda (e_\lambda P_{kl})^2 , \tag{5.40}$$

$$|H'_{kn_\lambda + 1, ln_\lambda}|^2 = 2\pi\hbar\omega_\lambda(n_\lambda + 1) \cos^2\theta P_{kl}^2 = 2\pi\hbar\omega_\lambda(n_\lambda + 1)(e_\lambda P_{kl})^2 . \tag{5.41}$$

The matrix elements (5.29)–(5.31) associated with the second term in (5.2) are calculated along the same lines. Factoring out the exponential functions in these expressions and seeing that the wave functions ψ_l, ψ_k are orthogonal, we obtain

$$H'_1 = H'_{k,n_\lambda + 1, n_\mu - 1; k, n_\lambda, n_\mu} = \frac{e^2}{\mu} \frac{2\pi\hbar}{\sqrt{\omega_\lambda\omega_\mu}} \sqrt{(n_\lambda + 1)n_\mu} \, (e_\lambda e_\mu) e^{i(\kappa_\mu - \kappa_\lambda)r} , \tag{5.42}$$

$$H'_2 = H'_{k,n_\lambda + 1, n_\mu + 1; k, n_\lambda, n_\mu} = \frac{e^2}{\mu} \frac{2\pi\hbar}{\sqrt{\omega_\lambda\omega_\mu}} \sqrt{(n_\lambda + 1)(n_\mu + 1)} \, (e_\lambda e_\mu) e^{-i(\kappa_\lambda + \kappa_\mu)r} , \tag{5.43}$$

$$H'_3 = H'_{k,n_\lambda - 1, n_\mu - 1; k, n_\lambda, n_\mu} = \frac{e^2}{\mu} \frac{2\pi\hbar}{\sqrt{\omega_\lambda\omega_\mu}} \sqrt{n_\lambda n_\mu} (e_\lambda e_\mu) e^{i(\kappa_\lambda + \kappa_\mu)r} . \tag{5.44}$$

The matrix elements H'_1, H'_2, H'_3 enable us to calculate the probabilities of four-photon processes with the participation of intermediate states. These processes are considered in Chapter IV.

The absorption or the emission of a photon $\hbar\omega_\lambda$ can be attributed to any of the numerous field oscillators, whose number density (i.e., number in unit volume) is given by Eq. (5.19). All these oscillators have the same frequency (falling within the interval $d\omega$), they are characterized by the same polarization and the same direction of propagation (within a solid angle element $d\Omega$). As we are always dealing with transition probabilities into some state in the interval $d\omega\, d\Omega$, Eqs. (5.40), (5.41) should be multiplied by the number of states in this interval $\rho(\omega)d\omega\, d\Omega$. As a result, n_λ is replaced by the mean number of photons $n(\omega, \Omega)$ of fixed polarization in unit volume (calculated for a unit frequency interval and a unit solid angle):

$$n(\omega,\Omega)\, d\omega\, d\Omega = \frac{n_\lambda \omega^2}{(2\pi c)^3}\, d\omega\, d\Omega .\tag{5.45}$$

After these manipulations, we get

$$\left|H'_{kl}\right|^2_{\text{abs}} d\omega\, d\Omega = 2\pi\hbar\omega\, n(\omega,\Omega)\,(eP_{kl})^2 d\omega\, d\Omega .\tag{5.46}$$

For the emission of a photon, the matrix element (5.41) is made up of two terms, the first proportional to the number of field photons n_λ (stimulated emission) and the second independent of n_λ (spontaneous emission). The matrix element is thus written in the form

$$\left|H'_{kl}\right|_{\text{em}} d\omega'd\Omega' = 2\pi\hbar\omega'\left[n'(\omega',\Omega',e';\omega,\Omega,e) + \frac{\omega'^2}{(2\pi c)^3}\right](e'P_{kl})^2 d\omega'd\Omega' .\tag{5.47}$$

Here n' is the number of emission-stimulating photons: ω', Ω', e' correspond to the emitted photon and ω, Ω, e to the stimulating photon. The function $n'(\omega',\Omega',e';\omega,\Omega,e)$ accounts for the correlation between the properties of the stimulating and the emitted radiation. An important property of stimulated radiation is that the emitted photons are identical to the stimulating photons, i.e., they have the same frequency, the same polarization, and propagate in the same direction. The function n' for the process of light emission may therefore be written in the form

$$n'(\omega',\Omega',e';\omega,\Omega,e) = n(\omega,\Omega,e)\delta(\omega'-\omega)\delta(\Omega'-\Omega)\delta(e'-e),\tag{5.48}$$

where $n(\omega,\Omega,e)$ is the number of stimulating photons.

Using the squares of the matrix elements (5.46), (5.47), we find the probabilities of the transitions considered in the previous sections. In case of light absorption, we use Eq. (4.89), where integration has been carried out over the frequency of the photon, assuming that the function

$$n(\omega,\Omega) = n_e\rho(\omega)\rho(\Omega)\tag{5.49}$$

has a sharp maximum at $\omega = \omega_e$. This gives

$$W_l(\infty) = \frac{2\pi n_e\omega_e}{\hbar}\, I_i(a_l)\int_\Omega (eP_{11})^2\rho(\Omega)\, d\Omega .\tag{5.50}$$

In case of Raman scattering, the squares of the matrix elements are inserted in (4.63) from (5.46), (5.47). Let us first consider the spontaneous emission, described by the second term in (5.47). When only this term is considered, we are dealing with "normal" Raman scattering. The frequency distribution, the angular distribution, and the polarization of this component of scattered radiation are described by the function $n'(\omega', \Omega', e')$, which in accordance with §2 through §4 depends on the frequency distribution, the angular distribution, and the polarization of the incident radiation (i.e., the functions $\rho(\omega)$ and $\rho(\Omega)$). If n' is sufficiently large, the first term in (5.47) describing stimulated emission becomes significant. In this case, it should be remembered that Raman scattering does not amount to successive independent absorption and emission events. The principles of energy and momentum conservation therefore apply only to the initial and the final states and thus establish a certain relation between ω', Ω', e' and ω, Ω, e. For example, energy conservation introduces the correlation factor $\delta(\omega' + \omega_i - \omega)$. As a result, a certain correlation is observed between the properties of the stimulated and the exciting radiation, and it is this correlation that is described by the function n'. We may thus take $n' = n'(\omega', \Omega', e'; \omega, \Omega, e)$. To simplify the mathematics, we further assume that the dependence of n' on the frequencies ω, ω' can be represented by a separate factor:

$$n' = n'(\omega', \omega)\,\rho(\Omega', e'; \Omega, e). \tag{5.51}$$

Inserting Eqs. (5.46), (5.47), (5.51) in the expression for the probability of Raman scattering, we consider the case $q_e \ll |q_l - q_1|$. Thus, the following factor is separated:

$$G(t) = \int_{-\infty}^{\infty} n'(\omega', \omega) \frac{\left[e^{-2q_k t} + e^{-2q_1 t} - 2e^{-(q_1 + q_k)t} \cos(xt)\right]}{x^2 + (q_k - q_1)^2} \rho(x - a)dx, \tag{5.52}$$

$$G(\infty) = \int_{-\infty}^{\infty} \frac{n'(\omega', \omega)}{x^2 + (q_k - q_1)^2} \rho(x - a)dx. \tag{5.52a}$$

For the probability of Raman scattering we obtain

$$W_R(\omega', \Omega', e)d\omega' d\Omega' =$$

$$= \frac{(2\pi\hbar)^2 \omega_e \omega' n_e}{\hbar^4} \left[G(\infty) \int_\Omega \rho'(\Omega', e'; \Omega, e)|S_{k1}|^2\, \rho(\Omega)d\Omega +$$

$$+ \frac{F_k(\infty)\omega'^2}{(2\pi c)^3} \int_\Omega |S_{k1}|^2 \rho(\Omega)d\Omega \right] d\omega' d\Omega', \tag{5.53}$$

where

$$S_{k1} = \sum_l \frac{(eP_{l1})(e'P_{kl})}{\omega_l^e - \omega_e + i(q_1 - q_l)} + \frac{(e'P_{l'1})(eP_{kl'})}{\omega_l^e + \omega' + i(q_1 - q_l)}, \tag{5.54}$$

and $F_k(\infty)$ is given by Eq. (4.94).

Eq. (5.53) is a generalization of Placzek's fundamental formula [7] for the probability of Raman scattering. Within the framework of our theory, the exact form of the function $n'(\omega', \Omega', e'; \omega, \Omega, e)$ remains arbitrary.* We will consider the resulting expression for the probability in two limiting cases.

a) The dependence of $n'(\omega', \omega)$ and $\rho'(\Omega', e; \Omega, e)$ on ω and Ω, respectively, is much less pronounced than the corresponding dependence of the distribution in the integrand. Then n' and ρ' can be factored out from the integrand for some $\omega = \omega_0$ and $\Omega = \Omega_0$. This gives

$$W_R(\omega', \Omega', e')\,d\omega'\,d\Omega' =$$

$$= \frac{(2\pi\hbar)^2 \omega_e \omega' n_e}{\hbar^4} F_k(\infty)\left[n'(\omega', \Omega', e'; \omega_0, \Omega_0, e) + \frac{\omega'^2}{(2\pi c)^3} \right] \times$$

$$\times \int_\Omega |S_{k1}|^2 \rho(\Omega)\,d\Omega\,d\omega'\,d\Omega' . \tag{5.53a}$$

Eq. (5.53a) is equivalent to Placzek's formula.

b) The dependence of $n'(\omega', \omega)$ and $\rho'(\Omega', e'; \Omega, e)$ on ω and Ω, respectively, is much more pronounced than the dependence of the other factors in the integrand. In the limit, we may write n' in a form similar to (5.48)

$$n'(\omega', \Omega', e'; \omega, \Omega, e) = n'_\infty \delta(\omega' + \omega_i - \omega)\,\delta(\Omega' - \Omega)\,\delta(e' - e) =$$

$$= n'_\infty \delta(x)\,\delta(\Omega' - \Omega)\,\delta(e' - e) . \tag{5.55}$$

Thus,

$$W_R(\omega', \Omega', e')\,d\omega'\,d\Omega' =$$

$$= \frac{(2\pi\hbar)^2 \omega_e \omega' n_e}{\hbar^4} \left[\frac{n'_\infty \rho(a)}{(q_k - q_1)^2} \rho(\Omega') |S_{k1}|^2 \delta(e' - e) + \right.$$

$$\left. + \frac{F_k(\infty)\omega'^2}{(2\pi c)^3} \int_\Omega |S_{k1}|^2 \rho(\Omega)\,d\Omega \right] d\omega'\,d\Omega' . \tag{5.53b}$$

We see that in this case the frequency distribution, the angular distribution, and the polarization of the scattered radiation as determined by the first term (stimulated Raman scattering) repeat in all details the frequency distribution, the angular distribution, and the polarization of the exciting radiation.

A detailed discussion of Eqs. (5.53a) and (5.53b) and their comparison with experimental findings will be given in Chapter IV.

---

* The analysis on pp. 55–56 is not to be considered as a consistent theory which leads to Eq. (5.53). This equation is nevertheless highly convenient for what follows.

Under the ordinary conditions of Raman scattering experiments, the number of scattered photons n' is small compared to $\omega'^2/(2\pi c)^3$. Indeed, according to our estimates [26], $\hbar\omega'n' = 3 \cdot 10^{-20}$ W $\cdot$ Hz^{-1} $\cdot$ rad^{-1} $\cdot$ cm^{-3} and $\hbar\omega'^3/(2\pi c)^3 = 10^{-14}$ W $\cdot$ Hz^{-1} $\cdot$ rad^{-1} $\cdot$ cm^{-3}, i.e., the first term in (5.53) is negligible.

Multiplying the transition probabilities by $\hbar\omega'$, we obtain the intensities corresponding to the various processes. Moreover, seeing that the product

$$I_e = \hbar\omega_e \cdot n_e \tag{5.56}$$

is the intensity of the exciting line, we find

$$I_R(\omega', \Omega') = \frac{I_e\omega'^4 F_k(\infty)}{2\pi\hbar^2 c^3} \int_\Omega |S_{k1}|^2 \rho(\Omega)\, d\Omega. \tag{5.57}$$

In dealing with absorption, let the absorbing layer thickness be dx. Then the product

$$\hbar\omega_e W_l(\infty)dx = dI_e(x) \tag{5.58}$$

describes the intensity decrement in this layer as a result of absorption. Using (5.50), we find

$$\frac{dI_e}{I_e} = -\frac{2\pi\omega_e}{\hbar[(\omega_l^e - \omega_e)^2 + q_l^2]} \int_\Omega (eP_{11})^2\rho(\Omega)d\Omega dx = -\kappa_l dx. \tag{5.59}$$

Here κ_l is the absorption coefficient at the frequency ω_e, associated with the transition of the molecule to the level l:

$$\kappa_l = \frac{2\pi\omega_e}{\hbar[(\omega_l^e - \omega_e)^2 + q_l^2]} \int_\Omega (eP_{11})^2\rho(\Omega)d\Omega. \tag{5.60}$$

For the intensity of the Raman lines, Eq. (5.57) gives for $\omega_l^e \gg \omega_e$ the usual dependence on frequency:

$$I_R = aI_e\omega'^4. \tag{5.61}$$

As ω_e approaches one of the electronic absorption bands, the function $I_R(\omega_e)$ becomes considerably more complicated. In the simplest case, when the absorbing substance has a single absorption band which is distinct from all the other bands, only one term need be retained near this band in the sum S_{k1}:

$$S_{k1} \approx \frac{(eP_{11})(e'P_{kl})}{\omega_l^e - \omega_e + i(q_1 - q_l)}. \tag{5.62}$$

Thus,

$$\frac{I_R}{I_e} = \frac{\omega'^4 F_k(\infty)(e'P_{kl})^2}{2\pi\hbar^2 c^3[(\omega_l^e - \omega_e)^2 + (q_1 - q_l)^2]} \int_\Omega (eP_{11})^2\rho(\Omega)d\Omega. \tag{5.63}$$

Comparison of (5.63) and (5.60) gives

$$\frac{I_R}{I_e} = \frac{\omega'^4 \kappa_l (e' P_{kl})^2}{4\pi^2 \hbar c^3 \omega_e} F_k(\infty).$$ (5.64)

In this simple case, the intensity of the Raman scattering line is thus proportional to the absorption coefficient at the frequency ω_e. In some cases, of course, the term of the sum S_{k1} corresponding to a transition through the l-th intermediate level may prove to be very small or even zero, since the factor $(e' P_{kl})$ is small (or zero). The intensity of these Raman scattering lines is then determined by the contribution from the other terms of S_{k1} which correspond to transitions through other intermediate levels. The "relevant" intermediate levels for a given Raman line are determined by assessing the maximum contribution of the l-th level to the line intensity. This contribution ($q_1 = 0$) is proportional to

$$(\Delta I_l)_{max} = \frac{(e' P_{kl})^2 (e P_{l1})^2}{q_l^2}.$$ (5.65)

If $(\Delta I_l)_{max} \ll I_R|_{\omega_e = \omega_l^e}$, the intensity of the corresponding Raman scattering line changes insignificantly as ω_e approaches the l-th electronic absorption band and (5.64) is broken. Lines with $(\Delta I_l)_{max} \simeq I_R|_{\omega_e = \omega_l^e}$ all follow the same dependence (5.64), and their intensity ratio therefore remains constant as $\omega_e \to \omega_l^e$.

If a molecule has several close absorption bands, the relation of the Raman scattering intensity to the absorption coefficient takes a more complex form. The sum S_{k1} for $\omega_e \to \omega_l^e$ can no longer be limited to a single term, and the dependence $S_{k1}(\omega_e)$ no longer coincides with the dependence $\kappa(\omega) = \Sigma \kappa_l(\omega)$ because the factors $(e' P_{kl})^2$ are different. Since the intensities of different Raman scattering lines are in general determined by different terms in the sum S_{k1}, the line intensity ratio changes when ω_e is varied. In particular, a different value may be obtained for the intensity ratio of the fundamental vibration frequencies and overtones.

The above theory is based on the assumption that a molecule is described by a set of levels whose width is small compared to the distances between them. This assumption is not justified, e.g., for molecules which have wide and partly overlapping vibrational levels in the excited state. In order to extend the theoretical conclusions to this case, the entire system of levels should be replaced by a single band of width Γ, which is the sum total of the widths of the component vibrational levels. The real profile of the absorption band in this case may noticeably differ from the theoretical dispersion curve (especially for condensed media). The width of the electronic absorption band Γ therefore may be regarded as some effective, formal parameter entering the theory. General considerations pertaining to the inevitability of absorption prior to secondary emission indicate that the Raman scattering intensity remains proportional to the absorption coefficient in the case of complex absorption bands, too. It is significant that experimental measurements of this dependence do not require knowledge of the exact position of the maximum and of the width of the electronic absorption band: it suffices to measure the absorption coefficient for various exciting lines. The above considerations and the resulting conclusions will apparently provide a closer approximation to reality as the vibrational structure of the electronic level becomes progressively more diffuse, since in the limit this leads to a structureless electron band.

The first experimental studies of the Raman scattering intensity as a function of the exciting frequency strove to establish that the intensity was proportional to ω'^4. Ornstein and Rekveld [27] studied CCl_4 in the visible spectrum and methyl alcohol in the visible and the near ultraviolet [28]. Sirkar [29] extended the intensity measurements of these compounds to the far ultraviolet. He also measured the benzene lines at 992 and 3062 cm^{-1}. Later, some of these measurements were repeated by Werth [30]. The results show that in the ultraviolet, the line intensity increases much faster than the fourth power of frequency.

Shorygin's measurements of the Raman scattering spectra near the absorption band and inside the band (resonance Raman scattering) [31, 32] stimulated renewed interest in the intensity–frequency dependence. Because of the high absorption, Shorygin used low-concentration solutions (0.0001 % scattering molecules).* The spectra generally showed few lines only. These results and later work of Shorygin and co-workers [33–37] and other authors [38–47] reveal a very rapid growth of intensity of some Raman scattering lines as the exciting line approaches the maximum of the electron absorption band.

Quantitative measurements of the Raman scattering intensity as a function of the exciting line frequency involve considerable experimental difficulties. One of the main problems is the measurement of intensities in a wide spectral region, including the vacuum ultraviolet. Reliable results in these measurements cannot be obtained unless certain precautions are observed. Since Raman scattering occurs in an absorbing medium, the absorption of the exciting line and the absorption of the Raman scattering line must be taken into consideration, not an easy task in high-absorption media. The absorption is often reduced by making measurements in solutions. This, however, involves a shift in the electron absorption bands and changes their profiles. Photochemical reactions, especially in the ultraviolet, are also significant. Partial neglect of these factors all but invalidates the results obtained by some authors.

In principle, the best policy is to carry out parallel measurements of the Raman scattering intensity and the absorption coefficient. Systematic measurements of this

---

* As the concentration is lowered, the absorption falls off exponentially, whereas the Raman scattering intensity decreases linearly, and therefore at low concentrations Raman scattering prevails.

kind were made by Zubov [24, 48–52], who also did his best to allow for the variety of factors distorting the results. The data in [24, 51] indicate that, within the experimental error, the Raman scattering intensity divided by ω'^4/ω_e is proportional to the absorption coefficient inside the absorption band, i.e., Eq. (5.64) is satisfied. As an illustration, Figures 14 and 15 plot the measurement results for hexadiene-2,4 and benzene.* The points corresponding to the Raman scattering lines closely follow the solid curve which represents the measured absorption coefficient for the exciting lines. In benzene, several Raman scattering lines were measured. Their behavior follows essentially the same pattern, and they are apparently all characterized by identical intermediate states.

The intensities of the second-order lines were measured as a function of the exciting frequency in [51, 52]. The measurements covered the overtones of the 1630–1650 cm^{-1} line associated with the $C=C$ bond stretching vibrations in the spectra of some unsaturated hydrocarbons. As the exciting line frequency was changed from 4358 Å to 3126 Å, the intensity of the fundamental line varied for various compounds by

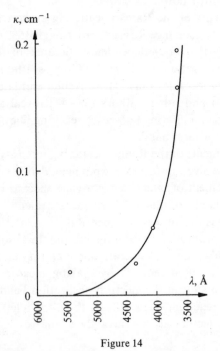

Figure 14

Intensity of the Raman scattering lines 1657 cm^{-1} and 1668 cm^{-1} (dots) and the absorption coefficient (solid curve) vs. the wavelength of the exciting light for hexadiene-2,4 [24, 51].

---

* The factor ω_e in Eq. (5.60) for the absorption coefficient was ignored in [24, 51]. The results presented in Figures 14 and 15 have been corrected accordingly.

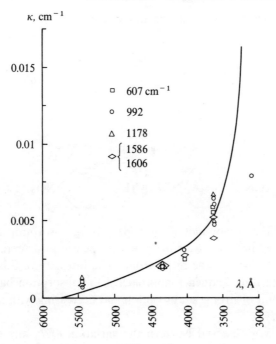

Figure 15

Intensity of Raman scattering lines (dots) and the absorption coefficient (solid curve) vs. the wavelength of exciting light for benzene [24, 51].

a factor ranging from 2–5 to 300–700. The overtone intensities changed by the same factor within the margin of experimental error, i.e., the overtone-to-fundamental line intensity ratio remained approximately constant.

Similar results were obtained for carbon tetrachloride and chloroform (see Table 1).

Table 1

THE RATIO OF OVERTONE INTENSITY TO FUNDAMENTAL LINE
INTENSITY VS. THE EXCITING FREQUENCY [51]

Compound	Line type	Δv, cm^{-1}	I_{ov}/I_f			
			5461 Å	4358 Å	4047 Å	3650–3663 Å
CCl_4	Overtone	~1540	0.9	1.2	1.1	1.0
	Fundamental	760–790				
$CHCl_3$	Overtone	~1520	0.9	0.8	1.2	1.0
	Fundamental	762				

Ivanova /53/ studied the two stilbene devivatives

4-nitro-4′-dimethylaminostilbene

$$Me_2N\text{—}\bigcirc\text{—}CH\text{=}CH\text{—}\bigcirc\text{—}NO_2$$

and

4-nitroaminostilbene

$$H_2N\text{—}\bigcirc\text{—}CH\text{=}CH\text{—}\bigcirc\text{—}NO_2.$$

The spectra of these compounds show wide, strong absorption bands between 4000 and 4500 Å. The 1340 cm^{-1} Raman scattering line was measured, corresponding to the symmetric vibration of the nitro group. The intensity of this line was seen to increase as the exciting frequency approached the absorption band, reaching a maximum at the point of strongest absorption and decreasing with further increase in exciting frequency.

A qualitative fit was observed between the variation of I_R and the absorption coefficient κ. The Raman scattering spectra of these compounds differ from normal spectra only in the very high intensity of the fundamental lines; the overtone intensities are at least two orders of magnitude less than the intensities of the fundamental frequencies.

It follows from the preceding data that the ratio $I_R/(\omega'^4/\omega_e)$ is proportional to the absorption coefficient for a sufficiently large group of compounds.

As we have noted on p. 58, identical variation of the Raman intensity with the frequency of the exciting line is observed only when the transitions involve the same "relevant" intermediate level. For lines of different origin, e.g., those associated with π-electrons and those with σ-electrons, the intensity as a function of ω_e may follow different curves. This effect was indeed observed [50]. It was established that the lines associated with the vibrations of the CH groups (σ-electrons) in the spectra of benzene and toluene preserve a constant intensity as λ_e varies from 5461 to 3021 Å, and in the spectra of unsaturated hydrocarbons their intensity varies substantially more slowly than the intensity of the ~ 1640 cm^{-1} lines (associated with π-electrons).

An even more pronounced change in the dependence of line intensity on $\omega_l^e - \omega_e$ was observed by Shorygin and Ivanova [54]. They studied the spectra of diphenyl-polyenes of the type

$$C_6H_5(\text{—}CH\text{=}CH\text{—})_nC_6H_5,$$

with $n = 2, 3, \ldots, 7$. For $\omega_e \rightarrow \omega_l^e$, a marked increase in line intensity was observed at ~ 1600 cm^{-1} and ~ 1100 cm^{-1}. For $\omega_l^e - \omega_e \approx 3000$ cm^{-1}, the Raman spectrum consists of virtually these two lines. In diphenylpolyenes with $n > 5$, the vibrational structure of the absorption bands was observed. If ω_e falls in the region where the vibrational bands overlap, the resonance Raman spectrum substantially changes in appearance. Alongside with the lines at $\sim$ 1140 cm^{-1} and $\sim$ 1550 cm^{-1}, the spectrum shows high-intensity overtones and compound frequencies of these lines (Figure 16). The frequency dependence of the intensity of the 1140 and 1550 cm^{-1} lines in this case has several maxima, whose position is different for the 1140 cm^{-1} line and the 1550 cm^{-1} line. No correlation is observed between the variation of I_R and that of the total absorption coefficient. This case of resonance Raman scattering apparently corresponds to the conditions described on p. 58.*

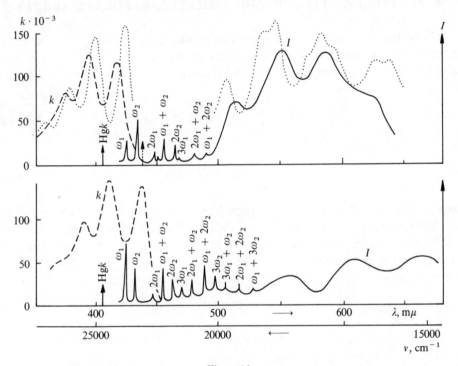

Figure 16

Absorption spectra (k) and resonance Raman spectra (I) for diphenyldecapentaene (top) and diphenyl-dodecahexaene (bottom) in acetone solutions at 25°C. The dotted curves on top give the absorption spectrum at -70°C (left) and the fluorescence bands at -196°C (right) [54].

* Some authors, proceeding from the semiclassical theory of polarizability, suggest that the marked increase in the relative intensity of overtones in the absorption band constitutes a general rule [45, 55]. This general assumption, however, is inconsistent with the experimental results described above. The increase in overtone intensity reported in [54] may be associated with the complex structure of the electron absorption band (see §7).

The depolarization ρ of the lines of some aromatic and unsaturated hydrocarbons was studied as a function of the exciting frequency in [49]. The exciting wavelengths were varied from 5461Å to 3021Å. The depolarization of the 1655 cm^{-1} line of pentadiene-1,3 varied in this interval from 0.29 to 0.48; the ρ of the 1638 cm^{-1} line of 2-metalbutadiene-1,3 varied from 0.23 to 0.53. Both these lines are associated with π-electrons. The lines associated with σ-electrons showed an insignificant change in depolarization. These results are attributed to the increase in the contribution from π-electrons to the line intensity as ω_e increases.

6. SCATTERING TENSOR AND MOLECULAR POLARIZABILITY

In the previous section we derived expressions for the absorption coefficient (5.60) and the Raman line intensity (5.57) assuming a general angular distribution of the exciting radiation. For further applications, we will require the integrals entering these expressions,

$$i_a = \int_\Omega (eP_{l1})^2 \rho(\Omega) \, d\Omega, \tag{6.1}$$

$$i_R = \int_\Omega |S_{k1}|^2 \rho(\Omega) \, d\Omega, \tag{6.2}$$

with certain restrictive assumptions regarding the form of the function $\rho(\Omega)$. The incident radiation is assumed to have a definite direction of propagation, i.e., it is confined to a very narrow solid angle around the axis $\boldsymbol{n}$ and has a definite direction of polarization (the direction of the electric vector $\boldsymbol{e}$). The integrals i_a and i_R, with the normalization condition (4.61), are then written in the form

$$i_a = \tfrac{1}{2}(eP_{l1})^2, \tag{6.3}$$

$$i_R = \tfrac{1}{2}|S_{k1}|^2 = \frac{1}{2}\left| \sum_l \frac{(eP_{l1})(e'P_{kl})}{\omega_l^e - \omega_e + i(q_1 - q_l)} + \frac{(e'P_{l'1})(eP_{kl'})}{\omega_l^e + \omega' + i(q_1 - q_l)} \right|^2. \tag{6.4}$$

In Eq. (6.4), the two possible states of polarization of the scattered light should be taken into account. Consider a certain fixed system of axes in which the scattered light is observed (see §2). The axis Z points along $\boldsymbol{n'}$, the axis X lies in the plane through the vectors $\boldsymbol{n'}$ and $\boldsymbol{e}$, and the axis Y is perpendicular to this plane (see Figure 2). In these axes, the vector $\boldsymbol{e'}$ has two allowed values, e'_X and e'_Y. Introducing for simplicity the vector

$$\boldsymbol{B} = \sum_l \frac{(eP_{l1})P_{kl}}{\omega_l^e - \omega_e + i(q_1 - q_l)} + \frac{(eP_{kl'})P_{l'1}}{\omega_l^e + \omega' + i(q_1 - q_l)}, \tag{6.5}$$

we may write

$$(i_R)_X + (i_R)_Y = \tfrac{1}{2}\{|Be'_X|^2 + |Be'_Y|^2\} = \tfrac{1}{2}(|B_X|^2 + |B_Y|^2). \tag{6.6}$$

For the scattered intensity we have from (5.57)

$$I_R(\omega', \Omega') = \frac{\omega'^4 I_e \cdot F_k(\infty)}{4\pi c^3 \hbar^2}(|B_X|^2 + |B_Y|^2). \tag{6.7}$$

Comparison of (6.7) with Eq. (2.16), written in the same axes, clearly shows that the vector $B/\hbar$ coincides with the induced classical moment P. Therefore, for the scattering tensor $\beta_{\rho\sigma}$ which has been previously defined by Eq. (2.1), we find

$$(\beta_{\rho\sigma})_{k1} = \frac{1}{\hbar} \sum_l \frac{(P_{kl})_\rho (P_{l1})_\sigma}{\omega_l^e - \omega_e + i(q_1 - q_l)} + \frac{(P_{l'1})_\rho (P_{kl'})_\sigma}{\omega_l^e + \omega' + i(q_1 - q_l)} \tag{6.8}$$

$$(\rho, \sigma = X, Y, Z).$$

All the classical results of §2 and §3 can therefore be extended to the quantum-mechanical expression (6.8), which gives the explicit form of the scattering tensor.

For the absorption coefficient we similarly find from (6.1) and (5.60)

$$\kappa_l = \frac{\pi\omega_e}{\hbar\left[(\omega_l^e - \omega_e)^2 + q_l^2\right]}[(P_e)_{l1}]^2, \tag{6.9}$$

where $(P_e)_{l1} = (eP_{l1})$.

Eqs. (6.8) and (6.9) contain the matrix elements of the dipole moment components of the scattering (or the absorbing) molecule. These matrix elements are formed using the complete set of the eigenfunctions of the molecule, whose explicit expressions are not known. Therefore, the matrix elements are calculated using approximative expressions for the wave functions, which can be obtained, say, from the following considerations.

The movement of the nuclei is very slow compared to the motion of the electrons. Therefore, when a molecule interacts with a radiation field, the electronic configuration changes before the nuclei manage to move from their initial positions. However, the state of the molecule and its characteristics, including the energy distribution between the electron shell and the nuclei, are altered by the interaction with the radiation field. As a result, energy is exchanged between the exciting light and the nuclei, although because of the high mass of the nuclei, light is scattered by the electrons only. It is the coupling between the movements of the nuclei and the electrons that leads to Raman scattering.

To every instantaneous position of the nuclei corresponds a certain electron polarizability of the molecule that characterizes its behavior in an electromagnetic field. This polarizability does not remain constant as the nuclei vibrate: it varies in time with the frequency of these vibrations. The scattered radiation is thus modulated by the movement of the nuclei, in accordance with the classical picture described in §1. The scattering intensity, on the other hand (see [7], §14), appears to be independent of the movement of the nuclei, and at any time it is determined by their instantaneous configuration. For example, the scattering intensity for a molecule with moving nuclei is instantaneously the same as for a molecule with fixed nuclei having the same configuration.

Since the atomic nuclei move much more slowly than the electrons, we have a tool for probing into the properties of molecules. Indeed, to first approximation, the atomic nuclei can be regarded as stationary, and in higher approximations perturbation theoretical methods are applied to allow for their motion. This approximative method is known as the *adiabatic approximation* (see, e.g., [56]). Without going into details, we will only describe the main result of this method. In the adiabatic approximation, the molecular wave function $\psi(\xi, x)$ can be written as a product of the electronic function $\phi(\xi, x)$ and the nuclear function $u(x)$:

$$\psi_{nv}(\xi, x) = \phi_n(\xi, x)u_{nv}(x). \tag{6.10}$$

Here ξ is the set of all the electronic coordinates, x is the set of all the nuclear coordinates, n and v are the corresponding quantum numbers. The function $\phi_n(\xi, x)$ contains x as a parameter. According to (6.10), the electron and the nuclear motions of the molecule are separable to certain approximation.

In accordance with Eq. (6.10) we have for the matrix elements

$$(P_{11})_\sigma = \int u_{n_1v_1}^*(x)\,\phi_{n_1}^*(\xi, x)\,P_\sigma\phi_{n_1}(\xi, x)\,u_{n_1v_1}(x)\,d\xi\,dx, \tag{6.11}$$

$$(P_{kl})_\rho = \int u_{n_kv_k}^*(x)\,\phi_{n_k}^*(\xi, x)\,P_\rho\phi_{n_l}(\xi, x)\,u_{n_lv_l}(x)\,d\xi\,dx. \tag{6.12}$$

The functions ϕ_{n_1} and $\phi_{n_k}^*$ describe the same electron state of the molecule, and they may therefore be regarded as identical, i.e., $n_1 = n_k$.

Let

$$\Phi_{l\sigma}(x) = \int \phi_{n_l}^*(\xi, x)P_\sigma\phi_{n_1}(\xi, x)d\xi, \tag{6.13}$$

$$\Phi_{l\rho}^*(x) = \int \phi_{n_l}^*(\xi, x)P_\rho\phi_{n_1}(\xi, x)d\xi. \tag{6.14}$$

Hence

$$(P_{11})_\sigma = \int u_{n_1v_1}^*(x)\Phi_{l\sigma}(x)u_{n_1v_1}(x)dx, \tag{6.15}$$

$$(P_{kl})_\rho = \int u_{n_lv_l}(x)\Phi_{l\rho}(x)u_{n_1v_k}^*(x)dx. \tag{6.16}$$

Inserting (6.15), (6.16) in the first term in (6.8) and separating the sums over the electron quantum numbers l and the nuclear quantum numbers v_l, we find

$$[(\beta_{\rho\sigma})_{k1}]_1 = \frac{1}{\hbar} \sum_l \sum_{v_l} \frac{\int u_{n_l v_l} \Phi_{l\rho} u^*_{n_1 v_k}\, dx \int u^*_{n_l v_l}\Phi_{l\sigma}u_{n_1 v_1}\,dx}{\omega^e_{l v_l} - \omega_e - i(q_{l v_l} - q_1)}. \tag{6.17}$$

This expression can be rewritten in the form

$$[(\beta_{\rho\sigma})_{k1}]_1 = \frac{1}{\hbar} \sum_l \int\int u^*_{n_1 v_k}(x)\Phi_{l\rho}(x)\left[\sum_{v_l} \frac{u_{n_l v_l}(x)u^*_{n_l v_l}(x')}{\omega^e_{l v_l} - \omega_e - i(q_{l v_l} - q_1)}\right] \times$$
$$\times\, \Phi_{l\sigma}(x')u_{n_1 v_1}(x')\,dx\,dx'. \tag{6.18}$$

When summing over v_l in (6.18), we should remember that the denominator in this expression depends on v_l:

$$\omega^e_{l v_l} - \omega_e - i(q_{l v_l} - q_1) = \bar\omega^e_l - \omega_e - i(\bar q_l - q_1) + \omega_{v_l} + i\Delta q_{v_l}; \tag{6.19}$$

$\bar\omega^e_l$ and $\bar q_l$ are some mean values of the corresponding quantities,* ω_{v_l} and Δq_{v_l} are the deviations from the mean, which depend on v_l. We may often take

$$|\omega_{v_l} + i\Delta q_{v_l}| \ll |\bar\omega^e_l - \omega_e - i(\bar q_l - q_1)|, \tag{6.20}$$

so that approximately

$$\sum_{v_l} \frac{u_{n_l v_l}(x)u^*_{n_l v_l}(x')}{\omega^e_{l v_l} - \omega_e - i(q_{l v_l} - q_1)} = \frac{\sum_{v_l} u_{n_l v_l}(x)u^*_{n_l v_l}(x')}{\bar\omega^e_l - \omega_e - i(\bar q_l - q_1)} +$$

$$+ \frac{\sum_{v_l}(\omega_{v_l} + i\Delta q_{v_l})u_{n_l v_l}(x)u^*_{n_l v_l}(x')}{[\bar\omega^e_l - \omega_e - i(\bar q_l - q_1)]^2} = \frac{\sum_{v_l} u_{n_l v_l}(x)u^*_{n_l v_l}(x')}{\bar\omega^e_l - \omega_e - i(\bar q_l - q_1)} + R(x,x'), \tag{6.21}$$

where $R(x,x')$ is of the order of $(\omega_{v_l} + i\Delta q_l)/[\bar\omega^e_l - \omega_e - i(\bar q_l - q_1)]$. As the functions $u_{n_l v_l}(x)$ are by definition a complete orthonormal set of wave functions, we have by the general rules of quantum mechanics (see [20])

$$\sum_{v_l} u_{n_l v_l}(x)u^*_{n_l v_l}(x') = \delta(x - x'). \tag{6.22}$$

This condition remains in force when the nuclear states have a continuous spectrum of eigenvalues.

---

* The quantities $\bar\omega^e_l$ and $\bar q_l$ are often attributed to the electron transition satisfying the Franck–Condon principle; in general, this interpretation is not quite valid, although the Franck–Condon transitions are indeed the most probable.

Using (6.22), we rewrite (6.18) in the form

$$[(\beta_{\rho\sigma})_{k1}]_1 = \frac{1}{\hbar} \sum_l \frac{\int u^*_{n_1 v_k}(x)\,\Phi_{l\rho}(x)\,\Phi_{l\sigma}(x)\,u_{n_1 v_1}(x)\,dx}{\bar{\omega}^e_l - \omega_e - i(\bar{q}_l - q_1)} + \bar{R}. \tag{6.23}$$

The second term in (6.8) can be similarly rewritten, and the additional term of the form R may be ignored, since the denominator is always $|\omega^e_l + \omega' - i(q_l - q_1)| \gg \omega_{v_l}$. We thus find for the scattering tensor

$$(\beta_{\rho\sigma})_{k1} = \int u^*_{n_1 v_k}(x) \left[\frac{1}{\hbar} \sum_l \frac{\Phi_{l\rho}(x)\,\Phi_{l\sigma}(x)}{\bar{\omega}^e_l - \omega_e - i(\bar{q}_l - q_1)} + \right.$$

$$\left. + \frac{\Phi_{l\rho}(x)\,\Phi_{l\sigma}(x)}{\bar{\omega}^e_l + \omega' - i(\bar{q}_l - q_1)} \right] u_{n_1 v_1}(x)\,dx + \bar{R}. \tag{6.24}$$

The expression in brackets,

$$\alpha_{\rho\sigma}(x) = \frac{1}{\hbar} \sum_l \frac{\Phi_{l\rho}(x)\,\Phi_{l\sigma}(x)}{\bar{\omega}^e_l - \omega_e - i(\bar{q}_l - q_1)} + \frac{\Phi_{l\rho}(x)\,\Phi_{l\sigma}(x)}{\bar{\omega}^e_l + \omega' - i(\bar{q}_l - q_1)}, \tag{6.25}$$

is a symmetrical tensor—the polarizability of a molecule. In general, $\alpha_{\rho\sigma}(x)$ is a complex-valued tensor, but for exciting light frequencies which are far from the electron absorption frequency, the term $i(\bar{q}_l - q_1)$ can be omitted from the denominator, which gives a real polarizability tensor.

Using (6.25), we obtain for the scattering tensor

$$(\beta_{\rho\sigma})_{k1} = \int u^*_{n_1 v_k}(x)\alpha_{\rho\sigma}(x)u_{n_1 v_1}(x)\,dx + \bar{R}. \tag{6.26}$$

When the exciting frequency is far from the electron absorption frequency, $\bar{R}$ can be ignored. Eq. (6.26) then gives the main result of Placzek's polarizability theory [7]: the scattering tensor for a transition between two nuclear states which belong to the same electron state of the molecule is equal to the matrix element of the polarizability tensor formed using the wave functions of the corresponding nuclear states. The limits of application of this theory are determined by (6.20). Note that since the polarizability tensor is symmetric, the scattering tensor is also symmetric.

The above derivation of Eq. (6.26) did not use any particular assumptions regarding the nuclear motion of the molecule in the intermediate electron states. It therefore remains valid when the intermediate electron states do not have a continuous vibrational structure.

Some properties of the scattering tensor in the electron absorption band can be established by the following approximative method. Suppose there is a single sharp resonance, so that one of the terms in the sum over v_l considerably differs in its magnitude from the other terms. Then,

$$\sum_{v_l} \frac{u_{n_1 v_l}(x) u_{n_1 v_l}^*(x')}{\omega_{l v_l}^e - \omega_e - i(q_{l v_l} - q_1)} = \frac{\left[\sum_{v_l} u_{n_1 v_l}(x) u_{n_1 v_l}^*(x')\right]}{\bar\omega_l^e - \omega_e - i(\bar q_l - q_1)} - \frac{u_{n_1 v_r}(x) u_{n_1 v_r}^*(x')}{\bar\omega_l^e - \omega_e - i(\bar q_l - q_1)} +$$

$$+ \frac{u_{n_1 v_r}(x) u_{n_1 v_r}^*(x')}{\omega_r^e - \omega_e - i(q_r - q_1)} + R_1(x_1 x') =$$

$$= \frac{\sum_{v_l} u_{n_1 v_l}(x) u_{n_1 v_l}^*(x')}{\bar\omega_l^e - \omega_e - i(\bar q_l - q_1)} + \frac{u_{n_1 v_r}(x) u_{n_1 v_r}^*(x')}{\omega_r^e - \omega_e - i(q_r - q_1)}. \tag{6.27}$$

We have thus isolated the term of the sum which causes the peaked resonance, and the polarizability theory is assumed to apply to all the other terms. In this case, for the additional term in (6.26) we have

$$\bar R = \frac{1}{\hbar} \frac{\int u_{n_1 v_r}(x) \Phi_{l\rho}(x) u_{n_1 v_k}^*(x) dx \int u_{n_1 v_r}^*(x) \Phi_{l\sigma}(x) u_{n_1 v_1}(x) dx}{\omega_r^e - \omega_e - i(q_r - q_1)}. \tag{6.28}$$

Since $\bar R$ is not a symmetric tensor, the total scattering tensor in the electron absorption band is not symmetric, either.

Under conditions in which the polarizability theory is applicable, Eq. (6.26) has the form

$$(\beta_{\rho\sigma})_{k1} = \int u_{v_k}^*(x) \alpha_{\rho\sigma}(x) u_{v_1}(x) dx, \tag{6.29}$$

where the functions $u_{v_k}^*(x)$ and $u_{v_1}(x)$ correspond to the same electronic state n_1. The invariants of the symmetric tensor (6.29), β_c and γ^2, determine the intensity and the depolarization of the Raman line (see §2) corresponding to the transition of the molecule from state 1 to state k.

For the same $1 \to k$ transition, according to (6.9), the absorption coefficient is determined by $[(P_e)_{k1}]^2$. For transitions between various nuclear states of the same electron state n_1, the matrix element $(P_e)_{k1}$ has the form

$$(P_e)_{k1} = \int u_{v_k}^*(x) \Phi_e(x) u_{v_1}(x) dx, \tag{6.30}$$

where

$$\Phi_e(x) = \int \phi_{n_1}^*(\xi, x) P_e \phi_{n_1}(\xi, x) d\xi.$$ (6.31)

The frequency of the $1 \to k$ transition generally lies in the infrared. It follows from (6.30) that the intensity in the infrared absorption spectra is determined by the matrix elements of the molecular dipole moment.

7. QUANTUM THEORY OF VIBRATIONAL TRANSITIONS

In the preceding section, a substantial simplification of the scattering tensor was achieved by separating between the electronic and the nuclear motion in the molecule. Further calculations, however, require explicit expressions for the nuclear wave functions. In the electronic ground state, the vibrational and the rotational motions of the molecule can be separated to fair approximation. We will therefore represent the nuclear wave function of the molecule in the electronic ground state as a product of a rotational and a vibrational function:

$$u_{v_k}(x_1, x_2, \ldots, x_n, \vartheta) = V_{v_k}(x_1, x_2, \ldots, x_n) \Theta_{v_k}(\vartheta).$$ (7.1)

The vibrational wave function V depends only on the relative nuclear coordinates x_i, and the rotational wave function Θ depends on the orientation of the molecule, i.e., on the Euler angles designated by the one letter ϑ. In this section we will consider pure vibrational transitions only. The nuclear coordinate x entering Eqs. (6.26)–(6.30) stands for the entire set of coordinates $x_1, x_2, \ldots, x_n$ corresponding to the ground state of the molecule which characterize the deviations of the respective coordinates from their equilibrium values. Rotational and vibration-rotational transitions will be considered in §8 and §16.

Application of Eq. (7.1) to excited electron states may involve certain difficulties if these states do not possess a discrete vibrational structure. In a number of cases, however, this aspect is of no significance, since the explicit form of the nuclear functions of the excited electron states is not used in calculations. On the other hand, the rotational motion can be separated from the general nuclear motion of the molecule even if the function $V(x)$ does not describe vibrations of the molecule.

In the simplest case, the vibrational motion of a polyatomic molecule can be represented as a combination of normal modes, each a function of one normal coordinates (see §10). The nuclear eigenfunction therefore can be written as a product of the vibrational eigenfunctions of the different normal modes,

$$V(x_1, x_2, \ldots, x_n) = V_1(x_1) V_2(x_2) \ldots V_n(x_n),$$ (7.2)

and the vibrational energy as a sum of the energies of these modes,

$$E_v = \sum_i \left(v_i + \frac{d_i}{2} \right) \hbar \omega_i , \tag{7.2a}$$

where d_i is the multiplicity of the mode ω_i. The functions $V_i(x_i)$ are the harmonic oscillator eigenfunctions. If ω_i is the eigenfunction of the i-th normal mode and $m_i \omega_i^2 x_i^2 / 2$ is its potential energy, the normalized wave function of this mode for the quantum state k is (see [20])

$$V_k(x_i) = \left(\frac{1}{\pi a_i^2} \right)^{1/4} \frac{1}{\sqrt{2^k k!}} e^{-x_i^2 / 2 a_i^2} H_k \left(\frac{x_i}{a_i} \right) . \tag{7.3}$$

Here

$$a_i^2 = \frac{\hbar}{m_i \omega_i} , \tag{7.4}$$

$H_n(\xi)$ are the Hermite polynomials, i.e., polynomials of degree n in ξ. They are defined by the equality (see, e.g., [20])

$$H_n(\xi) = (-1)^n e^{\xi^2} \frac{d^n e^{-\xi^2}}{d\xi^n} . \tag{7.5}$$

Some of the low-order Hermite polynomials are given here in explicit form:

$$H_0 = 1, \quad H_1 = 2\xi, \quad H_2 = 4\xi^2 - 2, \quad H_3 = 8\xi^3 - 12\xi . \tag{7.6}$$

We see from (7.3) and (7.5) that the vibrational eigenfunctions can be divided into even and odd with regard to the parity of the respective Hermite polynomials. The following recursion relations for the Hermite polynomials will be useful:

$$\xi H_n(\xi) = n H_{n-1}(\xi) + \tfrac{1}{2} H_{n+1}(\xi) , \tag{7.7}$$

$$\frac{dH_n}{d\xi} = 2n H_{n-1}(\xi) . \tag{7.8}$$

Let us apply the wave functions (7.3) to calculate the matrix elements of polarizability and dipole moment. Expanding $\alpha_{\rho\sigma}(x_1, x_2, \ldots, x_n)$ in (6.29) and $\Phi_e(x_1, x_2, \ldots, x_n)$ in (6.30) into power series in the normal coordinates, we get

$$\alpha_{\rho\sigma} = \alpha_{\rho\sigma}(0) + \sum_i \left(\frac{\partial \alpha_{\rho\sigma}}{\partial x_i} \right)_0 x_i + \frac{1}{2} \sum_{i,j} \left(\frac{\partial^2 \alpha_{\rho\sigma}}{\partial x_i \partial x_j} \right)_0 x_i x_j + \ldots , \tag{7.9}$$

$$\Phi_e = \Phi_e(0) + \sum_i \left(\frac{\partial \Phi_e}{\partial x_i} \right)_0 x_i + \frac{1}{2} \sum_{i,j} \left(\frac{\partial^2 \Phi_e}{\partial x_i \partial x_j} \right)_0 x_i x_j + \ldots . \tag{7.10}$$

Inserting these expansions in (6.29) and (6.30), we obtain expressions which contain integrals of the following types:

$$A_0 = \int V_{v_k}(x_i) V_{v_1}(x_i) dx_i, \tag{7.11}$$

$$A_1 = \int V_{v_k}(x_i) x_i V_{v_1}(x_i) dx_i, \tag{7.12}$$

$$A_2 = \int V_{v_k}(x_i) x_i^2 V_{v_1}(x_i) dx_i, \ldots \tag{7.13}$$

Seeing that the functions $V_{v_k}(x_i)$ are orthonormal, we conclude that integrals of the form A_0 do not vanish only when the vibrational quantum number of the i-th normal mode does not change ($v_k = v_1$); then $A_0 = 1$. Integrals of the form A_1 can be evaluated using the recursion formula (7.7). Inserting for $V_{v_k}(x_i)$ and $V_{v_1}(x_i)$ their expressions from (7.3), we get

$$A_1 = \left(\frac{1}{\pi a_i^2}\right)^{1/2} \frac{1}{\sqrt{2^{v_k} v_k!} \sqrt{2^{v_1} v_1!}} \int_{-\infty}^{\infty} e^{-x_i^2/a_i^2} x_i H_{v_k}\left(\frac{x_i}{a_i}\right) H_{v_1}\left(\frac{x_i}{v_i}\right) dx_i =$$

$$= \left(\frac{1}{\pi a_i^2}\right)^{1/2} \frac{1}{\sqrt{2^{v_k} v_k!} \sqrt{2^{v_1} v_1!}} \left[v_k a_i \int_{-\infty}^{\infty} e^{-x_i^2/a_i^2} H_{v_k-1}\left(\frac{x_i}{a_i}\right) H_{v_1}\left(\frac{x_i}{a_i}\right) dx_i + \right.$$

$$\left. + \frac{a_i}{2} \int_{-\infty}^{\infty} e^{-x_i^2/a_i^2} H_{v_k+1}\left(\frac{x_i}{a_i}\right) H_{v_1}\left(\frac{x_i}{a_i}\right) dx_i \right]. \tag{7.14}$$

This expression does not vanish in two cases only: if $v_k - 1 = v_1$, the first integral (see, e.g., [57]) gives

$$\int_{-\infty}^{\infty} e^{-x_i^2/a_i^2} H_{v_1}^2\left(\frac{x_i}{a_i}\right) dx_i = 2^{v_1} v_1! \sqrt{\pi} a_i, \tag{7.15}$$

and the second integral is zero; if $v_k + 1 = v_1$, the first integral is zero and the second is expressed by (7.15). Thus,

$$A_1 = \frac{a_i}{\sqrt{2}} \left[\sqrt{v_1 + 1}\, \delta_{v_k-1, v_1} + \sqrt{v_k + 1}\, \delta_{v_k+1, v_1} \right]. \tag{7.16}$$

The first term in this relation corresponds to $v_1 \to v_1 + 1$ transitions, and the second term to $v_1 \to v_1 - 1$ transitions. In either case, the vibrational quantum number changes by unity. In all the other transitions, this integral is zero.

Integrals of the form A_2 are reduced by recursion relation (7.7) to integrals of the form A_1. Acting along the same lines as before, we find (for $v_k \neq v_1$)

$$A_2 = \tfrac{1}{2} a_i^2 \left[\sqrt{(v_1 + 2)(v_1 + 1)} \delta_{v_k - 2, v_1} + \sqrt{(v_k + 2)(v_k + 1)} \delta_{v_k + 2, v_1} \right]. \quad (7.17)$$

Using the expressions for A_0, A_1, A_2, we can find $(\beta_{\rho\sigma})_{k1}$ and $(P_e)_{k1}$ for transitions of various types. For vibrational transitions of first and second order, to terms of second order in a_i, we obtain

$$(\beta_{\rho\sigma})_{v_1 + 1, v_1} = \sqrt{v_1 + 1} \left(\frac{\partial \alpha_{\rho\sigma}}{\partial x_i} \right)_0 \frac{a_i}{\sqrt{2}}, \quad (7.18)$$

$$(\beta_{\rho\sigma})_{v_1 - 1, v_1} = \sqrt{v_1} \left(\frac{\partial \alpha_{\rho\sigma}}{\partial x_i} \right)_0 \frac{a_i}{\sqrt{2}}, \quad (7.19)$$

$$(\beta_{\rho\sigma})_{v_1 + 2, v_1} = \tfrac{1}{2} \sqrt{(v_1 + 2)(v_1 + 1)} \left(\frac{\partial^2 \alpha_{\rho\sigma}}{\partial x_i^2} \right)_0 \frac{a_i^2}{2}, \quad (7.20)$$

$$(\beta_{\rho\sigma})_{v_1 - 2, v_1} = \tfrac{1}{2} \sqrt{v_1(v_1 - 1)} \left(\frac{\partial^2 \alpha_{\rho\sigma}}{\partial x_i^2} \right)_0 \frac{a_i^2}{2}, \quad (7.21)$$

$$(\beta_{\rho\sigma})_{v_1 + 1, v_1' + 1, v_1 v_1'} = \tfrac{1}{2} \sqrt{(v_1 + 1)(v_1' + 1)} \left(\frac{\partial^2 \alpha_{\rho\sigma}}{\partial x_i \partial x_j} \right)_0 \frac{a_i a_j}{2}, \quad (7.22)$$

$$(P_e)_{v_1 + 1, v_1} = \sqrt{v_1 + 1} \left(\frac{\partial \Phi_e}{\partial x_i} \right)_0 \frac{a_i}{\sqrt{2}}. \quad (7.23)$$

The calculation of the matrix elements of each transition involves series expansion of the polarizability (or the dipole moment) in powers of $a_i/\sqrt{2}$, which replaces the vibrational coordinate in Eqs. (7.9), (7.10). This variable has a simple physical meaning. Indeed, let us calculate the root mean square deviation of the coordinate x_i from the equilibrium value in a state with vibrational quantum number v_i. By definition,

$$\overline{(x_i^2)}_{v_i} = \int_{-\infty}^{\infty} V_{v_i} x_i^2 V_{v_i} dx_i . \quad (7.24)$$

Inserting $V_{v_i}(x_i)$ from (7.3) and acting along the same lines as in the calculation of A_2 (Eq. (7.17)), we find

$$\overline{(x_i^2)}_{v_i} = (2v_i + 1) \frac{a_i^2}{2} . \quad (7.25)$$

For the state $v_i = 0$ we thus have

$$\overline{(x_i^2)}_0 = \frac{a_i^2}{2},$$

i.e., (see (7.4))

$$\sqrt{\overline{(x_i^2)}_0} = \frac{a_i}{\sqrt{2}} = \sqrt{\frac{\hbar}{2m_i\omega_i}}. \tag{7.26}$$

Thus, the expansion parameter in (7.18)–(7.23) is a variable characterizing the root mean square deviation of the vibrational coordinate from its equilibrium value in the unperturbed (zeroth) vibrational state. This parameter is properly known as the *zero amplitude*.

Using Eqs. (7.18)–(7.22), we can find the intensity of the Raman scattering line corresponding to a given vibrational transition. We have already mentioned before that Eq. (6.7) for the scattering intensity is equivalent to the classical equation (2.16), with the quantum-mechanical expression (6.8) inserted for the scattering tensor. When the theory of polarizability applies, the scattering tensor is symmetric and for first-order (and second-order) lines corresponding to pure vibrational transitions it is expressed in terms of the first- (or second-) order derivatives of the polarizability tensor according to Eqs. (7.18)–(7.22). Having calculated the invariants $\beta_c(\alpha'_{\rho\sigma})$, $\gamma^2(\alpha'_{\rho\sigma})$, $\beta_c(\alpha''_{\rho\sigma})$ etc., of the derivative tensors of the polarizability tensor (primes denote differentiation with respect to the vibrational coordinate) in accordance with Eqs. (2.47), (2.48) for linearly polarized incident light, we find for the $v_i \rightarrow v_i + 1$ transition

$$dI(\beta_c) = \frac{I_e\omega'^4 F_k(\infty)}{15c^3} 5\beta_c(\alpha'_{\rho\sigma}) \sin^2\theta \frac{(v_i + 1)a_i^2}{2} d\Omega', \tag{7.27}$$

$$dI(\gamma^2) = \frac{I_e\omega'^4 F_k(\infty)}{15c^3} \frac{1}{2} \gamma^2(\alpha'_{\rho\sigma})(6 + \sin^2\theta) \frac{(v_i + 1)a_i^2}{2} d\Omega'. \tag{7.28}$$

For natural incident light and observation at right angles to the direction of incidence, we have from (3.19)

$$I_n\left(\frac{\pi}{2}\right) = \frac{I_e\omega'^4 F_k(\infty)}{60c^3} [10\beta_c(\alpha'_{\rho\sigma}) + 13\gamma^2(\alpha'_{\rho\sigma})] \frac{(v_i + 1)a_i^2}{2}. \tag{7.29}$$

Similar relations are obtained for the other transitions also.

Since in real systems the molecules are randomly distributed over the vibrational levels $v_i = 0, 1, 2, \ldots$, the observed intensities of the Raman scattering lines are obtained by summing expressions of the form (7.27)–(7.29) over all the possible levels v_i. As a result, the intensity of the Raman lines is a function of temperature. We will consider this temperature dependence for transitions of the first order.

In thermodynamic equilibrium, the number of molecules N_{v_i} in a state with energy E_{v_i} is expressed by Boltzmann's equation

$$N_{v_i} = CNg_{v_i}e^{-E_{v_i}/kT} . \tag{7.30}$$

Here g_{v_i} is the degeneracy of the i-th normal mode, v_i is the vibrational quantum number (for each normal model, v_i takes the values $v_i = 0, 1, 2, ...,$), T is the absolute temperature, k is Boltzmann's constant, N is the total number of molecules in the system.

In the harmonic approximation, all the normal modes are entirely independent and the vibrational energy is a sum of energies of the individual normal modes. Therefore, the statistical distribution of molecules over the vibrational numbers of a given normal mode is independent of the vibrational quantum numbers of other normal modes which the molecules happen to occupy at that instant. Thus, summation of (7.30) over all the vibrational numbers of the i-th normal mode gives the total number of molecules in the system in the left-hand side of the equality:

$$N = \sum_{v_i} N_{v_i} = CNg_{v_i} \sum_{v_i} e^{-E_{v_i}/kT} . \tag{7.31}$$

Using (7.30), we find

$$N_{v_i} = \frac{e^{-E_{v_i}/kT}}{\sum_{v_i} e^{-E_{v_i}/kT}} . \tag{7.32}$$

Inserting for the vibrational energy E_{v_i} in (7.32) its expression from

$$E_{v_i} = \hbar\omega_i(v_i + \tfrac{1}{2}) , \tag{7.33}$$

we get

$$N_{v_i} = \frac{e^{-\hbar\omega_i v_i/kT}}{\sum_{v_i} e^{-\hbar\omega_i v_i/kT}} . \tag{7.34}$$

The sum in the denominator is a geometrical progression, so that

$$\sum_{v_i} e^{-\hbar\omega_i v_i/kT} = (1 - e^{-\hbar\omega_i/kT})^{-1} . \tag{7.35}$$

Thus,

$$N_{v_i} = (1 - e^{-\hbar\omega_i/kT}) e^{-\hbar\omega_i v_i/kT} . \tag{7.36}$$

To find the intesity of the Raman line corresponding to the $v_i \to v_i + 1$ transition, we should multiply (7.27)–(7.29) by N_{v_i} and sum over all the v_i. This gives

$$I = K(1 - e^{-\hbar\omega_i/kT}) \sum_{v_i} (v_i + 1)e^{-\hbar\omega_i v_i/kT} = Kf_1(T)_{st} , \tag{7.37}$$

where K incorporates all the factors which are independent of the vibrational quantum number v_i, and $f_1(T)_{st}$ is the temperature factor for the first Stokes transition (it is the same for all the equations in (7.27)–(7.29)). The sum in (7.37) can be readily found by differentiating (7.35) with respect to $\kappa = \hbar\omega_i/kT$. This gives

$$\sum_{v_i} (v_i + 1)\, e^{-\hbar\omega_i v_i/kT} = (1 - e^{-\hbar\omega_i/kT})^{-2} . \tag{7.38}$$

Hence for the temperature factor

$$f_1(T)_{st} = \frac{1}{(1 - e^{-\hbar\omega_i/kT})} . \tag{7.39}$$

This temperature dependence is also characteristic, according to (7.23), of the absorption coefficient in the infrared at the vibrational frequency ω_i (fundamental frequency).

For the first anti-Stokes transition, $v_i \to v_i - 1$, we similarly have

$$f_1(T)_{ast} = \frac{e^{-\hbar\omega_i/kT}}{(1 - e^{-\hbar\omega_i/kT})} . \tag{7.40}$$

The intensities of the Stokes and the anti-Stokes lines according to (7.27)–(7.29) and (7.39), (7.40) differ only in the frequency factors ω'^4 and the temperature factors. Hence it follows, in particular, that the Stokes and the anti-Stokes lines have the same depolarization. The intensity ratio for anti-Stokes and Stokes lines is

$$\frac{I_{1\,ast}}{I_{1\,st}} = \frac{(\omega_e + \omega_i)^4}{(\omega_e - \omega_i)^4}\, e^{-\hbar\omega_i/kT} . \tag{7.41}$$

The above relations were derived assuming strictly harmonic vibrations in the molecule. The anharmonicity of the actual vibrations somewhat modifies the eigenfunctions and introduces a certain coupling between the normal modes: the normal modes are no longer independent. When the anharmonicity is low, however, this does not cause a noticeable change in the line intensities (some characteristic changes in spectra associated with the anharmonicity of vibrations are considered in §15). The temperature dependence of the line intensity is significantly affected by the fact that in the anharmonic case, the frequency of the $v_i \to v_i \pm 1$ transition depends on the quantum number v_i, since the spacing between levels is variable. The vibrational line as a result may have a fairly complex structure.

The temperature factors for the overtones can be readily found by differentiating Eq. (7.38) with respect to the parameter κ. For the $v_i \to v_i + 2$ transition, we have from (7.20)

$$f_2(T)_{st} = \frac{2}{(1 - e^{-\hbar\omega_i/kT})^2} . \tag{7.42}$$

Similarly, for the anti-Stokes overtone

$$f_2(T)_{ast} = \frac{2e^{-2\hbar\omega_i/kT}}{(1 - e^{-\hbar\omega_i/kT})^2} .$$

(7.43)

The intensity ratio for the anti-Stokes and the Stokes overtones is

$$\frac{I_{2ast}}{I_{2st}} = \frac{(\omega_e + 2\omega_i)^4}{(\omega_e - 2\omega_i)^4} e^{-2\hbar\omega_i/kT} .$$

(7.44)

We see that the overtones and the fundamental lines have different temperature dependences.

Various authors studied experimentally the temperature dependence of the intensities of Raman lines. The data for gases appear to be consistent with the above theory. These data, however, are very scanty [58]. In liquids, the temperature dependence of the Raman scattering intensity is markedly different from the theoretical prediction. This is undoubtedly the result of intermolecular interactions and their effect on line intensities and the distribution of molecules over vibrational levels. These topics are treated in §17. Crystals, alongside with lines whose intensity follows the theoretical temperature dependence, show lines with an anomalous temperature dependence (see §20).

Let us now consider the intensity of vibrational Raman scattering lines under conditions where the theory of polarizability does not apply. In the resonance region, according to (6.28), the line intensity is determined by a product of integrals of the form

$$I_{rk} = \int u_{n_1v_r}(x)\Phi_{l\rho}(x)u^*_{n_1v_k}(x)dx ,$$

(7.45)

$$I_{r1} = \int u^*_{n_1v_r}(x)\Phi_{l\sigma}(x)u_{n_1v_1}(x)dx .$$

(7.46)

Here $u^*_{n_1v_k}(x)$ and $u_{n_1v_1}(x)$ are the vibrational wave functions of the form (7.3), $x = x_i$ is one of the normal coordinates. Expanding the nuclear wave function of the excited electronic state $u_{n_1v_r}(x)$ in the vibrational functions of the electronic ground state, we have

$$u_{n_1v_r}(x) = \sum_j b_j u_{n_1v_j} = \sum_j b_j V_{v_j}(x) ,$$

(7.47)

where

$$b_j = \int u_{n_1v_r}(x)V_{v_j}(x)dx .$$

(7.48)

The functions $\Phi_{l\rho}(x)$ and $\Phi_{l\sigma}(x)$, as before, are expanded in powers of x:

$$\Phi_{l\rho}(x) = \Phi_{l\rho}(0) + \left(\frac{\partial\Phi_{l\rho}}{\partial x}\right)_0 x + \frac{1}{2}\left(\frac{\partial^2\Phi_{l\rho}}{\partial x^2}\right)_0 x^2 + \ldots, \tag{7.49}$$

$$\Phi_{l\sigma}(x) = \Phi_{l\sigma}(0) + \left(\frac{\partial\Phi_{l\sigma}}{\partial x}\right)_0 x + \frac{1}{2}\left(\frac{\partial^2\Phi_{l\sigma}}{\partial x^2}\right)_0 x^2 + \ldots \tag{7.50}$$

Inserting expansions (7.47)–(7.50) in (7.45), (7.46), seeing that the functions $V_{v_j}(x)$ are orthonormal, and using the recursion relations (7.7), we find

$$I_{rk} = \Phi_{l\rho}(0)b_{v_k} + \frac{a_i}{\sqrt{2}}\left(\frac{\partial\Phi_{l\rho}}{\partial x}\right)_0\left[b_{v_k+1}\sqrt{v_k+1} + b_{v_k-1}\sqrt{v_k}\right] +$$

$$+ \frac{a_i^2}{4}\left(\frac{\partial^2\Phi_{l\rho}}{\partial x^2}\right)_0\left[\sqrt{(v_k+2)(v_k+1)}\,b_{v_k+2} + \right.$$

$$\left. + \sqrt{v_k(v_k-1)}\,b_{v_k-2} + (2v_k+1)b_{v_k}\right] + \ldots, \tag{7.51}$$

$$I_{r1} = \Phi_{l\sigma}(0)b_{v_1}^* + \frac{a_i}{\sqrt{2}}\left(\frac{\partial\Phi_{l\sigma}}{\partial x}\right)_0\left[\sqrt{v_1+1}\,b_{v_1+1}^* + \sqrt{v_1}\,b_{v_1-1}^*\right] +$$

$$+ \frac{a_i^2}{4}\left(\frac{\partial^2\Phi_{l\sigma}}{\partial x^2}\right)_0\left[\sqrt{(v_1+2)(v_1+1)}\,b_{v_1+2}^* + \right.$$

$$\left. + \sqrt{v_1(v_1-1)}\,b_{v_1-2}^* + (2v_1+1)b_{v_1}^*\right] + \ldots. \tag{7.52}$$

As in the expansion of polarizability, this expression is a power series in the small parameter $a_i/\sqrt{2}$. In what follows, we will limit the discussion to the linear terms only, and thus proceed to evaluate the integrals I_{r1}, I_{rk} for the main transitions in this approximation. To simplify the notation, we write in what follows

$$\Phi_\rho = \Phi_{l\rho}(0), \quad \Phi_\rho' = (\partial\Phi_{l\rho}/\partial x)_0, \quad \text{etc.}$$

For the transition $v_1 = 0 \to v_k = 1$ (the first Stokes transition) we have

$$(I_{rk})_{01} = \Phi_\rho b_1 + \frac{a_i}{\sqrt{2}}\Phi_\rho'(\sqrt{2}b_2 + b_0), \tag{7.53}$$

$$(I_{r1})_{01} = \Phi_\sigma b_0^* + \frac{a_i}{\sqrt{2}} \Phi_\sigma' b_1^* . \tag{7.54}$$

Multiplying (7.53) and (7.54) and inserting the product in (6.28), we find, retaining only terms linear in a_i,

$$\bar{R}_{01} = \frac{\Phi_\rho \Phi_\sigma b_1 b_0^* + \dfrac{a_i}{\sqrt{2}} [\Phi_\rho \Phi_\sigma' b_1 b_1^* + \Phi_\sigma \Phi_\rho' (\sqrt{2}\, b_0^* b_2 + b_0 b_0^*)]}{\hbar [\omega_r^e - \omega_e - i(q_r - q_1)]_{01}} . \tag{7.55}$$

The tensor $\bar{R}_{01}$ can be decomposed into a symmetric and a skew-symmetric component:

$$\bar{R}_{01} = (\bar{R}_{01})_s + (\bar{R}_{01})_a , \tag{7.56}$$

$$(\bar{R}_{01})_s = \frac{\Phi_\rho \Phi_\sigma b_1 b_0^* + \dfrac{a_i}{2\sqrt{2}} [\Phi_\rho \Phi_\sigma' + \Phi_\sigma \Phi_\rho'](b_1 b_1^* + \sqrt{2}\, b_0^* b_2 + b_0 b_0^*)}{\hbar [\omega_r^e - \omega_e - i(q_r - q_1)]_{01}} , \tag{7.57}$$

$$(\bar{R}_{01})_a = \frac{a_i [\Phi_\rho \Phi_\sigma' - \Phi_\sigma \Phi_\rho'] (b_1 b_1^* - \sqrt{2}\, b_0^* b_2 - b_0 b_0^*)}{2\sqrt{2}\hbar [\omega_r^e - \omega_e - i(q_r - q_1)]_{01}} . \tag{7.58}$$

For the transition $v_1 = 1 \rightarrow v_k = 0$ (the first anti-Stokes transition), we similarly find

$$(\bar{R}_{10})_s = \frac{\Phi_\rho \Phi_\sigma b_0 b_1^* + \dfrac{a_i}{2\sqrt{2}} [\Phi_\rho \Phi_\sigma' + \Phi_\sigma \Phi_\rho'](b_1 b_1^* + \sqrt{2}\, b_0 b_2^* + b_0 b_0^*)}{\hbar [\omega_r^e - \omega_e - i(q_r - q_1)]_{10}} , \tag{7.59}$$

$$(\bar{R}_{10})_a = \frac{a_i [\Phi_\rho \Phi_\sigma' - \Phi_\sigma \Phi_\rho'] (b_0 b_0^* + \sqrt{2}\, b_0 b_2^* - b_1 b_1^*)}{2\sqrt{2}\, \hbar [\omega_r^e - \omega_e - i(q_r - q_1)]_{10}} . \tag{7.60}$$

Finally, for the second-order transition $v_1 = 0 \rightarrow v_k = 2$, we have

$$(\bar{R}_{02})_s = \frac{\Phi_\rho \Phi_\sigma b_2 b_0^* + \dfrac{a_i}{2\sqrt{2}} [\Phi_\rho \Phi_\sigma' + \Phi_\sigma \Phi_\rho'] (b_2 b_1^* + \sqrt{3}\, b_0^* b_3 + \sqrt{2} b_0^* b_1)}{\hbar [\omega_r^e - \omega_e - i(q_r - q_1)]_{02}} , \tag{7.61}$$

$$(\bar{R}_{02})_a = \frac{a_i [\Phi_\rho \Phi_\sigma' - \Phi_\sigma \Phi_\rho'] (b_2 b_1^* - \sqrt{3}\, b_0^* b_3 - \sqrt{2}\, b_0^* b_1)}{2\sqrt{2}\, \hbar [\omega_r^e - \omega_e - i(q_r - q_1)]_{02}} . \tag{7.62}$$

It follows from the above expressions that in case of a sharp peaked resonance, the scattered radiation contains an antisymmetric component whose angular dependence and polarization properties (see §2) markedly differ from those of the symmetrical component. The intensity of the antisymmetric scattered component according to (6.8) and (2.49), (3.19) is

$$dI(\beta_a) = \frac{I_e \omega'^4 F_k(\infty)}{15c^3} \frac{5}{2} \beta_a (1 + \cos^2\theta) d\Omega', \tag{7.63}$$

$$I_n\left(\frac{\pi}{2}\right) = \frac{I_e \omega'^4 F_k(\infty)}{6c^3} \frac{5}{6} \beta_a, \tag{7.64}$$

where for the $0 \to 1$ transition (see (2.44))

$$\beta_a = \frac{a_i^2 \, (b_1 b_1^* - \sqrt{2} \, b_0^* b_2 - b_0 b_0^*) \, (b_1 b_1^* - \sqrt{2} \, b_0 b_2^* - b_0 b_0^*)}{4\hbar^2 [(\omega_r^e - \omega_e)^2 + (q_r - q_1)^2]_{01}} \times$$

$$\times [(\Phi_1 \Phi_2' - \Phi_2 \Phi_1') (\Phi_2^* \Phi_1^{*'} - \Phi_1^* \Phi_2^{*'}) + (\Phi_1 \Phi_3' - \Phi_3 \Phi_1') (\Phi_3^* \Phi_1^{*'} - \Phi_1^* \Phi_3^{*'}) +$$

$$+ (\Phi_2 \Phi_3' - \Phi_3 \Phi_2') (\Phi_3^* \Phi_2^{*'} - \Phi_2^* \Phi_3^{*'})]. \tag{7.65}$$

Similar expressions can be readily derived for other transitions. Experimental observations of antisymmetric scattering would be of considerable interest.* Note that for certain types of vibrations, symmetry considerations allow only those modes which are associated with the skew-symmetric part of the scattering tensor.

Comparison of the expressions for Stokes and anti-Stokes transition components shows that the intensity ratio of the corresponding lines does not follow Eq. (7.41) in the resonance region. If we limit the discussion to the transitions $0 \to 1$ and $1 \to 0$ only, the intensity ratio is given by

$$\frac{I_{ast}}{I_{st}} = \frac{(\omega_e + \omega_i)^4 \, [(\omega_r^e - \omega_e)^2 + (q_r - q_1)^2]_{st}}{(\omega_e - \omega_i)^4 \, [(\omega_r^e - \omega_e)^2 + (q_r - q_1)^2]_{ast}} e^{-\hbar\omega_i/kT}. \tag{7.66}$$

The resonance regions for the Stokes and the anti-Stokes lines do not coincide, and the intensity ratio of these lines may therefore markedly vary depending on the position of ω_e relative to the frequency of the resonance level. In particular, the anti-Stokes line may be much stronger than the Stokes line.

In the resonance region, the intensity ratio of lines corresponding to transitions

---

* The antisymmetry of the Raman scattering tensor for electron transitions was discovered in [59].

of different orders is also substantially different from that observed when the theory of polarizability was applicable. Comparison of (7.57), (7.58) with (7.61), (7.62) shows that the intensities of first- and second-order lines in the resonance region have the same dependence on the small parameter a_i. The difference in the intensities of lines of different order is associated, first, with the relationship between the coefficients b_0, b_1, b_2 and, second, with the resonance denominators. Therefore, in the resonance region, second-order lines may easily prove to be of higher intensity than the first-order lines (note, however, that this is by no means always so).

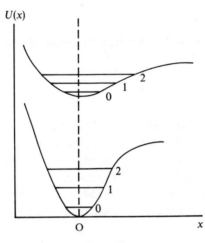

Figure 17

Potential energy profiles in electronic ground state and excited state.

As an example, consider the case of an electronic ground state and excited state with potential energy minima aligned precisely one above the other (Figure 17). The nuclear wave function of the excited state is

$$u_{n_l v_r}(x) = V_{v_r}(x),$$ (7.67)

i.e., it differs from the corresponding ground-state function only in the value of the parameter, which we designate a_i'. If the resonance level is even, the odd coefficients $b_1, b_3, \ldots$ vanish according to (7.48); if the level is odd, the even coefficients $b_0, b_2, \ldots$ are zero. We thus have:

even resonance level

$$(\bar{R}_{01})_s = \frac{a_i [\Phi_\rho \Phi_\sigma' + \Phi_\sigma \Phi_\rho'] (b_0 b_0^* + \sqrt{2} b_0^* b_2)}{2\sqrt{2} \hbar [\omega_r^e - \omega_e - i(q_r - q_1)]_{01}},$$ (7.68)

$$(\bar{R}_{02})_s = \frac{\Phi_\rho \Phi_\sigma b_2 b_0^*}{\hbar \left[\omega_r^e - \omega_e - i(q_r - q_1)\right]_{02}},\tag{7.69}$$

odd resonance level

$$(\bar{R}_{01})_s = \frac{a_i \left[\Phi_\rho \Phi_\sigma' + \Phi_\sigma \Phi_\rho'\right] b_1 b_1^*}{2\sqrt{2}\,\hbar \left[\omega_r^e - \omega_e - i(q_r - q_1)\right]_{01}},\tag{7.70}$$

$$(\bar{R}_{02})_s = 0.\tag{7.71}$$

Ignoring the resonance denominators, we have for the case of an even resonance level

$$\frac{(\bar{R}_{02})_s}{(\bar{R}_{01})_s} \sim \frac{1}{a_i} \gg 1,$$

whereas in the case of an odd resonance level the component $(\bar{R}_{02})_s$ is zero. The resonance denominators lead to a more complex intensity ratio for lines of different orders, which may vary substantially as ω_e moves into the resonance region.

This theoretical analysis provides a straightforward explanation of the experimental results obtained by Shorygin and Ivanova [54], who observed a substantial increase in the overtone intensity in the resonance region (see §5).

CHAPTER II

Raman Spectra and Molecular Structure

8. ROTATIONAL RAMAN SPECTRA

Rotational Raman spectra provide information for calculating the moments of inertia of molecules, which in the simplest cases yield the geometrical parameters of the molecule, i.e., the bond lengths and the bond angles. In some cases, the spin and the statistics of the nuclei can also be determined. In the present section, we consider pure rotational Raman spectra. The rotational structure of vibrational bands is treated in §16.

To first approximation, a molecule can be treated as a spinning rigid body. Its properties are described by the inertia tensor. This tensor can be transformed to the principal axes, and the corresponding three moments of inertia $\mathscr{I}_A$, $\mathscr{I}_B$, $\mathscr{I}_C$ about the principal axes are appropriately called the principal moments of intertia of the molecule.

The values of the three principal moments of inertia completely specify the properties of rigid rotation of a molecule. We accordingly distinguish between four different types of molecules:

1) linear molecules (one of the principal moments of inertia is zero, $\mathscr{I}_A = 0$, $\mathscr{I}_B = \mathscr{I}_C$);

2) symmetric top molecules (two principal moments of inertia are equal, $\mathscr{I}_A \neq \mathscr{I}_B = \mathscr{I}_C$);

3) asymmetric top molecules (all the three principal moments of inetria are different);

4) spherical top molecules (all the three principal moments of inertia are equal).

Spherical top molecules do not produce rotational Raman spectra. On the other hand, asymmetric top molecules have hardly been studied so far, since the common practice is to reduce the problem to one involving a symmetric top molecule. In the following, we will therefore consider mainly molecules of the first two types.

Substantial simplification in the manipulations with rigid spinning tops is attained by changing over to conservative quantities. These are the angular momentum M and the rotational energy E. In accordance with the laws of quantum mechanics (see, e.g., [20]), the angular momentum and the rotational energy are quantized and may take on a discrete set of values only. The square of the angular momentum is described by the quantum condition

$$M^2 = \hbar^2 J (J + 1), \tag{8.1}$$

where J is the rotational quantum number,

$$J = 0, 1, 2, 3, \ldots . \tag{8.2}$$

The projection of the angular momentum on some preferred direction in space is also quantized. The quantization axis may coincide, say, with the direction of an external electric or magnetic field. Let the quantization axis in a fixed system of coordinates be z. Then, from quantum mechanics,

$$M_z = \hbar m, \tag{8.3}$$

where the "magnetic" quantum number m takes on the values

$$m = 0, \pm 1, \pm 2, \ldots, \pm J . \tag{8.4}$$

For linear molecules, the rotational energy is related by a very simple expression to the angular momentum. Indeed, a linear molecule spins around an axis perpendicular to the molecule center line, which passes through the center of mass of the molecule. The angular momentum M is directed along the rotation axis and is given by

$$M = \mathscr{I}\Omega , \tag{8.5}$$

where Ω is the angular rotation velocity. The rotational energy is

$$E = \frac{1}{2} \mathscr{I}\Omega^2 = \frac{1}{2\mathscr{I}} M^2 . \tag{8.6}$$

Here $\mathscr{I} = \mathscr{I}_a$ is the moment of inertia about the rotation axis, expressed by

$$\mathscr{I} = \sum_i m_i r_i^2 , \tag{8.7}$$

where r_i is the distance of the i-th atomic nucleus of mass m_i from the center of mass of the molecule.

Inserting the square of the angular momentum from (8.1) in (8.6), we get

$$E = \frac{h^2}{2\mathscr{I}} J(J + 1) = BJ(J + 1).$$ (8.8)

Here

$$B = \frac{h^2}{2\mathscr{I}} = \frac{h}{8\pi^2 c\mathscr{I}} \, \text{cm}^{-1} = \frac{2.80 \cdot 10^{-39}}{\mathscr{I}} \, \text{cm}^{-1}$$ (8.9)

is called the *rotational constant* of the molecule. To each value of the rotational quantum number J correspond $2J + 1$ values of the quantum number m, so that the rotational levels are always $(2J + 1)$-fold degenerate.

Eq. (8.8) was derived assuming the molecule to be a perfect rigid body. However, the centrifugal forces in a spinning molecule slightly alter the distance between the nuclei. A more precise formula, which makes allowance for this increase in the internuclear distances, has the form (see, e.g., [60])

$$E = BJ(J + 1) - DJ^2(J + 1)^2,$$ (8.10)

where D is a constant which characterizes the non-rigidity of the molecule.

For symmetric top molecules, the rotational energy is given by a more complex expression:

$$E = \frac{1}{2\mathscr{I}_B}(M_x^2 + M_y^2) + \frac{1}{2\mathscr{I}_A}M_z^2,$$ (8.11)

where M_z is the projection of the angular momentum on the quantization axis, (i.e., on the symmetry axis of the molecule). This equation can be written in a form more suitable for quantization:

$$E = \frac{1}{2\mathscr{I}_B}M^2 + \frac{1}{2}\left(\frac{1}{\mathscr{I}_A} - \frac{1}{\mathscr{I}_B}\right)M_z^2.$$ (8.12)

Inserting for M^2 and M_z their quantum-mechanical expressions from (8.1) and (8.3), we find

$$E = \frac{h^2}{2\mathscr{I}_B}J(J + 1) + \frac{h^2}{2}\left(\frac{1}{\mathscr{I}_A} - \frac{1}{\mathscr{I}_B}\right)K^2.$$ (8.13)

Here $K = 0, \pm 1, \pm 2, \ldots, \pm J$. Introducing the rotational constants

$$A = \frac{h}{8\pi^2 c\mathscr{I}_A}, \quad B = \frac{h}{8\pi^2 c\mathscr{I}_B},$$ (8.14)

we find for the rotational energy

$$E = BJ(J + 1) + (A - B)K^2.$$ (8.15)

The second term in this expression depends on the quantum number K, which determines the projection of the angular momentum on the symmetry axis of the molecule. Since for a given J, the number $|K|$ may take on $J + 1$ values, each rotational level is split into $J + 1$ sublevels.

In the case of a deformable top, the expression for the rotational energy contains small correction terms:

$$E = BJ(J + 1) + (A - B) K^2 - D_J J^2 (J + 1)^2 - D_{JK} J (J + 1) K^2 - D_K K^4 .$$

(8.16)

Here D_J, D_{JK}, D_K are constants that are small compared to A and B.

Note that for a spherical top, Eq. (8.15) coincides with the expression for the rotational energy of a linear molecule, (8.8). However, the degeneracy of the energy levels is substantially different in these two cases. The rotational levels of a linear molecule are $(2J + 1)$-fold degenerate, since for a given J there are $2J + 1$ allowed values of the projection of the angular momentum on a fixed quantization axis in space. These projections correspond to different values of the magnetic quantum number m. For a spherical top, J and m have the same meaning as before, but a third quantum number K is added, which gives the projection of the angular momentum on a moving quantization axis linked with the molecule. The number K may also take $2J + 1$ values for a given J, and each rotational energy level of a spherical top is therefore $(2J + 1)^2$-fold degenerate.

To find the intensities and the selection rules in the rotational Raman spectra, we have to calculate the matrix elements of polarizability for the corresponding transitions (see §6). We thus require the polarizability components α_{ik} in a fixed system of coordinates. These are related to the polarizability components $\alpha_{i'k'}$ in the molecule's moving axes by the following equalities (see §3):

$$\alpha_{ik} = \sum_{i'k'} \alpha_{i'k'} \cos (i', i) \cos (k', k) .$$

(8.17)

The line intensities in a pure rotational spectrum are determined by the matrix elements of these polarizability components, formed using the rotational eigenfunctions $\psi_{J,m}$. The polarizabilities $\alpha_{i'k'}$ in the moving axes are independent of the angular variables, i.e., the calculations reduce to finding the matrix elements of the products of direction cosines of the form

$$H_{J',K'}^{J,K} = \int \psi_{J',K'}^* \cos(i', i) \cos (k', k) \psi_{J,K} \, d\tau .$$

(8.18)

The matrix elements (8.18) vanish if the integrand is an odd function of the variables of integration. The rotational eigenfunctions have the same parity as the rotational quantum number J, i.e., $(- 1)^J$. The transitions $J \to J'$ corresponding to non-zero matrix elements (8.18) are thus readily found by analyzing the parity of the various products of the direction cosines. The differences of the rotational quantum numbers

$\Delta J = J' - J$ for which the matrix elements (8.18) do not vanish are listed in Table 2. They determine the selection rules in pure rotational Raman spectra for various types of rotating molecules.

Table 2

SELECTION RULES IN PURE ROTATIONAL RAMAN
SPECTRA [61]

Type of molecule	Selection rule $(J' + J'' \geq 0)$
Linear	$\Delta J = 0, \pm 2$
Symmetric top	$\Delta J = 0, \pm 1, \pm 2; \Delta K = 0$
Spherical top	$\Delta J = 0$
Asymmetric top	$\Delta J = 0, \pm 1, \pm 2$

Note that the scalar part of the polarizability tensor is spherically symmetric, and is therefore independent of the spatial orientation of the molecule. The matrix elements of this part of the polarizability tensor therefore vanish in all transitions which involve a change in the rotational quantum number. The polarization of the rotational line is consequently determined by the properties of the anisotropic part of the polarizability tensor (see §2), i.e., these lines are depolarized.

The expression for the frequency change $|\Delta v|$ in the rotational spectra of linear molecules is obtained from the equality

$$|\Delta v| = E(J') - E(J), \tag{8.19}$$

where the rotational energy E should be inserted from (8.10) and $J' = J + 2$ (the rotational constant is expressed in cm^{-1}). This gives

$$|\Delta v| = (4B - 6D)\left(J + \frac{3}{2}\right) - 8D\left(J + \frac{3}{2}\right)^3. \tag{8.20}$$

Since $D \ll B$, we have to fair approximation

$$|\Delta v| = 4B\left(J + \frac{3}{2}\right). \tag{8.21}$$

The rotational Raman spectra of linear molecules are thus a succession of almost equally spaced lines arranged on either side of the exciting line. Specimen photographs of these spectra are shown in Figure 18. Since for all lines of this spectrum $\Delta J = 2$, we have only one branch, the S-branch.*

---

* The lines in the rotational spectrum corresponding to $\Delta J = +2, +1, 0, -1, -2$ are generally designated as S, R, Q, P, O.

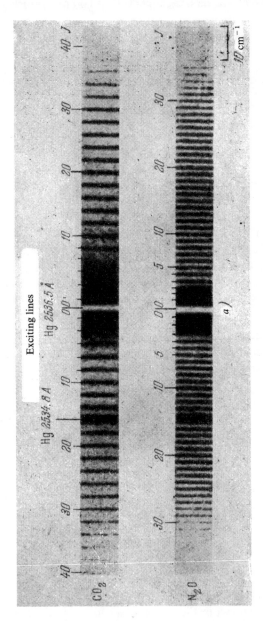

Figure 18

Rotational spectra of molecules:

a Linear molecules. The exciting line (2537 Å) is absorbed by mercury vapor.

b Symmetrical top molecules.

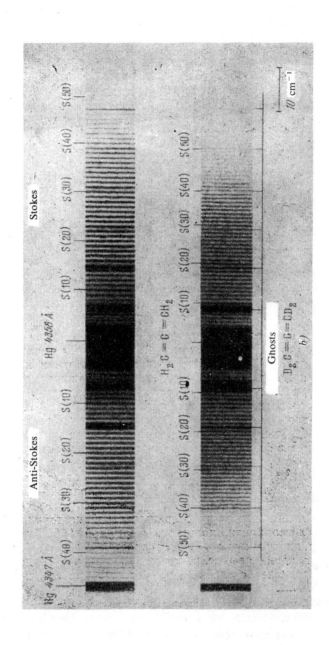

Since the rotational lines are almost uniformly spaced, the quantum number J can be readily found from (8.21) for any rotational line by measuring its distance from the exciting line. Note that the simplicity and the high reliability of the identification of the rotational lines makes Raman spectra particularly attractive compared to other complex spectra.

Once the quantum numbers of the rotational lines have been determined, the constants B and D in Eq. (8.20) can be found with higher precision. To this end, the plot of $v' = |\Delta v|/(J + \frac{3}{2})$ vs. $(J + \frac{3}{2})^2$ is drawn (Figure 19). The vertical intercept gives the value of $4B - 6D$, and the slope of the line gives the value of $8D$.

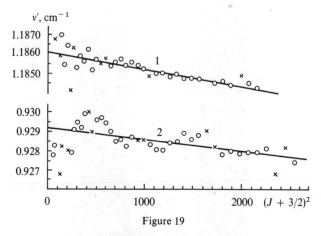

Figure 19

Graphs for the determination of the constants B and D:

1) allene,   2) allene-d_4.

If the rotational constant B is known, we can apply Eq. (8.9) to calculate the moment of inertia of the molecule $\mathscr{I}$. For the simplest molecules, when all r_i are equal, the moment of inertia is uniquely determined by the interatomic distance r_i; it is found from Eq. (8.7). If the r_i take different values, $\mathscr{I}$ alone is not sufficient to determine all the r_i. The difficulty can be partly avoided in the analysis of hydrocarbons by taking the spectra of deuterized compounds. Assuming that the interatomic distances do not change when D is substituted for H, we obtain another set of values for the moments of inertia and hence additional equations for r_i. The assumption of equal C—H and C—D distances (when using the parameter r_0, see below), however, is valid only to within about 0.002Å (see [62]). Moreover, in most cases, the data on deuterized derivatives are still insufficient for determining all the r_i. Therefore, some r_i values often have to be borrowed from data obtained for other molecules with similar bonds (mostly, data obtained by rf spectroscopy).

The rotational constant B and the moment of inertia $\mathscr{I}$ derived from rotational Raman spectra do not correspond to the equilibrium position of the nuclei r_e, but rather to the lowest vibrational state associated with the zero vibration of the molecule. The difference between the r_0 obtained from the rotational spectrum and the r_e falls within the limits of measurement error (about $0.001\,Å$). However, in diatomic molecules, N_2 for instance, we have $r_0 = 1.1000_6 \pm 0.0001\,Å$, $r_e = 1.0975_8 \pm 0.0001\,Å$, i.e., the difference $r_0 - r_e$ is significantly measureable.

For symmetric top molecules, the analysis of the spectra is more involved, since the rotational levels depend on two quantum numbers J and K, and the selection rules (see Table 2) allow a greater number of transitions than in linear molecules. Each value of K corresponds to two series of equally spaced lines, one with $\Delta J = 1$ (the R branch) and the other with $\Delta J = 2$ (the S branch), arranged on either side of the exciting line. Since the rotational levels with different K for a rigid symmetric top have exactly the same profile, the corresponding lines of the branches with different K coincide. Thus, only two branches, S and R, can actually be observed in the spectrum. For the frequency shift we have

$$|\Delta v| = (4B - 6D_J - 4D_{J,K}K^2)(J + \tfrac{3}{2}) - 8D_J(J + \tfrac{3}{2})^3 \qquad (8.22)$$

for the S branch, and

$$|\Delta v| = (2B - 2D_{J,K}K^2)(J + 1) - 4D_J(J + 1)^3 \qquad (8.23)$$

for the R branch. To first approximation, the constants D_J can be dropped. The lines of the R branch with even J are seen to coincide with the lines of the S branch.

The experimentally observed spectra are analyzed as in the case of linear molecule. The various data are summarized in Stoicheff's review [63]. Note that most authors studied only the S-branches, since the lines of the R-branches were too weak to allow reliable measurements.

The experimental material relating to the rotational Raman spectra is still highly limited. Conventional spectral instruments will measure only the rotational spectra of the simplest gases (N_2, O_2, H_2, CO_2). The spectra of these gases were obtained by Rasetti and co-workers [64, 65] (see also [63]) back in 1929. Subsequently, new measurement techniques had to be developed for observing rotational Raman spectra in gases at relatively low pressure. High dispersion and resolution were required to resolve the rotational structure. All this, however, drastically lowered the intensity of the lines. The recent advances in measurements of the rotational Raman spectra, mainly due to Stoicheff and co-workers (see [63]), were largely attributed to their success in stepping up the scattered intensity.

The experimental techniques concerned with the rotational Raman spectra are described in detail in [63]. The main experimental problem is how to obtain spectra with narrow lines. The observed line widths in Raman spectra are determined by three principal factors: the width of the instrumental function, the width of the exciting line, and the intrinsic width of the Raman line associated with the scattering gas pressure. Modern instruments with dispersions of $1.25\,Å/mm$, spectral bandwidths of 0.2 cm^{-1}, and exciting line widths of about 0.2 cm^{-1} (the 4358Å Hg line) have a practical resolution limit of about 0.4 cm^{-1} at gas pressures from 0.5 to 2 atm. This resolution limit for linear molecules corresponds to a rotational constant $B = 0.1$ cm^{-1} or to a moment of inertia $\mathscr{I} = 280 \cdot 10^{-40}$ g $\cdot$ cm^2.

The bond lengths derived from the rotational Raman spectra are of obvious interest, despite the limited scope of experimental data, as they enable us to trace the effect of molecular structure on bond length. Note that Raman scattering is applicable to both polar and apolar molecules. The data obtained by this method therefore constitute a significant addition to the data of microwave spectroscopy, which apply only to polar molecules. A detailed summary of the experimental findings will be found in [63], and we therefore consider some examples only.

Table 3 lists the bond lengths of some double-bond (unsaturated) hydrocarbons. These data clearly show that the C=C double bond is shorter when it adjoins another double bond. Further bond shortening is observed when the double bond is situated between two other double bonds, as in butatriene, say.

Table 3

GEOMETRICAL PARAMETERS OF DOUBLE-BOND HYDROCARBON MOLECULES

Compound	Parameter	Bond length (Å) and bond angle
Ethylene	C=C	1.339
	C—H	1.086
	∠HCH	117°34′
trans-Butadiene-1,3*	C=C	1.337
	C—C	1.464
	∠C=C—C	123.2°
Allene	C=C=	1.309
	C—H	1.07
	∠HCH	177°
Butatriene	=C=C=	1.284
	C=C=	1.309
	C—H	1.07

* From the data of [74].

The results regarding the effect of nearby bonds on bond length are borne out by the findings obtained for triple-bond compounds (Table 4). It is clear from the table that the length of a C—C bond is markedly contracted if it is conjugate to a triple bond. If the single bond is located between two triple bonds, the contraction is even greater. We see from Table 4 that the length of the C—C bond hardly depends on the particular atom attached to the triple bond, whether carbon or nitrogen. On the other hand, the length of the C≡C triple bond hardly changes when the conjugate C—H bond is replaced with C—C. A certain effect of the atom attached to the adjoining bond is observed for halogenated hydrocarons [66].

Table 4

BOND LENGTHS (Å) IN TRIPLE-BOND MOLECULES

Compound	C≡C	C≡N	C—C	C—H
Ethane*	—	—	1.543	1.095
Acetylene H—C≡C—H	1.207	—	—	1.061
Dimethylacetylene** H_3C—C≡C—CH_3	1.207	—	1.460	1.097
Diacetylene H—C≡C—C≡C—H	1.205	—	1.376	1.046
Dicyanogen N≡C—C≡N	—	1.157†	1.380	—

(Ethane structure:)

$$\begin{array}{c} H \quad\quad H \\ H-C-C-H \\ H \quad\quad H \end{array}$$

* From the data of [69].
** Largely based on the data of [70] for the microwave spectrum of methylacetylene.
† From the microwave spectrum of cyanoacetylene [71].

Table 5 lists data for two ring systems. Note that the rotational Raman spectra of benzene do not provide a direct proof in favor of any of the alternative models with the symmetries D_{6h}, D_{3h}, C_{6h}, or D_{3d}, since all these models are classified as a symmetric top molecule and their rotational spectra are identical. The authors of [67, 68] in their study of the rotational spectra of C_6H_6, C_6D_6, and the symmetric $C_6H_3D_3$ proceeded from the widely accepted model with D_{6h} symmetry. The resulting bond length was found to fall between the C—C and C≡C bond lengths.

In the case of triazine, the rotational structure of the spectrum was analyzed assuming a planar molecule of D_{3h} symmetry, in accordance with X-ray diffraction findings. The molecules of s-triazine and s-triazine-d_3 were studied. The C—H distance was taken equal to 1.084Å. The triazine ring was found to have a distorted

Table 5

BOND LENGTHS IN RING MOLECULES

Compound	Bond	Bond length, Å
Benzene		
	C—C, C=C	1.397
	C—H	1.084
Triazine 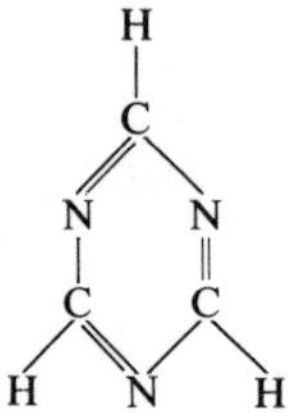	C—N	1.338
	C—H	1.084

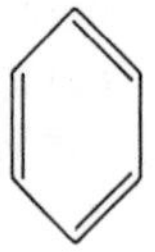

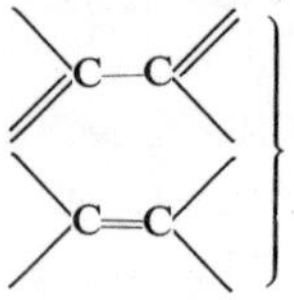

hexagonal structure with

$$\angle \ CNC = 113.2°, \qquad \angle \ NCN = 126.8°.$$

It follows from Tables 2–5 that the C—H bond length also depends on vicinal factors, i.e., the conjugate bonds, but this dependence is less pronounced than for the C—C bonds.

The experimental material reveals an obvious effect of the conjugate bonds on bond lengths (the results obtained by other methods are discussed, e.g., in [72]). The effect of the atom at the end of the conjugate bond is less pronounced, at least in the case of hydrocarbons. Note that the effect of a conjugate double bond, although noticeable, is by no means as marked as it was usually assumed. According to the accepted notion, systems with conjugate multiple bonds, i.e., alternating single and multiple bonds, display a certain "equalization" of bond lengths: the single bonds are contracted and the multiple bonds are stretched compared to the corresponding lengths of nonconjugate bonds. The bond lengths obtained from the rotational Raman spectra, however, do not bear out this point of view [73]. Thus, the length of the C=C bond in allene should have been the same as in ethylene, since allene has no conjugate bonds. In fact, however, the C=C bond in allene is contracted. In diacetylene— a molecule with conjugate bonds—we could have expected a longer C≡C bond than in acetylene. In fact, however, a slight contraction is again observed (Table 4).

True, the single C—C bond in diacetylene is shorter than in other molecules, but it is even shorter than in ethane; it is also contracted in dimethylacetylene, where no conjugate bonds are observed. In all these cases the contraction of the C—C single bond can be associated with the effect of nearby bonds, without resorting to the conjugation effect.

Let us now consider the line intensities in the rotational Raman spectra. The intensity distribution in the rotational spectrum is of independent interest, and it also assists in elucidating some fine details of molecular structure.

The intensity of a given spectral line depends on the transition probability, the frequency v, and also on the number of molecules in the initial state. In what follows we will only consider the case of thermodynamic equilibrium. The distribution of molecules over the various rotational states in this case is determined by the Boltzmann factor multiplied by the corresponding degeneracy (see §7). Thus, for linear molecules, the number of molecules N_J in a rotational state J at temperature T is given by

$$N_J = C(2J + 1)\exp\left(-E_J/kT\right) = C(2J + 1)\exp\left[-BJ(J + 1)/kT\right], \quad (8.24)$$

where C is a proportionality factor. This indeterminate factor can be eliminated if we remember that the true number of molecules in rotational states is obtained by multiplying the distribution function (8.24) and the total number of molecules N and then dividing the product by the sum over all states, i.e.,

$$N_J = \frac{N(2J + 1)\exp\left[-BJ(J + 1)/kT\right]}{\sum_J (2J + 1)\exp\left[-BJ(J + 1)/kT\right]}. \quad (8.25)$$

For sufficiently large T, the sum in the denominator can be replaced with an integral:

$$\sum_J (2J + 1)\exp\left[-BJ(J + 1)/kT\right] = \int_0^\infty (2J + 1)\exp\left[-BJ(J + 1)/kT\right]dJ = kT/B. \quad (8.26)$$

Thus,

$$N_J = \frac{NB}{kT}(2J + 1)\exp\left[-BJ(J + 1)/kT\right]. \quad (8.27)$$

This function has a maximum at

$$J = \sqrt{\frac{kT}{2B}} - \frac{1}{2}. \quad (8.28)$$

The line intensity distribution in the rotational Raman spectrum is mainly determined by the number of molecules N_J in the rotational state J. Another factor to be remembered is that in symmetrical molecules with equivalent nuclei, different rotational levels have different statistical weights g'_I differing in the nuclear spin I. For the line intensities in the rotational spectra of linear molecules we thus have

$$I_{lin} = Cv^4 g_I (2J + 1) \exp\left[- BJ(J + 1)/kT\right] |H^J_{J'}|^2 , \qquad (8.29)$$

where $H^J_{J'}$ is expressed by (8.18), v is the line frequency, C is a proportionality factor. For symmetric top molecules we have a similar expression:

$$I_{sym} = C'v^4 g_I 2(2J + 1) |H^{JK}_{J'K'}|^2 \exp\left[- \frac{BJ(J + 1) + (A - B)k^2}{kT}\right]. \qquad (8.30)$$

The substitution of the factor $2(2J + 1)$ for $(2J + 1)$ on passing from linear molecules to symmetric top molecules is associated with the two-fold degeneracy of each level with a given value of K (since the energy levels according to (8.15) depend on $|K|$ only). For a spherical top we could have applied Eq. (8.30) with a new factor $(2J + 1)^2$ substituted for $2(2J + 1)$, in accordance with the actual degeneracy of the energy levels in these molecules. However, as we have noted above, the spectrum of a spherical top, because of its inherently high symmetry, shows only the original unshifted line.

As an illustration, Figure 20 shows a schematic rotational Raman spectrum of NH_3—a symmetric top molecule [75]. The S and R branches overlap for even J, which results in a characteristic alternation of line intensities.

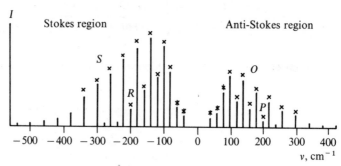

Figure 20

Theoretical intensity distribution in the rotational Raman spectrum of NH_3. × marks the observed lines; * identifies the lines overlapping with the mercury lines [75].

We have seen before that the line widths in rotational Raman spectra increase with increasing pressure, so that eventually the lines overlap and merge. Mikhailov's results [76] show that the pressure dependence of the rotational line widths is linear at moderate pressures (up to 50 atm). This result is in good agreement with the findings of the impact theory of line broadening in gases, developed by Sobel'man [77].

According to this theory, the line width 2δ is related to the pressure p by the equality

$$2\delta = \frac{Lv_r}{c}\rho^2 p. \qquad (8.31)$$

Here L is the Loschmidt number, c is the velocity of light, v_r is the relative velocity of the colliding molecules, ρ is the so-called Weisskopf radius, equal to the distance of the colliding atoms at which the relation between the atomic radiation before and after the collision is just broken. Mikhailov's measurements show that in oxygen and nitrogen, ρ is respectively equal to 4.43 and 4.9Å. These figures are somewhat larger than the gas-kinetic collision diameters, equal to 3.61Å for oxygen and 3.75Å for nitrogen.

Note that as the pressure increases, the intensity distribution between the rotational lines does not change. As an illustration, Figure 21 shows the rotational spectrum of oxygen at various pressures from [76].

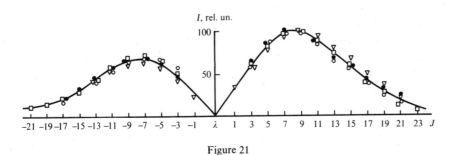

Figure 21

Intensity distribution in the O_2 rotational band at pressures of 7, 15, 25, and 50 atm (different points correspond to measurements at different pressures) [76].

Analysis of the rotational Raman spectra occasionally provides information on the nuclear spins. In symmetric molecules with equivalent nuclei, different rotational levels have different statistical weights g_I, which depend on the nuclear spin I. This leads to a typical alternation in the intensities of the rotational lines, an effect which is most pronounced for diatomic molecules.

According to the general laws of quantum mechanics, each energy level of a molecule is described by a certain wave function Ψ which depends on the coordinates of all the electrons and on the coordinates of the nuclei. We will consider symmetric diatomic molecules, i.e., molecules with identical nuclei. Thus, when the two nuclei are interchanged, the state of the electronic shell of the molecule, expressed by Ψ^2, remains unaltered. If x_1, y_1, z_1 are the coordinates of the first nucleus and x_2, y_2, z_2 those of the second nucleus, we have

$$[\Psi(x_1, y_1, z_1; x_2, y_2, z_2)]^2 = [\Psi(x_2, y_2, z_2; x_1, y_1, z_1)]^2. \qquad (8.32)$$

By (8.32), Ψ is either unaffected by the interchange of the nuclei or at most reverses its sign. A function which is not affected by the interchange is called symmetric (Ψ_s), and a function which reverses its sign is called antisymmetric (Ψ_a). Thus

$$\Psi_s(x_1, y_1, z_1 ; x_2, y_2, z_2) = \Psi_s(x_2, y_2, z_2; x_1, y_1, z_1), \qquad (8.33a)$$

$$\Psi_a(x_1, y_1, z_1; x_2, y_2, z_2) = - \Psi_a(x_2, y_2, z_2; x_1, y_1, z_1). \qquad (8.33b)$$

The total eigenfunction of a molecule is expressible to first approximation as a product of the electronic, the vibrational, and the rotational wave functions:

$$\Psi = \Psi_{el}\Psi_{vib}\Psi_{rot}. \qquad (8.34)$$

The vibrational eigenfunction Ψ_{vib} is never affected by the interchange of the nuclei, since it depends on the internuclear distance only. The behavior of the rotational wave functions, as we have noted before, depends on the parity of the rotational quantum number J. For even J, Ψ_{rot} is symmetric, and for odd J, Ψ_{rot} reverses its sign when the nuclei are interchanged (i.e., it is antisymmetric).

A rotational level with a given J is said to be symmetric or antisymmetric according as the total wave function Ψ is symmetric or antisymmetric under the interchange of nuclei. Thus, by (8.34), assuming a symmetric electronic wave function, the rotational level is symmetric for an even J and antisymmetric for an odd J. The situation is reversed for an antisymmetric electronic wave function. In what follows, we invariably assume a symmetric electronic wave function. The symmetry of the rotational levels is then determined by the parity of J.

A fundamental selection rule of Raman scattering states that only levels of equal symmetry can combine. This rule is compatible with the previously considered selection rules for the rotational Raman spectra of linear molecules, $\Delta J = 0$. Note that in infrared absorption spectra a different selection rule applies, viz., $\Delta J = \pm 1$.

In our analysis of rotational spectra, we will require the following quantum-mechanical rule: if the nuclear spins are ignored, all transitions between symmetric and antisymmetric states are absolutely forbidden [78]. Thus, if an assembly of identical molecules were initially all in symmetric states, no transition will change the symmetry, i.e., the molecules will indefinitely remain in symmetric states. As a result, some gases (H_2, D_2, N_2) may be treated as a mixture of two modifications— a para gas and an ortho gas, which in certain cases can actually be separated. The Raman spectra of the symmetric component show no lines corresponding to transitions between levels with odd J. The spectra of the antisymmetric component similarly show no lines corresponding to transitions between levels with even J. The infrared spectrum, with the selection rule $\Delta J = \pm 1$, is thus forbidden for symmetric linear molecules, as IR absorption induces symmetry-changing transitions.

A more detailed analysis of the rotational spectrum (see [60]) makes it possible to identify the symmetry of the gas. Figure 22 shows a line drawing of a rotational

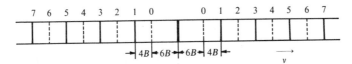

Figure 22

The rotational Raman spectrum of a molecule with identical nuclei. The dashed lines correspond to even rotational levels. The thick line at the center is the exciting line.

Raman spectrum. If all the lines are present, the distance between the first (dashed) Stokes and anti-Stokes lines should be $12B$ in accordance with (8.21), and the distance between the first dashed and the first solid line on either side of the exciting line should be $4B$. If the even rotational levels vanish, all lines with even J, i.e., all the dashed lines, should disappear from the spectrum. Therefore, the distance from the first Stokes line to the first anti-Stokes line will be $2(6 + 4)B = 20B$, whereas the distance between neighboring lines will increase to $8B$. Conversely, if all the lines with odd J are missing (the solid lines in the drawing), the distance between the first Stokes and anti-Stokes line is $12B$, and the distance between neighboring lines is again $8B$. The distances between the first Stokes and anti-Stokes lines and between the neighboring lines in these three cases are thus in a ratio of 6:2, 5:2, and 3:2, respectively. Therefore, without even measuring the rotational constant B, we can establish, by examining the rotational spectrum, which of the three different cases are actually observed. For example, this ratio in the O_2 spectrum was found to be 5:2, i.e., the even levels are missing.

In real rotational Raman spectra, every second line is greatly attenuated, without actually missing from the spectrum. This alternation of line intensities is vividly observed for N_2 (Figure 23). The effect is associated with the nuclear spin: some atomic nuclei, like the electron, have an intrinsic angular momentum, a nuclear spin. The nuclear spin has a very slight direct influence on the molecular levels, leading to a certain splitting of the levels. Its indirect effect, however, is most significant, and as a result rotational spectra can be used to measure the nuclear spins.

In case of a non-zero nuclear spin, the symmetry-changing transitions are no longer absolutely forbidden. Indeed, if the nuclei have a non-zero spin, their interchange in the molecule does not always produce an entirely identical state of the molecule, since the two nuclei may have differently aligned spins.

The spin vectors I of the two nuclei combine to give a resultant vector j—the total nuclear spin of the molecule. In the simplest case, when $I = \frac{1}{2}$, we have either $j = 1$ (parallel nuclear spins) or $j = 0$ (antiparallel nuclear spins). Two alternatives should thus be considered: 1) molecules with total spin 0 have a system of antisymmetric levels, and molecules with spin 1 have a system of symmetric levels; 2) spin 0 molecules have a system of symmetric levels and spin 1 molecules have anti-

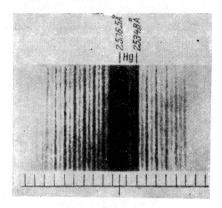

Figure 23

The Raman spectrum of N_2.

symmetric levels. According to the general rules of angular momentum quantization, spin 1 can have three different projections onto a certain direction in space (the z axis):

$$j_z = 0, \ \pm 1,$$

whereas spin 0 can have one projection only, $j_z = 0$. Hence, under alternative 1, the symmetric states are three times as frequent as the antisymmetric states, and under alternative 2 the antisymmetric states are three times as frequent as the symmetric states, i.e., the statistical weights of the symmetric and the antisymmetric states in either case differ by a factor of 3. Since symmetry-changing transitions are forbidden, the line intensities in Raman spectra should alternate in a ratio of 1:3.

The line intensity alternation is indeed observed in the spectra of some molecules. For example, in the spectrum of H_2, the odd lines are stronger than the even lines. Hence the conclusion that the nuclear spin of H (the proton spin) is $\frac{1}{2}$. The electronic eigenfunction of molecular hydrogen is symmetric [60], so that the even rotational levels are symmetric and the odd levels are antisymmetric. Therefore, seeing that the odd lines are the stronger ones, we conclude that the antisymmetric levels have a higher statistical weight, i.e., the nuclear spins are parallel. An analysis of the F_2 spectrum [79] has shown that the nuclear spin of F^{19} is also $\frac{1}{2}$.

If the nuclear spin is 1, the resultant molecular spin may take on the values 2, 1, 0. The statistical weights of these three states are 5, 3, 1. A more detailed analysis shows that the line intensity ratio in the spectra of these molecules is 1:2. Spectra with this intensity ratio are observed for the molecules N_2 and D_2. The nuclei N and D thus have a nuclear spin 1.

9. VIBRATIONAL SPECTRA AND MOLECULAR SYMMETRY

Analysis of vibrational spectra provides abundant information on molecular structure, starting with the chemical structure, as expressed by the chemical structural formulae, and all the way to the fine features of the spatial configuration of atoms and the nature of the chemical bonds.

The theory of vibrational spectra regards the molecule as a system of point masses (atomic nuclei) which vibrate with a small amplitude about the respective equilibrium positions. Raman scattering methods generally study the structure of molecules in the electronic ground state, and it is to ground-state molecules that our further discussion applies.

The vibrational spectra are highly sensitive to the molecular symmetry. We will therefore first give a brief review of the symmetry properties and their application to the vibrational spectra of molecules. A more detailed discussion of this topic can be found in [7, 20, 80–83].

A molecule, or any other three-dimentional object, is said to be symmetric if some transformation of coordinates carries it from one configuration to another, absolutely equivalent, configuration (it is assumed that identical atoms and chemical bonds are indistinguishable). These coordinate transformations are called symmetry operations, and their geometrical representations are known as the symmetry elements. Symmetry operations involve linear orthogonal transformations. Successive application of two (or more) symmetry operations leads to a certain result which can be achieved by one of the other possible symmetry operations. In case of molecules, we are dealing only with symmetry operations which leave one of the points in space fixed. These are the so-called point symmetry operations, which are the general subject of the group theory. In what follows, we use the mathematical apparatus of the group theory on a very limited scale, and all the relevant background information is given in the text.

The symmetry elements of molecules are the center of symmetry, the plane of symmetry, the axis of symmetry, and the reflection–rotation axis; they are designated as i, σ, C_p, S_p, respectively, where the subscript p identifies the order of the axis. The symmetry operations corresponding to the various symmetry elements are indicated by the same symbols.

Consider a few examples. A water molecule (Figure 24) has two planes of symmetry: one is the plane of the molecule (the plane σ_x) and the other is the plane (σ_y) perpendicular to the plane of the molecule and passing through the oxygen atom. The water molecule also has a two-fold symmetry axis C_2, formed by the intersection of the two symmetry planes. Every molecule has a single trivial symmetry element which corresponds to a so-called "identity" operation e, i.e., an operation which leaves the molecule unchanged. The four symmetry elements σ_y, σ_x, C_2 and e

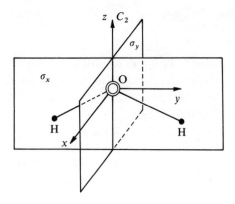

Figure 24

Plane of symmetry of a water molecule.

(and the corresponding symmetry operations) are related by the equalities

$$\sigma_x \sigma_y = C_2 , \tag{9.1}$$

$$\sigma_x^2 = \sigma_y^2 = C_2^2 = e . \tag{9.2}$$

Relation (9.1) signifies that reflection in the plane σ_y followed by reflection in the perpendicular plane σ_x is tantamount to a rotation C_2 through 180° around the vertical axis. Two successive reflections in one plane and two successive rotations through 180° around the same axis result in the same configuration, i.e., their final results is the identity operation e, as expressed in mathematical terms by (9.2).

To any symmetry operation there corresponds an inverse operation, which converts the new configuration to the original one. Thus, the inverse of the rotation $C(\phi)$ through an angle ϕ is the rotation $C(-\phi)$ through an angle $-\phi$:

$$C(-\phi) C(\phi) = C_1 = e . \tag{9.3}$$

The inverse of the symmetry operation a is designated a^{-1}. Thus, $C(-\phi) = C^{-1}(\phi)$. By (9.2),

$$\sigma_x^{-1} = \sigma_x, \quad \sigma_y^{-1} = \sigma_y, \quad C_2^{-1} = C_2 . \tag{9.4}$$

The set of the four symmetry element σ_y, σ_x, C_2, and e or the corresponding symmetry operations constitute the symmetry group of the water molecule. In general, a group is an assembly of abstract elements satisfying the following group conditions (see, e.g., [84–87]):

1) The product of any two group elements is an element of the group; the "product" here is understood as some prescription which assigns a certain element of the group to a combination of any two group elements. In general, the result of this group

multiplication depends on the order in which the factors are combined, i.e., in general

$$ab \neq ba .$$ (9.5)

2) The group multiplication is associative, i.e., for any three group elements

$$a(bc) = (ab)c .$$ (9.6)

3) The group should have at least one element e such that for any element a of the group

$$ae = a .$$ (9.7)

4) For any element a the group contains the inverse element a^{-1}, such that

$$aa^{-1} = e .$$ (9.8)

It is readily seen that the symmetry operations of the water molecule satisfy these requirements, i.e., they indeed constitute a group.

The example of a molecule with a center of symmetry is shown in Figure 25. Molecules with a center of symmetry also have a two-fold rotation axis C_2 and a plane of symmetry σ_h perpendicular to C_2. Simple examination of the symmetry properties of these molecules leads to the following relations:

$$C_2\sigma_h = \sigma_h C_2 = i ,$$ (9.9)

$$C_2 i = iC_2 = \sigma_h ,$$ (9.10)

$$i\sigma_h = \sigma_h i = C_2 .$$ (9.11)

A more complex symmetry is characteristic of molecules of the type X_2Y_6. These molecules have a six-fold reflection–rotation axis S_6 (Figure 26). The symmetry operation S_6 for this molecule entails a rotation through an angle $2\pi/6 = \phi$ with simultaneous reflection in a plane perpendicular to this axis. Rotation through $60°$ in this case is not a symmetry operation, i.e., the molecule does not have a C_6

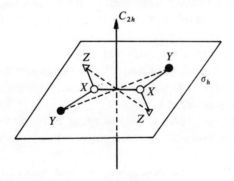

Figure 25

An $X_2Y_2Z_2$ molecule with a center of symmetry.

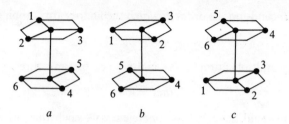

Figure 26

A molecule with a six-fold reflection–rotation axis:

a starting configuration,   *b* rotated through 60°,   *c* rotated through 60° and reflected.

axis. Examination of Figure 26 leads to the following relations:

$$S_p^2 = C_{p/2}, \text{ i.e., } [S(\phi)]^2 = C(2\phi), \tag{9.12}$$

$$S_p^{p/2} = i. \tag{9.13}$$

If the molecule has a rotation axis C_p and also a plane of symmetry through this axis, the notation used for the axis of symmetry is C_{pv} and for the plane of symmetry, σ_v; if alongside with a rotation axis C_p there is also a plane of symmetry perpendicular to the axis, the notation used is C_{ph} and σ_h.

A molecule which has a C_p axis and a perpenducular two-fold axis is classified in the dihedron group D_p. It is readily seen that these molecules have not one but p two-fold axes, all of which cross the C_p axis at one point and make a constant angle $2\pi/p$ with one another. If the molecule also has planes of symmetry, a more complex group is involved. By adding to the D_p group all the planes of symmetry through the C_p axis which bisect the angles between the C_2 axes, we obtain a D_{pd} symmetry group. Molecules with this symmetry have a reflection–rotation axis S_{2p}, and for odd p they have a center of symmetry i. If we add to D_p a plane of symmetry perpendicular to C_{pv}, the result is a group D_{ph}. For even p, the molecule also has a center of symmetry i and a reflection–rotation axis S_p.

Below, we list some important particular cases:

a) The group $D_2 = V$, with three mutually perpendicular two-fold axes.

b) $D_{2h} = V_h$, the group V plus a center of symmetry; three planes of symmetry through the axes are thus defined.

c) $D_{2d} = V_d$, the group V plus a vertical plane bisecting the angle between the two-fold axes; there is evidently another plane with this property and also a S_4 axis.

Finally, let us consider even more complex cubic symmetry groups. Molecules with symmetry of this kind are very common (methane CH_4, carbon tetrachloride CCl_4, etc.). These symmetry groups can be derived from a cube with two-fold axes passing through the centers of the cube faces (these axes themselves form the group $V = D_2$).

1) The tetrahedron group T. This group is obtained from the group V by adding a three-fold axis directed along the spatial diagonal of the cube.

2) The group T_d. If one of the two-fold axes of the T group is a reflection–rotation axis, all other two-fold axes are automatically reflection–rotation axes. As a result, there are 6 planes of symmetry, each passing through two diagonals of the cube. Figure 27 is a diagram showing a reflection–rotation symmetry axis S_4 of the methane molecule.

3) The group T_h, T plus a center symmetry at the center of the cube.

4) The octahedron group O. This group is obtained from the group T when the two-fold axes are upgraded to four-fold symmetry axes.

5) The group O_h, O with a center of symmetry at the center of the cube.

We have considered the principal symmetry groups used in the classification of molecular vibrations. A more comprehensive and systematic classification of these topics will be found in [80–83].

The total number of symmetry operations, including the identity operation e, is called the order of the group. Groups of order 2 have a single symmetry element: a center of symmetry i (C_i), a plane of symmetry σ (C_s), or a two-fold axis (C_2). The groups C_p, S_p are of order p; the groups C_{pv}, C_{ph}, D_p are of order $2p$; groups D_{ph}, D_{pd} are of order $4p$; T is a twelfth-order group; T_d, O, T_h are groups of order 24; O_h is a group of order 48.

If a subset of group elements (including the identity e) form an independent group, it is called a subgroup of the original group. For example, C_4, C_2, C_i, C_{1h}, C_{2h} are

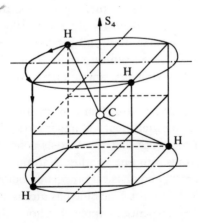

Figure 27

The T_d symmetry of the methane molecule. The arrows mark the paths traced by one of the hydrogen atoms under the symmetry operation S_4; the molecule is first rotated through 90°, and then reflected in the horizontal plane through the carbon atom.

subgroups of C_{4h}. The theory of groups of finite order leads to the conclusion (see, e.g., [84]) that the order of any subgroup is a divisor of the order of the group. The inverse proposition, namely that to any divisor h of the group order g corresponds a subgroup of order h, is in general not true. It is only when h is a power of a prime number that a subgroup of order h exists. For example, the group T of order 12 has subgroups of orders 2, 4, 3, but no subgroup of order 6.

Another important concept in group theory is that of a conjugate class of elements. This concept is formulated in mathematical terms as follows. Elements a and b of a group belong to the same class if there exists some element c of the group such that

$$b = cac^{-1}. \tag{9.14}$$

The elements a and b are called conjugate elements. If the group multiplication in (9.14) is a commutative operation, i.e., if $ca = ac$, we have from (9.14) $b = a$. Thus, in commutative groups,* any element is only the conjugate of itself, so that each element forms a separate class. For non-commutative groups, there are elements for which $ca \neq ac$, and hence in (9.14) $b \neq a$. As a result, these groups can be partitioned into classes, some of which will certainly contain more than one element. The number of elements in each class is a divisor of the group order (see [87]).

As an example, let us consider the ammonia molecule NH_3, which belongs to the symmetry group C_{3v} (Figure 28). This molecule contains equivalent symmetry elements—the symmetry planes $\sigma_v^{(1)}$, $\sigma_v^{(2)}$, and $\sigma_v^{(3)}$, which transform into one another by rotation. Equivalent symmetry operations—i.e., symmetry operations of the same kind which can be transformed into one another by rotations and reflections—constitute one class. For this group, reflections in the planes $\sigma_v^{(1)}$, $\sigma_v^{(2)}$, $\sigma_v^{(3)}$ are operations of the same class; there are three such operations, so that the class consists of three elements. Another class is the class of rotations through 120°. It consists of two elements, rotation C_3 through 120° and rotation $C_3^2 = C_3^{-1}$ through $-120°$. The identity operation $e = C_1$ constitutes a class in itself.

The number of classes of symmetry operations is an important characteristic of a group.

In terms of molecular symmetry, the atoms can be divided into different species, so that atoms of one species are equivalent with regard to symmetry. This equivalence should be understood in the sense that there exists a set of symmetry operations carrying the equivalent atoms into one another. Naturally, these equivalent atoms should have identical chemical and physical properties, but it is by no means certain that all chemically identical atoms are classified as atoms of one symmetry species. Note that the concept of equivalence is applicable not only to atoms, but also to chemical bonds, bond angles, etc.

Certain symmetry operations leave individual atoms in the same position, i.e.,

---

* If every two elements of a group commute, the group is said to be commutative or Abelian.

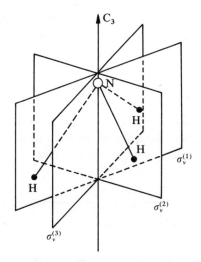

Figure 28

The symmetry of the NH_3 molecule (symmetry group C_{3v}).

these atoms are carried into themselves. For example, in the NH_3 molecule (Figure 28), the atom N is transformed into itself by each and every symmetry operation. Thus, alongside with the symmetry of the molecule as a whole, we can discuss the intrinsic symmetry of the atoms; here, intrinsic symmetry is to be understood as the set of symmetry operations transforming a particular atom into itself. In the case of ammonia, the intrinsic symmetry of the atom N is also the symmetry of the molecule. In general, the intrinsic symmetry is a subgroup of the symmetry group of the molecule. For example, in the water molecule (Figure 24), the H atoms are carried into themselves by the reflection in the σ_x plane (and naturally also by the identity operation e). The two operations σ_x and e constitute a subgroup of the total symmetry group of the water molecule (the group C_{2v}).

The number of equivalent atoms of one particular species is equal to the ratio of the molecular symmetry group order g to the order h of the intrinsic symmetry subgroup (see, e.g., [82]):

$$r = \frac{g}{h}. \tag{9.15}$$

For water, we have for the H atoms $r = 4/2 = 2$.

So far we have considered the molecular symmetry properties assuming a molecule at rest. Before taking up the actual discussion of molecular vibrations, we have to establish the effect of symmetry operations on a molecule with vibrating atoms. The instantaneous configuration of such a molecule is deformed relative to the equilibrium configuration.

The deformation of a molecule can be described in terms of the displacement vectors of the atoms from their equilibrium positions. The configuration of a deformed molecule is transformed by symmetry operations into a new configuration. These transformations are conveniently considered as transformations interchanging and distorting the displacement vectors of the equivalent atoms, but not the atoms themselves. Let us consider for instance the vibrations of a CO_2 molecule (Figure 29). Reflection in the symmetry plane perpenducular to the axis of the molecule can be regarded as interchanging the displacements of the equivalent atoms 1 and 2, without altering the position of these atoms.

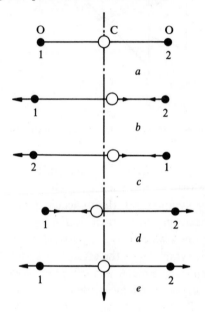

Figure 29

The results of the application of symmetry operations to a vibrating CO_2 molecule:

a the equilibrium configuration,   *b* a deformed molecule,   *c* the result of interchanging atoms 1 and and 2 in a deformed molecule,   *d* reflection in a plane perpendicular to the axis of the molecule;   *e* totally symmetric vibration of the same molecule.

The vibrations of a molecule with n degrees of freedom are described by n normal modes, each of which is entirely independent of the other modes (in the harmonic approximation). The displacements from the equilibrium positions of the atoms can be converted into the "normal" coordinates x_j by some linear transformation (see §10). The Hamiltonian of the molecule in normal coordinates is written in the form

$$H = T + U = \frac{1}{2} \sum_j x_j^2 + \frac{1}{2} \sum_j m_j \omega_j^2 x_j^2 . \tag{9.16}$$

Here the potential energy U is a function of the interatomic distances only, and it is therefore unaffected by symmetry operations which are compatible with the equilibrium configuration. Indeed, a molecule in one of its deformed configurations has the same potential energy as that in any other deformed configuration obtained from the former by symmetry operations, since the application of symmetry operations to a deformed molecule is equivalent to interchanging the atomic displacements. The same considerations apply to the kinetic energy. The Hamiltonian (9.16) thus remains invariant under symmetry operations.

The invariance of the Hamiltonian under all the symmetry operations of the molecule indicates that the normal coordinates are divisible into a number of classes with different transformation properties under symmetry operations.

For any molecular symmetry, there is a class of vibration modes whose normal coordinates are invariant under all the symmetry operations. These vibrations preserve the symmetry of the entire molecule. Vibrations of this kind are called totally symmetric.

For molecules whose symmetry group consists of two operations (one of the operations σ, i, C_2 and the identity operation e), two different classes of vibration modes are possible. The normal coordinates of one class of modes are not affected by symmetry operations, whereas the normal coordinates of the other class reverse their sign under symmetry operations. These are known as symmetric and anti-symmetric modes, respectively. An antisymmetric mode of CO_2 is shown in Figures 29b, c, d. The same figure also shows a symmetric mode of this molecule.

If the symmetry group of a molecule has more than two elements, but no rotation axes of higher than second order, the vibrations are either symmetric or antisymmetric relative to each element.

Vibrations which are symmetric relative to all the symmetry elements are classfied as totally symmetric.

More complex relations are obtained for molecules which have rotation axes of higher than second order. Modes with degenerate frequencies—two- and three-fold—are possible in this case (see §10). The normal coordinates of degenerate modes are transformed jointly and not separately by the symmetry operations (pairs of coordinates for two-fold degenerate modes and triads for three-fold degenerate modes).

The following notation is used for the normal modes of various symmetry classes. Letters A and B are reserved for nondegenerate modes, E designates a doubly degenerate mode, and F a triply degenerate mode. In general, A is assigned to symmetric modes and B to antisymmetric modes (relative to the preferential axis of the molecule). For symmetry groups without preferential axes (the groups $D_2 = V$, $D_{2h} = V_h$ and the cubic groups), the letter A signifies symmetry relative to three mutually perpenducular two-fold axes, and the letter B for the groups V and V_h signifies antisymmetry relative to two out of the three two-fold axes.

Symmetry or antisymmetry relative to the other symmetry elements is designated by subscripts. The subscrips g and u designate symmetry or antisymmetry relative to the center of symmetry i; a prime and a double prime indicate symmetry or anti-symmetry relative to a plane of symmetry σ. If there are several planes of symmetry, this notation refers to the plane which is perpendicular to the preferential axis. The indices plus and minus for degenerate modes indicate symmetry relative to an axis of rotation. If the system has another symmetry element, the subscript 1 is general-ly introduced to indicate symmetry relative to this additional element. Note that for the degenerate modes E and F, the various indices are often introduced for the sake of convenience, and do not identify the symmetry, as in nondegenerate modes. For the point group C_p, the letter A is used as a base for the prime and the double prime.

If a molecule has certain symmetry properties, the appropriate selection rules can be established from Eqs. (6.29) and (6.30), i.e., one can find the transitions with non-zero matrix elements and non-zero line intensities in Raman spectra or in IR absorption spectra.

A matrix element

$$(f_\lambda)_{kn} = \int_{-\infty}^{\infty} \psi_n^* f_\lambda \psi_k \, dx \tag{9.17}$$

does not vanish only if the integrand in (9.17) is invariant under a symmetry trans-formation. The wave functions ψ_n^*, ψ_k have definite transformation properties under symmetry operations, which depend only on the symmetry of the system and are well known for any symmetry type. The derivation of selection rules thus reduces to the determination of the symmetry properties of the triple products of the form $\psi_n^* f_\lambda \psi_k$, proceeding from the symmetry properties of the three components. A transition is allowed if the product is not affected by symmetry operations, and it is forbidden if the product reverses its sign (then the integrand in (9.17) is an odd function and we have $(f_\lambda)_{kn} = 0$). Hence it follows that if f_λ does not reverse its sign under a symmetry operation, the two wave functions ψ_n^* and ψ_k must be either both symmetric or both antisymmetric under the same operation. If, however, f_λ reverses its sign under a symmetry operation, one of the wave functions should be antisym-metric and the other symmetric.

The function f_λ may be a tensor, a vector, or a component of a tensor or a vector. To derive the selection rules for Raman scattering, we have to consider the behavior of the components of the scattering tensor under symmetry operations. The selection rules of infrared absorption are determined by the behavior of the components of the dipole moment vector. Comparison of the selection rules for Raman scattering and infrared absorption is of the greatest interest, since in a number of cases the molecular symmetry can then be derived from the vibrational spectra.

As an example, consider a molecule with a center of symmetry, e.g., the molecule $X_2Y_2Z_2$ (Figure 25). A transformation of coordinates corresponding to reflection through the center (inversion), reverses the sign of all the vector components. Therefore, a transition involving IR absorption is allowed only if the product $\psi_k^*\psi_n$ also reverses its sign under the corresponding symmetry transformation. A transition is thus allowed if the states k and n have different parities, and it is forbidden for states of the same parity.

The selection rules of Raman scattering can be found if we remember that the tensor components are not affected by inversion. The product $\psi_k^*\psi_n$ therefore should conserve its sign, which means that only transitions between states of equal parity are allowed in Raman scattering.

Thus, in systems with a center of symmetry, transitions which are allowed in IR absorption spectra are forbidden in Raman spectra, and vice versa. This is known as the *principle of mutual exclusion.*

In general, the scattering tensor can be decomposed into three components (see (2.38)), which produce three different types of scattered radiation: scalar scattering, anisotropic scattering, and antisymmetric scattering (see §2). We will now establish the selection rules for each of the three scattering components.*

The scalar part of the scattering tensor is a scalar and is therefore invariant under all the symmetry transformations. The product $\psi_n^*\psi_k$ is thus also invariant, which is possible only for transitions between levels of the same symmetry class. Of the main interest are the vibrational transitions between two states one of which is unexcited (the ground state). As unexcited states are totally symmetric states, the second state should also be totally symmetric. We thus conclude that scalar Raman scattering is allowed only for totally symmetric vibrations.

Let us now consider the anisotropic component of the scattering tensor. As we have noted before, scattering of this type (just like the scalar scattering) is forbidden for vibrations which are antisymmetric in relation to the center of symmetry. Moreover, if the molecule has symmetry axes of third and higher orders, certain vibrations which are antisymmetric in relation to reflection in the planes of symmetry are also forbidden. For example, A_2 vibrations, antisymmetric with regard to reflection in the plane σ_v, are forbidden for the molecules of the C_{3v} group.

For partially symmetric vibrations for which anisotropic scattering is allowed, the depolarization is expressed by Eqs. (2.60) and (3.20) with $\beta_c = 0$, and so for a scattering tensor without the antisymmetric part β_a, we have

$$\bar{\rho} = \tfrac{3}{4}, \qquad \rho = \tfrac{6}{7}.$$

Thus, when the polarizability theory is applicable, i.e., when $\beta_a = 0$, the change in the depolarization of a Raman line makes it possible to identify the line with one of the partially symmetric modes.

---

* In what follows, only selection rules for first-order lines are considered. A more rigorous derivation of the selection rules and selection rules for second-order lines will be found in §10.

In the case of totally symmetric modes, the scattering tensor in general has a scalar and an anisotropic component (without β_a). Therefore, by (2.60) and (3.20) we have

$$0 \leq \bar{\rho} \leq \tfrac{3}{4}, \quad 0 \leq \rho \leq \tfrac{6}{7}. \tag{9.18}$$

For cubic symmetry molecules, these inequalities are considerably strengthened, since in this case the anisotropic part of the scattering tensor does not contribute to the totally symmetric lines, i.e., for totally symmetric lines of cubic symmetry molecules we have

$$\bar{\rho} = 0, \quad \rho = 0. \tag{9.19}$$

To prove this proposition, let us consider the initial state of a molecule with cubic symmetry. If this is the ground state of the molecule, as is usually assumed, the total vibrational function has the same symmetry as the molecule, i.e., it contains all the symmetry elements of the tetrahedron group. For totally symmetric vibrations, as we have noted before, the final state of the molecule is also totally symmetric. For the product $\psi_n^* \beta \psi_k$ to remain invariant under symmetry operations, β should also have the symmetry of T_d. In this case, however, the tensor β reduces to a scalar— the trace of β, i.e., the scattered radiation contains only the scalar component.

The conclusion regarding the zero depolarization of the cubic symmetry molecules is of the greatest importance for checking the measurements of this parameter.

Before passing to selection rules in IR spectra, note that the dipole moment components are transformed like the corresponding coordinates. Since inversion is equivalent to a coordinate transformation of the form

$$x' = -x, \quad y' = -y, \quad z' = -z,$$

this symmetry operation reverses the sign of all the dipole moment components. If the vibration transition involves two totally symmetric states, the product $\psi_n^* P \psi_k$ is not invariant, the corresponding matrix element vanishes, and the transition is forbidden in the IR spectrum. For reflection in a plane of symmetry perpendicular to the z axis we have

$$x' = x, \quad y' = y, \quad z' = -z.$$

This symmetry operation leaves the sign of P_x, P_y unchanged, whereas P_z reverses its sign, and on the whole the transition is forbidden in the infrared spectrum. Finally, for rotation about a two-fold symmetry axis directed along the z axis, we have

$$x' = -x, \quad y' = -y, \quad z' = z.$$

P_x and P_y reverse their sign, and the component P_z is not affected. The transition on the whole is allowed in the IR spectrum. In more complex symmetry groups, vibrational transitions in IR spectra are forbidden if the vibration is symmetric about the center of symmetry or if it is symmetric relative to some additional symmetry elements. Triply degenerate modes of the type F_1 are also forbidden.

The selection rules for the antisymmetric tensor β_a can be derived remembering that this tensor is equivalent to an axial vector and its transformation properties are those of a cross product of two vectors. In rotations, β_a behaves like an ordinary polar vector, i.e., like the dipole moment P, and in reflections it behaves like a symmetric tensor.

The selection rules for some symmetry groups are listed in Tables 6 and 7. In these tables, the plus identifies allowed vibrations and the minus indicates that the vibration is forbidden for the corresponding type of scattered radiation or for IR absorption. More detailed tables will be found in [7, 80–83]. Note that in some cases the selection rules are not quite exact, since they are based on the assumption that the scattering molecule is in the vibrational ground state (i.e., unexcited). In practice, this assumption hardly affects the validity of the selection rules, since the number

Table 6

SELECTION RULES FOR THE SIMPLEST GROUPS

Group	Vibration mode	β_c	β_γ	β_a	P
C_i	A_g	+	+	+	−
	A_u	−	−	−	+
C_s	A'	+	+	+	+
	A''	−	+	+	+
$C_{2h}(C_2)^*$	A_g	+	+	+	−
	A_u	−	−	−	+
	B_g	−	+	+	−
	B_u	−	−	−	+
C_{2v}	A_1	+	+	−	+
	A_2	−	+	+	−
	B_1	−	+	+	+
	B_2	−	+	+	+
$D_{2h} = V_h$	A_{1g}	+	+	−	−
	A_{1u}	−	−	−	−
$(D_2 = V)^*$	B_{1g}	−	+	+	−
	B_{1u}	−	−	−	+
	B_{2g}	−	+	+	−
	B_{2u}	−	−	−	+
	B_{3g}	−	+	+	−
	B_{3u}	−	−	−	+

* For the groups C_2 and $D_2 = V$, drop the indices g and u and combine the corresponding rows.

Table 7

SELECTION RULES FOR GROUPS WITH A SINGLE
THREE-FOLD AXIS AND FOR THE T_d GROUP

Group	Vibration mode	β_c	β_γ	β_a	P
C_{3v}	A_1	+	+	−	+
	A_2	−	−	+	−
	E	−	+	+	+
D_{3h}	A'_1	+	+	−	−
	A''_1	−	−	−	−
	A'_2	−	−	+	−
	A''_2	−	−	−	+
	E'	−	+	−	+
	E''	−	+	+	−
D_{3d}	A_{1g}	+	+	−	−
	A_{1u}	−	−	−	−
	A_{2g}	−	−	+	−
	A_{2u}	−	−	−	+
	E_g	−	+	+	−
	E_u	−	−	−	+
T_d	A_1	+	−	−	−
	A_2	−	−	−	−
	E	−	+	−	−
	F_1	−	−	+	−
	F_2	−	+	−	+

of molecules in excited vibrational states is insignificant. The probabilities of violation of the selection rules because of this factor must be allowed for in studying low-frequency vibrations and in high-temperature studies.

When sufficiently comprehensive experimental data are available on the molecular vibrational spectra, the selection rules can be applied in a number of cases to determine the symmetry of the molecule. The appearance of a certain vibrational frequency in the Raman spectra or in the IR absorption spectrum or in both, and the numerical value of the depolarization of that line, identify the corresponding vibration mode and thus provide information regarding the symmetry of the molecule. The problem is particularly simple for molecules with a center of symmetry, since the principle of alternative forbiddenness is applicable to this case. Often, valuable information can be obtained from depolarization measurements of Raman lines. In practice, however, certain ambiguities arise, since the limited accuracy of laboratory measurements is not always sufficient for deciding whether or not the line is depolarized

($\rho = 6/7$), i.e., whether or not it is associated with a partially symmetric vibration. The question of complete polarization of a line ($\rho = 0$), indicatory of the cubic symmetry of the molecule, is also difficult to settle. Measurements of vibrational spectra are therefore generally suplemented by other physical and chemical data on molecular structure.

Note that measurements of Raman spectra around the electron absorption bands may in principle broaden our knowledge of molecular symmetries, since in this region vibrations with $\beta_a \neq 0$ are observed.

If certain vibrations are forbidden in relation to scalar and anisotropic scattering, e.g., the A_2 vibrations of C_{3v} molecules or A_{2g} vibrations of D_{3d} molecules, the depolarization of the corresponding lines is $\rho = 2$ (see (3.20)). Measurements of lines with this unusual depolarization are of obvious independent interest.

As an example of the derivation of molecular symmetry from symmetry rules, let us consider the case of XY_3 molecules. Two models can be proposed for these molecules: the pyramidal model with C_{3v} symmetry and the planar model with D_{3h} symmetry. The total number of vibration modes is six. Examination of the C_{3v} model (see Figure 28) readily reveals two totally symmetric modes: in one of these modes the three Y atoms vibrate along the XY bonds, and in the other the three angles YXY vary symmetrically. These are A_1 vibrations. The other vibrations are the doubly degenerate E modes (see Table 7). All these vibration modes are allowed both in the Raman spectrum and in the IR spectrum, i.e., four lines, two of which are polarized, can be expected in each spectrum. In case of the D_{3h} symmetry, there is one totally symmetric vibration A_1' (the atom X is fixed, and the triangle spanned by the three atoms Y expands and contracts symmetrically); this mode is forbidden in the IR spectrum (see Table 7). The second mode is an A_2'' vibration, antisymmetric relative to the plane of the molecule (the atom X vibrates along an axis perpendicular to the plane of the molecule, and the three Y atoms vibrate in the opposite direction); this mode does not contribute to Raman scattering. The two degenerate E' modes are allowed in both spectra. For this model, we can thus expect three lines in the Raman spectrum (one of them is polarized) and three lines in the IR spectrum.

The Raman spectrum of PCl_3 shows four lines, two of which are polarized (Table 8). Two of the frequencies observed in the IR spectrum correspond to a totally symmetric (polarized) and a degenerate mode, respectively. The two polarization lines in the Raman spectrum indicate that the PCl_3 molecule has the C_{3v} symmetry. This conclusion is further borne out by the fact that the 511 cm^{-1} line in the IR spectrum coincides with the frequency of the polarized Raman line.

The IR spectrum of the $B^{11}F_3$ molecule (Table 8) does not show the 888 cm^{-1} totally symmetric line, and the 691.3 cm^{-1} line is observed only in the IR spectrum. This pattern corresponds to D_{3h} symmetry.

The above examples show that the total number of modes of the different symmetries is required before we can decide on the symmetry of the molecule. In the

Table 8

DERIVATION OF MOLECULAR SYMMETRY FROM VIBRATIONAL SPECTRA

	PCl_3				$B^{11}F_3$	
	RS [88]		IR [89]		RS [90]	IR [91]
vibration mode	Δv, cm^{-1}	ρ	v, cm^{-1}	vibration mode	Δv, cm^{-1}	v, cm^{-1}
A_1	510 (10)	0.14	511	A'_1	888(s)	—
A_1	257 (6)	0.29	—	A''_2	—	691.3 (s)
E	480 (3)	0.86	488	E'	480.4 (m)	480.4 (s)
E	190 (10)	0.86	—	E'	—	1445.9 (vs)

Note. The vibrational frequencies differ for the molecules $B^{10}F_3$ and $B^{11}F_3$, and therefore the data for B^{11} are given. The intensity is indicated in parentheses: s for strong, m for medium, vs for very strong; the numbers in parentheses correspond to visual intensity estimates on a ten-point scale.

simplest cases, this question can be settled from model considerations. However, for molecules with more than 4 or 5 atoms, more general methods are needed for determining the number of modes of a given symmetry. These general methods are presented in the next section.

10. METHODS OF CALCULATION OF MOLECULAR VIBRATIONS

1. Small vibrations of a system of point masses

A number of conclusions pertaining to molecular structure and the properties of molecular vibration can be obtained from the classical problem of small vibrations of a system of point masses. If a molecule consists of N atoms, the number of vibrational degrees of freedom is $r = 3N - 6$ in general and $r = 3N - 5$ in the particular case of linear molecules. To each vibrational degree of freedom corresponds a certain vibration mode of the molecule with a definite frequency ω_j ($j = 1, 2, ..., r$). The vibrtational state of the molecule is characterized by r independent vibrational coordinates x^k which describe the displacement of the atoms from their equilibrium positions. Any particular vibration mode in general affects all the r vibrational coordinates, and they all vary with frequency ω_j, i.e.,

$$x_j^k = a_j^k e^{i\omega_j t} \quad (k = 1, 2, ..., r; \quad j = 1, 2, ... r). \quad (10.1)$$

The ratio of the amplitudes a_j^k for the j-th mode determines its actual form. To obtain a complete description of the vibrations of some molecule, we should determine the frequencies and the amplitude ratios for all the r vibration modes.

Although the general problem of small vibrations was considered by Lagrange back in 1765, its practical solution met with insurmountable difficulties even for the simplest molecules before the development of effective computation methods which could be applied to any molecule. These methods were developed for the purposes of molecular spectroscopy by El'yashevich and Stepanov [92–95]. Wilson et al. [96–98] also worked in this direction. The computational work was greatly simplified with the advent of large computers [99, 100].

As the numerical methods for the computation of molecular vibrations have been developed in considerable detail by various authors [80–83, 101], we will only give a brief discussion of the material necessary for easy understanding of what follows.

The first step toward the solution of the problem of small vibrations of a system of point masses is to determine the potential and the kinetic energy of the system. An appropriate choice of the starting coordinates in which the potential and the kinetic energy are expressed is of the greatest importance for the subsequent stages in the solution of the problem of vibrations of complex polyatomic molecules. The *natural* vibrational coordinates for molecules are the changes in the interatomic distances q_λ and in the bond angles α_μ relative to their equilibrium values. Since the natural coordinates are introduced as relative coordinates, the rotational and the translational motion of the molecule can be ignored, and the problem is thus greatly simplified.

The potential energy of the molecule (i.e., its electron energy for a given configuration of the nuclei, see §6) is a function of the natural vibrational coordinates. For small vibrations about the equilibrium, we expand the potential energy in a series in vibrational coordinates and retain only the quadratic terms:*

$$U(x_1, x_2, \ldots, x_r) = \frac{1}{2} \sum_{\lambda\mu} K_{\lambda\mu} x_\lambda x_\mu . \tag{10.2}$$

Terms of higher order are responsible for the anharmonic vibrations (see §15).

Differentiation of (10.2) with respect to the vibrational coordinate x_λ gives the force corresponding to this coordinate. Let $x_\lambda = q_i$ be the change in the i-th chemical bond. The force altering the length of the i-th bond is then

$$f_i = -\frac{\partial U}{\partial q_i} = -K_{ii}q_i - K_{ij}q_j - K_{il}\alpha_l - \ldots \tag{10.3}$$

The first term on the right in (10.3) is the quasielastic force for the given bond, and the coefficient K_{ii} is the force constant characterizing the "rigidity" of the bond. The second and the third term depend on the change of length of the j-th bond and

---

* The linear term in (10.2) vanishes by virtue of the equilibrium conditions $(\partial U/\partial x_\lambda)_0 = 0$ which are satisfied for all natural coordinates. If the potential energy is reckoned from the minimum, $U_0 = 0$.

the l-th angle, respectively. They are associated with the "coupling" between the i-th bond, on the one hand, and the j-th bond and the l-th angle on the other. The coefficients K_{ij} and K_{il} characterize the "feedback" effect of the changes in the j-th bond and the l-th angle on the i-th bond.

If $x_\mu = \alpha_l$ is the change in the l-th angle between the bonds (in general, between the vectors joining a pair of atoms), K_{ll} is the coefficient characterizing the "rigidity" of the l-th angle, and the meaning of the coefficients $K_{li} = K_{il}$ is as before: they describe the "coupling" between the various coordinates.

The coordinates q_λ and α_μ do not cover the entire variety of vibrational coordinates. In various complex molecules, one has to consider torsion of one part of the molecule relative to another (see §14). These torsional effects are described by angular coordinates χ_ν. Molecules with at least four atoms in a plane can vibrate so that some of the bonds emerge from the common plane. This vibrational mode is described by the angles ϕ_ρ between the bonds and their projections onto the molecular plane.

Coefficients of the form $K_{\lambda\mu}$ where $\lambda \neq \mu$ are known as *dynamic coupling coefficients*.

Let us now consider the kinetic energy T of a molecule. The kinetic energy is a quadratic function of the velocities:

$$T = \frac{1}{2} \sum_{\lambda\mu} M_{\lambda\mu} \dot{x}_\lambda \dot{x}_\mu \quad \left(\dot{x}_\lambda = \frac{dx_\lambda}{dt} \right). \tag{10.4}$$

Just as the potential energy of a molecule is described by the matrix of the dynamic coefficients $\| K_{\lambda\mu} \|$, the kinetic energy is described by the matrix of the coefficients $\| M_{\lambda\mu} \|$. For our purposes, the matrix $\| M_{\lambda\mu} \|$ is conveniently replaced by its inverse matrix

$$\| A_{\lambda\mu} \| = \| M_{\lambda\mu} \|^{-1}, \quad \| A_{\lambda\mu} \| \cdot \| M_{\lambda\mu} \| = E, \tag{10.5}$$

where E is the unit matrix. The matrices $\| A_{\lambda\mu} \|$ and $\| M_{\lambda\mu} \|$ are evidently symmetric. $\| A_{\lambda\mu} \|$ is known as the matrix of the *kinematic coupling coefficients*. The coefficients $A_{\lambda\mu}$ depend on the atomic masses and the relative configuration of bonds and angles, i.e., on the geometry of the molecule. The kinematic coefficients can be obtained in explicit form for various combinations of bonds and angles, without using the expression for the kinetic energy.

It is significant that the value of each coefficient $A_{\lambda\mu}$ depends only on the properties of those bonds and angles whose changes are described by the coordinates x_λ and x_μ. The only non-zero coefficients $A_{\lambda\mu}$ are those describing the kinematic coupling between bonds or angles which have at least one common atom.

For non-cyclic molecules, there is a total of eleven types of kinematic coefficients. The explicit formulas for all these coefficients were first derived by El'yashevich [80, 81].

The matrix of the kinematic coefficients thus can be written as soon as a particular model of the molecule has been chosen. The determination of the dynamic coefficients is a much more difficult problem. For the simplest molecules, these coefficients are derived from experimental data on vibration frequencies (see below). In subsequent calculations it is generally assumed that similar dynamic coefficients, i.e., dynamic coefficients describing the coupling between similar bonds and angles, retain a constant value in simple and complex molecules. Many of these coefficients are generally set equal to zero. As a result, the calculation of the vibration modes is inherently a highly approximate and semiempirical problem. Nevertheless, calculations of frequencies and vibration modes provide valuable information for the interpretation of the experimental spectra and lead to important conclusions concerning molecular structure.

The compilation of the matrices of kinematic and dynamic coupling coefficients was the first step toward the calculation of molecular vibrations. The next step is the derivation of the equations from which the frequencies and the vibration modes can be determined.

The Lagrange equations constitute the starting point in the problem of small vibrations of a system of point masses. These equations have the form

$$\frac{d}{dt}\left(\frac{\partial L}{\partial \dot{x}_\lambda}\right) - \frac{\partial L}{\partial x_\lambda} = 0 , \tag{10.6}$$

where x_λ are the generalized coordinates of a system with r degrees of freedom ($\lambda = 1, 2, \ldots, r$), and

$$L = T - U \tag{10.7}$$

is the Lagrangian of the system. From (10.2) and (10.4) we have

$$\frac{\partial L}{\partial \dot{x}_\lambda} = \frac{\partial T}{\partial \dot{x}_\lambda} , \quad \frac{\partial L}{\partial x_\lambda} = -\frac{\partial U}{\partial x_\lambda} = F_\lambda . \tag{10.8}$$

Eqs. (10.6) now take the form

$$\frac{d}{dt}\left(\frac{\partial T}{\partial \dot{x}_\lambda}\right) + \frac{\partial U}{\partial x_\lambda} = 0 . \tag{10.9}$$

Inserting for T and U the appropriate expressions, we find

$$\sum_{\mu=1}^{r} (M_{\lambda\mu}\ddot{x}_\mu + K_{\lambda\mu}x_\mu) = 0 . \tag{10.10}$$

These equations can be transformed to a simpler form. First we multiply (10.10) by the previously defined coefficients $A_{\nu\lambda}$ and sum over all λ:

$$\sum_{\lambda\mu} A_{\nu\lambda}(M_{\lambda\mu}\ddot{x}_\mu + K_{\lambda\mu}x_\mu) = 0 . \tag{10.11}$$

Using the standard rule of matrix multiplication, we find from (10.5)

$$\sum_\lambda A_{\nu\lambda} M_{\lambda\mu} = \delta_{\nu\mu}, \tag{10.12}$$

and hence

$$\ddot{x}_\nu + \sum_{\lambda\mu} A_{\nu\lambda} K_{\lambda\mu} x_\mu = 0 \quad (\nu = 1, 2, \ldots, r). \tag{10.13}$$

Eqs. (10.13) are a system of r linear homogeneous differential equations with constant coefficients. According to the general methods of solution of such equations, we seek r unknown functions $x_\nu(t)$ in the form

$$x_\nu(t) = a_\nu e^{i\omega t}. \tag{10.14}$$

Insertion of (10.14) in (10.13) gives (after cancelling out $e^{i\omega t}$) a system of linear homogeneous algebraic equations for the constants a_ν:

$$\sum_{\lambda\mu} (A_{\nu\lambda} K_{\lambda\mu} - \delta_{\nu\mu}\omega^2) a_\mu = \sum_\mu \left[\left(\sum_\lambda A_{\nu\lambda} K_{\lambda\mu} \right) - \delta_{\nu\mu}\omega^2 \right] a_\mu = 0. \tag{10.15}$$

This system is solvable, i.e., has non-zero solutions, if its determinant vanishes,

$$\left| \left(\sum_\lambda A_{\nu\lambda} K_{\lambda\mu} \right) - \delta_{\nu\mu}\omega^2 \right| = 0, \tag{10.16}$$

or in expanded form

$$\left| \begin{array}{cccc} \left(\sum_\lambda A_{1\lambda} K_{\lambda 1} \right) - \omega^2 & \sum_\lambda A_{1\lambda} K_{\lambda 2} & \cdot & \cdot & \cdot \\ \sum_\lambda A_{2\lambda} K_{\lambda 1} & \left(\sum_\lambda A_{2\lambda} K_{\lambda 2} \right) - \omega^2 & \cdot & \cdot \\ \cdot & \cdot & \cdot & \cdot & \cdot & \cdot \end{array} \right| =$$

$$= \left| \begin{array}{cccc} D_{11} - \omega^2 & D_{12} & \cdot & \cdot & \cdot \\ D_{21} & D_{22} - \omega^2 & \cdot & \cdot & \cdot \\ \cdot & \cdot & \cdot & \cdot & \cdot & \cdot \end{array} \right| = 0.$$

Here

$$\left\| \begin{array}{c} D_{11} \, D_{12} \ldots \\ D_{21} \, D_{22} \ldots \\ \cdot \quad \cdot \quad \cdot \quad \cdot \end{array} \right\| = \left\| \begin{array}{c} A_{11} \, A_{12} \ldots \\ A_{21} \, A_{22} \ldots \\ \cdot \quad \cdot \quad \cdot \quad \cdot \end{array} \right\| \cdot \left\| \begin{array}{c} K_{11} \, K_{12} \ldots \\ K_{21} \, K_{22} \ldots \\ \cdot \quad \cdot \quad \cdot \quad \cdot \end{array} \right\|$$

is the matrix of the "total" coupling coefficients. Unlike $\|A_{\lambda\mu}\|$ and $\|K_{\lambda\mu}\|$, this is not a symmetric matrix, i.e., $D_{ik} \neq D_{ki}$.

If the matrices $\|A_{\lambda\mu}\|$ and $\|K_{\lambda\mu}\|$ are "quasidiagonal", i.e., the non-zero elements are arranged in square cells along the main diagonal, the matrix $\|D_{\lambda\mu}\|$ is also quasi-diagonal, e.g.:

$$\begin{Vmatrix} A_{11} & A_{12} & 0 & 0 \\ A_{21} & A_{22} & 0 & 0 \\ 0 & 0 & A_{33} & A_{34} \\ 0 & 0 & A_{43} & A_{44} \end{Vmatrix} \cdot \begin{Vmatrix} K_{11} & K_{12} & 0 & 0 \\ K_{21} & K_{22} & 0 & 0 \\ 0 & 0 & K_{33} & K_{34} \\ 0 & 0 & K_{43} & K_{44} \end{Vmatrix} =$$

$$= \begin{Vmatrix} D_{11} & D_{12} & 0 & 0 \\ D_{21} & D_{22} & 0 & 0 \\ 0 & 0 & D_{33} & D_{34} \\ 0 & 0 & D_{43} & D_{44} \end{Vmatrix} .$$

Eq. (10.16) then separates into several equations corresponding to the different squares of the matrix. We can write in a shorter notation

$$\begin{vmatrix} D_{11} - \omega^2 & D_{12} \\ D_{21} & D_{22} - \omega^2 \end{vmatrix} = 0, \quad \begin{vmatrix} D_{33} - \omega^2 & D_{34} \\ D_{43} & D_{44} - \omega^2 \end{vmatrix} = 0 .$$

Eq. (10.16) is an equation of r-th degree in ω^2. It is called the characteristic or the secular equation of the system. The quantities ω satisfying this equation are known as the eigenfrequencies of the molecule. An algebraic equation of degree r is known to have r roots. The molecule thus has r eigenfrequencies, some of which may co-incide (multiple frequencies). Physical considerations indicate that all the roots of the secular equation are real and positive. Mathematically, the same conclusion follows from the fact that the kinetic energy of the system is a positive-definite bilinear form (see, e.g., [102]).

Having found all the r eigenfrequencies $\omega_1, \omega_2, \ldots, \omega_r$, they are inserted succes-sively in Eqs. (10.15) to find the coefficients $a_{\mu j}$ corresponding to each ω_j. We know from the theory of linear equations that if all the eigenfrequencies are different, the coefficients $a_{\mu j}$ are proportional to the minors of the determinant (10.16), with ω_j substituted for ω:

$$a_{\mu j} \sim \Delta_{\mu j} . \tag{10.17}$$

Thus, one of the particular solutions of the system of differential equations (10.13) has the form

$$x_\mu(t) = C_j \Delta_{\mu j} e^{i\omega_j t} , \tag{10.18}$$

where C_j is an arbitrary constant, which in general may be a complex number, $\mu = 1, 2, \ldots, r$. The general solution is the sum of all the r particular solutions:

$$x^\mu(t) = \sum_{j=1}^{r} C_j \Delta_{\mu j} e^{i\omega_j t} . \tag{10.19}$$

In accordance with (10.19), each vibrational motion of the molecule is a super-position of r simple periodic vibrations of the form

$$Q_j = Q_{j0} e^{i\omega_j t}. \tag{10.20}$$

The vibrations Q_j $(j = 1, 2, \ldots, r)$ are the vibration *modes* of the molecule, discussed at the beginning of this section. If Q_j are chosen as the vibrational coordinates of the system, our problem is greatly simplified.

Indeed, the normal coordinates according to (10.20) satisfy the equations

$$\ddot{Q}_j + \omega_j^2 Q_j = 0 \quad (j = 1, 2, \ldots, r). \tag{10.21}$$

Thus, if we can write the equations of motion in normal coordinates, the result is r independent equations, each describing one mode.

The Lagrangian of a molecule in normal coordinates is a sum of the Lagrangians of the different modes:

$$L = \tfrac{1}{2} M_0 \sum_j (\dot{Q}_j^2 - \omega_j^2 Q_j^2), \tag{10.22}$$

where M_0 is a constant with the dimension of mass; the normal coordinates then have the dimension of length. Comparison of (10.22) with the general expressions (10.7), (10.2), (10.4) shows that the kinetic and the potential energy of a molecule expressed in normal coordinates are written as a sum of squares,* i.e., there is no "coupling" between different coordinates. The secular equation (10.16) in normal coordinates has the form

$$\begin{vmatrix} A_1 K_1 - \omega^2 & 0 & \ldots \\ 0 & A_2 K_2 - \omega^2 \ldots \\ \cdot \quad \cdot \quad \cdot \quad \cdot \quad \cdot \quad \cdot \quad \cdot \end{vmatrix} = 0, \tag{10.23}$$

i.e., it is diagonalized.

We have assumed so far that all the r eigenfrequencies ω_j are different. If some of the eigenfrequencies are equal to one another, the general form of the solution of the equations of motion remains the same. The coefficients $\Delta_{\mu j}$ corresponding to the multiple frequencies, however, are no longer minors of the secular determinant (these minors vanish for multiple frequencies). A frequency of multiplicity s (or, as we say, an s-fold degenerate frequency) corresponds to s normal coordinates. The choice of these normal coordinates is not single-valued, since the normal coordinates corresponding to the same frequency ω_j can be subjected to any linear transformation which leaves invariant the sum of the squares $\dot{Q}_j^2$ and Q_j^2 in the kinetic and the potential energy.

---

* Mathematically, this means that the transformation (10.19) from the coordinates x^μ to the normal coordinates Q_j is a transformation which simultaneously diagonalizes the two bilinear forms T and U to a sum of squares.

Let us now return to Eqs. (10.19), which establish a relation between the natural coordinates x^μ and the normal coordinates Q_j. Using (10.20), we rewrite this system in the form

$$x^\mu(t) = \sum_{j=1}^{r} R_{\mu j} Q_j. \tag{10.24}$$

The coefficients $R_{\mu j}$, which by (10.19) are proportional to the minors $\Delta_{\mu j}$ and can be obtained by solving the system of linear equations (10.15), determine the shape of the vibration mode. The coefficients $R_{\mu j}$ for a given j-th mode, according to (10.18), determine the relative amplitudes of the coordinate changes x_μ. Each normal mode is thus characterized by the frequencies ω_j and by the set of mode coefficients $R_{\mu j}$.

We distinguish between stretching vibrations and bending vibrations. Stretching vibrations mainly involve a change in bond lengths. Bending vibrations mainly alter the bond angles. Thus, for stretching vibrations

$$q_{\lambda j} \neq 0, \quad \alpha_{\mu j} \approx 0. \tag{10.25}$$

For bending vibrations

$$q_{\lambda j} \approx 0, \quad \alpha_{\mu j} \neq 0. \tag{10.26}$$

Each vibration mode, strictly speaking, is a vibration of the entire molecule. Often, however, the vibrations are localized in individual parts of the molecule or in groups of atoms and bonds (possibly even in one bond). The vibration mode therefore characterizes those structural elements of the molecule which take active part in the vibration.

Experimental and theoretical studies of vibrational spectra of molecules established that in some cases certain bonds, groups of bonds, or other structural features of the molecule are invariably associated with certain fixed frequencies in the spectra. The presence of these characteristic frequencies leads to certain conclusions regarding the molecular structure; this technique is widely used in molecular spectroscopy. The specificity of vibrations is discussed in some detail in §11.

2. Calculation of frequencies and mode coefficients

We see from the above that the solution of the problem of molecular vibrations can be divided into the following stages:
1) Assembling the matrix of kinematic and dynamic coefficients.
2) Setting up and solving the secular equation.
3) Calculating the mode coefficients.

In principle, these are fairly elementary operations, but the problem becomes very complex for systems with numerous degrees of freedom.

The vibration problem is greatly simplified by introducing the symmetry of the molecule into consideration. As a result of this symmetry, some of the kinematic and dynamic coefficients are equal or are related by simple relationships, which are moreover the same for both matrices. Therefore, certain linear transformations of the coordinates—symmetry transformations—will reduce both matrices to quasidiagonal form and the r-th degree secular equation separates into several lower order secular equations, each corresponding to a certain symmetry class of vibrations.

Consider a simple example, a nonlinear symmetric triatomic molecule of the H_2O type. This molecule has three vibrational degrees of freedom. The natural vibrational coordinates in this case are the changes q_1 and q_2 in bond lengths and the change α in the bond angle (Figure 30). The potential energy of the molecule in these coordinates takes the form

$$U = \tfrac{1}{2}(K_q q_1^2 + K_q q_2^2 + 2hq_1q_2 + K_\alpha \alpha^2 + 2aq_1\alpha + 2aq_2\alpha). \tag{10.27}$$

Because of the symmetry of this molecule, the coefficients before q_1^2 and q_2^2 are equal to each other, and so are the coefficients before $q_1\alpha$ and $q_2\alpha$. This enables us to simplify the general expression for the potential energy. Indeed, let us change over to new variables q_a and q_s using the linear transformation

$$q_a = \frac{1}{\sqrt{2}}(q_1 - q_2), \qquad q_s = \frac{1}{\sqrt{2}}(q_1 + q_2). \tag{10.28}$$

Because of the factor $1/\sqrt{2}$, the sum of the squares of the coordinates is an invariant of the transformation:

$$q_a^2 + q_s^2 = q_1^2 + q_2^2. \tag{10.29}$$

Transformations with this property are orthogonal and normalized. The inverse transformation is given by

$$q_1 = \frac{1}{\sqrt{2}}(q_a + q_s), \qquad q_2 = \frac{1}{\sqrt{2}}(-q_a + q_s). \tag{10.30}$$

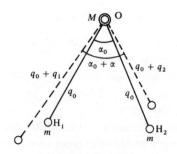

Figure 30

Vibrations of an H_2O molecule.

The matrices of transformations (10.28) and (10.30) are

$$C = \left\| \begin{matrix} \dfrac{1}{\sqrt{2}} & -\dfrac{1}{\sqrt{2}} \\ \dfrac{1}{\sqrt{2}} & \dfrac{1}{\sqrt{2}} \end{matrix} \right\|, \quad C^{-1} = \left\| \begin{matrix} \dfrac{1}{\sqrt{2}} & \dfrac{1}{\sqrt{2}} \\ -\dfrac{1}{\sqrt{2}} & \dfrac{1}{\sqrt{2}} \end{matrix} \right\|.$$

It is readily seen that the matrix product CC^{-1} actually gives the unit matrix. On the other hand, the matrices C and C^{-1} are obtained from one another by interchanging rows and columns, i.e., C^{-1} is equal to the transpose C^{+}:

$$C^{-1} = C^{+}. \tag{10.31}$$

Relation (10.31) expresses a fundamental property of orthogonal transformations (with real coefficients). It is readily seen that det $C = \pm 1$. Inserting (10.30) in (10.27), we get

$$U = \tfrac{1}{2}[(K_q + h)q_s^2 + \sqrt{2}\,aq_s\alpha + K_\alpha\alpha^2 + (K_q - h)q_a^2]. \tag{10.32}$$

The new expression for the potential energy does not contain terms with "crossproducts" of the coordinates q_a and q_s, or q_a and α. We have thus managed to separate the coordinate q_a from the other two coordinates.

The coordinates q_s and q_a have a simple physical meaning. If the vibrations are such that only the coordinate q_s varies, i.e., $q_a = 0$, we have from (10.30)

$$q_1 = \frac{1}{\sqrt{2}}q_s, \quad q_2 = \frac{1}{\sqrt{2}}q_s, \quad q_1 = q_2. \tag{10.33}$$

This is a vibration mode which does not change the symmetry of the molecule. If we perform a symmetry operation, e.g., reflection in a plane of symmetry perpendicular to the plane of the molecule, or rotation through 180° about the two-fold symmetry axis, the configuration of the vibrating molecule does not change. It is clear from Figure 30 that the coordinate α has the same property. As a result, q_s and α are called symmetric coordinates, and the vibrations involving a change in these two coordinates are classified as totally symmetric modes.

Let us consider another case, when only q_a changes, and $q_s = 0$. From (10.30) we have

$$q_1 = \frac{1}{\sqrt{2}}q_a, \quad q_2 = -\frac{1}{\sqrt{2}}q_a, \quad q_1 = -q_2. \tag{10.34}$$

The above symmetry operations reverse the sign of the displacement of the atoms from the equilibrium positions. Therefore q_a is called an antisymmetric coordinate, and the mode entailing a variation in q_a is classified as an antisymmetric mode.

We have considered a useful transformation of the potential energy. The kinetic energy is similarly transformed to the coordinates q_s, q_a, and the results are again advantageous, because the particular transformation is prescribed by the symmetry properties of the molecule, and not by an accidental juggling of the coefficients. This also applies to the kinematic coefficients, whose matrix is simply the inverse of the kinetic energy matrix.

Sometimes, instead of simplifying or diagonalizing the actual expressions for the potential and the kinetic energy, it is more convenient to transform the matrices of the kinematic and the dynamic coefficients. In our case of H_2O molecule, we have

$$K = \left\| \begin{array}{ccc} K_q & h & a \\ h & K_q & a \\ a & a & K_\alpha \end{array} \right\|. \tag{10.35}$$

The coordinate transformation (10.30) is equivalent to the following transformation of the matrix elements. Multiply the elements of the first and the second row by $1/\sqrt{2}$, add up the first and the second row, and subtract the first row from the second. This gives

$$K' = \left\| \begin{array}{ccc} \dfrac{1}{\sqrt{2}}(K_q + h) & \dfrac{1}{\sqrt{2}}(K_q + h) & \sqrt{2}a \\[2mm] -\dfrac{1}{2}(K_q - h) & \dfrac{1}{\sqrt{2}}(K_q - h) & 0 \\[2mm] a & a & K_\alpha \end{array} \right\|.$$

A similar transformation is applied to the first and the second column. The final result is*

$$K'' = \left\| \begin{array}{ccc} K_q + h & 0 & \sqrt{2}a \\ 0 & K_q - h & 0 \\ \sqrt{2}a & 0 & K_\alpha \end{array} \right\| \tag{10.36}$$

---

* These step-by-step transformations of the matrix K can be represented as a result of multiplying K by the transformation matrix

$$C^{-1} = \left\| \begin{array}{ccc} \dfrac{1}{\sqrt{2}} & \dfrac{1}{\sqrt{2}} & 0 \\[2mm] -\dfrac{1}{\sqrt{2}} & \dfrac{1}{\sqrt{2}} & 0 \\[2mm] 0 & 0 & 1 \end{array} \right\|,$$

and then by C, i.e., $K'' = C^{-1}KC$.

Finally, interchanging the second and the third row and the second and the third column, we get

$$K''' = \begin{Vmatrix} K_q + h & \sqrt{2}a & \vdots & 0 \\ \sqrt{2}a & K_\alpha & \vdots & 0 \\ \cdots & \cdots & \cdots & \cdots \\ 0 & 0 & \vdots & K_q - h \end{Vmatrix}. \tag{10.37}$$

The matrix K''' corresponds to the quasidiagonalized potential energy matrix (10.32). This is also a quasidiagonal matrix, made up of the two squares marked with dashed curves along the main diagonal.

The matrix of kinematic coefficients is written in the form

$$A = \begin{Vmatrix} A_q & A_h & A_a \\ A_h & A_q & A_a \\ A_a & A_a & A_\alpha \end{Vmatrix}. \tag{10.38}$$

The above transformation reduces it to the quasidiagonal form

$$A''' = \begin{Vmatrix} A_q + A_h & \sqrt{2}A_a & 0 \\ \sqrt{2}A_a & A_\alpha & 0 \\ 0 & 0 & A_q - A_h \end{Vmatrix}. \tag{10.39}$$

The secular equation (10.16) separates into two equations: for the symmetric vibrations

$$\begin{Vmatrix} A_q + A_h & \sqrt{2}A_a \\ \sqrt{2}A_a & A_\alpha \end{Vmatrix} \cdot \begin{Vmatrix} K_q + h & \sqrt{2}a \\ \sqrt{2}a & K_\alpha \end{Vmatrix} - \begin{Vmatrix} \omega^2 & 0 \\ 0 & \omega^2 \end{Vmatrix} = 0 \tag{10.40}$$

and for the antisymmetric vibrations

$$(A_q - A_h)(K_q - h) - \omega^2 = 0. \tag{10.41}$$

Symmetry considerations thus reduced the vibration problem of the H_2O molecule to two simpler problems, one for a symmetric vibration and the other for an antisymmetric vibration. The second problem is trivial, and its solution gives the frequency of the antisymmetric mode:

$$\omega_a^2 = (A_q - A_h)(K_q - h). \tag{10.42}$$

Let us continue our calculations of the vibrational spectrum of the H_2O molecule.

Using the tables in [80, 81], we find for the kinematic coefficients

$$A_q = \frac{1}{m} + \frac{1}{M}, \quad A_h = \frac{1}{M}\cos\alpha_0, \quad A_a = -\frac{1}{M\rho_0}\sin\alpha_0,$$

$$A_\alpha = \frac{2}{\rho_0^2}\left[\frac{1}{m} + \frac{1}{M}(1 - \cos\alpha_0)\right]$$

(10.43)

(for notation, see Figure 30). Using the geometrical parameters of the water molecule [103]

$$\rho_0 = 0.9572 \text{ Å}, \quad \alpha_0 = 104.52°$$

and inserting the masses $m_H = 1.008$, $M = 16.0$, we find $A_q = 1.0546$, $A_h = -0.0604$, $A_a = -0.0167$, $A_\alpha = 2.3700$.

We will also calculate the kinematic coefficient of heavy water D_2O. Taking $m_d = 2.015$, we find (the prime indicates that the coefficients refer to D_2O molecule)

$$A'_q = 0.5587, \quad A'_\alpha = 1.3158.$$

The other coefficients do not change.

To find the dynamic coefficients, we need the experimental frequencies. Here, however, two serious difficulties are encountered: 1) the number of frequencies is always less than the number of unknown dynamic coefficients; this difficulty is partly avoided by using the spectra of isotope-substituted molecules; 2) the experimental frequencies actually correspond to anharmonic vibrations. Anharmonicity effects as such constitute a fairly difficult problem (see §15). Anharmonicity is generally assumed to be small, and the observed frequencies are identified with the harmonic frequencies. This naturally results in intractable errors.

The experimental frequencies of H_2O and D_2O are listed in Table 9. Using these frequencies, we will first find the constant $K_q - h$ from Eq. (10.42). We have

$$K_q - h = \frac{\omega_a^2}{A_q - A_h} = 12.65 \,(H_2O), \quad (K_q - h)' = 12.56 \,(D_2O). \quad (10.44)$$

The slight difference in the $K_q - h$ values for H_2O and D_2O is apparently associated with anharmonicity effects.

Let us now consider the equation for the symmetric vibrations (10.40). This equation contains three unknown dynamic coefficients; to determine these coefficients, we need experimental data on the frequencies of both molecules. In practice, it is better to use the sum frequencies $\omega_q^2 + \omega_\alpha^2$, $\omega_q'^2 + \omega_\alpha'^2$ and one of the products $\omega_q^2\omega_\alpha^2$ or $\omega_q'^2\omega_\alpha'^2$. Writing the secular equation in the form

$$\begin{vmatrix} (A_q + A_h)(K_q + h) + 2A_a a - \omega^2 & (A_q + A_h)\sqrt{2a} + \sqrt{2A_a K_\alpha} \\ \sqrt{2A_a}(K_q + h) + \sqrt{2A_a a} & 2A_a a + A_\alpha K_\alpha - \omega^2 \end{vmatrix} = 0$$

Table 9

VIBRATIONAL SPECTRA OF H_2O AND
DEUTERIZED WATER IN THE GASEOUS STATE[83]

Molecule	Frequencies, cm$^{-1} \cdot 10^{-3}$		
	ω_{sq}	$\omega_{s\alpha}$	ω_a
H_2O	3.6545	1.595	3.7558
	RS	IR	IR
D_2O	2.666	1.179	2.789
	RS	IR	IR
HDO*	2.719	1.402	(3.710)

* For this molecule, symmetry considerations do not apply. The frequency in parentheses was calculated using Sverdlov's sum rule [105].

and expanding it, we find

$$\omega^4 - [(A_q + A_h)(K_q + h) + (4A_a a + A_\alpha K_\alpha)]\omega^2 + D = 0. \tag{10.45}$$

Here D is the determinant of the total coupling matrix:

$$D = \begin{vmatrix} K_q + h & \sqrt{2}a \\ \sqrt{2}a & K_\alpha \end{vmatrix} \begin{vmatrix} A_q + A_h & \sqrt{2}A_a \\ \sqrt{2}A_a & A_\alpha \end{vmatrix} = D(K)\,D(A). \tag{10.46}$$

According to the standard theorem relating the roots of an algebraic equation to the coefficients before the unknowns, we have

$$D = \omega_q^2\omega_\alpha^2, \qquad D' = \omega_q'^2\omega_\alpha'^2. \tag{10.47}$$

The coefficient before ω^2 is equal to the sum of the roots of the equation, so that

$$(A_q + A_h)(K_q + h) + 4A_a a + A_\alpha K_\alpha = \omega_q^2 + \omega_\alpha^2, \tag{10.48}$$

$$(A_q' + A_h)(K_q + h) + 4A_a a + A_\alpha' K_\alpha = \omega_q'^2 + \omega_\alpha'^2. \tag{10.48'}$$

Note that this coefficient is a sum of the diagonal terms of the matrix $\|D\|$. Solving simultaneously Eqs. (10.48), (10.48'), and the first equation in (10.47), we obtain two sets of constants, the more probable of which is

$$K_q + h = 6.139, \quad a = -1.97, \quad K_\alpha = 3.61.$$

Using (10.44), we finally obtain

$$K_q = 9.40, \quad h = -3.26.$$

By making use of the sum $D' = \omega_q'^2 + \omega_\alpha'^2$, we find

$$K_q' = 9.30, \quad h' = -3.16, \quad a' = -1.90, \quad K_\alpha' = 3.63.$$

Although the constants have close values, the above calculation should be considered as a mere illustration of the method for the determination of molecular force constants, since we ignored the considerable anharmonicity of the vibrations (see §15).

The relation that we have noted above between the sum of the roots of the secular equation and the sum of the diagonal elements of the total coupling matrix, and between the product of the roots and the determinant of this matrix, is applicable to equations of any order and it can be used to derive useful relations between the frequencies of isotope-substituted molecules. For the product of the roots of two isotopic molecules, we have

$$D = D(K)D(A) = \omega_1^2\omega_2^2\ldots\omega_r^2,$$

$$D' = D(K)D'(A) = \omega_1'^2\omega_2'^2\ldots\omega_r'^2.$$

Hence we find

$$\frac{\omega_1^2\omega_2^2\ldots\omega_r^2}{\omega_1'^2\omega_2'^2\ldots\omega_r'^2} = \frac{D(A)}{D'(A)}. \tag{10.49}$$

This relation is known as the *product rule* of Teller and Redlich [104].

Let us now make use of the equality

$$\sum_{k=1}^{r} \omega_k^2 = \sum_{k=1}^{r} d_{kk}. \tag{10.50}$$

Suppose that the molecule contains several identical atoms, H atoms say. Let the original molecule be identified as a; if we substitute D atoms for some of the H atoms, the result is a molecule b. A molecule obtained by substituting D atoms for the complement group of H atoms is designated c. Finally, the molecule d is obtained if the H atoms of both groups have been replaced with D atoms. These substitutions affect only those matrix elements of $\|d_{ik}\|$ which refer to the substituted atoms. Let m be the number of substituted D atoms in molecule b and n the number of substituted atoms in molecule c. For each molecule, we draw up the sums of the squares of the frequencies and the diagonal matrix elements of $\|d_{ik}\|$, suitably isolating the terms which correspond to the substituted hydrogen atoms. We thus find

$$\sum_{k=1}^{r} \omega_{ak}^2 = \sum_{k=1}^{m} d_{kk} + \sum_{k=m+1}^{n} d_{kk} + \sum_{k=n+1}^{r} d_{kk},$$

$$\sum_{k=1}^{r} \omega_{bk}^2 = \sum_{k=1}^{m} d'_{kk} + \sum_{k=m+1}^{n} d_{kk} + \sum_{k=n+1}^{r} d_{kk},$$

$$\sum_{k=1}^{r} \omega_{ck}^2 = \sum_{k=1}^{m} d_{kk} + \sum_{k=m+1}^{n} d'_{kk} + \sum_{k=n+1}^{r} d_{kk},$$

$$\sum_{k=1}^{r} \omega_{dk}^2 = \sum_{k=1}^{m} d'_{kk} + \sum_{k=m+1}^{n} d'_{kk} + \sum_{k=n+1}^{r} d_{kk}.$$

These relations readily show that

$$\sum_{k=1}^{r} \omega_{ak}^2 + \sum_{k=1}^{r} \omega_{dk}^2 = \sum_{k=1}^{r} \omega_{bk}^2 + \sum_{k=1}^{r} \omega_{ck}^2. \qquad (10.51)$$

This equality is known as Sverdlov's *sum rule* [105].

The product rule and the sum rule may be applied to check the identification of frequencies and to calculate the missing frequencies, if all the other modes are known. Applying the sum rule to the molecules H_2O, D_2O and HDO, we find

$$\sum \omega_i^2 (H_2O) + \sum \omega_i^2 (D_2O) = 2 \sum \omega_i^2 (HDO).$$

Using Table 9, we get

$$\omega_3 = 3710 \text{ cm}^{-1}.$$

The product rule gives $\omega_3 = 3730 \text{ cm}^{-1}$.

We have considered a water molecule with a relatively low symmetry. For higher symmetry molecules, symmetry considerations simplify the problem to an even greater extent. As an example, let us consider a methane molecule CH_4, with T_d symmetry.

The natural coordinates of a methane molecule are the increments q_i in the four C—H bond lengths (q_1, q_2, q_3, q_4) and the increments α_{ik} in the corresponding six H—C—H bond angles (Figure 31). The angular coordinates α_{ik} in this case are not entirely independent. They are related by one equality

$$\alpha_{12} + \alpha_{13} + \alpha_{14} + \alpha_{23} + \alpha_{24} + \alpha_{34} = 0. \qquad (10.52)$$

Thus, in our statement of the problem of vibration modes, we have introduced one "redundant" coordinate, and the frequency corresponding to this coordinate is zero. The redundant coordinate will be automatically eliminated by an appropriate transformation of coordinates (see below).

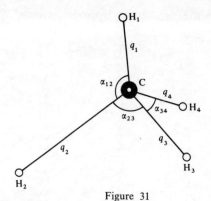

Figure 31

Natural vibrational coordinates of the methane molecule.

The methane molecule has tetrahedral bond angles ($\alpha_0 = 109°28'$, $\cos \alpha_0 = -\frac{1}{3}$, $\sin \alpha_0 = \sqrt{8/3}$). The C—H bond length is 1.09 Å. Proceeding from the geometrical structure of the methane molecule, we can find the kinematic coupling coefficients. Because of the high symmetry, there are only seven different kinematic and dynamic coefficients. All these are listed in Table 10a.

The kinematic and dynamic matrices are best simplified using the same technique as previously for the H_2O molecule. We multiply the first and the second row of the kinematic matrix by $1/\sqrt{2}$, add up the first two rows, and then subtract the first row from the second. The same operation is repeated for all the other pairs of rows, i.e., the 3rd and the 4th, the 5th and the 6th, etc. The same operations are then applied to the matrix columns. Symbolically, this transformation can be written as

$$\frac{1}{\sqrt{2}}(1 + 2),\ \frac{1}{\sqrt{2}}(2 - 1),\ \frac{1}{\sqrt{2}}(3 + 4),\ \frac{1}{\sqrt{2}}(4 - 3),\ \frac{1}{\sqrt{2}}(5 + 6),$$

$$\frac{1}{\sqrt{2}}(6 - 5),\ \frac{1}{\sqrt{2}}(7 + 8),\ \frac{1}{\sqrt{2}}(8 - 7),\ \frac{1}{\sqrt{2}}(9 + 10),\ \frac{1}{\sqrt{2}}(10 - 9).$$

The numbers in parentheses identify the rows and the columns. As a result of this transformation, numerous matrix elements vanish. Further transforming

$$\frac{1}{\sqrt{2}}(1 + 3),\ \frac{1}{\sqrt{2}}(3 - 1),\ \frac{1}{\sqrt{2}}(5 + 9),\ \frac{1}{\sqrt{2}}(9 - 5),\ \frac{1}{\sqrt{2}}(6 + 10),$$

$$\frac{1}{\sqrt{2}}(10 - 6),$$

we obtain a substantially simpler matrix, which is reduced to a quasidiagonal form by a simple interchange of rows and columns. Tables 10a and 10b illustrate this

Table 10a

TRANSFORMATION OF THE KINEMATIC MATRIX OF THE METHANE MOLECULE

		1	2	3	4	5	6	7	8	9	10
		q_1	q_2	q_3	q_4	α_{12}	α_{13}	α_{23}	α_{14}	α_{24}	α_{34}
1	q_1	A_q	A_h	A_h	A_h	A_1	A_1	A_2	A_1	A_2	A_2
2	q_2	A_h	A_q	A_h	A_h	A_1	A_2	A_1	A_2	A_1	A_2
3	q_3	A_h	A_h	A_q	A_h	A_2	A_1	A_1	A_2	A_2	A_1
4	q_4	A_h	A_h	A_h	A_q	A_2	A_2	A_2	A_1	A_1	A_1
5	α_{12}	A_1	A_1	A_2	A_2	A_α	γ_1	γ_1	γ_1	γ_1	γ_2
6	α_{13}	A_1	A_2	A_1	A_2	γ_1	A_α	γ_1	γ_1	γ_2	γ_1
7	α_{23}	A_2	A_1	A_1	A_2	γ_1	γ_1	A_α	γ_2	γ_1	γ_1
8	α_{14}	A_1	A_2	A_2	A_1	γ_1	γ_1	γ_2	A_α	γ_1	γ_1
9	α_{24}	A_2	A_1	A_2	A_1	γ_1	γ_2	γ_1	γ_1	A_α	γ_1
10	α_{34}	A_2	A_2	A_1	A_1	γ_2	γ_1	γ_1	γ_1	γ_1	A_α

Note: Symbols used (the corresponding dynamic coefficients are given in parentheses):

$$A_q = \varepsilon_H + \varepsilon_C(K_q) ; \quad A_h = -\frac{1}{3}\varepsilon_C(h) ;$$

$$A_1 = -\frac{\sqrt{8}}{3}\varepsilon_C(a_1) ; \quad A_2 = \frac{\sqrt{8}}{3}\varepsilon_C(a_2) ; \quad A_\alpha = 2\varepsilon_H + \frac{8}{3}\varepsilon_C(K_\alpha) ;$$

$$\gamma_1 = -\frac{1}{2}\varepsilon_H(l_1) ; \quad \gamma_2 = -\frac{8}{3}\varepsilon_C(l_2) ;$$

$$\varepsilon_H = \frac{1}{m_H} ; \quad \varepsilon_C = \frac{1}{m_C} .$$

Relations: $A_1 + A_2 = 0, \quad A_\alpha + 4\gamma_1 + \gamma_2 = 0.$

transformation for the kinematic matrix. The dynamic matrix undergoes a similar transformation. The 3×3 matrix in Table 10b is reduced by the transformation

$$\frac{\sqrt{2}}{\sqrt{3}}(5) + \frac{1}{\sqrt{3}}(7), \quad \frac{\sqrt{2}}{\sqrt{3}}(7) - \frac{1}{\sqrt{3}}(5)$$

to the form

	1	5	7
1	$A_q + 3A_h$	$\sqrt{6}(A_1 + A_2)$	0
5	$\sqrt{6}(A_1 + A_2)$	$A_\alpha + 4\gamma_1 + \gamma_2$	0
7	0	0	$A_\alpha - 2\gamma_1 + \gamma_2$

Table 10b

	1	5	7	2	3
1	$A_q + 3A_h$	$2(A_1 + A_2)$	$\sqrt{2}(A_1 + A_2)$		
5	$2(A_1 + A_2)$	$A_\alpha + 2\gamma_1 + \gamma_2$	$2\sqrt{2}\gamma_1$		
7	$\sqrt{2}(A_1 + A_2)$	$2\sqrt{2}\gamma_1$	$A_\alpha + \gamma_2$		
2				$A_q - A_h$	0
3				0	$A_q - A_h$
4				0	0
6				$-\dfrac{1}{\sqrt{2}}(A_1 - A_2)$	$A_1 - A_2$
8				$A_1 - A_2$	0
9				$\dfrac{1}{\sqrt{2}}(A_1 - A_2)$	$A_1 - A_2$
10					

Because of the mathematical relations between the kinematic coefficients (see Table 10a), all the coefficients in the fifth column and the fifth row are zero. This row and this column correspond to the "redundant" coordinate, and they can be crossed out from the dynamic matrix. We are thus left with only the diagonal coefficients $A_q + 3A_h$ and $A_\alpha - 2\gamma_1 + \gamma_2$, and the latter is identical to the coefficient entering the 10th row of the quasidiagonal matrix in Table 10b. We thus end up with two first-order secular equations:

$$(A_q + 3A_h)(K_q + 3h) - \omega^2 = 0 \tag{10.53}$$

(this equation gives the frequency of the totally symmetric modes),

$$(A_\alpha - 2\gamma_1 + \gamma_2)(K_\alpha - 2l_1 + l_2) - \omega^2 = 0 \tag{10.54}$$

(this equation gives the frequency of the doubly degenerate modes).

The 6×6 matrix in Table 10b is reduced to quasidiagonal form by the transformation

$$\frac{1}{\sqrt{2}}(2 + 4), \ \frac{1}{\sqrt{2}}(4 - 2), \ \frac{1}{\sqrt{2}}(6 + 9), \ \frac{1}{\sqrt{2}}(9 - 6).$$

4	6	8	9	10
0	$-\dfrac{1}{\sqrt{2}}(A_1 - A_2)$	$A_1 - A_2$	$\dfrac{1}{\sqrt{2}}(A_1 - A_2)$	
0	$A_1 - A_2$	0	$A_1 - A_2$	
$A_q - A_h$	$-\dfrac{1}{\sqrt{2}}(A_1 - A_2)$	$-(A_1 - A_2)$	$\dfrac{1}{\sqrt{2}}(A_1 - A_2)$	
$-\dfrac{1}{\sqrt{2}}(A_1 - A_2)$	$A_\alpha - \gamma_2$	0	0	
$-(A_1 - A_2)$	0	$A_\alpha - \gamma_2$	0	
$\dfrac{1}{\sqrt{2}}(A_1 - A_2)$	0	0	$A_\alpha - \gamma_2$	
				$A_\alpha - 2\gamma_1 + \gamma_2$

The transformed matrix and the corresponding dynamic matrix give three identical second-order secular equations for the triply degenerate modes,

$$
\left\| \begin{matrix} A_q - A_h & \sqrt{2}\,(A_1 - A_2) \\ \sqrt{2}\,(A_1 - A_2) & A_\alpha - \gamma_2 \end{matrix} \right\| \cdot \left\| \begin{matrix} K_q - h & \sqrt{2}\,(a_1 - a_2) \\ \sqrt{2}\,(a_1 - a_2) & K_\alpha - l_2 \end{matrix} \right\| -
$$

$$
- \left\| \begin{matrix} \omega^2 & 0 \\ 0 & \omega^2 \end{matrix} \right\| = 0. \qquad (10.55)
$$

The problem of vibration modes for a methane molecule has thus been reduced by symmetry considerations to two first-order equations and one quadratic equation. These equations contain only five independent combinations of the dynamic coefficients, which should be determined from experimental data on the vibration frequencies of CH_4 and isotope-substituted molecules.

The results of numerical calculations for CH_4, CD_4, and CT_4, with allowance for anharmonicity, are given in §15.

The above method for simplifying the kinematic and dynamic matrices proves to be even more effective if the original matrices can be broken up into separate blocks or squares, some of which may be identical because of the peculiar symmetry properties of the molecule. Matrices of this kind occur when the molecule is made up of relatively few characteristic atomic groupings. Each square then corresponds to the coupling of the vibrational coordinates within one atomic grouping or between two nearby groupings, etc. The squares remain unaltered or change insignificantly when we pass from one molecule to the next in a series of analogous compounds or from one rotational isomer to another. The square-block structure of the matrices, like the symmetry considerations, greatly simplifies the solution of secular equations [100].

The manipulations with square-block matrices will be considered for the case of cyclohexane C_6H_{12}. This molecule has 48 vibrational degrees of freedom. It shows a characteristic "chair" configuration with D_{3d} symmetry (Figure 32). The alternative "boat" configuration is unstable at room temperature, but may prove relatively significant at high temperatures [106]. Note that in the "chair" configuration of cyclohexane, the hydrogen atoms surrounding each of the carbons are not entirely equivalent. One of these atoms lies in the "equatorial" belt which runs around the ring (the equatorial hydrogen atoms), whereas the other hydrogen atom is situated above or below this belt (the "polar" hydrogen atoms). This gives rise to a complicated stereoisomerism of the cyclohexane derivatives, which will be considered at a later stage.

The natural coordinates for a cyclohexane molecule are the 12 increments q_i of the C—H bond lengths, the 6 increments Q_i of the C—C bond lengths, and the 36 increments of the corresponding bond angles which are related by six equalities of the form

$$\alpha_i + 4\beta_i + \gamma_i = 0 . \tag{10.56}$$

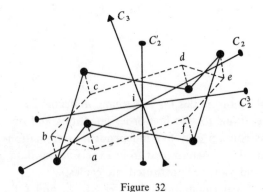

Figure 32

Schematic diagrams of the cyclohexane molecule.

Here α_i is the angle between C_i—H bonds, β_i is the angle between the C_i—H and C_i—C bonds, γ_i is the angle between the C_i—C bonds; the subscript i identifies the carbon atoms. The kinematic coupling coefficients can be found using the tables in [80, 81]. The result is a 54×54 matrix, which can be written in the following schematic form using square blocks (see [100]):

$$
A = \begin{Vmatrix}
H & F & C & 0 & C' & F' \\
F' & H & F & C & 0 & C' \\
C' & F' & H & F & C & 0 \\
0 & C' & F' & H & F & C \\
C & 0 & C' & F' & H & F \\
F & C & 0 & C' & F' & H
\end{Vmatrix}. \tag{10.57}
$$

Here H, F, C, are 9×9 matrices with one "zero" row, or 8×8 matrices if the "redundant" coordinate is eliminated using Eq. (10.56). It is readily seen that the matrix A can be simplified further by using larger blocks, i.e.,

$$
A' = \begin{Vmatrix} \alpha & \beta \\ \beta & \alpha \end{Vmatrix}, \tag{10.58}
$$

where

$$
\alpha = \begin{Vmatrix} H & F & C \\ F' & H & F \\ C' & F' & H \end{Vmatrix}, \quad
\beta = \begin{Vmatrix} 0 & C' & F' \\ C & 0 & C' \\ F & C & 0 \end{Vmatrix}. \tag{10.59}
$$

The matrix A' (10.58) is diagonalized by the transformation

$$
\frac{1}{\sqrt{2}}(1 + 2), \quad \frac{1}{\sqrt{2}}(2 - 1)
$$

and takes the form

$$
A' = \begin{Vmatrix} \alpha + \beta & 0 \\ 0 & \alpha - \beta \end{Vmatrix}. \tag{10.60}
$$

The original matrix A, (10.57), thus separates into two matrices:

$$
\alpha + \beta = \begin{Vmatrix}
H & F + C' & F' + C \\
F' + C & H & F + C' \\
F + C' & F' + C & H
\end{Vmatrix},
$$

$$
\alpha - \beta = \begin{Vmatrix}
H & F - C' & -(F' - C) \\
F' - C & H & F - C' \\
-(F - C') & F' - C & H
\end{Vmatrix}. \tag{10.61}
$$

The matrix $\alpha + \beta$ can be reduced to quasidiagonal form by a tranformation

$$\frac{1}{\sqrt{2}}(2+3),\ \frac{1}{\sqrt{2}}(3-2),\ \text{followed by}\ \frac{\sqrt{2}}{3}(1)-\frac{1}{\sqrt{3}}(2),\ \frac{\sqrt{2}}{\sqrt{3}}(2)+\frac{1}{\sqrt{3}}(1):$$

$$\alpha + \beta = \begin{Vmatrix} H+F+F'+C+C' & 0 & 0 \\ 0 & H-\frac{1}{2}(F+F'+C+C') & -\frac{\sqrt{3}}{2}(F-F'-C+C') \\ 0 & \frac{\sqrt{3}}{2}(F-F'-C+C') & H-\frac{1}{2}(F+F'+C+C') \end{Vmatrix}.$$

$$(10.62)$$

Similarly, the transformation $\dfrac{1}{\sqrt{2}}(2+3),\ \dfrac{1}{\sqrt{2}}(3-2)$ followed by

$$\frac{\sqrt{2}}{\sqrt{3}}(1)-\frac{1}{\sqrt{3}}(3),\ \frac{\sqrt{2}}{\sqrt{3}}(3)+\frac{1}{\sqrt{3}}(1)$$

reduces the matrix $\alpha - \beta$ to the quasidiagonal form

$$\alpha - \beta = \begin{Vmatrix} H-(F+F')+(C+C') & 0 & 0 \\ 0 & H+\frac{1}{2}(F+F'-C-C') & \frac{\sqrt{3}}{2}(F-F'+C-C') \\ 0 & -\frac{\sqrt{3}}{2}(F-F'+C-C') & H+\frac{1}{2}(F+F'-C-C') \end{Vmatrix}.$$

$$(10.63)$$

Subsequent transfomations break the 2×2 matrices in (10.62) and (10.63) each into two identical matrices. Thus, the original 48×48 matrix breaks up into six 8×8 matrices, i.e., the problem of vibration modes is greatly simplified. The two pairs of identical matrices give each eight E_g modes (the $\alpha + \beta$ matrix) and eight E_u modes (the $\alpha - \beta$ matrix). The matrix $H + F + F' + C + C'$ leads to six normal modes A_{1g} (totally symmetric) and two A_{2g} modes. The matrix $H - (F + F') + C + C'$ similarly gives five A_{2u} modes and three A_{1u} modes.

The above transformation technique automatically breaks the normal modes into separate classes corresponding to the symmetry properties of the molecule. The high-order secular equation as a result breaks up into several low-degree secular equations for each class of normal modes, and the solution of the problem is greatly simplified. The transformation from natural to normal coordinates thus includes a highly important stage in which the transformation to the symmetry coordinates is computed. The complete solution of the problem gives a full set of vibration frequencies for each symmetry class, which can be compared with the experimental frequencies to check on the initial assumptions concerning molecular symmetry. Such calculations have been carried out for numerous molecules and many valuable results have been obtained regarding molecular structure and the interpretation of vibrational spectra. In practice, the actual computations and especially the symmetry considerations may follow an entirely different path from that used in our example. Nowadays, these computations are usually carried out using a digital computer, so that the numerical material (the matrices and the computation procedure) is usually adapted for the particular requirements of the individual computer.

A computer solution of the problem of vibration modes is not always required for the analysis of molecular structure and the interpretation of the vibrational spectra. Sometimes it is sufficient to know the number of modes in each symmetry class. This simple problem can be solved easily using the methods of the theory of group representations. We will briefly consider some basic propositions of this theory, which has a significant bearing not only on the calculation of the number of vibration modes in various symmetry classes but also on the exact derivation of the selection rules discussed in §9. The theory of representations provides a particularly valuable tool in studying the vibrations of crystals (see Chapter III).

We recall that a group G of order g has g independent elements. The elements of symmetry groups are the symmetry operations. Each symmetry operation corresponds to a certain linear transformation of coordinates, defined by the matrix of the appropriate coefficients. The group product of two symmetry operations corresponds to a multiplication of the two linear-transformation matrices describing these symmetry operations. The identity operation e corresponds to a unit matrix, and the inverse operation corresponds to the inverse matrix. The entire set of the linear-transformation matrices corresponding to the elements of a given symmetry group is itself a group, whose properties are equivalent to the properties of the original symmetry group. The group of the linear-transformation matrices π_i which are in one-to-one correspondence with the elements of some other group constitutes the *representation* of the latter group. The number of variables whose linear transformations constitute the representation determines the rank of the representation matrix and is known as the *dimension* of the representation. The variables themselves form the *basis* of the representation.

To make all these concepts more tangible, let us consider the case of an ammonia molecule (C_{3v} symmetry). In the natural coordinates q_1, q_2, q_3, the six possible symmetry operations correspond to six linear transformations of coordinates.

Rotation C_3 through 120° has the representation (Figure 33)

$$q'_1 = q_3 = 0 \cdot q_1 + 0 \cdot q_2 + 1 \cdot q_3,$$
$$q'_2 = q_1 = 1 \cdot q_1 + 0 \cdot q_2 + 0 \cdot q_3, \qquad (10.64)$$
$$q'_3 = q_2 = 0 \cdot q_1 + 1 \cdot q_2 + 0 \cdot q_3.$$

The symmetry element C_3 thus corresponds to the matrix

$$\pi(C_3) = \begin{Vmatrix} 0 & 0 & 1 \\ 1 & 0 & 0 \\ 0 & 1 & 0 \end{Vmatrix}.$$

Figure 33 shows the symbols of the transformation matrices corresponding to each of the symmetry elements of the NH_3 molecule:

$$e = \begin{Vmatrix} 1 & 0 & 0 \\ 0 & 1 & 0 \\ 0 & 0 & 1 \end{Vmatrix} = \begin{Vmatrix} 1 & 0 & 0 \\ 0 & 1 & 0 \\ 0 & 0 & 1 \end{Vmatrix}, \quad C_3 = \begin{Vmatrix} 0 & 0 & 1 \\ 1 & 0 & 0 \\ 0 & 1 & 0 \end{Vmatrix} = \begin{Vmatrix} 1 & 0 & 0 \\ 0 & -\dfrac{1}{2} & -\dfrac{\sqrt{3}}{2} \\ 0 & \dfrac{\sqrt{3}}{2} & -\dfrac{1}{2} \end{Vmatrix},$$

$$C_3^{-1} = \begin{Vmatrix} 0 & 1 & 0 \\ 0 & 0 & 1 \\ 1 & 0 & 0 \end{Vmatrix} = \begin{Vmatrix} 1 & 0 & 0 \\ 0 & -\dfrac{1}{2} & \dfrac{\sqrt{3}}{2} \\ 0 & -\dfrac{\sqrt{3}}{2} & -\dfrac{1}{2} \end{Vmatrix}$$

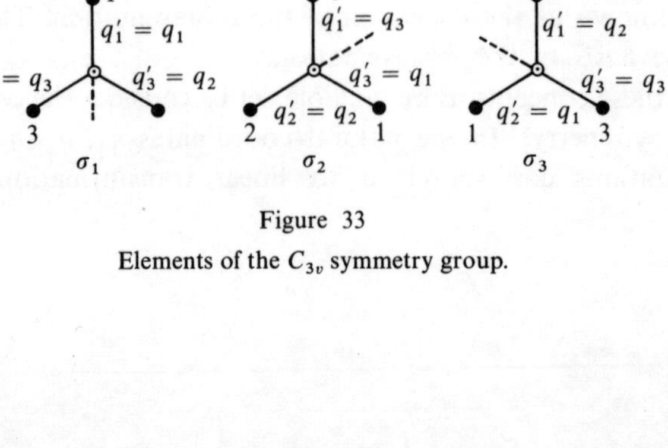

Figure 33

Elements of the C_{3v} symmetry group.

$$\sigma_1 = \begin{vmatrix} 1 & 0 & 0 \\ 0 & 0 & 1 \\ 0 & 1 & 0 \end{vmatrix} = \begin{vmatrix} 1 & \vdots & 0 & 0 \\ \hdots & & & \\ 0 & \vdots & \dfrac{1}{2} & \dfrac{\sqrt{3}}{2} \\ 0 & \vdots & \dfrac{\sqrt{3}}{2} & -\dfrac{1}{2} \end{vmatrix},$$

$$\sigma_2 = \begin{vmatrix} 0 & 0 & 1 \\ 0 & 1 & 0 \\ 1 & 0 & 0 \end{vmatrix} = \begin{vmatrix} 1 & \vdots & 0 & 0 \\ \hdots & & & \\ 0 & \vdots & -\dfrac{1}{2} & -\dfrac{\sqrt{3}}{2} \\ 0 & \vdots & -\dfrac{\sqrt{3}}{2} & -\dfrac{1}{2} \end{vmatrix},$$

$$\sigma_3 = \begin{vmatrix} 0 & 1 & 0 \\ 1 & 0 & 0 \\ 0 & 0 & 1 \end{vmatrix} = \begin{vmatrix} 1 & \vdots & 0 & 0 \\ 0 & \vdots & -1 & 0 \\ 0 & \vdots & 0 & 1 \end{vmatrix}.$$

These six matrices form the representation of the C_{3v} group, and the dimension of this representation is 3.

A topic of considerable interest is the transformation of the representation matrices of some group to an identical quasidiagonal form. If some orthogonal transformation of the coordinates will simultaneously reduce all the representation matrices to quasidiagonal form, the representation is said to be *reducible*; if no such transformation exists, the representation is said to be *irreducible*. For the C_{3v} group, a transformation of the form

$$C = \begin{Vmatrix} \dfrac{\sqrt{2}}{\sqrt{3}} & 0 & \dfrac{1}{\sqrt{3}} \\ 0 & 1 & 0 \\ -\dfrac{1}{\sqrt{3}} & 0 & \dfrac{\sqrt{2}}{\sqrt{3}} \end{Vmatrix} \cdot \begin{Vmatrix} \dfrac{1}{\sqrt{2}} & \dfrac{1}{\sqrt{2}} & 0 \\ -\dfrac{1}{\sqrt{2}} & \dfrac{1}{\sqrt{2}} & 0 \\ 0 & 0 & 1 \end{Vmatrix} = \begin{Vmatrix} \dfrac{1}{\sqrt{3}} & \dfrac{1}{\sqrt{3}} & \dfrac{1}{\sqrt{3}} \\ -\dfrac{1}{\sqrt{2}} & \dfrac{1}{\sqrt{2}} & 0 \\ -\dfrac{1}{\sqrt{6}} & -\dfrac{1}{\sqrt{6}} & \dfrac{\sqrt{2}}{\sqrt{3}} \end{Vmatrix}$$

$$(10.65)$$

reduces all the representation matrices to the quasidiagonal form shown on pp. 140, 141, e.g.,

$$C\pi(C_3)C^{-1} = \left\| \begin{array}{ccc} 1 & 0 & 0 \\ 0 & -\dfrac{1}{2} & -\dfrac{\sqrt{3}}{2} \\ 0 & \dfrac{\sqrt{3}}{2} & -\dfrac{1}{2} \end{array} \right\| .$$

A similar reduction is observed for all the other elements of the group. Note that transformation (10.65) was previously used in connection with the cyclohexane molecule.

The reduction broke up the three-dimension representation Γ into a sum of two representations,

$$\Gamma = \Gamma^1 + \Gamma^2, \tag{10.66}$$

where Γ^1 is a one-dimensional representation and Γ^2 is a two-dimensional representation. The significance of irreducible representations is in that the vibration modes from different symmetry classes are described by coordinates which transform according to different irreducible representations. In other words, the entire set of coordinates under a given linear transformation breaks into several subsets, and each is transformed according to a certain irreducible representation by the symmetry operations of the group. It may turn out, however, that several different subsets (say, m) transform according to the same irreducible representation. In this case we say that the particular irreducible representation is contained (or accommodated) m times in a reducible representation.

It can be shown that the number of different irreducible representations of a group is equal to the number n of classes in the group. The dimensions l_i of the irreducible representations Γ_i of the group are related by a simple equality to the group order g (see, e.g., [5]):

$$\sum_{i=1}^{n} l_i^2 = g. \tag{10.67}$$

For the C_{3v} group, the number of classes is $n = 3$ (see §9), the order of the group is $g = 6$, and we have

$$1^2 + 1^2 + 2^2 = 6, \tag{10.67'}$$

i.e., there should be two one-dimensional representations and one two-dimensional representation. The previous analysis gives a one-dimensional identity representation A_1, which may be regarded as totally symmetric, and a two-dimensional representation E, which corresponds to doubly degenerate vibrational coordinates.

The third irreducible representation—the antisymmetric representation A_2—should be one-dimensional according to (10.67').* Eq. (10.67) thus predicts the partition of the representation Γ of the C_{3v} group into three irreducible representations:

$$\Gamma = A_1 + A_2 + E. \tag{10.68}$$

Groups with several symmetry axes of third or higher order may have a three-dimensional representation F, which corresponds to triply degenerate modes. For the T_d group (the symmetry group of the methane molecule), we have

$$g = 24, \quad n = 5.$$

Eq. (10.67) yields

$$1^2 + 1^2 + 2^2 + 3^2 + 3^2 = 24. \tag{10.69}$$

The corresponding group representation is thus reduced to the form

$$\Gamma = A_1 + A_2 + E + F_1 + F_2 \tag{10.70}$$

(see Table 7).

The decompositions of group representations into irreducible representations are known for all the symmetry groups, but they are hardly even used in explicit form because each matrix can be adequately characterized by a certain number, known as the *character* of the matrix. The character of a matrix is defined as the sum of its diagonal elements.

$$\chi(z) = \sum \pi_{mm}(z), \tag{10.71}$$

where z is a group element. The great significance of the characters stems from the following facts: a) they do not change under orthogonal transformations of coordinates, b) they have the same numerical value for all the group elements which belong to one class. For the C_{3v} group, for example, we have the following range of characters (see Figure 33):

group elements:	C_1	C_3, C_3^{-1}	$\sigma_1, \sigma_2, \sigma_3$
characters:	3	0	1

It follows from the definition of a character and from property a above that if some reducible representation is decomposable into irreducible representations,

$$\Gamma = \sum \Gamma^i, \tag{10.72}$$

---

* The coordinates transforming according to this representation emerge if we consider rotation and translation of the molecule. They also turn up in vibrations of more complex molecules of this symmetry group.

the character of the element z also can be decomposed into a sum of characters,

$$\chi(z) = \sum \chi_i(z).$$ (10.73)

The character for the unit element e is evidently equal to the dimension of the representation. The characters of some symmetry groups are listed in Table 11.

It is demonstrated in group theory (see, e.g., [86]) that the characters of irreducible non-equivalent representations satisfy an orthogonality relation

$$\sum_z \chi_k(z)\chi_i^*(z) = g \cdot \delta_{kl},$$ (10.74)

where g is the order of the group. Since the elements of one class have the same character, the sum over the elements in (10.74) can be replaced with a sum over the classes. Indeed, let N_j be the number of elements in class j, n the number of different classes. Then each character $\chi_k(z_j)$ appears N_j times in the sum (10.74). Hence,

$$\sum_{j=1}^{n} N_j\chi_k(z_j)\chi_i^*(z_j) = g \cdot \delta_{kl}.$$ (10.75)

Table 11

CHARACTERS OF IRREDUCIBLE REPRESENTATIONS
OF SOME POINT GROUPS*

C_i	e	i	C_s	e	σ_h	C_2	e	C_2	C_3	e	$2C_3$
A_g	1	1	A'	1	1	A	1	1	A	1	1
A_u	1	-1	A''	1	-1	B	1	-1	E	2	-1

T_d	e	$8C_3$	$3C_2$	$6S_4$	$6\sigma_d$

O	e	$8C_3$	$3C_2$	$6C_4$	$6C_2'$	$D_{2d} = V_d$	e	$2S_4$	C_2	$2C_2'$	$2\sigma_d'$
A_1	1	1	1	1	1	A_1	1	1	1	1	1
A_2	1	1	1	-1	-1	A_2	1	1	1	-1	-1
E	2	-1	2	0	0	B_1	1	-1	1	1	-1
F_1	3	0	-1	1	-1	B_2	1	-1	1	-1	1
F_2	3	0	-1	-1	1	E	2	0	-2	0	0

D_{3d}	e	$2C_3$	$3C_2$	i	$2S_6$	$3\sigma_d$
A_{1g}	1	1	1	1	1	1
A_{2g}	1	1	-1	1	1	-1
E_g	2	-1	0	2	-1	0
A_{1u}	1	1	1	-1	-1	-1
A_{2u}	1	1	-1	-1	-1	1
E_u	2	-1	0	-2	1	0

* More detailed tables of characters will be found in [44, 82, 83].

Using the orthogonality relation (10.74), we can decompose the character of any reducible representation of a group into a sum of characters of irreducible representations. Let m_i be the number of times some i-th irreducible representation is contained in the given reducible representation. Then

$$\chi(z) = \sum_i m_i \chi_i(z). \tag{10.76}$$

The sum in (10.76) is over all the irreducible representations. It is readily seen that (10.76) is in fact an alternative form of writing (10.73). The coefficients m_i are given according to (10.74), (10.75) by the formula

$$m_i = \frac{1}{g} \sum_z \chi(z)\chi_i^*(z) = \frac{1}{g} \sum_{j=1}^n N_j\chi(z_j)\chi_i^*(z_j). \tag{10.77}$$

Eq. (10.77) provides the basic formula for calculating the number of normal modes of each symmetry class of a given molecule. The characters of the irreducible representations $\chi_i(z_j)$ entering this equation can be found in tables [44, 82, 83]. The number N_j of symmetry operations of the j-th class is indicated in the tables by a coefficient before the symbol of the symmetry operation of the corresponding class. We thus only have to count the characters $\chi(z_j)$ of the representations of the symmetry operations of the molecule.

In normal coordinates the energy of a molecule can be written in the form

$$E = \frac{1}{2} \sum_\alpha \sum_{i=1}^{f_\alpha} \dot{Q}_{\alpha i}^2 + \frac{1}{2} \sum_\alpha \omega_\alpha^2 \sum_{i=1}^{f_\alpha} Q_{\alpha i}^2, \tag{10.78}$$

where the subscript α identifies the different eigenfrequencies, and the subscript i enumerates the coordinates corresponding to the same f_α-fold degenerate frequency. This expression is ivariant under symmetry transformations. Hence, under any symmetry transformation, the normal coordinates with every given α, i.e., the co-ordinates $Q_{\alpha 1}, Q_{\alpha 2}, \ldots, Q_{\alpha f_\alpha}$, are only intermixed between themselves and the sums $\sum_{i=1}^{f_\alpha} Q_{\alpha i}^2$ remain unaltered. This implies that the normal coordinates $Q_{\alpha 1}, Q_{\alpha 2}, \ldots, Q_{\alpha f_\alpha}$ are transformed according to a certain irreducible representation of the symmetry group of the molecule, and f_α can be interpreted as the dimension of this representation. If each element z of the symmerty group is made to correspond to a matrix $\pi(z)$ of the appropriate linear transformation of the vibrational coordinates, we obtain the *vibrational representation* Γ_v of the group G (see [86]). In general, the dimension of this representation is $3N - 6$, where N is the number of atoms in the molecule. Γ_v may contain every irreducible representation of the given symmetry group more than once. In some cases, a more general representation Γ_m has to be considered; it is generated by supplementing Γ_v with the three-dimensional representation Γ_t

corresponding to the translational motion of the molecule and the three-dimensional representation Γ_Ω corresponding to the molecular rotation:

$$\Gamma_m = \Gamma_v + \Gamma_t + \Gamma_\Omega. \tag{10.79}$$

Γ_m is known as the *mechanical representation* [86].

In calculating the characters $\chi(z)$ of Γ_m and Γ_v, we should remember that only the atoms whose equilibrium positions are not altered by a given symmetry operation z contribute to these characters. To prove this proposition (see [20, 86, 107]), it is better to change over from vibrational coordinates to displacements of atoms from their equilibrium positions. Since the representation characters are invariant under orthogonal linear transformations, this does not affect the magnitude of the characters.

Let $r_i, r_k, \ldots$ be the displacement vectors of the atoms $i, k, \ldots$ from their equilibrium positions. The cartesian components of these vectors are x_i, y_i, z_i, etc. Suppose a given symmetry operation z moves the atom i to a new position, previously occupied by another atom k of the same species. Under this transformation, the displacement components x_i', y_i', z_i' are expressible in terms of x_k, y_k, z_k, i.e., they do not contain the components x_i, y_i, z_i. As a result, the corresponding matrix rows $\pi_{ik}(z)$ have no diagonal elements and the contribution from these atoms to $\chi(z)$ is indeed nil.

If, on the other hand, the symmetry operation z does not alter the equilibrium position of the i-th atom, the components of the displacement vector are only inter-mixed between themselves by this operation. Let us first consider a rotation C_ϕ through an angle ϕ about some symmetry axis, which we assume to point along the axis z. By assumption, the equilibrium position of the atom i is on this axis. As a result of the rotation, the components of the vector r_i are transformed as follows:

$$x_i' = x_i \cos \phi + y_i \sin \phi,$$
$$y_i' = - x_i \sin \phi + y_i \cos \phi, \tag{10.80}$$
$$z_i' = z_i.$$

The character, i.e., the sum of the diagonal elements of the transformation matrix (10.80), is

$$\chi(C_\phi) = 1 + 2 \cos \phi. \tag{10.81}$$

If there are $a(C_\phi)$ atoms of one species, the overall character of the representation Γ_m for this symmetry operation is

$$\chi_m(C_\phi) = a(C_\phi)(1 + 2 \cos \phi). \tag{10.82}$$

For translational motion, described by the displacement vector r_t of the center of inertia of the molecule (which lies on the symmetry axis), the character is also given by

$$\chi_t(C_\phi) = 1 + 2 \cos \phi. \tag{10.83}$$

Similarly, for the rotation of the entire molecule* through a small angle $\delta\Omega$ we have

$$\chi_\Omega(C_\phi) = 1 + 2\cos\phi. \tag{10.84}$$

The character of the vibrational representation Γ_v for the symmetry operation C_ϕ is thus

$$\chi_v(C_\phi) = \chi_m - \chi_t - \chi_\Omega = [a(C_\phi) - 2](1 + 2\cos\phi). \tag{10.85}$$

Let us now consider the reflection–rotation transformation S_ϕ, which can be treated as a rotation through an angle ϕ around the axis z followed by mirror reflection in the plane x, y. Under this symmetry operation we have

$$x'_i = x_i \cos\phi + y_i \sin\phi,$$

$$y'_i = - x_i \sin\phi + y_i \cos\phi, \tag{10.86}$$

$$z'_i = - z_i.$$

For the representation characters under this operation we have, as before,

$$\chi_m(S_\phi) = a(S_\phi)(- 1 + 2\cos\phi), \tag{10.87}$$

$a(S_\phi)$ is the number of atoms whose equilibrium positions are not altered by S_ϕ,

$$\chi_t(S_\phi) = - 1 + 2\cos\phi, \tag{10.88}$$

$$\chi_\Omega(S_\phi) = - (- 1 + 2\cos\phi). \tag{10.89}$$

Thus, for S_ϕ we have

$$\chi_v(S_\phi) = \chi_m(S_\phi) = a(S_\phi)(- 1 + 2\cos\phi). \tag{10.90}$$

Particular cases of the operation S_ϕ are reflection σ in a plane ($\phi = 0$), when

$$\chi_v(S_0) = \chi_v(\sigma) = a(\sigma), \tag{10.91}$$

and inversion i ($\phi = \pi$),

$$\chi_v(S_\pi) = \chi_v(i) = - 3a(i). \tag{10.92}$$

In general (excepting linear molecules), the character of the vibrational representation corresponding to the identity transformation is

$$\chi_v(e) = 3N - 6. \tag{10.93}$$

This is a particular case of expression (10.85) for $\phi = 0$, when $a(C_\phi) = a(e) = N$.

---

* A small rotation angle can be regarded as a vector of magnitude $\delta\Omega$ directed along the rotation axis. The vector $\delta\Omega$ defined in this way is an axial vector. The following expressions for the characters of representations of the polar vector r_i and the axial vector $\delta\Omega$ can be applied to other vectors of the same kind.

Eqs. (10.85) and (10.90) thus cover the entire range of symmetry operations of non-linear molecules.

Let us apply the above results to calculate the number of modes in each symmetry class. Inserting for $\chi(z_j)$ in (10.77) their expressions from (10.85) and (10.90), we find

$$m_i = \frac{1}{g} \left\{ \sum_{j=1}^{n'} N_j [a(C_{\phi j}) - 2] (1 + 2 \cos \phi_j) \chi_i^* (C_{\phi j}) + \right.$$

$$\left. + \sum_{j'=n'+1}^{n} N_{j'} a(S_{\phi j'}) (-1 + 2 \cos \phi_{j'}) \chi_i^* (S_{\phi j'}) \right\}. \tag{10.94}$$

This is the solution of our problem. As an example, let us consider the cyclohexane molecule (see Figure 32) with D_{3d} symmetry. The symmetry elements of this group are

$$e, \ 2C_3, \ 3C_2, \ i, \ 2S_6, \ 3\sigma_d \ (g = 12).$$

Figure 32 readily shows that only e and σ_d leave certain atoms without changing their equilibrium positions, namely $a(e) = 18$, $a(\sigma_d) = 6$. For the other symmetry operations $a(C_3) = a(C_2) = a(i) = a(S_6) = 0$. As a result, the sum in (10.94) contains three terms only. The characters of the irreducible representations are borrowed from Table 11. We thus have

$$m(A_{1g}) = \tfrac{1}{12} \left[1 \cdot (18 - 2) \cdot 3 \cdot 1 + 3 (-2)(-1) \cdot 1 + 3 \cdot 6 \cdot 1 \cdot 1 \right] =$$

$$= \tfrac{1}{12} [48 \cdot 1 + 6 \cdot 1 + 18 \cdot 1] = 6,$$

$$m(A_{2g}) = \tfrac{1}{12} [48 \cdot 1 + 6 (-1) + 18 (-1)] = 2,$$

$$m(E_g) = \tfrac{1}{12} [48 \cdot 2 + 6 \cdot 0 + 18 \cdot 0] = 8,$$

$$m(A_{1u}) = \tfrac{1}{12} [48 \cdot 1 + 6 \cdot 1 + 18 (-1)] = 3,$$

$$m(A_{2u}) = \tfrac{1}{12} [48 \cdot 1 + 6 (-1) + 18 \cdot 1] = 5,$$

$$m(E_u) = \tfrac{1}{12} [48 \cdot 2 + 6 \cdot 0 + 18 \cdot 0] = 8.$$

We obtain the following decomposition of the vibrational representation of the cyclohexane molecule into irreducible representations:

$$\Gamma_v = 6A_{1g} + 2A_{2g} + 3A_{1u} + 5A_{2u} + 8E_g + 8E_u. \tag{10.95}$$

Let us consider now the linear molecules. The total number of the vibrational degrees of freedom for these molecules in $3N - 5$, so that

$$\chi_v(e)_{\text{lin}} = 3N - 5. \tag{10.96}$$

The vibration modes of linear molecules can be divided into two types.

1) The vibrating atoms remain on one line. The number of such modes is $N - 1$, since the total number of the degrees of freedom for the motion of N atoms along a

straight line is N, and one of these degrees of freedom corresponds to the translational motion of the center of inertia of the molecule. These vibration modes correspond to nondegenerate frequencies of class A_1.

2) The vibrating atoms do not remain on one line. The number of these modes is

$$(3N - 5) - (N - 1) = 2(N - 2).$$

The corresponding frequencies are the doubly degenerate frequencies of class E. Each frequency is associated with two similar normal modes in mutually perpendicular planes.

The theory of group representations gives a more rigious tool for the derivation of the selection rules advanced in §9. We first have to define the direct product of two representations. Consider two vectors R^α and R^β with the components $R_1^\alpha, \ldots,$ $R_{f_\alpha}^\alpha$ and $R_1^\beta, \ldots, R_{f_\beta}^\beta$ which transform according to two irreducible representations of some group G. We can assign to these two vectors another vector $R^{\alpha\beta}$ with the components $R_i^\alpha R_k^\beta$. The number of these components is evidently $f_\alpha f_\beta$, so that $R^{\alpha\beta}$ is an $f_\alpha f_\beta$-dimensional vector. If Γ^α and Γ^β are the representations of G whose respective bases are the coordinates of R^α and R^β, the representation

$$\Gamma^{\alpha\beta} = \Gamma^\alpha \times \Gamma^\beta, \tag{10.97}$$

whose basis are the coordinates of the vector $R^{\alpha\beta}$, is called the *direct product* of representations Γ^α and Γ^β. In general, $\Gamma^{\alpha\beta}$ is a reducible representation.

Consider some element z of G. Under the symmetry operation corresponding to z, the components of R^α and R^β transform as follows:

$$(R_i^\alpha)' = zR_i^\alpha = \sum_l z_{li}^\alpha R_i^\alpha,$$

$$(R_k^\beta)' = zR_k^\beta = \sum_m z_{mk}^\beta R_m^\beta. \tag{10.98}$$

For the components of $R^{\alpha\beta}$ we similarly have

$$z(R_i^\alpha R_k^\beta) = \sum_{l,m} z_{li}^\alpha z_{mk}^\beta R_l^\alpha R_m^\beta. \tag{10.99}$$

For the characters of Γ^α, Γ^β, and $\Gamma^{\alpha\beta}$ we find

$$\chi^\alpha(z) = \sum_i z_{ii}^\alpha, \quad \chi^\beta(z) = \sum_k z_{kk}^\beta,$$

$$\chi^{\alpha\beta}(z) = \sum_{ik} z_{ii}^\alpha z_{kk}^\beta = \sum_i z_{ii}^\alpha \sum_k z_{kk}^\beta = \chi^\alpha(z)\chi^\beta(z). \tag{10.100}$$

The character of a direct product of representations is thus equal to the product of the characters of the constituent representations.

The following fundamental property of direct products will be required in later discussion. The decomposition of a direct product of two *different* irreducible rep-

resentations into irreducible components does not contain the unit representation.*
On the other hand, the decomposition of the direct product of an irreducible representation with itself (or in general, with its conjugate representation) always
contains the unit representation, but only once.

To prove this proposition, let us count how many times the unit representation
e occurs in $\Gamma^{\alpha\beta}$. Using (10.77) and (10.100), we find

$$m(e) = \frac{1}{g} \sum_z \chi^{\alpha\beta}(z)\,\chi^e(z) = \frac{1}{g} \sum_z \chi^\alpha(z)\chi^\beta(z)\chi^e(z).$$

By definition, all $\chi^e(z) = 1$, so that

$$m(e) = \frac{1}{g} \sum_z \chi^\alpha(z)\chi^\beta(z),$$

and, in virtue of the orthogonality relation (10.74),

$$m(e) = \delta_{\alpha\beta}. \tag{10.101}$$

Thus, $m(e) = 1$ if $\alpha = \beta$, and $m(e) = 0$ if $\alpha \neq \beta$, which was to be proved.

The wave functions of a quantum-mechanical system in some stationary states
can always be chosen as the basis of a representation. Indeed, the Schroedinger
equation of a molecule should remain invariant under symmetry transformations
of the molecule. The eigenfunctions corresponding to some energy eigenvalue are
therefore intermixed between themselves under symmetry transformations, i.e.,
they transform according to some irreducible representation of the symmetry group.
Thus, each energy level of the system can be made to correspond to some representation of its symmetry group. The degeneracy of this energy level determines the dimension of the representation.

As we have noted in §9, the selection rules for a transition characterized by a vector
or tensor component f_λ follow from the properties of the matrix element

$$(f_\lambda)_{\alpha\beta} = \int_{-\infty}^{\infty} \psi_\beta^* f_\lambda \psi_\alpha\, dx. \tag{10.102}$$

Because of the invariance of the Schroedinger equation under symmetry transformations, the integral (10.102) does not change under these transformations.
This means that the matrix element $(f_\lambda)_{\alpha\beta}$ either transforms according to the unit
representation of the given symmetry group or vanishes. Suppose the wave functions
ψ_α and ψ_β transform according to the irreducible representations Γ^α and Γ^β, respectively, whereas f_λ transforms according to Γ^λ; the integrand in (10.102) then trans-

---

* The unit representation is the trivial one-dimensional representation which assigns the unit matrix
  to every element z of G. All the characters of the unit representation are 1.

forms according to the direct-product representation

$$\Gamma^{\beta\lambda\alpha} = \Gamma^{\beta} \times \Gamma^{\lambda} \times \Gamma^{\alpha}. \tag{10.103}$$

In general, $\Gamma^{\beta\lambda\alpha}$ is reducible. If the decomposition of this representation contains the unit representation, we have $(f_{\lambda})_{\alpha\beta} \neq 0$ and the transition is "allowed". If, on the other hand, $\Gamma^{\beta\lambda\alpha}$ does not contain the unit representation, $(f_{\lambda})_{\alpha\beta} = 0$ and the transition is "forbidden".

These general selection rules can be formulated in a slightly different form. According to (10.101), the direct product of two representations contains the unit representation only if the two representations are identical. Hence, a transition is allowed only if the respective decompositions of the direct product $\Gamma^{\beta} \times \Gamma^{\lambda}$ and of the representation Γ^{α} (or $\Gamma^{\lambda} \times \Gamma^{\alpha}$ and Γ^{β}, or $\Gamma^{\beta} \times \Gamma^{\alpha}$ and Γ^{λ}) contain at least one common irreducible representation.*

The selection rule is greatly simplified in the highly important case when the initial state α or the final state β of the system is the ground (unexcited) state. The ground state is always totally symmetric, i.e., it transforms according to the identity representation. The transition is thus allowed if the representation Γ^{λ}, governing the transformation of f_{λ}, contains the representation governing the transformation of the excited state.

In vibrational transitions, the wave functions in the integrand in (10.102) are products of the harmonic oscillator eigenfunctions (7.3), i.e.,

$$\psi_{\beta} = \prod_i V_{v_i}(Q_i) = C \exp\left\{ -\frac{1}{2} \sum_i \frac{Q_i^2}{a_i^2} \right\} \prod_i H_{v_i}\left(\frac{Q_i}{a_i}\right). \tag{10.104}$$

Here the subscript i identifies the normal mode and v_i is the quantum state. The exponential factor in (10.104) is invariant under all symmetry transformations. The symmetry properties of the wave function ψ_{β} are therefore determined by a product of the form

$$\psi_{\beta} \sim \prod_j \left[\prod_{k=1}^{d_j} H_{v_{kj}}\left(\frac{Q_{kj}}{a_{kj}}\right) \right], \tag{10.105}$$

where d_j is the multiplicity of the eigenfrequency ω_j:

$$\sum_{k=1}^{d_j} v_{kj} = v_j. \tag{10.106}$$

The wave functions corresponding to the same degenerate vibration frequency ω_j consititute, as we have noted before, a certain representation of the symmetry group of the molecule, whereas the wave functions corresponding to different frequencies transform independently of one another. The representation for a given

* The direct product of representations does not depend on the order and the sequence of multiplication.

excited state β is therefore a product of representations, each corresponding to one of the different frequencies ω_j.

In the Hermite polynomials $H_{v_{kj}}(Q_{kj}/a_{kj})$, terms of the same degree are only inter-mixed between themselves. Since the symmetry properties of the polynomials are entirely determined by the symmetry properties of their leading terms, the symmetry properties of the vibrational state β are expressed by the product

$$\psi_\beta \sim \prod_j \left(\prod_{k=1}^{d_j} Q_{kj}^{v_{kj}} \right). \tag{10.107}$$

Let the coordinate Q_{kj} transform according to an irreducible representation π_{d_j}. Then the product $\prod_{k=1}^{d_j} Q_{kj}^{v_{kj}}$ transforms according to a representation which is the symmetric product of π_{d_j} multiplied v_j times by itself.* We will use the symbol $[\pi_{d_j}]^{v_j}$ for these representations. The representation of the state β according to (10.107) has the form

$$\Gamma^\beta = [\pi_{d_1}]^{v_1} \times [\pi_{d_2}]^{v_2} \times \dots \tag{10.108}$$

(note that $\pi_{d_i} \times \pi_{d_i} \neq [\pi_{d_i}]^2$).

The prescriptions for the calculation of the symmetric products of representations and direct products of irreducible representations are given in Tables 12 and 13 (see [81–83, 108]).

Let us now find the representation Γ^λ of the component f_λ, which may be regarded as a scalar, a polar vector, an axial vector (antisymmetric tensor), or a symmetric tensor. If f_λ is a scalar, then by definition f_λ is invariant under all symmetry trans-formations, i.e., it invariably corresponds to a totally symmetric representation.

The characters of the representations of the vector r_t and the axial vector (anti-symmetric tensor) r_Ω were calculated before (Eqs. (10.83), (10.84), (10.88), (10.89)). Decomposing these characters according to Eq. (10.77), we can find the representa-tions of the vector and the axial vector for the corresponding symmetry group.

Once we have found the representation of a vector for some symmetry group, the representation of a tensor can be obtained as a direct product of two vectors (see [86]). The representation of a tensor for any symmetry group is readily de-composed into two components corresponding to the symmetric and the anti-

---

* Consider the direct product of an irreducible representation with itself. In this case, the same representa-tion is realized by two different sets of functions $\psi_1, \dots, \psi_d$ and $\phi_1, \dots, \phi_d$, so that the direct product of a representation with itself is realized by the d^2 functions $\psi_i\phi_k$. This reducible representation can be decomposed into two representations of lower dimension. One of these representations is realized by the functions $\psi_i\phi_k + \psi_k\phi_i$ and the other by the functions $\psi_i\phi_k - \psi_k\phi_i$ ($i \neq k$). The former is known as the *symmetric product* of the representation by itself, and the latter as the *antisymmetric product* (see [20, 86]). For the characters of these representations we have

$$[\chi(z)]_s^2 = \tfrac{1}{2}\{[\chi(z)]^2 + \chi(z^2)\}, \quad [\chi(z)]_a^2 = \tfrac{1}{2}\{[\chi(z)]^2 - \chi(z^2)\}. \tag{10.109}$$

Table 12

RULES FOR THE CALCULATION OF THE SIMPLEST SYMMETRIC PRODUCTS
OF REPRESENTATIONS

General rules

$$[g]^v = g, \ [u]^v = g, \ [']^v = ['], \ ['']^v = ['], \text{ if } v \text{ is even};$$

$$[g]^v = g, \ [u]^v = u, \ [']^v = ['], \ ['']^v = [''], \text{ if } v \text{ is odd.}$$

Nondegenerate frequencies

$$[A_1]^2 = [A_1]^3 = [A_1]^4 = A_1, \ [A_2]^2 = A_1, \ [A_2]^3 = A_2, \ [A_2]^4 = A_1,$$

$$[B_1]^2 = A_1, \ [B_1]^3 = B_1, \ [B_1]^4 = A_1, \ [B_2]^2 = A_1, \ [B_2]^3 = B_2, \ [B_2]^4 = A_1.$$

Doubly degenerate frequencies

1) Groups $C_3, C_{3v}, C_{3h}, D_3, D_{3h}, T, T_d, T_h, O, O_h$:

$$[E]^2 = A_1 + E, \ [E]^3 = A_1 + A_2 + E, \ [E]^4 = A_1 + 2E.$$

2) Groups $C_6, C_{6v}, C_{6h}, D_6, D_{3d}, D_{6h}, S_6$:

$$[E_1]^2 = A_1 + E_2, \ [E_1]^3 = B_1 + B_2 + E_1, \ [E_1]^4 = A_1 + 2E_2,$$

$$[E_2]^2 = A_1 + E_2, \ [E_2]^3 = A_1 + A_2 + E_2, \ [E_2]^4 = A_1 + 2E_2.$$

3) Groups $C_4, C_{4v}, C_{4h}, D_4, D_{2d}, D_{4h}, S_4$:

$$[E]^2 = A_1 + B_1 + B_2, \ [E]^3 = 2E, \ [E]^4 = 2A_1 + A_2 + B_1 + B_2.$$

4) Groups $D_{5h}, D_5, C_5, C_{5h}, C_{5d}$:

$$[E_1]^2 = A_1 + E_2, \ [E_1]^3 = E_1 + E_2, \ [E_1]^4 = A_1 + E_1 + E_2,$$

$$[E_2]^2 = A_1 + E_1, \ [E_2]^3 = E_1 + E_2, \ [E_2]^4 = A_1 + E_1 + E_2.$$

5) Groups D_{4d}, C_{8v}, D_8 :

$$[E_1]^2 = A_1 + E_2, \ [E_1]^3 = E_1 + E_3, \ [E_1]^4 = A_1 + B_1 + B_2 + E_2,$$

$$[E_2]^2 = A_1 + B_1 + B_2, \ [E_2]^3 = 2E_2, \ [E_2]^4 = 2A_1 + A_2 + B_1 + B_2,$$

$$[E_3]^2 = A_1 + E_2, \ [E_3]^3 = E_1 + E_3, \ [E_3]^4 = A_1 + B_1 + B_2 + E_2.$$

6) Linear molecules (groups $C_{\infty v}, D_{\infty h}$):

$$[E_1]^2 = A_1 + E_2, \ [E_1]^3 = E_1 + E_3, \ [E_1]^4 = A_1 + E_2 + E_4,$$

where

$$A_1 = \Sigma^+, \ E_1 = \Pi, \ E_2 = \Delta, \ E_3 = \Phi, \ E_4 = \Gamma.$$

Triply degenerate frequencies

Groups T_d, O, O_h :

$$[F_1]^2 = A_1 + E + F_2, \ [F_1]^3 = A_2 + 2F_1 + F_2, \ [F_1]^4 = 2A_1 + 2E + F_1 + 2F_2,$$

$$[F_2]^2 = A_1 + E + F_2, \ [F_2]^3 = A_1 + F_1 + 2F_2, \ [F_2]^4 = 2A_1 + 2E + F_1 + 2F_2.$$

Note: For the groups T, T_h the subscripts 1 and 2 are omitted.

Table 13

RULES FOR THE MULTIPLICATION OF IRREDUCIBLE REPRESENTATIONS

General rules

$A \times A = A$, $B \times B = A$, $A \times B = B$, $A \times E = E$, $B \times E = E$,

$A \times F = F$, $B \times F = F$,

$g \times g = g$, $u \times u = g$, $u \times g = u$, $'\times' = '$, $"\times" = '$, $'\times" = "$,

$A_{1,2} \times E_1 = E_1$, $A_{1,2} \times E_2 = E_2$, $B_{1,2} \times E_1 = E_2$, $B_{1,2} \times E_2 = E_1$.

Subscripts of *A* or *B*:

$1 \times 1 = 1$; $2 \times 2 = 1$; $1 \times 2 = 2$ for all groups except $D_2 = V$ and $D_{2h} = V_h$, where
$B_1 \times B_2 = B_3$, $B_2 \times B_3 = B_1$, $B_1 \times B_3 = B_2$.

Doubly degenerate representations

1) Groups C_3, C_{3h}, C_{3v}, D_3, D_{3h}, D_{3d}, C_6, C_{6h}, C_{6v}, D_6, D_{6h}, S_6, O, O_h, T, T_d, T_h :

$E_1 \times E_1 = E_2 \times E_2 = A_1 + A_2 + E_2$, $E_1 \times E_2 = B_1 + B_2 + E_1$.

2) Groups C_4, C_{4v}, C_{4h}, D_{2d}, D_4, D_{4h}, S_4 :

$E \times E = A_1 + A_2 + B_1 + B_2$.

3) Groups D_{5h}, D_5, C_5, C_{5h}, C_{5v} :

$E_1 \times E_1 = A_1 + A_2 + E_2$, $E_2 \times E_2 = A_1 + A_2 + E_1$, $E_1 \times E_2 = E_1 + E_2$.

4) Groups D_{4d}, C_{8v}, D_8 :

$E_1 \times E_1 = A_1 + A_2 + E_2$, $E_1 \times E_2 = E_1 + E_3$, $E_1 \times E_3 = B_1 + B_2 + E_2$,

$E_2 \times E_2 = A_1 + A_2 + B_1 + B_2$, $E_2 \times E_3 = E_1 + E_3$, $E_3 \times E_3 = A_1 + A_2 + E_2$.

Triply degenerate representations

$E \times F_1 = E \times F_2 = F_1 + F_2$,

$F_1 \times F_1 = F_2 \times F_2 = A_1 + E + F_1 + F_2$, $F_1 \times F_2 = A_2 + E + F_1 + F_2$

Note: For groups where the symbols *A*, *B*, *E*, *F* have no subscripts, the corresponding subscripts in the formulae are omitted.

symmetric product of the representation of a vector with itself, using the formulae of Tables 12 and 13. The first component is the representation of a symmetric tensor (i.e., the sum of the scalar and the anisotropic parts of the scattering tensor) and the second component is the representation of an antisymmetric tensor. The decomposition of the representations of a tensor corresponds to a decomposition of characters. Indeed, by (10.83), (10.88), and (9.12) we have

$$\chi_{P}(C_\phi) = 1 + 2\cos\phi, \quad \chi_P(S_\phi) = -1 + 2\cos\phi,$$
$$C_\phi^2 = C_{2\phi}, \quad S_\phi^2 = C_{2\phi}.$$

Using (10.109), we find

$$\chi_{\beta_c+\beta_y}(C_\phi) = [\chi_P(C_\phi)]_c^2 = \tfrac{1}{2}\{[\chi_P(C_\phi)]^2 + \chi_P(C_{2\phi})\},$$

or

$$\chi_{\beta_c+\beta_y}(C_\phi) = 2\cos\phi\,(1 + 2\cos\phi). \tag{10.110}$$

Similarly,

$$\chi_{\beta_c+\beta_y}(S_\phi) = 2\cos\phi\,(-1 + 2\cos\phi). \tag{10.111}$$

These relations were derived in [107] by a direct examination of the transformations of the components of a symmetric tensor under the symmetry operations C_ϕ and S_ϕ. For the characters of an antisymmetric tensor, we obtain in the same way

$$\chi_{\beta_z}(C_\phi) = 1 + 2\cos\phi\,, \qquad \chi_{\beta_z}(S_\phi) = 1 - 2\cos\phi\,,$$

and these equalities evidently coincide with (10.84) and (10.89), respectively.

Table 14 lists the representations for f_λ of four different kinds for various symmetry groups. This table also gives the corresponding selection rules for transitions from the ground (totally symmetric) state to a state where a single quantum of one of the normal modes is excited. The allowed transitions are those for which the representation Γ^λ of f_λ contains an irreducible representation according to which the particular normal mode transforms. To derive the selection rules for overtones and combination frequencies, and also for transitions between excited states, we should form the product $\Gamma^\alpha \times \Gamma^\beta$ according to (10.103), decompose it into irreducible components and, using the formulae of Tables 12 and 13, compare this decomposition with the representations of the various f_λ. The allowed transitions are those for which $\Gamma^\alpha \times \Gamma^\beta$ and Γ^λ contain common irreducible representations. (A general derivation of the selection rules for overtones and composite frequencies on the basis of the theory of characters is given in [109, 110], and a derivation based on a straightforward determination of representations will be found in [108]).

As an example, let us consider the selection rules for some lines in the spectra of molecules with T_d symmetry, assuming an unexcited initial state.

1) $v = 2v_E + v_{F_2}$.

From Table 12 we have

$$[E]^2 = A_1 + E\,.$$

Thus, for the given transition

$$\Gamma^\alpha \times \Gamma^\beta = \Gamma^\beta = (A_1 + E) \times F_2 = A_1 F_2 + E F_2 = F_2 + F_1 + F_2\,.$$

Comparison with Table 14 shows that this triple frequency can be observed in Raman scattering (the corresponding line is depolarized) and also in the infrared spectrum.

Table 14

REPRESENTATIONS OF THE SCALAR β_c, THE ANISOTROPIC β_γ, AND THE ANTISYMMETRIC β_a SCATTERING AND OF THE VECTOR P FOR THE PRINCIPAL SYMMETRY GROUPS*

Group	β_c	β_γ	β_a	P
C_i	A_g	A_g	A_g	A_u
C_s	A'	$A' + A''$	$A' + A''$	$A' + A''$
C_2	A	$A + B$	$A + B$	$A + B$
C_{2h}	A_g	$A_g + B_g$	$A_g + B$	$A_u + B_u$
C_{2v}	A_1	$A_1 + A_2 + B_1 + B_2$	$A_2 + B_1 + B_2$	$A_1 + B_1 + B_2$
D_2	A_1	$A_1 + B_1 + B_2 + B_3$	$B_1 + B_2 + B_3$	$B_1 + B_2 + B_3$
D_{2h}	A_{1g}	$A_{1g} + B_{1g} + B_{2g} + B_{3g}$	$B_{1g} + B_{2g} + B_{3g}$	$B_{1u} + B_{2u} + B_{3u}$
C_{3v}	A_1	$A_1 + E$	$A_2 + E$	$A_1 + E$
D_{3h}	A_1'	$A_1' + E' + E''$	$A_2' + E''$	$A_2'' + E'$
D_{3d}	A_{1g}	$A_{1g} + E_g$	$A_{2g} + E_g$	$A_{2u} + E_u$
D_{4h}	A_{1g}	$A_{1g} + B_{1g} + B_{2g} + E_g$	$A_{2g} + E_g$	$A_{2u} + E_u$
C_{4h}	A_g	$A_g + B_g + E_g$	$A_g + E_g$	$A_u + E_u$
D_{4d}	A_1	$A_1 + E_2 + E_3$	$A_2 + E_3$	$B_2 + E_1$
S_4	A	$A + B + E$	$A + E$	$A + E$
D_{5h}	A_1'	$A_1' + E_1'' + E_2'$	$A_2' + E_1''$	$A_2'' + E_1'$
D_{6h}	A_{1g}	$A_{1g} + E_{1g} + E_{2g}$	$A_{2g} + E_{1g}$	$A_{2u} + E_{1u}$
C_{6h}	A_g	$A_g + E_g$	$A_g + E_g$	$A_u + E_u$
$C_{\infty v}$	A_1	$A_1 + E_1 + E_2$	$A_2 + E_1$	$A_1 + E_1$
$D_{\infty h}$	A_{1g}	$A_{1g} + E_{1g} + E_{2g}$	$A_{2g} + E_{1g}$	$A_{1u} + E_{1u}$
T	A	$E + F$	F	F
T_d	A_1	$E + F_2$	F_1	F_2
O	A_1	$E + F_2$	F_1	F_2
O_h	A_{1g}	$E_g + F_{2g}$	F_{1g}	F_{2u}

* The numerical factors before the representation symbols are omitted.

2) $v = 2v_{F_1} + 2v_{F_2}$.

For this transition

$$\Gamma^\beta = [F_1]^2 \times [F_2]^2 = (A_1 + E + F_2) \times (A_1 + E + F_2) =$$

$$= 4A_1 + 4E + 3F_1 + 5F_2.$$

The line is allowed in the Raman spectrum, where it is partly polarized, and in the IR spectrum.

3) $v = v'_{F_2} - v''_{F_2}$.

In this case $\Gamma^\alpha = F_2$, $\Gamma^\beta = F_2$ and $\Gamma^\alpha \times \Gamma^\beta = F_2 \times F_2 = A_1 + E + F_1 + F_2$. This difference frequency is allowed in the Raman spectrum (partly polarized) and in the IR spectrum.

3. Calculation of line intensities in Raman spectra

Once it has been established that a certain line is "allowed" in the Raman spectrum by the selection rules, we have to find its intensity I and also the numerical value of the depolarization ρ (this only for partially polarized lines). The general theory is not very helpful in this respect: an "allowed" line may turn to have a vanishingly small intensity in practice.

Direct calculation of line intensities in the vibrational spectra of molecules on the basis of quantum-mechanical treatment still presents insurmountable difficulties. Therefore, the only practicable approach to this problem is the determination of I and ρ by semiempirical computation methods. Valuable results are also obtained by comparative analysis of the spectra of analogous compounds (see §11). We will describe an approximate method for the calculation of intensities, which is known as the *valence–optical theory of intensities*. This method, originally proposed by Vol'kenshtein [111] and later developed in cooperation with El'yashevich [112], is adequate for fairly accurate calculations of intensities and depolarizations of lines in the spectra of complex molecules [113–119].

The valence–optical theory of intensities stems from the concept of additivity of various molecular properties. In other words, the properties of a molecule can be represented as a sum of the properties of the various structural units, which are preserved on passing from one molecule to another. In modern chemistry, the atomic valent bonds are generally regarded as the structural unit. It should be emphasized, however, that the constituent structural units cannot be defined in an abstract way: the definition must closely rely on the experimental findings. In vibrational spectra, the additivity is often seen to break down, and this effect can be generally attributed to "coupling" or "interaction" between the structural units. As a result, the chemical bonds in certain cases cannot be regarded as the basic structural units of the molecule, and more complex groupings have to be dealt with (see §11). Nevertheless, the additivity hypothesis associated with the use of valent chemical bonds generally provides a satisfactory "zero" approximation.

With regard to molecular polarizability, the additivity hypothesis prescribes an independent polarizability tensor α_{ik}^p to every chemical bond, and the overall polarizability is taken equal to the sum of the polarizabilities of the individual bonds:

$$\alpha_{ik} = \sum_{p=1}^{N} \alpha_{ik}^p, \tag{10.112}$$

where N is the number of chemical bonds. It is naturally assumed that the bond direction coincides with one of the principal axes of the tensor α_{ik}^p, and the two other principal axes are taken perpendicular to the bond. As in §2, the subscripts $i, k = x,$ y, z are associated with the molecule's moving system of axes, and the subscript

λ ($\lambda = 1, 2, 3$) identifies the principal axes of the bond polarizability tensor. Thus (see (2.21))

$$\alpha_{ik}^p = \sum_{\lambda=1}^{3} \alpha_\lambda^p n_{\lambda i}^p n_{\lambda k}^p ,\tag{10.113}$$

where $n_{\lambda i}^p = \cos(\lambda, i)$, $n_{\lambda k}^p = \cos(\lambda, k)$ for the p-th bond.

To extend the additivity hypothesis to vibrational spectra, we have to introduce a further assumption, namely that the additivity is preserved in a vibrating molecule. Then for the derivatives of the polarizability tensor we have

$$\frac{\partial \alpha_{ik}}{\partial Q_j} = \sum_{p=1}^{N} \frac{\partial \alpha_{ik}^p}{\partial Q_j} = \sum_{p=1}^{N} \left\{ \sum_{t=1}^{N} \frac{\partial \alpha_{ik}^p}{\partial q_t} \frac{\partial q_t}{\partial Q_j} + \sum_{s=1}^{2N} \frac{\partial \alpha_{ik}^p}{\partial \gamma_s} \frac{\partial \gamma_s}{\partial Q_j} \right\} ,\tag{10.114}$$

where q_t, γ_s are the bond stretching and the bond bending natural coordinates, respectively. Inserting for α_{ik}^p their expressions from (10.113), we initially assume α_λ^p to depend only on the variation in the length of the p-th bond and the direction cosines $n_{\lambda i}^p$, $n_{\lambda k}^p$ to depend only on the variation of the bond angles γ_s. In this approximation*

$$\frac{\partial \alpha_\lambda^p}{\partial q_t} = 0 \ (t \neq p), \qquad \frac{\partial \alpha_\lambda^p}{\partial \gamma_s} = 0, \qquad \frac{\partial n_{\lambda i}^p}{\partial q_t} = 0 .\tag{10.115}$$

Using (10.115), we write (10.114) in the form

$$\frac{\partial \alpha_{ik}}{\partial Q_j} = \sum_{p=1}^{N} \sum_{\lambda=1}^{3} \left\{ \frac{\partial \alpha_\lambda^p}{\partial q_p} n_{\lambda i}^p n_{\lambda k}^p \frac{\partial q_p}{\partial Q_j} + \alpha_\lambda^p \frac{\partial}{\partial \gamma_s} (n_{\lambda i}^p n_{\lambda k}^p) \frac{\partial \gamma_s}{\partial Q_j} \right\} .\tag{10.116}$$

Each term in (10.116) contains two factors, an electrooptical factor dependent on α_λ^p, $n_{\lambda i}^p$ and their derivatives, and a mechanical factor—the derivatives of the natural coordinates with respect to the normal coordinates. The derivatives $\partial q_p/\partial Q_j$ and $\partial \gamma_s/\partial Q_j$ can be found by solving the mechanical problem of vibrations. The calculation according to the valence–optical scheme thus makes it possible to differentiate between the electrooptical and the mechanical factors influencing the intensity and the polarization of the Raman lines and also to reach certain conclusions regarding molecular structure and the nature of the chemical bond.

Eq. (10.116) automatically separates into a bond-stretching and a bond-bending part. In case of pure stretching vibrations, i.e., when $\gamma_s = 0$, the line intensity and the polarization depend only on the derivatives $\partial \alpha_\lambda^p/\partial q_p$; in case of pure bond-bending

---

* To follow Vol'kenshtein's terminology [80], this is the zeroth approximation of the valence–optical scheme. We recall that since the vibrational angular momentum is zero, the direction cosines actually depend also on the variation of the bond lengths.

vibrations ($q_p = 0$), these magnitudes depend only on α_λ^p. In real vibrations, both q_p and γ_s are variable, so that in general, bond stretching is combined with bond bending. However, to a certain approximation, we can treat separately the electro-optical properties of stretching and bending vibrations. In this way, we derive new (approximate) selection rules [80].

The direction cosines are linked by the orthogonality relations:

$$\sum_{\lambda=1}^{3} n_{\lambda i}^{p} n_{\lambda k}^{p} = \delta_{ik} .$$

(10.117)

Hence

$$n_{1i}^{p} n_{1k}^{p} = \delta_{ik} - n_{2i}^{p} n_{2k}^{p} - n_{3i}^{p} n_{3k}^{p} ,$$

(10.118)

$$\frac{\partial}{\partial \gamma_s} \sum_{\lambda=1}^{3} n_{\lambda i}^{p} n_{\lambda k}^{p} = \frac{\partial \delta_{ik}}{\partial \gamma_s} = 0 .$$

(10.119)

Let direction 1 lie along the bond. Directions 2 and 3, perpendicular to the bond direction, may be regarded as equivalent for σ bonds (this is of course only true in the zeroth approximation). Thus

$$\alpha_2^p = \alpha_3^p , \qquad \frac{\partial \alpha_2^p}{\partial q_p} = \frac{\partial \alpha_3^p}{\partial q_p} .$$

(10.120)

In this approximation, Eq. (10.116) after simple manipulations takes the form

$$\frac{\partial \alpha_{ik}}{\partial Q_j} = \sum_{p=1}^{N} \left\{ \left[\left(\frac{\partial \alpha_1^p}{\partial q_p} - \frac{\partial \alpha_2^p}{\partial q_p} \right) n_{1i}^p n_{1k}^p + \frac{\partial \alpha_2^p}{\partial q_p} \delta_{ik} \right] \frac{\partial q_p}{\partial Q_j} + \right.$$

$$\left. + \sum_s (\alpha_1^p - \alpha_2^p) \frac{\partial}{\partial \gamma_s} (n_{1i}^p n_{1k}^p) \frac{\partial \gamma_s}{\partial Q_j} \right\} .$$

(10.121)

Using (10.121), we find the trace of the tensor $\partial \alpha_{ik}/\partial Q_j$. Thus

$$b = \sum_i \frac{\partial \alpha_{ii}}{\partial Q_j} = \sum_{p=1}^{N} \frac{\partial (\alpha_1^p + \alpha_2^p + \alpha_3^p)}{\partial q_p} \frac{\partial q_p}{\partial Q_j} .$$

(10.122)

The trace of the bond bending part of the tensor $\partial \alpha_{ik}/\partial Q_j$ is clearly zero. Hence follows the first approximate selection rule, derived by Vol'kenshtein [80, 120]:

1. The depolarization for pure bond-bending, totally symmetric vibrations of molecules of any symmetry group is

$$\rho_{\text{bend}} = \frac{6}{7} .$$

(10.123)

This rule readily follows from (10.122). Indeed, in the case of pure bond-bending vibrations, the bond stretching part of the tensor $\partial\alpha_{ik}/\partial Q_j$ vanishes. Hence, the trace of this part is zero. Then from (10.122) we have $b = 0$, so that

$$\rho_{\text{bend}} = \frac{6g^2}{5b^2 + 7g^2} = \frac{6}{7}.$$

Let us now consider another important case of totally symmetric vibrations of a group of N identical bonds making equal angles ϕ with one another. In this case all q_p and $\partial q_p/\partial Q_j$ are equal and the subscripts can be dropped. We further introduce the shorter notation

$$\frac{\partial\alpha_1^p}{\partial q_p} = \frac{\partial\alpha_1}{\partial q} = \alpha_1', \qquad \frac{\partial\alpha_2^p}{\partial q_p} = \frac{\partial\alpha_2}{\partial q} = \alpha_2'.$$

Restricting the discussion to pure bond-stretching vibrations, we find from (10.121), (10.122), using (2.40a), (2.40b),

$$b_N = N(\alpha_1' + 2\alpha_2')\frac{\partial q}{\partial Q} = Nb_1\frac{\partial q}{\partial Q}, \tag{10.124}$$

$$g_N^2 = \frac{3}{2}\sum_{ik}(\alpha_{ik}')^2 - \frac{1}{2}b^2 = N^2(\alpha_1' - \alpha_2')^2\left[1 - \frac{N-1}{2N}3\sin^2\phi\right]\left(\frac{\partial q}{\partial Q}\right)^2 =$$

$$= N^2g_1^2\left[1 - \frac{N-1}{2N}3\sin^2\phi\right]\left(\frac{\partial q}{\partial Q}\right)^2. \tag{10.125}$$

Here $b_1 = \alpha_1' + 2\alpha_2'$ and $g_1 = \alpha_1' - \alpha_2'$ are the trace and the anisotropy of the tensor α_{ik}' for an isolated σ bond.

For the depolarization we have

$$\rho_N = \frac{6\rho_1\left[1 - \dfrac{N-1}{2N}3\sin^2\phi\right]}{6 - 7\rho_1\dfrac{N-1}{2N}3\sin^2\phi}, \tag{10.126}$$

where ρ_1 is the depolarization for the vibration of an isolated bond. By (10.126),

$$\rho_N \leqq \rho_1, \tag{10.127}$$

and the equality corresponds to the case $\sin\phi = 0$, i.e., a linear molecule.

Let us analyze ρ_1. Using the expression for b_1 and g_1, we find

$$\rho_1 = \frac{6(\alpha_1' - \alpha_2')^2}{5(\alpha_1' + 2\alpha_2')^2 + 7(\alpha_1' - \alpha_2')^2}. \tag{10.128}$$

For diatomic molecules and for the vibrations of isolated bonds, we may take $\alpha'_1 > 0$, $\alpha'_2 > 0$ (see [80]). Then, from (10.128), $0 \leq \rho_1 \leq \frac{1}{2}$. Hence

$$\rho_N \leq \frac{1}{2}. \tag{10.129}$$

Inequality (10.129) is an expression of Vol'kenshtein's second approximate selection rule:

2. The depolarization for the vibration of a diatomic molecule or a pure bond-stretching, totally symmetric vibration mode of an isolated bond or a group of equivalent bonds is at most equal to $\frac{1}{2}$.

Let us consider separately the case of tetrahedral angles ($\sin^2 \phi = \frac{8}{9}$). Eq. (10.126) yields in this case

$$\rho_2 = \frac{3\rho_1}{9 - 7\rho_1}, \qquad \rho_3 = \frac{3\rho_1}{27 - 28\rho_1}, \qquad \rho_4 = 0. \tag{10.130}$$

Table 15 lists the values of ρ_N calculated from (10.130) and obtained experimentally [100] for totally symmetric lines of the groups CH_3, CH_2, and CH. The fit is quite satisfactory.

Table 15

DEPOLARIZATIONS FOR TOTALLY SYMMETRIC
BOND-STRETCHING VIBRATIONS OF THE CH
GROUP IN HYDROCARBONS

Number of bonds N	ρ_N	
	experimental	calculated
1	0.35	—
2	0.2	0.16
3	~0.1	0.04
4	0	0

Another case of totally symmetric bond-stretching vibrations deserves special mention. These are the vibrations of planar molecules made up of identical bonds which belong to the D_{nh} symmetry group. The polarizability tensor of these molecules has the form

$$\alpha_{ik} = \begin{Vmatrix} a_1 & 0 & 0 \\ 0 & a_2 & 0 \\ 0 & 0 & a_2 \end{Vmatrix}, \tag{10.131}$$

where a_1 is the polarizability component at right angles to the plane of the molecule. If the molecule with D_{nh} symmetry has $N \geq 3$ bonds, the valence–optical scheme leads to the relations

$$a_1 = N\alpha_3, \qquad a_1 + 2a_2 = N(\alpha_1 + \alpha_2 + \alpha_3). \tag{10.132}$$

The tensor α_{ik} can be written in the form

$$\alpha_{ik} = \frac{1}{2}N \begin{Vmatrix} 2\alpha_3 & 0 & 0 \\ 0 & \alpha_1 + \alpha_2 & 0 \\ 0 & 0 & \alpha_1 + \alpha_2 \end{Vmatrix}. \tag{10.133}$$

For totally symmetric vibrations of these molecules we have $q = CQ$. Hence

$$\alpha'_{ik} = \frac{1}{2}NC \begin{Vmatrix} 2\alpha'_3 & 0 & 0 \\ 0 & \alpha'_1 + \alpha'_2 & 0 \\ 0 & 0 & \alpha'_1 + \alpha'_2 \end{Vmatrix}. \tag{10.134}$$

Thus

$$\rho_N = \frac{6(\alpha'_1 + \alpha'_2 - 2\alpha'_3)^2}{20(\alpha'_1 + \alpha'_2 + \alpha'_3)^2 + 7(\alpha'_1 + \alpha'_2 - 2\alpha'_3)^2}. \tag{10.135}$$

We have thus derived Vol'kenshtein's third approximate selection rule:

3. The depolarizations for totally symmetric vibrations are equal for all the plane molecules of D_{nh} symmetry made up of identical bonds, irrespective of the actual number of bonds in the molecule.

In the simplest case $\alpha'_2 = \alpha'_3$, we get

$$\rho_N = \frac{2\rho_1}{6 - 7\rho_1}, \tag{10.136}$$

and since $\rho_1 \leqq \frac{1}{2}$, we see that $\rho_N \leqq \frac{2}{5}$.

The data for some plane ring molecules of hydrocarbons [100, 118] show that rule 3 is satisfied for molecules without π bonds. Molecules with π bonds have a higher depolarization [121, 122].

The above data (see also [80, 120]) show that the zeroth approximation of the valence–optical scheme gives quite satisfactory results for qualitative treatment of Raman spectra. For numerical calculations of intensity and depolarization, however, this approximation is much too crude and the next higher approximation should be used [113, 115]. This naturally introduces considerable difficulties, mainly associated with the zero angular momentum of the molecule. Without going into details, we will only say that these difficulties notwithstanding, quite satisfactory calculations have been performed even for the more complex molecules [113–118].

11. CHARACTERISTIC LINES IN VIBRATIONAL RAMAN SPECTRA

In the two preceding sections we have shown that the vibrational Raman spectra provide a wealth of information on molecular structure. Raman spectra present clear indications of molecular symmetry. The molecules fall into several classes according to the symmetry of their vibration modes. Each class is characterized by its own selection rules, which decide whether the particular frequency will appear in the infrared spectrum or in the Raman spectrum. The class of vibration modes also determines (at least qualitatively) the intensity of the lines and their state of polarization. The number of vibration modes in each symmetry class and the number of corresponding lines in the spectrum can be calculated by methods of group theory. Vibrational spectra thus provide a tool for selecting the true model among several alternative models of a certain molecule (see § 9).

The identification of molecular symmetry from the vibrational spectra is based on the general relations which are derived in group theory. The generality of the method is its main advantage. The method has yielded valuable information on the structure of various molecules, and the nature of the technique makes its conclusions indisputable. This method, however, is not very effective for any but relatively simple molecules. As the complexity of the molecule increases, the results based on the relation of the vibrational spectra to molecular symmetry become less reliable: in vibrational spectra containing numerous lines, the identification of the symmetry class of the observed vibrational lines is no longer single-valued.

A more detailed theory of vibrational spectra uses the model of a molecule as an assembly of point masses (nuclei, atoms) oscillating with small amplitudes about their equilibrium states. In this theory, the vibration frequencies measured from the line frequencies in the spectrum can be related to the quasielastic constants which characterize the atomic interaction in molecules. This theory also provides a tool for determining the electrooptical parameters of the molecule from line intensity and polarization. The existing computation methods (see § 10) will give the vibration frequencies, the mode shapes, etc., for a certain molecular model. Comparison of the theoretical results with the experimental findings makes it possible to improve the molecular constants used in calculations and to develop a detailed interpretation of the observed spectrum.

The application of digital computers enabled the spectroscopists to carry out calculation for fairly complex molecules, containing some 20–25 atoms. Further development of computation techniques will undoubtedly raise this "ceiling", which is determined mainly by the storage capacity of the computer. Computers are successfully taking over in yet another field: programs have been developed which enable the computer itself to draw up the equations of molecular vibrations before proceeding with their solution. This activity, however, is again limited by the complexity of the molecules. Further limitation is imposed by the unfortunate fact that for complex molecules the results of the calculation of vibration modes are not readily amenable to interpretation. Thus, a lengthy computation of the vibration modes of a complex molecule will often produce a series of numbers which are not very meaningful.

Because of these limitations of the numerical methods, considerable efforts are being devoted to the experimental study of the Raman spectra, which helps to disclose various empirical relationships in these spectra. The comparative method is particularly popular in the study of the vibrational spectra of molecules: its purpose is to bring out certain regular features which emerge from a comparison of the spectra of a number of close compounds. Another point to be remembered is that the regular features manifested in the spectra of complex molecules are definitely specific. The physics and the significance of the various details observed in the spectra of complex molecules have not been established conclusively so far. The reliability and the generality of these results naturally depends on the quality and the volume of the experimental material used in the analysis. Unfortunately, we are often faced with examples of blatant overestimation of the significance of the observed features, which may lead to wrong conclusions and, in some cases, to long, fruitless arguments.

The main result produced by the comparative study of the vibrational spectra at the very first stages was the discovery of the so-called *characteristic group frequencies*. The spectra of molecules containing the same characteristic groups of atoms or bonds often show certain common or slightly shifted frequencies. These frequencies associated with certain chemical groups entering the composition of various molecules became known as the characteristic group frequencies.

The initial oversimplified interpretation of the characteristic group frequencies as the frequencies of vibration with the participation of a single bond or a small group of atoms proved to be largely incorrect. This oversimplified approach led to numerous errors and discrepancies.* However, fundamentally, the comparative method of analysis is a sound technique, and the existence of the characteristic frequencies undoubtedly reflects important properties of polyatomic molecules. If carefully used, the concept of characteristic group frequencies provides valuable results about molecular structure. The main technique of this method calls for a systematic examination of large classes of compounds with molecular structure of progressively increasing complexity.

Initially, the inadequacy of the experimental methods limited the measurements of vibrational spectra to one parameter only, the frequency. As a result, the potential of the comparative method was only partly tapped in Raman spectroscopy. It was only after the development of rigorous methods for measurements of intensities,

---

* A critical analysis of the simplified concept of characteristic frequencies and a vigorous theory of characteristic frequencies are given by Mayants [101, 123].

depolarizations, and line widths, which provided results for quantitative comparison of these spectroscopic parameters, that the comparative method received a great impetus.

The comparison of the spectra of compounds with common structural features established that in a number of cases the frequency is not the only molecular parameter which is conserved on passing from one molecule to another. It is significant that the behavior of various characteristic parameters in Raman spectra is interrelated. This interrelationship made it possible to extend the concept of characteristic frequencies to a wider concept of characteristic lines, which are formed by a set of several characteristic parameters [124]. The concept of characteristic lines is a natural generalization of the original concept of characteristic group frequencies.

The study of spectra have shown [100] that characteristic lines in Raman spectra are by no means associated with every branching, combination of branchings, or other structural feature of a molecule which repeats itself in a number of analogous compounds. Only certain specific groups of atoms or bonds (and in some cases individual atoms or isolated bonds) are associated with characteristic spectral lines. These structural elements, whose presence in a molecule produces a stable, persistent series of characteristic spectral lines, may be referred to as characteristic structural elements of molecules.

The special significance of the characteristic structural elements is that they are the actual structural units of molecules which take active part in vibrations and thus leave their impression in the vibrational spectra. This aspect should be stressed because in complex branched molecules one can quite arbitrarily define various combinations of branchings, atomic groupings, etc., which do not correspond to any characteristic group frequencies in Raman spectra of the molecules. This remark is even more applicable to infrared spectra. The extensive lists of the characteristic group frequencies in vibrational spectra published, e.g., in [125] are rather deficient in this respect and, although highly valuable, they must be used with some reservation.

The spectra of complex polyatomic molecules with several characteristic structural elements are often formed by additive superposition of the spectra of the individual structural elements. If the molecule contains several identical characteristic structural elements, the frequencies of the corresponding characteristic lines often coincide. As a result, the intensity of these lines is proportional to the number of the identical structural elements. Numerous examples of this additivity in Raman spectra will be considered below.

It is highly significant, however, that this additivity is by no means a universal feature. In some cases, a complex "interaction" of the characteristic structural elements is observed, which breaks the additivity. The most typical breakdown of additivity in molecules with several characteristic structural elements is observed when the characteristic lines of only one element appear in full strength, whereas the lines of the other elements are markedly attenuated or not visible at all. The molecules thus often contain a dominant characteristic structural element, whose presence determines the main features of the Raman spectrum. This dominant element as if "suppresses" the other characteristic structural elements present in the molecule.

The above remarks regarding the Raman spectra of complex molecules, based on the analysis of extensive experimental material [100], suggest a general method for detecting correlations between Raman spectra and molecular structure. The underlying idea of this method is the study of the characteristic lines corresponding to various characteristic structural elements of molecules.

The identification of the characteristic structural elements with the corresponding characteristic lines is the first step in this procedure. The second step calls for a careful study of the changes in the characteristic parameters, i.e., possible deviations from characteristic behavior. Since every characteristic structural element is a constituent of the molecule, its vibrations, strictly speaking, are the vibrations of the entire molecule. Therefore, any change in molecular structure is reflected to a certain extent in the parameters of the characteristic lines. In this sense, the significance of the method of the characteristic structural elements is in that it provides a valid first approximation to the interpretation of the spectra of complex molecules.

As an illustration of the method of the characteristic structural elements and characteristic lines, we will now examine the experimental results obtained for the Raman spectra of paraffins.

The spectral properties of paraffins are of considerable importance for the molecular analysis of liquid motor fuel, especially gasoline, and also of other natural and synthetic products. Paraffins have therefore been studied in considerable detail. In addition to the experimental study of the spectra of individual paraffins, extensive work has been done with regard to computations and theoretical interpretation of the paraffin spectra. The main contributions in this field are those of El'yashevich and Stepanov [92, 93, 126, 127] (see also [80]).

The theoretical and experimental studies of the Raman spectra of paraffins have identified the following characteristic structural elements with their corresponding characteristic lines: a) a quaternary carbon atom, b) two adjacent tertiary carbon atoms, c) a tertiary carbon atom, d) a free chain of carbon atoms (Figure 34). These skeletal structure elements of the paraffins should be supplemented by three additional groups, CH_3, CH_2, and CH, whose characteristic lines emerge in the C—H stretching region. The characteristic structural elements of these hydrocarbons are shown in Figure 34.

A quaternary carbon in the paraffin molecule leads to fairly characteristic changes in the entire spectrum, irrespective of the presence of other characteristic structural elements in the molecule. A quaternary carbon thus may be regarded as a "dominant" characteristic structural element in the paraffin spectra.

In the region of totally symmetric stretching vibrations of the paraffin skeleton,

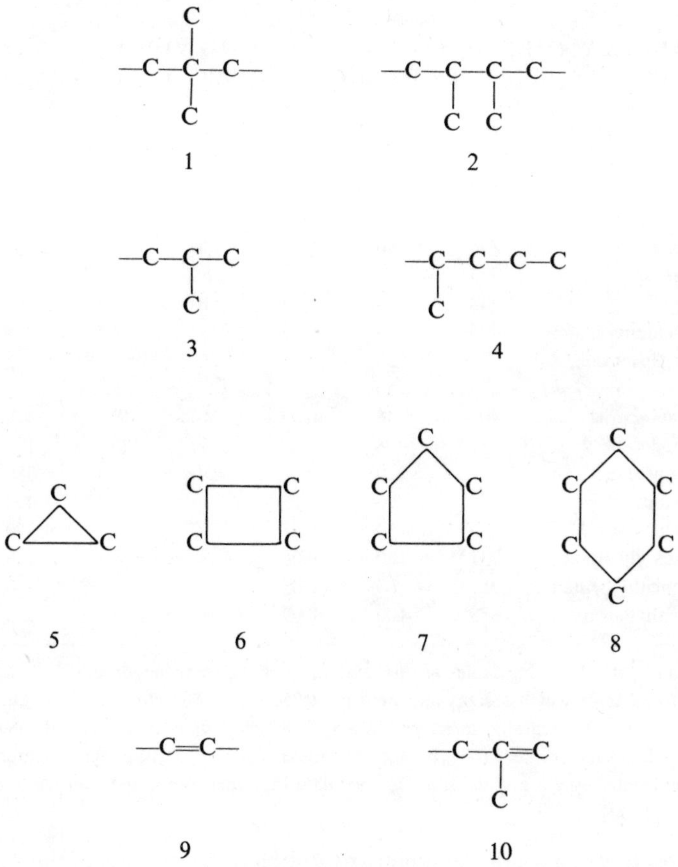

Figure 34

Characteristic structural elements of hydrocarbons:

1) quaternary carbon,   2) adjacent tertiary carbons,   3) tertiary carbon,   4) free chain,   5, 6, 7, 8) rings, 9) double bond,   10) semiquaternary atom.

the quaternary carbon produces lines of outstanding intensity (Table 16). These lines are mostly confined in a narrow range between 710 and 750 cm^{-1}. Some of the most symmetric molecules show a certain shift of these lines to lower frequencies (670–700 cm^{-1}). Paraffins with two adjacent quaternary carbons show an even more pronounced red shift of the totally symmetric vibrations: the corresponding lines occur at 650–670 cm^{-1}.

The integrated intensity of these lines (per 1 g-mole) remains constant to first approximation on passing from one paraffin with a single quaternary carbon to another such molecule; it is doubled if the molecule contains two quaternary carbons.

Table 16

TOTALLY SYMMETRIC BOND-STRETCHING VIBRATIONS OF THE
PARAFFIN SKELETON WITH QUATERNARY CARBON ATOMS

Compound	Δv	I_0	ρ	I_∞	δ	I'_∞	References
Tetramethylmethane	733	25	P	—	—	—	[128]
2,2-Dimethylbutane	712	100	0.02	310	3.8	350	[100, 121]
2,2-Dimethylpentane	746	80	0.05	240	8.8	360	[100, 121]
2,2-Dimethylhexane	733	9	—	60	— }	280	[100, 121]
	748	28	0.13	110	9.8 }		
3,3-Dimethylpentane	695	75	0.05	250	6.5	360	[100, 121]
3-Methyl-3-ethylpentane	679	50	— }	240	—	380	[100, 121]
	686	50	— }				
3-Methyl-3-ethylhexane	707	46	0.09	240	19	420	[100, 121]
5,5-Dimethylundecane	757	8	—	60	20	150	[100, 121]
2,2,4-Trimethylpentane	746	120	0.02	230	3.8	380	[100, 121]
2,2,3-Trimethylbutane	688	75	0.03	330	8.3	490	[100, 121]
2,2,3-Trimethylpentane	716	50	0.04	250	7.7	390	[100, 121]
2,2,4,4-Tetramethylpentane	731	120	0.06	—	—	600	[129]
2,2,4,6,6-Pentamethylheptane	757	80	0.08	—	—	500	[129]
3,3,4,4-Tetramethylhexane	658	100	0.09	—	—	570	[129]

Note: Here and in the following tables of this section, Δv is the frequency in cm^{-1}, I_0 is the maximum line intensity (on a scale which assigns an intensity of 250 to the 802 cm^{-1} cyclohexane line), ρ is the depolarization, I_∞ is the integrated intensity (on a scale which assigns an integrated intensity of 500 to the 802 cm^{-1} cyclohexane line, see [100]), δ is the line width in cm^{-1}, I'_∞ is the integrated intensity computed allowing for molecular weight and density. Detailed data for some compounds not included in this table can be found in [100].

This indicates that the totally symmetrical stretching vibrations of the paraffin chain are largely identifiable with the vibrations of a local atomic grouping linked with the quaternary carbon atom. The splitting of the quaternary carbon lines in different spectra can be attributed to the existence of rotational isomers.

The symmetrical lines of the quaternary carbon are fairly narrow. The width of these lines shows a tendency to increase with the increasing chain length of the substituent radicals. This trend is particularly noticeable in the spectrum of 5,5-dimethylundecane (the 757 cm^{-1} line). An increase in molecular symmetry and the appearance of new branchings conversely makes the symmetrical lines narrower (e.g., the 746 cm^{-1} line of 2,2,4-trimethylpentane). The line widths of the relevant lines are generally measured simultaneously with depolarization measurements. The above three features in the variation of the width of the symmetrical lines are also observed in the spectra of other hydrocarbons with structural elements which show highly pronounced characteristic properties. These features are a reflection of a more general law, which is discussed in some detail in §17.

In addition to the symmetrical skeletal vibrations, paraffins with quaternary carbons show highly characteristic lines at 925 cm^{-1} and at 1200–1250 cm^{-1}. The corresponding data are arranged in Table 17. According to Stepanov's detailed calculations [80] and our results for the spectrum of tetramethylmethane [100], both these lines (in tetramethylmethane) are associated with triply degenerate modes. As a result of a strong coupling between Q and β_{CH_3}, both these coordinates are variable during vibration.*

Table 17

TRIPLY DEGENERATE VIBRATION MODES OF PARAFFINS WITH
QUATERNARY CARBON ATOMS

Compound	Δv	I_0	ρ	Δv	I_0	ρ	References
Tetramethylmethane	921	40	dep	1249	60	dep	[128]
2,2-Dimethylbutane	929	19	0.76	1218	13	0.86	[100, 121]
				1254	11	0.76	
2,2-Dimethylpentane	927	22	0.70	1208	18	0.56	[100, 121]
				1248	15	0.64	
3,3-Dimethylpentane	913	14	0.76	1196	10	0.85	[100, 121]
	934	11	0.8	1220	10	0.8	
				1240	8	0.8	
3,3-Diethylpentane	909	20	0.92	—	—	—	[129]
2,2,4-Trimethylpentane	929	23		1207	13	0.76	[100, 121]
			0.82	1250	14	0.76	
2,2,3-Trimethylbutane	919	36 ⎫		1209	8	—	[100, 121]
	927	33 ⎭	0.65	1224	13	0.86	
2,3,3-Trimethylpentane	930	38	0.66	1254	12	0.82	
				1210	14	0.7	[100, 121]
				1233	10	0.9	
2,2,3,4-Tetramethylpentane	922	35	0.71	1227	20	1.0	[129]
				1244	17	0.68	
2,2,4,4-Tetramethylpentane	920	46	0.73	1249	55	0.73	[129]
2,2,3,3-Tetramethylhexane	920	38	0.89	1229	42	0.65	[129]
				1239	40	0.78	

Examination of the experimental material in Table 17 shows that the frequency 1250 cm^{-1} appears persistently only in the spectra of paraffins which have three free methyl groups attached to the quaternary carbon. This group includes all the paraffins with the quaternary atom at the terminal position in the chain and an additional branching in position 4 and farther. If the quaternary atom is located in the middle of the chain, the 1250 cm^{-1} line is not observed altogether. In molecules with an "interfering" branching next to a terminal quaternary carbon, this frequency is

* According to Stepanov's terminology, the vibration β_{CH_3} is a mode in which the angles between the C—H bonds of the CH$_3$ group and the C—C bond vary.

sometimes observed, although not persistently, and mostly it is shifted toward the red by 10–15 cm^{-1}. Molecules with 2,2,3 branchings (without any other branchings) show three characteristic lines at 1200–1250 cm^{-1}.

The second line (near 925 cm^{-1}) is much less persistent. In some cases, this line is found to split into two components.

The properties of a tertiary carbon as a characteristic structural element are much less pronounced than those of the quaternary atom. An isolated tertiary carbon in a paraffin molecule will sometimes produce lines at lower frequencies (730–800 cm^{-1}) than the lines of normal paraffins (800–900 cm^{-1}). In most cases, however, the lines which can be associated with the symmetrical skeletal stretching vibrations of the paraffin are observed in the same region for normal paraffins and for paraffins with isolated tertiary carbons (800–900 cm^{-1}). Lines in this spectral region are therefore not characteristic of the tertiary carbon.

Experimental data and calculated frequencies [80, 130] show that the principal characteristic lines of paraffins with isolated tertiary carbons occur at 950, 1145, and 1170 cm^{-1}. Table 18 lists the relevant data for the spectra of some paraffins.

Table 18

FUNDAMENTAL CHARACTERISTIC LINES OF PARAFFINS WITH
TERTIARY CARBON ATOMS

Compound	Δv	I_0	ρ	Δv	I_0	ρ	Δv	I_0	ρ	References
Isobutane	966	16	dep	—	—	—	1169	15	dep	[131]
Isopentane	909	10	0.5	1147	8	0.7	1177	8	0.6	[100, 121]
	954	5	0.7							
2-Methylpentane	942	4	—	1149	12	0.6	1174	9	0.8	[100, 121]
	958	12	0.6							
2-Methylhexane	940	4	—	1144	10	0.6	1172	8	0.7	[100, 121]
	956	8	0.9							
3-Methylpentane	952	13	0.6	1156	12	0.5	1174	10	0.5	[100, 121]
	966	13	0.6							
	988	13	0.6							
4-Methylheptane	910	6	—	1151	10	0.5	1171	3	—	[100, 121]
3-Ethylpentane	903	13	0.88	1152	8	0.9	1168	8	0.9	[100, 121]
3-Ethylheptane	934	2	—	1154	7	—	—	—	—	[100, 121]
	951	2	—							
2,5-Dimethylhexane	907	7	0.7	1148	19	0.7	1172	19	0.7	[100, 121]
	941	7	—							
	961	22	0.82							
2,4,7-Trimethyloctane	915	12	—	1149	23	—	1172	25	—	[132]
	956	23	—							
	968	8	—							
	996	2	—							

The calculation of the vibration frequencies of the simplest paraffin molecule with a tertiary carbon—isobutane—carried out by Stepanov [80] (see also [130]) shows that the 965 and 1172 cm^{-1} lines of this hydrocarbon are doubly degenerate; the 965 cm^{-1} line is associated mainly with the variation of the angles β, whereas the 1172 cm^{-1} line is a mix of the variation of the angles β and the bonds Q approximately in equal measures. In isopentane, according to Stepanov's calculations, each of these frequencies is split into two; the 965 cm^{-1} line splits into 909 and 954 cm^{-1}, and the 1172 cm^{-1} line splits into 1147 and 1177 cm^{-1}. As the molecule becomes more complex, the frequencies around 1145 and 1170 cm^{-1} do not change. The behavior of the frequencies at 950 cm^{-1} is more complex: in molecules without a tertiary carbon at the end of the chain, the strong 950 cm^{-1} line disappears; in molecules with tertiary carbons separated by two links of the chain, one of the frequencies (960 cm^{-1}) splits into two because of a resonance interaction (910 and 990 cm^{-1}), whereas the other frequency is conserved. There are certain exceptions to these general rules (see [80]).

We see from Table 18 that Stepanov's rules are on the whole satisfied. The regular pattern, however, is somewhat obscured by the presence of a number of extraneous lines in the relevant region (in Table 18, some of the weak lines have been omitted).

A topic of considerable interest is the behavior of the characteristic lines associated with a tertiary carbon in the presence of a "stronger" characteristic structural element —a quaternary carbon—in the molecule. Data for such lines are listed in Table 19. Note the considerable decrease in the intensity of these lines. Often the characteristic lines of tertiary carbon are not observed altogether. Thus the quaternary carbon, acting as a dominant characteristic structural element, as if "suppresses" the weaker structural element—the tertiary carbon. It should be stressed that the identification of the lines in Table 19 with tertiary atoms is not completely certain. There is a

Table 19

CHARACTERISTIC LINES OF TERTIARY CARBON ATOMS IN THE SPECTRA
OF PARAFFINS WITH QUATERNARY ATOMS

Compound	Δv	I_0	ρ	Δv	I_0	ρ	References
2,2,4-Trimethylpentane	955	4	0.9	1173	3	0.8	[100, 121]
2,2,4-Trimethylhexane	—	—	—	1161	5	—	[129]
2,2,4-Trimethylheptane	963	4	0.8	1158	4	—	[129]
2,2,4-Trimethyloctane	—	—	—	1147	3	1.0	[129]
2,2,5-Trimethylhexane	958	12	0.8	—	—	—	[129]
2,2,6-Trimethylheptane	—	—	—	—	—	—	[129]
2,2,3-Trimethylbutane	959	0	—	1159	1	—	[100, 121]
2,2,3-Trimethylpentane	975	12	0.5	—	—	—	[100, 121]
2,2,3-Trimethylpentane	959	4	—	1196	14	—	[100, 121]

possibility that the relevant spectral region contains lines of some entirely different origin: similar (weak) lines are observed in some cases in the spectra of molecules which have no tertiary carbons altogether. Our purpose in citing these data, however, was to illustrate the unquestionable breakdown of additivity: in a molecule with several characteristic structural elements, the lines of one of these elements appear as if there were no other elements in the molecule, whereas the lines of the other characteristic structural elements are greatly attenuated or do not show at all. This breakdown of additivity, often observed in the spectra of complex molecules with characteristic structural elements of different "strength", will be described as a "suppression" of some characteristic structural elements by others. The vibrations of the inferior structural elements may be enhanced by increasing the chain length, introducing additional branchings in the molecule, and by other techniques which distort the vibrations of the dominant structural element. Similar effects are observed in other classes of compounds also.

Qualitative conclusions based on the relative evaluation of the role of various characteristic structural elements in the vibrations of complex molecules thus present a valid picture of the Raman spectrum and even predict some of its features.

A group of compounds with adjacent tertiary atoms is important enough to be considered separately among the paraffins with only tertiary carbons. When a molecule of this kind vibrates, the adjacent tertiary carbons reveal a strong coupling, and therefore lose to a certain extent the characteristic properties of independent structural units. As a result, the Raman spectra of paraffins with adjacent tertiary carbons are substantially different from the spectra of paraffins with isolated tertiary atoms. The Raman spectra of these paraffins do not show any of the characteristic lines of an isolated tertiary carbon. Instead, a new stable series of characteristic lines is observed. We may therefore consider a branched chain of the form

$$
\begin{array}{c}
-\text{C}-\text{C}-\text{C}-\text{C}- \\
\phantom{-\text{C}-}|| \\
\phantom{-\text{C}-}\text{C}\text{C}
\end{array}
$$

as a new characteristic structural element [100].

The characteristic frequencies of this group were determined by Stepanov [80]. A detailed calculation of the vibration modes of the simplest compound with adjacent tertiary carbons—2,3-dimethylbutane—was carried out in [133]; the vibration modes of several different rotational isomers of this compound were calculated. This calculation accounted for the presence of several strong and highly polarized lines between 720 and 760 cm^{-1} in the spectrum of 2,3-dimethylbutane and related compounds. These lines are characteristic of the symmetrical stretching vibrations of the paraffin skeleton, and each of these lines corresponds to a certain rotational isomer. The strong coupling between the adjacent tertiary carbons thus primarily causes a marked shift of the entire region of symmetrical stretching vibrations of the paraffin skeleton. The frequencies decreased on the average by 80 cm^{-1} compared to those in less branched paraffins.

Another remarkable feature is the considerable stability of the symmetrical stretching frequencies of paraffins with adjacent tertiary carbons. They all show at least one strong and highly polarized line in a relatively narrow region between 720 and 760 cm^{-1}. The occasional presence of several lines in this region is associated with the existence of several rotational isomers. The relatively small splitting and the insignificant frequency shift on passing from one paraffin to the next point to an unusually slight effect of the structure of the entire molecule on the symmetrical skeletal vibrations, which can thus be taken as characteristic of the particular structural element being considered.

According to Stepanov [80] and the present author [133], the main characteristic lines of paraffins with adjacent tertiary carbons are the lines at 950, 1160, and 1190 cm^{-1}. Some additional features in the spectra of slightly branched paraffins, which are helpful in identifying the constituent elements of the molecule from Raman spectra, are given in the next section.

Interesting conclusions regarding the position of the branching can be drawn from an examination of the lines in the deformation region of a carbon chain. This region (150–500 cm^{-1}) generally contains several lines, and the frequencies alone do not reveal any regular pattern in their arrangement. However, by using the entire set of line parameters, one can identify the line corresponding to the bending vibrations of the longest free chain in the molecule. This line has the highest intensity, the smallest width, and the greatest polarization among all the lines in this spectral region. The frequency of this line is related to the free chain length by a simple equality [100]:

$$\Delta v = \frac{a}{m_C + 6}. \tag{11.1}$$

Here m_C is the number of carbon atoms in the free chain (including the branching atom). The constant a slightly varies depending on the type of the branching. In the case of a branching with a tertiary carbon, $a = 3250$, and in the case of a quaternary carbon $a = 3350$. Figures 35 and 36 plot the experimental findings against the results of Eq. (11.1).

We also tried to trace the dependence of Δv on the total number n_C of carbon atoms in a chain with a substituent radical attached to it. Figure 35 shows that as n_C increases (for a fixed m_C), the vibration frequency of the chain somewhat decreases, but this dependence is very slight. Other features of molecular structure hardly affect the frequency of the spectral line, and it can therefore be regarded as a characteristic line of the free chain. Note that Eq. (11.1) is valid not only for paraffins but for other hydrocarbons too. This dependence is of the utmost importance in structural analysis: it expresses the free chain length in terms of the measured frequency, and thus makes it possible to pinpoint the position of the branching.

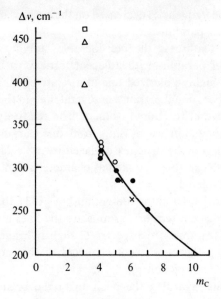

Figure 35

The frequency of the skeletal deformation vibrations in paraffins with tertiary carbons vs. the length of the chain for different branch points:

$\square$ $n_C = 4$, $\triangle$ $n_C = 5$, $\bigcirc$ $n_C = 6$, $\bullet$ $n_C = 7$, $\times$ $n_C = 8$. The solid curve is calculated from (11.1).

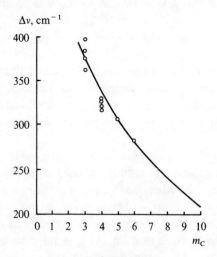

Figure 36

The frequency of the skeletal deformation vibrations in paraffins with quaternary carbons vs. the length of the free chain.

With regard to the groups CH_3, CH_2, and CH, their stretching vibrations occupy a sharply defined region between 2850 and 2970 cm^{-1}. As a result of the weak coupling of the C—H stretching vibrations with other vibration modes, the spectra of hydrocarbons in this region are made up additively from the spectra of the constituent CH_3, CH_2, and CH groups in the molecule of the compound. However, the frequencies of the lines associated with CH_3, CH_2, and CH, respectively, are not strictly constant. The interaction between the hydrogen atoms in the geometrically nearest groups causes a certain shift and splitting of the frequencies [100]. The structure of the spectrum in the C—H stretching region is therefore fairly complex, changing from one compound to the next.

The 2965 cm^{-1} line corresponding to the degenerate vibrations of the CH_3 group shows the greatest stability in the spectrum. The intensity of this line (per one CH_3 group) is fully characteristic. Therefore, the intensity of the 2965 cm^{-1} line in the spectrum of any given compound is proportional to the number of CH_3 groups. Figure 37 plots the corresponding proportionality, which emerges with maximum clarity from measurements conducted in polarized light. This technique eliminates the polarized lines which are partly superimposed on the 2965 cm^{-1} line (this line is depolarized).

Among the other hydrocarbons, systematic results are available only for the Raman spectra of compounds which are significant in petroleum chemistry [134, 135], e.g., five-membered and six-membered naphthenes [121, 136–142] and unsaturated hydrocarbons [121, 143–158]. Some indications relating to the structural analysis of these hydrocarbons are given in §12. The data available for other classes of compounds are unfortunately incomplete and we can only point to occasional structural features emerging in their Raman spectra.

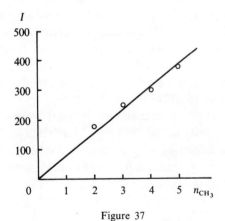

Figure 37

The intensity of the 2965 cm^{-1} line vs. the number of CH_3 groups in paraffin molecules.

12. STRUCTURAL ANALYSIS USING RAMAN SPECTRA

Structural analysis is based on the identification of structural units in molecules which are associated with stable series of characteristic lines in Raman spectra. However, certain characteristic elements are known to "suppress" other elements, so that the general appearance of the spectrum and the presence of certain characteristic lines in it are primarily determined by the "strongest" characteristic structural element in the molecule. No general procedure for structural analysis can be devised unless this coupling between the characteristic structural elements is taken into full consideration. Without this coupling, we are left with a random assembly of structural features which, although leading to meaningful results in some cases, do not provide a general solution of the entire problem.

1. Structural analysis of paraffins

The characteristic structural elements of paraffins are the quaternary carbon, the tertiary carbon, two adjacent tertiary carbons, and a free carbon chain. The C—H stretching region also has to be considered.

We distinguish between four groups of paraffins according to the different characteristic structural elements in the molecule. Supplementary secondary features are sought for each of these groups in order to fully describe the structure of the molecule. As we have stressed repeatedly, the entire range of spectral features must be taken into consideration if we are to come up with a valid model of the molecule.

Group I. Paraffins with a quaternary carbon

These paraffins are characterized by strong, highly polarized, narrow (4–6 cm^{-1} wide) lines between 650 and 760 cm^{-1} and fairly strong depolarized lines around 925 cm^{-1} and 1200–1250 cm^{-1}. The number of quaternary atoms is derived from the intensity of the symmetrical lines (the integrated line intensity per quaternary carbon is approximately 300).* In high-symmetry molecules, the symmetrical line is located at 670–700 cm^{-1}, and it is very narrow; in molecules with adjacent quaternary atoms, this line shifts to 650–670 cm^{-1}.

The total number of CH_3 groups in the molecule and thus the number of branchings are inferred from the intensity of the 2965 cm^{-1} line (for one CH_3 group, $I = 80$). If the paraffin contains a single quaternary atom, without any additional branchings, the position of the quaternary atom is determined from the frequency of the strongest polarized line in the deformation region (200–400 cm^{-1}) and from empirical curves (Figure 36).

---

* The molecular weight and the density of the paraffin are assumed known.

Additional features: *a*) symmetrical lines at $870–890$ cm^{-1} are indicatory of a free chain consisting of two (the 890 cm^{-1} line) or three and more (the 870 cm^{-1} line) carbon atoms; *b*) a quaternary atom at the end of the chain is characterized by the 1250 cm^{-1} line.

If the molecule also contains tertiary carbons, their number can be found from the intensity of the 2965 cm^{-1} line, which is proportional to the number of CH_3 groups. The presence of adjacent quaternary and tertiary atoms leads to the appearance of a line at 530 cm^{-1} and suppresses the 1250 cm^{-1} line. If this complex branching is located at the end of the molecule, three lines (rather than two) appear at $1200–1250$ cm^{-1}. Ethyl groups in the branchings are characterized by a strong depolarized line ($I_0 \sim 7–20$) at $1020–1080$ cm^{-1}.

Additional features of tertiary atoms include weak lines at 950 cm^{-1} and $1140–1170$ cm^{-1}. The additional features *a* and *b* pertaining to a free chain and a terminal quaternary atom (see above) are also observed.

Group II. Paraffins with adjacent tertiary carbons (without quaternary carbons)

This group of paraffins are characterized by symmetrical lines at $720–750$ cm^{-1} and by lines at 950, 1160, and 1190 cm^{-1}. Ethyl groups in the branching produce a strong line at $1020–1080$ cm^{-1}. The free chain features (lines at $870–890$ cm^{-1}) are conserved. The overall number of branchings is determined, as before, from the intensity of the 2965 cm^{-1} line. The presence of three adjacent tertiary atoms is characterized by the appearance of three (rather than two) lines at $1160–1190$ cm^{-1}.

Group III. Paraffins with isolated tertiary carbons

These paraffins are characterized by lines at 950, 1145, and 1170 cm^{-1}. Symmetrical lines are observed at $800–900$ cm^{-1} (the only exception are the high-symmetry molecules, whose symmetrical lines are narrower and shifted to $730–800$ cm^{-1}). The intensity of the 2965 cm^{-1} line gives the number of CH_3 groups. Additional data are obtained from the intensity of the 1300 cm^{-1} line, which is proportional to the number of CH_2 groups, and the intensity of the 1340 cm^{-1} line, proportional to the number of CH groups. The 1340 cm^{-1} line is stronger when the branching is located at the end of the chain; the intensity of the 1300 cm^{-1} line markedly drops when the CH_2 group is located between two branchings.

In the case of paraffins with one branching, the position and the type of the branching can be determined from the frequency of the strongest line with the highest polarization in the deformation region, using the empirical curve (Figure 35).

Additional features of the free chain include lines at $870–890$ cm^{-1} (see above). Ethyl groups in the branching produce an enhancement of the line at $1020–1080$ cm^{-1}. Disappearance of the 950 cm^{-1} line is characteristic of molecules without terminal branching, and three lines at $900–950$ cm^{-1} are indicatory of branchings in the 2,4 position (these features are unreliable).

Group IV.   Normal paraffins

These paraffins are characterized by a number of symmetrical lines at $800-900$ cm^{-1}, a strong line at 1300 cm^{-1}, and a strong higly polarized line in the deformation region ($200-400$ cm^{-1}), whose intensity decreases as the chain becomes longer. Additional features include lines at 1070 and 1140 cm^{-1}.

In all cases, the general character of the spectrum should be taken into consideration. A decrease in the number of lines in the spectrum and a reduction in the width of symmetrical lines is characteristic of high-symmetry hydrocarbons.

This scheme for the structural analysis of paraffins uses most of the features first established by Stepanov from his analysis of frequencies ([80], Vol. II). At the same time, a wide use of all the parameters of the Raman lines helped to establish a number of new structural features, while previously known features received a better and more precise definition. Of course, it is always assumed that the spectroscopist carrying out the structural analysis is able to measure all the parameters that are needed.

2. Structural analysis of naphthenes [100]

A given compound generally can be identified as a naphthene without using Raman spectroscopy, by examining such physical constants as the boiling point, the density, and the refractive index. When using Raman spectroscopy, however, certain difficulties may arise because of the uncertain distinction between naphthenes and paraffins: as we have mentioned earlier, the spectra of some naphthenes are on the whole similar to the spectra of paraffins. The distinctive feature of naphthenes is provided by the structure of the spectrum in the C—H stretching region. Because of the numerous "naphthene"-type CH_2 groups in the molecule, the intensities of the lines associated with CH_3 groups and the "paraffin" CH_2 groups do not correspond to the molecular weight (the molecular weight of the compound is assumed known). Thus, alongside with the relatively low intensity of the 2960 cm^{-1} line characteristic of the CH_3 group, the naphthene spectra show weak lines at 2908 cm^{-1} and 1304 cm^{-1} (these frequencies are characteristic of slightly branched paraffins). The measurements are best carried out on photographs taken in polarized light. The determination of the number of CH_3 groups (from the intensity of the depolarized line at about 2960 cm^{-1}) is also highly significant for the further stages of the analysis.

Once the compound has been identified as a naphthene, the ring type has to be determined. Cyclopropane derivatives can be identified from the strong lines at $2990-3080$ cm^{-1}, which are in general characteristic of unsaturated hydrocarbons; in distinction from unsaturated hydrocarbons, however, cyclopropane derivatives do not show the characteristic line at 1600 cm^{-1}. Cyclohexane derivatives are readily identified from the lines at $1030-1050$, $1160-1190$, 1260, and 1350 cm^{-1}, characteristic of the six-membered ring. If on the basis of these signs the hydrocarbon is definitely not suspected as a three-membered or a six-membered naphthene, sharp and strong lines in the region below 1200 cm^{-1} identify it as a cyclobutane derivative. Fairly weak diffuse lines in this region are characteristic of five-membered naphthenes. The spectra of cycloheptane, cyclooctane and other derivatives have been little studied, and no characteristic features of these naphthenes are known. In general appearance, the spectra of these naphthenes are close to cyclopentane hydrocarbons. This unfortunately lowers the reliability of the structural analysis of naphthenes.

The subsequent stages of the structural analysis will be illustrated only for the two best known groups of naphthenes, namely the five-membered and the six-membered naphthenes. The currently available data for other naphthenes are insufficient for a systematic structural analysis.

Let us first consider the five-membered naphthenes. These naphthenes can be divided into two groups according as the spectrum contains or lacks the strong polarized line at around 890 cm^{-1}. The spectra of the first group, which includes the monosubstituted naphthenes, the 1,1- and 1,2-disubstituted naphthenes, and the 1,1,2-trisubstituted naphthenes, show this line; the spectra of the five-membered naphthenes of the second group (1,3-disubstituted naphthenes and all the trisubstituted naphthenes, except 1,1,2) do not show the 890 cm^{-1} line.

The first group of five-membered naphthenes

If the 890 cm^{-1} line is observed jointly with a strong polarized line at 680–700 cm^{-1}, the molecule is a 1,1,2-trisubstituted naphthene; a similar line at 750–780 cm^{-1} identifies a 1,2-disubstituted naphthene. *Gem*-substituted five-membered naphthenes and other naphthenes with a quaternary carbon in the branching are characterized by lines at 930–950 cm^{-1} and 1230–1250 cm^{-1}. Naphthenes with a quaternary atom in the branchings are also characterized by a strong highly polarized line at 710–730 cm^{-1}, whereas in 1,1-*gem*-substituted naphthenes this line is fairly weak. Moreover, 1,1-*gem*-substituted naphthenes and monosubstituted naphthenes with a quaternary atom in the branching have a different number of CH$_3$ groups, and this difference is reflected in the intensity of the 2960 cm^{-1} line.

If the spectrum does not show the characteristic line of a quaternary carbon and of adjacent tertiary atoms, the hydrocarbon is identified as a monosubstituted five-membered naphthene. In the case of monosubstituted five-membered naphthenes with an unbranched radical, the frequency of the strongest, narrowest and most polarized line in the region below about 500 cm^{-1} gives the position of the atom to which the five-membered ring is attached. The frequency of this line obeys the general empirical relation (11.1).* Some details of the structure of the substituent radical can also be derived from the general features established for paraffins.

---

* For cyclopentanes with a normal structure of the substituent radical, $a = 3400$; if the five-membered ring is attached to one of the inner atoms in the chain, $a = 3000$.

The second group of five-membered naphthenes

The 1,1,3-trisubstituted five-membered naphthenes show the characteristic lines of the quaternary carbon at 930–950 cm^{-1} and at 1230–1250 cm^{-1} and a strong polarized line at 740–800 cm^{-1}. The 1,3-disubstituted five-membered naphthenes differ from the 1,2,3- and the 1,2,4-trisubstituted naphthenes in the respective positions of the strongest polarized lines. These trisubstituted naphthenes have adjacent tertiary carbon atoms, and their symmetrical lines accordingly fall at 740–780 cm^{-1}, whereas the symmetrical lines of the 1,3-disubstituted naphthenes, which do not have this characteristic structural element, fall at 800–840 cm^{-1}. Lines at 960–990 cm^{-1} and 1150–1190 cm^{-1} are also higly characteristic of the 1,2,3-trisubstituted five-membered napthenes. These lines are also observed in the spectra of 1,2,4-trisubstituted five-membered naphthenes, but they are much weaker there. An additional distinguishing feature between disubstituted and trisubstituted naphthenes of these types is provided by the intensity of the 2960 cm^{-1} line, which is proportional to the number of CH$_3$ groups in the molecule.

Raman spectra thus provide means for distinguishing between the different types of substitution in five-membered naphthenes, with from one to three substituents. For naphthenes with a higher number of substituents, no data are available as yet.

The longest of the unbranched substituent radicals can be described from the frequency of the strongest, narrowest, and most polarized line in the region below 600 cm^{-1}. If the molecule only contains methyl groups, the frequency of this line falls at 480–570 cm^{-1}. The corresponding frequency intervals for longer substituent radicals are the following: ethyl group, 360–420 cm^{-1}; propyl group, 310–325 cm^{-1}; butyl group, 270–300 cm^{-1}. The length of still longer groups can be calculated from Eq. (11.1).

Let us now consider the *six-membered naphthenes*. The spectra of relatively few naphthenes of this group have been studied, and we may therefore propose nothing but a tentative schedule for the structural analysis of these compounds. This schedule uses the spectral characteristics of a number of structural elements (a quaternary atom, adjacent tertiary atoms, etc.) established in the analysis of hydrocarbons of other classes.

The total number of CH$_3$ groups in the molecule can be determined from the intensity of the 2960 cm^{-1} line, as before. This number characterizes the branchings in the molecule and is significant for the further stages of the analysis.

The exact position of the symmetrical skeletal lines, which are comparatively strong and sharp for the six-membered naphthenes, is of the greatest importance for identifying the substitution mode. Monosubstituted six-membered naphthenes have their strongest polarized lines at around 760–800 cm^{-1}. The strong polarized line at 840–850 cm^{-1} is also highly characteristic of these naphthenes. *Gem*-substituted six-membered naphthenes have their strongest symmetrical lines at 680–730 cm^{-1}. At 820–850 cm^{-1}, they generally have two lines of medium intensity. The lines of the quaternary carbon at 900–950 cm^{-1} and 1200–1250 cm^{-1} are also characteristic of *gem*-substituted naphthenes. An additional feature of monosubstituted and *gem*-substituted six-membered naphthenes is the very strong unpolarized line at 1030–1040 cm^{-1}. Similar lines are observed in the spectra of other six-membered naphthenes also, but they are scattered over a much wider frequency interval there.

Six-membered naphthenes with adjacent tertiary carbons (1,2-disubstituted naphthenes and the corresponding trisubstituted naphthenes) are distinguished by a strong, sharp, and highly polarized line at 730–750 cm^{-1}. The characteristic lines of the adjacent tertiary carbons at 950–990 cm^{-1} and 1150–1190 cm^{-1} are unstable and may only be used as a secondary character. These lines are expected to be stronger in the spectra of 1,2,3-trisubstituted six-membered naphthenes.

The spectra of six-membered naphthenes without *gem*-atoms and adjacent tertiary carbons (1,3- and 1,4-disubstituted naphthenes and 1,3,5-trisubstituted naphthenes) have symmetrical lines at 750–780 cm^{-1} for the disubstituted naphthenes and at 790–800 cm^{-1} for the trisubstituted. The 1,4-disubstituted six-membered naphthenes have no strong lines at 820–850 cm^{-1}, whereas the 1,3,5-trisubstituted naphthenes show an exceptionally strong line at this frequency, but the lines at 790–800 cm^{-1} are relatively weak.

Disubstituted six-membered naphthenes show an additional feature which can be used to determine with higher precision the spatial position of the substituents [100, 138, 139]: isomers with substituents in the polar position are characterized by a strong line at 600–640 cm^{-1}. A similar line is also characteristic of substituents in the polar position in more complex six-membered naphthenes.

Additional data on the longest free chain in the molecule are provided by the frequency of the strongest, narrowest, and most polarized deformation line in the region below 400 cm^{-1}. The frequency of this line is related to the length of the substituent chain by Eq. (11.1) with $a = 3100$.

3. Structural analysis of unsaturated hydrocarbons [100]

Unsaturated hydrocarbons with isolated C=C bonds are readily distinguishable from hydrocarbons of other classes according to the intensity of the polarized line at 1640–1680 cm^{-1}, which is characteristic of the C=C stretching. If the compound contains two or more equivalent C=C bonds (not conjugated), the intensity of these lines increases in proportion to the number of bonds (the per bond intensity is $I'_{\infty} = 400$–500). If the C=C bonds are not equivalent, e.g., one is terminal and the other in the middle of the molecule, two distinct lines are observed in this region. The appearance of two lines at 1640–1680 cm^{-1} may also indicate that the test sample is a mixture of stereoisomers (see below). A marked increase in the intensity of the lines at 1640–1680 cm^{-1} (by a factor of 5–10 compared to the intensity of a single C=C bond) points to conjugation of C=C bonds.

The type of the substitution is identified using the following features (Figure 38).

1. Unsaturated hydrocarbons of groups 1 and 2 (double bond at the end of the chain) are characterized by lines at around 3000 cm^{-1} and 3080 cm^{-1}, which are associated with the stretching vibrations of the $=CH_2$ group. The first line is polarized, and the second is depolarized. These hydrocarbons are also characterized by a line at about 1414 cm^{-1}, which is associated with bending vibrations of the same group. In unsaturated hydrocarbons of group 1 (α-olefins), the frequency of the double bond is 1642 cm^{-1}, and in unsaturated hydrocarbons of group 2 (two substituents at the same carbon) this frequency is about 1650 cm^{-1}.

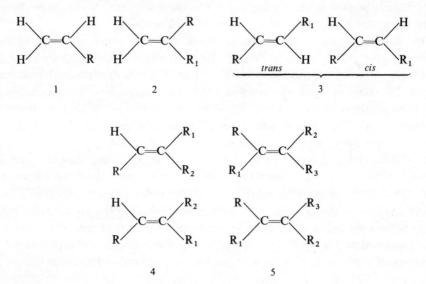

Figure 38

Various groups of open-chain unsaturated hydrocarbons.

Additional features of unsaturated hydrocarbons of group 1: medium intensity line at around 912 cm^{-1}, weak lines at around 430, 630, 990, and 1295 cm^{-1}.

Additional features of unsaturated hydrocarbons of group 2: medium intensity line at around 888 cm^{-1}, weak lines at around 435, 700, and 1000 cm^{-1}. Moreover, unsaturated hydrocarbons of this group show the characteristic signs of a "semiquaternary" carbon (see Figure 34): lines at 900–950 cm^{-1} and 1200–1250 cm^{-1} and a shift of the symmetrical chain frequencies to 730–770 cm^{-1} (in the absence of other characteristic structural elements).

2. In unsaturated hydrocarbons of group 4 (trisubstituted unsaturated hydrocarbons), the frequency of the double bond is 1670–1680 cm^{-1}, and the spectra show the characteristic lines of this type of substitution at 500–530 cm^{-1} and 1340–

$1360 \ cm^{-1}$. Additional features: weak lines at about $250-260 \ cm^{-1}$, $300 \ cm^{-1}$, and $1210 \ cm^{-1}$. Furthermore, the unsaturated hydrocarbons of this group show all the characteristic features of the semiquaternary carbon.

3. For unsaturated hydrocarbons of group 5 (quadrisubstituted unsaturated hydrocarbons) with double bond frequency of about $1670 \ cm^{-1}$, strong characteristic lines are observed at $680-690 \ cm^{-1}$, $\sim 505 \ cm^{-1}$, and $\sim 1390 \ cm^{-1}$. An additional feature is the absence of lines at $1200-1250 \ cm^{-1}$.

4. If the spectrum with a double bond frequency of $1655-1675 \ cm^{-1}$ shows no signs of unsaturated hydrocarbons of groups 4 and 5, the compound belongs to group 3 (unsaturated hydrocarbons with two substituents at different carbon atoms). The frequency of the double bond of cis-isomers in this case is $1655-1660 \ cm^{-1}$, and of the trans-isomers $1670-1675 \ cm^{-1}$. If the spectrum shows both these lines and their combined integrated intensity does not markedly exceed the intensity of a single $C{=}C$ bond, the compound can be regarded as a mixture of stereoisomers.

Additional features of cis-isomers: a strong line at about $1260 \ cm^{-1}$, medium intensity lines at about 580 and $960 \ cm^{-1}$, and weak lines at 300 and $400 \ cm^{-1}$.

Additional features of trans-isomers: strong lines at $1300-1310$, $1060-1100$, $470-490 \ cm^{-1}$, weak lines at ~ 745, $965 \ cm^{-1}$.

The structure of the substituent radicals is established mainly from the spectral features associated with the characteristic structural elements of these radicals. We can therefore retain the general procedure of structural analysis described for paraffins and the same subdivision into groups.

1. An isolated quaternary carbon is represented by strong highly polarized lines at $700-760 \ cm^{-1}$ and strong lines at 925 and $1200-1250 \ cm^{-1}$. These features are fairly close to the spectral features of the semiquaternary carbon, but they are more prominent for the quaternary atom, for which all these lines are much stronger; moreover, the lines between 900 and $950 \ cm^{-1}$ show a more pronounced clustering around $925 \ cm^{-1}$ and the lines at $1200-1250 \ cm^{-1}$ a more pronounced clustering around $1200 \ cm^{-1}$ than the corresponding lines of the semiquaternary carbon.

Note that semiquaternary atoms can occur only in unsaturated hydrocarbons of groups 2 and 4. Therefore, if all the above lines are present in the spectra of unsaturated hydrocarbons of groups 1, 3, and 5, this provides a direct indication of a quaternary atom in the molecule. On the other hand, unsaturated hydrocarbons of groups 2 and 4 are a priori known to carry a semiquaternary atom, and the question to be considered is therefore whether or not the molecule also contains an isolated quaternary atom. This question can be readily answered by examining the line intensities. If the molecule only contans a semiquaternary atom, the line intensities I'_0 at $900-950 \ cm^{-1}$ are of the order of $10-15$ units, whereas the region $1190-1210$ cm^{-1} contains only weak lines with $I'_0 \approx 3$. If the molecule also contains a quaternary atom, the spectrum shows lines at around $925 \ cm^{-1}$ and in the region $1190-1210$ cm^{-1} with intensity $I'_0 \approx 20$ (or higher).

If the molecule contains adjacent quaternary and tertiary or quaternary and semiquaternary atoms, the frequency of the symmetrical skeletal vibrations shifts to $660-700$ cm^{-1}, two lines appear at $900-950$ cm^{-1}, and one line remains in the region $1200-1250$ cm^{-1} (near 1200 cm^{-1}). Moreover, lines generally appear at $520-530$ cm^{-1}.

2. Adjacent tertiary atoms (without quaternary atoms in the molecule) are characterized by symmetrical lines at $700-750$ cm^{-1}, and also by fairly strong lines at $900-950$ cm^{-1} and $1160-1190$ cm^{-1}.

3. Unsaturated hydrocarbons with only isolated tertiary carbons are characterized by symmetrical skeletal lines at $760-850$ cm^{-1}, by medium intensity lines at $900-950$ cm^{-1}, and by a line at $1145-1170$ cm^{-1}.

In all the three cases above, a free chain with $m_C \geq 3$ in the molecule is characterized by a line between $1020-1080$ cm^{-1}. If the double bond is located at the end of the chain, this line is very weak. The number of links in the longest free chain extending from the branching is determined from the frequency of the strongest, most polarized, and narrowest bending line, using Eq. (11.1) with $a = 3600$.

The presence of CH_3 groups attached directly to the double-bond carbon is characterized by a strong line at 2916 cm^{-1} and a line at $2990-3030$ cm^{-1}. This feature is of the greatest significance for unsaturated hydrocarbons of groups 3, 4, and 5.

4. Normal unsaturated hydrocarbons have symmetrical skeletal lines at $800-900$ cm^{-1}. The terminal position of the double bond is readily established using the spectral features of the unsaturated hydrocarbons of group 1. In the case of unsaturated hydrocarbons of group 3 with a *trans*-configuration, the position of the double bond in the chain can be determined from the frequency of the strongest, narrowest, and most polarized line in the deformation region, using Eq. (11.1), where m_C should be replaced with m'_C, the number of carbon atoms in the chain after the double bond (including the double-bond carbon itself). Additional data point to lines at $1070-1130$ cm^{-1}. The dependence of the line frequency on m'_C is plotted in Figure 30. This curve is applicable to both *trans*- and *cis*-isomers.

The above spectral features often provide sufficient information for a complete determination of the molecular structure of unsaturated hydrocarbons. This scheme of structural analysis of unsaturated hydrocarbons, as in the case of hydrocarbons of other classes, allows for the coupling of the individual structural elements and for the possible "suppression" of some elements by stronger ones. On the whole, the structural analysis of unsaturated hydrocarbons is more complicated than the analysis of paraffins owing to the appearance of a new structural element—the double bond. Therefore, in some cases, the unraveling of the molecular structure from Raman spectra cannot be carried out to completion. In highly branched compounds, isolated tertiary atoms may escape our notice, since the total number of CH_3 groups in unsaturated hydrocarbons cannot be determined with the same reliability as in paraffins, and the characteristic lines of the tertiary atoms may be "sup-

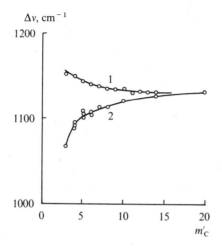

Figure 39

The "maximum vibration frequency" of a chain vs. chain length:

1) n-paraffins,   2) normal unsaturated hydrocarbons.

pressed" by stronger characteristic structural elements. These specific properties of the structural analysis of unsaturated hydrocarbons must be taken into consideration in structural analysis.

The above schedules of structural analysis have been tried by the author for some compounds of relatively complex structure. We worked with hydrocarbons of known molecular weight, without any additional information about their structure and composition. Figure 40 shows the structural formulae of these compounds. For all the compounds, except one, a correct determination of the structure was obtained. For compound 6, the formula obtained experimentally is the one in brackets, i.e., we missed an additional short substituent. This error was attributable to the fact that relatively few six-membered naphthenes had been studied.

A necessary stepping stone toward the development of structural analysis schedules for compounds of other classes is the systematic study of Raman spectra of the simplest representatives of the respective classes, the identification of their characteristic structural elements, and the measurement of the basic parameters of the characteristic lines. It is hoped that work in this direction will be done on an increasing scale. At present, because of the lack of essential data, we can only give some tables summarizing the characteristic frequencies that may be useful for the determination of the structure of hydrocarbons from Raman spectra (Tables 20–23). The reliability of the extensive lists of characteristic frequencies in infrared and Raman spectra published in a number of handbooks [125, 44] is unfortunately doubtful. As we have noted before, complex molecules can be arbitrarily split into various combinations

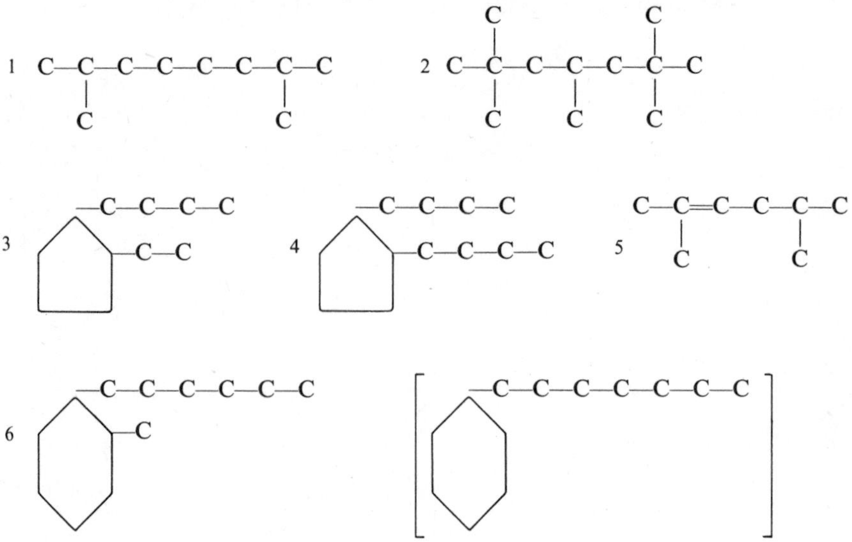

Figure 40

Some compounds whose structure was determined from Raman spectra.

of branchings, atomic groups, etc., which do not correspond to any real characteristic features in the vibrational spectra. The structural analysis should naturally proceed from the identification of the characteristic structural elements as structural units of molecules which can be tagged to specific features in the molecular spectra. The coupling of the structural elements also must be taken into consideration.

Some information on the molecular structure can be obtained from examination of the physical constants (boiling point, density, refractive index, etc.). Infrared spectroscopy also provides valuable data. Extensive use of all the different kinds of information is naturally conducive to a speedy and successful completion of the structural analysis.

13. INTERACTION OF ATOMS AND ATOMIC GROUPS IN COMPLEX MOLECULES AS REFLECTED IN RAMAN SPECTRA

1. Conjugation of multiple bonds

We have noted in § 11 that the C=C double bond corresponds in Raman spectra to a characteristic line near 1640 cm^{-1}. If the scattering molecule has two such double bonds, with several single bonds interposed between them, the frequency of the corresponding line is conserved and its intensity is approximately doubled,

Table 20

CHARACTERISTIC LINES OF X—H BONDS

Bond	Frequency range, cm^{-1}	Remarks*	References
C—H	2850–2980	Paraffins, naphthenes,	[88, 121]
—CH$_3$	2965	$\rho = 6/7$	[100]
$\triangle^{-H}$	3000; 3080	Cyclopropane derivatives	[100, 121]
=C—H	3000; 3080	Unsaturated hydrocarbons	[121]
⬡—H	3000–3080	Aromatic hydrocarbons	[121]
≡C—H	3270–3305		[159]
—O—H	3600–3680	Unassociated molecules	[88, 160]
—O—H	3400 (band)	Associated molecules	[88, 160]
S—H	2570		[88]
Se—H	2300		[88]
Si—H	2100–2200	Organosilicon compounds	[161]
P—H	2400–2440	Structures with P(V)	[162, 163]
=N—H	3330–3340		[88, 159]
—NH$_2$	3350–3370; 3300–3310		[88, 159]
N—H	3400–3500	RNH$_2$, R$_2$NH (unassociated molecules)	[164]
N—H	3300–3400	RNH$_2$, R$_2$NH (associated molecules)	[164]
N—H	3470	RCONHR' (unassociated molecules)	[164]
N—H	3300	RCONHR' (associated molecules)	[164]

* Here and in the following tables R stands for an alkyl radical, C_nH_{2n+1}, Ar stands for an aryl radical, C_6H_5.

i.e., the intensities are additive in this case. New interesting features are observed in the case of conjugated C=C bonds, i.e., when the molecule contains a characteristic structural element of the form C=C—C=C. The bonds are strongly coupled, and the properties of the entire molecule change. In Raman spectra, this conjugation effect somewhat lowers the line frequency corresponding to the C=C bond and markedly increases its intensity [171, 172, 80, Vol. II]. A significant increase in intensity is observed not only for conjugation of C=C bonds between themselves, but also in case of conjugation with multiple bonds of other types (C=O, C=N, C≡C, etc.); conjugation of multiple bonds with aromatic rings and of rings with rings produces a similar effect. This topic has been studied by various authors [171–176]. Conjugation of double bonds also affects the depolarization of the Raman lines: the depolarization of lines corresponding to the vibration of multiple bonds increases in the presence of conjugation [177, 178].

The simplest case of conjugation of C=C bonds is observed in unsaturated hydrocarbons. Experimental data for some compounds of this form from the measurements of [178] are listed in Table 24; in some cases, the intensities and the depolarizations are given for several exciting lines. We see from the table that conjugation of double bonds greatly increases the intensity of the lines around $1600 \, cm^{-1}$ (for the same exciting line). The dependence of the line intensities on the exciting frequency does not follow the relation $I = cv'^4$. To eliminate the effect of the trivial factor v'^4, we also list the values of I'_∞/v'^4 in the table. Note that in branched molecules, the conjugation effect is largely suppressed: the line enhancement is less pronounced, and the intensity vs. exciting frequency curve is not so steep.

Table 24 also lists depolarization data, which show that as the conjugated chain

Table 21

CHARACTERISTIC LINES OF ISOLATED MULTIPLE BONDS

Bond	Frequency range, cm^{-1}	Remarks	References
—C≡C—	2100–2300		[159, 165–167]
—C≡C—	2220–2300; 365	Dialkylacetylenes	[159, 165–167]
—C≡C—	2118; 630; 340	Monoalkylacetylenes	[159, 165–167]
—C≡N	2250; 2330	Nitriles	[159]
—C≡N	2150	RSC≡N, RN≡C	[44, 159]
—C=C—	1640–1680	Unsaturated hydrocarbons (see text)	[100, 144, 145]
C=O	1650–1800	Carbonyl compounds	[159, 164]
C=O	1690	$NH_2 \cdot CO \cdot OR$	[164]
C=O	1705–1725	$R \cdot CO \cdot R'$	[159, 164]
C=O	1720–1740	$R \cdot CO \cdot H$	[159]
C=O	1776	$Cl \cdot CO \cdot OR$	[159]
C=O	1792	$R \cdot CO \cdot Cl$	[159]
C=O	1745; 1804	$R \cdot CO \cdot O \cdot COR$	[159]
C=N	1630–1670		[159]
N=O	1610	$R \cdot NO$	[159]
N=O	1640	$R \cdot O \cdot NO$	[159]
R\ SO$_2$ /R	1270; 1130		[125]
R\ SO /R	1030–1050		[125]
P=O	1200–1320		[163]
P=S	550–750		[163]

Table 22

CHARACTERISTIC LINES OF SOME ATOMIC AND BOND GROUPINGS

Atomic (bond) grouping	Frequency range, cm^{-1}	Remarks	References
$RC \equiv C - C \equiv CR'$	2250		[44, 159]
$-N = N \equiv N$	2104; 1276		[44, 159]
$-C = C = C-$	1980	Allene and its derivatives	[125]
$RN = C = S$	2105; 2180		[159]
$C = C = O$	2049	Ketene	[125]
$-NO_2$	1623	Nitric acid esters	[159]
$-NO_2$	1550; 1380	$R \cdot NO_2$	[159]
$-NO_2$	1520; 1340	$Ar \cdot NO_2$	[159]
$-NO_2$	1620; 1270	$RO \cdot NO_2$	[164]
$-N = C = O$	1409–1434	Alkylisocyanates	[125]
$C = N - N = C$	1627		[159]
$C = C - C \equiv N$	2228		[164]
$-C \equiv N$	2224		[159]
$C = C - C = C$	1620–1670		[100, 121]
$C - I$	480–500	Alkyl derivatives	[159]
$C - Br$	510–560	Alkyl derivatives	[159]
$C - Cl$	570–650	Alkyl derivatives	[159]
$O - Si - O$	610–660		[168]

becomes longer, the depolarization increases. This result is consistent with Vol'-kenshtein's theoretical findings [80, Vol. II].

In Raman spectroscopy of conjugated compounds, an important factor to remember is that conjugation introduces radical changes in the electron envelope of the molecule. In the electronic spectra, this effect is reflected in a certain decrease in the frequency of electronic transitions and an increase in the frequency of the absorption bands. The changes in Raman spectra of conjugated molecules are thus associated with two different factors: 1) the changes in the polarizability derivative tensor α' associated with structural changes in the molecular skeleton; 2) deformation of the molecular electron cloud. We will mainly concern ourselves with the changes in the tensor α', and the deformation of the electron cloud will be treated as a secondary factor.

In principle, the contributions from these two factors cannot be considered separately. However, the electron cloud deformation in conjugated molecules mainly alters the electronic absorption band, and the effect of this factor on Raman

Table 23

CHARACTERISTIC LINES OF CYCLIC COMPOUNDS

Ring	Frequency range, cm^{-1}	Remarks	References
	890	Monosubstituted, 1,1- and 1,2-disubstituted, and 1,1,2-trisubstituted five-membered naphthenes	[100]
	1030–1050; 1160–1190; 1260; 1350	Six-membered naphthenes	[100]
	842	Monosubstituted six-membered naphthenes	[100, 169]
	621; 1002; 1031; 1156; 1182; 1205	Monosubstituted benzene	[169]
	586; 714; 1039; 1220	1,2-Disubstituted benzene	[169]
	525; 716; 1002; 1247	1,3-Disubstituted benzene	[169]
	642; 780–810; 1204	1,4-Disubstituted benzene	[169]
	482; 532; 652; 994; 1097	1,2,3-Trisubstituted benzene	[169]
	458–485; 548; 738; 1245	1,2,4-Trisubstituted benzene	[169]
	513; 574; 990; 1297	1,3,5-Trisubstituted benzene	[169]

Table 23 (continued)

Ring	Frequency range, cm^{-1}	Remarks	References
	1500	Cyclopentadiene, furan, pyrrol, and their derivatives	[159]
	1380	Naphthalene derivatives	[159]
	1270–1285	Diphenyl derivatives	[165, 169]

spectra is confined to a change in the absorption coefficient. Thus, using the results of §5, we can eliminate the contribution from this factor and isolate those changes of α' in Raman spectra which are directly traceable to changes of skeletal structure. This reasoning is borne out by the fact that the depolarization changes only insignificantly as the exciting frequency is changed (Table 24). Indeed, the constancy of ρ, despite extreme changes in I'_∞, probably indicates that all the scattering tensor components have the same dependence on the exciting frequency, i.e., the different components all contain the same frequency factor. Eliminating these frequency factors, we can find the trace and the anisotropy of the tensor α', which do not depend explicitly on the frequency of the exciting light.

Having eliminated the frequency dependence (which is different for different compounds), we obtained comparable reduced intensities I_r for the lines of compounds with isolated or conjugated C=C bonds (see [100]). The reduced intensities I_r and the averaged values of ρ for some unsaturated hydrocarbons are listed in Table 25. Using the data for I_r and ρ, we can calculate the trace b and the anisotropy g^2:

$$b^2 = \frac{I_r(6 - 7\rho)}{6C \cdot 5(1 + \rho)}, \quad g^2 = \frac{I_r\rho}{6C \cdot (1 + \rho)} \tag{13.1}$$

(C is a constant which depends on the measurement conditions). These parameters are also listed in Table 25. We see that conjugation leads to a steep increase in the

Table 24

THE PARAMETERS OF RAMAN SCATTERING LINES AS A FUNCTION
OF THE EXCITING FREQUENCY

Compound	Formula	$\Delta\nu$, cm^{-1}	λ_{ex}, Å	I'_∞	I'_∞/ν'^4	ρ
Pentene-1	C=C—C—C—C	1642	4358	370	—	0.12
2-Methylpentene-2	C—C=C—C—C (C)	1677	5461	110	1	—
			4358	500	1.70	0.12
			3663	2700	4.46	—
Diallyl	C=C—C—C—C=C	1642	5461	160	1	—
			4358	950	2.22	0.14
			3663	2600	3.58	—
Hexadiene-2,4 (dipropenyl)	C—C=C—C=C—C		5461	1150	1	—
		1657	4358	10,000	3.40	0.34
		1668	3663	88,700	13.6	0.33
2-Methylpentadiene-2,4	C—C=C—C=C (C)	1623 } 1654	4358	4700	—	— 0.33
Heptadiene-2,4	C—C=C—C=C—C—C	1654 } 1663	4358	7600	—	0.34
Alloocimene	C—C=C—C=C—C—C=C—C (C) (C)		5461	15,800	1	0.41
		1628 } 1649	4358	183,000	4.45	0.38
				—	—	0.43
			4047	—	—	0.40
			3663	1,490,000	16.7	0.40

Table 25

INVARIANTS OF THE POLARIZABILITY DERIVATIVE TENSOR FOR UN-
SATURATED HYDROCARBONS WITH ISOLATED AND CONJUGATED
DOUBLE BONDS

Compound	Characteristic structural element	I_r	ρ	b	g
2-Methylpentene-2	C=C	390	0.12	1	1
Diallyl	C=C	325*	0.14		
Dipropenyl	C=C—C=C	1440	0.34	1.6	3.5
Alloocimene	C=C—C=C—C=C	6700	0.40	3.1	7.9

* Per one C=C bond.

anisotropy g^2. This is apparently so because in conjugated molecules, the characteristic structural element is the C=C—C=C group, which is greatly stretched
compared to the isolated double bond C=C. In alloocimene which has three conjugated bonds, a further increase of the anisotropy is observed.

The trace b also increases in conjugated molecules. To first approximation, according to Table 25, conjugation leads to "addition" of the traces of the individual double bonds, whereas without conjugation the squares of the traces b^2 are added (the latter corresponds to additive intensity).

Assuming that the tensors α' are axially symmetric for the structural elements C=C and C=C—C=C, we can find the stretching coefficients of the tensor axes for the two structural elements. The relevant expressions are given in [177]. The following ratios of the ellipsoid axes were obtained in [177] for the transition from alkenes to alkadienes with conjugated bonds:

$$\frac{(a_1)_2}{(a_1)_1} = 3.5, \qquad \frac{(a_2)_2}{(a_2)_1} = 0.9. \qquad (13.2)$$

Here $(a_1)_2$ and $(a_1)_1$ are the longitudinal axes, $(a_2)_1 = (a_3)_1$ and $(a_2)_2 = (a_3)_2$ are the transversal axes of the ellipsoids for the structural elements C=C—C=C and C=C, respectively. The ellipsoid of the polarizability derivative for the former element is thus markedly stretched compared to the ellipsoid of the C=C bond. Similar conclusions were reached in [176, 179], where more complex compounds were studied.

2. Conjugation in complex systems

Conjugation in complex molecules containing a benzene ring, a nitro group, etc., has been studied by numerous authors [171–184]. We will consider some recent data obtained by Bobovich and co-workers using rigorous quantitative methods [180–184].

A comparison of the data listed in Table 26 reveals the effect of molecular structure and conjugation on the intensity of the Raman lines. For the simplest nitro compound, nitromethane (I), the intensity of the symmetrical stretching vibration of the nitro group is 0.02.* For compound II, where the NO_2 group is conjugated with the C=C bond, the intensity of this vibration increases to 0.33. In compound III, where conjugation with a benzene ring is added, the intensity jumps to 5.5. Finally, in compound V the intensity is as high as 45. In compound IX, where a five-membered furan ring takes part in conjugation together with the two C=C bonds, the intensity reaches 255.

Conjugation has an even more pronounced effect on the antisymmetrical vibration of the benzene ring. Comparing the data for compounds III, V, VIII, and X, we see that the intensity of the 1340 cm^{-1} line changes by a factor of 8 in this series, and the intensity of the 1600 cm^{-1} line changes by a factor of 20. The intensity of

* Bobovich used a system of units assigning the value of 0.01 to the intensity of the 1710 cm^{-1} acetone line.

Table 26

INTENSITIES IN SPECTRA OF CONJUGATED SYSTEMS* [180–184]

	Compound	Vibration of nitro group		Vibration of benzene ring	Vibration of C=C bond
		totally symmetric	antisym- metric		
I	CH_3NO_2	1380–1400 (0.02)	1500 (0.003)	—	—
II	$CH_3CH_2CH_2CH=CH—NO_2$	1340 (0.33)	—	—	1650 (0.125)
III	⟨benzene⟩CH=CH—NO₂	1320 (5.5)	—	1580 (2.4)	1630 (4.3)
IV	⟨benzene⟩CH=C—NO₂ | CH₃	1325 (4.2)	—	1600 (1.3)	1660 (2.3)
V	CH₃O⟨benzene⟩CH=CH—NO₂	1325 (45)	1500 (3.7)	1600 (19)	1625 (10)
VI	(NO₂)⟨benzene⟩CH=CH—NO₂	1335 (3.5)	—	1590 (3.5)	1630 (3.5)
VII	(NO₂)⟨benzene⟩CH=C—NO₂ | CH₃	1345 (2.8)	—	1600 (3)	1655 (3)
VIII	(NO₂)⟨benzene⟩CH=CH—CH=CH NO₂	1340 (25)	—	1590 (30)	1630 (20)
IX	⟨furan-O⟩CH=CH—CH=CH—NO₂	1335 (255)	—	—	1620 (95)
X	HC=CH⟨benzene⟩CH=CH NO₂ NO₂	1335 (16.8)	1510 (2.5)	1600 (50)	1625 (18)
XI	HC=CH⟨benzene⟩CH=CH | NO₂ NO₂	1340 (8)	1510 (1)	1595 (3.5)	1630 (5.4)

* The numbers in parentheses are the intensities per one C=C bond and one NO_2 group.

the 1340 cm^{-1} line is maximum for compound V, and the intensity of the 1600 cm^{-1} is maximum for compound X. For the C=C bond vibrations, the intensity is maximum in compound VIII. Thus the conjugation effect is a fairly complex function of molecular structure, and this function has its own characteristic features for each type of bonding.

Let us now trace the effect of symmetrical groups and bonds in the molecule on the intensity of Raman lines. Comparison of the spectra of compounds III and X reveals an increase in intensity. For nonsymmetrical dinitro derivatives, the intensity of the benzene ring and the C=C bond increases, whereas the intensity of the nitro group decreases. This is evident from a comparison of the spectra of compounds VI and VII with those of compounds III and IV. On passing from para derivatives to meta derivatives (compounds X and XI), the intensity decreases, which is particularly obvious for the ring vibrations. A similar effect is observed for the aromatic compounds [171].

A remarkable feature is the exceptionally high intensity of the lines in the spectrum of compound IX, where the benzene ring has been replaced with a furan ring. This suggests that the furan ring is substantially less "aromatic", i.e., it can be treated as a system of two double bonds. (Extensive data on the spectrum of furan derivatives are contained in the work of Eidus [183]).

3. Relation between spectral characteristics and reactivity of some aromatic compounds

According to Hammett [185], reactions with the participation of aromatic derivatives are governed by a universal relation linking the properties of the substituent X in the para or the meta position of the benzene ring with the reactivity of the side chain Y. This relation has the form

$$\log K - \log K_0 = \rho\sigma, \qquad (13.3)$$

where K and K_0 are the reaction rate constants for the substituted and the unsubstituted (standard) compound, ρ is a constant characterizing the type of the reaction, the physical conditions, and the properties of the side chain Y, σ is Hammett's factor, which generally depends only on the nature and the position of the substituent X. Hammett's factor can be regarded as a measure of the substituent effect on the activation energy of the reaction for the standard compound [185, 186].

Any possible correlation between molecular spectra and the reactivity of compounds is of obvious interest. This topic has been treated by a number of authors [187–192]. In the infrared spectra, a relation has been established between the frequency and the log intensity, on the one hand, and Hammett's factor, on the other [193, 194]. Similar relations obtain in Raman spectra [184, 195].

Figure 41a plots the log intensity of a Raman line corresponding to a symmetrical

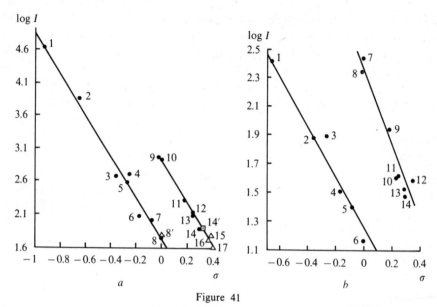

Figure 41

Raman line intensities vs. Hammett factors:

a for the symmetrical vibration of the nitro group; *b* for the antisymmetrical vibration of the benzene ring. Substituents X: 1) N (CH₃); 2) NH₂; 3) OH; 4) OC₂H₅; 5) OCH₃; 6) CH₃; 7) CH₂COOH; 8) H; 9) NHCCH₃; 10) C₆H₅; 11) I; 12) Br; 13) Cl; 14) COOH; 15) CHO; 16) COCl. Substituents in the meta position are marked with a prime. (After Ya. S. Bobovich).

stretching of the nitro group in aromatic nitro compounds vs. Hammett's factor for substituents in the para and meta positions of the benzene ring. Solutions in acetone were used. The log intensity and Hammett's factor are clearly linked by a linear relation. The bottom line corresponds to compounds with electropositive substituents, and the top line to compounds with electronegative substituents. A similar dependence is observed for the intensity of the antisymmetrical line of the para-substituted benzene ring (Figure 41*b*).

14. ROTATIONAL ISOMERISM AND INTERNAL ROTATION

1. Vibrational spectra and rotational isomerism

As we have noted before, vibrational spectra provide information not only about the chemical structure but also about the geometrical configuration of the molecules. Vibrational spectra are particularly popular for the study of rotational isomerism. The very existence of rotational isomerism was originally established by K. Kohlrausch from measurements of Raman spectra [196].

The rotation of one part of the molecule relative to another about a joining chemical bond involves a change in the potential energy U of the system. If the potential energy U is plotted as a function of the rotation angle ϕ, the resulting curve shows a number of peaks and valleys (Figure 42). The valleys correspond to the most stable configurations of the molecule, schematically shown in Figure 43.

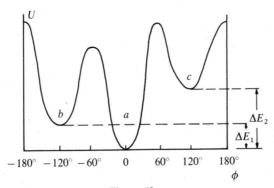

Figure 42

Potential energy U vs. the angle of rotation.

The behavior of the molecule is largely decided by the height of the potential barrier (the difference between the adjoining peak and valley) and by the energy difference ΔE between various peaks. We distinguish between three different cases, depending on the relative values of these energy parameters and the product kT characterizing the thermal energy of the molecule:

1. If all the potential barriers are large compared to kT, the molecule does not change spontaneously from one stable configuration to another. The geometrical isomers therefore can be separated. An example of this isomerism is provided by the *cis*- and *trans*-isomers of naphthenes and unsaturated compounds.

2. If the barrier is comparable with kT, stable configurations may rapidly change

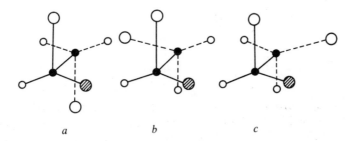

a   b   c

Figure 43

Stable configurations of rotational isomers. Isomers a, b, and c correspond to the valleys of the potential energy curve in Figure 42.

into one another. A dynamic equilibrium is established between the individual rotational isomers, which cannot be separated. Typical examples of this isomerism are provided by ethane derivatives in which some of the hydrogen atoms have been replaced with atoms of another monovalent element (e.g., Cl, F, Br) or radicals (e.g., CH_3). These molecules show hindered rotation about the C—C bond.

3. If the change in U caused by rotation is small compared to kT, almost free rotation is observed.

Raman spectroscopy is particularly useful in the study of rotational isomers which cannot be separated and analyzed by the conventional techniques (case 2). The study of rotational isomerism is highly significant for the determination of the thermo-dynamic properties of molecules, the theory of structure of macromolecules [197, 198], and various questions related to reaction rates and mechanisms. Moreover, insofar as the rotations are hindered mainly by forces between atoms or groups of atoms which are not bonded chemically, rotational isomerism provides a new means for the study of these intramolecular forces.

The existence of rotational isomers of any given compound can be established by comparing the observed Raman spectrum of the compound with the theoretically expected spectrum. Each isomer has its own range of Raman lines. Although the frequencies of numerous lines coincide and these lines overlap in the spectrum, there are always a few lines with markedly different frequencies. Therefore, the total number of lines in a given spectral region will exceed the theoretically expected number, and this provides a sure indication of two or several rotational isomers. A classical example of rotational isomerism is the case of 1,2-dichloroethane, whose Raman spectra are given in Table 27. Figure 44 schematically shows the rotational isomers of this compound.

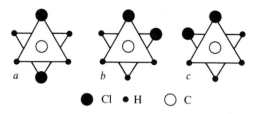

Figure 44

Rotational isomers of 1,2-dichloroethane:

a trans form,   *b* and *c* skew forms.

A more complex problem is the identification of the rotational isomers which are actually present in the mixture and the assignment of the various lines to the corresponding isomers. Measurements of Raman spectra at various temperatures constitute an indispensible step on the way toward the solution of this problem. A change in temperature alters the equilibrium conditions and modifies the relative

Table 27

VIBRATION FREQUENCIES OF THE ROTATIONAL ISOMERS OF THE
1,2-DICHLOROETHANE MOLECULE

sym-metry	v_{calc}	v_{exp}		sym-metry	v_{calc}	v_{exp}	
		RS	IR			RS	IR
A_g	330	302 (1 pol)	—	A	230	263 (2 pol)	—
	775	754 (15 pol)	—		675	654 (10 pol)	656 (s)
	1055	1052 (1 pol)	—		970	940 (2 pol)	940 (m)
	1300	1302 (3 pol)	—		1055	1031 (1)	1015 (w)
	1430	1429 (3 dep)	—		1275	1302 (3 pol)	—
					1440	1440 (0.5 dep)	1400
B_g	985	989 (1)	—				
	1270	1262 (1 dep)	—	B	460	411 (3 dep)	—
					705	675 (3 dep)	676 (s)
B_u	320	—	—		800	880 (1 dep)	878 (m)
	765	—	707 (s)		1175	1144 (0.5 dep)	—
	1260	—	1243 (w)		1235	1206 (2 dep)	—
	1450	—	1400		1375	1393 (0.5)	—
					1450	1440 (0.5 dep)	1400
A_u	730	—	759 (w)				
	1150	—	1092 (w)				

Note: v_{calc} from [80], v_{exp} from [199, 200]. The numbers in parentheses are line intensities obtained from visual estimates; pol—polarized, dep—depolarized, s—strong, m—medium, w—weak.

concentrations of the rotational isomers. To first approximation, the intensities I_i of Raman lines can be assumed proportional to the concentrations N_i of the corresponding rotational isomers (possible departures from this rule are discussed in §18). Thus,

$$\frac{I_1}{I_2} = K \frac{N_1}{N_2} = K \frac{g_1 \, \Pi f_1}{g_2 \, \Pi f_2} e^{-\Delta E/RT}, \tag{14.1}$$

independent of temperature. A comparison of the intensity ratios at two different where Πf_1 and Πf_2 are the products of the sums over states for the 1st and the 2nd isomer; g_1 and g_2 are the respective statistical weights, ΔE is the difference of the internal energy of the isomers, K is a constant which depends on the properties of the spectral lines under discussion. The pre-exponential factor in (14.1) is generally temperatures T_1 and T_2 thus gives the following equation, which can be solved for the energy difference of the isomers:

$$\frac{(I_1/I_2)_{T_2}}{(I_1/I_2)_{T_1}} = \exp \left[\frac{\Delta E}{R} \left(\frac{1}{T_1} - \frac{1}{T_2} \right) \right]. \tag{14.2}$$

This method has been used to determine the energy differences of the rotational isomers of numerous molecules. Appropriate summaries of results were published in [201, 202]. Sosinskii [203] applied this method to solutions of 1,2-dichloroethane in various solvents, and was thus able to study the molecular interactions.

Crystallization conducted from a liquid phase often preserves only one isomer, which happens to be the most stable under the particular conditions. The Raman spectrum is thus greatly simplified (only the lines of that one isomer are retained).* As an example, Figure 45 shows the spectra of n-butane at various temperatures (from [204]). The actual geometrical configuration of the isomer which remains stable in the solid phase can be determined by X-ray diffraction or other methods. If the isomer possesses a certain symmetry, its geometrical configuration can be derived without difficulty from the vibrational spectra (see §9). For normal paraffins, the most stable isomer in the solid phase is the one in the form of a planar stretched zigzag chain (*trans*-configuration). Figure 46 shows various possible isomers of the simplest paraffin with rotational isomerism—n-butane. A confirma-

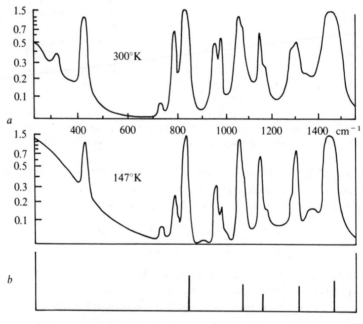

Figure 45

The spectra of n-butane at different temperatures:

a liquid,   *b* solid state (schematic).

---

* In some cases, the spectrum of the crystal is actually more involved because of the special conditions governing the vibration of molecules in the crystal unit cell (see Chapter III).

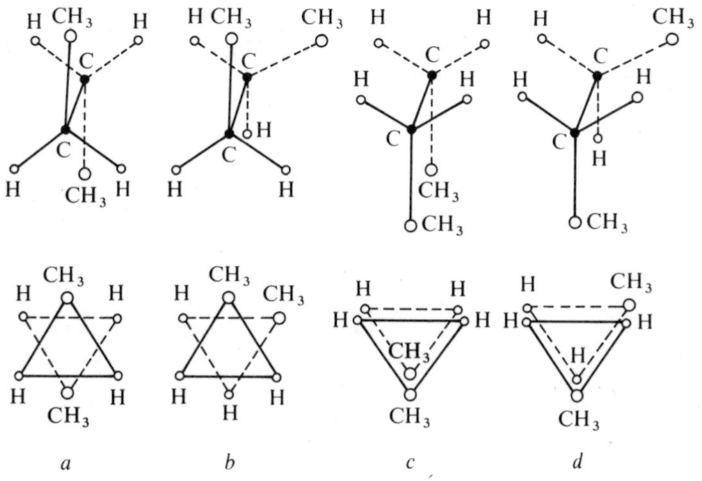

Figure 46

Various rotational isomers of n-butane:

a the "basic" staggered *trans*-isomer ($\phi = 0$); b the skew form ($\phi = 120°$); c the fully eclipsed *cis*-isomer ($\phi = 180°$); d the eclipsed form ($\phi = 60°$). Top, general view, bottom, projection onto a plane perpendicular to the C—C axis.

tion of the *trans*-configuration in the solid state can be obtained by calculating the characteristic frequencies of the various isomers [80, 100].

The calculation of the frequencies of the various models of rotational isomers also provides a solution to a more complex problem, namely the determination of the real geometrical configuration of the rotational isomers which are present simultaneously in a liquid or a solid phase. Systematic calculations of this kind were carried out by the author for the molecules of n-butane and 2,3-dimethylbutane [205, 206]; the frequencies were calculated for the inherently unstable *cis*-configuration, as well as for the staggered and the skew *trans*-configurations. The calculations established the dependence of the most characteristic frequencies on the rotation angle ϕ. As an example, Table 28 lists the results for some frequencies of 2,3-dimethylbutane. Comparison with experimental data definitely shows that one of the isomers has a staggered *trans*-configuration ($\phi = 0$). The second isomer present in the liquid phase apparently has an intermediate configuration between a skew isomer and a fully eclipsed *cis*-isomer. The rotation angle of this configuration is $120° < \phi < 180°$. As the accuracy of the calculations is improved, this method will give the position of the valleys on the $U(\phi)$ curve (see Figure 42), an obviously valuable contribution.

Table 28

FREQUENCY SHIFT IN THE ROTATIONAL ISOMERS OF 2,3-DIMETHYLBUTANE

Frequency (trans-isomer)	Δ_{calc}, cm^{-1}				Δ_{exp}, cm^{-1}
	$\phi = 0$	$\phi = 60°$	$\phi = 120°$	$\phi = 180°$	
432	0	−136	−109	0	−53
505	0	3	−8	−106	−26
756	0	2	−10	−22	−28
1151	0	−69	−110	−118	−117

Note: $\phi = 0$, trans-isomer; $\phi = 60°$, eclipsed isomer; $\phi = 120°$, skew isomer; $\phi = 180°$, fully eclipsed cis-isomer (see Figure 46).

2. Internal rotation in Raman spectra

The origin of the potential barrier hindering the rotation of the atomic groups in molecules is not completely clear. The barriers for the internal rotation are small compared to the other forms of molecular energy, and it is therefore exceedingly difficult to calculate them theoretically with sufficient accuracy. Rigorous quantum-mechanical calculations of the barriers were only carried out for ethane, the simplest molecule showing internal rotation. The results of these calculations are far from successful [207–209]. Repeated attempts were made to apply the simpler theory of the electrostatic bond interaction to account for the existence of the potential barrier [210–212]. The theory of Lassetre and Dean [210], which analyzes this intermolecular interaction in terms of dipole and quadrupole moments of the molecular bonds, appeared quite promising for a time. It was later established, however, that the numerical values of the quadrupole moments of the molecular bonds derived from the Lassetre and Dean theory are much too high compared to experimental data obtained from microwave spectroscopy.

In a number of studies, the interaction of atoms or atomic groups without chemical bonds between them is replaced with the interaction of isoelectronic or free atoms and molecules estimated from experimental data [213–215]. This approach, however, again fails as far as the main purpose is concerned. Thus, Mason and Kreevoy [213] have shown that the van der Waals interaction of chemically unbonded atoms can account only for approximately half the potential barrier to internal rotation.

As the calculations based on general physical arguments proved inadequate, a number of authors tried to determine the rotation-hindering potential barriers by simple semiempirical methods. These methods are based on the assumption that the potential barrier is equal to the difference of the repulsion energies between the two rotating parts of the molecule in positions with minimum and maximum repulsion. For the case of n-butane, this is the difference of the repulsion energies of the *trans*- and the *cis*-isomers (see Figure 46). Using the experimental values of the potential barriers of some simple molecules, the potential barriers of more complex molecules can be calculated with fair accuracy [216–221].

The determination of the potential barriers from the internal rotation frequencies in Raman spectra thus acquires particular significance. The general procedure is described below (see [80, Ch. 28], [220–223]).

Consider a bond which serves as an axis for internal rotation. Because of the interaction of atoms which do not lie on the bond axis, there are certain rotation angles ϕ which correspond to the most stable positions. This effect breaks the cylindrical symmetry of the rotation axis (as originally assumed by van't Hoff) and a lower symmetry results, i.e., the rotation axis is an axis of finite order C_n. The potential energy of the molecule may thus be considered as a periodic function of period $2\pi/n$, and to first approximation we write

$$U(\phi) = \tfrac{1}{2} U_0 (1 - \cos n\phi), \tag{14.3}$$

where U_0 is the potential barrier. The most important case is that of a rotation axis of symmetry C_{3v}. Then

$$U(\phi) = \tfrac{1}{2} U_0 (1 - \cos 3\phi). \tag{14.4}$$

The measurements of Fateley and Miller in the far infrared [224] have shown that the deviations of the potential function from (14.4) in the case of internal rotation of methyl groups are insignificant even when the molecular skeleton is non-symmetrical. For example, if the potential function of the chloroethane molecule CH_2Cl—CH_3 is written in the form

$$U(\phi) = \tfrac{1}{2} U_0 (1 - \cos 3\phi) + \tfrac{1}{2} U' (1 - \cos 6\phi), \tag{14.5}$$

the term with U' amounts to no more than 3% of the first term. Note that the second term does not affect the height of the potential barrier: it only changes its shape. In what follows, we will therefore use the simple expression (14.4) (a more detailed discussion of the theory will be found in [80, Ch. 28]).

If the geometrical parameters of the rotating group and the molecular skeleton, as well as the potential function $U(\phi)$ are known, we can solve the quantum-mechanical problem of internal rotation. Inserting the potential function (14.4) in the Schroedinger equation for a one-dimensional rotator, we reduce the problem to a solution of the Mathieu equation

$$\frac{d^2\psi}{dx^2} + (\lambda + q \cos 2x)\psi = 0, \tag{14.6}$$

where λ and q depend on the molecular parameters and the height of the potential barrier. The corresponding solutions of the Mathieu equation are tabulated in [225], and the tables include the parameter

$$\Delta b = \frac{v}{2.25F}, \quad F = \frac{\hbar^2}{2\mathscr{I}_r},$$ (14.7)

where v is the internal rotation frequency, $\mathscr{I}_r$ is the reduced moment of inertia of the rotating groups. Given Δb, we can find from the tables the parameter S, which is directly related to the potential barrier U_0:

$$U_0 = 2.25F \cdot S.$$ (14.8)

For a high barrier U_0, the rotation angle ϕ is small, and $\cos 3\phi$ can be expanded in a series, retaining the quadratic terms only. In this limiting case, the potential function (14.4) reduces to a parabola, i.e., internal rotation is described by the equation of harmonic oscillations. The relation of the potential barrier U_0 to the internal rotation frequency in this case takes the simple form

$$v \, (\text{cm}^{-1}) = \frac{3}{2\pi c} \sqrt{\frac{U_0}{2\mathscr{I}_r}}.$$ (14.9)

We see from the above expressions, that the calculations require knowledge of the reduced moment of inertia $\mathscr{I}_r$ of the molecule. If the molecule is made up of a skeleton and a rotating group of the symmetrical top type, the reduced moment of inertia can be determined from Crawford's formula [226]

$$\mathscr{I}_r = \mathscr{I}_\phi \left[1 - \mathscr{I}_\phi \sum_j \frac{\lambda_j^2}{\mathscr{I}_j} \right],$$ (14.10)

where $j = 1, 2, 3$, $\mathscr{I}_j$ are the principal moments of inertia of the entire molecule, λ_j are the direction cosines of the top axis relative to the principal axes of inertia, $\mathscr{I}_\phi$ is the moment of inertia of the top relative to the axis of rotation.

In the case of two asymmetrical rotating groups, the reduced moment of inertia can be found with fair accuracy from Zirnit's formula [220, 227]

$$\mathscr{I}_r = \frac{\mathscr{I}_1 \mathscr{I}_2}{\mathscr{I}_1 + \mathscr{I}_2},$$ (14.11)

where $\mathscr{I}_1$ and $\mathscr{I}_2$ are the moments of inertia of each group about an axis parallel to the rotation axis and passing through the center of mass of the corresponding group. If the molecule contains several symmetrical rotating groups, the internal rotation modes in general fall into distinct symmetry classes in accordance with molecular symmetry. Internal rotations of various symmetry classes correspond to lines of slightly different frequencies [228]. Every symmetry class has its own reduced moment of inertia.

The determination of the potential barriers from the internal rotation frequencies clearly constitutes a significant addition to, and improvement of, the data obtained by other methods. The internal rotation frequencies are generally low, and the corresponding Raman lines lie close to the exciting lines. This greatly facilitates the identification of the observed lines with internal rotations, but seriously interferes with spectroscopic measurements, since the internal rotation lines (in liquids) lie in the wing of the Rayleigh line. Moreover, the aureole of the exciting line introduces additional errors, etc. In practice, lines with frequencies of about $70-80$ cm^{-1} can be detected in liquids under favorable conditions [220]. As an example, Figure 47 shows schematic spectra of four methyl-substituted butanes, which are analogous to the halogen derivatives of ethane with regard to internal rotation (the halogen atom is replaced in methyl-substituted butanes by the CH_3 group). We see from Figure 47 that the lines of the lowest frequency are removed far from other lines which can be associated with ordinary deformation vibrations. Therefore, the identification of the lines between 80 and 120 cm^{-1} with internal rotations is quite reliable. Table 29 lists the measured internal rotation frequencies and the potential barriers calculated from these frequency data. These barriers are consistent with the available thermodynamic results [230, 231]. For the more complex case of methyl-substituted pentanes, the data will be found in [220].

This direct method for the determination of the potential barriers from the experimental internal rotation frequencies meets with a fundamental difficulty: it is not always that the observed lines can be assigned unambiguously to this mode of intramolecular motion. The low-frequency spectral region, where the internal rotation frequencies lie, also contains some molecular deformation frequencies. The currently attainable accuracy of frequency calculations is still insufficient to ensure a reliable distinction between bending and internal rotation (in the existing com-

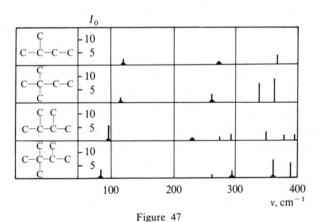

Figure 47

A schematic diagram of the low-frequency Raman spectrum of methyl-substituted butanes [220, 229].

Table 29

INTERNAL ROTATION FREQUENCIES AND POTENTIAL BARRIERS OF
METHYL-SUBSTITUTED BUTANES

Compound	ν, cm^{-1}	$\mathscr{I}_r$, amu · Å^2	U, cal/mole
Isopentane	120	16.5	4500
2,2-Dimethylbutane	116	18.6	4700
2,3-Dimethylbutane	98	31.8	5800
2,2,3-Trimethylbutane	86	40.4	5600

putational techniques, internal rotation is generally ignored). The low-frequency region also contains the frequencies of some complexes, primarily those attributable to the hydrogen bond (see § 17). We thus require some minimum preliminary information about the internal rotation frequencies to facilitate the tentative interpretation of the observed spectrum.

This difficulty can be unraveled if we first calculate the potential barrier using the previously mentioned semiempirical methods. As an example, let us apply this procedure to methyl-substituted cyclohexanes [220, 221].

In hydrocarbons, there are two different types of interaction between chemically unbonded atoms that have a bearing on the calculation of potential barriers: these are the H...H coupling and the H...C coupling. Magnasco [232] proposed a Morse repulsion potential to describe these interactions. For the repulsion of hydrogen atoms, he took (r is the interatomic distance)

$$U_0 = 923.2 \exp(-1.944r) - 1951 \exp(-2 \cdot 1.944r). \tag{14.12}$$

The author assumed a repulsion potential between C and H, too. However, a separate check for a number of compounds whose geometrical parameters were known with sufficient accuracy and whose potential barrier was available from microwave (and other) measurements established that the assumed interaction between C and H atoms produced an exaggerated result for the potential barriers. If, however, we consider the H...H coupling only, extending it for distant atoms also,* the calculated potential barriers fit the experimental results to within ±15%. It should be emphasized that Eq. (14.12) is applicable only to a limited range of r values. For small r, the function $U_0(r)$ is not available.

As we have observed in § 10, the cyclohexane molecule may have C—H bonds of two kinds: some parallel to the symmetry axis of the ring (polar, or p-bonds), and some aligned approximately in the ring "plane" (equatorial, or e-bonds). Methyl groups substituting the hydrogen atoms may also occupy p- and e-positions, de-

---

* In [232], even the interaction of moderately distant hydrogen atoms is ignored.

pending on the original position of the H atoms. In methylcyclohexane, the only methyl group is preferably located in the e-position, which is energetically more favorable: in the p-position, the nearby hydrogen atoms experience strong repulsion. In dimethylcyclohexanes, the methyl groups may occupy both e- and p-positions.

Because of the great proximity of the hydrogen atoms in the methyl groups in p-position, the potential function (14.12) proved to be inapplicable to these groups. The potential barriers were thus calculated only for the equatorial groups. The results for the potential barriers U_0 and the calculated internal rotation frequencies are listed in Table 30. The table also lists the experimentally observed frequencies which are closest to the calculated figures. The fit is quite satisfactory. For cis-1,2-dimethylcyclohexane, however, the theoretical frequency range includes two experimental frequencies, and the identification of the internal rotation frequency is impossible. For other compounds, the experimental data make it possible to improve the numerical value of U_0.

Table 30

POTENTIAL BARRIERS AND INTERNAL ROTATION FREQUENCIES OF CYCLOHEXANE DERIVATIVES

Compound	Possible position of CH_3 groups	U_0, cal/mole	ν_{calc}, cm^{-1}	ν_{exp}, cm^{-1}
Methylcyclohexane	e	4000	240	237
1,1-Dimethylcyclohexane	e, p	4800	265	247
Cis-1,2-dimethylcyclohexane	e, p	2400	190	{181 / 236}
Cis-1,3-dimethylcyclohexane	e, e	4000	240	278
Trans-1,3-dimethylcyclohexane	e, p	4000	240	257
Cis-1,4-dimethylcyclohexane	e, p	3700	230	256
Trans-1,4-dimethylcyclohexane	e, e	4000	240	258
Cis-1,3,5-trimethylcyclohexane	e, e, e	4000	240	253

Note that cis-1,3-dimethylcyclohexane, trans-1,4-dimethylcyclohexane, and cis-1,3,5-trimethylcyclohexane have several methyl groups in the e-position, and in principle several internal rotation frequencies are possible. For the last two compounds, however, the selection rules of Raman scattering allow only one line for each. In cis-1,3-dimethylcyclohexane, the two allowed lines should have very close frequencies because of the insignificant coupling between internal rotation and other vibration modes; they both apparently coincide with the observed line at 278 cm^{-1}.

Note that for some of the compounds, equal values of U_0 were obtained (see Table 30). Therefore, the internal rotation frequencies for these compounds should be close even if the original potential function (14.12) is not quite accurate. We see from the table that this conclusion holds for frequencies around 240 cm^{-1}, which clearly confirms the validity of the general procedure.

15. SECOND-ORDER SPECTRA AND ANHARMONICITY OF MOLECULAR VIBRATIONS

1. Second-order Raman spectra

Second-order Raman lines are generally very weak, and this greatly interferes with their experimental study. As a result, second-order Raman spectra were studied only on very few occasions. After the original work of Landsberg and Malyshev [233] and Ananthakrishnan [234], we can mention only the study of Welsh, Crawford, and Scott [235], who published quantitative data on frequencies, intensities, and depolarizations of the second-order lines for CCl_4, $SnCl_4$, and $SnBr_4$ molecules. Later they published limited results on overtones in $TiCl_4$ [236], $CHCl_3$, $C_2H_2Cl_2$, $C_2H_4Cl_2$, CH_3OH, C_6H_5Cl and CS_2 [237] molecules. A systematic study of second-order Raman spectra was carried out only recently [238–243]. Cyclohexane, benzene, chloroform, their deutero derivatives, and some other molecules were studied. The success of these studies was largely due to the development of a new exciting source in the form of low-pressure lamps with a comparatively low background.

The interpretation of second-order spectra is closely linked with the general problem of anharmonicity of molecular vibrations. We will first consider the question of anharmonicity for the case of a diatomic molecule. Assuming a small anharmonicity,* we may write the potential energy of a diatomic molecule in the form

$$U(x) = \tfrac{1}{2} Kx^2 + \alpha x^3 + \beta x^4 . \tag{15.1}$$

We introduce the reduced molecular mass

$$m = \frac{m_1 m_2}{m_1 + m_2} , \tag{15.2}$$

where m_1 and m_2 are the masses of the constituent atoms. The molecular Hamiltonian is then written in the form

$$\hat{H} = \frac{\hat{p}^2}{2m} + \tfrac{1}{2} Kx^2 + \alpha x^3 + \beta x^4 . \tag{15.3}$$

The wave equation with this Hamiltonian can be solved by the method of the perturbation theory. First we drop the correction terms αx^3 and βx^4. This gives

---

* The current experimental material shows that this assumption is mostly valid for molecular vibrations.

the standard quantum-mechanical equation of a harmonic oscillator

$$\left(\frac{\hat{p}^2}{2m} + \tfrac{1}{2} K x^2 \right) \psi = E \psi . \tag{15.4}$$

The allowed energy values are

$$E_n = \hbar \omega \left(n + \tfrac{1}{2} \right), \tag{15.5}$$

where $\omega = \sqrt{K/m}$ is the frequency of the oscillator vibrations. The normalized eigenfunctions $\psi_n(x)$ of the harmonic oscillator were given in §7 (Eq. (7.3)).

We will now treat the second and the third term in (15.3) as a "perturbation":

$$\hat{V} = \alpha x^3 + \beta x^4 . \tag{15.6}$$

The matrix elements of the perturbation operator are

$$V_{nm} = \int \psi_n(x) \, \hat{V} \psi_m(x) \, dx . \tag{15.7}$$

First- and second-order corrections to the n-th energy eigenvalue, according to the general perturbation theory (see [203]), are

$$\Delta' E_n = V_{nn} = \int \psi_n(x) \, \hat{V} \psi_n(x) \, dx , \tag{15.8}$$

$$\Delta'' E_n = \sum_{m \neq n} \frac{|V_{mn}|^2}{E_n - E_m} . \tag{15.9}$$

The matrix elements with the wave functions of the harmonic oscillator were also considered in §7. From the general form of (15.8) we readily see that the energy correction contributed by the term αx^3 is zero in the first approximation. The first-approximation correction introduced by the term βx^4 is (see [20], [80, Ch. 16])

$$\Delta' E_n = \tfrac{3}{2} \beta \left(\frac{\hbar}{m\omega} \right)^2 (n^2 + n + \tfrac{1}{2}). \tag{15.10}$$

The second-approximation corrections introduced by the term αx^3 are of the same order. Writing, as in (7.4),

$$a = \frac{\hbar}{m\omega} , \tag{15.11}$$

we obtain for the non-zero matrix elements of x^3

$$(x_{n,\,n+1})^2 = \tfrac{9}{8} a^3 (n + 1)^3 , \qquad (x_{n,\,n-1})^2 = \tfrac{9}{8} a^3 n^3 , \tag{15.12}$$

$$(x_{n,\,n+3})^2 = \tfrac{1}{8} a^3 (n + 3)(n + 2)(n + 1) , \qquad (x_{n,\,n-3})^2 = \tfrac{1}{8} a^3 (n - 2)(n - 1) n . \tag{15.13}$$

Inserting these expressions in (15.9), we obtain the second-approximation energy associated with the term αx^3 in the potential energy:

$$\Delta'' E_n = - \frac{15\alpha^2 a^3}{4\hbar\omega} (n^2 + n + \tfrac{11}{30}).$$

(15.14)

The total energy of an anharmonic oscillator can be written by combining (15.5), (15.10), and (15.14) in the form

$$E_n = \hbar\omega (n + \tfrac{1}{2}) + \hbar\kappa(n^2 + n) + C,$$

(15.15)

where

$$\kappa = - \frac{15\alpha^2 a^3}{4\hbar^2\omega} + \frac{3\beta a^3}{2\hbar}, \qquad C = - \frac{11\alpha^2 a^3}{8\hbar^2\omega} + \frac{3\beta a^2}{4\hbar}.$$

(15.16)

Here κ is the anharmonicity coefficient. It can be readily found experimentally, if the fundamental vibration frequency v and the first overtone v_1 are known. Indeed, from (15.15) we have

$$E_2 - 2E_1 = \hbar(v_1 - 2v) = 2\hbar\kappa$$

Hence

$$\kappa = \frac{v_1 - 2v}{2}.$$

(15.17)

Generally $\kappa < 0$, which corresponds to a condensation of the successive energy levels

$$E_{n+1} - E_n = \hbar\omega + 2\hbar\kappa (n + 1)$$

(15.18)

with increasing n.

The problem of anharmonic vibrations for polyatomic molecules is solved along the same lines as for diatomic molecules. Third- and fourth-order terms of the form $\alpha_{ijk} x_i x_j x_k$ and $\beta_{ijkl} x_i x_j x_k x_l$ should be introduced in the expression for the potential energy (10.2). When expressed in the normal coordinates Q_j (see §10), the anharmonic part of the potential energy contains terms of the form $\alpha'_{ijk} Q_i Q_j Q_k$ and $\beta'_{ijkl} Q_i Q_j Q_k Q_l$. These terms determine the dynamic coupling between the various normal coordinates, associated with the anharmonicity of the vibrations. Hence it follows that the very concept of normal coordinates is applicable only in the absence of anharmonicity. When anharmonicity is considered, the normal coordinates are used only as coordinates ensuring an *approximate* separation of the energies of the various modes.

Further solution of the problem requires the application of the perturbation theory, as for the diatomic molecule. Third- and fourth-order terms are considered as a "perturbation". The "unperturbed" solution gives a selection of "harmonic" frequencies ω_i and harmonic oscillator eigenfunctions ψ_i, corresponding to the normal modes $Q_i (i = 1, 2, \ldots, n)$. The corresponding problem has been treated in some detail in §7 and §10. The total wave function of the unperturbed system is represented as a product of the respective eigenfunctions of the individual normal modes (see (7.2)). Using this function, we can find the first- and second-approximation corrections to the unperturbed energy in accordance with Eqs. (15.8) and (15.9). The first-approximation correction due to the cubic terms is zero, since the product of $Q_i Q_j Q_k$ contains at least one normal coordinate in an odd degree. The second-approximation correction due to the cubic terms and the first-approximation correction due to the fourth-order terms are of the same order. Using these corrections, we obtain for the vibrational energy (see [83])

$$E(v_1, v_2, v_3, \ldots) = \sum_i \hbar\omega_i \left(v_1 + \tfrac{1}{2} d_i\right) +$$

$$+ \sum_i \sum_{k \geq i} \hbar\kappa_{ik} \left(v_i + \tfrac{1}{2} d_i\right)\left(v_k + \tfrac{1}{2} d_k\right) + C. \tag{15.19}$$

Here v_i are the vibrational quantum numbers, ω_i is the harmonic frequency, d_i is the degeneracy of the i-th normal mode, κ_{ik} is the anharmonicity coefficient, C is a constant. In general, to allow for degenerate modes, Eq. (15.19) should contain an additional term of the form $\sum_i \sum_{k \geq i} g_{ik} l_i l_k$, where g_{ik} are coefficients characterizing the coupling between vibrations and rotations, l_i are quantum numbers, $l_i = v_i$, $v_i - 2, v_i - 4, \ldots, 1$ (or 0). This term may cause splitting of the degenerate frequencies. This splitting, however, has not been observed experimentally in Raman spectra. This term will be discussed in more detail in §16.

From (15.19) we obtain for the transitions corresponding to the fundamental frequencies, overtones, and combination frequencies:

$$E(1, 0, 0, \ldots) - E(0, 0, 0, \ldots) = E(1, 0, 0, \ldots) - E_0 =$$

$$= \hbar v = \hbar \left(\omega_1 + \kappa_{11} + d_1\kappa_{11} + \tfrac{1}{2}\kappa_{12}d_2 + \tfrac{1}{2}\kappa_{13}d_3 + \ldots\right),$$

$$E(2, 0, 0, \ldots) - E_0 = \hbar v_1 = \hbar\left(2\omega_1 + 4\kappa_{11} + 2\kappa_{11}d_1 + \kappa_{12}d_2 + \ldots\right),$$

$$E(3, 0, 0, \ldots) - E_0 = \hbar v_2 = \hbar\left(3\omega_1 + 9\kappa_{11} + 3\kappa_{11}d_1 + \tfrac{3}{2}\kappa_{12}d_2 + \ldots\right),$$

$$E(0, 1, 0, \ldots) - E_0 = \hbar v' = \hbar\left(\omega_2 + \kappa_{22} + \kappa_{22}d_2 + \tfrac{1}{2}\kappa_{12}d_1 + \tfrac{1}{2}\kappa_{23}d_2 + \ldots\right),$$

$$E(1, 1, 0, \ldots) - E_0 = \hbar v_{12} = \hbar\left(\omega_1 + \omega_2 + \kappa_{11} + \kappa_{22} + \kappa_{11}d_1 + \right.$$

$$\left. + \kappa_{22}d_2 + \kappa_{12} + \tfrac{1}{2}\kappa_{12}(d_1 + d_2) + \tfrac{1}{2}\kappa_{13}d_3 + \tfrac{1}{2}\kappa_{23}d_3 + \ldots\right). \tag{15.20}$$

After simple manipulations we obtain

$$E(2, 0, 0, \ldots) - 2E(1, 0, 0, \ldots) = \hbar(v_1 - 2v) = 2\hbar\kappa_{11},$$

$$\kappa_{11} = \tfrac{1}{2}(v_1 - 2v); \tag{15.21}$$

$$E(3, 0, 0, \ldots) - 3E(1, 0, 0, \ldots) = \hbar(v_2 - 3v) = 6\hbar\kappa_{11},$$

$$\kappa_{11} = \tfrac{1}{6}(v_2 - 3v); \tag{15.22}$$

$$E(1, 1, 0, \ldots) - E(1, 0, 0, \ldots) - E(0, 1, 0, \ldots) = \hbar(v_{12} - v - v') = \hbar\kappa_{12},$$

$$\kappa_{12} = v_{12} - (v + v'). \tag{15.23}$$

Here v, v' are the measured fundamental frequencies, v_1 is the measured frequency of the first overtone, v_2 is the frequency of the second overtone, v_{12} is the measured combination frequency corresponding to the sum $v + v'$. It follows from (15.20)–(15.23) that the observed frequencies v do not coincide with the harmonic frequencies ω, and the overtones and combination frequencies are not whole multiples of the fundamental frequencies and combinations of these frequencies.

Experimental studies of second-order spectra in principle make it possible to determine the anharmonicity coefficients κ_{ik} and the harmonic frequencies ω_i. In practice, however, this problem involves great difficulties. Alongside with experimental difficulties attributable to the weakness of the Raman spectra, we have to face serious difficulties in the interpretation of the spectra. In complex molecules with numerous vibrational degrees of freedom, we can form several combinations of the fundamental frequencies which are consistent with the selection rules and are fairly close to the frequency of the observed line. Therefore, the identification of the observed lines is not unambiguous. Generally, the identification scheme leading to a minimum anharmonicity coefficient is adopted. This identification principle is quite arbitrary. The only supporting argument is that the anharmonicity of molecular vibrations is generally small. However, if we reject the principle of the least anharmonicity coefficients, we are left without any guiding line for the interpretation of the Raman spectra. Some additional data for interpretation are supplied by simultaneous measurements of ordinary molecules and their deutero derivatives. Such measurements were carried out in [239–243] for three pairs of molecules: cyclohexane, benzene, chloroform and their respective deutero derivatives. In most cases, the lines in the spectra of these pairs could be identified as combinations of fundamental frequencies of the same symmetry class and same mode shape. Moreover, second-order lines of a common origin for the ordinary molecule and its deutero derivative have close intensities both in Raman spectra and in IR spectra. The anharmonicity coefficients of line pairs of common origin in most cases were found to have the same sign and close values.

This analogy in the behavior of lines of common origin in isotope-substituted molecules can be interpreted as a reflection of certain characteristic features of second-order spectra. A more immediate proof of the existence of such characteristic behavior is provided by measurements of compounds with prominent characteristic structural elements. Table 31 lists some compounds with dominant bonds. The anharmonicity coefficients of these bonds are quite characteristic.

Table 31

ANHARMONICITY COEFFICIENTS OF SOME CHARACTERISTIC
MOLECULAR VIBRATIONS [241]

Compound	Bond	Spectrum	v, cm^{-1}	$-\kappa$, cm^{-1}
Chloroform CHCl$_3$	C—H	IR	$v_1 = 5921$	57
		RS	$v = 3018$	58
		IR	$v_2 = 8703$	
Deuterochloroform CDCl$_3$	C—D	IR	$v_1 = 4439$	33
		RS	$v = 2253$	32
		IR	$v_2 = 6568$	
Methyldichlorosilane CH$_3$Cl$_2$SiH	Si—H	IR	$v_1 = 4384$	
		RS	$v = 2221$	29
Ethyldichlorosilane C$_2$H$_5$Cl$_2$SiH	Si—H	IR	$v_1 = 4353$	
		RS	$v = 2210$	33
Acetone (CH$_3$)$_2$CO	C=O	IR	$v_1 = 3409$	
		IR	$v = 1711$	6
		IR	$v_2 = 5102$	6
Methylethylketone CH$_3$C$_2$H$_5$CO	C=O	IR	$v_1 = 3414$	
		IR	$v = 1716$	9
		IR	$v_2 = 5100$	8
Diethylamine (C$_2$H$_5$)$_2$NH	N—H	IR	$v_1 = 6480$	
		RS	$v = 3311$	71
		IR	$v_2 = 9444$	81
Acetonitrile CH$_3$C≡N	C≡N	IR	$v_1 = 4520$	
		RS	$v = 2246$	-14
		IR	$v_2 = 6870$	-22
Pentene-1 C—C—C—C=C	C=C	RS	$v_1 = 3279$	
		RS	$v = 1642$	3
Diallyl C=C—C—C—C=C	C=C	RS	$v_1 = 3278$	
		RS	$v = 1642$	3
Pentadiene-1,3 C=C—C=C—C	C=C—C=C	RS	$v_1 = 3301$	
		RS	$v = 1655$	5
Dipropenyl C—C=C—C=C—C	C=C—C=C	RS	$v_1 = 3320$	
		RS	$v = 1668$	8
Isobutadiene C=C—C=C $\vert$ C	C=C—C=C	RS	$v_1 = 3265$	
		RS	$v = 1638$	6

Although the experimental material on second-order spectra is still highly limited, we will try to present a general analysis of the data available. We selected 118 second-order lines which had been measured and identified with the greatest accuracy and reliability (lines associated with resonance splitting were not included). Of these, 73 lines were found to have small anharmonicity coefficients between 0 and 6 cm^{-1}, 27 lines had anharmonicity coefficients between 6 and 11 cm^{-1}, and 18 lines had anharmonicity coefficients exceeding 11 cm^{-1}. These results confirm the conclusion regarding the generally small anharmonicity of molecular vibrations. Note that the anharmonicity coefficients of overtones are smaller than those of combination frequencies.

The anharmonicity coefficients were found to be largly of one sign (negative): of the 118 lines, 92 lines had $\kappa < 0$, and 26 lines, $\kappa > 0$. This result is highly significant for estimating the effect of anharmonicity on the observed vibration frequencies. Indeed, every observed frequency v_i is representable as a sum of the form

$$v_i = \omega_i + 2\kappa_{ii} + \tfrac{1}{2} \sum_{i \neq k} \kappa_{ik}, \tag{15.24}$$

where ω_i is the harmonic frequency, and the last term is the sum of the anharmonicity coefficients of the combination frequencies. This sum for polyatomic molecules includes very numerous terms, and since they are mostly of the same sign, the sum may give a substantial contribution to the observed frequency (although each of the coefficients is small).

2. Introduction of anharmonicity in the calculation of molecular vibrations

The theory of molecular vibrations (§10) is based on the assumption of strictly harmonic vibrations. In practice, however, we always use the experimental frequencies, since no complete data are available on the anharmonicity constants, not even for the simplest of molecules. Therefore, considerable uncontrollable errors are introduced from the very start into the system of the dynamic coupling constants. These errors are subsequently transferred to the results of the frequency calculations for complex molecules from known force constants of simpler molecules. The accuracy of the calculated vibrational frequencies is therefore still limited (the errors reach 10–20 cm^{-1}, and in some cases even up to 50 cm^{-1}), despite the widespread use of computers.

The replacement of the harmonic frequencies ω_i with the observed frequencies v_i also invalidates such rigorous theoretical relations as the sum rule and the product rule. As an example, Table 32 lists the corresponding data for chloroform and deuterochloroform. The complete set of the anharmonicity coefficients had been determined for these molecules [242], and the harmonic frequencies therefore could be found. The results in Table 32 show that the product rule is satisfied with

Table 32

OBSERVED AND HARMONIC FREQUENCIES OF $CHCl_3$ AND $CDCl_3$

Vibration mode	$CHCl_3$		$CDCl_3$		$\Pi_{(H)}/\Pi_{(D)}$		
	ν_i	ω_i	ν_i	ω_i	observed frequencies	harmonic frequencies	theoretical
A	3018	3140	2254	2333			
	669	679	649	659	1.91	1.99	2.01
	366	380	365	374			
E	1219	1300	903	963			
	764	793	736	780	2.00	1.96	1.95
	264	276	260	272			

Note: $\Pi_{(H)}$ is the product of the chloroform frequencies squared; $\Pi_{(D)}$ ditto for deuterochloroform.

higher accuracy for the harmonic frequencies than for the observed frequencies. We see from the table that in a number of cases the harmonic frequencies are markedly different from the observed frequencies.

The problem of anharmonic corrections in the calculation of frequencies is one of the most difficult topics in the theory of molecular vibrations. The most popular method which allows for the effects of anharmonicity is the so-called *method of spectroscopic masses* proposed by Hemptinne and Mannenback [244]. This technique was adopted by El'yashevich and Stepanov in their calculations [80, 81]. In a number of cases, it ensures a good fit between the experimental and the calculated frequencies, but its principal disadvantage is that it is definitely known to give a distorted molecular force field. Moreover, the method of spectroscopic masses is inapplicable to second-order spectra.

A number of recent publications tried to get over the various difficulties by establishing certain relations between the anharmonicity coefficients. These relations, however, were introduced either without any justification or on the basis of not very convincing arguments [245–247]. This approach apparently ensures only an accidental fit between theory and experiment.

A general approximate method for deriving anharmonicity corrections can be obtained from the following considerations [248]. The first studies which dealt with the calculations of molecular vibrations used a highly simplified molecular force field: only the diagonal elements of the dynamic coupling matrix were considered. In this approximation, the calculations of the molecular frequencies often led to gross errors, and the off-diagonal elements had to be introduced in later work. However, many of the coupling coefficients are taken as zero to this day. In our opinion, the problem of anharmonicity should be tackled initially in the same way, i.e., by considering the anharmonicity constants for the principal types of interaction only. A partial experimental justification of this approach is provided by the previously noted fact that the anharmonicity coefficients are characteristic of the dominant bonds .

Applying this technique to our problem in natural coordinates, we have to add to the potential function of the molecule terms of the form $\alpha_i q_i^3$ and $\beta_i q_i^4$, which correspond to the anharmonicity corrections of the diagonal elements in the dynamic coupling matrix. In this way, we ensure an approximate correction to the principal diagonal coupling coefficients while introducing a very limited number of new constants. Conceptually, this step is equivalent to the "zero" approximation of the scheme which used only the diagonal coupling coefficients. Despite the highly approximate character of this technique, it seems to constitute a logical and, more-over, an indispensable step toward the solution of the general anharmonicity problem. In this method, the anharmonicity constants found for some molecules may also be used for other molecules with the same dynamic coupling.

The application of this method in practice will be illustrated for the case of a methane molecule and its isotope-substituted derivatives [248]. To the expression for the potential function of this molecule in natural coordinates (see §10), we add third- and fourth-order terms of the form

$$\Delta U = \tfrac{1}{6}\alpha_q \left(q_1^3 + q_2^3 + q_3^3 + q_4^3\right) + \tfrac{1}{6}\alpha_y \left(\gamma_{12}^3 + \gamma_{13}^3 + \gamma_{14}^3 + \gamma_{23}^3 + \gamma_{24}^3 + \gamma_{34}^3\right) +$$

$$+ \tfrac{1}{24}\beta_q \left(q_1^4 + q_2^4 + q_3^4 + q_4^4\right) +$$

$$+ \tfrac{1}{24}\beta_y \left(\gamma_{12}^4 + \gamma_{13}^4 + \gamma_{14}^4 + \gamma_{23}^4 + \gamma_{24}^4 + \gamma_{34}^4\right). \tag{15.25}$$

We thus introduce a total of four anharmonicity constants, α_q, α_y, β_q, β_y. The expression for the potential energy U in natural coordinates should now be transformed to normal coordinates. The general transformation technique has been described in §10. Third- and fourth-order terms in (15.25) are also transformed. The potential energy correction ΔU expressed in normal coordinates makes it possible to calculate the vibrational energy correction ΔE_v. For the total vibrational energy of a molecule we thus find [248]

$$\frac{E_v}{h} = \omega_A \left(v_A + \tfrac{1}{2}\right) + \omega_E \left(v_E + 1\right) + \omega_q \left(v_q + \tfrac{3}{2}\right) + \omega_y \left(v_y + \tfrac{3}{2}\right) - \kappa_{AA} \left(v_A + \tfrac{1}{2}\right)^2 -$$

$$- \kappa_{Aq} \left(v_A + \tfrac{1}{2}\right)\left(v_q + \tfrac{3}{2}\right) - \kappa_{Ay} \left(v_A + \tfrac{1}{2}\right)\left(v_y + \tfrac{3}{2}\right) - \kappa_{qq} \left[\left(v_{q1} + \tfrac{1}{2}\right)^2 + \right.$$

$$\left. + \left(v_{q2} + \tfrac{1}{2}\right)^2 + \left(v_{q3} + \tfrac{1}{2}\right)^2\right] - \kappa_{yy} \left[\left(v_{y1} + \tfrac{1}{2}\right)^2 + \left(v_{y2} + \tfrac{1}{2}\right)^2 + \left(v_{y3} + \tfrac{1}{2}\right)^2\right] -$$

$$- Y_{qq} \left[\left(v_{q1} + \tfrac{1}{2}\right)\left(v_{q2} + \tfrac{1}{2}\right) + \left(v_{q1} + \tfrac{1}{2}\right)\left(v_{q3} + \tfrac{1}{2}\right) + \left(v_{q2} + \tfrac{1}{2}\right)\left(v_{q3} + \tfrac{1}{2}\right)\right] -$$

$$- Y_{\gamma\gamma} \left[(v_{\gamma 1} + \tfrac{1}{2})(v_{\gamma 2} + \tfrac{1}{2}) + (v_{\gamma 1} + \tfrac{1}{2})(v_{\gamma 3} + \tfrac{1}{2}) + (v_{\gamma 2} + \tfrac{1}{2})(v_{\gamma 3} + \tfrac{1}{2})\right] -$$

$$- Y_{q\gamma} (v_q + \tfrac{3}{2})(v_\gamma + \tfrac{3}{2}) - Y_{q1\gamma 1} \left[(v_{q1} + \tfrac{1}{2})(v_{\gamma 1} + \tfrac{1}{2}) + (v_{q2} + \tfrac{1}{2})(v_{\gamma 2} + \tfrac{1}{2}) + \right.$$

$$+ \left. (v_{q3} + \tfrac{1}{2})(v_{\gamma 3} + \tfrac{1}{2})\right] - 3Y_{EE} \left[(v_{E1} + \tfrac{1}{2})^2 + (v_{E2} + \tfrac{1}{2})^2\right] -$$

$$- 4Y_{EE} (v_{E1} + \tfrac{1}{2})(v_{E2} + \tfrac{1}{2}). \tag{15.26}$$

Here the anharmonicity coefficients κ_{AA}, Y_{EE}, etc. are known functions of the anharmonicity constants entering (15.25) and of harmonic frequencies and molecular parameters; v_{E1} and v_{E2} are the vibrational quantum numbers of the individual doubly degenerate vibration modes, such that $v_{E1} + v_{E2} = v_E$; v_{q1}, v_{q2}, v_{q3} and $v_{\gamma 1}$, $v_{\gamma 2}$, $v_{\gamma 3}$ are the vibrational quantum numbers for triply degenerate vibrations, such that $v_{q1} + v_{q2} + v_{q3} = v_q$, $v_{\gamma 1} + v_{\gamma 2} + v_{\gamma 3} = v_\gamma$. Using (15.26) we can readily find expressions for the observed fundamental frequencies, overtones, and combination frequencies.

In numerical calculations, we used the experimental material for first- and second-order frequencies of the molecules CH_4, CD_4 and CT_4 assembled in [246]. The calculations were carried out by successive approximations. The results are listed in Table 33, which shows that the fit between theory and experiment is quite satisfactory. Note that the number of experimental frequencies (25 frequencies) is much higher than the number of the theoretical constants (9 constants).

Table 33

CALCULATED AND EXPERIMENTAL FREQUENCIES FOR CH_4, CD_4, AND CT_4 MOLECULES (in cm^{-1})

Frequency	CH_4		CD_4		CT_4	
	calc.	exp.	calc.	exp.	calc.	exp.
v_A	2929	2916.5	2099	2107.8	1773.5	—
v_E	1538	1534	1089.5	1092.2	893.5	—
v_q	3023.5	3018.7	2260	2258.6	1931.5	1937
v_γ	1309	1306	995	996.0	857	858
$2v_A$	5792	—	4165	—	3427	—
$2v_E$	3071	—	2176	—	1780	—
$2v_q$	6007	6004.7	4498	4496.4	3846.5	3855
$2v_\gamma$	2608	2600	1984	1986.8	1710	—
$v_A + v_E$	4467	—	3188.5	—	2615.5	—
$v_A + v_q$	5880.5	5861	4321.5	4331	3629	—
$v_A + v_\gamma$	4238	4222	3094	3105	2581.5	—
$v_E + v_q$	4561.5	4546	3349.5	3338	2822.5	—
$v_E + v_\gamma$	2847	2826	2084.5	2084	1748	—
$v_q + v_\gamma$	4332.5	4313	3255	3255	2788.5	—

The following values were obtained for the force constants and the anharmonicity constants:

$$K_q = 9.275 \cdot 10^6 \text{ cm}^{-2}, \quad K_\gamma = 0.741 \cdot 10^6 \text{ cm}^{-2}, \quad a = 0.36 \cdot 10^6 \text{ cm}^{-2}$$

$$h = 0.045 \cdot 10^6 \text{ cm}^{-2}, \quad l = -0.027 \cdot 10^6 \text{ cm}^{-2}, \quad a_q = 35.8 \cdot 10^6 \text{ cm}^{-5/2},$$

$$\alpha_\gamma = 0, \quad b_q = -82.3 \cdot 10^6 \text{ cm}^{-3}, \quad b_\gamma = -0.76 \cdot 10^6 \text{ cm}^{-3},$$

where

$$a_q^2 = \frac{\hbar \alpha_q^2}{64^2 \pi^4 M_0^3}, \qquad b_q = \frac{\hbar \beta_q}{16 \cdot 64 \pi^4 M_0^2}, \qquad b_\gamma = \frac{\hbar \beta_\gamma}{16 \cdot 64 \pi^4 M_0^2}.$$

These force constants are seen to be markedly different from the corresponding constants calculated by the method of spectroscopic masses [80].

3. The intensity of second-order lines

According to the general theory of §6, the intensity and the polarization of second-order lines when the polarizability theory is applicable is determined by the invariants β_c and γ^2 of the tensor

$$(\beta_{\rho\sigma})_{2,0} = \int u_2^*(x) \alpha_{\rho\sigma}(x) u_0(x) dx . \tag{15.27}$$

The polarizability $\alpha_{\rho\sigma}(x)$ can be series-expanded in powers of the coordinate x (see (7.9)). The calculation of the tensor $\beta_{\rho\sigma}$ then reduces to calculating the matrix elements of the various powers of x. For the case when the wave functions $u_k(x)$ are the harmonic oscillator eigenfunctions, this problem was solved in §7. For the $0 \to 2$ transition, we have by (7.20)

$$(\beta_{\rho\sigma})_{2,0} = \frac{1}{4} \sqrt{2} \left(\frac{\partial^2 \alpha_{\rho\sigma}}{\partial x_i^2} \right)_0 a_i^2 . \tag{15.28}$$

Eq. (15.28) gives the intensity of the overtone of frequency ω_i assuming strictly harmonic vibrations. To use Vol'kenshtein's terminology [80, Ch. 23], the contribution of Eq. (15.28) to the overtone intensity may be termed the *electrooptical anharmonicity*. For the combination frequencies $\omega_1 + \omega_j$, we similarly find, using (7.22),

$$(\beta_{\rho\sigma})_{11,00} = \frac{1}{4} \left(\frac{\partial^2 \alpha_{\rho\sigma}}{\partial x_i \partial x_j} \right)_0 a_i a_j . \tag{15.29}$$

The anharmonicity of the molecular vibrations also causes a certain shift of the energy levels, as we have mentioned before. The eigenfunctions of the system are thus changed. According to the general perturbation theory (see [20]), the first-approximation correction to the wave function ψ_n is

$$\Delta\psi_n = \sum_m \frac{V_{mn}}{E_n - E_m} \psi_m \qquad (m \neq n), \qquad (15.30)$$

where ψ_m are the unperturbed eigenfunctions (in our case, products of the harmonic oscillator wave functions, see (7.2)). Thus, in the anharmonic case, the functions $u_2(x)$ and $u_0(x)$ in the polarizability matrix elements in (15.27) have the form

$$u_2(x) = \psi_2 + \Delta\psi_2,$$

$$u_0(x) = \psi_0 + \Delta\psi_0,$$

where the corrections $\Delta\psi_2$ and $\Delta\psi_0$ are expressed by (15.30). The correction to $(\beta_{\rho\sigma})_{2,0}$ has the form

$$\Delta(\beta_{\rho\sigma})_{2,0} = \int [\psi_2(x)\Delta\psi_0(x) + \psi_0(x)\Delta\psi_2(x) + \Delta\psi_0(x)\Delta\psi_2(x)]\,\alpha_{\rho\sigma}(x)\,dx. \qquad (15.31)$$

The contribution to the overtone intensity associated with this correction is termed by Vol'kenstein the *mechanical anharmonicity*.* It is readily seen that the mechanical anharmonicity is zero for harmonic oscillations, when the potential energy corrections in (15.1) are zero, whereas the electrooptical anharmonicity is retained in this case also.

In (15.31) we write

$$\alpha_{\rho\sigma}(x) = \alpha_{\rho\sigma}(0) + \sum_i \left(\frac{\partial\alpha_{\rho\sigma}}{\partial x_i}\right)_0 x_i.$$

For the overtone of frequency ω_j, retaining only the lowest order terms with V_{mn}, we find

$$\Delta(\beta_{\rho\sigma})_{2,0} = \alpha_{\rho\sigma}(0) \sum_{v_j} \frac{V_{v_j,2} V_{v_j,0}}{(E_2 - E_{v_j})(E_0 - E_{v_j})} +$$

$$+ \frac{a_j}{\sqrt{2}} \left(\frac{\partial\alpha_{\rho\sigma}}{\partial x_i}\right)_0 \left[\frac{V_{1,2}}{E_2 - E_1} + \frac{\sqrt{2}V_{1,0}}{E_0 - E_1} + \frac{\sqrt{3}V_{3,0}}{E_0 - E_3}\right] +$$

$$+ \sum_k \frac{a_k}{\sqrt{2}} \left(\frac{\partial\alpha_{\rho\sigma}}{\partial x_k}\right)_0 \left[\frac{V_{v_k=1,\,v_j=2;\,00}}{E_{00} - E_{v_k=1,\,v_j=2}} + \frac{V_{v_k=1,\,v_j=0;\,v_k=0,\,v_j=2}}{E_{v_k=0,\,v_j=2} - E_{v_k=1,\,v_j=0}}\right], \qquad (15.32)$$

* Vol'kenshtein [80, 249] considered the mechanical anharmonicity within the framework of the classical theory, and his expressions are therefore somewhat different from what follows.

where $v_j \neq 0$, $v_j \neq 2$, $k \neq j$. The subscripts specify only those vibrational quantum numbers which do not remain zero in the particular transition. For the combination frequency $\omega_i + \omega_j$, we similarly have

$$\Delta(\beta_{\rho\sigma})_{11,00} = \alpha_{\rho\sigma}(0) \sum_{v_i,v_j} \frac{V_{v_iv_j,\,11}V_{v_iv_j,\,00}}{(E_{00} - E_{v_iv_j})(E_{11} - E_{v_iv_j})} +$$

$$+ \frac{a_i}{\sqrt{2}} \left(\frac{\partial \alpha_{\rho\sigma}}{\partial x_i}\right)_0 \left[\frac{V_{v_i=1,\,v_j=0;\,11}}{E_{11} - E_{v_i=1,\,v_j=0}} + \frac{\sqrt{2}V_{v_i=0,\,v_j=1;\,00}}{E_{00} - E_{v_i=0,\,v_j=1}} + \frac{\sqrt{3}V_{v_i=2,\,v_j=1;\,00}}{E_{00} - E_{v_i=2,\,v_j=1}}\right] +$$

$$+ \frac{a_j}{\sqrt{2}} \left(\frac{\partial \alpha_{\rho\sigma}}{\partial x_j}\right)_0 \left[\frac{V_{v_i=0,\,v_j=1;\,11}}{E_{11} - E_{v_i=0,\,v_j=1}} + \frac{\sqrt{2}V_{v_i=1,\,v_j=0;\,00}}{E_{00} - E_{v_i=1,\,v_j=0}} + \frac{\sqrt{3}V_{v_i=1,\,v_j=2;\,00}}{E_{00} - E_{v_i=1,\,v_j=2}}\right] +$$

$$+ \sum_k \frac{a_k}{\sqrt{2}} \left(\frac{\partial \alpha_{\rho\sigma}}{\partial x_k}\right)_0 \left[\frac{V_{v_k=1,\,v_i=0,\,v_j=0;\,011}}{E_{011} - E_{v_k=1,\,v_i=0,\,v_j=0}} + \frac{V_{v_k=1,\,v_i=1,\,v_j=1;\,000}}{E_{000} - E_{111}}\right], \qquad (15.33)$$

where

$$v_i,\ v_j \neq 0,\, 0,\quad v_i,\ v_j \neq 1,\, 1,\quad k \neq i,\, k \neq j.$$

By (15.32) and (15.33) we see that the contribution of the mechanical anharmonicity to the intensity of the second-order lines increases as the matrix elements V_{mn} increase and the vibration frequencies decrease, i.e., as the relative anharmonicity increases. We can therefore expect a certain correlation between the anharmonicity coefficients and the intensity of second-order lines. Some supporting evidence will be found in [243].

4. Resonance splitting of lines in vibrational spectra (Fermi resonance)

The previous theory is applicable only if the correction term $\Delta\psi_n$ in (15.30) is small, i.e., when

$$V_{mn} \ll E_n - E_m. \qquad (15.34)$$

Condition (15.34) may be broken if the distance between some perturbed levels accidentally happens to be small (i.e., in the case of accidental degeneracy). A problem of this kind was first considered by Fermi for the CO_2 molecule [250]. The accidental coincidence of energy levels is therefore known as the Fermi resonance.

The problem can be solved by the theory of perturbations of degenerate systems (see [20], §39). Let E_m^0 be an energy level of multiplicity f. Let $\psi_1^0, \psi_2^0, \ldots, \psi_f^0$ be the eigenfunctions corresponding to this energy. The choice of these functions is not single-valued, since they always can be replaced by any f independent linear combinations of these functions. This ambiguity is eliminated, however, if an additional condition is imposed on the wave functions, namely that they change insignificantly under the applied perturbation. Let the wave functions satisfying this additional requirement have the form

$$\psi_k = c_1^0 \psi_1^0 + c_2^0 \psi_2^0 + \ldots + c_f^0 \psi_f^0 \quad (k = 1, 2, \ldots, f).$$ (15.35)

We will now use the general equation of the perturbation theory, (4.18), inserting in the first approximation $\lambda = E_m = E_m^0 + E'$ and taking for c_m their zero-approximation values:

$$c_1 = c_1^0, c_2 = c_2^0, \ldots, c_f = c_f^0; \quad c_m = 0 \quad \text{for} \quad m \neq 1, 2, \ldots, f.$$

This gives

$$E' c_k^0 = \sum_l H'_{kl} c_l^0,$$ (15.36)

where $k = 1, 2, \ldots, f$. This system of linear homogeneous equations for the unknowns c_k^0 has a nontrivial solution if

$$\begin{vmatrix} H'_{11} - E' & H'_{21} & \cdots & H'_{ff} \\ H'_{12} & H'_{22} - E' & \cdots & H'_{f2} \\ \cdot & \cdot & \cdots & \cdot \\ H'_{1f} & H'_{2f} & \cdots & H'_{ff} - E' \end{vmatrix} = 0.$$ (15.37)

The roots of this equation give the sought first-approximation corrections to the energy eigenvalues. Successively inserting the roots of Eq. (15.37) in (15.36), we find the coefficients c_k^0 and hence the zero-approximation eigenfunctions.

For the case of vibrational energy levels with a two-fold degeneracy, the secular equation (15.37) takes the form

$$\begin{vmatrix} V_{11} - E' & V_{12} \\ V_{21} & V_{22} - E' \end{vmatrix} = 0.$$ (15.37')

Solving this equation, we find

$$E' = \tfrac{1}{2} \left[(V_{11} + V_{22}) \pm \sqrt{(V_{11} - V_{22})^2 + 4V_{12}^2} \right].$$ (15.38)

A doubly degenerate energy level E_m^0 thus splits into two levels:

$$E_{m1} = E_0 \pm \tfrac{1}{2} \kappa = E_0 \pm \tfrac{1}{2} \sqrt{\Delta^2 + 4V_{12}^2},$$ (15.39)

$$E_{m2} = E_0 \mp \tfrac{1}{2} \kappa = E_0 \mp \tfrac{1}{2} \sqrt{\Delta^2 + 4V_{12}^2}.$$

Here,

$$E_0 = E_m^0 + \tfrac{1}{2}(V_{11} + V_{22}) = \tfrac{1}{2}(E_{m1} + E_{m2}),$$

$$\Delta = V_{11} - V_{22}, \quad \kappa = \sqrt{\Delta^2 + 4V_{12}^2} = E_{m1} - E_{m2},$$

(15.40)

and we should take the upper or the lower sign in (15.39) according as $\Delta > 0$ or $\Delta < 0$. Having calculated the coefficients c_1^0, c_2^0 for the energies E' from (15.38), we find the zero-approximation eigenfunctions

$$u_1 = \frac{1}{\sqrt{2\kappa}}\left[\sqrt{\kappa + |\Delta|}u_1^0 \pm \sqrt{\kappa - |\Delta|}u_2^0\right],$$

(15.41)

$$u_2 = \frac{1}{\sqrt{2\kappa}}\left[\sqrt{\kappa - |\Delta|}u_1^0 \mp \sqrt{\kappa + |\Delta|}u_2^0\right].$$

The upper sign is taken when Δ and V_{12} are of the same sign, and the lower sign when Δ and V_{12} are of opposite signs.

It follows from (15.41) that the matrix element

$$V_{12} = \int u_1^0(x)\,\hat{V}u_2^0(x)\,dx$$

(15.42)

determines to what extent the eigenfunctions u_1, u_1^0 and u_2, u_2^0 differ from one another.

In this expression, $\hat{V}$ is the sum of anharmonic terms (terms of third, fourth, and higher degree) of the potential energy,* and u_1^0 and u_2^0 are the eigenfunctions of two coupled vibrational levels in the zero approximation. The potential energy of the molecule is invariant under any symmetry operation belonging to the molecule point group, i.e., the function $\hat{V}$ is totally symmetric. Hence it follows that $u_1^0(x)$ and $u_2^0(x)$ should belong to the same symmetry class. Thus two vibrational levels may perturb each other only if they belong to the same symmetry class. This rule severely limits the occurrence of a resonance interaction between levels (Fermi resonance) in molecules possessing symmetry elements.

When the interacting levels satisfy the above symmetry rule, the matrix element of the perturbation (15.42) may substantially exceed its value in molecules without resonance interaction between energy levels. Indeed, in distinction from (15.8), the first-approximation correction to the energy eigenvalue in case of resonance does not vanish for the cubic terms of the potential energy, whereas in the non-resonance case a finite correction is only contributed by the fourth-degree terms.

* Strictly speaking, the perturbation operator $\hat{V}$ also includes additional terms of the kinetic energy operator which do not enter the zeroth-approximation expression. However, the contribution of these terms to the matrix element V_{12} is generally small (these terms will be considered in greater detail in the next section).

As an example, let us consider the case of two vibrational levels in a molecule whose frequencies are related as follows:

$$\omega_1 \approx 2\omega_2 . \tag{15.43}$$

In the expression for the potential energy, we need only consider a perturbing term of the form $\alpha'_{122}Q_1Q_2^2$, and for the perturbation matrix element we have (see (7.18)–(7.20))

$$V_{12} = V_{10,02} = \tfrac{1}{2}\alpha'_{122}a_1a_2^2 , \tag{15.44}$$

where (see (7.11)) $a_1^2 = \hbar/M\omega_1$, $a_2^2 = \hbar/M\omega_2$ (the unchanging vibrational quantum numbers have been omitted).

The observed frequency difference $\omega_1 - 2\omega_2$ according to (15.40) is determined by two constants, Δ and V_{12}. For $\Delta^2 \ll V_{12}^2$ (a sharp resonance), we have approximately

$$\kappa = 2V_{12}\left(1 + \frac{\Delta^2}{8V_{12}^2}\right). \tag{15.45}$$

In this case, the perturbed eigenfunctions have the form

$$u_1 = \frac{1}{\sqrt{2}}(u_1^0 + u_2^0), \qquad u_2 = \frac{1}{\sqrt{2}}(u_1^0 - u_2^0). \tag{15.46}$$

In the other extreme case, $\Delta^2 \gg V_{12}^2$, we have

$$\kappa = \Delta\left(1 + \frac{2V_{12}^2}{\Delta^2}\right), \tag{15.47}$$

and the eigenfunctions reduce to the unperturbed functions u_1^0, u_2^0. The displacement of the levels due to their interaction and the mixing of the wave functions are the characteristic effects of the Fermi resonance which are determined by the relationship between V_{12}^2 and Δ^2. They may remain insignificant even for very small Δ, provided that the corresponding anharmonicity constant α'_{122} is small. This point should be borne in mind in the interpretation of the observed spectra. Note that in the literature, the Fermi resonance is often used without any obvious justification in explaining various experimental data.

Let us now calculate the line intensities for the case of resonance interaction between vibrations. According to the general rules, we should first find the matrix elements of polarizability. Let $(\alpha'_{10})_0$, $(\alpha''_{02})_0$ be the matrix elements of the first and the second term in the expansion of polarizability for the case of zero coupling between the vibrations for transitions corresponding to the frequencies ω_1, $2\omega_2$. Using the eigenfunctions (15.41) to compute the polarizability matrix elements for the coupled vibrations, we find (see [7], §20)

$$\alpha'_{10} = \frac{1}{\sqrt{2\kappa}} \left\{ \sqrt{\kappa + |\Delta|} \, (\alpha'_{10})_0 \pm \sqrt{\kappa - |\Delta|} \, (\alpha''_{02})_0 \right\},$$

$$(15.48)$$

$$\alpha''_{02} = \frac{1}{\sqrt{2\kappa}} \left\{ \sqrt{\kappa - |\Delta|} \, (\alpha'_{10})_0 \mp \sqrt{\kappa + |\Delta|} \, (\alpha''_{02})_0 \right\}.$$

To calculate the line intensities and the depolarizations, we should form the invariants $\beta_c = \frac{1}{3} b^2$ and γ^2 of the tensors α'_{10} and α'_{02} (see §2, §3). The first invariant is readily found from (15.48) if the traces b_1 and b_2 of the tensors $(\alpha'_{10})_0$ and $(\alpha''_{02})_0$ are known. Writing

$$b_{10} = b(\alpha'_{10}), \quad b_{02} = b(\alpha''_{02}), \quad k_1 = \sqrt{\frac{\kappa + |\Delta|}{2\kappa}}, \quad k_2 = \sqrt{\frac{\kappa - |\Delta|}{2\kappa}},$$

we find*

$$b_{10} = k_1 b_1 + k_2 b_2, \quad b_{02} = k_2 b_1 - k_1 b_2. \quad (15.49)$$

The anisotropy is more difficult to calculate, since this invariant cannot be expressed directly in terms of the anisotropies γ_1^2 and γ_2^2 of the original tensors. From (2.40) we have

$$\gamma_{10}^2 = k_1^2 \gamma_1^2 + k_2^2 \gamma_2^2 + 2k_1 k_2 \sigma,$$

$$\gamma_{02}^2 = k_2^2 \gamma_1^2 + k_1^2 \gamma_2^2 - 2k_1 k_2 \sigma,$$

$$(15.50)$$

where

$$\sigma = \frac{2}{3} \left(\sum_i \alpha'_i \alpha''_i - \sum_{i \neq k} \alpha'_i \alpha''_k \right), \quad (15.51)$$

α'_i, α''_i are the principal values of the tensors $(\alpha'_{10})_0, (\alpha''_{02})_0$.

From (15.49) and (15.50), seeing that $k_1^2 + k_2^2 = 1$, we find

$$b_{10}^2 + b_{02}^2 = b_1^2 + b_2^2, \quad \gamma_{10}^2 + \gamma_{02}^2 = \gamma_1^2 + \gamma_2^2. \quad (15.52)$$

The trace squared is proportional to the intensity of scalar scattering, and γ^2 is proportional to the intensity of anisotropic scattering. Therefore, by (15.52),

$$I_{10} + I_{02} = I_1 + I_2, \quad (15.53)$$

and this equality is satisfied separately for the scalar and the anisotropic parts of scattering. The total intensity of the coupled lines is thus equal to the sum of the

---

* In what follows we use the top signs in (15.48).

respective line intensities in the unperturbed case. The perturbation only causes a certain redistribution of intensity between the two lines.

In what follows, we will only consider highly polarized lines. The contribution of the anistropic scattering to line intensities in this case is fairly small, and Eq. (15.48) can be replaced by approximate expressions for calculating the anisotropy.

1. For $k_2 \ll k_1$, we have

$$\alpha'_{10} \approx k_1(\alpha'_{10})_0, \qquad \alpha''_{02} \approx -k_1(\alpha''_{02})_0, \tag{15.48a}$$

$$\gamma^2_{10} = k_1^2 \gamma_1^2, \qquad \gamma^2_{02} = k_1^2 \gamma_2^2. \tag{15.54}$$

Therefore, approximately,

$$I_{10} = \left(k_1 \sqrt{I_1} + k_2 \sqrt{I_2}\right)^2, \qquad I_{02} = \left(k_2 \sqrt{I_1} - k_1 \sqrt{I_2}\right)^2, \tag{15.55}$$

$$\rho_{10} = \frac{k_1^2 I_1 \rho_1}{I_{10}}, \qquad \rho_{02} = \frac{k_1^2 I_2 \rho_2}{I_{02}}. \tag{15.56}$$

2. If k_2 and k_1 are of the same order of magnitude, the terms associated with the overtone can be dropped in calculating the anisotropy, since usually $I_2 \ll I_1$. Then

$$\alpha'_{10} \approx k_1(\alpha'_{10})_0, \qquad \alpha''_{02} \approx k_2(\alpha'_{10})_0, \tag{15.48b}$$

$$\gamma^2_{10} = k_1^2 \gamma_1^2, \qquad \gamma^2_{02} = k_2^2 \gamma_1^2. \tag{15.57}$$

Thus,

$$\rho_{10} = \frac{k_1^2 I_1 \rho_1}{I_{10}}, \qquad \rho_{02} = \frac{k_2^2 I_1 \rho_1}{I_{02}}. \tag{15.58}$$

Eqs. (15.55) are retained for I_{10} and I_{02}.

In the limit of a sharp resonance ($k_1 \approx k_2$)

$$\frac{I_{02}}{I_{10}} = \frac{\left(k_2 \sqrt{I_1} - k_1 \sqrt{I_2}\right)^2}{\left(k_1 \sqrt{I_1} + k_2 \sqrt{I_2}\right)^2} \approx \frac{\left(\sqrt{I_1} - \sqrt{I_2}\right)^2}{\left(\sqrt{I_1} + \sqrt{I_2}\right)^2}, \tag{15.59}$$

$$\rho_{10} = \frac{k_1^2 I_1 \rho_1}{\left(k_1 \sqrt{I_1} + k_2 \sqrt{I_2}\right)^2} \approx \frac{I_1 \rho_1}{\left(\sqrt{I_1} + \sqrt{I_2}\right)^2}, \tag{15.60}$$

$$\rho_{02} = \frac{k_2^2 I_1 \rho_1}{\left(k_2 \sqrt{I_1} - k_1 \sqrt{I_2}\right)^2} \approx \frac{I_1 \rho_1}{\left(\sqrt{I_1} - \sqrt{I_2}\right)^2}.$$

Seeing that generally $I_2 \ll I_1$, we conclude from (15.59) and (15.60) that as we come closer to the resonance (as $|\Delta|$ decreases), the line intensities I_{10} and I_{02} are equalized, and the depolarizations ρ_{10} and ρ_{02} approach ρ_1, one remaining less than ρ_1 and the other greater than ρ_1. Note that the monotonic increase of the overtone intensity I_{02} is observed when V_{12} and Δ have the same sign. If these parameters have different signs, I_{02} first drops to zero and only then starts increasing monotonically.

We have considered the Fermi resonance for the case $\omega_1 \approx 2\omega_2$. Similar effects are also observed when three frequencies satisfy the relation $\omega_1 + \omega_2 \approx \omega_3$, since the law of transformation for the vibrations of the class ω_3 can be derived as the product of the corresponding laws of transformation for the vibrations ω_1 and ω_2. Other approximate relations between frequencies, e.g., $\omega_1 \approx n\omega_2$ for $n > 2$, lead to resonance interaction only via fourth- and higher order terms in the potential energy. Resonance effects in these cases are therefore not very pronounced.

A classical example of a resonance interaction between vibrations is provided by the spectrum of CO_2 [7, 80, 83, 250]. In accordance with the symmetry of this molecule, one totally symmetrical vibration of frequency ω_1 is allowed in the Raman spectrum, whereas actually two strong lines are observed with frequencies $\omega_1' = 1285.5$ cm^{-1} and $\omega_1'' = 1388.3$ cm^{-1}. The appearance of an extra line is explained as follows: the doubly degenerate infrared frequency $\omega_2 = 667.3$ cm^{-1} satisfies the approximate relation $2\omega_2 \approx \omega_1$, and Fermi resonance is observed.

Detailed studies of Raman spectra and IR absorption spectra of CO_2 established the complete set of anharmonicity coefficients of this molecule. According to Dennison [251], $V_{12} = 50.4$ cm^{-1} in Eq. (15.38) (see also [83, p. 70]). In this case, $\kappa = \omega_1'' - \omega_1' = 102.8$ cm^{-1}. Using these values of V_{12} and κ, we find from (15.40) $\Delta = 17.5$ cm^{-1}, $k_1 = 0.765$, $k_2 = 0.644$.

For the experimentally observed line intensity ratio we have from [252] (see also [88], p. 299) $I_{02}/I_{01} = I'/I'' = 0.61$. Using this figure, we find from (15.59) $\sqrt{I_2}/\sqrt{I_1} = 0.04$, and then from (15.60)

$$\rho_{10} = \rho'' = 0.93\rho_1 , \qquad \rho_{02} = \rho' = 1.10\rho_1 , \qquad \frac{\rho_{10}}{\rho_{02}} = 0.84 .$$

Experimental results give

$$\rho'' = 0.14 , \qquad \rho' = 0.18 , \qquad \frac{\rho''}{\rho'} = 0.78 ,$$

i.e., the calculated and the experimental depolarization ratios show a good fit.

16. ROTATIONAL STRUCTURE OF LINES IN VIBRATIONAL RAMAN SPECTRA

So far, rotation and vibration have been treated as two independent modes of molecular motion. In practice, however, vibration and rotation occur simultaneously in a molecule. As a result, the vibrational lines acquire a distinct rotational structure.

In the simplest molecules, the rotational structure of the lines can be resolved, and it yields remarkably accurate data on the molecular structure. In the majority of cases, however, the rotational structure remains unresolved and only broadens the vibrational lines.

We have seen (§8) that the bond lengths slightly change in a rotating molecule, and as a result, the moments of inertia and the corresponding rotational constants of the molecule are altered. Additional terms have to be introduced in the expressions for the rotational energy (8.10) and (8.16) to allow for these centrifugal effects, irrespective of whether the molecule vibrates or not. In the case of a vibrating molecule, however, the rotational constant $D = D(v)$ slightly changes on passing from one vibrational level v to the next. This is so because vibration changes the moment of inertia $\mathscr{I}$ in such a way that its mean value does not coincide with the corresponding equilibrium value $\mathscr{I}_e$, calculated for the equilibrium distances between the nuclei r_e. Although in harmonic vibrations the mean interatomic distance is equal to the equilibrium distance, $r = r_e$, the anharmonicity of the real vibrations leads to a situation where the r in a vibrating molecule is not equal to r_e. This effect necessitates still another correction in the expression for energy, but both corrections are relatively small. In practice, the most significant coupling between molecular vibrations and rotation is associated with Coriolis effects [7, 61, 82].

A point mass moving with a velocity v relative to a system of axes which rotates with a constant angular velocity Ω experiences a centrifugal force

$$F_c = m[\Omega[\rho\Omega]] \tag{16.1}$$

and a Coriolis force

$$F_{cor} = 2m[v\Omega] \tag{16.2}$$

(m is the mass, ρ is the distance of the moving point from the axis of rotation). These two forces in general produce an additional vibrational angular momentum l and alter the energy of the molecule.

In our study of the vibration–rotation structure of the Raman lines we thus have to consider three factors: the centrifugal bond stretching, anharmonicity of vibrations, and a Coriolis coupling between molecular vibrations and rotation.

In complex molecules, it is not easy to separate between the vibrational and the rotational components of motion. The quantum-mechanical treatment requires the Hamiltonian of a molecule which rotates while its constituent atoms vibrate. This Hamiltonain contains the angular momentum of the system, which vanishes if the molecule does not rotate. However, when the atoms vibrate, the concept of a "nonrotating" molecule should be defined in clear mathematical terms.

The radius-vectors r_i of the vibrating particles can be written in the form

$$r_i = r_{0i} + u_i, \tag{16.3}$$

where r_{0i} are the radius-vectors of the equilibrium states of the particles, u_i are the displacements of the particles from their equilibrium states. As a definition of a nonrotating molecule, we may adopt the condition (see [20, §104], [82])

$$\sum_i m_i [r_{0i} v_i] = 0.\qquad(16.4)$$

Suppose that the translational motion of the molecule has been separated by an appropriate choice of the coordinates. Then $v_i = \dot{r}_i = \dot{u}_i$. Integration of Eq. (16.4) with respect to time gives the equality

$$\sum_i m_i [r_{0i} u_i] = 0.\qquad(16.5)$$

In view of the above, the motion of a molecule can be treated as a combination of "pure vibrational" motion, satisfying conditions (16.4) or (16.5), and rotation of the molecule as a whole. The total angular momentum M of the molecule may then be written in the form

$$M = \sum_i m_i [r_i v_i] = \sum_i m_i [r_{0i} v_i] + \sum_i m_i [u_i v_i].\qquad(16.6)$$

The first term on the right in (16.6) can be treated as the angular momentum of the rotational motion,

$$M' = \sum_i m_i [r_{0i} v_i],\qquad(16.7)$$

so that the angular momentum of the vibrational motion is defined by the sum

$$l = \sum_i m_i [u_i v_i] = \sum_i [u_i p_i].\qquad(16.8)$$

Thus,

$$M' = M - l.\qquad(16.9)$$

Inserting M' for the rotational angular momentum in the expressions for the rotational energy of a molecule (8.6), (8.12), we obtain an explicit expression of the coupling between molecular vibrations and rotation. This is the Coriolis coupling effect we have mentioned earlier. Additional vibration–rotation coupling effects are associated with the dependence of the moments of inertia on the normal coordinates and the anharmonicity of vibrations.

It should be stressed that the vibrational angular momentum l in itself does not satisfy any conservation laws. Therefore, according to the general principles of quantum mechanics (see, e.g., [20]), this component of the angular momentum does not have a definite value in stationary states of the system. For a particular vibrational state, we can only find the mean value of the vibrational angular momentum. This mean value is zero for nondegenerate states of the molecule ([20], §26), and we may therefore omit from further analysis all the nondegenerate vibrations.

Degenerate vibration modes are possible only if the molecule has at least one symmetry axis of order $p > 2$ (see §10). A molecule with such a symmetry axis is classified as a symmetrical top (see §8). Let the axis z of the molecule's moving system be directed along the symmetry axis of the molecule; then $\mathscr{I}_B = \mathscr{I}_C$. Symmetry considerations show that the mean values of the components l_x and l_y of the vibrational angular momentum, perpendicular to the molecular symmetry axis, are both zero, and they will therefore be ignored in the following. The component directed along the symmetry axis is given by

$$l_z = \sum_i m_i (u_{ix} v_{iy} - u_{iy} v_{ix}) = \sum_i (u_{ix} p_{iy} - u_{iy} p_{ix}). \tag{16.10}$$

Changing over to normal coordinates, we find

$$l_z = l_\zeta = \sum_{i<k} \zeta_{ik} (\xi_i p_k - \xi_k p_i), \tag{16.11}$$

where ζ_{ik} are the Coriolis coupling constants, which in general depend on the masses, the equilibrium distances between the atoms, and the force constants; p_i and p_k are the momentum components corresponding to the degenerate normal coordinates ξ_i and ξ_k. Thus, for symmetrical top molecules, the vibration–rotation energy of the molecule is given by (E' is the vibrational energy)

$$E = \frac{M^2}{2\mathscr{I}_B} + \left(\frac{1}{\mathscr{I}_A} - \frac{1}{\mathscr{I}_B}\right) \frac{M_\zeta^2}{2} - \frac{M_\zeta l_\zeta}{\mathscr{I}_A} + \frac{l_\zeta^2}{2\mathscr{I}_A} + E'. \tag{16.12}$$

Quantizing as before for the case of pure rotational motion of a symmetrical top (see §8), we find the energy levels

$$E = \frac{\hbar^2 J (J+1)}{2\mathscr{I}_B} + \left(\frac{1}{\mathscr{I}_A} - \frac{1}{\mathscr{I}_B}\right) \frac{\hbar^2 K^2}{2} - \frac{\hbar K}{\mathscr{I}_A} \overline{l_\zeta} +$$

$$+ \frac{\overline{l_\zeta^2}}{2\mathscr{I}_A} + \Delta_1 + \Delta_2 + \sum_\alpha \hbar \omega_\alpha (v_\alpha + \tfrac{1}{2}). \tag{16.13}$$

Here the term $\hbar K \overline{l_\zeta}/\mathscr{I}_A$ is the Coriolis effect contribution, Δ_1 is the contribution due to bond stretching* (see (8.16)), Δ_2 is the anharmonicity correction. For non-degenerate vibrations, as we have noted before, $\overline{l_\zeta} = 0$.

---

* An elegant method for calculating the centrifugal stretching constants from the geometrical parameters of the molecule, the atomic masses, and the force constants was proposed by Aliev and Aleksanyan [253].

For linear molecules, inserting M' from (16.9) for M in (8.6), we find

$$E = \frac{1}{2\mathscr{I}}(M^2 - 2M_\zeta l_\zeta + l_\zeta^2) + E'. \tag{16.14}$$

In this case $M'_\zeta = 0$, and therefore $M_\zeta = l_\zeta$, so that

$$E = \frac{1}{2\mathscr{I}}(M^2 - l_\zeta^2) + E'. \tag{16.15}$$

Since the projection of the total angular momentum onto the molecular axis, M_ζ, has definite values in the stationary states of the molecule, the component l_ζ of the vibrational angular momentum should also have definite values

$$l_\zeta = \hbar l, \tag{16.16}$$

where l is an integer. For the energy levels of a linear molecule we find

$$E = \frac{\hbar^2}{2\mathscr{I}}[J(J+1) - l^2] + \Delta_1 + \Delta_2 + \sum_\alpha \hbar\omega_\alpha(v_\alpha + \tfrac{1}{2}). \tag{16.17}$$

Here Δ_1 is a second-order correction which can be written in the form (see [83])

$$\Delta_1 = -D(v)[J(J+1) - l^2]^2, \tag{16.18}$$

and Δ_2 is the anharmonicity correction (see below).

The allowed values of the quantum numbers J and l are described by the equality

$$J = |l|, \quad |l| + 1, \ldots \tag{16.19}$$

This signifies that states with $J = 0, 1, 2, \ldots, |l| - 1$ do not exist.

Linear molecules may have doubly degenerate vibrations perpendicular to the molecule axis (see §10). If one of these vibration modes has been excited, we find for the quantum number l (see [20], §104)

$$l = v, \ v - 2, \ v - 4, \ldots, \ -v,$$

where v is the vibrational quantum number of the degenerate mode. If now several degenerate modes with quantum numbers v_α have been excited, we have

$$l = \sum_\alpha l_\alpha, \tag{16.20}$$

where l_α are no longer integers.

When anharmonicity is taken into consideration, terms quadratic in l_α have to be introduced, in addition to terms quadratic in v_α, in the expression for the vibration–rotation energy levels (16.17) of degenerate vibration modes. This produces a correction term of the form

$$\Delta_2 = \sum g_{\alpha\beta} l_\alpha l_\beta, \tag{16.21}$$

where $g_{\alpha\beta}$ are constants. Note that by (16.20), Eq. (16.17) does not depend explicitly on l_α, i.e., the vibration–rotation levels are degenerate with respect to these numbers. This degeneracy is removed, however, when the vibrations are anharmonic (see (16.21)). The levels nevertheless retain a twofold degeneracy, since the energy of the molecule does not change when the sign of all l_α and l is reversed. This degeneracy is removed only when the constituent atoms in a real molecule are slightly displaced so that an asymmetrical top results. Each vibration–rotation level therefore splits into two sublevels. This effect is known as l-doubling. The distance $\Delta\omega$ between the sublevels increases with increasing rotational quantum number J (see [83]):

$$\Delta\omega = qJ(J+1),\tag{16.22}$$

where q is a constant.

Let us now consider spherical top molecules, which include molecules with the symmetry of cubic point groups (in practice, only molecules of the group T_d are of any interest). The nondegenerate vibration modes of these molecules are supplemented by doubly and triply degenerate modes. Doubly degenerate vibrational states, however, do not show the Coriolis splitting, and their vibration–rotation energy levels have the same form as the levels of the nondegenerate vibrational states. This follows from the symmetry properties of cubic molecules. Indeed, suppose that the vectors of the mean vibrational angular momenta do not vanish in two states corresponding to the same doubly degenerate energy level. These vectors then transform into each other under all the symmetry transformations of the molecule. In cubic symmetry groups, however, there are always at least three directions which transform simultaneously into one another, and no isolated pair of directions transforming into each other can exist.

Thus in symmetrical top molecules, the Coriolis effect is observed only for triply degenerate vibrational states. Using (16.9), we find for the vibration–rotation energy of a spherical top molecule

$$E = \frac{1}{2\mathscr{I}}(\mathbf{M} - \mathbf{l})^2 + E'.\tag{16.23}$$

Symmetry considerations show (see [20], §104) that the angular momentum l of a triply degenerate vibrational state corresponds to an operator of the form $\zeta\hat{l}_1$, where ζ is a constant characteristic of the particular vibrational state, and $\hat{l}_1$ is an operator corresponding to a unit vibrational angular momentum. The Hamiltonian in this case has the form

$$\hat{H} = \frac{\hbar^2}{2\mathscr{I}}(\hat{\mathbf{M}} - \zeta\hat{l}_1)^2 + \hat{H}' = \frac{\hbar^2}{2\mathscr{I}}\hat{\mathbf{M}}^2 + \frac{\hbar^2}{2\mathscr{I}}\zeta^2\hat{l}_1^2 - \frac{\hbar^2}{\mathscr{I}}\zeta\hat{\mathbf{M}}\hat{l}_1 + \hat{H}'.\tag{16.24}$$

The eigenvalues of the first term constitute the pure rotational energy of a spherical top, which coincides with the values obtained from (8.8). The second term, after averaging over the vibrational state, gives a result which is independent of the rotational quantum number and is therefore of no relevance for our analysis. The last term represents the pure vibrational energy. The Coriolis interaction energy is obtained by averaging the operator

$$\hat{H}_{\text{cor}} = -\frac{\hbar^2}{\mathscr{I}} \zeta \hat{M} \hat{I}_1 .$$

(16.25)

The operator $\hat{M}\hat{I}_1$ for a given rotational quantum number J may have three eigenvalues: $J, -1, -(J+1)$. The vibration–rotation level is therefore split into three sublevels with the following Coriolis interaction energies:

$$(E_{\text{cor}})_1 = -\frac{\hbar^2}{\mathscr{I}} \zeta J , \quad (E_{\text{cor}})_2 = \frac{\hbar^2}{\mathscr{I}} \zeta , \quad (E_{\text{cor}})_3 = \frac{\hbar^2}{\mathscr{I}} \zeta (J+1) . \quad (16.26)$$

The structure of the vibration–rotation bands is determined by the selection rules for the quantum numbers J, K, l in the particular transition. The selection rules for the rotational quantum number J are particularly significant. As in pure rotational spectra, for $\Delta J = -2, -1, 0, 1, 2$ we have the O-, P-, Q-, R-, S-branches of the vibration–rotation band.

Generally we may assume with fair accuracy that the selection rules of a pure vibrational spectrum and those of a pure rotational spectrum remain valid for the vibration–rotation spectra, irrespective of the interaction between the two modes of motion.

The selection rules are attractively simple for the isotropic part of the scattering tensor. Because of the spherical symmetry of this scattering component, $\Delta J = 0$, i.e., all the isotropic scattering is concentrated in the Q-branch. A summary of the selection rules for the vibration–rotation lines of various types is given in Table 34.

Symmetrical top molecules

The selection rules for the symmetrical Raman lines coincide with the selection rules in a pure rotational spectrum (see §8, Table 2). For antisymmetrical and degenerate vibrations, transitions with $\Delta K \neq 0$ are also allowed.

The intensities of the individual components of the vibration–rotation band depend on integrals of the form (8.18). The factors

$$b_{J',K'}^{J,K} = |H_{J',K'}^{J,K}|^2 ,$$

(16.27)

which give the relative intensities of the individual rotational lines in the anisotropic scattering component for the $J, K \to J', K'$ transitions, were calculated by Placzek and Teller [61]. The values of the coefficients $b_{J',K'}^{J,K}$ can be found in [63]. The intensities of the rotational components in symmetrical vibration–rotation bands are expressed by Eq. (8.30). The relative intensities of the various branches in the

Table 34

SELECTION RULES FOR VIBRATION–ROTATION LINES IN RAMAN SPECTRA

Type of molecule	Mode	Nonzero polarization component	Selection rules
Symmetrical top	Symmetric	$\alpha_{xx} + \alpha_{yy}; \alpha_{zz}$	$\Delta J = 0, \pm 1, \pm 2; \Delta K = 0$
	Antisymmetric	$\alpha_{xx} - \alpha_{yy}; \alpha_{xy}$	$\Delta J = 0, \pm 1, \pm 2; \Delta K = \pm 2$
	Degenerate	$\alpha_{xx} - \alpha_{yy}; \alpha_{xy}$	$\Delta J = 0, \pm 1, \pm 2; \Delta K = \pm 2$
		α_{yz}, α_{zx}	$\Delta J = 0, \pm 1, \pm 2;$
			$\Delta K = \pm 1 \, (J' + J'' \geqq 2)$
Linear	Symmetric	$\alpha_{xx} + \alpha_{yy}; \alpha_{zz}$	$\Delta J = 0, \pm 2$
	Degenerate	α_{yz}, α_{zx}	$\Delta J = 0, \pm 1, \pm 2$
			$(J' + J'' \geqq 0)$
Spherical top	Symmetric	$\alpha_{xx} + \alpha_{yy} + \alpha_{zz}$	$\Delta J = 0$
	Doubly degenerate	$\alpha_{xx} + \alpha_{yy} + 2\alpha_{zz}; \alpha_{xx} - \alpha_{yy}$	$\Delta J = 0, \pm 1, \pm 2$
	Triply degenerate	$\alpha_{xy}, \alpha_{yz}, \alpha_{xz}$	$\Delta J = 0, \pm 1, \pm 2$
			$(J' + J'' \geqq 2)$
Asymmetric top	Symmetric	$\alpha_{xx}, \alpha_{yy}, \alpha_{zz}$	$\Delta J = 0, \pm 1, \pm 2$
			$(J' + J'' \geqq 2)$

anisotropic scattering component of symmetrical bands are plotted in Figure 48 as a function of the ratio $\mathscr{I}_A/\mathscr{I}_B$.

In degenerate vibration–rotation bands, the Coriolis coupling leads to a certain additional band splitting (see [83]).

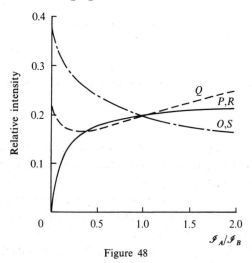

Figure 48

Relative intensities of the branches in a symmetrical vibration–rotation band of symmetrical top molecules vs. the ratio $\mathscr{I}_A/\mathscr{I}_B$ [61].

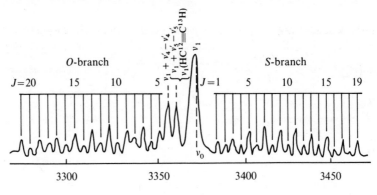

Figure 49

A microphotometric tracing of the symmetrical band v_1 of the acetylene molecule [254].

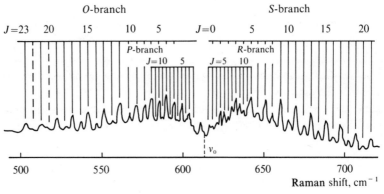

Figure 50

A microphotometric tracing of the doubly degenerate band v_4 of the acetylene molecule [254].

Linear molecules

The K of a symmetrical top and the l of a linear molecule are the angular momenta about the figure axis. This analogy suggests that the transitions $\Delta K = 1$ and $\Delta l = 1$ have identical intensity factors.

As an illustration, Figures 49 and 50 show microphotometric tracings of the symmetrical band $v_1 = 3372.5$ cm^{-1} and the doubly degenerate band $v_4 = 613.5$ cm^{-1} in the Raman spectrum of acetylene from the data of Feldman, Shepherd, and Welsh [254]. The band v_1 is associated with the transitions $\Delta J = 0, \pm 2$ between two Σ_g^+ levels schematically shown in Figure 51. The statistical weight of the anti-symmetrical levels is three times that of the symmetrical levels, and this leads to the

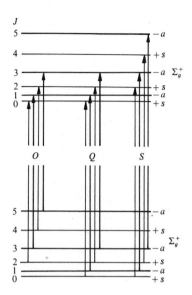

Figure 51

A diagram of $\Sigma_g^+ \to \Sigma_g^+$ transitions of linear molecules.

characteristic alternation of line intensities. Figure 49 shows the very strong Q-branch characteristic of symmetrical bands. Two Raman lines are observed near the Q-branch. The band $v_4(\Pi_g)$ has a characteristic structure with a very weak Q-branch (Figure 50). The rotational energy of the upper level of this band is described by Eqs. (16.17), (16.18), with $l = 1$. The transition diagram is shown in Figure 52.

In an excited (degenerate) vibrational state, to every value of the rotational quantum number J correspond two sublevels $-a$ and $+s$. This l-doubling increases with the increasing J. According to general rules, $J = l, l + 1 \ldots = 1, 2, \ldots$, i.e., in the upper state there is no level with $J = 0$. The selection rules (see §8) in general allow only transitions between levels of the same symmetry, i.e., transitions of the form $+ \leftrightarrow +$, $- \leftrightarrow -$. We see from Figure 51 that the l-doubling now allows transitions with $\Delta J = \pm 1$. However, the lines $Q(0)$, $P(1)$, and $O(2)$ should be missing from the spectrum. The observed spectrum indeed has a very weak Q-branch, and the lines $P(1)$ and $O(2)$ are missing. The branches O, P, R, S show a characteristic alternation of intensities.

Spherical top molecules

The symmetrical Raman lines of spherical tops show no rotational structure, since only the Q-branch is allowed ($\Delta J = 0$). Transitions into a doubly degenerate vibrational state may produce five branches. The vibration–rotation bands cor-

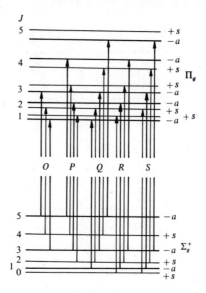

Figure 52

A diagram of $\Sigma_g^+ \to \Pi_g$ transitions of linear molecules.

responding to transitions into a triply degenerate state have an exceedingly complex structure. In accordance with the Coriolis splitting into three sublevels and the selection rules $\Delta J = 0, \pm 1, \pm 2$, these transitions produce fifteen branches.

Experimental data for spherical top molecules are available for methane only. The band v_2 corresponding to the doubly degenerate vibration of this molecule has been studied in [254]. This band is observed as a vibration–rotation band with the branches O, P, Q, R, S corresponding to the appropriate selection rules. An interesting feature was detected in the spectrum of this band: the distance between two successive lines in the O- and S-branches was not equal to double the corresponding distance in P- and R-branches. Analysis of the spectrum showed that the excited vibrational state with a given J splits into two sublevels, α and β in this case, with selection rules of the form $\Delta J = 0, \pm 1$ for sublevel α, and $\Delta J = \pm 2$ for sublevel β.

The triply degenerate vibrational band v_3 of the methane molecule was studied under high resolution by Stoicheff [63]. The complex structure of this band fits the theory, but no complete analysis has been carried out.

No consistent theory has been developed so far for the structure of the vibration–rotation bands in the Raman spectra of asymmetrical top molecules. The analysis of the experimental material for these molecules is generally based on the symmetrical top model, and the real molecule is only assumed to be "slightly asymmetrical."

Extensive material is available about the structure of vibration–rotation bands in IR spectra. A survey of the various data will be found in [255].

The reason for the fairly large width of the highly polarized vibrational lines should be established. For these lines, the Q-branch of the isotropic part of the scattering tensor is the most significant. For linear molecules and symmetrical top molecules, in accordance with the selection rule $\Delta K = 0$, the individual components of the Q-branch with different J overlap, forming a sharp line. The width of these lines was first measured by Sterin [256], who used a Fabry–Perot interferometer. He studied the benzene 992 cm^{-1} line and the cyclohexane 802 cm^{-1} line; both these molecules are symmetrical tops. The width of these lines was found to be about 2 cm^{-1}, and it hardly changed on passing from liquid to vapor.

In view of the low depolarization of these lines $\rho \approx 0.05$, the contribution from anisotropic scattering to the Q-branch is negligible and cannot produce a considerable broadening. Sterin considered several alternative broadening mechanisms, including collisional broadening, Doppler effect, and anharmonicity. He came to the conclusion that none of these factors could account satisfactorily for the observed line widths. On the other hand, if we assume that the line widths characterize the mean lifetime of the corresponding excited vibrational states, we are up against serious difficulties. For a line width of 2 cm^{-1}, the lifetime of the vibrational state should be about 10^{-11} sec. The ordinary radiational losses give much higher lifetimes for the symmetrical vibrational states. Energy transfer between vibrational and other degrees of freedom also gives mean lifetimes of 10^{-5}–10^{-7} sec.

An acceptable interpretation of the observed width of these Raman lines was offered by Sobel'man [77]. He argued that the vibrational and the rotational energy of a molecule are separable to first approximation only. Significantly, the moments of inertia in the excited vibrational states of a molecule do not coincide with the moments of inertia in the unexcited states. Calculations allowing for this factor and the anharmonicity of vibrations lead to a splitting of the Q-branch into several components, corresponding to the various values of the rotational quantum number J. For diatomic molecules, according to [20], §82, this splitting is described by an additional term in the expression for the vibration–rotation energy,

$$\Delta E = \alpha \left(v + \tfrac{1}{2}\right) J \left(J + 1\right), \tag{16.28}$$

where

$$\alpha = \frac{6B^2}{\hbar\omega} - \frac{6B^2 a}{M\omega^3} \sqrt{\frac{2}{MB}}. \tag{16.29}$$

Here $B = \hbar^2/2\mathscr{I}_0$ is the rotational constant for the equilibrium configuration of the molecule, M is the molecular mass, a is the coefficient before the cubic term in the expansion of the potential energy in powers of the normal coordinate. In accordance with (16.28), the J-component of the Q-branch is displaced by $\alpha J\,(J+1)$ from the zero component. The intensity of this component is proportional to the probability of excitation of a level with a given J,

$$W(J) = c\,(2J+1)\exp\left[\frac{-\,BJ\,(J+1)}{kT}\right].\tag{16.30}$$

The intensity distribution in the Q-branch is described by the relation

$$I = I_0\sqrt{1 + 4\,\frac{\Delta\omega}{\alpha}}\,\exp\!\left(\frac{-\,B\Delta\omega}{\alpha kT}\right),\tag{16.31}$$

where $\Delta\omega = \omega_J - \omega_0$.

For symmetrical top molecules, such as the benzene and cyclohexane molecules studied by Sterin, the expression for the vibration–rotation energy also acquires an additional term ΔE_i described by a formula analogous to (16.28). This case was studied in detail by Sobel'man [77] and by Kovner and Chaplik [257]. The additional term for the symmetrical vibrations of symmetrical top molecules is

$$\Delta E_i = \alpha^i\,(v_i + \tfrac{1}{2})\left[J\,(J+1) - \tfrac{1}{2}K^2\right],\tag{16.32}$$

where $\alpha^i = \alpha^i_1 + \alpha^i_2 + \alpha^i_3$, and

$$\alpha^i_1 = \frac{\hbar}{2m_i\omega_i}\left(\frac{\partial^2 B}{\partial q_i^2}\right)_0,\qquad \alpha^i_2 = -\,\frac{3\hbar a_i}{m_i^2\omega_i^3}\left(\frac{\partial B}{\partial q_i}\right)_0,$$

$$\alpha^i_3 = -\sum_{j\neq i}\frac{\hbar a_{jii}}{m_i m_j\omega_i\omega_j^2}\left(\frac{\partial B}{\partial q_j}\right)_0.\tag{16.33}$$

Here q_i, q_j are the normal coordinates, a_i, a_{jii} are the coefficients before q_i^3 and $q_j q_i^2$ in the expansion of the potential energy in normal coordinates, ω_i, ω_j are the normal frequencies, m_i, m_j are the harmonic oscillator masses, $B = \hbar^2/2\mathscr{I}_B$, where $\mathscr{I}_B$ is the smaller of the two principal moments of inertia (for benzene $B = 2A$).

The intensity distribution in the Q-branch has the form

$$I = I_0\exp\left(-\,\frac{\hbar B\,\Delta\omega_i}{\alpha^i kT}\right).\tag{16.34}$$

For the line width we have the approximate expression

$$\delta_i = \frac{\alpha^i kT\ln 2}{\hbar B}.\tag{16.35}$$

Expressions for the doubly degenerate vibrations of the benzene molecules were derived by Kovner and Chaplik [257].

An estimate of the constant α_1^i gives $\alpha_1^i = 0.12 \cdot 10^{-3}$ cm^{-1} for the 992 cm^{-1} line, and this leads to a correct order of magnitude for the line width. Calculation of the constants α_2^i, α_3^i involves considerable difficulties, since the anharmonicity coefficients a_i, a_{jii} are not known. Tentative estimates will be found in [77, 257].

After Sterin's work, extensive experimental studies of the widths of the vibrational Raman lines were carried out by Mikhailov [76], who measured the lines of N_2, O_2, and CH_4 at various pressures and temperatures.

The 1555 cm^{-1} vibrational line of oxygen was studied at $t = 27°C$ at pressures between 15 and 125 atm. The Raman spectrum showed a sharp Stokes line corresponding to the Q-branch. The O- and S-branches allowed by the selection rules were seldom observed (at high pressures, a weak diffuse wing appeared in place of the S-branch). Figure 53 shows the observed profile of this oxygen line. The line is clearly asymmetric, with a wing extending toward the exciting line. The observed line width is about 3 cm^{-1}. It is remarkable that neither the line width nor the profile changes as the pressure is raised. The maximum was not observed to shift either.

The spectrum of nitrogen was studied at the same temperature at pressures from 14 to 114 atm. Only the Q-branch of the 2345 cm^{-1} vibrational band was observed, its width being about 3 cm^{-1}. As in the spectrum of oxygen, the line width and profile hardly changed with the increase in pressure.

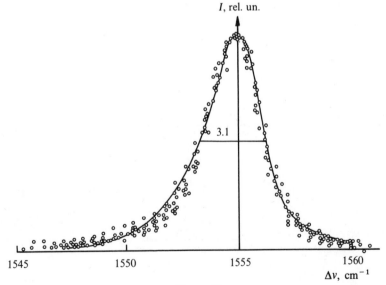

Figure 53

The observed profile of the Q-branch of a vibrational oxygen band excited by the 4358 Å mercury line at pressures from 15 to 125 atm [76]. The dots mark the results of measurements at various pressures, and the solid curve presents the calculated profile.

Thus the width of the vibrational lines is independent of pressure, whereas the width of the rotational Raman lines markedly increases with increasing pressure (see §8). This fact appears to be quite puzzling. Mikhailov treated this behavior of the vibrational lines as a certain hitherto unexplained property of the vibrational transitions. However, this result follows directly from (4.91) if we consider t to be of the order of magnitude of the mean time between molecular collisions. According to this theory, the width of a Raman line is determined by the difference in the widths of the initial and the final levels. In the case of the Q-branch, the initial and the final levels constitute the same rotational level, and it is therefore quite natural that, despite the broadening of this level, the line width remains unchanged.

The profile of the Q-branch of O_2 and N_2 was calculated in [76] assuming that this branch had an unresolved structure associated with the superposition of individual J-components (see (16.28)). The calculation revealed a satisfactory fit with the experimental profile.

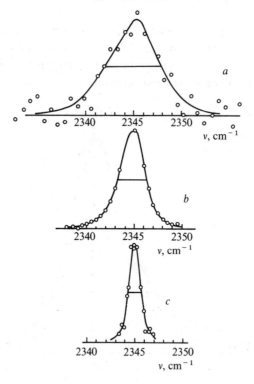

Figure 54

The observed profile of the Q-branch of a vibrational nitrogen band (exciting line, Hg 4358 Å) at various temperatures [76]:

a 200°C, $\delta = 5.7$ cm^{-1}, b 27°C, $\delta = 3.1$ cm^{-1}, c −196°C, $\delta = 1.4$ cm^{-1}.

The results obtained for the Q-branch of the nitrogen vibrational band at various temperatures show that the width markedly increases with the increase in temperature. Figure 54 shows the observed line profiles at various temperatures according to Mikhailov [76]. Note that because of the considerable width of the instrumental function ($\delta_{inst} = 1.0\,\text{cm}^{-1}$), the observed line profile in liquid nitrogen does not correspond to the true line profile: the true line width is substantially less than that appearing in the figure. The observed changes in the width of the Q-branch may be attributed to a change in the distribution of molecules over the rotational levels, described by Eq. (16.30). The growth of line width with temperature fits Eq. (16.35). Line broadening in Raman spectra due to molecular interactions will be considered in the next section.

It follows from the above that the width of the individual J-components of the Q-branch of diatomic molecules in gases at moderate pressures is probably the minimum permissible for Raman lines. Direct experimental detection of these components and measurement of their widths still fall beyond the possibilities of our instruments. Sterin's theoretical estimates [256] give widths of the order of $0.1\,\text{cm}^{-1}$ for these lines. This is considerably greater than the radiation line width, amounting to about $5 \cdot 10^{-4}\,\text{cm}^{-1}$ (see, e.g., [258]). The conditions of applicability of the perturbation theory, formulated in §4, are thus valid even at high exciting power levels.

17. RAMAN SPECTRA AND MOLECULAR INTERACTION

The interaction of molecules in condensed media affects virtually all the parameters of Raman lines. Comparison of the spectra of liquids and gases reveals significant differences. The differentiation is even more pronounced when the Raman spectra of gases and liquids are compared with the spectra of crystals, which possess a number of unique features (see Chapter III).

So far we have considered Raman scattering by an isolated molecule. In most cases, the assumption of an isolated molecule leads to substantial errors in the treatment of condensed media. The molecular interaction can be considered to some approximation as a perturbation which leads to relatively small corrections in the parameters of the Raman lines in rarefied gases. This approach, however, is not always applicable. For example, the temperature dependence of the intensity of Raman lines in liquids is qualitatively different from the theoretical dependence for rarefield gases.

Theoretical analysis of the characteristic features of the Raman spectra in condensed media requires knowledge of the motion and the interaction of molecules in these media. No such analysis is possible with adequate completeness at this stage. Therefore in this section we will mainly consider the experimental data pertaining to Raman spectra in condensed media and only briefly review the principal directions of theoretical interpretation of these data.

1. The effect of molecular interaction on the frequencies of Raman lines

The differences between the vibrational frequencies in gases and in condensed phases (liquid, solution, crystal) have been repeatedly noted in the literature. Vol'kenshtein [259] analyzed the experimental material and came to the conclusion that the frequencies generally decrease on passing to the condensed phase, and the frequency lowering is particularly noticeable for polar compounds (where the relative frequency shift may sometimes reach about 5%). The effect of the solvent on the vibration frequencies of the solute becomes more pronounced as the dipole moment of the solvent molecule increases. Shorygin [260] also found that the frequency of the C=O vibration in solutions depends on the polarity of the solvent. In nonpolar solvents, the frequency of this vibration is close to its value in the gaseous phase.

Systematic studies of the effect of phase transitions and temperature on vibration frequencies were carried out by Sechkarev [261–264]. Polar compounds containing the groups C—Hal, C=O, O—H and others were investigated. Alongside with the previously noted lowering of the frequency from gases to liquids (e.g., the frequencies of the C=O and O—H stretching), an increase of frequency was often observed (Table 35).

A typical dependence of the Raman scattering frequency of a polar substance on temperature and the state of aggregation is shown in Figure 55. We see that the frequency shift in phase transitions is considerably larger than the change in frequency associated with temperature variation.

Raman spectra of zero dipole moment molecules also show a certain phase shift as a result of changes in temperature and phase transitions, although the effects are less pronounced than in the spectra of polar molecules. When the temperature is kept constant, the frequency shift is determined by two factors: the change in density and the change in the state of aggregation. As an example, Figure 56 shows the results of measurements of the methane frequency v_1 [265]. At a constant density, v_1 in the gaseous phase is about 2910 cm^{-1}, in the liquid 2905.2 cm^{-1}, and in the solid state 2903.9 cm^{-1}. The minimum on the frequency vs. density curve is apparently a characteristic feature.

Theoretical analyses of the effect of molecular interaction on the vibrational frequencies have been carried out on several occasions. Nevertheless, no complete theory of these phenomena is avialable so far, and the calculations amount to no more than plausible estimates.

Molecular interactions are generally divided into universal and specific. Universal interactions include the van der Waals forces; after various averaging operations, they can be described as the resultant effect of the dielectric medium on the molecule which is immersed in it. Specific interactions are localized in a group of bonds or molecules. They are clearly directional and lead to the establishment of physico-chemical (as distinct from chemical) bonds between the molecules [266, 267].

Table 35

CHANGES IN VIBRATION FREQUENCIES OF POLAR GROUPS BETWEEN GAS
AND LIQUID PHASE AND AS A RESULT OF TEMPERATURE VARIATION [261–264]

Compound	Polar group	Mode	v_0, cm^{-1}	Δv_{obs}	Δv_{calc}	$\|dv/dT\|_0 \cdot 10^2$, cm^{-1}/deg
Fluorobenzene	C—F	Out-of-plane deformation	220	21	30	6.1
		In-plane deformation	351	14	17	6.9
		Breathing	485	16	5	0.9
Chlorobenzene	C—Cl	Out-of-plane deformation	174	19	17	4.4
		In-plane deformation	271	28	9	2.2
		Breathing	413	6	6	1.1
Bromobenzene	C—Br	Out-of-plane deformation	167	7	10	4.9
		In-plane deformation	239	14	6	1.6
		Breathing	309	2	5	2.7
Toluene	C—CH$_3$	Out-of-plane deformation	214	1	2	1.0
		Breathing	533	-12	-3	<0.4
Acetone	C=O	Deformation	376	14	12	<0.5
		Stretching	1740	-30		3.0
Acetaldehyde	C=O	Deformation	505	5	8	
		Stretching	1740	-10		
Acetyl chloride	C=O	Deformation	429	7	6	1.2
		Stretching	1824	-21		<0.5
	C—Cl	Stretching	606	-14		<0.5
Acetamide	C=O	Deformation	439	9	11	<0.7
		Stretching	1750	-20		<0.7
Acetophenone	C=O	Out-of-plane deformation	145	10	6	5.3
		In-plane deformation	370	0	1	1.1
		Stretching	1700	-14		2.1

Note: $\Delta v = v - v_0$ (v_0 is the frequency in gas, v the frequency in liquid near the boiling point); $|dv/dT|_0$ is the mean temperature change of frequency in the liquid.

The effect of the van der Waals forces on the vibrational frequencies has been treated in some detail by Vol'kenshtein [80, 268] and Sechkarev [261–264]. These authors considered the interaction of molecules whose vibrations are coupled by van der Waals forces. The general procedure is as follows:

Consider a system of n identical molecules. The Langrangian of this system expressed in normal coordinates q can be written in the form

$$L = \tfrac{1}{2} M \sum_{i=1}^{n} \dot{q}_i^2 - \tfrac{1}{2} M \omega_0^2 \sum_{i=1}^{n} q_i^2 - U(q_1, q_2, \ldots, q_n). \qquad (17.1)$$

Here M is a coefficient which depends on the atomic masses and the geometrical

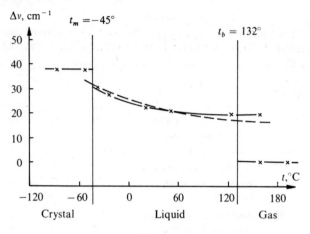

Figure 55

The frequency of a Raman line of a polar compound (chlorobenzene, $v_0 = 174$ cm^{-1}) vs. temperature and state of aggregation [264].

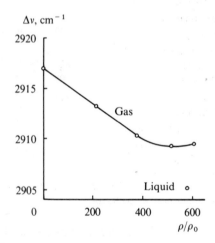

Figure 56

The methane frequency v_1 vs. density and state of aggregation [265].

configuration of the molecule, U is the potential energy of the molecular interaction; the sums are taken over all the molecules. In a noninteracting system, each molecule has the same normal frequency ω_0, which in a system of n molecules can be considered as an n-fold degenerate frequency. The molecular interaction relieves this degeneracy, and the frequency ω_0 splits into n components (and also shifts).

The Lagrangian (17.1) leads to the following set of n equations of motion:

$$M\ddot{q}_i + M\omega_0^2 q_i + \frac{\partial U}{\partial q_i} = 0. \tag{17.2}$$

Series-expanding $\partial U/\partial q_i$ in powers of q_i and retaining only the linear terms, we find

$$\frac{\partial U}{\partial q_i} = C_i - B_i q_i - \sum_{i \neq j} (A_i)_j q_j. \tag{17.3}$$

Here $A_{ji} = A_{ij}$, since the molecules are equivalent with regard to binary interactions. The constant term C_i in (17.3) can be dropped, since it only shifts the equilibrium value q_i, and this is of no consequence at this stage.

Inserting (17.3) in (17.2), we find

$$M\ddot{q}_i + (M\omega_0^2 - B_i)\, q_i - \sum_{i \neq j} A_{ij} q_j = 0. \tag{17.4}$$

The solutions of these differential equations can be written in the form (see §9)

$$q_i = q_{i0} e^{i\omega t}.$$

Inserting this solution in (17.4), we obtain a system of homogeneous linear algebraic equations for the amplitudes q_{i0}, which have a nonzero solution if

$$\begin{vmatrix} \lambda - B_1 & -A_{12} \ldots -A_{1n} \\ -A_{21} & \lambda - B_2 \ldots -A_{2n} \\ \cdot & \cdot \quad \cdot \quad \cdot \quad \cdot \\ -A_{n1} & -A_{n2} \ldots \lambda - B_n \end{vmatrix} = 0. \tag{17.5}$$

Here, for simplicity, we wrote

$$\lambda = M(\omega_0^2 - \omega^2). \tag{17.6}$$

Thus, the original frequency ω_0 is replaced in an interacting system with a set of n close frequencies $\omega_1, \omega_2, \ldots, \omega_n$ corresponding to the roots $\lambda_1, \lambda_2, \ldots, \lambda_n$ of Eq. (17.5). The distribution of the roots ω_i determines the width $\Delta\omega$ and the shape of the Raman line.

The sum of the diagonal elements of the secular determinant (17.5) is equal to the sum of the roots of the corresponding equation. Thus,

$$\sum_{i=1}^{n} \lambda_i \approx 2M\omega_0 \sum_{i=1}^{n} (\omega_0 - \omega_i) = \sum_{i=1}^{n} B_i. \tag{17.7}$$

The mean frequency is defined by the relation

$$\omega = \frac{1}{n} \sum_{i=1}^{n} \omega_i .$$ (17.8)

For the line shift $\delta\omega = \omega - \omega_0$ due to the molecular interaction we thus find

$$\delta\omega = - \frac{1}{2nM\omega_0} \sum_{i=1}^{n} B_i .$$ (17.9)

In particular, for the interaction of two identical molecules (a case treated in [80, 268]), we have

$$B_1 = B_2 = B , \qquad A_{12} = A_{21} = A$$

and Eq. (17.5) takes the form

$$\begin{vmatrix} \lambda - B & - A \\ - A & \lambda - B \end{vmatrix} = 0 .$$

The roots of this equation are

$$\omega = \omega_0 - \frac{B}{2M\omega_0} \pm \frac{A}{2M\omega_0} .$$ (17.10)

The line is thus shifted by the amount

$$\delta\omega = - \frac{B}{2M\omega_0}$$ (17.11)

and splits into two components with spacing

$$\Delta\omega = \frac{A}{M\omega_0} .$$ (17.12)

In a system with numerous interacting molecules, line splitting gives way to line broadening, which is measured as before in terms of the parameter $\Delta\omega$. To first approximation, the interaction of a given molecule with all the adjacent molecules will multiply $\delta\omega$ and $\Delta\omega$ by a factor which is equal to the number of the immediate neighbors of that molecule. For the closest spherical packing, the number of the immediate neighbors is 12. Therefore, the numerical values of $\delta\omega$ and $\Delta\omega$ derived from (17.11) and (17.12) should be multiplied approximately by a factor of 10.

Van der Waals forces are mainly determined by the dipole moment, the polarizability, and the molecular ionization potential. In some cases, the quadrupole moment probably also makes a certain contribution. In the first approximation, the following molecular interactions should be considered.

1. *Orientation interaction*, whereby a molecule of permanent dipole moment μ

is oriented in a certain way in the field of another dipole molecule. Thermal motion counteracts this effect, and the orientation interaction therefore decreases with increasing temperature.

An i-th molecule of dipole moment μ_i sees the electric field E_i of all the other molecules. The potential energy of this interaction is therefore

$$U_i = - E_i \mu_i \cos \phi_i, \tag{17.13}$$

where ϕ_i is the angle between the dipole moment and the direction of the field. Generally it is assumed that

$$U_i \ll kT. \tag{17.14}$$

Averaging the interaction energy over all the possible orientations of a dipole, we obtain the following expression for the potential energy of the orientation interaction of the i-th and k-th molecules with dipole moments μ_i and μ_k (see, e.g., [259]):

$$U_{\mathrm{or}} = - \frac{2}{3R^6} \frac{\mu_i^2 \mu_k^2}{kT}, \tag{17.15}$$

where R is the distance between the interaction molecules.

According to Frenkel [269], relation (17.14) is not true for liquids, and we may actually have a reverse inequality

$$U_i > kT. \tag{17.16}$$

Then the angles ϕ_i may be regarded as sufficiently small, and for the mean specific energy of the orientation interaction of a molecule in a liquid we have [259, 270]

$$U'_{\mathrm{or}} = - s(T) \frac{\mu_i \mu_k}{R^3}. \tag{17.17}$$

Here $s(T)$ is a coefficient which we call the degree of mutual orientation of molecules.

2. *Induction interaction*, associated with the polarizing action of a permanent dipole on the electron cloud of another molecule. This interaction is proportional to the dipole moment μ_i of the i-th molecule and the polarizability α_k of the k-th molecule. If R is much greater than the size of the molecule, we have for the mean energy of the induction interaction [259]

$$U_{\mathrm{ind}} = - \frac{2}{R^6} \mu_i^2 \alpha_k. \tag{17.18}$$

3. *Dispersion interaction*, with a mean binary interaction energy [259]

$$U_{\mathrm{d}} = - \frac{3}{2R^6} \frac{Y_i Y_k}{(Y_i + Y_k)} \alpha_i \alpha_k; \tag{17.19}$$

Y_i, Y_k are the ionization potentials of the two molecules. This interaction is independent of the molecular dipole moment, and is therefore observed for polar and nonpolar molecules alike. The dispersion interaction of molecules is basically a quantum effect.

Note that for large kT, the dependence of the mean interaction energy on the intermolecular distance R is the same in all the three cases: the mean energy is proportional to R^{-6}.

4. *Quadrupole interaction*, which unlike the preceding effects is proportional to R^{-5}. Averaging over all the possible relative orientations of the molecules gives a mean quadrupole energy which is proportional to R^{-10} [20]. This interaction is therefore ignorable compared to the dispersion interaction.

A particular case is observed when one of the molecules is excited (resonance interaction). The mean energy of the dipole interaction is then proportional to R^{-3}, and that of the quadrupole interaction is proportional to R^{-5} (see [20, 56]).

If the mean energy of molecular interaction is known, the Raman frequency shift $\delta\omega$ and the Raman line broadening $\Delta\omega$ can be found without difficulty. Thus, using Eq. (17.15) and expanding $\mu_i(q_i)$, $\mu_k(q_k)$, we find

$$U_{or} = -\frac{2}{2R^6 kT}\left[2\mu_i\mu_k^2\frac{\partial\mu_i}{\partial q_i}q_i + 2\mu_i^2\mu_k\frac{\partial\mu_k}{\partial q_k}q_k + \mu_k^2\left(\frac{\partial\mu_i}{\partial q_i}\right)^2 q_i^2 + \right.$$

$$\left. + \mu_i\mu_k^2\frac{\partial^2\mu_i}{\partial q_i^2}q_i^2 + 4\mu_i\mu_k\frac{\partial\mu_i}{\partial q_i}\frac{\partial\mu_k}{\partial q_k}q_i q_k + \mu_i^2\left(\frac{\partial\mu_k}{\partial q_k}\right)^2 q_k^2 + \mu_i^2\mu_k\frac{\partial^2\mu_k}{\partial q_k^2}q_k^2\right].$$

For the interaction of identical molecules

$$U_{or} = -\frac{2}{3kTR^6}\left[2\mu^3\frac{\partial\mu}{\partial q}(q_i + q_k) + \right.$$

$$\left. + \left(\mu^2\left(\frac{\partial\mu}{\partial q}\right)^2 + \mu^3\frac{\partial^2\mu}{\partial q^2}\right)(q_i^2 + q_k^2) + 4\mu^2\left(\frac{\partial\mu}{\partial q}\right)^2 q_i q_k\right]. \tag{17.20}$$

Comparison with (17.3) yields

$$A_{or} = \frac{8}{3kTR^6}\mu^2\left(\frac{\partial\mu}{\partial q}\right)^2, \qquad B_{or} = \frac{4}{3kTR^6}\left[\mu^2\left(\frac{\partial\mu}{\partial q}\right)^2 + \mu^3\frac{\partial^2\mu}{\partial q^2}\right]. \tag{17.21}$$

Similarly from (17.18) and (17.19) we have

$$A_{ind} = \frac{4}{R^6}\mu\frac{\partial\mu}{\partial q}\frac{\partial\alpha}{\partial q}, \qquad B_{ind} = \frac{2}{R^6}\left[\alpha\left(\frac{\partial\mu}{\partial q}\right)^2 + \alpha\mu\frac{\partial^2\mu}{\partial q^2} + \mu^2\frac{\partial^2\alpha}{\partial q^2}\right], \tag{17.22}$$

$$A_d = \frac{3Y}{4R^6}\left(\frac{\partial \alpha}{\partial q}\right)^2, \qquad B_d = \frac{3Y}{4R^6}\,\alpha\,\frac{\partial^2 \alpha}{\partial q^2}. \tag{17.23}$$

Inserting (17.21)–(17.23) in (17.11) and (17.12), we find the line shift and the line broadening. Vol'kenshtein, in his previously mentioned publications, carried out a tentative calculation for HCl. He found 2% for $\delta\omega/\omega_0$ of the orientation forces, 0.01% for the induction forces, and 0.24% for the dispersion forces. The line broadening was of the same order of magnitude. The results thus show that the shift and the broadening of the vibrational Raman lines are mainly caused by the van der Waals orientation interaction (dipole–dipole interaction).

The significance of the dipole – dipole orientation interaction increases even further if its energy is sufficiently high for the inequality (17.16) to be satisfied. The calculations for this case were carried out by Sechkarev [261–264].

The electrostatic interaction energy of i-th and k-th polar molecules can be written in the form [271]

$$U_{ij} = S_{ij}\Phi_{ij}, \tag{17.24}$$

where

$$S_{ij} = -\,\mu_i\mu_j/R_{ij}^3, \tag{17.25}$$

$$\Phi_{ij} = 2\cos\alpha_{ij}\cos\alpha_{ji} - \sin\alpha_{ij}\sin\alpha_{ji}\cos\psi_{ij}\,; \tag{17.26}$$

α_{ij} and α_{ji} are the angles between the polar axes of the molecules and the vector R_{ij}, ψ_{ij} is the dihedral angle between the two planes through the vector R_{ij} and the vectors μ_i and μ_j, respectively. The total energy of molecular interaction is

$$U = \tfrac{1}{2}\sum_{i,j} U_{ij} = \tfrac{1}{2}\sum_{i,j} S_{ij}\Phi_{ij}. \tag{17.27}$$

Let us expand the function U in powers of q_i, q_j, assuming that the relative position of the molecules does not change significantly during one period of vibration, i.e., R_{ij} may be treated as constant. In this expansion, we need only consider the quadratic terms.

$$[U] = \tfrac{1}{2}\sum_{i,j}\Phi_{ij}\frac{\partial^2 S_{ij}}{\partial q_i^2}q_i^2 + \sum_{i,j}\Phi_{ij}\frac{\partial^2 S_{ij}}{\partial q_i\partial q_j}q_iq_j + \tfrac{1}{2}\sum_{i,j}S_{ij}\frac{\partial^2 \Phi_{ij}}{\partial q_i^2}q_i^2 + \sum_{i,j}S_{ij}\frac{\partial^2 \Phi_{ij}}{\partial q_i\partial q_j}q_iq_j. \tag{17.28}$$

Since for identical molecules $\mu_i = \mu_j = \mu$, we obtain

$$\frac{\partial^2 S_{ij}}{\partial q_i^2} = \frac{1}{\mu}\,S_{ij}\frac{\partial^2\mu}{\partial q_i^2}, \qquad \frac{\partial^2 S_{ij}}{\partial q_i\partial q_j} = \frac{1}{\mu^2}\,S_{ij}\left(\frac{\partial\mu}{\partial q_i}\right)^2. \tag{17.29}$$

To simplify the problem we take $\cos \psi_{ij} = 1$ in (17.26). Then $\Phi_{ij} = \Phi_{ji}$, and also

$$\frac{\partial^2 \Phi_{ij}}{\partial \alpha_{ij}^2} = -\Phi_{ij}, \qquad \frac{\partial^2 \Phi_{ij}}{\partial \alpha_{ij} \partial \alpha_{ji}} = 2 \sin \alpha_{ij} \sin \alpha_{ji} - \cos \alpha_{ij} \cos \alpha_{ji} .$$

For small angles α_{ij} and α_{ji}, we have approximately

$$\frac{\partial^2 \Phi_{ij}}{\partial \alpha_{ij} \partial \alpha_{ji}} = -\tfrac{1}{2} \Phi_{ij} .$$

Then

$$\frac{\partial^2 \Phi_{ij}}{\partial q_i^2} = -\Phi_{ij} \left(\frac{\partial \alpha}{\partial q_i} \right)^2, \qquad \frac{\partial^2 \Phi_{ij}}{\partial q_i \partial q_j} = -\tfrac{1}{2} \Phi_{ij} \left(\frac{\partial \alpha}{\partial q_i} \right)^2 . \tag{17.30}$$

Inserting (17.29) and (17.30) in (17.28), we find

$$[U] = \frac{1}{2\mu} \left(\frac{\partial^2 \mu}{\partial q_i^2} \right)_0 \sum_{i,j} S_{ij} \Phi_{ij} q_i^2 + \frac{1}{\mu^2} \left(\frac{\partial \mu}{\partial q_i} \right)_0^2 \sum_{i,j} S_{ij} \Phi_{ij} q_i q_j -$$

$$- \frac{1}{2} \left(\frac{\partial \alpha}{\partial q_i} \right)_0^2 \sum_{i,j} S_{ij} \Phi_{ij} q_i^2 - \frac{1}{2} \left(\frac{\partial \alpha}{\partial q_i} \right)_0^2 \sum_{i,j} S_{ij} \Phi_{ij} q_i q_j . \tag{17.31}$$

Differentiating with respect to q_i, we obtain for the coefficients A_i, B_i in (17.3)

$$B_i = -\left[\frac{1}{\mu} \left(\frac{\partial^2 \mu}{\partial q_i^2} \right)_0 - \left(\frac{\partial \alpha}{\partial q_i} \right)_0^2 \right] \sum_{j=1}^{n} S_{ij} \Phi_{ij} , \tag{17.32}$$

$$A_i = -\left[\frac{1}{\mu^2} \left(\frac{\partial \mu}{\partial q_i} \right)_0^2 - \frac{1}{2} \left(\frac{\partial \alpha}{\partial q_i} \right)_0^2 \right] \sum_{j=1}^{n} S_{ij} \Phi_{ij} . \tag{17.33}$$

Hence

$$\sum_{i=1}^{n} B_i = -2 \left[\frac{1}{\mu} \left(\frac{\partial^2 \mu}{\partial q^2} \right)_0 - \left(\frac{\partial \alpha}{\partial q} \right)_0^2 \right] U . \tag{17.34}$$

For the frequency shift we have from (17.9)

$$\delta \omega = \left[\frac{1}{\mu} \left(\frac{\partial^2 \mu}{\partial q^2} \right)_0 - \left(\frac{\partial \alpha}{\partial q} \right)_0^2 \right] \frac{U}{n M \omega_0} . \tag{17.35}$$

The ratio $U' = U/n$ is the mean interaction energy per one molecule. Using (17.17) and (17.35), we find

$$\delta \omega = -\left[\frac{1}{\mu} \left(\frac{\partial^2 \mu}{\partial q^2} \right)_0 - \left(\frac{\partial \alpha}{\partial q} \right)_0^2 \right] \frac{s \mu^2}{M \omega_0 R^3} . \tag{17.36}$$

Eq. (17.36), according to Sechkarev [261–264], gives a better fit to measurement results than Eq. (17.21). Calculations based on (17.36) give correct orders of magnitude for the frequency shift $\delta\omega$ between gas and liquid. Moreover, this relation explains the frequency shifts toward both higher and lower frequencies.

The frequency shift caused by the molecular interaction can be presented in a slightly different form, namely as the result of the interaction of the vibrating molecule with the internal field E_i set up by all the other molecules. In accordance with this interpretation, we replace U/n in (17.35) with U_i from (17.13); then

$$\delta\omega = -\left[\frac{1}{\mu}\left(\frac{\partial^2\mu}{\partial q^2}\right)_0 - \left(\frac{\partial\alpha}{\partial q}\right)_0^2\right]\frac{\mu E_i}{M\omega_0} \tag{17.37}$$

(in (17.13) we took $\cos\phi = 1$).

The problem of the internal field is one of the most involved topics in the theory of liquids and other condensed media. We cannot discuss it here in any detail. According to Kirkwood's approximate theory [272, 80]

$$E_i = \frac{(\varepsilon - 1)}{(2\varepsilon + 1)}\frac{2\mu}{R^3}, \tag{17.38}$$

where ε is the dielectric constant of the medium. Inserting this expression in (17.37), we find

$$\frac{\delta\omega}{\omega_0} = C\frac{\varepsilon - 1}{2\varepsilon + 1}, \tag{17.39}$$

$$C = -\left[\left(\frac{\partial^2\mu}{\partial q^2}\right)_0 - \mu\left(\frac{\partial\alpha}{\partial q}\right)_0^2\right]\frac{2\mu}{M\omega_0^2 R^3}. \tag{17.40}$$

Eq. (17.39) was originally derived by Kirkwood. The expression in brackets in (17.40) changes depending on the actual assumptions regarding the magnitude of the internal field. Comparison of Eq. (17.39) with experimental data, assuming that $U_i \ll kT$ and

$$C = -\left[\frac{1}{\mu}\left(\frac{\partial\mu}{\partial q}\right)_0^2 + \left(\frac{\partial^2\mu}{\partial q^2}\right)_0\right]\frac{2\mu}{M\omega_0^2 R^3}, \tag{17.41}$$

gives a correct order of magnitude for $\delta\omega/\omega_0$. However, the numerical values of $\delta\omega/\omega_0$ and the sign of the frequency shift do not agree with the experimental findings [267].

2. Molecular interaction and Raman line widths in liquids

The Raman line width in liquids varies between wide limits: from $1.5-2.0 \text{ cm}^{-1}$ to $15-20 \text{ cm}^{-1}$ and wider. The line width is sensitive to the symmetry and the shape of the vibration mode, and also to temperature. In gas–liquid and liquid–crystal phase transitions, the line width generally changes abruptly and discontinuously.

A typical temperature curve of the Raman line width is shown in Figure 57 (according to Rakov [273]). The temperature dependence of the line width for depolarized lines is much more prominent than for polarized lines. The abrupt change in line width in liquid-to-crystal phase transitions is also more significant for depolarized lines. As an example, Table 36 lists the results of line width measurements for two compounds in liquid and solid state (δ_{liq} and δ_{cr}) [273]. Similar results were derived in [274–278]. Raman spectra of polar compounds show wider lines than nonpolar compounds, and the increase of line width with temperature follows a steeper curve [264].

The relation of the Raman line width to the viscosity of liquids, observed by Rakov [273, 278], is a highly significant effect. The width of depolarized and weakly polarized lines is proportional to $1/\eta$, where η is the viscosity (Figure 58).

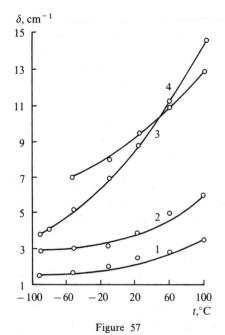

Figure 57

The width of the Raman line of toluene vs. temperature [273]:

1) $v = 786 \text{ cm}^{-1}$, $\rho = 0.09$;   2) $v = 1211 \text{ cm}^{-1}$, $\rho = 0.13$;   3) $v = 217 \text{ cm}^{-1}$, $\rho = 0.87$;
4) $v = 623 \text{ cm}^{-1}$, $\rho = 0.73$.

Table 36

CHANGES IN RAMAN LINE WIDTH IN LIQUID-TO-CRYSTAL PHASE TRANSITION

Compound	Δv, cm^{-1}	ρ	δ_{liq}, cm^{-1}	δ_{cr}, cm^{-1}	$\delta_{liq}-\delta_{cr}$, cm^{-1}
Benzene	606	0.86	6.6	1.9	4.7
	992	0.06	1.7	0.9	0.8
	1586	0.81	12.5	2.3	10.2
	3062	0.30	7.8	3.6	4.2
Paradichlorobenzene	298	0.73	6.0	1.0	5.0
	331	0.21	3.0	1.0	2.0
	627	0.86	2.5	1.0	1.5
	747	0.06	2.5	2.0	0.5
	1578	0.67	5.0	4.0	1.0
	3064	0.86	11.0	6.0	5.0
	3072	0.39	8.5	5.0	3.5

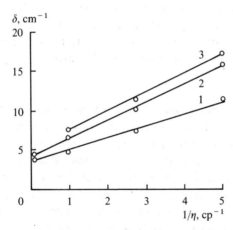

Figure 58

The line width of isopentane vs. $1/\eta$:

1) $v = 954$ cm^{-1}, $\rho = 0.5$; 2) $v = 909$ cm^{-1}, $\rho = 0.7$; 3) $v = 1147$ cm^{-1}, $\rho = 0.7$.

A number of regular features pertaining to the Raman line widths in liquids can be interpreted on the basis of the theory of thermal movement of molecules in liquids. According to Frenkel [269], the thermal movement of molecules in liquids consists of irregular oscillations about a temporary, unstable state of equilibrium. The mean oscillation frequency $1/\tau'$ is close to the vibration frequencies of particles in crystals, and the amplitude of the oscillation depends on the dimensions of the "void" between the given particle and its neighbors. The center of these oscillations is determined by the field of the neighboring particles, and it moves together with these particles.

Because of the high density in liquids and the strong interaction between the liquid molecules, the particles are restrained from moving continuously, and they mainly move by abrupt jerks, suddenly overcoming the potential barrier which separates between the two allowed regions of oscillation of one particle. The mean "sessile" lifetime τ of a molecule in a temporary state of equilibrium between two successive jumps satisfies the inequality

$$\tau \gg \tau'. \tag{17.42}$$

From general statistical considerations

$$\tau = \tau' e^{U/kT}, \tag{17.43}$$

where U is the potential barrier that the molecule should overcome before it can change its equilibrium position. If the molecule has anisotropic properties, its rotation, i.e., change of its orientation, has to be considered in conjunction with the translational motion. Then τ' is interpreted as the period of rotation about some equilibrium orientation, $\tau = \tau_{or}$ is the mean time to change the orientation and $U = U_{or}$ is the potential barrier to be overcome by the molecule if it is to change the orientation. Eq. (17.43) in this case takes the form

$$\tau_{or} = \tau' e^{U_{or}/kT}. \tag{17.44}$$

Sobel'man [279] has shown that the rotatory Brownian movement of molecules accompanied by changes in their orientation leads to a certain broadening of the Raman lines. Sobel'man assumes an anisotropic tensor $\alpha'_{jk} = \partial \alpha_{jk}/\partial q_i$. Then the amplitude E of the scattered light wave is modulated by the rotatory Brownian movement of the molecules. The higher the anisotropy of the tensor α'_{jk}, the greater is the effect of the random orientation changes of the molecules on the amplitude $E(t)$, which may be treated as a random function of time. The relationship between the isotropic and the anisotropic parts of the tensor α'_{jk} also determines the depolarization ρ of the Raman line. Rotatory Brownian movement thus has the maximum effect on depolarized Raman lines and does not affect highly polarized lines.

If a line is completely depolarized, the amplitude of the scattered light wave $E(t)$, being a random function of time, is characterized by the correlation function [280]

$$\phi(\tau) = \overline{E(t)E^*(t+\tau)}. \tag{17.45}$$

The function $\phi(\tau)$ has a maximum for $\tau = 0$ and monotonically decreases with increasing τ. For $\tau \to \infty$, $\phi(\tau) \to 0$. In practice, the correlation vanishes for some $\tau = \tau_{cor}$. For such processes as the process of random orientation changes, the theory generally uses the equation

$$\phi(\tau) = \overline{E^2} e^{-|\tau|/\tau_{cor}} . \tag{17.46}$$

From the correlation function we can find the distribution of line intensities in the spectrum. According to the theory of random stationary processes [280], the correlation function is related to the spectral density of the process, or the line shape in our case, by the equality

$$I(\omega - \omega_0) = \frac{1}{\pi} \operatorname{Re} \int_{-\infty}^{\infty} \phi(\tau) e^{-i(\omega - \omega_0)\tau} \, d\tau . \tag{17.47}$$

Inserting $\phi(\tau)$ from (17.46), we obtain for the line width associated with the rotatory Brownian movement

$$\Delta\omega_{or} = \frac{2}{\tau_{cor}} . \tag{17.48}$$

In this case, the correlation function describes the process of orientation change. The time τ_{cor} is therefore the mean lifetime of a molecule in a certain orientation, $\tau_{cor} = \tau_{or}$.

If the line is partly polarized ($\rho < 6/7$), the anisotropic part should be separated in the tensor α'_{jk}, and the line width $\Delta\omega_{or}$ is assigned by (17.48) to this part of the scattered radiation only. Inserting (17.44) in (17.48), we find

$$\Delta\omega_{or} = \frac{2}{\tau'} e^{U_{or}/kT} , \tag{17.49}$$

i.e., the part of the line width associated with rotatory Brownian movement increases exponentially with the increase in temperature. At low temperatures, $\Delta\omega_{or}$ is negligibly small compared to the "residual" line width $\Delta\omega_{res}$ attributable to other factors. This variation of line width with temperature fits the measurement results of Rakov [273]. According to his data, τ_{or} is of the order of magnitude of 10^{-12} sec, which is in good agreement with the findings of other methods. U_{or} is close to the potential barrier U_v which determines, in Frenkel's theory, the viscosity of the liquid:

$$\eta = \text{const} \cdot e^{U_v/kT} .$$

This accounts for the dependence of line width on the viscosity coefficient (see above).

The theory of line widths in Raman spectra was developed further by Valiev [281–284]. He considered the following factors leading to line broadening:

1) dissipative loss of a vibrational quantum by the molecule, i.e., conversion of vibrational energy into thermal motion;

2) interaction of vibrations with a vicinal force field;

3) Brownian rotation of the molecule;

4) interaction of molecular vibrations with rotation.

The Brownian rotation was considered for a nonspherical rotating molecule in the shape of a symmetrical or an asymmetrical top (see §8). Estimates of the contribution from the various factors to line broadening have shown that for depolarized lines the interaction of molecular vibrations with a vicinal force field produces the same effect as the Brownian rotation. For polarized lines, on the other hand, the interaction factor is the most important.

Estimates of line broadening due to the van der Waals interaction can be obtained by analyzing Eq. (17.5). Tentative calculations [261–264] confirm the significant contribution of this factor to the broadening of Raman lines.

Experimental measurements of the line widths of the polarized components in Raman spectra provided information on the actual contribution of Brownian rotation to the widths of partly polarized lines. As we have noted earlier, Brownian rotation of molecules may affect only the width of the component which corresponds to the anisotropic part of the tensor α'. The other broadening factors may alter the width of both components. Therefore, the difference $\delta_{||} - \delta_{\perp}$ of the two components* characterizes the line broadening associated with Brownian rotation alone.

The Raman line widths of chloroform and deuterochloroform corresponding to the C—H and C—D stretching were measured in [286]. These lines are particularly convenient in that their depolarization is fairly high. The width of each polarized component therefore could be measured separately. Having calculated the ratio I_{isotr}/I for the perpendicular component, the entire line, and the parallel component (associated with the anisotropic part of the tensor α'), we can find by graphical extrapolation the width associates with the isotropic part of the tensor α' (Figure 59). The results are listed in Table 37. We see that Brownian rotation is not particularly significant for these line widths.

In connection with the general problem of line widths in Raman spectra (and especially the widths of polarized lines), let us consider the empirical regularities observed in the spectra of close compounds. The variation of line widths corresponding to symmetrical stretching vibrations in a series of molecules possessing a sufficiently stable characteristic structural element follows a definitely systematic pattern. The widths of the characteristic lines of a given structural element of the molecule (we are dealing with symmetrical stretching lines, which are always highly polarized) vary regularly with changes in the molecular structure. This regular variation can be described as follows [100]:

1) the line width increases as the substituent chain becomes longer; this feature is observed for substituents of moderate chain length;

---

* The subscripts $||$ and $\perp$ represent the orientation of the polaroids which make the electrical vector of the exciting light respectively parallel and perpendicular to the cell axis, in the usual system for photographing the polarized Raman spectra with tubular polaroids.

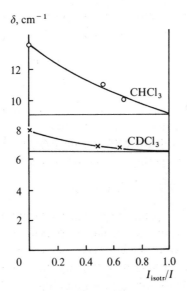

Figure 59

Line width vs. the fraction of isotropic scattering in the total scattered radiation for the 3018 cm^{-1} CHCl$_3$ line and the 2254 cm^{-1} CDCl$_3$ line.

Table 37

THE WIDTH OF DIFFERENT LINE COMPONENTS

	CHCl$_3$	CDCl$_3$
Δv, cm^{-1}	3018	2254
ρ	0.28	0.31
δ_{tot}, cm^{-1}	10	7
$\delta_{\parallel}$, cm^{-1}	13	9
$\delta_{\perp}$, cm^{-1}	9	7
$\delta_{\parallel} - \delta_{\perp}$, cm^{-1}	4	2

2) the line width decreases with an increase in molecular symmetry and with the appearance of additional branch points;

3) the line width varies in the same direction as the depolarization.

These features are qualitative and are not observed exactly. Their importance is that they reveal a definite relationship between line width and molecular structure. (All the spectra were compared under identical conditions).

A more rigorous quantitative formulation of the relationship between the Raman line width and molecular structure can be derived using the invariants of the tensor

α'. The trace b and the anisotropy g^2 of this tensor can be found experimentally for every line by measuring its intensity and depolarization (see §2):

$$g^2 = \frac{I}{6C} \frac{\rho}{(1 + \rho)}, \quad b^2 = \frac{I}{6C} \frac{(6 - 7\rho)}{5(1 + \rho)}. \tag{17.50}$$

Here C is a quantity which was assumed to remain constant for a series of close compounds with identical characteristic elements.

Comparison of the line width δ with the invariants g^2 and b^2 has shown that for highly polarized lines this parameter is related to the anisotropy by the equality

$$\delta = A + Bg^4. \tag{17.51}$$

The coefficients A and B depend on the particular characteristic element in the molecule. Figure 60 plots the curves calculated from (17.51). The experimental points cluster closely around the calculated curves. Deviations from (17.51), apart from measurement errors, are associated with the fact that the anisotropy is apparently not the only factor affecting the width of Raman lines. In particular, the coefficient

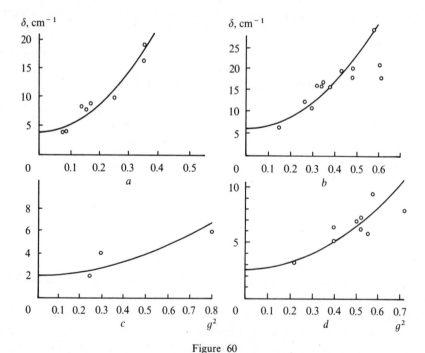

Figure 60

The width of symmetrical lines vs. the anisotropy of the polarizability derivative tensor:

a a quaternary carbon, $\delta = 3.8 + 120g^4$;   *b* a five-membered ring, $\delta = 6.0 + 66g^4$;   *c* a six-membered ring, $\delta = 2.0 + 7.5g^4$;   *d* a double bond C=C, $\delta = 2.5 + 16g^4$.

A is not zero, and this definitely proves that other factors, in addition to anisotropy, affect the line width.

Proceeding from the general relationship expressed by Eq. (17.51), we can readily understand the three qualitative trends of line width variation noted above. Indeed, as the substituent becomes longer, the anisotropy of the tensor α, and hence, for symmetrical lines, of the tensor α', increases, i.e., the line width should also increase. An increase in molecular symmetry and in the number of branch points generally makes the molecule less stretched in one direction, i.e., the anisotropy diminishes and the line width decreases. Finally, the parallel variation of line width and de-polarization follows directly from (17.51), using the expression for the anisotropy (17.50)

We thus conclude that the line widths in the Raman spectra of liquids are affected both by molecular interactions and by molecular structure. The relative significance of the structural factors may vary between wide limits depending on the symmetry and the shape of vibrations.

3. The effect of molecular interaction on the intensity of Raman lines

The effect of molecular interactions is most clearly reflected in the dependence of the intensity of Raman lines on temperature, concentration, and state of aggregation.

As we have noted in §7, the temperature dependence of the line intensities of Raman scattering in liquids shows no fit whatsoever with the theoretical curve. The theory developed for rarefield gases indicates that the line intensity should increase with increasing temperature; it has been experimentally established, however, that in liquids an increase in temperature definitely lowers the intensity of the Raman lines. Note that since an increase in temperature also increases the line width, the only useful characteristic of line intensity is the integrated intensity. When measuring the temperature dependence of Raman line intensities, we should naturally consider such factors as the volume expansion of the liquid on heating and the variation of its refractive index and absorption coefficient; the individual features of the experimental equipment used are also of some relevance. Since the authors were not always careful to allow for all the relevant factors, reliable data on the temperature dependence of line intensities in Raman spectra are very limited.

As an example of the observed temperature dependence of the intensity of Stokes lines in Raman spectra, Figures 61 and 62 plot data for some of the benzene and CCl_4 lines from the measurements of Kondilenko and Babich [286, 287]. As the tempera-ture increases, the line intensity at first drops steeply, but then the decrease is slowed down. The relative change in the intensity of different lines in the same temperature range varies between wide limits. Thus, the intensity of the benzene 1178 cm^{-1} line drops by approximately 50% (see Table 38), whereas the intensity of the 992 cm^{-1} line of the same compound decreases a few percent only. Contrary to the

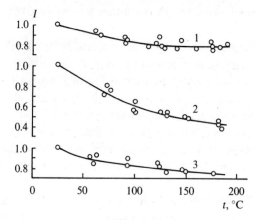

Figure 61

The intensity of the benzene Raman lines vs. temperature [286, 287]:

1) $v = 3060\ \text{cm}^{-1}$, 2) $v = 1178\ \text{cm}^{-1}$, 3) $v = 992\ \text{cm}^{-1}$.

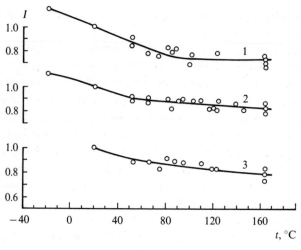

Figure 62

The intensity of the CCl_4 Raman lines vs. temperature [286, 287]:

1) $v = 459\ \text{cm}^{-1}$, 2) $v = 313\ \text{cm}^{-1}$, 3) $v = 217\ \text{cm}^{-1}$.

predictions of some authors, the changes in intensity do not appear to correlate with the type of vibrations. Thus, in [288] it was suggested that deformation vibrations were more sensitive to changes in temperature than the stretching vibrations. However, the experimental data of [287] show that in CCl_4 the intensity of the

Table 38

THE INTENSITY OF STOKES LINES IN THE RAMAN SPECTRA OF BENZENE
AND ITS MONOSUBSTITUENTS AT VARIOUS TEMPERATURES

Compound	$\Delta\nu$, cm^{-1}	ρ	I, relative units				ΔI, % for 100°C
			25°C		70°C		
Benzene	607	0.88	15		13		28
	992	0.11	100		74		52
	1586	0.81	16		14		26
	1606	0.80	10		9		26
			−10°C	25°C	60°C	100°C	
Toluene	521	0.61	33	30	29	27	18
	623	0.73	25	23	23	19	27
	786	0.09	63	57	53	50	19
	1004	0.07	110	100	94	89	17
	1031	0.10	32	29	27	26	16
	1211	0.13	35	35	33	31	15
	1586	0.76	19	17	16	14	25
	1606	0.70	42	38	35	31	25
			25°C	80°C	125°C		
Hexylbenzene C—C—C—C—C—C	623	0.90	21	20	19		7
	1003	0.11	100	96	94		6
	1031	0.09	34	34	33		4
	1584	0.77	19	18	18		6
	1606	0.76	57	55	53		7

symmetrical 459 cm^{-1} line decreases by 25% when the liquid is heated from 20 to 165°C, whereas the intensity of the deformation lines at 313 and 217 cm^{-1} decreases by 7 and 16%, respectively. Similar conclusions emerge in the work of Bazhulin and Sokolovskaya [289–292] and of Rea [293].

It would seem that the temperature dependence of line intensities in Raman spectra should be more pronounced for polar molecules, but the measurements of Sokolovskaya fail to detect any effect of this kind. In [292], the line intensities were measured at various temperatures for a number of compounds with different dipole moments μ. The results of these measurements are listed in Table 39. We see from the table that the largest temperature changes in line intensity were observed in the spectrum of CS_2, which has $\mu = 0$. The spectra of molecules with substantially

Table 39

STOKES AND ANTI-STOKES LINE INTENSITIES IN RAMAN SPECTRA AS A FUNCTION OF TEMPERATURE (I in relative units)

Δv, cm^{-1}	t, °C	I_{st}		I_{ast}		I_{st}/I_{ast} exp.	$\left(\dfrac{v-v_j}{v+v_j}\right)^4 \times$ $\times e^{hv_j/kT}$
		exp.	theor.	exp.	theor.		
				CCl$_4$			
217	−20	100	81	31	25	3.2	3.2
	+25	87	87	33	32	2.6	2.7
	+70	75	96	37	40	2.0	2.4
314	−20	105	91	19	17	5.5	5.4
	+25	97	97	23	24	4.2	4.0
	+70	83	104	26	31	3.2	3.4
459	−20	104	96	9	8.3	11.6	11.5
	+25	100	100	11	11	9.1	9.1
	+70	85	104	12	18	6.8	5.8
				CHCl$_3$			
366	−40	114	91	13.7	10.6	8.3	8.6
	+25	98	98	20	19	4.8	5.1
	+60	88	103	22	24	4.0	4.3
665	+25	100	110	5.1	4.9	19.4	20.4
	+60	94	103	7	7.4	13.5	14.0
				C$_6$H$_6$			
992	+25	100	100	1.1	1.15	91	87
	+70	74	103	1.8	2.3	42	45
				CS$_2$			
656	−50	198	98	2.4	1.8	80	66
	−20	155	99	3.4	3.0	46	39
	+25	100	100	7.1	5.2	14	12

different dipole moments showed fairly constant changes in intensity. The dipole moment of the scattering molecule therefore cannot be related directly to the observed temperature effect.

The above data referred to Stokes lines in Raman spectra. The intensity of the anti-Stokes lines does not change with the increase in temperature or increases more slowly than the theoretical rate (see §7). The intensity ratio of the Stokes and the anti-Stokes line components, however, is close to the theoretical figure [292]. As an example, Table 39 lists the results of measurements [292] for some compounds at various temperatures. We see that the experimental intensity ratio I_{st}/I_{ast} coincides with the theoretical figure (within the margin of experimental error). Hence it follows that the relative population of the vibrational levels of molecules in liquids corresponds to the theoretical population calculated for noninteracting molecules. The effect of molecular interaction on line intensities, according to these data, is thus the same for the Stokes and the anti-Stokes components, and the change in molecular interaction with temperature is not reflected in the intensity ratio of these components. In vapors, where the molecular interaction is very small, the temperature dependence of the intensity of Raman lines is close to the theoretical figure (see §7).

Sokolovskaya [292] is so far the only author who studied the change in the intensity of Raman lines between liquid and vapor. Sokolovskaya's measurements show that the line intensity (per one molecule) in the liquid is higher than the line intensity in the vapor phase. The ratio I_{liq}/I_v is a function of temperature. At $t = 60°C$, this ratio ranges from 1.42 (the $CHCl_3$ 665 cm^{-1} line) to 2.50 (the benzene 992 cm^{-1} line). At $t = 120°C$, the corresponding ratios are 1.24 and 1.40. For CS_2, the intensity ratio of the 656 cm^{-1} line in liquid and in vapor was found to be substantially higher: 7.40 at $t = 40°C$ and 3.30 at $t = 80°C$.

The variation of line intensity in solutions as a function of concentration should provide valuable information about the effect of molecular interaction on line intensities in Raman spectra. In the absence of molecular interaction, the line intensities are proportional to the number of scattering molecules, i.e., generally, to the volume concentration c of the scattering component in the mixture:

$$I = Kc, \qquad (17.52)$$

where K is a constant. This dependence is often observed in liquid mixtures also, e.g., in mixtures of structurally close hydrocarbons [294–299].

Deviations from the linear dependence (17.52) are possible because the volume of the mixture is not equal to the combined volume of the component and because the refractive index changes upon mixing. These "apparent" changes in intensity are readily corrected for, and we will not consider them here. In some cases, apparent changes in intensity may be produced by partial overlapping of the lines of different components [294].

A "true" breakdown of proportionality between the intensity of Raman lines and the concentration of the scattering molecules is possible when molecular compounds are formed [300, 301]. Frequent deviations from the linear relation (17.52) are also associated with the effect of molecular interaction [302–308].

Deviations from proportionality between line intensity and concentration are most pronounced at low concentrations. As an example, Figure 63 shows the results of intensity measurements for the CCl_4 459 cm^{-1} line in various solvents [308].

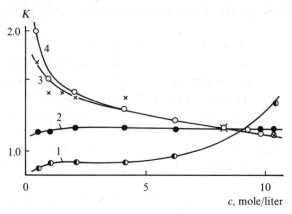

Figure 63

The intensity of the CCl_4 459 cm^{-1} line vs. concentration in various solvents [308]:

1) methyl alcohol,   2) chloroform,   3) benzene,   4) toluene.

We see that the ratio $K = I/c$ at low concentrations may decrease, increase, or remain constant depending on the particular solvent used.

4. Specific molecular interactions and their effect on Raman spectra

The so-called hydrogen bond is a special type of molecular interaction whose spectroscopic features have been studied in considerable detail. Compounds containing the O—H group show a number of anomalous properties, which are attributable to the strong forces acting between the molecules [160, 309, 310]. Generally it is assumed that a special "hydrogen bond" is formed between molecules containing O—H groups, and as a result molecular aggregates occur in the medium. Estimates of the energy of the hydrogen bond give figures ranging from 4 to 8 kcal/mole, i.e., several times higher than the energy of the ordinary van der Waals interaction (1–2 kcal/mole). Note that a hydrogen bond is formed not only between molecules with O—H groups, but also between molecules with F—N, N—H and some other groups.

The spectra of compounds with molecules containing the O—H group show certain characteristic changes in phase transitions. Thus, the Raman spectrum of water has a wide band (some 400 cm^{-1} wide) with a maximum around 3460 cm^{-1}, which is attributable to the vibrations of the O—H group. On the other hand, in the spectrum of water vapor, at low pressures, only a narrow line is observed at 3654 cm^{-1}. The frequency shift in this case amounts to some 200 cm^{-1}, or about 6%. Similar changes are observed in the spectra of other compounds with OH groups, whereas other frequencies, e.g., those of CH_2 and CH_3 groups, hardly change.

Landsberg and Ukholin [311, 312] carried out systematic measurements of the effect of density and temperature on the vibrations of the OH group. They studied the frequency variation of the Raman line of the OH group in water and methanol with increasing temperature of the liquid, i.e., with increasing mean intermolecular distance. As water was gradually heated from 60 to 320°C and the density varied from 0.98 to 0.66, the maximum of the wide hydroxyl band shifted from 3448 cm^{-1} to 3530 cm^{-1}, and the band became narrower. At 350°C, the maximum of the band occurred at 3530 cm^{-1}. In the critical state (380° C, density 0.33), the maximum was observed at the same frequency, i.e., despite the considerable change in density on passing through the critical point, no spectral changes were observed. In superheated steam, at 360°C and density 0.133, still no changes in the spectrum were observed. It was only at a density of 0.096 that a narrow line at 3646 cm^{-1} appeared, supplementing the wide band with a maximum at 3630 cm^{-1}. At 330°C and density of 0.055, only this narrow line remained in the spectrum. Finally, at 250°C and density of 0.0135, this line split into two components, 3639 cm^{-1} and 3653 cm^{-1}.

The wide band is apparently attributable to the presence of associated molecules, whereas the narrow line corresponds to isolated molecules. The simultaneous presence of the band and the line in the spectrum under certain conditions therefore points to the existence of an equilibrium state between isolated and associated molecules. Temperature variation only displaces this equilibrium, but does not break the bonds in the molecular aggregates. The most significant parameter in this respect is apparently the mean intermolecular distance. As the density ρ of water decreases from 1 to 0.06, the mean intermolecular distance increases from 3 to 8 Å. In this range of densities, the spectrum shows a wide band, which indicates that a considerable proportion of the molecules occur in the associated state. It is only at mean intermolecular distances in excess of 10 Å that all the molecules are virtually isolated and the band disappears.

Associations of molecules containing OH groups can be broken up by dissolving the compound in solvents without OH groups. Extensive studies in this direction were carried out by Landsberg and Malyshev [160, 313–316]. This method proved exceedingly fruitful for studying the effect of the solvent on the vibrations of the O—H bond. Molecular interactions were studied from the changes in the spectra of OH groups which were observed when the compound was dissolved in various solvents.

If the interaction of solute molecules with solvent molecules is not pronounced, the change of solute concentration leads only to effects associated with the change in the mean distance between OH groups. Thus a decrease of methanol concentration in CCl_4 produces spectral changes not unlike those observed when the steam density is lowered. The spectrum of pure methanol shows a characteristic wide band peaked around 3370 cm^{-1}. The spectrum of a 1 vol. % solution of methanol in CCl_4 shows a sharp line at 3647 cm^{-1}, replacing the wide band (Figure 64). At

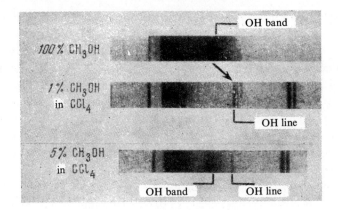

Figure 64

Raman spectra of methanol and 1 % and 5 % solutions of methanol in CCl_4 [160, 313–316].

methanol concentrations of 2 % and higher, both the band and the line are observed simultaneously, and their relative intensity varies smoothly as a function of concentration. When methanol is dissolved in other neutral nonpolar solvents, the general changes in Raman spectra follow the same pattern, although the exact frequency of the line of isolated molecules and the width of this line are seen to change. Thus, in 5 % solutions of methanol in cyclohexane and hexane at 50°C, the molecular line occurs at 3653 cm^{-1} and is about 20 cm^{-1} wide, whereas in benzene this line is observed at 3611 cm^{-1} and its width is 40 cm^{-1}. Hence the conclusion that the interaction between benzene and methanol molecules is stronger than the interaction between methanol molecules and the other two solvents.

If the solvent molecules are permanent dipoles, the vibration lines of the OH groups of unassociated methanol molecules show a certain frequency shift and become broader. In the spectrum of a 2 % solution of methanol in chloroform ($\mu = 1.15 \cdot 10^{-18}$ CGSE), the frequency of this line is 3630 cm^{-1} and its width is about 30 cm^{-1}. However, the dipole moment of the chloroform molecule has a much stronger effect on the intensity of the band of associated molecules. For equal methanol concentrations, the intensity of this band relative to the intensity of the sharp line is much higher in CCl_4 solutions than in $CHCl_3$ solutions. Therefore the dipole moment of the chloroform molecules markedly displaces the equilibrium between associated and free molecules toward free molecules. The dipole moment of the solvent molecules probably interacts with the dipole moment of the methanol molecules, and as a result the latter are restrained from orienting themselves in a way conducive to the formation of associated aggregates.

If the solvent molecules contain an oxygen atom, the maximum of the wide band of associated molecules is markedly shifted. For example, in the spectrum of the solution of methanol in acetone CH_3—CO—CH_3, this maximum corresponds to 3530 cm^{-1}. A similar situation is observed when methanol is dissolved in dioxane $(C_4H_8O_2)$, ethyl ether $((C_2H_5)_2O)$, and other oxygen-containing solvents [314, 315].

A large shift of the band of associated molecules indicates that the interaction of the methanol molecules with the oxygen-containing solvent molecules is strong enough to be regarded as association between the respective molecules. This solvent–solute association competes with the normal association of methanol molecules. The above interpretation of the various changes observed in the Raman spectra is borne out by the studies of ternary mixtures [315, 316]. We have previously noted that a 2% solution of methanol in CCl_4 shows a strong line of isolated methanol molecules and a weak band of associated methanol molecules. If a few percent of acetone is added to this mixture, the spectrum changes: the intensity of the line of isolated molecules drops sharply, and a new band appears at 3530 cm^{-1}, corresponding to the interaction of the methanol OH groups with the acetone oxygen.

Thus studies of Raman spectra reveal the existence of two different interactions— interaction between hydroxyl groups (*hydroxyl bond*) and interaction between an OH group and an oxygen atom (*hydrogen bond*). Schematically, these two interactions can be regarded as two different dimers:

| Hydroxyl bond | Hydrogen bond |

In a number of cases, these simple dimers may form complex aggregates.

Oxygen-containing molecules (acetone, etc.) can be replaced with nitrogen-containing solvents (pyridine C_5H_5N, etc.). In both cases, the spectra show qualitatively similar changes, but the band corresponding to the formation of nitrogenous aggregates is peaked around 3400 cm^{-1} (as compared to 3530 cm^{-1} for oxygen-containing aggregates).

Association of molecules through a hydrogen bond is possible only when the two hydroxyl groups are oriented in a definite way. If certain factors prevent the molecules from approaching one another close enough or from assuming the necessary mutual orientation, the proportion of isolated molecules in the mixture should increase and that of associated molecules decrease. This conclusion was confirmed by the findings of Malyshev and Shishkina [317], who studied the Raman spectra of a number of monobasic alcohols from ethanol (C_2H_5OH) to octanol $(C_8H_{17}OH)$. These authors measured the relative intensity of the line of isolated molecules and the peak intensity of the band of associated molecules; their results are given in Table 40. The measurements were carried out under identical conditions at $75°C$.

Table 40

RELATIVE INTENSITIES OF THE LINES OF ISOLATED MOLECULES AND THE BANDS OF ASSOCIATED MOLECULES IN ALCOHOLS

Alcohol	I_{line}/I_{band}	Alcohol	I_{line}/I_{band}
n-Propanol C_3H_7OH	0.11	n-Octanol $C_8H_{17}OH$	0.54
n-Butanol C_4H_9OH	0.19	Isobutanol C_4H_9OH	0.22
n-Hexanol $C_6H_{13}OH$	0.35	Primary isoamyl alcohol $C_5H_{11}OH$	0.30
n-Heptanol $C_7H_{15}OH$	0.39	Secondary isoamyl alcohol $C_5H_{11}OH$	0.37

We see that an increase in the length of the hydrocarbon radical and in the number of branch points (two factors which hinder the mutual orientation of the hydroxyl groups) lowers the relative intensity of the band of associated molecules.

The hydrogen bond in carboxylic acids deserves special attention. The Raman spectra of these compounds show a band of associated molecules peaked at around 3000 cm^{-1}, i.e., it is markedly displaced compared to the analogous band in alcohols (3370 cm^{-1}). This strong shift may be attributed to the formation of exceptionally stable dimers of the form

$$R-C \underset{O-H...O}{\overset{O...H-O}{\Big\langle \quad \Big\rangle}} C-R,$$

whose existence is borne out by other data. The heat of dissociation of carboxylic acids according to Shubin [318] (see also [320]) is equal to 13.9 kcal/mole for formic acid and 16–17 kcal/mole for the other acids, which gives about 8 kcal/mole for the heat of formation of a single hydrogen bond.

The exceptional stability of the carboxylic acid dimers suggests that the vibration frequencies of this molecular aggregate can probably be observed. The vibrations of one half of the dimer relative to the other should fall in the low-frequency part of the spectrum, since the dimer bond energy is small compared to the usual chemical bond energies. The most comprehensive study of the Raman spectra of carboxylic acids was carried out by Kohlrausch [88]. However, he failed to observe any lines at frequencies below 250 cm^{-1}, except for formic acid which showed a wide band around 200 cm^{-1}. Halford [321] attributed this band to symmetrical stretching vibrations of one half of the dimer relative to the other. Halford's model made it possible to determine the force constant of the hydrogen bond, proceeding from the experimentally observed vibration frequency. The result fitted the value of force constant determined by other methods.

Low-frequency Raman spectra of six carboxylic acids were studied in [322]. Wide lines, whose frequencies are listed in Table 41, were observed in the low-frequency region of the spectrum. Because of the obvious similarity in the position and the width of these lines, they were identified with hydrogen bond vibrations. To check this identification, a simple model of the molecular aggregate was considered, not unlike Halford's model for formic acid. All the dimers of these carboxylic acids can be regarded as composed of two rigid components joined by hydrogen bonds. The dimers of formic and acetic acids have C_{2h} symmetry. The symmetry of the dimers of higher acids may be lower because of stereoisomerism. Of the four possible normal modes of C_{2h} symmetry, the Raman spectrum will show only three (two A_g modes and one B_g mode). Following Halford, the symmetrical stretching vibration of the dimer can be approximately treated as a vibration of a diatomic molecule, where the atomic masses M are each equal to the molecular weight of the corresponding carboxylic acid; the same force constant is assumed for all the acid molecules. (The approximation of the antisymmetrical stretching vibration of the dimer as a vibration of a diatomic molecule, presented in [323], is not convincing in our opinion). Solving the harmonic oscillations of such a diatomic molecule, we find

$$v_1 = v_2 \sqrt{M_2/M_1} ,$$

where v_1 is the vibration frequency of the dimer of one acid, v_2 the vibration frequency of the dimer of another acid, M_1 and M_2 the corresponding molecular weights of the two acids. Taking $v = 197$ cm^{-1} for formic acid (this is a firmly established figure), we calculated the frequencies for other carboxylic acids using the above equality. The experimental and the calculated frequencies, together with the corresponding molecular weights, are listed in Table 41. A satisfactory qualitative fit is observed between the experimental and theoretical frequencies. The 123 cm^{-1} frequency observed in the spectrum of acetic acid apparently does not belong to A_g stretching vibrations. This line can be interpreted only with the aid of the more

Table 41

VIBRATION FREQUENCIES OF DIMERS OF CARBOXYLIC ACIDS

Acid	M, amu	v_{calc}, cm^{-1}	v_{exp}, cm^{-1}
Formic	46	(197)	197
Acetic	60	172	— (A_g)
Acetic	60	—	123 (B_g)
Propionic	74	156	155
Oleic	88	143	143
Isooleic	88	143	134
Isovaleric	102	132	133

detailed calculations of the acetic acid dimer carried out by Miyazawa and Pitzer [324]. According to these authors, the Raman spectrum may show A_g lines at 193 cm^{-1} and 81 (or 95) cm^{-1} and a B_g line at 116 (or 128) cm^{-1} (the different frequencies correspond to different methods of calculation). The last frequency fits the experimentally observed frequency of 123 cm^{-1} [322]. Note that these authors also obtained 180 cm^{-1} for the frequency of the B_u vibrations, which again fits the 176 cm^{-1} frequency observed in the far infrared [323]. This fit bears out the fundamental validity of the calculations in [324].

No A_g line at 170–180 cm^{-1} was observed in the spectrum of acetic acid, apparently because of its low intensity.

Alongside with the direct spectroscopic manifestations of hydrogen bond in the region of stretching vibrations of the O—H group and in the low-frequency region, there are also numerous examples of the effect of this bond on the internal rotations of interacting molecules. Because of the relatively high energy of the hydrogen bond, the force constants of the bonds near the interaction centers are altered, so that the frequencies change and the lines split. The force constants are affected to a particularly great extent if the interaction center is part of a π-electron system. In this respect, the changes in the Raman spectra of pyridine are of considerable interest, since this compound is the strongest known proton acceptor.

The various solvents can be divided into two groups in terms of their effect on pyridine. In CCl$_4$, dioxane, and chloroform, the frequencies of the pyridine lines do not change, and these solvents apparently hardly interact with pyridine. In the spectra of pyridine solutions in water [325–327], alcohols [328–331], and carboxylic acids [326, 327, 332–336], the parameters of some lines change and new lines appear; all this points to a strong interaction of the solvent with pyridine. The changes of the 990 cm^{-1} breathing vibration of the pyridine ring are particularly characteristic in this respect. In aqueous and alcoholic solutions of pyridine, a 997 cm^{-1} line appears next to the 990 cm^{-1} line, its intensity and width varying with the concentration of the solution. As an example, Figure 65 shows the spectra of pyridine and its methanolic solutions according to the data of Rezaev and Vasil'eva [331]. The 997 cm^{-1} line is naturally attributed to the ring vibration of a pyridine molecule associated with solvent molecules. As the pyridine concentration is lowered, the fraction of its molecules in the monomeric state decreases and the proportion of associated molecules increases, which leads to the observed changes in the relative intensities of the 990 and 997 cm^{-1} lines, while the total intensity of these lines remains constant (see [331]).

The effect of temperature on the formation of molecular aggregates in solutions was also investigated in [331]. Ternary mixtures of pyridine, alcohol (or water), and CCl$_4$ were used. With the increase in temperature, a redistribution of intensities between the 990 and 997 cm^{-1} lines was observed. The energy of formation of the hydrogen bond was determined from intensity measurements.

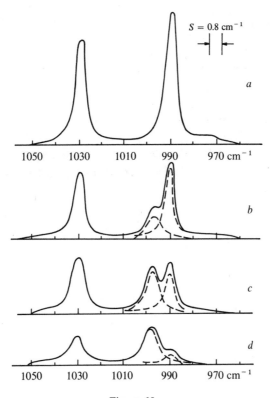

Figure 65

A part of the Raman spectrum of pure pyridine (*a*) and of methanolic solutions of pyridine at concentrations of 4:1 (*b*), 1:1 (*c*), and 1:4 (*d*).

The spectra of pyridine solutions in carboxylic acids show two shifted lines: at 1006 and 1021 cm^{-1}. The effect is explained as follows. First, solvation takes place,

$$C_5H_5N + HO(CO)R = C_5H_5NHO(CO)R ,$$

and the 990 cm^{-1} frequency is changed to 1006 cm^{-1}. At high dilutions, the solvated aggregate dissociates,

$$C_5H_5NHO(CO)R = C_5H_5NH^+ + [O(CO)R]^- ,$$

and the ring frequency rises to 1021 cm^{-1}.

Association of carboxylic acids also alters the frequency of the C=O bond. This effect has been investigated by numerous authors [337–339]. Carboxylic acid monomers are characterized by the highest vibration frequency of the C=O bond (1730–1740 cm^{-1}), cyclic dimers show the lowest frequency (1660–1670 cm^{-1}), and chain molecules occupy the intermediate position.

We have discussed the changes occurring in Raman spectra due to the formation of hydrogen bonds. Similar spectroscopic effects are observed in the more general case of formation of so-called associative aggregates. Associative aggregates are formed without the participation of the physical bridges characterizing the hydrogen bond. Bonds not unlike the hydrogen bond may form if one atomic group is a proton donor while another group (or a single atom) is a proton acceptor. The proton acceptor is characterized by an excess negative charge, e.g., it may have a free electron pair.

Donor–acceptor interaction apparently plays a dominant role in many solutions. Interactions of this kind were studied by methods of Raman spectroscopy by Borod'ko and Syrkin [301].

CHAPTER III

Raman Spectra of Crystals

18. SYMMETRY OF THE CRYSTAL LATTICE

So far we have dealt with light scattering by isolated molecules. Molecular interaction was considered, when necessary, as a certain perturbation. This approach,
however, is generally inapplicable to the scattering by crystals. In crystals, the atoms,
molecules, or ions* are set at small distances from one another and their displacements from the equilibrium positions are correspondingly small. The intermolecular
forces can no longer be treated as a weak perturbation, since they are essentially
responsible for the very existence of the crystal. Moreover, crystals are characterized
by a regular three-dimensional arrangement of atoms and thus show a typical symmetry. This symmetry largely determines the particular properties of the crystal.

We will start with an infinitely extended crystal lattice, ignoring the finite physical
dimensions of the real crystal. Because of the spatial periodicity in the arrangement
of the atoms, parallel translations of the lattice over certain distances and in certain
directions will bring the lattice to coincide with itself. These translations are responsible for what is known as the translational symmetry of the crystal lattice. The
lattice may also be symmetric relative to various rotations and reflections. The
corresponding symmetry elements are identical to those of a molecule (see §9):
these are axes and planes of symmetry and reflection–rotation axes.

Combinations of translations with rotations and reflections constitute special

* For simplicity, we will only use the word atoms for the crystal constituents in the future.

273

symmetry elements of the crystal lattice, not applicable to isolated molecules. Combination of a rotation about an axis with translation along the same axis produces a *screw axis*: a lattice has an n-fold screw axis if it is brought to coincide with itself by a rotation through an angle of $2\pi/n$ around the axis combined with a translation over a certain distance d along the same axis. Combination of reflection with translation in a direction which lies in the plane of mirror reflection produces a *glide-reflection plane*: the lattice has a glide-reflection plane if it can be brought to coincide with itself by a reflection in this plane combined with a translation over a certain distance d in a certain direction lying in the plane of reflection.

Detailed descriptions of crystal structures will be found in various textbooks of physics and crystallography, notably [280, 340–344]. We will therefore give only a very concise survey of the basic concepts, needed for a better understanding of the conventional terminology.

Because of translational symmetry of a crystal, we can choose three basis vectors a_1, a_2, a_3 such that the lattice is invariant under translations by any vector a which is a linear combination of the basis vectors with integral coefficients:

$$a = l_1 a_1 + l_2 a_2 + l_3 a_3. \tag{18.1}$$

The choice of the basis vectors is clearly not single-valued.

The arrangement of atoms in the entire crystal can be defined by specifying the structure of a single unit cell, e.g., the parallelepiped formed by the basis vectors a_1, a_2, a_3. The entire lattice can be treated as an assembly of these unit cells, stacked in some regular manner. The vertices of the unit cells are occupied by identical atoms, i.e., these vertices are equivalent points of the lattice. The set of all these equivalent lattice points which can be brought to coincide with one another by suitable translations constitutes a so-called *Bravais lattice*.

The choice of the unit cell is not single-valued either. An elementary cell can be formed by any triad of basis vectors, resulting in different unit cell shapes.

As an example, let us consider in some detail a body-centered cubic lattice (Figure 66). This structure may be regarded as a cubic lattice with two atoms in the unit cell, or as two interpenetrating simple cubic lattices described by the equations

$$a = l_x a_x + l_y a_y + l_z a_z, \tag{18.2}$$

$$a' = (l_x + \tfrac{1}{2}) a_x + (l_y + \tfrac{1}{2}) a_y + (l_z + \tfrac{1}{2}) a_z, \tag{18.3}$$

where l_x, l_y, l_z are integers. If, however, we write

$$a_1 = \tfrac{1}{2}(-a_x + a_y + a_z),$$

$$a_2 = \tfrac{1}{2}(a_x - a_y + a_z), \tag{18.4}$$

$$a_3 = \tfrac{1}{2}(a_x + a_y - a_z),$$

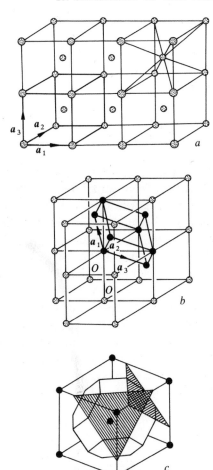

Figure 66

Body-centered cubic lattice:

a) cubic unit cell,   b) basis vectors of the Bravais cell,   c) Wigner–Seitz cell.

the vectors of all the points of the two sublattices are given by

$$a = l_1 a_1 + l_2 a_2 + l_3 a_3 , \qquad (18.5)$$

where l_1, l_2, l_3 are integers. If the sum $(l_1 + l_2 + l_3)$ is odd, the vector defines the cube center, and if the sum is even, we have a vector to one of the cube vertices. This is indeed an example of a Bravais lattice (Figure 66b).

The cubic unit cell can be replaced by the *Wigner–Seitz cell* shown in Figure 66c. The Wigner–Seitz cell is formed by cutting off the cube vertices with planes passing half-way between the vertex and the cube center. The resulting solid has the same symmetry as the cube.

A lattice with the basis vectors

$$b_1 = \frac{1}{v}[a_2 a_3], \qquad b_2 = \frac{1}{v}[a_3 a_1],$$

$$b_3 = \frac{1}{v}[a_1 a_2], \qquad v = a_1[a_2 a_3],$$

(18.6)

is called a *reciprocal lattice*. The so-called Brillouin zone is generally chosen as the unit cell of a reciprocal lattice. To construct the Brillouin zone, we draw vectors to all the points of the reciprocal lattice from the origin and erect perpendicular planes bisecting these vectors. The minimum volume delimited by these planes which contains the origin can be shown to be completely equivalent to the unit cell. The symmetrical polyhedron constructed in this way is known as the *first Brillouin zone*, or simply *Brillouin zone*. It is readily seen that the Brillouin zone is the Wigner–Seitz cell of the reciprocal lattice.

The concepts of a direct and a reciprocal lattice are mutually reciprocal. For example, the body-centered cubic lattice is the reciprocal of the face-centered cubic lattice shown in Figure 67, and *vice versa*. The Brillouin zone of a face-centered lattice is the Wigner–Seitz cell of the body-centered cubic lattice in Figure 66c.

The main applications of the theory of symmetry of crystal lattices involve extensive uses of the mathematical apparatus of the theory of space groups [85–87].

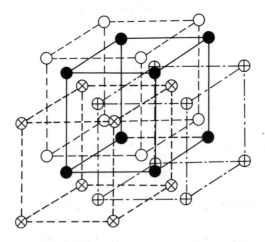

Figure 67

Face-centered cubic lattice represented as a combination of four interpenetrating sublattices.

The set of all the transformations of the space occupied by the crystal which do not alter the equilibrium configuration (merely interchanging identical atoms) is known as the *symmetry group* of the crystal. A lattice always has a certain translational symmetry, and it may also have axes and planes of symmetry.* The set of all the symmetry elements of a crystal lattice constitutes the *space group* of the lattice. Different space groups are classified into crystal classes. There is a total of 230 different space groups.

Each space group contains a translation subgroup which includes all the possible translations moving the lattice onto itself. The elements of the translation subgroup can be written in the form $\{\varepsilon_1 \,|\, a\}$, where ε_1 is the unit element of the group of directions of the crystal, $a = l_1 a_1 + l_2 a_2 + l_3 a_3$.

Space groups are infinite groups. However, the symmetry groups of a crystal may be treated as finite groups if we accept Born's condition of periodicity [345]. According to Born, a sufficiently large number L of translations along each of the vectors a_1, a_2, a_3 will bring the crystal to coincide with itself, i.e.,

$$\{\varepsilon_1 \,|\, a_1\}^L = \{\varepsilon_1 \,|\, a_2\}^L = \{\varepsilon_1 \,|\, a_3\}^L = \{\varepsilon_1 \,|\, 0\}. \tag{18.7}$$

From the condition of periodicity, we have

$$0 \leqq l_1, \, l_2, \, l_3 < L. \tag{18.8}$$

The translation subgroup can thus be treated as a finite group of order $N = L^3$. Moreover, all the translations are commutative, so that this is an Abelian group and all its irreducible representations (N in number) are one-dimensional. These irreducible representations are conveniently treated in the space of the wave vectors k or in the "reciprocal" space defined by the unit vectors

$$b_1 = 2\pi \frac{[a_k a_l]}{(a_i a_k a_l)} \quad (i, \, k, \, l = 1, \, 2, \, 3) \tag{18.9}$$

(these vectors differ from the basis vectors of the reciprocal lattice (18.6) by a factor 2π).

Two vectors in the reciprocal space are called equivalent if their difference is equal to a whole number of basis vectors b_i. The set of the nonequivalent vectors in the reciprocal space can be obtained by considering only the points of the reciprocal space contained in the Brillouin zone spanned by the basis vectors (18.9). The number of these points and the corresponding number of vectors k is equal to N, and each of them corresponds to a certain irreducible representation of the translation group,

---

* The set of rotations and reflections in the symmetry planes of the crystal (proper and improper rotations, § 10) constitutes the *group of directions F*, or the *group of macroscopic symmetry* of the crystal [86]. This group is also known as the *rotation–reflection group, rotation–inversion group*, of the *full orthogonal group*.

whose operators are scalar numbers of the form

$$T(g) = T(\{\varepsilon_1 \,|\, a\}) = e^{ika},$$ (18.10)

and the basis functions are

$$\psi_k = e^{ika}.$$ (18.11)

The reciprocal space has a simple physical meaning. In the system of units with $\hbar = 1$, it coincides with the momentum space of the crystal quasiparticles whose quasimomentum may assume N discrete values only (see §20).

The complete space group G is obtained if the translation subgroup is supplemented with f elements of the form

$$g_j = \{h_j \,|\, \alpha_j\} \quad (j = 1, 2, \ldots, f).$$ (18.12)

Here h_j are the elements of the group of directions,

$$\alpha_j = p_1 a_1 + p_2 a_2 + p_3 a_3 \quad (0 \leqq p_1, p_2, p_3 \leqq 1).$$ (18.13)

In the particular case when all $\alpha_j = 0$, the space group is called symmorphic. The proper and the improper rotations in the crystal are the elements of the symmetry group of the entire crystal, moving into one another the equivalent points, as well as the equivalent directions, in the crystal. If, however, $\alpha_j \neq 0$, the elements of the crystal group include screw axes or glide-reflection planes.

The theory of irreducible representations of the group of directions F enables us to tackle a number of problems which arise in the study of the Raman scattering of crystals. Often, however, we are forced to use representations of the complete space group G. A description of the irreducible representations of the space groups can be found in a number of sources [86, 280, 346–348].

Every representation T of a space group G is characterized by a set $\{k\}$ of vectors from the reciprocal space, such that the entire set is invariant under the rotational elements of the space group. Thus, if $k_i \subset \{k\}$, then also $h_j k_i \subset \{k\}$ ($j = 1, 2, \ldots, f$). This set of vectors $\{k\}$ is known as the *star* of the representation T. The star $\{k\}$ is said to be irreducible if for any two vectors $k_i, k_j \subset \{k\}$ there exists a rotation transforming k_j into k_i. An irreducible star $\{k\}$ corresponds to an irreducible representation of the group G.

To every vector k of the star corresponds a certain subgroup of the group G consisting of elements whose rotation part does not change the vector k. The set of these elements is designated as the group G_k of the vector k or the "small" group. The irreducible representations of the group G_k will be denoted by $\tau_k \{h_j \,|\, \alpha_j\}$. Knowledge of these irreducible representations is in fact sufficient for finding the matrix elements of the entire irreducible representation of the group G. Moreover, in applications, knowledge of the characters of the irreducible representations of G_k is often sufficient.

A group $\hat{G}_k$ whose elements are the rotation elements h_j of the group G_k leaving the vector k invariant is of considerable practical significance. For $k = 0$, $\hat{G}_k$ coincides with the group of directions F.

The irreducible representations of G_k are conveniently constructed by the method of "loaded representations" of $\hat{G}_k$, described in detail in [86, 346]. If every element g of some group G is assigned an operator $T(g)$, such that

$$T(g_1)T(g_2) = T(g_1 g_2)\psi(g_1, g_2), \tag{18.14}$$

where $\psi(g_1, g_2)$ is some function, the resulting correspondence defines a *loaded representation* of the group G. For $\psi \equiv 1$, the loaded representation reduces to an ordinary representation.

To every element h_j of the group $\hat{G}_k$ we assign an operator

$$h_j \rightarrow \hat{\tau}(h_j) = \tau_k \{h_j \mid \alpha\} e^{-ik\alpha}, \tag{18.15}$$

where $\alpha = \alpha_j + a$.

The operators $\hat{\tau}(h_j)$ satisfy the following relation (see [86]):

$$\hat{\tau}(h_s h_t) = \hat{\tau}(h_s)\hat{\tau}(h_t) e^{i(k - h_s^{-1}k, \alpha_t)} \quad (s, t = 1, 2, \ldots, h), \tag{18.16}$$

i.e., they constitute a loaded representation of the group $\hat{G}_k$ with a load

$$\psi(h_s h_t) = \exp[-i(k - h_s^{-1}k, \alpha_t)]. \tag{18.17}$$

Tables of irreducible loaded representations for all the space groups were published by Kovalev [346].

Once the irreducible representations of the group G_k of the vector k have been determined, the matrices of the operators of the irreducible representation T of the entire space group G can be readily found (they have a square-block form) [86].

19. VIBRATIONAL SPECTRA OF CRYSTALS

1. Vibrations of a one-dimensional lattice

Numerous important properties of vibrations of crystals can be elucidated by analyzing the simple model of a one-dimensional lattice [249, 350].

Consider a chain of identical atoms of mass m, distant a from each other. Let u_n be the displacement of the n-th atom from its state of equilibrium. If we only allow interaction between the immediate neighbors, the force F_n on the n-th atom can be written in the form

$$F_n = f(u_{n+1} - u_n) - f(u_n - u_{n-1}), \tag{19.1}$$

where f is the force constant of the lattice. The equation of motion of the n-th atom can be written in the form

$$m\ddot{u}_n = f(u_{n+1} + u_{n-1} - 2u_n).$$ (19.2)

The solution of this equation is sought in the form

$$u_n = u_0 e^{i(\omega t + kna)}.$$ (19.3)

Substituting (19.3) in (19.2), we obtain the condition

$$\omega = \pm 2 \sqrt{\frac{f}{m}} \sin\left(\frac{ka}{2}\right).$$ (19.4)

Eq. (19.4) relating the vibration frequency ω to the wave number k is the *dispersion relation* of our problem. It follows from (19.4) that the maximum frequency ω_m attainable in a chain of identical atoms is $\omega_m = 2\sqrt{f/m}$. This frequency corresponds to wave numbers $k_m = \pm \pi/a$. The range of k values between $-\pi/a$ and $+\pi/a$ is evidently the Brillouin zone of the particular lattice. In crystals, $|k_m| = \pi/a \approx 10^8$ cm^{-1}, $\omega_m \approx 10^{13}$ sec^{-1}. This maximum frequency lies in the infrared.

If the one-dimensional chain consists of N atoms, we have N solutions of the form (19.3) and correspondingly N allowed values of the wave number k lying in the Brillouin zone. This result is consistent with the number of the degrees of freedom of the chain, which is also N. The length L of such a chain is clearly $L = (N - 1)a$.

We have considered a limited chain. However, if L is sufficiently large, we may consider a chain of arbitrarily large length, introducing an additional requirement that the solutions remain periodic over the length L, i.e., we have to assume a condition of periodicity

$$u(na + L) = u(na).$$ (19.5)

Here $L = Na$. The allowed values of k obtained from (19.3) for this case are

$$k = \pm \frac{2\pi}{L}, \quad \pm \frac{4\pi}{L}, \quad \ldots, \quad \pm \frac{(N/2)2\pi}{L}.$$ (19.6)

These values of k define the N vibration modes of the chain.

Let us find the distribution of the number of modes according to the frequencies of the vibrational spectrum. Let $g(\omega)\,d\omega$ be the number of frequencies in an interval from ω to $\omega + d\omega$, and $W(k)\,dk$ the number of modes in an interval between k and $k + dk$. Then

$$g(\omega)\,d\omega = W(k)\left(\frac{dk}{d\omega}\right)d\omega.$$ (19.7)

The derivative $dk/d\omega$ is readily obtained from (19.4):

$$\frac{dk}{d\omega} = \frac{2}{a\sqrt{\omega_m^2 - \omega^2}}.$$ (19.8)

Thus, since the interval $2\pi/L$, according to (19.6), contains only one mode, we find

$$g(\omega)\,d\omega = \frac{N}{\pi\sqrt{\omega_n^2 - \omega^2}}\,d\omega. \tag{19.9}$$

Let us now consider a more complex case: a linear chain of equally spaced alternating atoms of two species, with masses m_1 and m_2. The force constant between the immediate neighbors is f, as before. The unit cell in this case contains two atoms, and the equations of motion grow more complicated. Eq. (19.2) is replaced by a set of two equations (only the interactions between the immediate neighbors are considered)

$$m_1\ddot{u}_{2n} = f(u_{2n+1} + u_{2n-1} - 2u_{2n}),$$

$$m_2\ddot{u}_{2n+1} = f(u_{2n+2} + u_{2n} - 2u_{2n+1}). \tag{19.10}$$

The solutions of these equations are sought in the form

$$u_{2n} = A_1 e^{i(\omega t + 2nka)},$$

$$u_{2n+1} = A_2 e^{i[\omega t + (2n+1)ka]}. \tag{19.11}$$

Inserting this solution in (19.10), we obtain a set of two homogeneous equations

$$-\omega^2 m_1 A_1 = f A_2 (e^{ika} + e^{-ika}) - 2f A_1,$$

$$-\omega^2 m_2 A_2 = f A_1 (e^{ika} + e^{-ika}) - 2f A_2. \tag{19.12}$$

This system has nontrivial solutions for A_1 and A_2 if

$$\begin{vmatrix} 2f - m_1\omega^2 & -2f\cos ka \\ -2f\cos ka & 2f - m_2\omega^2 \end{vmatrix} = 0. \tag{19.13}$$

This gives

$$\omega^2 = f\left(\frac{1}{m_1} + \frac{1}{m_2}\right) \pm f\left[\left(\frac{1}{m_1} + \frac{1}{m_2}\right)^2 - \frac{4\sin^2 ka}{m_1 m_2}\right]^{1/2} \tag{19.14}$$

The dependence of ω on k described by (19.14) is plotted in Figure 68 (it is assumed that $m_1 > m_2$). We see that the dispersion curve has two branches in this case. One of them is the *acoustic branch*, and the other is the *optical branch*. Similar branches are obtained for two-dimensional and three-dimensional lattices.

For a three-dimensional lattice consisting of N unit cells, we have $3Nn$ vibration frequencies which are grouped into $3n$ branches, where n is the number of particles in a unit cell. Three of these branches have frequencies which go to zero for $k \to 0$. These are the three acoustic branches. The remaining $3n - 3$ branches have frequencies which remain finite for $k = 0$. These are the optical branches of the crystal.

The methods for theoretical calculations of the vibration spectrum originally

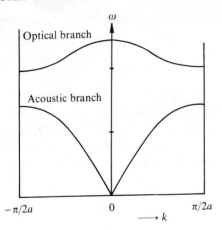

Figure 68

Vibration frequencies of a biatomic chain.

developed for the one-dimensional model were subsequently generalized to three-dimensional lattices. Numerous authors also tried to derive analytical expressions for the frequency distribution function $g(\omega)$. This aspect is discussed in §21.

2. General theory of harmonic vibrations of crystals [351]

Consider a crystal with n particles in its unit cell and $N = L^3$ unit cells inside the volume of periodicity. The position of any atom in the crystal may be described by the vector

$$R\begin{pmatrix} l \\ \kappa \end{pmatrix} = X\begin{pmatrix} l \\ \kappa \end{pmatrix} + u\begin{pmatrix} l \\ \kappa \end{pmatrix} = l + x_\kappa + u\begin{pmatrix} l \\ \kappa \end{pmatrix}, \qquad (19.15)$$

where $l = l_1 a_1 + l_2 a_2 + l_3 a_3$ is a vector defining the position of the unit cell which contains the particular atom, l_i are integers satisfying the inequality $0 \le l_i < L$. The vector x_κ defines the equilibrium position of the atom κ ($\kappa = 1, 2, \ldots, n$) in the

unit cell defined by the vector l; the vector $u\begin{pmatrix} l \\ \kappa \end{pmatrix}$ characterizes the deviation of this

atom from the equilibrium position.

Suitable generalized coordinates for this mechanical system are the $3Nn$ displace-

ments $u_\alpha\begin{pmatrix} l \\ \kappa \end{pmatrix}$ of the atoms from their equilibrium positions in the direction of the

α ($\alpha = 1, 2, 3$) axis in the cartesian system of coordinates. The Hamiltonian and the

Lagrangian of the system in the harmonic approximation have the form

$$H = T + \Phi = \frac{1}{2} \sum_{l\kappa\alpha} m_\kappa \left[\dot{u}_\alpha \begin{pmatrix} l \\ \kappa \end{pmatrix} \right]^2 +$$

$$+ \frac{1}{2} \sum_{\substack{l\kappa\alpha \\ l'\kappa'\alpha'}} \Phi_{\alpha\alpha'} \begin{pmatrix} ll' \\ \kappa\kappa' \end{pmatrix} u_\alpha \begin{pmatrix} l \\ \kappa \end{pmatrix} u_{\alpha'} \begin{pmatrix} l' \\ \kappa' \end{pmatrix}, \tag{19.16}$$

$$L = T - \Phi = \frac{1}{2} \sum_{l\kappa\alpha} m_\kappa \left[\dot{u}_\alpha \begin{pmatrix} l \\ \kappa \end{pmatrix} \right]^2 -$$

$$- \frac{1}{2} \sum_{\substack{l\kappa\alpha \\ l'\kappa'\alpha'}} \Phi_{\alpha\alpha'} \begin{pmatrix} ll' \\ \kappa\kappa' \end{pmatrix} u_\alpha \begin{pmatrix} l \\ \kappa \end{pmatrix} u_\alpha \begin{pmatrix} l' \\ \kappa' \end{pmatrix}. \tag{19.17}$$

Here m_κ is the mass of the atom κ, $\Phi_{\alpha\alpha'} \begin{pmatrix} ll' \\ \kappa\kappa' \end{pmatrix}$ are the second-order coefficients in the expansion of the potential energy in powers of the displacements of the atoms.
The equations of motion take the form

$$m_\kappa \ddot{u}_\alpha \begin{pmatrix} l \\ \kappa \end{pmatrix} + \sum_{l'\kappa'\alpha'} \Phi_{\alpha\alpha'} \begin{pmatrix} ll' \\ \kappa\kappa' \end{pmatrix} u_{\alpha'} \begin{pmatrix} l' \\ \kappa' \end{pmatrix} = 0. \tag{19.18}$$

The solution of (19.18) is sought in the form

$$u_\alpha \begin{pmatrix} l \\ \kappa \end{pmatrix} = u_\alpha^0 \begin{pmatrix} l \\ \kappa \end{pmatrix} e^{-i\omega t}. \tag{19.19}$$

Inserting (19.19) in (19.18), we obtain

$$\sum_{l'\kappa'\alpha'} \left[\Phi_{\alpha\alpha'} \begin{pmatrix} ll' \\ \kappa\kappa' \end{pmatrix} - \omega^2 m_\kappa \delta_{\alpha\alpha'} \delta_{\kappa\kappa'} \delta_{ll'} \right] u_{\alpha'}^0 \begin{pmatrix} l' \\ \kappa' \end{pmatrix} = 0. \tag{19.20}$$

Eqs. (19.20) have a nontrivial solution if the determinant vanishes:

$$\left| \Phi_{\alpha\alpha'} \begin{pmatrix} ll' \\ \kappa\kappa' \end{pmatrix} - \omega^2 m_\kappa \delta_{\alpha\alpha'} \delta_{\kappa\kappa'} \delta_{ll'} \right| = 0. \tag{19.21}$$

Eq. (19.21) is an algebraic equation of degree $3Nn$ in the unknown ω^2. The solution of Eq. (19.20) is a set of $3Nn$ eigenvectors corresponding to the solution of the characteristic equation (19.21) (see §10).

The displacements $u_\alpha^0 \begin{pmatrix} l \\ \kappa \end{pmatrix}$ can be transformed to other, more convenient variables. Because of translational symmetry, suitable variables are the Fourier coefficients $u_\alpha^0 \begin{pmatrix} k \\ \kappa \end{pmatrix}$ in the expansion of $u_\alpha^0 \begin{pmatrix} l \\ \kappa \end{pmatrix}$ in plane waves: ·

$$u_\alpha^0 \begin{pmatrix} l \\ \kappa \end{pmatrix} = \sum_k \frac{1}{\sqrt{m_\kappa N}} u_\alpha^0 \begin{pmatrix} k \\ \kappa \end{pmatrix} e^{ikl}. \tag{19.22}$$

From (19.22),

$$u_\alpha^0 \begin{pmatrix} k \\ \kappa \end{pmatrix} = \sqrt{\frac{m_\kappa}{N}} \sum_l u_\alpha^0 \begin{pmatrix} l \\ \kappa \end{pmatrix} e^{-ikl}. \tag{19.23}$$

Because of the periodic boundary conditions, the vector k may assume a finite number of discrete values:

$$k_x = \pm \frac{2\pi}{La_1}, \quad \pm \frac{4\pi}{La_1}, \quad \dots, \quad \pm \frac{2\pi}{La_1} \frac{L}{2},$$

$$k_y = \pm \frac{2\pi}{La_2}, \quad \pm \frac{4\pi}{La_2}, \quad \dots, \quad \pm \frac{2\pi}{La_2} \frac{L}{2},$$

$$k_z = \pm \frac{2\pi}{La_3}, \quad \pm \frac{4\pi}{La_3}, \quad \dots, \quad \pm \frac{2\pi}{La_3} \frac{L}{2},$$

where a_1, a_2, a_3 are the linear dimensions of the unit cell.

Inserting (19.22), (19.19) in (19.18), we find

$$\sum_{\alpha'\kappa'} \left[D_{\alpha\alpha'} \begin{pmatrix} k \\ \kappa\kappa' \end{pmatrix} - \omega^2 \delta_{\alpha\alpha'} \delta_{\kappa\kappa'} \right] u_{\alpha'}^0 \begin{pmatrix} k \\ \kappa' \end{pmatrix} = 0, \tag{19.24}$$

where

$$D_{\alpha\alpha'} \begin{pmatrix} k \\ \kappa\kappa' \end{pmatrix} = \frac{1}{\sqrt{m_\kappa m_{\kappa'}}} \sum_l \Phi_{\alpha\alpha'} \begin{pmatrix} l \\ \kappa\kappa' \end{pmatrix} e^{-ikl},$$

$$\Phi_{\alpha\alpha'} \begin{pmatrix} l \\ \kappa\kappa' \end{pmatrix} = \Phi_{\alpha\alpha'} \begin{pmatrix} 0 & l \\ \kappa & \kappa' \end{pmatrix}.$$

Eqs. (19.24) are solvable if

$$\left| D_{\alpha\alpha'}\begin{pmatrix} k \\ \kappa\kappa' \end{pmatrix} - \omega^2 \delta_{\alpha\alpha'}\delta_{\kappa\kappa'} \right| = 0 \,. \tag{19.25}$$

Writing $l\left(\kappa \left|\begin{matrix} k \\ j \end{matrix}\right.\right)$ for the eigenvectors of (19.24) and $\omega^2\begin{pmatrix} k \\ j \end{pmatrix}$ for the corresponding

eigenvalues, we obtain

$$\sum_{\kappa'\alpha'} D_{\alpha\alpha'}\begin{pmatrix} k \\ \kappa\kappa' \end{pmatrix} l_{\alpha'}\left(\kappa' \left|\begin{matrix} k \\ j \end{matrix}\right.\right) = \omega^2\begin{pmatrix} k \\ j \end{pmatrix} l_{\alpha}\left(\kappa \left|\begin{matrix} k \\ j \end{matrix}\right.\right) . \tag{19.26}$$

Eq. (19.25) is of order $3n$, so that $j = 1, 2, \ldots, 3n$.

Thus, a three-dimensional lattice consisting of $3nN$ particles has $3nN$ vibration frequencies which are grouped into $3n$ branches. The dependence $\omega = \omega(k)$ obtained from (19.25) is a multivalued function which has $3n$ different values of ω for each value of the vector k (in the absence of degeneracy), and each of these frequencies corresponds to one of the $3n$ branches. The three "acoustic" branches have frequencies ω_{ac} which go to zero for $k \to 0$. The other $3n - 3$ branches are the optical branches.

Eqs. (19.24) give the eigenvectors $l\left(\kappa\left|\begin{matrix} k \\ j \end{matrix}\right.\right)$, apart from a constant factor. We may

therefore choose the eigenvectors so that they are orthonormal:

$$\sum_{\kappa\alpha} l_{\alpha}^*\left(\kappa\left|\begin{matrix} k \\ j \end{matrix}\right.\right) l_{\alpha}\left(\kappa\left|\begin{matrix} k \\ j' \end{matrix}\right.\right) = \delta_{jj'} \,,$$

$$\tag{19.27}$$

$$\sum_{j} l_{\alpha'}^*\left(\kappa'\left|\begin{matrix} k \\ j \end{matrix}\right.\right) l_{\alpha}\left(\kappa\ \begin{matrix} k \\ j \end{matrix}\right) = \delta_{\alpha\alpha'}\delta_{\kappa\kappa'} \,.$$

The Hamiltonian of a crystal is a sum of two quadratic forms which can be diagonalized simultaneously (see §10). This transformation can be accomplished using the expansion

$$u_{\alpha}\begin{pmatrix} l \\ \kappa \end{pmatrix} = \frac{1}{\sqrt{Nm_{\kappa}}} \sum_{kj} l_{\alpha}\left(\kappa\left|\begin{matrix} k \\ j \end{matrix}\right.\right) Q\begin{pmatrix} k \\ j \end{pmatrix} e^{ikl} \,. \tag{19.28}$$

Since $u_{\alpha}\begin{pmatrix} l \\ \kappa \end{pmatrix}$ are real, we have

$$Q^*\begin{pmatrix} k \\ j \end{pmatrix} = Q\begin{pmatrix} -k \\ j \end{pmatrix} . \tag{19.29}$$

Inserting (19.28) in the Hamiltonian and the Lagrangian, we find

$$H = \frac{1}{2} \sum_{kj} \left[\dot{Q}^* \begin{pmatrix} k \\ j \end{pmatrix} \dot{Q} \begin{pmatrix} k \\ j \end{pmatrix} + \omega^2 \begin{pmatrix} k \\ j \end{pmatrix} Q^* \begin{pmatrix} k \\ j \end{pmatrix} Q \begin{pmatrix} k \\ j \end{pmatrix} \right],$$

$$L = \frac{1}{2} \sum_{kj} \left[\dot{Q}^* \begin{pmatrix} k \\ j \end{pmatrix} \dot{Q} \begin{pmatrix} k \\ j \end{pmatrix} - \omega^2 \begin{pmatrix} k \\ j \end{pmatrix} Q^* \begin{pmatrix} k \\ j \end{pmatrix} Q \begin{pmatrix} k \\ j \end{pmatrix} \right]. \qquad (19.30)$$

This leads to the equation of motion

$$\ddot{Q} \begin{pmatrix} k \\ j \end{pmatrix} + \omega^2 \begin{pmatrix} k \\ j \end{pmatrix} Q \begin{pmatrix} k \\ j \end{pmatrix} = 0 \qquad (19.31)$$

whose solution is

$$Q \begin{pmatrix} k \\ j \end{pmatrix} = Q^0 \begin{pmatrix} k \\ j \end{pmatrix} e^{-i\omega t + \phi_0}, \qquad (19.32)$$

where $Q^0 \begin{pmatrix} k \\ j \end{pmatrix}$ is the amplitude of the particular normal mode, and ϕ_0 is the initial

phase. $Q \begin{pmatrix} k \\ j \end{pmatrix}$ are the normal coordinates, and the vibration modes of the atoms

with frequency $\omega \begin{pmatrix} k \\ j \end{pmatrix}$ are the normal modes of the crystal.

The normal coordinates $Q \begin{pmatrix} k \\ j \end{pmatrix}$ and the corresponding canonic conjugate mo-

menta $P \begin{pmatrix} k \\ j \end{pmatrix}$ are in general complex-valued. We can change over to real coordinates

using the transformation

$$Q \begin{pmatrix} k \\ j \end{pmatrix} = \frac{1}{2} \left[q \begin{pmatrix} -k \\ j \end{pmatrix} + q \begin{pmatrix} k \\ j \end{pmatrix} \right] + \frac{i}{2\omega \begin{pmatrix} k \\ j \end{pmatrix}} \left[\dot{q} \begin{pmatrix} k \\ j \end{pmatrix} - \dot{q} \begin{pmatrix} -k \\ j \end{pmatrix} \right]. \qquad (19.33)$$

This is a canonical transformation, as is readily seen. The variables $q \begin{pmatrix} k \\ j \end{pmatrix}$ and

$\dot{q} \begin{pmatrix} k \\ j \end{pmatrix}$ are canonic conjugates.

Substitution from (19.33) reduces the Hamiltonian to the form

$$H = \frac{1}{2} \sum_{kj} \left[p^2 \binom{k}{j} + \omega^2 \binom{k}{j} q^2 \binom{k}{j} \right],$$

where $p \binom{k}{j} = \dot{q} \binom{k}{j}$, and the variables $p \binom{k}{j}$ and $q \binom{k}{j}$ are real.

In the quantum-mechanical treatment, the variables $u_\alpha \binom{l}{\kappa}, p_\alpha \binom{l}{\kappa}$ are regarded as operators $\hat{u}_\alpha \binom{l}{\kappa}, \hat{p}_\alpha \binom{l}{\kappa}$ satisfying the following commutation relations:

$$\left[\hat{u}_\alpha \binom{l}{\kappa}, \hat{p}_{\alpha'} \binom{l'}{\kappa'} \right] = i\hbar \delta_{ll'} \delta_{\kappa\kappa'} \delta_{\alpha\alpha'} .$$

The variables $Q \binom{k}{j}, P \binom{k}{j}$ and $q \binom{k}{j}, p \binom{k}{j}$ are also regarded as operators, and from (19.27) we have

$$\left[\hat{Q} \binom{k}{j}, \hat{P} \binom{k'}{j} \right] = i\hbar \Delta (k - k') \delta_{jj'} ,$$

$$\left[\hat{q} \binom{k}{j}, \hat{p} \binom{k'}{j'} \right] = i\hbar \Delta (k - k') \delta_{jj'} ,$$

(19.34)

(if $k = 0$ or is equal to a reciprocal lattice vector, we have $\Delta(k) = 1$; otherwise, $\Delta(k) = 0$).

In the coordinate representation, we have the standard relations

$$\hat{p} \binom{k}{j} = - i\hbar \frac{\partial}{\partial q \binom{k}{j}}, \quad \hat{q} \binom{k}{j} = q \binom{k}{j},$$

so that the Schroedinger equation takes the form

$$\frac{1}{2} \sum_{kj} \left\{ - \hbar^2 \frac{\partial^2}{\partial q^2 \binom{k}{j}} + \omega^2 \binom{k}{j} q^2 \binom{k}{j} \right\} \psi = E\psi.$$

The standard solutions of this equation are written in the form

$$\psi = \prod_{kj} \psi_m \binom{k}{j}\left[q\binom{k}{j}\right],$$

where $m\binom{k}{j}$ is the vibrational quantum number of the oscillator identified as $\binom{k}{j}$. Each of the functions $\psi_m\binom{k}{j}$ satisfies the equation

$$\left\{-\frac{h^2}{2}\frac{\partial^2}{\partial q^2\binom{k}{j}} + \frac{1}{2}\omega^2\binom{k}{j}q^2\binom{k}{j}\right\}\psi_m\binom{k}{j} = E_m\binom{k}{j}\psi_m\binom{k}{j}. \qquad (19.35)$$

The total energy $E_{\{m\}}$ of the crystal in a state described by the $3Nn$ quantum numbers $m\binom{k}{j}$ is

$$E_{\{m\}} = \sum_{kj} E_m\binom{k}{j}.$$

The solution of Eq. (19.35) has the form

$$\psi_m(q) = \left(\frac{\beta}{\pi^{\frac{1}{2}}2^m m!}\right)^{\frac{1}{2}}\exp\left(-\tfrac{1}{2}\beta^2 q^2\right)H_m(\beta q), \qquad (19.36)$$

where $\beta^2 = \beta_j^2(k) = \frac{1}{h}\omega^2\binom{k}{j}$, and $H_m(x)$ is the Hermite polynomial of degree m (see §10).

The corresponding energy levels are given by

$$E_m = \left[m\binom{k}{j} + \frac{1}{2}\right]\hbar\omega\binom{k}{j},$$

where $m\binom{k}{j} = 0, 1, 2, \ldots$ The matrix elements of the operators $\hat{q}\binom{k}{j}, \hat{p}\binom{k}{j}$

computed using the wave function (19.36) have the form

$$\langle m|q|m'\rangle = \sqrt{\frac{\hbar}{2\omega}}\,(\sqrt{m+1}\,\delta_{m',m+1} + \sqrt{m}\,\delta_{m',m-1}),$$

(19.37)

$$\langle m|p|m'\rangle = -i\sqrt{\frac{\hbar\omega}{2}}\,(\sqrt{m+1}\,\delta_{m',m+1} - \sqrt{m}\,\delta_{m',m-1}).$$

Let us now consider the second-quantization representation. We will first have to introduce new canonic variables $a\begin{pmatrix}k\\j\end{pmatrix}$, $a^*\begin{pmatrix}k\\j\end{pmatrix}$ defined by the relations

$$a\begin{pmatrix}k\\j\end{pmatrix} = \left[\left(\frac{\omega\begin{pmatrix}k\\j\end{pmatrix}}{2\hbar}\right)^{\frac{1}{2}} Q\begin{pmatrix}k\\j\end{pmatrix} + i\left(\frac{1}{2\hbar\omega\begin{pmatrix}k\\j\end{pmatrix}}\right)^{\frac{1}{2}} P\begin{pmatrix}k\\j\end{pmatrix}\right]$$

(19.38)

$$a^*\begin{pmatrix}k\\j\end{pmatrix} = \left[\left(\frac{\omega\begin{pmatrix}k\\j\end{pmatrix}}{2\hbar}\right)^{\frac{1}{2}} Q^*\begin{pmatrix}k\\j\end{pmatrix} - i\left(\frac{1}{2\hbar\omega\begin{pmatrix}k\\j\end{pmatrix}}\right)^{\frac{1}{2}} P^*\begin{pmatrix}k\\j\end{pmatrix}\right]$$

In the quantum-mechanical treatment, the variables $a\begin{pmatrix}k\\j\end{pmatrix}$, $a^*\begin{pmatrix}k\\j\end{pmatrix}$ are replaced with operators. Using (19.34), we readily find

$$\left[\hat{a}\begin{pmatrix}k\\j\end{pmatrix}, \hat{a}^*\begin{pmatrix}k'\\j\end{pmatrix}\right] = \Delta(k-k')\,\delta_{jj'},$$

$$\left[\hat{a}\begin{pmatrix}k\\j\end{pmatrix}, \hat{a}\begin{pmatrix}k'\\j'\end{pmatrix}\right] = \left[\hat{a}^*\begin{pmatrix}k\\j\end{pmatrix}, \hat{a}^*\begin{pmatrix}k'\\j'\end{pmatrix}\right] = 0.$$

Thus $\hat{a}$ may be treated as Bose operators. The matrix elements of these operators in the representation (19.36) can be found using (19.38), (19.33), (19.37):

$$\langle m|a^*|m'\rangle = \sqrt{m}\,\delta_{m',m-1},$$

$$\langle m|a|m'\rangle = \sqrt{m+1}\,\delta_{m',m+1},$$

(19.39)

The Hamiltonain thus takes the form

$$H = \sum_{kj} \hbar\omega \begin{pmatrix} k \\ j \end{pmatrix} \left[\hat{a}^* \begin{pmatrix} k \\ j \end{pmatrix} \hat{a} \begin{pmatrix} k \\ j \end{pmatrix} + \frac{1}{2} \right].$$

Since any stationary state of the crystal is defined by specifying the $3nN$ quantum numbers $\left\{ m \begin{pmatrix} k \\ j \end{pmatrix} \right\}$, any quantum state of the system may be described by the set of these numbers. The corresponding wave function $\psi \left\{ m \begin{pmatrix} k \\ j \end{pmatrix} \right\}$ depends on $3nN$ variables and defines the second quantization representation. From (19.39) we see that $\hat{a}^* \begin{pmatrix} k \\ j \end{pmatrix} \hat{a} \begin{pmatrix} k \\ j \end{pmatrix}$ is a diagonal operator in the second-quantization representation, and

$$\hat{a}^* \begin{pmatrix} k \\ j \end{pmatrix} \hat{a} \begin{pmatrix} k \\ j \end{pmatrix} \psi \left\{ m \begin{pmatrix} k \\ j \end{pmatrix} \right\} = m \begin{pmatrix} k \\ j \end{pmatrix} \psi \left\{ m \begin{pmatrix} k \\ j \end{pmatrix} \right\}. \tag{19.40}$$

Operating with the Hamiltonian on the function $\psi \left\{ m \begin{pmatrix} k \\ j \end{pmatrix} \right\}$, we obtain

$$\hat{H}\psi \left\{ m \begin{pmatrix} k \\ j \end{pmatrix} \right\} = E_{\{m\}} \psi \left\{ m \begin{pmatrix} k \\ j \end{pmatrix} \right\},$$

where

$$E_{\{m\}} = \sum_{kj} \hbar\omega \begin{pmatrix} k \\ j \end{pmatrix} \left[m \begin{pmatrix} k \\ j \end{pmatrix} + \frac{1}{2} \right].$$

The last expression can be interpreted as the energy of an assembly of noninteracting oscillators, each corresponding to $m \begin{pmatrix} k \\ j \end{pmatrix}$ quasiparticles of energies $\hbar\omega \begin{pmatrix} k \\ j \end{pmatrix}$ plus the energy of the vacuum $E_0 = \frac{1}{2} \sum_{kj} \hbar\omega \begin{pmatrix} k \\ j \end{pmatrix}$.

These quasiparticles are called *phonons*. The matrix elements (19.39) lead to the following results:

$$\hat{a}^* \begin{pmatrix} k \\ j \end{pmatrix} \psi \left\{ m \begin{pmatrix} k \\ j \end{pmatrix} \right\} = \sqrt{m \begin{pmatrix} k \\ j \end{pmatrix} + 1} \, \psi \left\{ m \begin{pmatrix} k \\ j \end{pmatrix} + 1 \right\},$$

$$\hat{a} \begin{pmatrix} k \\ j \end{pmatrix} \psi \left\{ m \begin{pmatrix} k \\ j \end{pmatrix} \right\} = \sqrt{m \begin{pmatrix} k \\ j \end{pmatrix}} \, \psi \left\{ m \begin{pmatrix} k \\ j \end{pmatrix} - 1 \right\}. \tag{19.41}$$

This explains why $\hat{a}* \begin{pmatrix} k \\ j \end{pmatrix}$ and $\hat{a} \begin{pmatrix} k \\ j \end{pmatrix}$ are generally called the *creation* and *de-*

struction operators of quasiparticles; the operator $\hat{m} \begin{pmatrix} k \\ j \end{pmatrix} = \hat{a}* \begin{pmatrix} k \\ j \end{pmatrix} \hat{a} \begin{pmatrix} k \\ j \end{pmatrix}$, in ac-

cordance with (19.40), is the *number operator* of quasiparticles.

3. General classification of the normal modes of crystals

In the general theory of small oscillations, the normal modes (when all the particles oscillate with the same velocity) are classified according to the irreducible representations of the symmetry group G of the equilibrium configuration of the system [86]. This classification is done as follows. Every element of the symmetry group, when applied to a system displaced from its equilibrium state, will move the system from one configuration to another, in general different, configuration. The space $u_i(r)$ ($i = 1$, $2, \ldots, 3s$, s is the number of particles in the system, r is the vector of the equilibrium position) of the deviations of the particles from the equilibrium positions is called the mechanical space L_m (see §10). Under symmetry transformations, the displacements $u_i(r)$ change into $\sum_{i'} T_{ii'}(g) u_{i'}(gr)$, where g is an element of the symmetry group of the system, $T_{ii'}(g)$ are the coefficients of a matrix which depends on the elements of the group G.

If we introduce linear operators $T(g)$ defined by the equality

$$T(g) u_i(r) = \sum_{i'} T_{ii'}(g) u_{i'}(gr), \tag{19.42}$$

and assign to every element g of G the operator $T(g)$,

$$g \rightarrow T(g),$$

we obtain a mechanical representation T_m of the group G. The mechanical representation T_m is reducible, and the mechanical space of displacements L_m is also reducible.

The main results of the group-theoretical classification are the following.

Every normal mode is made to correspond to a basis vector of some space L_j transforming according to an irreducible representation T_j of the group G; L_j is one of the subspaces into which the reducible space L_m is decomposed, $L_m = \sum_j L_j$ (the sum here is to be understood in the sense of a direct sum of spaces). All the normal modes associated in this way with the same representation T_j and the same space L_j have the same frequency. Moreover, if T_j is not a real representation, all the normal modes corresponding to the complex conjugate of T_j have the same frequency as the normal modes corresponding to T_j. Therefore, if T_j is a real representation, the degeneracy of the corresponding frequency is equal to the dimension of the space L_j; if T_j is not a real representation, the degeneracy of this frequency is double the dimension of the space L_j.

According to the above, the group-theoretical classification of normal modes requires that the reducible mechanical representation T_m be decomposed into irreducible representations T_j whose character (whether real or complex) is then established.

The normal modes of a crystal have been classified by a number of authors. Bhagavantam [352] used a classfication based on the irreducible representations of the group of directions F (this corresponds to the case $k = 0$) and the irreducible representations of the finite group of the Raman supercell (see below). Last [353] developed a classification by considering groups of several equivalent atoms in the crystal. He treated these groups as molecules. Further analysis required application of the techniques developed for free molecules. Neither approach is strict from the point of view of the general theory of classification of normal modes, since both authors ignore the overall symmetry of the crystal lattice.

A classification of the normal modes using all the symmetry elements of the crystal was developed by Lyubarskii [86]. His final expressions, however, are not particularly convenient for actual computations. Poulet [354] considers a classification of the normal modes of a crystal for $k \neq 0$, but working expressions have been derived for the simplest cases only.

In view of the great importance of the general classification of the normal modes of crystals for $k \neq 0$, we will consider this topic in some detail using the results of [355].

The mechanical space L_m of crystals is the $3nN$-dimensional space of the displacements $u_\alpha \begin{pmatrix} l \\ \kappa \end{pmatrix}$. The mechanical representation operators are defined by the relation

$$T_m (g) u_\alpha \begin{pmatrix} l \\ \kappa \end{pmatrix} = \sum_\beta A_{\alpha\beta} (h_j) u_\beta \left[g \begin{pmatrix} l \\ \kappa \end{pmatrix} \right], \qquad (19.43)$$

where g is an element of the group G, $A_{\alpha\beta} (h_j)$ are the elements of the transformation matrix for the components of a vector; $\alpha, \beta = 1, 2, 3$. Then

$$g \begin{pmatrix} l \\ \kappa \end{pmatrix} = g (l + x_\kappa) = \{h_j | \alpha\} (l + x_\kappa) = h_j l + h_j x_\kappa + \alpha = l' + x_{\kappa'} = \begin{pmatrix} l' \\ \kappa \end{pmatrix}. \qquad (19.44)$$

Here $\begin{pmatrix} l' \\ \kappa' \end{pmatrix}$ is a vector defining the position to which the symmetry transformation moves the atom originally occupying the position $\begin{pmatrix} l \\ k \end{pmatrix}$. Therefore

$$T_m(\{h_j \,|\, \alpha\})\, u_\alpha \begin{pmatrix} l \\ \kappa \end{pmatrix} = \sum_\beta A_{\alpha\beta}\,(h_j)\, u_\beta \begin{pmatrix} l' \\ \kappa' \end{pmatrix}. \tag{19.45}$$

A general displacement $u_\alpha \begin{pmatrix} l \\ \kappa \end{pmatrix}$ can be decomposed in basis vectors transforming

according to irreducible representations of the translation group,

$$u_\alpha \begin{pmatrix} l \\ \kappa \end{pmatrix} = \sum_k \frac{1}{\sqrt{m_\kappa N}}\, u_\alpha^0 \begin{pmatrix} k \\ \kappa \end{pmatrix} e^{ikl} = \sum_k u_\alpha \begin{pmatrix} k \\ l \\ \kappa \end{pmatrix}, \tag{19.46}$$

where m_κ is the mass of the corresponding atom.

The functions $u_\alpha^0 \begin{pmatrix} k \\ \kappa \end{pmatrix}$ depend on the vectors x_κ, but they do not depend on l,

i.e., they are constant for all the points of the direct lattice.

Expansion (19.46) shows that the star of the representation T_m is a reducible star $\{k\}$ whose irreducible components are all the irreducible stars of the Brillouin zone. We also conclude from (19.46) that the mechanical space L_m can be decomposed into N subspaces L_k, each invariant under the group G_k of the vector k (the "small" group), although not invariant under all the elements of the group G.

Consider the mechanical space L_m containing an invariant subspace L_k. Every vector from L_k is transformed by the operator $T_m(g)$ into a vector from the same space. Therefore, in L_k, the operators $\tau_k(g)$ can be defined by the relation

$$\tau_k(g)\, u_\alpha \begin{pmatrix} k \\ l \\ \kappa \end{pmatrix} = T_m(g)\, u_\alpha \begin{pmatrix} k \\ l \\ \kappa \end{pmatrix}.$$

We say that the operator $\tau_m(g)$ is induced by the operator $T_m(g)$ in the invariant subspace L_k (see [86]).

To decompose $\tau_k(g)$ into irreducible components, we require the corresponding characters $\chi_k(g)$. Acting with the operator $\tau_k(g)$ on the basis vector of the space L_k $(g \subset G_k)$, we obtain

$$\tau_k(g)\, u_\alpha \begin{pmatrix} k \\ l \\ \kappa \end{pmatrix} = \tau_k(g)\, \frac{1}{\sqrt{m_\kappa N}}\, u_\alpha^0 \begin{pmatrix} k \\ \kappa \end{pmatrix} e^{ikl} =$$

$$= \frac{1}{\sqrt{m_\kappa N}} \sum_\beta A_{\alpha\beta}(h_j)\, u_\beta^0 \begin{pmatrix} k \\ \kappa' \end{pmatrix} e^{ikl} =$$

$$= \frac{1}{\sqrt{m_\kappa N}} \sum_\beta A_{\alpha\beta}(h_j)\, u_\beta^0 \begin{pmatrix} k \\ \kappa' \end{pmatrix} e^{ikl} e^{ik(l'-l)} =$$

$$= \sum_\beta A_{\alpha\beta}(h_j)\, u_\beta \begin{pmatrix} k \\ l' \\ \kappa' \end{pmatrix} e^{ik(l'-l)}.$$

For the character $\chi_k(g)$ of the representation $\tau_k(g)$ we thus find

$$\chi_k(\{h_j\,|\,\alpha\}) = (\pm 1 + 2\cos\phi) \sum_\kappa \delta(\kappa)\, e^{ik(l'-l)}, \qquad (19.47)$$

where the signs are chosen according as the rotation is proper or improper; the sum is taken over all the nonequivalent atoms of the unit cell; the symbol $\delta(\kappa)$ is defined in the following way: $\delta(\kappa) = 1$ if the atom is displaced from its position by pure translations only, and $\delta(\kappa) = 0$ if identical nonequivalent atoms are interchanged. Eq. (19.47) coincides with the result of [86] (with a slight change in notation). The shortcoming of the last formula is that it contains implicitly the dependence on the translation α, and this complicates the transition to loaded representations; another tedious aspect is the calculation of the vector $l' - l$ for every atom of the unit cell. It is therefore advisable to transform (19.47) to the following form. Seeing that

$$l' - l = \begin{pmatrix} l' \\ \kappa' \end{pmatrix} - \begin{pmatrix} l \\ \kappa \end{pmatrix} - x_{\kappa'} + x_\kappa, \text{ we can write (19.47) in the form}$$

$$\chi_k(\{h_j\,|\,\alpha\}) = (\pm 1 + 2\cos\phi) \sum_\kappa \delta(\kappa)\, \exp\left\{ ik\left[\begin{pmatrix} l' \\ \kappa' \end{pmatrix} - \begin{pmatrix} l \\ \kappa \end{pmatrix} \right] \right\} =$$

$$= (\pm 1 + 2\cos\phi) \sum_\kappa \delta(\kappa)\, \exp\left\{ ik\left[h_j \begin{pmatrix} l \\ \kappa \end{pmatrix} - \begin{pmatrix} l \\ \kappa \end{pmatrix} + \alpha \right] \right\} =$$

$$= (\pm 1 + \cos\phi) \left[\sum_\kappa \delta(\kappa)\, \exp\left\{ i(h_j^{-1}k - k) \begin{pmatrix} l \\ \kappa \end{pmatrix} \right\} \right] e^{ik\alpha} =$$

$$= (\pm 1 + 2\cos\phi) \left[\sum_\kappa \delta(\kappa)\, \exp\{ i(h_j^{-1}k - k) x_\kappa \} \right] e^{ik\alpha}. \qquad (19.48)$$

Writing $k_0 = h_j^{-1}k - k$ (the vector k_0 is a vector of the reciprocal space or zero, since $\{h_j \,|\, \alpha\} \subset G_k)$, we obtain

$$\chi_k(\{h_j \,|\, \alpha\}) = (\pm 1 + 2 \cos \phi) \left[\sum_\kappa \delta(\kappa) e^{i k_0 x_\kappa} \right] e^{i k \alpha}. \tag{19.49}$$

If $k_0 = 0$ (this is true, in particular, for all the points inside the Brillouin zone), Eq. (19.49) takes a simpler form, which coincides with the corresponding result of [354]:

$$\chi_k(\{h_j \,|\, \alpha\}) = (\pm 1 + 2 \cos \phi) n_0 e^{i k \alpha}, \tag{19.50}$$

where n_0 is the number of nonequivalent atoms inside a unit cell which remain in their original position under the symmetry transformation, apart from pure translation. There is thus no contradiction between the results of [86] and [354].

On the other hand, the general equation (19.49) is free from the previously mentioned shortcomings and enables us to change over without difficulty to the characters of the loaded representation $\hat{\tau}_k(h_j)$ of the group $\hat{G}_k$ (the point group of the vector k):

$$\hat{\chi}_k(h_j) = \chi_k(\{h_j \,|\, \alpha\}) e^{-i k \alpha} = (\pm 1 + 2 \cos \phi) \left(\sum_\kappa \delta(\kappa) e^{i k_0 x_\kappa} \right). \tag{19.51}$$

For the number n_p of irreducible loaded representations of character $\hat{\chi}^p(h_j)$ contained in the reducible representation $\hat{\tau}_k(h_j)$ we find, taking the load into consideration,

$$n_p = \frac{1}{f'} \sum_{h_j \subset \hat{G}_k} \hat{\chi}_k(h_j) \, \overline{\hat{\chi}^p(h_j)} \, e^{i(k - h_j k, \alpha)}, \tag{19.52}$$

where $\chi_k(h_j)$ is obtained from (19.51), f' is the number of elements of the group $\hat{G}_k$.

Let us consider in some detail the final expression (19.52). If the wave vector k lies inside the Brillouin zone, then $k - h_j k = h_j^{-1} k - k = 0$ (loaded representations are no different from the ordinary representations of the point group $\hat{G}_k$) and (19.52) takes the form

$$n_p = \frac{1}{f'} \sum_{h_j \subset \hat{G}_k} (\pm 1 + 2 \cos \phi) n_0 \overline{\chi^p(h_j)}, \tag{19.53}$$

where $\chi^p(h_j)$ is the character of the ordinary representation of the point group $\hat{G}_k$.

In the particular case $k = 0$, Eq. (19.53) takes the simpler form

$$n_p = \frac{1}{f} \sum_{h_j \subset F} (\pm 1 + 2 \cos \phi) n_0 \overline{\chi^p(h_j)}, \tag{19.54}$$

where F is the group of directions of the crystal, f is the number of elements of this group.

Eq. (19.54) coincides with the analogous results of Bhagavantam [87, 352], who classified the normal modes of a crystal using the irreducible representations of the point group F. We thus see that the classification of normal modes according to the irreducible representations of the group F is the classification of photons with $k = 0$.

Once we have found the irreducible representations of the group τ_k^p entering the reducible representation τ_k, we can proceed with the construction of the irreducible representations of the entire space group which enter T_m. To this end, we have to combine all the representations corresponding to the same star $\{k\}$, in accordance with the standard [86] of constructing the irreducible representations of a space group. To every normal mode of the crystal, corresponds an irreducible representation $\tau_{\{k\}}^p$ obtained in this way.

It now remains to establish that the irreducible representations $\tau_{\{k\}}^p$ according to which the spaces $L_{\{k\}}^p$ transform are real. According to the realness criterion [86, 356]

$$\frac{1}{f'} \sum_{h_j k = -k} \chi_k(g^2) = \begin{cases} 1, & \text{if } \tau_{\{k\}}^p \text{ is real,} \\ 0 \text{ or } -1 & \text{if } \tau_{\{k\}}^p \text{ is not real.} \end{cases} \tag{19.55}$$

The sum is taken over all the elements of the point group F for which $h_j k = -k$, where k is any vector of the star $\{k\}$.

The degeneracy of a normal mode is equal to the dimension of the corresponding space $L_{\{k\}}^p$ if $\tau_{\{k\}}^p$ is real, and to double the dimension of this space if $\tau_{\{k\}}^p$ is not real. Physically, this means that all the discrete plane waves corresponding to the normal modes of a crystal characterized by a polarization index ρ and a direction of propagation k have the same frequency.

Note that the classification of vibrational levels corresponding to excitations with $k = 0$ has largely proved sufficient for the first stage of Raman scattering experiments, when the spectrum $\omega_i(0)$ of various optical branches was investigated. However, for some modes which are active in the IR absorption spectrum, the function $\omega(k)$ has significant features of its own even in the first approximation.

The classification of vibrational levels for a general nonzero wave vector is essential in the analysis of second-order spectra.

4. Vibrations of crystals containing complex atomic groups

The general theory of the previous sections enables us to classify the normal modes of a crystal with a unit cell containing any number of nonequivalent atoms. However, considering the actual properties of the interatomic forces, it is often advisable to isolate individual atomic groupings which can be treated as new structural units of the crystal. Complex ions and, in molecular crystals, individual molecules may be used as such groups. The normal modes in this case may be divided into external and internal. External modes correspond to vibrations of particles relative to one another. Internal modes are treated as the vibrations of idealized point masses inside each of the selected groups.

In the case of internal vibrations, the vector displacement from the equilibrium position characterizes the displacements inside the group. The displacement vectors of the external vibrations are three-dimensional if the particular group may be regarded as a geometrical point, and six-dimensional if the group has to be treated as a geometrical solid with six degrees of freedom.

The next step is the subdivision of the external vibrations into translational modes and orientation rotations. Note that this subdivision of the vibrational modes, as long as it is physically sound, induces a corresponding partition of the reducible spaces, L_k, although for certain values of the vectors k this partition may prove inapplicable. In practice, this partition is particularly important for the normal modes with $k = 0$. The expressions for the characters of the corresponding representations are given in Table 42.

5. Raman's theory of the lattice dynamics

Raman developed a theory of lattice vibrations [357] which significantly differs from Born's theory. We will briefly present the fundamental points of Raman's approach.

Raman dropped Born's periodic boundary conditions, maintaining that the normal modes of the lattice particles should not be identified with all the wave motions which are obtained from the periodic conditions. Raman postulated that, in normal modes, the displacement ratios α, β, γ of any two adjacent equivalent atoms located on any of the three principal axes of the Bravais lattice are real and equal for any pair of such atoms:

$$\alpha, \beta, \gamma = \pm 1 .$$

This implies that these atoms vibrate either in phase or in counterphase. If $\alpha = \beta = \gamma = 1$, i.e., the vibration modes of the equivalent atoms are identical, the n interpenetrating Bravais lattices corresponding to a primitive cell with n nonequivalent particles vibrate one relative to the other so that the adjacent equivalent atoms move in phase. There is a total of $3n$ such modes; the other seven possible values of α, β, γ give additional $21n$ degrees of freedom corresponding to modes in which only part of the adjacent planes consisting of equivalent atoms move in phase (some planes move in counterphase). It is thus assumed that the crystal has a total of $24n - 3$ degrees of freedom corresponding to real physical vibrations (among all the normal modes, there are always three modes which constitute simple translations of the entire crystal). The problem thus reduces to an analysis of the

Table 42

EXPRESSIONS FOR THE CHARACTERS OF VARIOUS REPRESENTATIONS

Object	Representation	Character
Unit cell with n point particles	Mechanical representation T_k, k belongs to the first Brillouin zone	$\hat{\chi}(h_\phi) = n_0(\pm 1 + 2 \cos \phi)$
	Vibrational representation ($k = 0$)	$\chi(h_\phi = (n_0 - 1)(\pm 1 + 2\cos \phi)$
Unit cell with n point particles. External vibration with the participation of m groups	External vibrational representation (without acoustic modes)	$\chi(C_\phi) = (2m_0 - 1)(1 + 2 \cos \phi)$ $\chi(S_\phi) = 1 - 2 \cos \phi$
	Internal vibrational representation	$\chi(C_\phi) = (n_0 - 2m_0)(1 + 2 \cos \phi)$ $\chi(S_\phi) = n_0(-1 + 2 \cos \phi)$
	Translation-vibrational representation	$\chi(C_\phi) = (m_0 - 1)(1 + 2 \cos \phi)$ $\chi(S_\phi) = (m_0 - 1)(-1 + 2 \cos \phi)$
	Rotation-vibrational representation	$\chi(C_\phi) = m_0(1 + 2 \cos \phi)$ $\chi(S_\phi) = m_0(1 - 2 \cos \phi)$
Unit cell with n point particles. External vibrations with the participation of m asymmetric groups and p point particles	External vibrational representation	$\chi(C_\phi) = (2m_0 + p_0 - 1)(1 + 2 \cos \phi)$ $\chi(S_\phi) = (p_0 - 1)(-1 + 2 \cos \phi)$
	Translation-vibrational representation	$\chi(C_\phi) = (p_0 + m_0 - 1)(1 + 2 \cos \phi)$ $\chi(S_\phi) = (p_0 + m_0 - 1)(-1 + 2 \cos\phi)$
	Rotation-vibrational representation	$\chi(C_\phi) = m_0(1 + 2 \cos \phi)$ $\chi(S_\phi) = m_0(1 - 2 \cos \phi)$
	Internal vibrational representation	$\chi(C_\phi) = (n_0 - p_0 - 2m_0)(1 + 2 \cos \phi)$ $\chi(S_\phi) = (n_0 - p_0)(-1 + 2 \cos \phi)$

Note. n_0, m_0, p_0 give the number of particles which remain stationary, apart from translation by a direct lattice vector.

vibrations of a system comprising $8n$ atoms in eight adjacent unit cells, and we may therefore apply the same reasoning as in the treatment of polyatomic molecules.

Group-theoretical classification of the Raman normal modes has been carried out by several authors [358–361]. The classification is generally accomplished in two stages. First, the $3n$ normal modes corresponding to $\alpha = \beta = \gamma = 1$ are classified. To this end, the nonequivalent atoms of a single unit cell are considered; a factor-group of G (i.e., the group of directions of the crystal) is taken as the symmetry group of the system, and expressions for the characters of the mechanical and other representations coincide with the corresponding relations of [87] for $k = 0$.

All the Raman normal modes are classified by considering eight adjacent elementary cells (a so-called supercell) and using as the symmetry group the group of directions of the crystal plus the translations moving adjacent equivalent atoms into one another. In diamond, for instance, this symmetry group contains 384 elements (of which only 48 elements belong to the group of directions of the crystal). The expressions for the characters of the mechanical representation are the same as (19.50) for $k = 0$ (see Table 42), provided all the atoms in the supercell are taken into consideration.

At first, the Raman and Born theories seemed to be mutually compatible. However, the development of the theory of critical points made it possible to establish a definite relationship between the two "conflicting" theories (see below).

A discussion of the experimental data on Raman scattering from the standpoint of Raman's theory will be given in §21.

6. Polar lattice vibrations

We have so far assumed that the ions vibrate independently of the electromagnetic modes propagating in the crystal. This is not so, however, for polar vibrations which entail changes in the dipole moment.

Polar vibrations of ions generate electromagnetic waves which are strongly coupled with pure mechanical vibrations. The equations of motion for these vibrations include both the relative displacements of the ions and the electromagnetic field components. The corresponding equations of motion for a polar diatomic lattice of a cubic crystal can be written in the form

$$w = b_{11}w + b_{12}E, \quad P = b_{21}w + b_{22}E,$$

$$\text{div } D = 0, \quad \text{div } H = 0, \tag{19.56}$$

$$\text{curl } E = -\frac{1}{c}\dot{H}, \quad \text{curl } H = \frac{1}{c}\dot{D},$$

where $w = u\sqrt{m_1 m_2/(m_1 + m_2)}$, u is the relative displacement vector of the two sublattices, m_1, m_2 are the atomic masses, $b_{11}, b_{12}, b_{21}, b_{22}$ are some coefficients. The remaining notation has the usual meaning.

The solution of Eqs. (19.56) is sought in the form of plane monochromatic waves:

$$\left.\begin{matrix} w = w_0 \\ P = P_0 \\ E = E_0 \\ H = H_0 \end{matrix}\right\} \cdot e^{i(kx - \omega t)}. \tag{19.57}$$

Inserting (19.57) in (19.56), we find

$$- \omega^2 w = b_{11} w + b_{12} E, \quad P = b_{21} w + b_{22} E,$$

$$k(E + 4\pi P) = 0, \quad kH = 0, \tag{19.58}$$

$$[kE] = \frac{\omega}{c} H, \quad [kH] = -\frac{\omega}{c}(E + 4\pi P).$$

From the first and the second equation in (19.58), we get

$$w = -\frac{b_{12} E}{b_{11} + \omega^2}, \tag{19.59a}$$

$$P = \left(-\frac{b_{12} b_{21}}{b_{11} + \omega^2} + b_{22}\right) E, \tag{19.59b}$$

$$D = \left(1 + 4\pi b_{22} - \frac{b_{12} b_{21}}{b_{11} + \omega^2}\right) E = \varepsilon E. \tag{19.60}$$

From (19.60) we see that

$$\varepsilon(\omega) = 1 + 4\pi b_{22} - \frac{b_{12} b_{21}}{b_{11} + \omega_2}. \tag{19.61}$$

Eq. (19.61) can be written in the form

$$\varepsilon(\omega) = \varepsilon_\infty + \frac{\varepsilon_0 - \varepsilon_\infty}{1 - (\omega/\omega_0)^2}. \tag{19.62}$$

The constants ω_0, ε_0, ε_∞ have a simple physical meaning and can be determined experimentally: $\varepsilon_0 = \varepsilon(0)$ is the static dielectric constant; $\varepsilon_\infty = \varepsilon(\infty)$ is the dielectric constant at frequencies much higher than the infrared frequencies, and yet lower than the electron absorption frequencies; ω_0 is the infrared dispersion frequency.

Comparison of (19.61) and (19.62) gives (according to the microscopic theory [345], $b_{12} = b_{21}$)

$$b_{11} = -\omega_0^2,$$

$$b_{12} = b_{21} = \left(\frac{\varepsilon_0 - \varepsilon_\infty}{4\pi}\right)^{1/2} \omega_0,$$

$$b_{22} = \frac{1}{4\pi}(\varepsilon_\infty - 1).$$

The solution of Eqs. (19.58) is a combination of longitudinal and transverse waves. Indeed, using (19.59), we rewrite the third equation in (19.58) in the form

$$(kE)\left(1 + 4\pi b_{22} - \frac{4\pi b_{12}b_{21}}{b_{11} + \omega^2}\right) = 0. \tag{19.63}$$

This leads to the following two alternatives:

$$a) \qquad 1 + 4\pi b_{22} - \frac{4\pi b_{12}b_{21}}{b_{11} + \omega^2} = 0 ; \tag{19.64}$$

$$b) \qquad (kE) = 0. \tag{19.65}$$

Let us first consider case a. By (19.64), (19.58), and (19.59b), $[kH] = 0$. Since also $kH = 0$, this equality implies that $H = 0$ and this, in its turn, leads to the equality $[kE] = 0$. Since $E \neq 0$ (if $E = 0$, Eqs. (19.58) only have a trivial solution), we conclude that $E \parallel k$. Then, from (19.59a), (19.59b), $P \parallel k$, $w \parallel k$. The frequencies are found from Eq. (19.64), which gives

$$\omega^2 = - b_{11} + \frac{4\pi b_{12}b_{21}}{1 + 4\pi b_{22}} = \frac{\varepsilon_0}{\varepsilon_\infty} \omega_0^2 = \omega_l^2 , \tag{19.66}$$

where ω_l is the frequency of the longitudinal vibration.

In case b, (19.65), we obtain, using (19.58),

$$\frac{k^2 c^2}{\omega^2} = 1 + 4\pi b_{22} - \frac{4\pi b_{12}b_{21}}{b_{11} + \omega^2} = \varepsilon_\infty + \frac{\varepsilon_0 - \varepsilon_\infty}{\omega_0^2 - \omega^2} \omega_0^2 . \tag{19.67}$$

Eq. (19.67) gives the frequencies of the transverse branches; the frequency is seen to be a function of the magnitude of the wave vector k.

The solutions of (19.58) are plotted by the solid curves in Figure 69; the dashed lines correspond to the case of two noninteracting electromagnetic and mechanical systems.

We have here a typical example of resonance between two coupled vibrational subsystems. To the right of the resonance point, the frequency of the electromagnetic oscillations (branch 1) is so high that the electromagnetic field fails to pump the heavy ions; the corresponding ionic vibrations (branch 2) are purely mechanical. Conversely, near the resonance point, the mechanical vibrations are "intermixed" with the electromagnetic modes. The quasiparticles of the crystal corresponding to the section of curve 5 near the resonance point are called *polarons*.

The equations of motion (19.56) were generalized for more complex cubic crystals

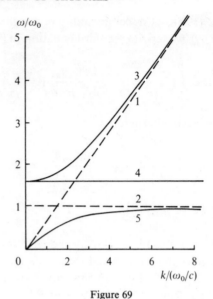

Figure 69

Optical and mechanical lattice vibrations:

1) optical wavelengths without dispersion,   2) mechanical vibrations of nuclei without interaction with electromagnetic field,   3) optical   wavelengths   with   dispersion,   4) longitudinal   lattice   vibrations, 5) transverse lattice vibrations.

in [362]. According to the results of Cochran and Cowley [362], each vector-type triply degenerate mode (i.e., a mode active in the infrared absorption spectrum) is split into a nondegenerate longitudinal vibration and a doubly degenerate transverse vibration. For a crystal with n vector-type optical modes, the following relation is obtained:

$$\prod_{j=1}^{n} \left(\frac{\omega_{lj}}{\omega_{tj}}\right)^2 = \frac{\varepsilon_0}{\varepsilon_\infty},$$

(19.68)

where ω_{lj}, ω_{tj} are the frequencies of the longitudinal and the transverse modes for sufficiently large values of the wave vector ($k \gg \omega/c$).

For noncubic crystals, the dispersion curves of the different vibrational branches are more complex. In this case, the frequencies of the polar vibrations depend both on the magnitude and the direction of the vector k; the separation of modes into longitudinal and transverse is valid only for certain directions of the vector k (those characterized by the highest symmetry). When the direction of k is changed, a transverse mode may convert to a longitudinal mode, or vice versa. Let us consider a uniaxial crystal in which only one of the three vibrational branches active in the IR spectrum is represented. As a result of the anisotropy of the crystal, the vibration frequency $\omega_{\parallel}$ in the direction of the z axis in the absence of long-wave electrical forces is substantially different from the frequency $\omega_\perp$ of the doubly degenerate mode confined to the xy plane.

A generalization of equations (19.56) to noncubic uniaxial crystals with three polar branches was given in [363, 364]. For any orientation of the phonon wave vector k relative to the z axis, we obtain two solutions. In one of these solutions, the vectors E and P are perpendicular both to the vector k and to the axis z. This solution corresponds to the *ordinary wave*, for which the following equality is satisfied:

$$\frac{k^2 c^2}{\omega^2} = \frac{\omega_\perp^2 \varepsilon_{0\perp} - \omega^2 \varepsilon_{\infty\perp}}{\omega_\perp^2 - \omega^2}. \tag{19.69}$$

The second solution corresponds to the *extraordinary wave*. The frequencies of the extraordinary wave depend on the angle θ between the vector k and the axis z:

$$\frac{k^2 c^2}{\omega^2} = \frac{\left(\dfrac{\omega_\parallel^2 \varepsilon_{0\parallel} - \omega^2 \varepsilon_{\infty\parallel}}{\omega_\parallel^2 - \omega^2}\right)\left(\dfrac{\omega_\perp^2 \varepsilon_{0\perp} - \omega^2 \varepsilon_{\infty\perp}}{\omega_\perp^2 - \omega^2}\right)}{\left(\dfrac{\omega_\parallel^2 \varepsilon_{0\parallel} - \omega^2 \varepsilon_{\infty\parallel}}{\omega_\parallel^2 - \omega^2}\right)\cos^2 \theta + \left(\dfrac{\omega_\perp^2 \varepsilon_{0\perp} - \omega^2 \varepsilon_{\infty\perp}}{\omega_\perp^2 - \omega^2}\right)\sin \theta}; \tag{19.70}$$

$\varepsilon_{0\perp}, \varepsilon_{\infty\perp}, \varepsilon_{0\parallel}, \varepsilon_{\infty\parallel}$ are the corresponding values of the dielectric constants.

Let

$$\omega_\parallel^l = \omega_\parallel \sqrt{\frac{\varepsilon_{0\parallel}}{\varepsilon_{\infty\parallel}}}, \qquad \omega_\perp^l = \omega_\perp \sqrt{\frac{\varepsilon_{0\perp}}{\varepsilon_{\infty\perp}}}. \tag{19.71}$$

From (19.69), (19.70) it follows that for $k = 0$ the phonon frequencies are $\omega_\parallel^l$ and $\omega_\perp^l$. For large wave vectors ($k \gg \omega/c$), Eqs. (19.69) and (19.70) give $\omega = \omega_\perp$ (an ordinary phonon) and

$$\left(\frac{\omega_\parallel^2 \varepsilon_{0\parallel} - \omega^2 \varepsilon_{\infty\parallel}}{\omega_\parallel^2 - \omega^2}\right)\cos^2 \theta + \left(\frac{\omega_\perp^2 \varepsilon_{0\perp} - \omega^2 \varepsilon_{\infty\perp}}{\omega_\perp^2 - \omega^2}\right)\sin^2 \theta = 0 \tag{19.72}$$

(extraordinary phonons).

Since, in general, the last equation has two different roots ω_1, ω_2, for $k \gg \omega/c$ we obtain three nondegenerate phonon branches with the frequencies $\omega_\perp, \omega_1, \omega_2$.

To analyze the general relation (19.72), let us consider two limiting cases.

Case 1. $|\omega_\parallel - \omega_\perp| \ll \omega_\parallel^l - \omega_\parallel, \omega_\perp^l - \omega_\perp$. The difference in the mechanical elastic coefficients of the vibrational branches associated with the anisotropy of the crystal is much less than the increments due to electrostatic forces. Examples of such crystals are provided by the hexagonal ZnO and SiC lattices, and others. Assuming that the difference between $\varepsilon_\parallel$ and $\varepsilon_\perp$ is insignificant, we obtain from (19.72)

$$\omega_1^2 = \omega_\parallel^2 \sin^2 \theta + \omega_\perp^2 \cos^2 \theta, \quad \omega_2^2 = (\omega_\parallel^l)^2 \cos^2 \theta + (\omega_\perp^l)^2 \sin^2 \theta. \quad (19.73)$$

The shape of the dispersion curves for various directions of the wave vector k is shown schematically in Figure 70, a, b, c.

Case 2. $|\omega_\parallel - \omega_\perp| \gg \omega_\parallel^l - \omega_\parallel$, $\omega_\perp^l - \omega_\perp$. The solutions of Eq. (19.72) take the form

$$\omega_1^2 = \omega_\parallel^2 \sin^2 \theta + (\omega_\parallel^l)^2 \cos^2 \theta, \quad \omega_2^2 = \omega_\perp^2 \cos^2 \theta + (\omega_\parallel^l)^2 \sin^2 \theta. \quad (19.74)$$

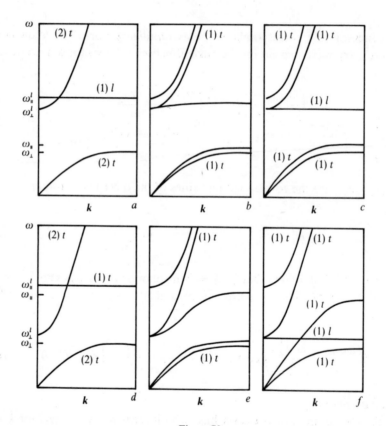

Figure 70

Dispersion curves of optical branches for small wave vectors k for a uniaxial crystal and various positions of the phonon wave vector:

a,d) phonon wave vector parallel to the z axis, c,f) phonon wave vector in the xy plane, b,e) intermediate position.   Curves d,e,f correspond to the case when anisotropic interatomic forces predominate over electrostatic forces; l and t identify the longitudinal and the transverse branches and the parenthetical numbers give the degeneracy of the vibrations.

The corresponding curves are shown in Figure 70, d, e, f. Expressions analogous to (19.73) and (19.74) were first derived in [365].

Further development of the theory for the case of three polar branches was given in [365]. In general, the polaron frequencies depend both on the direction and the magnitude of the wave vector.

A group-theoretical classification of the polar modes with $k = 0$ cannot be carried out using the relations of Table 42, since the mechanical system is no longer independent: it is strongly coupled with the electromagnetic field. For $k \neq 0$, however, all the previous results remain in force, since, strictly speaking, the anisotropic interatomic forces cause a splitting of the degenerate vibrational levels even for small k, and the electrostatic forces can only increase this splitting. In this case, the vector k lies inside the Brillouin zone, so that all the irreducible representations of the group $\hat{G}_k$ are ordinary (unloaded) and the expression for the characters of the mechanical representation is of the form (19.50).

7. An example of a group-theoretical classification of the lattice modes

Consider the cubic ZnS crystal, which belongs to the symmorphic symmetry group T_d^2 (see §18).

Figure 71, a, b, c show the unit cell and the Brillouin zone of the ZnS crystal. If $2l$ is the side of the cube, the translation vectors have the coordinates

$$a_1 = l(0, 1, 1), \quad a_2 = l(1, 0, 1), \quad a_3 = l(1, 1, 0).$$

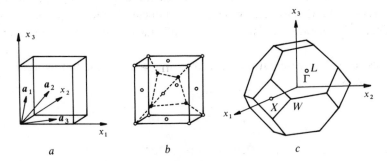

Figure 71

ZnS lattice (cubic modification):

a, b) unit cell, c) Brillouin zone.

The reciprocal lattice vectors are

$$b_1 = \frac{\pi}{l}(-1, 1, 1), \quad b_2 = \frac{\pi}{l}(1, -1, 1), \quad b_3 = \frac{\pi}{l}(1, 1, -1).$$

The vectors of the principal points of the Brillouin zone are (see [354])

$$k_2 = \mu(b_1 + b_2) + \mu_3 b_3 = \frac{\pi}{l}(\mu_3, \mu_3, (2\mu - \mu_3)),$$

$$k_5 = \mu(b_1 + b_2 + b_3) = \frac{\pi}{l}(\mu, \mu, \mu),$$

$$k_6 = \mu(b_1 + b_2) = \frac{\pi}{l}(0, 0, 2\mu),$$

$$k_7 = \tfrac{1}{2}(b_1 + b_3) + \mu(b_1 + b_2) = \frac{\pi}{l}(0, 1, 2\mu),$$

$$k_8 = \tfrac{1}{4}(b_1 + b_2) + \tfrac{1}{2}(b_2 + b_3) = \tfrac{1}{2}\pi(1, 0, \tfrac{1}{2}),$$

$$k_9 = \tfrac{1}{2}(b_1 + b_2 + b_3) = \frac{\pi}{l}(\tfrac{1}{2}, \tfrac{1}{2}, \tfrac{1}{2}),$$

$$k_{10} = \tfrac{1}{2}(b_1 + b_2) = \frac{\pi}{l}(0, 0, 1),$$

$$k_{11} = 0 = \frac{\pi}{l}(0, 0, 0).$$

They are characterized by different groups $\hat{G}_k$. Applying the elements of the group F to the vectors k, we obtain all the irreducible stars of the group G. The characters of the representations $\hat{\tau}_k(h_j)$ corresponding to these vectors are calculated from (19.51). Using (19.52), we decompose the reducible representations $\hat{\tau}_k(h_j)$ into irreducible representations. The results for all the above vectors are summarized in Table 43.

The mechanical representation T_m is thus made up of the following irreducible representations:

$$3\tau_{\{k_2\}}^{(1)} + 3\tau_{\{k_2\}}^{(2)},$$

$$\tau_{\{k_5\}}^{(1)} + \tau_{\{k_5\}}^{(2)} + 2\tau_{\{k_5\}}^{(3)},$$

$$2\tau_{\{k_6\}}^{(1)} + 2\tau_{\{k_6\}}^{(3)} + 2\tau_{\{k_6\}}^{(4)},$$

$$3\tau_{\{k_7\}}^{(1)} + 3\tau_{\{k_7\}}^{(2)},$$

$$2\tau_{\{k_8\}}^{(2)} + 2\tau_{\{k_8\}}^{(3)} + 2\tau_{\{k_8\}}^{(4)},$$

$$\tau_{\{k_9\}}^{(1)} + \tau_{\{k_9\}}^{(2)} + 2\tau_{\{k_9\}}^{(3)},$$

$$2\tau_{\{k_{10}\}}^{(1)} + 2\tau_{\{k_{10}\}}^{(3)} + 2\tau_{\{k_{10}\}}^{(4)},$$

$$2\tau_{\{k_{11}\}}^{(3)}.$$

Table 43

CHARACTERS OF REPRESENTATIONS FOR THE ZnS CRYSTAL

Vector $k_2 = \mu(b_1 + b_2) + \mu_3 b_3$			Vector $k_7 = \frac{1}{2}(b_1 + b_3) + \mu(b_2 + b_2)$		
G_k	E	σ	G_k	E	C_2
$\hat{\chi}^{(1)}$	1	1	$\hat{\chi}^{(1)}$	1	1
$\hat{\chi}^{(2)}$	1	-1	$\hat{\chi}^{(2)}$	1	-1
$\hat{\chi}_k$	6	2	$\hat{\chi}_k$	6	-2

$$\tau = 4\tau^{(1)} + 2\tau^{(2)} \qquad\qquad\qquad \tau = 2\tau^{(1)} + 4\tau^{(2)}$$

Vectors $k_5 = \mu(b_1 + b_2 + b_3)$ $k_9 = \frac{1}{2}(b_1 + b_2 + b_3)$ (L)				Vector $k_3 = \frac{1}{4}(b_1 + b_2) + \frac{1}{2}(b_2 + b_3)$ (W)				
G_k	E	$C_3^{\pm 1}$	3σ	G_k	E	C_2	S_4	S_4^3
$\hat{\chi}^{(1)}$	1	1	1	$\hat{\chi}^{(1)}$	1	1	1	1
$\hat{\chi}^{(2)}$	1	1	-1	$\hat{\chi}^{(2)}$	1	-1	i	$-i$
$\hat{\chi}^{(3)}$	2	-1	0	$\hat{\chi}^{(3)}$	1	1	-1	-1
$\hat{\chi}$	6	0	2	$\hat{\chi}^{(4)}$	1	-1	$-i$	i
				$\hat{\chi}_k$	6	-2	-2	-2

$$\tau_k = 2\tau^{(1)} + 2\tau^{(3)} \qquad\qquad \tau_k = \tau^{(1)} + 2\tau^{(2)} + 2\tau^{(3)} + \tau^{(4)}$$

Vectors $k_6 = \mu(b_1 + b_2)$ $k_{10} = \frac{1}{2}(b_1 + b_2)$ (X)					Vector $k_{11} = 0$					
G_k	E	C_2	σ_1	σ_2	G_k	E	$4C_3^{\pm 1}$	$3C_2$	6σ	$3S_4^{\pm 1}$
$\hat{\chi}^{(1)}$	1	1	1	1	$\hat{\chi}^{(1)}$	1	1	1	1	1
$\hat{\chi}^{(2)}$	1	1	-1	-1	$\hat{\chi}^{(2)}$	1	1	1	-1	-1
$\hat{\chi}^{(3)}$	1	-1	1	-1	$\hat{\chi}^{(3)}$	2	-1	2	0	0
$\hat{\chi}^{(4)}$	1	-1	-1	1	$\hat{\chi}^{(4)}$	3	0	-1	-1	1
$\hat{\chi}_k$	6	-2	2	2	$\hat{\chi}^{(5)}$	3	0	-1	1	-1
					$\hat{\chi}_k$	6	0	-2	2	-2

$$\tau_k = 2\tau^{(1)} + 2\tau^{(3)} + 2\tau^{(4)} \qquad\qquad \tau_k = 2\tau^{(5)}$$

Using the realness criterion (19.55), we can show that all these representations are real. Similar calculations were carried out by Poulet [354] for four points of the Brillouin zone: $\Gamma(k_{11})$, $X(k_{10})$, $L(k_9)$, $W(k_8)$. The general formulae of §19 can be applied to crystals of nonsymmorphic symmetry groups at any point of the Brillouin zone.

20. FIRST-ORDER RAMAN SCATTERING IN CRYSTALS

1. The theory of intensity of Raman scattering in crystals

The calculation of the scattered intensities is one of the basic tasks of the theory of Raman scattering, and it has led to the development of various mathematical methods of treatment.

One of the first studies in the theory of Raman scattering in crystals was published by Tamm [366]. Raman scattering was considered by Tamm as the outcome of the interaction of the normal modes of the electromagnetic waves with the mechanical normal modes of the crystal lattice — phonons. Formally, these processes arise when terms of third and higher orders in amplitudes of the crystal vibrations are included in the Hamiltonian of a system comprising electrons, nuclei, and a radiation field.

Despite the quite general approach, Tamm's theory was essentially semi-phenomenological, since the explicit expressions for the anharmonicity constants of the crystal remained unknown. Ovander [367] developed the microscopic theory for molecular crystals and calculated the actual anharmonicity coefficients. He applied the method of canonical transformation to isolate successively second and third-order terms in the Hamiltonian of a molecular crystal (assuming sufficiently small interaction between the crystal molecules). According to this theory

$$H = H^{(2)} + H^{(3)}, \tag{20.1}$$

where

$$H^{(2)} = \sum_{\rho k} E_\rho(k)\, \xi_\rho^+(k)\, \xi_\rho(k), \tag{20.2}$$

$$H^{(3)} = \sum_{\rho_1 \rho_2 \rho_3} Q_{\rho_1 \rho_2 \rho_3}(k_1, k_2)\, \xi_{\rho_1}(k_1)\, \xi_{\rho_2}(k_2)\, \xi_{\rho_3}^+(k_3) + \text{complex conjugates}. \tag{20.3}$$

Here $\xi_\rho^+(k)$, $\xi_\rho(k)$ are the Bose creation and destruction operators of quasiparticles in the crystal, ρ is the polarization index, k is the wave vector, $Q_{\rho_1 \rho_2 \rho_3}(k_1, k_2)$ are the anharmonicity coefficients. The Hamiltonian with second-order terms is used as the zero approximation; it provides the energy spectrum of quasiparticles obeying the Bose statistics, i.e., the spectrum of excitons. Introduction of third-order terms requires application of the methods of perturbation theory. These terms give rise to processes with the simultaneous participation of three quasiparticles (one quasi-particle decaying into two, and the reverse fusion process).

We will consider the Raman scattering of light within the framework of this theory. Let the incident photon of exciting radiation be characterized by the indices (ρ_0, k_0), the phonon taking part in Raman scattering by the indices (ρ, k), and the scattered photon by the indices (ρ', k') for the Stokes component and (ρ'', k'') for the anti-Stokes component. The corresponding constants in (20.3) have the form $Q_{\rho'\rho\rho_0}(k', k)$ and $Q_{\rho_0\rho\rho''}(k_0, k)$. The rate of change of the number of quasiparticles in these processes is described in the first order of the perturbation theory by the expressions

$$\frac{dn(\rho', k')}{dt} = \frac{2\pi}{\hbar} \sum_{\rho_0\rho} |Q_{\rho'\rho\rho_0}(k', k)|^2 \, n(\rho_0, k_0) \left[n(\rho', k') + 1 \right] \times$$

$$\times \left[n(\rho, k) + 1 \right] \delta \left\{ E(\rho_0, k_0) - E(\rho, k) - E(\rho', k') \right\}, \qquad (20.4)$$

$$\frac{dn(\rho'', k'')}{dt} = \frac{2\pi}{\hbar} \sum_{\rho_0\rho} |Q_{\rho_0\rho\rho''}(k_0, k)|^2 \, n(\rho_0, k_0) \, n(\rho, k) \times$$

$$\times \left[n(\rho'', k'') + 1 \right] \delta \left\{ E(\rho_0, k_0) + E(\rho, k) - E(\rho'', k'') \right\}. \qquad (20.5)$$

Here $n(\rho_0, k_0), n(\rho, k), n(\rho'_1, k'), n(\rho'', k'')$ are the number of exciting photons, the number of phonons, and the number of photons in the Stokes and anti-Stokes components of the scattered light, respectively.

The explicit form of the anharmonicity coefficient is highly complex, and will not be given here. The expressions for the scattered intensity derived in [367] are also very unwieldy, and are likewise omitted. The generalization of the exciton theory to semiconductor crystals was done in [368].

The distinctive feature of the theory of [367, 368] is that the interaction of the electromagnetic radiation with the electronic and the vibrational subsystems is not necessarily small. Raman scattering thus can be studied under conditions when the incident light frequency is close to the exciton absorption band.

Another approach to Raman scattering assumes a small perturbation of the electron subsystem of the crystal by the electromagnetic radiation field. The direct interaction of light with the vibrating nuclei is ignored because of the relatively large mass of the nuclei. It is assumed, however, that lattice vibrations may interact indirectly with the incident radiation, through the intermediacy of the electron subsystems. A detailed solution of the problem of Raman scattering under these assumptions is given in Chapter I. The specific features of Raman scattering in crystals are incorporated into this model in [369, 370].

Considering the crystal as a "giant molecule", we can use the general expression (5.57), which combined with (5.54) and (6.8) gives for the intensity of Raman scattering

$$I_R(\omega', \Omega') = \frac{I_e \omega'^4 F_k(\infty)}{4\pi c^3} |(\beta_{\rho\sigma})_{k1}|^2,$$
(20.6)

where ρ, σ are the subscripts identifying the fixed axes X, Y, Z in which the scattered light is observed (see §6). If the polarizability theory is applicable,* the scattering tensor $(\beta_{\rho\sigma})_{k1}$ is equal to the matrix element of the polarizability tensor $\alpha_{\rho\sigma}$ of the crystal (see §6). For the first-order vibrational transitions we have from (7.18) and (7.19)

$$(\beta_{\rho\sigma})_{v_1 + 1, \ v_1} = \sqrt{v_1 + 1} \left(\frac{\partial \alpha_{\rho\sigma}}{\partial x_i}\right)_0 \sqrt{(x_i^2)_0},$$
(20.7)

$$(\beta_{\rho\sigma})_{v_1 - 1, \ v_1} = \sqrt{v_1} \left(\frac{\partial \alpha_{\rho\sigma}}{\partial x_i}\right)_0 \sqrt{(x_i^2)_0}.$$
(20.8)

One of the shortcomings of the above methods, which treat Raman scattering in the second order of the perturbation theory, is that the eigenfunctions of the unperturbed electron subsystem correspond to the nonequilibrium configuration of the nuclei. The actual form of these functions remains unknown; therefore, the matrix elements entering the expressions for the scattering tensor cannot be evaluated. A better policy naturally would be to use the functions corresponding to the equilibrium configuration of the nuclei as the unperturbed eigenfunctions of the electron subsystem; the vibration of the nuclei can be allowed for in this case by introducing an additional perturbation associated with the electron–phonon interaction. This method was first applied to the description of Raman scattering by Sobel'man [371]. A detailed development of the method for simple crystals was carried out in [372, 373].

In this method, probability of Raman scattering does not vanish only in the third order of the perturbation theory. The probability of Stokes scattering in unit time is described by the expression

$$W_R = \frac{2\pi}{\hbar^6} \sum_{k_0 k'} \left| \sum_{a, b} \frac{\langle n_0 - 1, 1; n + 1; 0 | V | a \rangle \langle a | V | b \rangle \langle b | V | n_0, 0; n; 0 \rangle}{(\omega_a - \omega_0)(\omega_b - \omega_0)} \right|^2;$$
(20.9)

---

* When transforming the expressions for the matrix elements (5.26), (5.27), it should be remembered that the exponential factors $\exp(ikr)$, $\exp(-ikr)$ in a crystal are not constant and therefore cannot be factored out of the integral (see §5). This point, however, is of no consequence in the subsequent calculations leading to Eq. (6.26). The scattering and polarizability tensor of the crystal also depends on the vector k, i.e., we have here a case of spatial dispersion.

here a, b are the indices of the intermediate states of the entire system, k_0, k' are the wave vectors of the incident and scattered light, $V = H_{rad} + H_{lat}$ is the perturbation operator consisting of the perturbation of the electron subsystem by the radiation field H_{rad} and by the phonon field H_{lat}. Despite the complexity of Eq. (20.9), it was successfully applied to obtain particular estimates of the scattering cross section in simple crystals, since the values of electron–photon and electron–phonon coupling constants are known for some crystals.

The results of direct measurements of the absolute cross section of Raman scattering in crystals are given in §22.

2. Selection rules in first-order Raman spectra

Unlike gases and liquids, where the intensity of Raman lines depends on the invariants of the scattering tensor, crystals give scattered light whose intensity (for given directions of incidence and scattering) depends directly on the components of the scattering tensor. Therefore the selection rules for crystals have a somewhat more complex form than the selection rules for individual molecules, although the general principles leading to the derivation of selection rules are the same.

According to the general theory (see §10), the matrix element $(f_\lambda)_{ik}$ of some physical quantity f_λ does not vanish only if the direct product of representations $\Gamma^i \times \Gamma^\lambda \times \Gamma^k$ contains the unit representation. Here Γ^i is the representation of the symmetry group of the quantum system according to which the wave function ψ_i of the initial state is transformed, Γ^k is the representation according to which the wave function ψ_k of the final state is transformed (the initial and the final states are assumed to be different), Γ^λ is the representation according to which f_λ is transformed. In the case of Raman scattering in crystals, the wave functions ψ_i, ψ_k transform according to irreducible representations of the space group of the crystal, and f_λ in the approximation of the polarizability theory are the components of the symmetrical polarizability tensor $\alpha_{\rho\sigma}$.

From the conservation of quasimomentum in Raman scattering, we conclude that the wave vectors of the photons and phonons taking part in this process are of the same order of magnitude. Therefore, if $k_{phot} = 0$, we should also have $k_{phon} \approx 0$. In this case, the vibrational wave functions can be approximately classified according to the irreducible representations of the group F, i.e., we can use the mathematical apparatus developed for molecules (see §10). In particular, the number $n_{\Gamma k}$ of normal modes of the given group F for the component of the polarizability tensor is expressed by the equality

$$n_{\Gamma k} = \frac{1}{f} \sum_{n_j \subset F} \chi_{\alpha_{\rho\sigma}}(h_j)\, \chi_{\Gamma k}(h_j), \tag{20.10}$$

where $\chi_{\alpha_{\rho\sigma}}(h_j)$ is the character of the irreducible representation according to which the component $\alpha_{\rho\sigma}$ is transformed; f is the number of elements of the group F. If $n_{\Gamma k} = 0$, the particular vibration is forbidden for the component $\alpha_{\rho\sigma}$ of the polarizability tensor. Using (20.10), we can readily identify the nonzero components of the Raman scattering tensor for a given crystal. The form of these tensors for the main crystal systems is given in Table 44, following [373]. For each crystal system, the table lists the irreducible representations which are active in first-order Raman spectra.

Table 44

SELECTION RULES IN FIRST-ORDER RAMAN SPECTRA
OF THE MAIN SYMMETRY SYSTEMS OF CRYSTALS [373]

System		Class	Raman scattering tensor			
			$$\begin{pmatrix} a & d & \\ & b & \\ d & & c \end{pmatrix} \begin{pmatrix} & & e \\ & e & f \\ & f & \end{pmatrix}$$			
Monoclinic	2	C_2	$A(y)$	$B(x, z)$		
	m	C_s	$A'(x, z)$	$A''(y)$		
	$2/m$	C_{2h}	A_g	B_g		
			$$\begin{pmatrix} a & & \\ & b & \\ & & c \end{pmatrix} \begin{pmatrix} & d & \\ d & & \\ & & \end{pmatrix} \begin{pmatrix} & & e \\ & & \\ e & & \end{pmatrix} \begin{pmatrix} & & \\ & & f \\ & f & \end{pmatrix}$$			
Orthorhombic	222	D_2	A	$B_1(z)$ $B_2(y)$ $B_3(x)$		
	$mm2$	C_{2v}	$A_1(z)$	A_2	$B_1(x)$	$B_2(y)$
	mmm	D_{2h}	A_g	B_{1g}	B_{2g}	B_{3g}
			$$\begin{pmatrix} a & & \\ & a & \\ & & b \end{pmatrix} \begin{pmatrix} c & d & e \\ d & -c & f \\ e & f & \end{pmatrix} \begin{pmatrix} d & -c & -f \\ -c & -d & e \\ -f & e & \end{pmatrix}$$			
	3	C_3	$A(z)$	$E(x)$	$E(y)$	
	3	C_{3i}	A_g	E_g	E_g	
Trigonal			$$\begin{pmatrix} a & & \\ & a & \\ & & b \end{pmatrix} \begin{pmatrix} c & & \\ & -c & d \\ & d & \end{pmatrix} \begin{pmatrix} & -c & -d \\ -c & & \\ -d & & \end{pmatrix}$$			
	32	D_3	A_1	$E(x)$	$E(y)$	
	$3m$	C_{3v}	$A_1(z)$	$E(y)$	$E(-x)$	
	$\bar{3}m$	D_{3d}	A_{1g}	E_g	E_g	

Table 44 (continued)

System	Class		Raman scattering tensor

Tetragonal

$$\begin{pmatrix} a & & \\ & a & \\ & & b \end{pmatrix} \quad \begin{pmatrix} c & d & \\ d & -c & \\ & & \end{pmatrix} \quad \begin{pmatrix} & & e \\ & & f \\ e & f & \end{pmatrix} \quad \begin{pmatrix} & & -f \\ & & e \\ -f & e & \end{pmatrix}$$

4	C_4	$A(z)$	B	$E(x)$	$E(y)$
$\bar{4}$	S_4	A	$B(z)$	$E(x)$	$E(-y)$
$4/m$	C_{4h}	A_g	B_g	E_g	E_g

$$\begin{pmatrix} a & & \\ & a & \\ & & b \end{pmatrix} \quad \begin{pmatrix} c & & \\ & -c & \\ & & \end{pmatrix} \quad \begin{pmatrix} & d & \\ d & & \\ & & \end{pmatrix} \quad \begin{pmatrix} & & e \\ & & \\ e & & \end{pmatrix} \quad \begin{pmatrix} & & \\ & & e \\ & e & \end{pmatrix}$$

4mm	C_{4v}	$A_1(z)$	B_1	B_2	$E(x)$	$E(y)$
422	D_4	A_1	B_1	B_2	$E(-y)$	$E(x)$
$\bar{4}2m$	D_{2d}	A_1	B_1	$B_2(z)$	$E(y)$	$E(x)$
$4/mmm$	D_{4d}	A_{1g}	B_{1g}	B_{2g}	E_g	E_g

Hexagonal

$$\begin{pmatrix} a & & \\ & a & \\ & & b \end{pmatrix} \quad \begin{pmatrix} & & c \\ & & d \\ c & d & \end{pmatrix} \quad \begin{pmatrix} & & -d \\ & & c \\ -d & c & \end{pmatrix} \quad \begin{pmatrix} e & f \\ f & -e \end{pmatrix} \quad \begin{pmatrix} f & -e \\ -e & -f \end{pmatrix}$$

6	C_6	$A(z)$	$E_1(x)$	$E_1(y)$	E_2	E_2
$\bar{6}$	C_{3h}	A'	E''	E''	$E'(x)$	$E'(y)$
$6/m$	C_{6h}	A_g	E_{1g}	E_{1g}	E_{2g}	E_{2g}

$$\begin{pmatrix} a & & \\ & a & \\ & & b \end{pmatrix} \quad \begin{pmatrix} & & \\ & & c \\ & c & \end{pmatrix} \quad \begin{pmatrix} & & -c \\ & & \\ -c & & \end{pmatrix} \quad \begin{pmatrix} d & & \\ & & \\ & & d \end{pmatrix} \quad \begin{pmatrix} d & & \\ & -d & \\ & & \end{pmatrix}$$

622	D_6	A_1	$E_1(x)$	$E_1(y)$	E_2	E_2
6mm	C_{6v}	$A_1(z)$	$E_1(y)$	$E_1(-x)$	E_2	E_2
$\bar{6}m2$	D_{3h}	A'_1	E''	E''	$E'(x)$	$E'(y)$
$6/mmm$	D_{6h}	A_{1g}	E_{1g}	E_{1g}	E_{2g}	E_{2g}

Cubic

$$\begin{pmatrix} a & & \\ & a & \\ & & a \end{pmatrix} \quad \begin{pmatrix} b & & \\ & b & \\ & & \bar{b} \end{pmatrix} \quad \begin{pmatrix} b & & \\ & \bar{b} & \\ & & b \end{pmatrix} \quad \begin{pmatrix} & & \\ & & d \\ & d & \end{pmatrix} \quad \begin{pmatrix} & & d \\ & & \\ d & & \end{pmatrix} \quad \begin{pmatrix} & d & \\ d & & \\ & & \end{pmatrix}$$

23	T	A	E	E	$F(x)$	$F(y)$	$F(z)$
m3	T_h	A_g	E_g	E_g	F_g	F_g	F_g
432	O	A_1	E	E	F_2	F_2	F_2
$\bar{4}3m$	T_d	A_1	E	E	$F_2(x)$	$F_2(y)$	$F_2(z)$
m3m	O_h	A_{1g}	E_g	E_g	F_{2g}	F_{2g}	F_{2g}

As we have noted before, the Raman scattering tensor in general is not symmetrical. Ovander [367] gives the nonzero elements of the scattering tensor considered as a tensor of rank 2. These elements differ from those of Table 44 in that they contain additional terms.

To calculate the effective cross section σ or the intensity I of Raman lines with the aid of Table 44, we must use the relation

$$\sigma = A \left[\sum_{\rho, \sigma} e_\rho \beta_{\rho\sigma} e'_\sigma \right]^2 , \qquad (20.11)$$

where A is a proportionality coefficient, e_ρ, e'_σ are the components of the unit polarization vectors of the electric field of the incident and scattered radiation, $\beta_{\rho\sigma}$ are the components of the Raman scattering tensor.

As an example let us consider Raman scattering in the geometry shown in Figure 72.

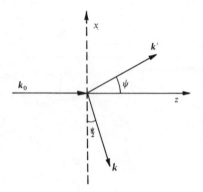

Figure 72

Geometrical conditions of scattering.

First let us consider the scattering by a B mode of the group C_4. The effective cross section for Raman scattering in this case is

$$\sigma = A(e_x\beta_{xx}e'_x + e_x\beta_{xy}e'_y + e_x\beta_{xz}e'_z + e_y\beta_{yx}e'_x + e_y\beta_{yy}e'_y + e_y\beta_{yz}e'_z)^2 .$$

According to Table 44, $\beta_{xz} = \beta_{yz} = 0$, $\beta_{xx} = c$, $\beta_{xy} = \beta_{yx} = d$, $\beta_{yy} = -c$. For scattered radiation polarized in the plane xz (parallel scattering), we obtain the effective cross section

$$\sigma_{\parallel} = A(e_x c + e_y d)^2 \cos^2 \psi .$$

For radiation polarized at right angles to the plane xz, we have

$$\sigma_{\perp} = A(e_x d - e_y c)^2 .$$

It is assumed that the scattered light wave is transversal.

Let us consider another example of scattering by a triply degenerate mode F_{2g} of the group O_h. The total effective cross section in this case may be written as a sum of three terms, each derived from the corresponding matrix in Table 44. After some calculations, we find

$$\sigma_{||} = Ad^2 \left[(e_x \sin \psi)^2 + e_y^2 \right],$$

$$\sigma_{\perp} = Ad^2 e_x^2 .$$

In the particular case $\psi = \frac{1}{2}\pi$, these expressions are considerably simplified.

An important characteristic of the scattered light is the depolarization ρ, defined as the ratio $\rho = \sigma_{||}/\sigma_{\perp}$.

The depolarization in general depends on the angle ψ and it provides an insight into the symmetry of the vibrations which are active in the scattering process. Depolarization calculations for various crystals and various illumination geometries were carried out in [374, 375].

A so-called two-dimensional intensity table [340] is generally constructed experimentally for the analysis of the Raman scattering tensor. The scattered intensities are measured for various orientations of the crystal and of the polarizing devices intercepting the incident and the scattered light. Observations are made at right angles to the direction of incidence. The components of the intensity table are calculated for nondegenerate modes by taking the square of the corresponding component of the Raman scattering tensor. For example, the component of the intensity table corresponding to a geometry in which the polarizing device, the detector, and the light source are all oriented along the x axis is proportional to β_{xx}^2, etc. If the vibration modes active in Raman scattering are degenerate, the component of the intensity table is obtained by adding up the corresponding squares of the components of the RS tensor.

The selection rules of Raman scattering are often broken in crystals. There are various reasons for this violation.

First, just like in Raman spectra of molecules, forbidden lines sometimes appear because, at sufficiently high temperatures, the crystal may scatter from an excited vibrational state [376–378]. Second, as we come close to the electronic absorption band, the RS tensor becomes nonsymmetrical, and additional vibration modes are allowed in Raman scattering (see §7). Third, the presence of impurities and vacancies in the crystal breaks the translational invariance and also violates the law of quasi-momentum conservation in Raman scattering [379]. As a result, Raman scattering is allowed with the participation of a single lattice phonon of an arbitrary quasi-momentum. In this case, the main contribution is from phonons corresponding to the critical points of the Brillouin zone. It is apparently this mechanism that produces the first-order lines in the spectrum of the $SrTiO_3$ crystal [376], for which all the vibration modes are forbidden in Raman scattering according to the strict selection rules. The appearance of additional sharp, but exceedingly weak lines near strong Raman lines [382] is also related to the breakdown of selection rules falling under this category.

Selection rules may be violated by application of external fields which lower the crystal symmetry. This method fact may be used to study modes which are normally inactive in Raman scattering [383].

3. First-order Raman spectra of the simplest crystals

Calcite $CaCO_3$

The Raman spectrum of calcite has been studied by numerous authors, since large single crystals of this mineral are relatively easily accessible; they are moreover transparent in a wide range of frequencies, homogeneous, and readily machined. The calcite unit cell is shown in Figure 73. It contains two $CaCO_3$ molecules. The notation and the coordinates of the atoms are as follows:

$$Ca (1;2): \tfrac{1}{4}, \tfrac{1}{4}, \tfrac{1}{4}; \tfrac{3}{4}, \tfrac{3}{4}, \tfrac{3}{4},$$

$$C (3;4): 0, 0, 0; \tfrac{1}{2}, \tfrac{1}{2}, \tfrac{1}{2};$$

$$O(5; 6, 7; 8; 9, 10).$$

The symmetry space group of the crystal is D_{3d}^6, the group of directions is D_{3d}. The limiting vibration modes ($k = 0$) of the unit cell can be classified as follows. The CO_3 groups may be treated as one whole; correspondingly, we distinguish between translational vibrations (the CO_3 groups moving relative to one another and relative to Ca atoms), orientation vibrations (the CO_3 groups rotating relative to one another in phase or in counterphase), and internal vibrations in the CO_3 groups. The characters of the corresponding representations and of the representations of a vector and a symmetrical tensor of rank 2 can be calculated using Figure 73 and Table 45.

Decomposing the reducible representations into irreducible representations, we find

$$\Gamma_{rot} = A_{2g} + A_{1u} + E_g + E_u,$$

$$\Gamma_{tr} = A_{2g} + A_{1u} + A_{2u} + 2E_u + E_g,$$

$$\Gamma_{int} = A_{1g} + A_{2g} + A_{1u} + A_{2u} + 2E_u + 2E_g,$$

$$\Gamma_{tot} = A_{1g} + 3A_{2g} + 3A_{1u} + 2A_{2u} + 5E_u + 4E_g. \qquad (20.12)$$

Comparison of (20.12) with the vector representation $\Gamma_v = A_{2u} + E_u$ and the tensor representation $\Gamma_{\alpha_{\rho\sigma}} = 2A_{1g} + 2E_g$ shows (see §10) that the modes A_{1g} and E_g are

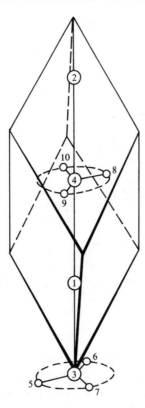

Figure 73

The unit cell of calcite.

active in the Raman spectrum and inactive in the IR absorption spectrum. At high frequencies (internal vibrations), we can expect three Raman lines, and at low frequencies, only two lines.

The Raman spectrum of calcite shows 5 lines at 155, 282, 712, 1086 and 1436 cm^{-1} [380–382]. The last three lines evidently correspond to the internal vibrations in the CO_3 group; the strongest line $\Delta v = 1086$ cm^{-1} is identified with the symmetrical A_{1g} mode, and the 712 and 1436 cm^{-1} lines with E_g modes. The two low-frequency lines correspond to E_g modes.

Later studies of the Raman spectrum of calcite [384, 385] have revealed a much more complex structure of the spectrum. Numerous weak sharp lines were discovered, and also a continuous background in certain regions of the spectrum. Thus, the 1086 cm^{-1} line has weak satellites with frequencies of 1067, 1072, and 1075 cm^{-1}; near the 1436 cm^{-1} line, there are additional lines at 1399, 1412, and 1418 cm^{-1}, etc.

Table 45

CHARACTERS OF REPRESENTATIONS FOR THE CALCITE CRYSTAL (D_{3d} GROUP)

Representation	e	$2S_6$	$2C_3$	i	$3\sigma_v$	$3C_2$
Vibrational representation	27	0	0	−3	−1	−3
Translation-vibrational representation	9	0	0	−3	−1	−1
Rotation-vibrational representation	6	0	0	0	0	−2
External vibrational representation	15	0	0	−3	−1	−3
Internal vibrational representation	12	0	0	0	0	0
Vector representation	3	0	0	−3	1	−1
Symmetrical tensor representation	6	0	0	6	2	2
A_{1g}	1	1	1	1	1	1
A_{1u}	1	−1	1	−1	−1	1
A_{2g}	1	1	1	1	−1	−1
A_{2u}	1	−1	1	−1	1	−1
E_g	2	−1	−1	2	0	0
E_u	2	1	−1	−2	0	0

The appearance of the additional lines has been accounted for on the basis of Raman's theory of lattice dynamics [382, 384]. These lines are associated with the scattering by the additional degrees of freedom of the Raman superlattice. Note that the appearance of the additional lines also can be interpreted within the framework of Born's theory, as a result of the nonconservation of the quasimomentum in an inhomogeneous lattice. We will return to this problem in connection with the theory of critical points in §21.

Quartz SiO_2

Numerous authors have studied the Raman scattering of quartz, so that not only the frequencies, but also the intensities, states of polarization, and widths of the various lines are known [1, 374, 386–392].

The α-quartz lattice is made up of Si—O tetrahedra: each silicon ion is bonded to four surrounding oxygen ions, and each oxygen ion is bonded to two silicon ions. The group of directions of α-quartz is D_3, the unit cell contains three SiO_3 molecules. The Raman spectrum for $k = 0$ therefore should contain four allowed A_1 modes and eight doubly degenerate E modes. The other degrees of freedom contribute four A_2 modes which are active in the IR spectrum and three acoustic branches.

The quartz crystals used in Raman scattering tests are generally cube-shaped, with the sides directed along the crystallographic axes. In what follows, we assume the optical axis of α-quartz to be directed along the z axis. According to Table 44, we thus have for the components of the scattering tensor $\beta_{xx} = \beta_{yy} \neq \beta_{zz}$, $\beta_{\rho\sigma} = 0$ for $\rho \neq \sigma$ (A_1 modes) and $\beta_{xx} = -\beta_{yy} = -\beta_{xy}$, $\beta_{xz} = -\beta_{yz}$, $\beta_{zz} = 0$ (E modes). Twelve lines have been observed experimentally in the Raman spectrum of α-quartz. Table 46 lists the results of photoelectric measurements of some parameters of α-quartz lines carried out in [388]. The Raman line intensities in [388] were measured for three different positions of the specimens, with each of the three axes successively pointing in the direction of scattering (other conditions remaining constant). The symbols Z, X, Y in Table 46 identify the measurement results obtained with the respective axis aligned in the direction of scattering under conditions of uniform illumination of the specimen in a plane perpendicular to this axis.

Using polarization measurements, Kiselev and Osipova [389] compiled intensity tables for the Raman lines of α-quartz. The polarization measurements can be carried out by several different methods.

1. The crystal is illuminated by linearly polarized light. The scattered light is intercepted by polaroids with the direction of polarization parallel and perpendicular to the spectrometer slit.

2. The crystal is alternately illuminated with polarized light with the direction of polarization parallel and perpendicular to the direction of observation; this method is generally implemented using "tubular" polaroids.

3. The crystal is illuminated by unpolarized light, and the scattered light is alternately intercepted by polaroids with the direction of polarization parallel and perpendicular to the slit.

The measured intensities in each of these methods can be arranged in a table whose entries are proportional to the squares of the scattering tensor components (the

Table 46

RELATIVE LINE INTENSITIES OF RAMAN SCATTERING OF α-QUARTZ

Symmetry class	Frequency $\Delta\nu$, cm^{-1}	Width δ, cm^{-1}	$I_\infty(Z)$	$I_\infty(X)$	$I_\infty(Y)$	$I_0(Z)$	$I_0(X)$	$I_0(Y)$
E	128	4.4	90	55	55	100	60	60
A	206	21	51	60	60	28	30	30
E	266	4.4	6.2	6.5	6.0	12	11	12
A	357	4	5.3	5.7	6.1	12	14	13
A	466	6.6	180	210	210	180	220	220
E	696	6.4	3.1	2.4	2.4	4.4	3	3
E	795	8.4 ⎫	7.3	6.4	6.2	3	3.4	3.4
E	805	11.3 ⎭				3.8	4.3	4.1
E	1061	7.9	2.7	1.8	1.5	3.1	1.9	2.1
A	1081	11.5	1.5	3.3	3.1	1.1	2.8	2.7
E	1159	8.4	10	7.2	7	10	6.9	6.5
E	1228	11.6	1.4	1.6	1.4	1.3	1.1	1.2

measurement methods, the calculations, and the essential corrections are described in [389, 393]; see also the supplement to [44]). Using the intensity table, we can readily find the absolute values of the scattering tensor components. The signs of the tensor component sometimes can be determined from simple symmetry considerations, but in a number of cases this requires additional calculations and measurements.

For α-quartz, the problem is significantly simplified by crystal symmetry considerations. If the optical axis of the crystal is aligned along the z axis, and the two second-order axes coincide with the axes x and y, respectively, the latter two axes are optically equivalent. Thus, in the intensity table, $I_{zx} = I_{zy}$, $I_{xx} = I_{yy}$. The intensity table and the scattering tensor thus contain only four components differing in the absolute magnitudes. For the lines of class A_1, all the components of the scattering tensor may be taken positive. For the strongest 466 cm^{-1} line, the Raman scattering tensor [389] is

$$\beta(466) = \begin{bmatrix} 103 \pm 3 & 14 \pm 12 & 22 \pm 2 \\ 14 \pm 12 & 103 \pm 3 & 22 \pm 2 \\ 22 \pm 2 & 22 \pm 2 & 100 \pm 2 \end{bmatrix}$$

Similar data are given in [389] for other lines of the class A_1. Note that the mixed components $\beta_{\rho\sigma}(\rho \neq \sigma)$ do not vanish, i.e., the selection rules are broken.

Measurements show [389] that the scattering tensors for the lines 206, 357, and 466 cm^{-1} are approximately spherically symmetrical ($\beta_{zz} \approx \beta_{xx} = \beta_{yy}$). The fourth line of class A_1 has a substantially different scattering tensor (the components are expressed on the same scale as those of the tensor $\beta(466)$):

$$\beta(1081) = \begin{bmatrix} 6 & 0 & 5 \\ 0 & 6 & 5 \\ 5 & 5 & 17.3 \end{bmatrix}.$$

The form of this tensor shows that the vibrations of the induced electric moment in this case occur mainly along the z axis.

The scattering tensor for the degenerate modes of α-quartz has been experimentally determined by Kiselev [390]. Two identical cube specimens were used, with differently oriented X and Y crystallographic axes. The axes of one specimen were directed along the cube sides, and the sides of the second specimen made an angle of 45° with the crystallographic axes X and Y.

Measurements showed that, within the margin of experimental error, the intensity tables of the two specimens coincide for the strongest E-type lines 128, 696, 795–805, and 1159 cm^{-1}.

The Raman scattering tensor for degenerate vibrations can be written in the form

$$\beta_{\rho\sigma} = \beta'_{\rho\sigma} + \beta''_{\rho\sigma},$$

where the tensors β' and β'' each correspond to one of the degenerate modes of the given frequency ω. Since two vibrations of class E with the same frequency ω are normal modes independent of each other, we may write

$$I_{\rho\sigma} = (\beta'_{\rho\sigma})^2 + (\beta''_{\rho\sigma})^2 = I'_{\rho\sigma} + I''_{\rho\sigma}.$$

The experimental findings were processed in [390] assuming that $I'_{\rho\sigma} = I''_{\rho\sigma}$, so that the scattering tensors β' and β'' differed only in the sign of some components. Scattering tensors for E-type lines were obtained in this way.

21. SOME TYPICAL CASES OF RAMAN SCATTERING IN CRYSTALS

Observation of Raman scattering in crystals involves considerable experimental difficulties. High-purity specimens of sufficient size are essential for these observations, and this severely limits the range of potential objects. Powders and poly-crystalline specimens may be used, but they introduce additional difficulties. The Raman lines in crystals are exceedingly weak. They moreover fall near the exciting line, which produces a strong background and, in diffraction grating instruments, "ghosts". All these difficulties notwithstanding, more than a hundred various crystals have been investigated by now, and the total number of papers published on the Raman scattering of crystals reaches several hundreds. We do not intend to present here a systematic review of all the publications, since several reviews with comprehensive bibliographies are already available [373, 394, 395]. We will only concentrate on some typical cases of Raman scattering in crystals, which in our opinion are of special physical interest.

1. Molecular crystals

Intensive studies of lattice vibrations of molecular crystals were begun following the discovery of the low-frequency Raman spectrum by Gross and Vuks [396]. The lines of this spectrum are distinguished by two important features:

1) their frequencies are very close to the exciting line, which means that the characteristic frequencies of the scattering molecule are very low;

2) distinct lines are observed in the spectrum of the crystal, whereas the same compound in the liquid state gives only a continuous spectrum in the relevant frequency region (wings of the Rayleigh line).

Gross and co-workers advanced the opinion that the low-frequency spectrum was due to intermolecular vibrations, or in other words vibrations of the crystal lattice. This conclusion was corroborated by a number of experimental findings [397].

To first approximation, the individual molecules in a molecular crystal lattice may be treated as rigid objects capable of translation and rotation (i.e., change in orientation). It is naturally important to consider the separability of these two modes of molecular motion. Anselm and Porfir'eva [398] computed the vibrations of a one-dimensional molecular lattice, and their results shed light on the significant features of the general problem.

Let us first consider a one-dimensional lattice with a single molecule in the unit cell. The position of the center of mass and the orientation of the n-th molecule are defined by the coordinates x_n and θ_n, respectively (the molecule may rotate in one plane only). The potential energy of the n-th molecule is thus

$$U_n = U_0 + \tfrac{1}{2} a(\theta_{n-1}^2 + \theta_n^2) + \tfrac{1}{2} b(\theta_n^2 + \theta_{n+1}^2) +$$
$$+ c(\theta_{n-1}\theta_n + \theta_n\theta_{n+1}) + \tfrac{1}{2} f[(x_{n-1} - x_n)^2 + (x_n - x_{n+1})^2] +$$
$$+ g[\theta_{n-1}(x_{n-1} - x_n) + \theta_n(x_n - x_{n+1})] +$$
$$+ h(\theta_n(x_{n-1} - x_n) + \theta_{n+1}(x_n - x_{n+1})] + \ldots \tag{21.1}$$

Here a, b, c, f, g, h are the usual dynamic constants. The equations of motion take the form

$$m\ddot{x}_n = - f(2x_n - x_{n-1} - x_{n+1}) - g(\theta_n - \theta_{n-1}) - h(\theta_{n+1} - \theta_n),$$
$$\tag{21.2}$$
$$\mathscr{I}\ddot{\theta}_n = - (a + b)\theta_n - c(\theta_{n-1} + \theta_{n+1}) - g(x_n - x_{n+1}) - h(x_{n-1} - x_n)$$

(m is the mass, $\mathscr{I}$ is the moment of inertia of the molecule).

The solution of these equations is sought in the form of rotation–translation waves

$$x_n = Xe^{i(\omega t - n\phi)}, \qquad \theta_n = \Theta e^{i(\omega t - n\phi)}, \tag{21.3}$$

where $\phi = 2\pi\delta/\lambda$ is the phase of the wave, δ is the lattice constant. Inserting (21.3) in (21.2), we obtain a system of two linear homogeneous equations for the amplitudes X, Θ:

$$[m\omega^2 - 2f(1 - \cos\phi)] X - [g(1 - e^{i\phi}) - h(1 - e^{-i\phi})] \Theta = 0,$$
$$[g(1 - e^{-i\phi}) - h(1 - e^{i\phi})] X - [\mathscr{I}\omega^2 - (a + b + 2c\cos\phi)] \Theta = 0. \tag{21.4}$$

Equating the determinant of this system to zero, we find

$$\omega^2 = \tfrac{1}{2}\Omega_1^2(1 - \cos\phi) + \tfrac{1}{2}\Omega_2^2(1 + q\cos\phi) \pm$$
$$\pm \{[\tfrac{1}{2}\Omega_2^2(1 + q\cos\phi) - \tfrac{1}{2}\Omega_1^2(1 - \cos\phi)]^2 +$$
$$+ (g_0 - h_0)^2 (1 - \cos\phi)^2 + (g_0 + h_0)^2 \sin^2\phi\}^{1/2}. \tag{21.5}$$

Here $g_0 = g/\sqrt{m\mathscr{I}}$, $h_0 = h/\sqrt{m\mathscr{I}}$, $\Omega_1^2 = 2f/m$, $\Omega_2^2 = (a + b)/\mathscr{I}$, $q = 2c/(a + b)$. Ω_1 and Ω_2 are the translation and the rotation frequencies of the molecule when its nearest neighbors are fixed in the equilibrium positions.

We see from (21.5) that in general the vibrations are a mixture of translation and rotation. The spectrum can be separated into rotation and translation frequencies only when

$$g = h = 0. \tag{21.6}$$

Then

$$\omega_{\text{rot}} = \omega_+ = \Omega_2 \sqrt{1 + q \cos \phi}, \qquad \omega_{\text{tr}} = \omega_- = \Omega_1 \sqrt{1 - \cos \phi}. \tag{21.7}$$

The limiting frequencies for long waves $\lambda \to \infty$ (or $\phi = 0$) are given by

$$\omega_{\text{rot}}^2 = \frac{a + b}{\mathscr{I}} (1 + q), \qquad \omega_{\text{tr}}^2 = 0. \tag{21.8}$$

The translation frequencies in this case form an ordinary acoustic branch (see §19.1).

For a linear molecular lattice with two molecules in the unit cell, the calculations of Ansel'm and Porfir'eva [398] lead to the following expressions for the limiting frequencies:

$$\omega_1^2 = 0, \qquad \omega_2^2 = \Omega_2^2 (1 - q),$$

$$\omega_3^2 = \tfrac{1}{2}(1 + q)\Omega_2^2 + \Omega_1^2 + [(\tfrac{1}{2}(1 + q)\Omega_2^2 - \Omega_1^2)^2 + 4(g_0 + h_0)^2]^{1/2},$$

$$\omega_4^2 = \tfrac{1}{2}(1 + q)\Omega_2^2 + \Omega_1^2 - [(\tfrac{1}{2}(1 + q)\Omega_2^2 - \Omega_1^2)^2 + 4(g_0 + h_0)^2]^{1/2}. \tag{21.9}$$

The first frequency corresponds to a pure translation acoustic branch, the second frequency refers to a pure rotation branch. The third and the fourth branches are mixed, and they only can be split into translation and rotation when $g_0 + h_0 = 0$.

In later work, Porfir'eva [399] considered two-dimensional and three-dimensional models of molecular lattices. The vibrations only separate into pure translation and rotation for the limiting frequencies when $g + h = 0$. The limiting frequencies of the acoustic branches of pure translation vibrations are zero, and those of pure rotation vibrations are proportional to $\sqrt{R_i/\mathscr{I}_i}$ ($i = x, y, z$). The limiting frequencies of the optical branches in this case are proportional to $\sqrt{f_i/m}$ (translation vibrations) and $\sqrt{R'_i/\mathscr{I}_i}$ (rotation). Here $\mathscr{I}_x, \mathscr{I}_y, \mathscr{I}_z$ are the moments of inertia of the molecule about the three axes, R_i, R'_i, f_i are some combinations of the quasielastic lattice constants. Similar conclusions were obtained in [400].

The total number of lines in the low-frequency spectrum is determined by the number of molecules m in the unit cell. Generally, only the limiting frequencies corresponding to $\lambda \to \infty$ are observed. The three acoustic branches have zero limiting frequencies. The spectrum should thus show $3(m - 1)$ "translation" frequencies and $3m$ "rotation" frequencies. Many of these frequencies will naturally remain undetected in the spectrum because of the extreme weakness of the corresponding lines.* For example, the spectrum of hexamethylbenzene, whose unit cell contains a single molecule, may show three "rotation" lines. Actually, only two lines at 53 cm^{-1}

---

* Some lines may be forbidden by selection rules.

and 95 cm^{-1} were observed [401]. In crystals with two molecules in the unit cell, the spectrum should contain nine lines. Of these, three can be roughly classified as translation lines and six as rotation lines (assuming that the separation into translation and rotation is meaningful to some approximation).

Comparison of the spectra of crystals with close quasielastic constants in principle permits assigning the observed lines to definite vibration modes. Systematic studies of this kind were carried out by Gross, Korshunov, Vuks, and co-workers [402–404]. They made a comparison of the low-frequency spectra of crystals with similar structure, mainly of isomorphic crystals. The regular frequency changes in the spectra of similar crystals consisting of molecules of different masses and moments of inertia lead to definite conclusions regarding the nature of the corresponding vibration modes.

A good example of the application of this method is provided by the low-frequency spectra of the isomorphous crystals of dihalogen derivatives of benzene in the para-position. Molecules of these compounds have the form

$$R_1 - \left\langle \!\!\!\bigcirc\!\!\! \right\rangle - R_2 \, .$$

Here R_1 and R_2 stand for the halogen atoms Cl, Br, I. The data of [403, 405] are listed in Table 47, where $\mathscr{I}_1$ is the principal moment of inertia about an axis perpendicular to the plane of the benzene ring, $\mathscr{I}_2$ is the moment of inertia about an axis in the plane of the benzene ring at right angles to the line joining the two halogen atoms, $\mathscr{I}_3$ is the moment of inertia about the axis through the two halogen atoms.

Lines grouped in the same column of Table 47 have close intensities and identical states of polarization. This is evidence of their common origin in different crystals. The frequencies v_9 and v_8 hardly change from one compound to the next, and this property definitely identifies them with rotation about the axis through the halogen atoms. The weak lines v_1, v_2, v_4 are assigned in [403] to translation modes, and the strong lines v_3, v_5, v_6, v_7 to rotation about the axes with the moments of inertia $\mathscr{I}_1$ and $\mathscr{I}_2$, which markedly change from one molecule to the next. The dependence of v^2 on $1/\mathscr{I}$ for the last four lines follows a straight line. As an example, Figure 74 gives the corresponding results for v_7. The moments of inertia $\mathscr{I}_1$ and $\mathscr{I}_2$ have very close values, and it is therefore impossible to unambiguously assign the frequencies to orientation rotations about each axis. The solid and the dashed lines in Figure 74 correspond to the two alternative interpretations. It is significant that these lines in Figure 74 do not pass through the origin. In [403] this is attributed to a certain regular change in the quasielastic constants from one molecule to the next.

Group-theoretical analysis of the vibration modes of the molecular crystals of benzene para-dihalogen derivatives can be based on the general theory of §19 and §20. These crystals are isomorphic and they all belong to the C_{2h}^5 space group with two

Table 47

LOW-FREQUENCY RAMAN SPECTRA OF BENZENE PARA-DIHALODERIVATIVES

Compound	ν_1	ν_2	ν_3	ν_4	ν_5	ν_6	ν_7	ν_8	ν_9
α-$C_6H_4Cl_2$	8	17	27.5	35	47.5	48.7	56	72	93
$\mathscr{I}_1 = 1384$ $\mathscr{I}_2 = 1234$	(2)	(2)	(10)	(2)	(10)	(10)	(10)	(1)	(6)
C_6H_4ClBr	7	13	22.4	29	42.3	41	44.7	70	94
$\mathscr{I}_1 = 2284$ $\mathscr{I}_2 = 2131$	(2)	(2)	(10)	(2)	(10)	(10)	(10)	(1)	(6)
C_6H_4ClI	—	—	18	—	40	34.5	37	64	90
$\mathscr{I}_1 = 2692$ $\mathscr{I}_2 = 2542$			(10)		(10)	(10)	(10)	(1)	(6)
$C_6H_4Br_2$	6	12	20.1	25	40	37.4	39.4	68	93
$\mathscr{I}_1 = 3182$ $\mathscr{I}_2 = 3030$	(2)	(2)	(10)	(2)	(10)	(10)	(10)	(1)	(6)
C_6H_4BrI	—	—	18	—	37	32	35.5	66	92
$\mathscr{I}_1 = 4162$ $\mathscr{I}_2 = 4012$			(10)		(10)	(10)	(10)	(1)	(6)

Note. Frequencies ν in cm^{-1} (the relative intensities are given in parentheses), the moments of inertia $\mathscr{I}$ are in 10^{-40} g·cm^2. For all the molecules in the table $\mathscr{I}_3 = 150 \cdot 10^{-40}$ g·cm^3.

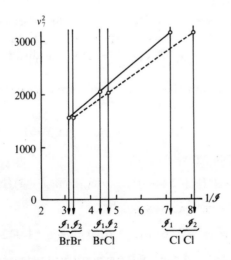

Figure 74

ν_7^2 vs. the reciprocal moment of inertia for crystals of para-dihaloderivatives of benzene.

molecules in the unit cell. The unit cell is thus described by twelve coordinates, which can be chosen as the six displacements of the centers of mass of the molecules along the axes coinciding with the sides of the unit cell and the six angles corresponding to the rotation of the molecules about the principal directions of the ellipsoid of inertia (Figure 75).

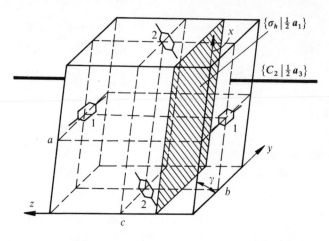

Figure 75

The unit cell of molecular crystals of para-dihaloderivatives of benzene:

$\{C_2|\frac{1}{2}a_3\}$ screw axis, $\{\sigma_h|\frac{1}{2}a_1\}$ mirror-glide plane, γ the angle between the unit cell axes.

The elements of the space group C_{2h}^5 are the unit transformation $\{e|0\}$, the two-fold screw axis $\{C_2|\frac{1}{2}a_3\}$, a mirror-glide plane $\{\sigma_h|\frac{1}{2}a_1\}$, and a center of inversion with partial translation $\{i|\frac{1}{2}(a_1 + a_3)\}$. The group of directions of these crystals is C_{2h}.

Using Table 42, we can find the characters of the vibrational representations: external vibrational representation

$$\chi(C_\phi) = (2m_0 - 1)(1 + 2 \cos \phi), \quad \chi(S_\phi) = 1 - 2 \cos \phi;$$

translation-vibrational representation

$$\chi(C_\phi) = (m_0 - 1)(1 + 2 \cos \phi), \quad \chi(S_\phi) = (m_0 - 1)(1 - 2 \cos \phi);$$

rotation-vibrational representation

$$\chi(C_\phi) = m_0(1 + 2 \cos \phi), \quad \chi(S_\phi) = m_0(-1 + 2 \cos \phi).$$

Table 42 also gives the characters of the symmetrical tensor representation

$$\chi(C_\phi) = 2 \cos \phi (1 + 2 \cos \phi), \quad \chi(S_\phi) = 2 \cos \phi (-1 + 2 \cos \phi);$$

and the vector representation

$$\chi(C_\phi) = 1 + 2 \cos \phi, \qquad \chi(S_\phi) = -1 + 2 \cos \phi.$$

The results of calculations are listed in Table 48.

Table 48

CHARACTERS OF REPRESENTATIONS FOR CRYSTALS OF
BENZENE PARA-DIHALODERIVATIVES

Representation	e	C_2	σ_h	i
External vibrational	9	1	−1	3
Translation-vibrational	3	1	−1	−3
Rotation-vibrational	6	0	0	6
Symmetrical tensor representation	6	2	2	6
Vector representation	3	−1	1	−3

Using the orthogonality relation (19.52) for the characters and the table of characters of the irreducible representations of the point group C_{2h} (see § 10), we can readily decompose all the reducible representations into irreducible ones. We thus find.

$$T_{ex} = 3A_g + 3B_g + 2A_u + B_u,$$

$$T_{rot} = 3A_g + 3B_g,$$

$$T_{tr} = 2A_u + B_u,$$

$$T_{vect} = A_u + 2B_u,$$

$$T_{s.\,ten} = 4A_g + 2B_g.$$

All the limiting vibration modes (corresponding to $k = 0$) are thus divided into twelve branches, of which three are acoustic branches, six rotation branches, and three translation branches. The six rotation modes are active in Raman spectra. The translation modes are forbidden in Raman spectra, although allowed in IR spectra.

The vibrations of the molecular crystals of benzene paradihalogen derivatives are treated in more detail in [399].

We have defined the conditions under which translation and rotation can be separated in the low-frequency spectra. Experimental data are generally analyzed assuming the different modes are indeed separable. However, the numerous violations of the selection rules in low-frequency Raman spectra call for extreme caution in the classification of vibrations.

One of the reasons for the breakdown of the selection rules is to be sought in the inhomogeneity of the crystal lattice. This, according to Loudon [379], leads to non-conservation of quasimomentum in Raman scattering and thus excites vibrations with $k \neq 0$. However, translation and rotation are separable only for the limiting frequencies ($k = 0$). Thus, in a real crystal, we are dealing with mixed translation–rotation modes even when the limiting frequencies are strictly separable.

Further note that the separation into internal and external vibrations is not exact either. The coupling between internal and external vibrations, which is generally uncontrollable, may shift the line frequencies and alter other parameters of the lines in low-frequency spectra. According to the theoretical results of Porfir'eva [406], the coupling between internal vibrations and orientation rotations of the molecule is significant even when the external limiting vibrations are totally separable into translation and rotation modes.

There are no data on the relationship of the numerical values of the translation and rotation vibrations. Bhagavantam [407] suggested that the translation frequencies are much lower than the rotation frequencies and are also of exceedingly low intensity in Raman spectra. Skripov [408] and Rakhimov [409] do not agree with this point of view: translation and rotation frequencies may have comparable orders of magnitude. Numerical calculations of Shur [410] for KH_2PO_4 also give translation frequencies which fall within the range of normal rotation frequencies.

The importance of low-frequency Raman spectra is not limited to similar (and primarily isomorphous) crystals: temperature and pressure dependence of these crystals is of considerable significance in the study of lattice dynamics. These studies often help to assign various lines to definite lattice vibrations.

According to [409, 411, 412], a decrease in temperature raises the frequencies. This effect is apparently associated with the decrease in the intermolecular distance due to the contraction of the crystal on cooling, leading to an increase in the quasi-elastic constants of the crystal. The frequency shift is smooth (almost linear), slightly slowing down at low temperatures. Figure 76 plots the temperature curves of the frequencies of stilbene and tolan from [412]. A similar effect is observed when the crystal is subjected to triaxial compression. According to Frühling [411], the lines of crystalline benzene, observed at 63 and 105 cm^{-1} under normal conditions, shift to 66 and 112 cm^{-1}, respectively, at pressures of 720 atm.

As the temperature is increased, the integrated intensity of the low-frequency Raman lines increases [409], and, unlike the temperature dependence of the scattering intensity in liquids (see §17), the temperature curve in this case follows the theoretical expression (7.39).

The line widths in low-frequency Raman spectra were studied in [413, 409, 414]. The line width measurements carried out at various temperatures are of special interest.

The main reasons for line broadening in the low-frequency spectrum are apparently anharmonicity of vibrations and the sudden jerky change in the orientation of

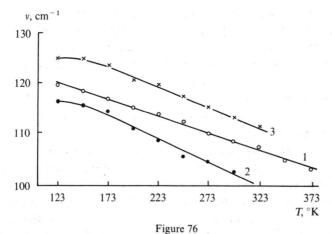

Figure 76

Frequency vs. temperature curves:

1) stilbene 110 cm^{-1} line, 2) toluene 105 cm^{-1} line, 3) tolan 116 cm^{-1} line.

molecules. The effect of anharmonicity on the temperature dependence of line width was considered qualitatively in [415]. The resulting expression for the line width is

$$\delta_{anh} = \frac{aTv}{f},\tag{21.10}$$

where a is a constant, T is the absolute temperature, v is the line frequency, f is quasielastic constant.

The effect of orientation changes of molecules in a liquid on the width of Raman lines with a nonzero anisotropic part of the scattering tensor has been studied experimentally and theoretically by a number of authors (see §17). Unlike liquids, where the molecules in principle may rotate through any angle, the crystals allow only those rotations which are consistent with the lattice symmetry. Rakov [273] was the first to demonstrate by the optical method that random orientation changes of molecules do occur in a number of crystalline substances, and he calculated the potential barriers for the change in orientation U_{cr}. The temperature dependence of the line width in crystals is expressed in the form

$$\delta_{or} = A \exp\left(-U_{cr}/kT\right).\tag{21.11}$$

Orientation changes of molecules in a crystal lattice can be effectively studied using the low-frequency spectra [409]. According to (21.10) and (21.11), the temperature dependence of the line width is in general determined by two terms, the anharmonic and the orientation:

$$\delta = \delta_{anh} + \delta_{or} = AT + B \exp\left(-U_{cr}/kT\right),\tag{21.12}$$

A and *B* being some constants. Depending on the ratio of these terms, the temperature dependence of the line width approaches a linear or an exponential curve.

Figure 77 shows a typical temperature dependence of line widths in a low-frequency spectrum [409]. For most lines, the temperature dependence is linear, but for the 90 cm^{-1} line, the curve is nearly exponential, i.e., for this line, the main effect is contributed by the orientation changes of the lattice molecules. The experimental data can be processed to yield the orientation barriers U_{cr} and the mean time to change the orientation τ_{cr}.

We have used a fairly rough qualitative treatment of the various factors affecting the line widths in low-frequency spectra. A more rigorous solution of the problem was advanced in [416] where the random walk theory was applied to the rotations of a molecule in a lattice. According to this approach, the first step is to consider the scattering by a free isolated molecule, and then the resultant scattering by all the molecules in the crystal is determined. Despite the distinctly classical approach, the correlation theory of [416] leads to a satisfactory agreement with the experiment. The quantum-mechanical theory was developed by Shelepin and Rakhimov [417]. The basic relations of the quantum-mechanical and the correlation theories have fundamentally the same physical meaning.

Let us now consider the perturbation of intramolecular vibrations by the crystal lattice field. These perturbations are generally small, and they can be attributed to two mechanisms:

a) The static crystal field shifts the frequencies and alters the selection rules for intramolecular vibrations (as a result some forbidden frequencies become active and the degenerate frequencies may split).

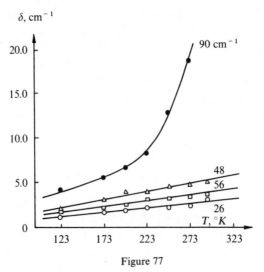

Figure 77

Line widths in the low-frequency spectrum of para-dichlorobenzene vs. temperature.

b) A resonance interaction between identical vibration modes of molecules in the unit cell leads to frequency splitting (the number of splitting components does not exceed the number of molecules in the unit cell).

The first effect is known as *static splitting*, and the second as *dynamical* or *Davydov splitting* (it was first advanced by A. S. Davydov to explain the structure of the electronic spectra of molecular crystals [418]).

The splitting of vibration frequencies due to these factors has been mainly studied in absorption spectra [419]. In some cases, splitting due to one of these two factors was observed. Thus Fialkovskii [420] studied the IR absorption spectrum of an anthracene single crystal, where he observed a splitting of the 740 cm^{-1} band into two components, 742 cm^{-1} and 728 cm^{-1}. The anthracene molecule has no degenerate vibration modes. The observed effect therefore constitutes pure Davydov splitting. Static splitting of degenerate lines in IR spectra is roughly of the same order of magnitude.

Cyclohexane crystals provide valuable information regarding the effect of lattice field on intramolecular vibrations. At $+ 6°C$, cyclohexane crystallizes in a cubic lattice (form I) with four molecules in the unit cell; no splitting of the fundamental lines is observed. At $- 87°C$, a first-kind temperature transition occurs, producing a monoclinic crystal (form II) with eight molecules in the unit cell. The IR spectrum of form II shows many split lines [139]. Similar splitting is observed in the Raman spectrum of form II. According to Ito [421], lines of type E_g, whose frequencies in liquid cyclohexane are 1025, 1266, 1345 and 1441 cm^{-1} split into 1023 and 1032 cm^{-1}, 1264 and 1276 cm^{-1}, 1335 and 1347 cm^{-1}, and 1439 and 1445 cm^{-1}, respectively. Microphotometer tracings of three lines at 77°K in a supercooled crystal of form I and in a crystal of form II are shown in Figure 78.

The spectrum of form II shows additional A_{2g}-type lines, 1059 cm^{-1} and 1422 cm^{-1}, which are forbidden by the selection rules in the liquid phase. These effects may be due to lowering of the lattice symmetry (static splitting) and thus provide additional information for establishing the exact symmetry group of the crystal [421].

2. Raman spectra of crystals in phase transitions

In one of their first studies of the Raman scattering in crystals, Landsberg and Mandelshtam [422] observed a change in the intensity and the width of quartz lines near the point of the $\alpha \rightleftarrows \beta$ phase transition at $T = 573°C$. They studied the lines at 207 cm^{-1} and 466 cm^{-1}. The 466 cm^{-1} line was found to become wider and more diffuse with increasing temperature, but the position of its maximum hardly changed above the transition point. The 207 cm^{-1} line became extremely diffuse with the increase in temperature and shifted toward the exciting line. This line was hardly distinguishable near the phase transition point, and it vanished altogether above the transition point, i.e., in β-quartz.

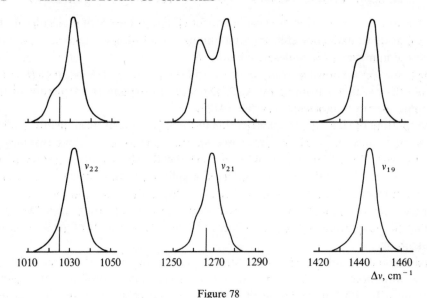

Figure 78

Microphotometric tracings of three lines of crystalline cyclohexane at 77° K.

Bottom, form I crystal; top, form II crystal. The vertical dashes mark the position of the line in liquid cyclohexane.

Because of experimental difficulties, no systematic studies on the subject appeared for a long time after the publication of [422]. Detailed studies of Raman spectra near points of phase transitions of the second kind began only following Ginzburg's report [423] regarding the peculiar behavior of some lines in phase transitions.

Phase transitions of the second kind between different crystal modifications either involve a definite displacement of the sublattices in the direction of one of the normal modes or lead to an ordering on the sublattices along some modes. These effects are significantly influenced by the shape of the potential curve of the normal mode. For a single-valley potential, the phase transition belongs to the displacement type, whereas a two-valley potential produces an order–disorder transition.

In ferroelectrics, the type of the phase transition can be identified from the value of the Curie–Weiss constant. For displacement transitions, this constant is about 10^5 deg, and for order–disorder transitions it is about 10^3 deg [424]. In particular, phase transitions in $BaTiO_3$, $SrTiO_3$, $KTaO_3$, and quartz crystals are classified as displacement transitions, and those in the crystals of $NaNO_2$, $NaClO_3$, KH_2PO_4, $NH_4 \cdot H_2PO_4$, Segnette salt, triglycine sulfate, etc., are order–disorder transitions.

The theory developed by Ginzburg and Levanyuk [423], relates the displacement transitions to the lattice dynamics. According to this theory, the frequency of one Raman line (or of several lines) goes to zero as the crystal approaches the phase transition point, and the intensity markedly increases. Similar results concerning the frequency shift of some lines emerge from Cochran's semiphenomenological theory of ferroelectrics [425].

The general assumptions of Ginzburg's theory are the following. According to the general theory of phase transitions of the second kind (see [280]), the thermo-dynamic potential of a system near the transition point can be expanded in powers of some parameter η, whose equilibrium value does not vanish for one of the phases only:

$$\Phi(p, T, \eta) = \Phi_0(p, T) + \alpha\eta^2 + \tfrac{1}{2}\beta\eta^4 + \ldots \tag{21.13}$$

The coefficients α and β in (21.13) are functions of temperature and pressure. In phase transitions of the second kind $\alpha(\Theta) = 0$, and we may take

$$\alpha(T) = \alpha'_\Theta(T - \Theta) \quad \text{for} \quad T > \Theta, \tag{21.14}$$

where Θ is the transition point. In equilibrium,

$$\frac{\partial\Phi}{\partial\eta} = \eta(2\alpha + 2\beta\eta^2) = 0, \tag{21.15}$$

$$\frac{\partial^2\Phi}{\partial\eta^2} = 2\alpha + 6\beta\eta^2 > 0. \tag{21.16}$$

The equilibrium values of the characteristic parameter $\eta = \eta_0$ are thus

$$\eta_0 = 0 \quad \text{for} \quad T > \Theta, \tag{21.17}$$

$$\eta_0^2 = -\frac{\alpha}{\beta} = \frac{\alpha'_\Theta(\Theta - T)}{\beta} > 0 \quad \text{for} \quad T < \Theta. \tag{21.18}$$

In phase transitions of the second kind in crystals, the parameter η characterizes the displacement of one sublattice relative to the other. In the symmetric phase, the atoms or groups of atoms in the lattice vibrate about some equilibrium position $\eta_0 = 0$; in the low-symmetry phase, $\eta_0 \neq 0$, and the equilibrium position changes. Since α vanishes at the transition point, the generalized elastic energy $\alpha\eta^2$ is also zero. Equilibrium is established when the generalized elastic force vanishes:

$$-\frac{\partial\Phi}{\partial\eta} = -\alpha\eta - \beta\eta^3 = 0. \tag{21.19}$$

Consider an oscillator of reduced mass μ and a damping coefficient γ (the damping is caused by the dissipation of the oscillator energy through interaction with other degrees of freedom). The equation of motion of this oscillator under the action of a general quasielastic force $(\alpha\eta + \beta\eta^3)$ and some driving force $f(t)$ has the form

$$\mu\ddot{\eta} + \gamma\dot{\eta} + \alpha\eta + \beta\eta^3 = f(t). \tag{21.20}$$

For small oscillations about the equilibrium position η_0, retaining only terms linear in $\Delta\eta = \eta - \eta_0$, we find

$$\mu\Delta\ddot{\eta} + \gamma\Delta\dot{\eta} + \mu\Omega_i^2\,\Delta\eta = f(t), \qquad (21.21)$$

where the frequency Ω_i is obtained from the conditions

$$\Omega_i^2 = \frac{\alpha}{\mu} = \frac{\alpha'_\Theta(T - \Theta)}{\mu} \qquad \text{for} \quad T > \Theta, \qquad (21.22)$$

$$\Omega_i^2 = \frac{2\,|\alpha|}{\mu} = \frac{2\alpha'_\Theta(\Theta - T)}{\mu} \qquad \text{for} \quad T < \Theta. \qquad (21.23)$$

We thus see that $\Omega_i = 0$ at the transition point.

So far, the vibrational spectra of crystals near phase transitions of the second kind have been studied mainly in connection with the ferroelectric properties of crystals. Ferroelectric crystals possess a spontaneous polarization in one or several directions, and the direction of this spontaneous polarization can be changed by application of an external electric field. The spontaneous polarization is observed in a certain temperature interval only. The temperature at which the crystal passes from un-polarized to polarized state is known as the Curie point. The phase transition in ferroelectrics may be of first or second kind. The dielectric constant ε generally has a large maximum at the phase transition point.

The state of a ferroelectric is characterized not only by the temperature T and the pressure p, but also by the polarization P, which is made up from the spontaneous polarization P_0 and the polarization P_{in} induced by the external electric field E. The spontaneous polarization is different from zero only in the ordered (pyro-electric) state.

In ferroelectrics, we may take $\Delta\eta = P_{in\ z}$, where $P_{in\ z}$ is the polarization induced by an external field $E_z = E_0 e^{i\Omega t}$. For small fields and large ε,

$$P_{in\ z} = \frac{\varepsilon - 1}{4\pi}\,E_z \approx \frac{\varepsilon}{4\pi}\,E_z. \qquad (21.24)$$

In the presence of an external field, a term $-P_{in\ z}E_z$ is added to expansion (21.13), and this introduces a generalized force E_z in the right-hand side of (21.20). The equation of vibrations (21.21) thus takes the form

$$\ddot{P}_{in\ z} + \left(\frac{\gamma}{\mu}\right)\dot{P}_{in\ z} + \Omega_i^2 P_{in\ z} = \frac{E_z}{\mu}. \qquad (21.25)$$

Inserting the field E_z in (21.25) and solving the equation, we obtain, using (21.24),

$$\varepsilon = \varepsilon' - i\varepsilon'' = \frac{(4\pi/\mu)}{\Omega_i^2 - \Omega^2 + i(\gamma/\mu)\Omega}, \qquad (21.26)$$

where $\Omega_i^2 = \alpha/\mu$ for $T > \Theta$ and $\Omega_i^2 = 2|\alpha|/\mu$ for $T < \Theta$; the frequency Ω_i in (21.26) is the characteristic frequency of the optical branch, and for this mode the polarization P below the transition point varies along the axis z. Above the transition point, the crystal is dielectrically isotropic.

The spectrum of the scattered light is determined by the kinetics of the fluctuations $\Delta\varepsilon$ which are related near a transition point of the second kind to the fluctuations of the parameter η. Near the transition point, we have approximately (see [423])

$$\Delta\varepsilon = 2a\eta_0\Delta\eta, \quad \text{where} \quad a = \left(\frac{\partial\varepsilon}{\partial\eta^2}\right)_{\rho,\,T} \tag{21.27}$$

The field of a scattered light wave with a wave vector k is proportional to $\Delta\varepsilon_k e^{i\omega_0 t} = 2a\eta_0\Delta\eta_k e^{i\omega_0 t}$, and the spectrum is expressed by the Fourier components

$$G_\Omega = \frac{1}{2\pi}\int_{-\infty}^{\infty} \Delta\eta_k(t)e^{-i\Omega t}\,dt, \tag{21.28}$$

where $\Omega = \omega - \omega_0$, ω is the scattered frequency, ω_0 is the incident frequency. For the spectral density of the scattered intensity we have $I(\Omega) \sim |G_\Omega|^2$.

Fluctuations of the parameter η are caused by thermal movements in the crystal. Solving (21.21) for $f(t)$ which is a random time function, we obtain

$$G_\Omega = \frac{f_\Omega}{\Omega_i^2 - \Omega^2 + i(\gamma/\mu)\Omega}, \quad f_\Omega = \frac{1}{2\pi}\int_{-\infty}^{\infty} f(t)e^{-i\Omega t}\,dt. \tag{21.29}$$

Thus,

$$I(\Omega) = \frac{(\gamma\Omega_i^2/\pi\mu)\,Y(T)}{(\Omega_i^2 - \Omega^2)^2 + (\gamma/\mu)^2\Omega^2}, \quad Y(T) = \int_{-\infty}^{\infty} I(\Omega)d\Omega, \tag{21.30}$$

where, according to normalization requirements, $Y(T)$ is the integrated light intensity scattered by the fluctuations.

For the Raman line corresponding to crystal vibrations of frequency Ω_i we have

$$\Omega_{\text{max}} = \pm\sqrt{\Omega_i^2 - \tfrac{1}{2}(\gamma/\mu)^2}. \tag{21.31}$$

The frequencies Ω_{max} correspond to the peaks of the function $I(\Omega)$ for $\Omega_i > \gamma/\sqrt{2\mu}$. For $\Omega_i \leq \gamma/\sqrt{2\mu}$, the function $I(\Omega)$ has a single peak at $\Omega = 0$. The peak intensity of a Raman line is determined by the expression

$$I(\Omega_{\text{max}}) = \frac{Y(T)}{(\pi\gamma/\mu)\left[1 - \gamma^2/4\mu^2\Omega_i^2\right]}. \tag{21.32}$$

As we approach the critical Curie point, the total scattered intensity $Y(T)$ increases. Therefore, the intensity of the Raman lines shifting toward the exciting line should also increase anomalously in these cases. Such a case apparently occurs in quartz, where $I(\Theta)/I(20°\text{C}) = 1.4 \cdot 10^4$, and critical opalescence is observed near the $\alpha \rightleftarrows \beta$ transition [426]. The 207 cm^{-1} line (at $20°\text{C}$) is completely polarized. Because of the increased contribution of this line to the total (Rayleigh and Raman) scattering, the depolarization of the scattered light (0.12 at $20°\text{C}$, at first increasing to 0.18 on heating) drops to 0.06 at the transition point. For $T > \Theta$, this mode is inactive in first-order Raman scattering, and the corresponding line is not observed.

The theoretical work of Ginzburg and Levanyuk [423] and Cochran [425] stimulated numerous experimental studies of the vibrational spectra of crystals near phase transition points.

One of the most remarkable objects of study is barium titanate $BaTiO_3$. In pure $BaTiO_3$, the ferroelectric phase transition is a transition of the first kind near the Curie point, and therefore $\Omega_i(\Theta) \neq 0$ (although this frequency is very low). This frequency corresponds to the vibration of the Ba atom relative to the TiO_3 group. The IR spectrum of the $BaTiO_3$ single crystal at room temperature shows lines at 12, 174, 182, and 491 cm^{-1} [427], the 174 cm^{-1} line vanishing above the transition point. Line splitting at 180 cm^{-1} may be attributed to a change in the lattice symmetry, which is cubic above the transition point ($\Theta \approx 120°\text{C}$) and tetragonal below that point. The lines 182 cm^{-1} and 491 cm^{-1} are not affected by the increase in temperature, whereas the frequency of the first line drops to 6 cm^{-1} near the transition point. Frequency changes near the phase transition were previously observed in [428] for polycrystalline $BaTiO_3$ specimens.

Raman spectra of barium titanate have been studied only at relatively high frequencies. In [377], lines at 235, 306, 512, and 718 cm^{-1} were observed in the tetragonal phase near the transition point. Only the frequency of the first line showed any significant variation with temperature, changing from 271 to 235 cm^{-1} with heating from 290 to $393°\text{K}$. The authors assign this frequency to a longitudinal mode associated with a low-frequency transverse ferroelectric vibration.

Bazhulin and Aref'ev [429] studied the Raman spectrum of another typical ferroelectric, KH_2PO_4, and also that of $NH_4H_2PO_4$. The measurements were carried out at room temperature and near the respective transition points ($\Theta = 123°\text{K}$ for KH_2PO_4 and $\Theta = 147°\text{K}$ for $NH_4H_2PO_4$). The spectra of both crystals showed a line at 34 cm^{-1}. When cooled to the transition point, the frequency of this line decreased by 4 cm^{-1} in both crystals. Note that according to Cochran's calculations [425], the frequency of the vibration associated with the ferroelectric transition in KH_2PO_4 should vary from 85 cm^{-1} at room temperature to $14 \text{ cm} -^1$ at the transition point. The actual effect observed in [429] shows a poor fit with the theory in this respect. It is moreover not clear why the intensity of these lines in KH_2PO_4 and $NH_4H_2PO_4$ crystals decreases, rather than increases, with the approach to the transition point [429].

The low-frequency spectra of triglycine sulfate and Segnette salt (both ferroelectrics) were studied in [430]. No changes were observed in the spectra of these single crystals with the increase in temperature and during the phase transition. Similar results were obtained in [431].

Some changes in Raman spectra near the phase transition point were observed in [378, 432] for $NaNO_2$ single crystals. The measurements carried out in [378] showed that all the lines of the $NaNO_2$ crystal shift toward the exciting line and become wider as the temperature is increased. These effects are most pronounced for the low-frequency lines $\Delta v_1 = 121 \text{ cm}^{-1}$, $\Delta v_2 = 158 \text{ cm}^{-1}$ and $\Delta v_3 = 184 \text{ cm}^{-1}$ (the frequencies correspond to room temperature). At the ferroelectric transition point ($\Theta = 160°C$), the frequencies of these lines are $\Delta v_1' = 110 \text{ cm}^{-1}$, $\Delta v_2' = 143 \text{ cm}^{-1}$, and the $\Delta v_3'$ line becomes so diffuse that it cannot be measured. Above the transition point, the low-frequency part of the spectrum has the form of an asymmetric band peaked around 110 cm^{-1}. The intensity of this band falls off uniformly with distance from the exciting line. Also, some of the higher frequency lines disappear above the transition point, in accordance with the selection rules.

The broadening of the Raman lines and their shift toward the exciting line at higher temperatures are attributed to normal temperature effects. No lines with anomalously low frequencies near the transition point were detected in [378]. The corresponding vibration modes should belong to the translation type (displacement of Na relative to NO_2 along the z axis), and below the transition point the intensity of the corresponding line is apparently very low. Above the transition point, all the translation modes are forbidden in Raman spectra (a group-theoretical analysis of the $NaNO_2$ crystal will be found in [378]).

Much more pronounced changes in the Raman spectrum were observed during the heating of $NaClO_3$ crystal [433]. This crystal shows a ferroelectric transition at $\Theta = 593°K$. The measurements were carried out between 83 and 483°K. Observations at higher temperatures were precluded, since the crystal melts at 573°K.

The observed lines in the spectrum of the $NaClO_3$ crystal can be divided into three groups: 1) weak lines of very low frequencies, $\Delta v_1 = 72 \text{ cm}^{-1}$, $\Delta v_2 = 81 \text{ cm}^{-1}$, and $\Delta v_3 = 107 \text{ cm}^{-1}$, apparently corresponding to translation modes; 2) the lines $\Delta v_4 = 123 \text{ cm}^{-1}$, $\Delta v_5 = 131 \text{ cm}^{-1}$, $\Delta v_6 = 179 \text{ cm}^{-1}$ corresponding to rotation vibrations; 3) lines of higher frequencies corresponding to internal vibrations of the $NaClO_3$ molecule (all the frequencies are given for 45°C). All these modes are active in the Raman spectrum.

When the crystal is heated, all the lines, except Δv_6, show but an insignificant frequency shift (3–5 cm^{-1}), although they definitely become broader. Significant temperature changes are observed for the line Δv_6. The measured parameters of the line Δv_6 are plotted in Figure 79. When the crystal is heated from 83 to 483°K, the Δv_6 line shifts 45 cm^{-1} toward the exciting line, and its width increases from 5 to 44 cm^{-1}. The integrated intensity of this line, approximately proportional to the product $I_0 \delta$, also increases with temperature.

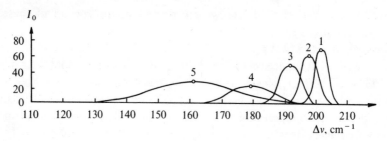

Figure 79

The parameters of the Δv_6 line of the NaClO$_3$ crystal as a function of temperature:

1) $T = 83°\,K$;   2) $T = 113°\,K$;   3) $T = 203°\,K$;   4) $T = 318°\,K$;   5) $T = 423°\,K$. I_0 is the peak intensity in relative units. The lines are plotted with allowance for their half-widths.

All the theoretically predicted effects [423] are thus borne out qualitatively. A new experimental effect [433] entails a substantial line broadening associated with the ferroelectric transition. At high temperatures, the line becomes so diffuse that the harmonic approximation apparently no longer applies to lattice vibrations in this case. The failure of the earlier attempts to detect theoretically predicted effects in Raman spectra is probably linked with the extreme width of the line near the transition point, which makes it hardly distinguishable from the continuous background.*

The discrepancy between experimental findings and the theoretical predictions [423, 425] in some cases is traceable to the fact that the theory deals with displacement transitions, whereas the experimental data mainly apply to order–disorder transitions (see p. 332). In view of this, special importance is attached to the work of Vaks et al. [434], who developed a theory of collective excitations near points of phase transition of the second kind. It is noted that the behavior of the frequency Ω_i associated with the ferroelectric transition depends on the shape of the potential curve. For single-valley potentials, Ω_i^2 goes to zero in proportion to $T - \Theta$ as we approach the transition point. For multivalley potentials, this function for $k = 0$ goes to a finite limit as $T \to \Theta$. A significant decrease in Ω_i will be observed in this case only for low potential barriers. (This result is derived only in the "classical" version of the theory [434].)

An anomalous shift of one of the Raman lines toward the exciting line near the phase transition point has been previously observed [383]. The vibration frequency associated with the ferroelectric transition moves as much as $60\ \mathrm{cm}^{-1}$ toward the exciting line when the crystal is cooled from 300 to 8°K. Although this vibration

---

* We recall that, according to (21.31), the intensity distribution in a Raman spectrum with wide lines has a single maximum at $\Omega = 0$.

mode is forbidden in the Raman spectrum, the selection rules were broken in [383] by application of an external electric field. Note that the frequency of this vibration, despite its significant decrease, does not vanish at the transition point.

3. Light scattering by piezoelectric crystals

We have so far dealt with light scattering by vibration modes which are inactive in the IR absorption spectrum. If the crystal has a center of symmetry, all the vibration modes active in the Raman spectrum are forbidden in the IR spectrum. However, if there is no center of symmetry in the crystal, as for piezoelectric crystals, scattering may be caused by polar vibrations of the lattice. Raman scattering by polar vibrations has a number of specific properties.

In accordance with the general features of the dispersion curves of the optical branches of polar vibrations, the scattered frequency changes depending on the magnitude and the direction of the wave vector of the vibrational quantum taking part in the scattering process. Excitation of various points in the reciprocal space enables us to study their dispersion curves in Raman scattering. This can be achieved by an appropriate choice of the scattering geometry. We see from Figure 72 that the magnitude of the scattered wave vector diminishes with a decrease in the angle θ between the incident and the scattered light. If this angle is very small, the scattering is longitudinal. Longitudinal Raman scattering excites not only mechanical vibrations, but also "mixed" vibrational quanta, polaritons, whose frequency markedly decreases with the decrease of the wave vector. Experimentally, Raman scattering by polaritons was discovered in [435] for a cubic piezoelectric GaP crystal. The considerable experimental difficulties in this case are associated with the necessity to ensure a very small divergence between the incident and the scattered beams (about 0.5°), and this greatly reduces the intensity of the scattered light; a helium-neon laser was used as a light source in [435]. The observed polaron frequency shift was found to be 20% for the angle θ varying from zero to a few degrees. Longitudinal Raman scattering was studied in [436] using an argon laser ($\lambda = 4880\,\text{Å}$) and a uniaxial ZnO crystal. The laser beam was directed along the axis x, and the scattered light propagated in the xz plane at an angle θ to the direction of incidence (Figure 80). Both the incident and the scattered light were polarized. The case of an ordinary exciting beam and extraordinary scattered beam is marked by yz in Figure 80a; zy stands for the opposite polarization of the incident and the scattered light.

For both polarizations of the incident and the scattered light, an ordinary transverse polariton polarized along the y axis was excited. The solid line in Figure 80a is the dispersion curve calculated from the relation

$$\frac{k^2 c^2}{\omega^2} = \frac{v_0^2 \varepsilon_{0\perp} - v_\perp^2 \varepsilon_{\infty\perp}}{v_0^2 - v^2},$$

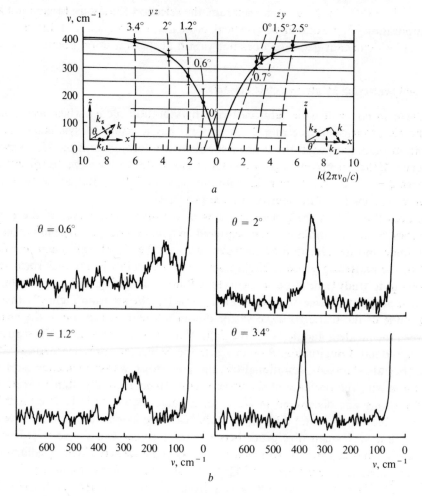

Figure 80

Dispersion curves (a) and Raman spectra of the ZnO crystal for various angles θ (b).

where $\omega = 2\pi v$, $\varepsilon_{0\perp} = 8.15$, $\varepsilon_{\infty\perp} = 4.0$ are the static and the high-frequency dielectric constant, respectively, v_0 is the dispersion frequency, equal to 407 cm^{-1}, k is expressed in units of $2\pi v_0/c$.

According to the law of energy and quasimomentum conservation, we have for small θ

$$k = \{[v_e(n_e - n_o) + vn_o]^2 + v_e(v_e - v)n_en_o\theta^2\}^{1/2}$$

for the case zy, and

$$k = -\{[vn_e - v_e(n_e - n_o)]^2 + v_e(v_e - v)n_on_e\theta^2\}^{1/2}$$

for the case yz. Here v_e is the laser frequency, n_o and n_e are the refractive indices of the ordinary and the extraordinary ray. The curves of energy and quasimomentum conservation corresponding to these relations are marked by dashed lines in Figure 80a. Figure 80b shows a spectrogram taken with yz polarization. The observed frequencies shift from $407 \, \text{cm}^{-1}$ to $160 \, \text{cm}^{-1}$ as the angle changes from $0°$ to $3.4°$.

In these experiments, Raman scattering was used to investigate the frequency of polar vibrations as a function of the magnitude of the wave vector. For noncubic crystals, however, as we have noted in §19.6, the polariton frequency also depends on the direction of the wave vector k. An effect of this kind was observed in Raman spectra of a number of crystals [437–439].

A characteristic property of Raman scattering in peizoelectric crystals is the anomalous depolarization of some lines [440], which does not agree with the theoretical depolarization values. A discussion of these anomalies will be found in [365, 367, 373]. As we have noted before, degenerate polar vibrations are split into longitudinal and transverse modes by external electrostatic forces (in a cubic crystal). The intensity of Raman scattering is different for the longitudinal and the transverse modes. This follows, in particular, from the form of the scattering tensor derived in the third-order perturbation theory [373], since the electron–phonon interaction is different for the longitudinal and the transverse vibrations. Indeed, a longitudinal vibration accompanied by an electric field involves an additional electron–phonon interaction which may prove substantially stronger than the ordinary electron–phonon interaction described by the deformation potential theory.

4. Second-order Raman spectra

Two phonons participate simultaneously in second-order Raman scattering. We distinguish between the following processes.

1. A photon of frequency ω_0 (incident radiation) decays into a photon of frequency ω' (scattered radiation) and two phonons of frequencies Ω_1 and Ω_2. The energy and quasimomentum conservation for this process are written in the form

$$\hbar\omega_0 = \hbar\omega' + \hbar\Omega_1 + \hbar\Omega_2 \, ,$$

$$\hbar k_0 = \hbar k' + \hbar k_1 + \hbar k_2 \, . \tag{21.33}$$

2. A photon of frequency ω_0 interacts with a phonon of frequency Ω_1. The scattering produces a photon of frequency ω' and a phonon of frequency Ω_2. The conservation laws take the form

$$\hbar\omega_0 + \hbar\Omega_1 = \hbar\omega' + \hbar\Omega_2 \, ,$$

$$\hbar k_0 + \hbar k_1 = \hbar k' + \hbar k_2 \, . \tag{21.34}$$

3. A photon of frequency ω_0 interacts simultaneously with two phonons of frequencies Ω_1 and Ω_2. The result is a photon of frequency ω'. The conservation laws take the form

$$\hbar\omega_0 + \hbar\Omega_1 + \hbar\Omega_2 = \hbar\omega',$$

(21.35)

$$\hbar k_0 + \hbar k_1 + \hbar k_2 = \hbar k'.$$

Since the absolute magnitude of the phonon wave vectors is small compared to the linear dimensions of the first Brillouin zone, we see from (21.33)–(21.35) that the wave vectors of the phonons participating in scattering approximately satisfy the equalities

$$k_1 + k_2 = 0 \quad \text{or} \quad k_1 - k_2 = 0,$$

(21.36)

It follows from (21.36) that second-order Raman scattering may involve phonons not only from the beginning of the first Brillouin zone, but actually from any point of the zone, and in particular from points on the zone boundary. Second-order Raman spectra thus provide information on the phonon spectrum of the entire first Brillouin zone.

Processes (21.33)–(21.35) can be studied by introducing into the crystal Hamiltonian fourth-order terms which describe processes with the simultaneous participation of four quasiparticles — two photons and two phonons. In particular, scattering process (21.33) is described by a term of the form

$$H^{(4)} = \sum_{\rho_0\rho'\rho_1\rho_2} Q_{\rho_0\rho'\rho_1\rho_2}(k_0, k', k_1, k_0 - k' - k_1) \times$$

$$\times \xi_{\rho_0}(k_0) \xi_{\rho'}^+(k') \xi_{\rho'}^+(k_1) \xi_{\rho_2}^+(k_0 - k' - k_1). \quad (21.37)$$

Here ξ, ξ^+ are the Bose quasiparticle destruction and creation operators, $\rho_0, \rho', \rho_1, \rho_2$ are the polarization indices of the corresponding quasiparticles with the wave vectors k_0, k', k_1, k_2. The increase in the number of scattered photons $n(\rho', k')$ in unit time can be found using the first-order perturbation theory:

$$\frac{dn(\rho', k')}{dt} = \frac{2\pi}{\hbar} \sum_{\rho'\rho_1\rho_2} |Q_{\rho_0\rho'\rho_1\rho_2}|^2 n(\rho_0, k_0) \{n(\rho', k') + 1\} \times$$

$$\times \{n(\rho_1, k_1) + 1\} \{n(\rho_2, k_2) + 1\} \delta \{E_{\rho_0 k_0} - E_{\rho' k'} - E_{\rho_1 k_1} - E_{\rho_2 k_2}\}. \quad (21.38)$$

Here $n(\rho, k)$ is the number of quasiparticles per oscillator (ρ, k). Similar expressions can be derived for processes (21.34) and (21.35). Explicit expressions for the fourth-order anharmonicity coefficients have not been derived so far. The corresponding formulae will probably be very unwieldy.

Second-order Raman scattering may also be described on the basis of the polarizability theory [441, 442]. As we have noted before, the principal results of the polarizability theory is the fact that the scattered intensities are expressed in terms of the matrix elements of the polarizability of the electron subsystem, which depends on the nuclear coordinates as parameters. For processes (21.33), the matrix element is evaluated between the crystal ground state and the state corresponding to a doubly excited vibrational level. The only nonzero matrix element in this case is that of the term $\frac{1}{2}(\partial^2\alpha_{\rho\sigma}/\partial Q_\mu\partial Q_\nu)_0\, Q_\mu O_\nu$ in the expansion of the electron polarizability in normal coordinates. The intensity of the second-order lines, as for molecules (see §15), is proportional to $(\partial^2\alpha_{\rho\sigma}/\partial Q_\mu\partial Q_\nu)_0$.

The intensity of second-order Raman scattering also can be computed using the electron wave functions corresponding to the equilibrium configuration of the nuclei; the motion of the nuclei is introduced as an additional small perturbation. In this method, a nonzero probability of scattering emerges only in the fourth-order perturbation-theoretical treatment. The final expressions of this method are too complicated to be of any use, but an important result of this approach is that the Raman scattering cross section is determined by the electron–phonon and the electron–photon interaction constants.

The actual computation of the cross section for second-order Raman scattering thus involves the following specific difficulties: 1) the fourth-order anharmonicity constants are not known, 2) the density of the two-phonon crystal states entering the final expression of the perturbation theory is not known (the scattering probability is proportional to the density of the final states, i.e., the number of states per unit energy interval).

The density function of one-phonon crystal states is derived from the secular equation (19.25) if the elastic constants characterizing the atomic (ionic) interaction in the crystal lattice are known. In general, this function has the form [351, 445]

$$g(\omega) = \frac{2\omega v_0}{3n} \int_{S(\omega^2)} \frac{dS}{\left|\mathrm{grad}_k\,\omega^2\,(k)\right|}, \tag{21.39}$$

where v_0 is the unit cell volume, n is the number of atoms in the unit cell, $S(\omega^2)$ is the surface in the Brillouin zone for which $\omega^2(k) = \omega^2$.

The final expression for the function $g(\omega)$ can be obtained only on the basis of various simplifying assumptions and only for the simplest lattices. (The function was computed for a one-dimensional lattice in §19.1). In [441, 442], computations of this kind were carried out for NaCl cubic lattices and the diamond lattice assuming that only the nearest neighbors interact. These computations show that the density of states as a function of frequency (the function $g(\omega)$) is a very smooth curve with several maxima. The second-order Raman spectrum should thus be quasi-continuous.

Recently it has been established that the density function of one-phonon crystal states always has a number of characteristic points, known as critical. A *critical* *point* is a point in the *k* space where each component grad $\omega(k)$ is either zero or changes its sign. According to (21.39), the density of states is infinite at such critical points.* This property of critical points was first noted in [443]. Later it was established [444] that the characteristic features of the one-phonon state density function coincide with the characteristic properties of the two-phonon state density function for $k = 0$, which is essential for calculating the probability of second-order Raman scattering. Knowledge of the critical points thus permits elucidating the contribution to scattering from various parts of the Brillouin zone without going into detailed calculations of the entire density function. Methods for the determination of the critical points have been worked out in [443, 445]. Thus for ZnS crystals (cubic symmetry) and the diamond lattice, the critical points are Γ, L, W, X (see Figure 71*c*). The existence of critical points will produce sharp intensity maxima in second-order Raman spectra; the contribution from the other points of the Brillouin zone amounts to a weak continuous background of scattered radiation.

Experimental data on second-order spectra are still interpreted from two different standpoints: from Born's theory of lattice dynamics and from Raman's theory. The most detailed information is available for the second-order spectra of alkali halides [446–451]. Specimen second-order spectra are shown in Figure 81, *a* and *b*. The sharp maxima in the second-order spectra are interpreted in [447] as a manifestation of the additional degrees of freedom of the Raman supercell. At the same time, the authors of [446, 448, 451] stress the quasicontinuous character of the second-order spectrum and point to the satisfactory agreement between the experimental spectrum and Born's state density function, although the number of the experimental sharp maxima is higher than the theoretical number.

The method of critical points is more fruitful than the theoretical computations based on simplified lattice models. It eliminates the apparent discrepancy between Born's theory of lattice dynamics and the experimental data. The analysis of critical points also explains the presence of the additional sharp lines of "zero" intensity which appear in the Raman spectra of a number of crystals (e.g., calcite [384, 385]). These lines are produced by one-phonon scattering processes and they are apparently associated with nonconservation of quasimomentum following the breakdown of the translational invariance of a crystal lattice with defects or impurities (see § 20). The scattering probability is the highest for the critical point, and the observed spectrum is correspondingly made up of discrete lines. On the other hand, the additional degrees of freedom of the Raman supercell may coincide with the normal modes of the crystal lattice corresponding to the critical points of the Brillouin zone.

Let us consider the normal modes of ZnS and diamond lattices corresponding to the critical points Γ, L, X. At the point $\Gamma (k = 0)$, the atoms (ions) of the adjacent cells

---

* Actually, the density of states is infinite at the critical point only for a one-dimensional lattice. In the three-dimensional case, the density of states has a maximum at these points.

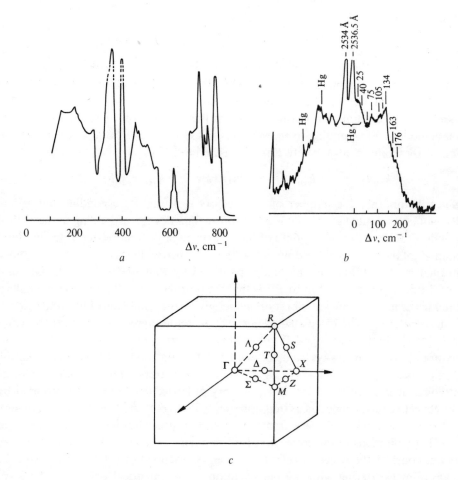

Figure 81

Second-order Raman spectra of some crystals:

a GaP [456];   *b* CsBr [451];   *c* the Brillouin zone of CsBr.

vibrate in phase, and thus satisfy Raman's requirement. Six normal modes correspond to this point (two atoms in a unit cell). At the point L,

$$k_9 = \tfrac{1}{2}(b_1 + b_2 + b_3) = \left\{\frac{\pi}{2\tau}, \ \frac{\pi}{2\tau}, \ \frac{\pi}{2\tau}\right\}.$$

Correspondingly

$$k_9 a_1 = \pi, \quad k_9 a_2 = \pi, \quad k_9 a_3 = \pi,$$

since

$$a_1 = \{0, \tau, \tau\}, \quad a_2 = \{\tau, 0, \tau\}, \quad a_3 = \{\tau, \tau, 0\}.$$

The atoms of the adjacent cells thus vibrate in counterphase and therefore again satisfy Raman's condition ($\alpha = \beta = \gamma = -1$). Since the star $\{k_9\}$ comprises four vectors, the points of the Brillouin zone corresponding to these vectors are associated with additional normal modes of the Raman type. The total number of these modes corresponding to the star $\{k_9\}$ is evidently 24. Vibrations correspond-ing to the point X also satisfy Raman's criterion:

$$k_{10}a_1 = \pi, \quad k_{10}a_2 = \pi, \quad k_{10}a_3 = 0, \quad k_{10} = \tfrac{1}{2}(b_1 + b_2).$$

Since in this case the number of star vectors is 3, the corresponding number of Raman normal modes is 18. Thus all the normal modes corresponding to the critical points Γ, L, X are normal modes of the Raman supercell; moreover, since the total number of the degrees of freedom of the Raman supercell in this case is 48, the above normal modes exhaust all the modes predicted by Raman's theory. The fact that saved Raman's theory in this case was that the postulated normal modes were indeed among the most significant vibration modes giving the main contribution to second-order scattering. The calculated frequencies therefore agree with the experimental data [452]. On the other hand, the normal modes corresponding to the critical points naturally need not always coincide with the Raman modes. In our example, the point $W(k_8 = \tfrac{1}{4}(b_1 + b_2) + \tfrac{1}{2}(b_2 + b_3))$ does not correspond to any Raman modes, although it is a critical point. Born's theory of lattice dynamics, supplemented by the concept of critical points, is thus apparently more consistent with the experiment.

Let us now consider the selection rules in second-order Raman spectra. According to (21.36), phonons of the entire first Brillouin zone take part in Raman scattering. Let us consider the selection rules for processes described by (21.33).* For overtone transitions (scattering with the participation of two identical phonons), the wave function of the final state is transformed according to the representation $[\tau]^2$, which is a symmetrical square of the physically irreducible representation τ according to which the particular normal mode of the crystal lattice is classified. On the basis of general rules (see §10), assuming that the initial state is the ground state of the crystal and is classified according to a totally symmetric representation, we obtain the selection rules in the form

$$[v]_\alpha^2 \times [\tau]^2 \supset A. \tag{21.40a}$$

For combination transitions we have

$$[v]_\alpha^2 \times \tau_1 \times \tau_2 \supset A. \tag{21.41a}$$

---

* The selection rules for the processes (21.34) and (21.35) are derived by the same method.

Selection rules (21.40a), (21.41a) can be written in the form

$$[\tau]^2 \supset [v]_\alpha^2, \tag{21.40b}$$

$$\tau_1 \times \tau_2 \supset [v]_\alpha^2. \tag{21.41b}$$

According to §19, the physically irreducible representation τ is either an irreducible real representation of the group G or can be expressed as a direct sum of two complex conjugate representations τ' and τ''. In the latter case, $[\tau]^2$ may be written in the form (see [86])

$$[\tau]^2 = [\tau']^2 + [\tau'']^2 + \tau'\tau''. \tag{21.42}$$

Then (21.40a) is equivalent to the relations

$$[\tau']^2 \supset [v]_\alpha^2, \tag{21.43a}$$

$$[\tau'']^2 \supset [v]_\alpha^2, \tag{21.43b}$$

$$[\tau'\tau''] \supset [v]_\alpha^2. \tag{21.43c}$$

The representation $\tau_1 \times \tau_2$ correspondingly may be written as a sum of products of irreducible representations of the group G. Therefore in both cases, the selection rules reduce to relations of the form (21.40b), (21.41b), where τ, τ_1, τ_2 are irreducible representations of the group G.

The problem of selection rules in second-order Raman spectra thus can be solved only if the structure of the products of the irreducible representations of the entire space group is known. Only in the particular case of the excitation of phonons with $k = 0$ in the process of scattering may τ be considered as a representation of the point group of directions of the crystal, F, to which the method originally developed for molecules is applicable (§10).

The problem of decomposition of a product of representations of space groups has been solved by a number of authors [453–455] in application to particular physical problems. In [454], a general procedure is developed for the decomposition of a product of two and three irreducible representations of a space group into irreducible representations and appropriate selection rules are derived for crystals of the T_d^2 group for Raman scattering with the participation of two and three phonons corresponding to critical points of the Brillouin zone. The method calls for the construction of the characters of the product of irreducible representations of the entire space group from the characters of small representations. However, the general method of [454] is fairly cumbersome, and it is not practicable for the calculation of the selection rules in second-order Raman spectra.

Let us consider in some detail the method developed by Gorelik [355], which is analogous to the technique applied in [86] to establish the possibility of phase transitions of the second kind. This method, in addition to being attractively simple in applications, has a further advantage: the final results are obtained in the form of expressions which are convenient for analyzing a number of particular cases and deriving general relations.

First we will describe a method for finding the common representations of the symmetric square $[\tau]^2$ of an irreducible representation of a group G and of the representation $[v]^2$ of a symmetrical tensor of rank two decomposable into irreducible representations $[v]_\alpha^2$. The star $\{k\}^2$ of the representation $[\tau]^2$ consists of all the possible vectors of the form $k_i + k_{i'}$ (k_i, $k_{i'}$ are the vectors of the star $\{k\}$ of the representation τ). If these vectors do not include the zero vector, condition (21.41) is a priori not satisfied, since the star of the representation $[v]^2$ is $\{0\}$. Thus, in order to satisfy (21.41), the vectors of the star $\{k\}$ should contain with any vector k_i its inverse vector $k_{i'} = -k_i$.* This requirement is a reflection of the quasi-momentum conservation in Raman scattering. If the representation τ meets this condition, the star $\{k\}^2$ is partitioned into two stars: one containing the zero vector alone, and the other all the nonzero vectors. The representation $[\tau]^2$ is thus also partitioned into two representations τ_0 and τ_1, where only τ_0 may have common representations with $[v]^2$, as is indeed necessary in order to satisfy (21.41). Let us first consider only those representations τ whose stars contain vectors k_i which are not equivalent to $-k_i$. For this case, we have from [86]

$$n([v]_\alpha^2) = \frac{l}{2f'} \sum_{h_j \subset \hat{G}_{k_1}} \{\chi^{(1)}(g)\,\chi^{(1)}(g_{11'}^{-1}gg_{11'})\,\chi_v(g) +$$

$$+ \chi^{(1)}(g_{11'}gg_{11'}g)\,\chi_v(g_{11'}g)\}, \qquad (21.44)$$

where $g = \{h_j | \alpha_j + a\}$, l is the number of vectors of the star $\{k\}$, f' is the number of elements of the point group of the vector $k_1 \subset \{k\}$, $g_{11'}k_1 = k_{1'} = -k_1$; $g_{11'} \subset G$, $\chi^{(1)}(g)$ are the characters of the small representation of the group G_{k_1}; χ_v is the character of the irreducible representation $[v]_\alpha^2$ entering the representation $[v]^2$; $n([v]_\alpha^2)$ is the number of irreducible representations $[v]_\alpha^2$ contained in the representation τ_0. If the vectors of the star of the representation τ are such that each vector k_1 is equivalent to $-k_1$, we have from [86]

$$n([v]_\alpha^2) = \frac{l}{2f'} \sum_{h_j \subset \hat{G}_{k_1}} \{[\chi^{(1)}(g)]^2 + \chi^{(1)}(g^2)\}\,\chi_v(g). \qquad (21.45)$$

The notation is the same as in (21.44).

To satisfy the relation $\tau_1 \times \tau_2 \supset [v]_\alpha^2$, where τ_1, τ_2 are irreducible representations of the group G, it is necessary that the star $\{k\}_1 \times \{k\}_2$ of the representation $\tau_1 \times \tau_2$

---

* Here and in what follows, wave vectors are considered equal if they coincide apart from a reciprocal lattice vector.

contain the star $\{0\}$. This will be so if the stars $\{k\}_1$ and $\{k\}_2$ can be written in the form

$$\{k\}_1 = \{k_1, k_2, \ldots, k_l\},$$

$$\{k\}_2 = \{-k_1, -k_2, \ldots, -k_l\}. \tag{21.46}$$

If there exists an element $g \subset G$ such that $gk_1 = -k_1$ ($k_1 \subset \{k\}_1$), the stars $\{k_1\}$ and $\{k_2\}$ consist of the same vectors k. In this case, the product $\tau_1 \times \tau_2$ is decomposed into a representation τ_0 with a star $\{0\}$ and a representation τ_1 whose star contains all the other vectors. The number of irreducible representations $[v]_\alpha^2$ contained in the representation $\tau_1 \times \tau_2$ is obtained from the equality

$$n([v]_\alpha^2) = \frac{l}{f'} \sum_{h_j k_1 = k_1} \chi^{(1)}(g) \chi^{(1)'}(g) \chi_v(g), \tag{21.47}$$

where $g = \{h_j \mid \alpha_j + a\} \subset G$; $\chi^{(1)}(g)$ is the character of the small representation $\tau_{k_1}(g)$; $\chi^{(1)'}(g)$ is the character of the small representation $\tau_{-k_1}(g)$.

Note that if τ_1 and τ_2 are complex-conjugate representations, we always have

$$\tau_1 \times \tau_2 \supset A, \tag{21.48}$$

i.e., the product of complex-conjugate representations always contains the unit representation.

Using (21.44), (21.46), (21.48), we can readily establish the selection rules for composite transitions. In the particular case when the vectors of the star $\{k\}$ are arbitrarily arranged inside the Brillouin zone, inversion is the only element of the point group F capable of moving the vector k over to the vector $-k$. Using the general relations (21.44), (21.47), we find in both cases

$$n([v]_\alpha^2) = \chi_v(\varepsilon_1) \neq 0,$$

i.e., Raman scattering is always allowed for overtone and combination transitions of the particular symmetry in crystals with an inversion center. This result is consistent with the analogous conclusion of [86], derived by a direct construction of the characters of irreducible representations of the entire space group. Also note that by (21.48), an overtone transition for a reducible representation τ consisting of two complex-conjugate irreducible representations is always allowed because of the scalar component of the polarizability tensor.

As an example, let us consider the selection rules in second-order Raman spectra for the C_{2h}^5 group. Each element of this group can be represented as a product of translation

$$\{e \mid a\} (a = n_1 a_1 + n_2 a_2 + n_3 a_3; n_1, n_2, n_3 = 0, \pm 1, \ldots)$$

and one of the elements of the form

$$\{e \mid 0\}, \quad \{C_2 \mid \alpha_1\}, \quad \{i \mid \alpha_2\}, \quad \{\sigma_h \mid \alpha_3\}. \tag{21.49}$$

Here $\alpha_1 = \frac{1}{2}a_3$, $\alpha_2 = \frac{1}{2}(a_1 + a_3)$, $\alpha_3 = \frac{1}{2}a_1$; a_1, a_2, a_3 are the elementary trans-lation vectors (see [86]). The group of directions of the crystal is the point group $C_{2h} = \{e, C_2, i, \sigma_h\}$. According to [86], the Brillouin zone of this group contains 14 characteristic points, each corresponding to a certain star of an irreducible representation of the group G. Let us consider some of these characteristic points.

1. The point $k_1 = \frac{1}{2}(b_1 + b_2)$. The corresponding star of the irreducible rep-resentation τ consists of a single vector ($l = 1$), since all the elements of the group F leave the vector k_1 invariant. The point group of the vector k_1 is therefore C_{2h}. It is readily seen that $k = -k$ (apart from equivalence). We thus have to apply the general relation (21.45). Using the results of [86], we find that the group C_{2h} has only one loaded two-dimensional representation $\hat{\tau}$ at the relevant point. Table 49 lists the matrix elements of the representations $\hat{\tau}$, τ_k and the characters of τ_k necessary for calculations using (21.45). From the realness criterion and Table 42 we obtain

$$\frac{1}{f'} \sum_{gk_1 = -k_1} \chi_{k_1}(g^2) = 1,$$

i.e., the irreducible representation τ of the space group G is real. Using (21.45) and (21.47), we obtain in this case

$$[\tau]^2 \supset A_g, \quad \tau \times \tau \supset A_g + B_g.$$

The overtone transition is thus allowed for the totally symmetric components of the polarizability tensor α_{xx}, α_{yy}, α_{zz}, α_{xy}; the combination transition is allowed for all the components of this tensor.

2. The point $k = \frac{1}{2}(b_1 + b_2 + b_3)$. This point, like the one before, lies on the boundary of the Brillouin zone. The point symmetry group in this case is C_{2h}. The loaded representations of this group for the vector $k = \frac{1}{2}(b_1 + b_2 + b_3)$ are one-dimensional (Table 49). Using the realness criterion (Table 49), we find that all the irreducible representations τ_1, τ_2, τ_3, τ_4 of the space group corresponding to $\hat{\tau}^{(1)}$, $\hat{\tau}^{(2)}$, $\hat{\tau}^{(3)}$, $\hat{\tau}^{(4)}$ are not equivalent to their complex conjugates. Combining the complex-conjugate representations, we obtain the physically irreducible representa-tions $\tau_I = \tau_1 + \tau_3$ and $\tau_{II} = \tau_2 + \tau_4$. From (21.48) we know that the overtone transitions are active in Raman scattering for the polarizability tensor components of symmetry A_g. Using the general relations (21.45), (21.47) and Table 49, we find

$$[\tau_I]^2 \supset A_g + B_g, \quad [\tau_{II}]^2 \supset A_g + B_g,$$

$$\tau_I \times \tau_I \supset A_g + B_g, \quad \tau_{II} \times \tau_{II} \supset A_g + B_g.$$

The overtones and the combination transitions in Raman spectra are thus allowed for all the components of the polarizability tensor.

Knowledge of the critical points and selection rules in Raman spectra, and data on IR absorption, neutron scattering, and the shape of dispersion curves permit

Table 49

MATRIX ELEMENTS AND CHARACTERS OF THE REPRESENTATIONS OF THE C_{2h}^5 GROUP

Vector $k = \frac{1}{2}(b_1 + b_2)$

$\hat{G} = C_{2h}$	e	C_2	i	σ_h
$\hat{\tau}$	$\begin{pmatrix} 1 & 0 \\ 0 & 1 \end{pmatrix}$	$\begin{pmatrix} 1 & 0 \\ 0 & -1 \end{pmatrix}$	$\begin{pmatrix} 0 & -1 \\ 1 & 0 \end{pmatrix}$	$\begin{pmatrix} 0 & 1 \\ 1 & 0 \end{pmatrix}$
G_k	$\{e\|0\}$	$\{C_2\|\frac{1}{2}a_3\}$	$\{i\|\frac{1}{2}(a_1+a_3)\}$	$\{\sigma_h\|\frac{1}{2}a_1\}$
τ_k	$\begin{pmatrix} 1 & 0 \\ 0 & 1 \end{pmatrix}$	$\begin{pmatrix} 1 & 0 \\ 0 & -1 \end{pmatrix}$	$\begin{pmatrix} 0 & -i \\ i & 0 \end{pmatrix}$	$\begin{pmatrix} 0 & i \\ i & 0 \end{pmatrix}$
$\chi(g)$	2	0	0	0

Vector $k = \frac{1}{2}(b_1 + b_2 + b_3)$

$\hat{\tau}^{(1)}$	1	1	1	-1
$\hat{\tau}^{(2)}$	1	1	-1	1
$\hat{\tau}^{(3)}$	1	-1	1	1
$\hat{\tau}^{(4)}$	1	-1	-1	-1
G_k	$\{e\|0\}$	$\{C_2\|\frac{1}{2}a_3\}$	$\{i\|\frac{1}{2}(a_1+a_3)\}$	$\{\sigma_h\|\frac{1}{2}a_1\}$
$\tau_k^{(1)}$	1	i	-1	$-i$
$\tau_k^{(2)}$	1	i	1	i
$\tau_k^{(3)}$	1	$-i$	-1	i
$\tau_k^{(4)}$	1	$-i$	1	$-i$
$\chi_1(g)$	1	i	-1	$-i$
$\chi_2(g)$	1	i	1	i
$\chi_3(g)$	1	$-i$	-1	i
$\chi_4(g)$	1	$-i$	1	$-i$

Application of the realness test

g	$\{e\|0\}$	$\{C_2\|\frac{1}{2}a_3\}$	$\{i\|\frac{1}{2}(a_1+a_3)\}$	$\{\sigma_1\|\frac{1}{2}a_1\}$
g^2	$\{e\|0\}$	$\{e\|a_3\}$	$\{e\|0\}$	$\{e\|a_1\}$
$k = \frac{1}{2}(b_1 + b_2)$ $\chi(g^2)$	2	2	2	-2
$k = \frac{1}{2}(b_1 + b_2 + b_3)$ $\chi_1(g^2), \chi_2(g^2),$ $\chi_3(g^2), \chi_4(g^2).$	1	-1	1	-1

classifying the observed lines in second-order spectra, although their identification naturally is not always single-valued. Let us consider some examples of the interpretation of second-order Raman spectra.

The second-order spectrum of the CsBr crystal has been studied in [451]. The unit cell of this crystal contains two nonequivalent atoms. The symmetry group is the space group O_{1h}^1. The Brillouin zone for this group is shown in Figure 81c. The classification of the vibrational levels is based on the compatibility relations for the irreducible representations of the group G . The vibrations are divided into transverse and longitudinal, depending on their polarization. According to the selection rules, the second-order Raman spectrum of this crystal is allowed for the overtones and for the combination frequencies at the points Γ, Δ, T, X, Λ, R, Σ, S, Z, M. Calculation of the dispersion curves [451] shows that the points Γ, M, X, Λ, R, S, Σ, and T are critical. The selection rules and the numerous critical points result in a substantial number of sharp maxima in the spectrum (Figure 81b). Using the calculated frequencies, the authors of [451] tried to identify all the observed lines (Table 50). The characteristic feature of this spectrum is that various phonon-pair combinations contribute to the same intensity peak, making it virtually unassignable.

The second-order Raman spectrum of the GaP crystal has been studied in [456].

Table 50

SECOND-ORDER RAMAN SPECTRUM OF THE CsBr CRYSTAL

Experimental Δv [451], cm^{-1}	Calculated Δv, cm^{-1}	Identification
25	24	$LA(M) - TA_2(M)$; $LO(T) - LA(T)$; $LO(S) - LA(S)$; $TO_1(Z) - TA_1(Z)$
40	41	$LO(\Gamma) - TO(\Gamma)$; $LO(X) - TO(X)$; $LO(T) - LA(T)$; $LO(S) - TA_2(S)$; $LO(Z) - TA_1(Z)$
54	52	$LO(M) - TA_2(M)$; $LO(X) - TA(X)$; $LO(S) - TA_1(S)$; $LO(Z) - TA_2(Z)$
75	83	$LA(M) + TA_2(M)$; $2LA(T)$; $TA(S) + TA_2(S)$
105	105	$2TO_2(M)$; $TO_1(T) + LA(T)$; $TO_2(S) + TA_1(S)$; $LA(Z) + TA_1(Z)$
125	125	$LO(X) + TA(X)$; $LO(T) + LA(T)$; $TO_1(S) + LA(S)$; $TO_1(S) + LA(S)$; $TO_1(Z) + TA_1(Z)$
134	134	$TO(X) + LA(X)$; $LO(M) + TO_2(M)$
134	135	$LO(M) + LA(M)$
134	133	$LO(R) + LA(R)$; $LO(T) + TO(T)$; $TO_1(S) + TA_1(T)$; $LO(Z) + TA_1(Z)$
—	155	$2LA(X)$; $2LO(T)$; $LO(S) + TO_1(S)$; $2TO_1(Z)$
163	163	$2LO(M)$; $2LO(T)$; $LO(S) + TO_1(S)$; $LO(Z) + TO_1(Z)$
176	182	$2LO(X)$; $2LO(S)$; $2LO(Z)$

Note. LO, LA longitudinal optical and acoustic branches; TO, TO_1, TO_2, TA, TA_1, TA_2 transverse optical and acoustic branches.

The crystal lattice of GaP is the same as that of the cubic modification of ZnS (Figure 71). Γ, L, X, W are the critical points of the Brillouin zone. According to [451], all the overtone and combination transitions are allowed in the Raman spectrum for each of these points. Figure 81a shows the spectrum of this crystal at $20°$K. According to the calculated dispersion curves of the GaAs crystal, the longitudinal optical branch (LO) and the transverse optical branch (TO) intersect, so that $LO > TO$ at the beginning of the Brillouin zone and $TO > LO$ at the end of the Brillouin zone; moreover, the longitudinal acoustic branch LA is fairly far from the transverse acoustic branch TA, almost catching up with the optical branch at the boundary of the Brillouin zone. In [456], the dispersion curves of the vibrational branches of GaP are assumed to have roughly the same form. If this is indeed so, the observed Raman spectrum can be interpreted as follows (see Figure 81a).

The observed spectrum can be divided into three regions. The region 670–800 cm^{-1} corresponds to sum transitions of pairs of optical phonons; the second region stretches from 293 to 613 cm^{-1}, and the corresponding lines are associated with sum combinations of pairs of optical and acoustic phonons; phonons of the transverse acoustic branch are apparently observed between 150 and 289 cm^{-1}. Difference combinations do not produce Raman scattering because of the sufficiently low temperature of the crystal. The 366 cm^{-1} and 422 cm^{-1} lines are the results of first-order Raman scattering by transverse and longitudinal long-wave optical vibrations. The 289 cm^{-1} intensity peak probably corresponds to the sum combination of phonon pairs at the end of the transverse acoustic branch. The 804 cm^{-1} peak corresponds to the overtone transition excited by a longitudinal long-wave optical vibration. The several maxima around 786 cm^{-1} indicate that the transverse optical branch is markedly displaced at the end of the Brillouin zone. Table 51 lists the probable identification of the other observed lines. Studies of second-order Raman spectra may thus yield valuable information on the dispersion curves of the vibrational branches of crystals.

22. RAMAN SPECTRA OF DISPERSE MEDIA

Application of molecular spectroscopy to disperse media (polycrystalline samples, powders, suspensions) is of considerable interest, since numerous natural and artificial products belong to this category. However, the spectra of these objects are very difficult to obtain, and there are correspondingly very few published reports in this field. Although the Raman spectroscopy of disperse media is by no means a new undertaking (the first techniques were described in [458–460]), large-scale application of these methods to various objects (including those showing absorption) has begun only in recent years [461–467]. The latest advances are largely due to the application of lasers as exciting sources [468–470].

Table 51

RAMAN SPECTRUM OF THE GaP CRYSTAL

Frequency, cm^{-1}	Identification	Frequency, cm^{-1}	Identification
804	Maximum of two-phonon density of states	548	Maximum of $TA + TO$ combinations
802	$2 \times TO(W)$	546	$TO_1(W) + TA_1(W)$
786	$2 \times TO(X)$	533	$TO_2(W) + TA_2(W)$
770	$2 \times TO(W)$	570	$2 \times LA(X)$
756	$2 \times TO(L)$	495	$TO(X) + TA(X)$
745	$TO(X) + LO(X)$	471	$2 \times LA(L)$
740	$TO(L) + LO(L)$	460	$LO(X) + TA(X)$
721	$2 \times LO(L)$	450	$TO(L) + TA(L)$
705	$2 \times LO(X)$	402 ⎫	First-order lines
687	$2 \times LO(W)$	366 ⎭	
650 ⎫		309	$TA(L) + LA(L)$
618 ⎪	$LA + TO$	289	Maximum of $2 \times TA$ combinations
613 ⎪			
607 ⎭		285	$2 \times TA(W)$
582 ⎫	$LA + LO$	209	$2 \times TA(X)$
567 ⎭		151	$2 \times TA(L)$

Note. LO, LA longitudinal optical and acoustic branches; TO, TA, TA_1, TA_2 transverse optical and acoustic branches.

Various methods have been proposed for effective Raman spectroscopy of disperse media (mainly absorbing powders). These methods can be broadly divided into two groups: "reflection" methods and "transmission" methods. In "reflection" methods, the scattered radiation is collected from the same surface which is exposed to the incident radiation; in "transmission" methods, the two relevant surfaces are separated by a layer of matter. "Reflection" methods give higher intensities, but the intensity ratio of the Raman lines to the background is much more advantageous in "transmission" methods. A comparison of the various methods will be found in [44, 471].

The most difficult problem in Raman spectroscopy of disperse media is how to measure the line intensities, which are complex functions of the material parameters and also of the dispersity characteristics of the medium, such as grain size. A similar problem arises in connection with the luminescence of disperse media. Ivanov [473] was the first to allow for the effect of dispersity on the luminescence intensity. Proceeding from the calculations of Gershun [472], he derived the luminescence intensity as a function of powder layer thickness. In these calculations, however, the absorption of the luminescence wavelengths was assumed to be negligible compared to the absorption of excitation wavelengths. This assumption is inapplicable to Raman scattering.

Shuvalov [474] advanced a general solution of the problem, without this restricting assumption. The principal results of his work are presented below.

Consider Raman scattering in a medium composed of a multitude of grains. If we assume that the number of grains in unit volume is so high that scattering by grain boundaries and absorption may be treated as continuous functions of the layer thickness, the problem can be solved by differential methods.

In general, the conditions of light propagation in a disperse medium depend on the conditions of illumination. For simplicity, we will consider a material layer between two infinite parallel planes illuminated by diffuse light. Any plane inside this layer parallel to its boundaries is illuminated from both sides.

Let E_1 and E_2 be the right and left illuminances, respectively. E_1 and E_2 are functions of the depth inside the layer, layer thickness, absorption, and scattering. Consider a lamina of thickness dx; let $r = s\,dx$ be the reflection coefficient and $t = 1 - (s + k)dx$ the transmission coefficient of the infinitesimal lamina. Here s is the scattering constant, which characterizes the flux reflected by the infinitesimal lamina, k is the absorption constant. This treatment of a diffuse medium was first proposed by Schuster [475]. If the structure of the object is assumed to remain constant throughout and the light inside the scattering layer remains ideally diffuse, s and k are determined by the properties of the material, being independent of the layer thickness. On the basis of this assumption, Gershun [472] obtained the following expressions for E_1 and E_2:

$$E_1(x) = \frac{\sinh\left[L(x_0 - x) - \ln R\right]}{\sinh\left[Lx_0 - \ln R\right]},\qquad (22.1)$$

$$E_2(x) = \frac{\sinh\left[L(x_0 - x)\right]}{\sinh\left[Lx_0 - \ln R\right]}.\qquad (22.2)$$

Here

$$L = \sqrt{k^2 + 2ks}, \qquad R = 1 + (k/s) - \sqrt{(k/s)^2 + 2(k/s)}.\qquad (22.3)$$

R is the reflection coefficient of an infinitely thick layer, L is the effective extinction coefficient.

Let dl be the intensity of Raman scattering emitted by a layer of thickness dx at a depth x from the surface. Then

$$dI = 2\kappa(E_1 + E_2)dx,\qquad (22.4)$$

where κ is the scattering coefficient for the given Raman line. Let $I_1(x)$ and $I_2(x)$ be the luminous flux densities of Raman scattering incident on a plane inside the layer from the right and the left, respectively. The luminous energy balance on this plane can be expressed by the equalities (see Figure 82)

$$I_1(x + dx) = tI_1(x) + rI_2(x + dx) + \kappa(E_1 + E_2)dx, \qquad (22.5)$$

$$I_2(x)dx = tI_2(x + dx) + rI_1(x) + \kappa(E_1 + E_2)dx. \qquad (22.6)$$

Inserting for r and t their explicit expressions, we find

$$\frac{dI_1}{dx} = -(s' + k')I_1 + s'I_2 + \kappa(E_1 + E_2), \qquad (22.7)$$

$$\frac{dI_2}{dx} = -s'I_1 + (s' + k')I_2 - \kappa(E_1 + E_2) \qquad (22.8)$$

(primed quantities refer to Raman scattering). It is assumed that the infinitesimal lamina emits equal luminous fluxes in both directions.

Seeing that $I_1(0) = 0$, $I_2(l) = 0$ (l is the layer thickness), we obtain the solution of Eqs. (22.7), (22.8) in the form

$$I_1(l) = \frac{(1 + R')(1 + R)\kappa}{(\delta^2 - R^2)(\delta'^2 - R'^2)}\left[\frac{(\delta - \delta')(\delta\delta' + RR')}{L - L'} - \right.$$

$$\left. - \frac{(\delta'R + R'\delta)(\delta\delta' - 1)}{L + L'}\right], \qquad (22.9)$$

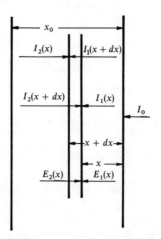

Figure 82

Illustrating the determination of scattering intensity in a disperse medium.

I_0 is the exciting intensity, I_1 and I_2 are the Raman scattering intensities, E_1 and E_2 are the illuminances of a plane distant x from the surface.

$$I_2(0) = \frac{(1 + R')(1 + R)\kappa}{(\delta^2 - R^2)(\delta'^2 - R'^2)} \left[\frac{(\delta\delta' + RR')(\delta\delta' - 1)}{L + L'} \right.$$

$$\left. - \frac{(\delta - \delta')(\delta'R + R'\delta)}{L - L'} \right]. \qquad (22.10)$$

Here $\delta = e^{Ll}$, $\delta' = e^{L'l}$.

The parameters s and k are the effective characteristics of the scattering medium; under certain additional assumptions, they can be expressed in the form (see [473])

$$s = \frac{2Cr}{\Delta}, \quad k = 2k_0 C, \qquad (22.11)$$

where C is the packing coefficient, Δ is the mean grain size, k_0 is the absorption coefficient of the crystal.

Eqs. (22.9). (22.10) give a general solution for the intensity of Raman scattering in a disperse absorbing media. $I_1(l)$ corresponds to the intensity of Raman scattering in "reflection" measurements (in a plane cuvette), and $I_2(0)$ to the intensity in "transmission" measurements. Note, however, that the particular assumptions used in the derivation of these relations are largely inapplicable to actual conditions. Therefore, the main task in practice is to establish under exactly what conditions these relations do apply.

Let us first consider some particular cases. In case of Raman scattering at moderate vibration frequencies, we may take $k = k'$, $s = s'$. Then

$$I_1(l) = \frac{(1 + R)^2 \kappa \delta}{L(\delta^2 - R^2)^2} \left[lL(\delta^2 + R^2) - R(\delta^2 - 1) \right], \qquad (22.12)$$

$$I_2(0) = \frac{(1 + R)^2 \kappa}{2L(\delta^2 - R^2)^2} \left[(\delta^2 + R^2)(\delta^2 - 1) - 4lLR\delta^2 \right] \qquad (22.13)$$

For $s = s' = 0$, $k \neq k'$, we have

$$I_1(l) = \frac{\kappa}{k - k'} e^{-k'l} \left[e^{(k - k')l} - 1 \right], \qquad (22.14)$$

$$I_2(0) = \kappa \left[\frac{1}{k + k'} + \frac{2k'}{k^2 - k'^2} e^{-(k - k')l} - \frac{1}{k - k'} e^{-2kl} \right]. \qquad (22.15)$$

For $k = k'$, $s = s' = 0$, we have from (22.12), (22.13)

$$I_1(l) = \kappa l e^{-kl}, \qquad (22.16)$$

$$I_2(0) = \tfrac{1}{2} \kappa (1 - e^{-2kl}). \qquad (22.17)$$

The last relations evidently correspond to scattering in an absorbing medium which, however, is not disperse. Some authors use in their treatment a single effective parameter — the turbidity — and this approach also leads to relations of the form (22.16). Although this method sometimes leads to satisfactory agreement with the experiment [471], its application is naturally more limited than the application of the previous, more general method which describes the disperse medium in terms of two effective parameters.

In what follows, we will use (22.12), which can be written in the form

$$\frac{I}{l} = \frac{(1 + R)^2 \kappa \delta}{(\delta^2 - R^2)^2} \left[\delta^2 + R^2 - \frac{R(\delta^2 - 1)}{Ll} \right] = f(R, Ll)\kappa. \tag{22.18}$$

Eq. (22.18) is convenient in that it contains only two variables, R and Ll. L can be found by measuring the dependence of the exciting line intensity on the cuvette thickness. Indeed, taking for this case $\kappa = 0$ and solving Eqs. (22.7), (22.8), we find

$$I_e(l) = I_e(0) e^{-l}. \tag{22.19}$$

Measuring the ratio $I_e(l)/I_e(0)$ for several values of l, we can readily find L for the given powder, and R remains the only unknown in (22.18). This parameter also can be determined experimentally by measuring the Raman line intensity for various cuvette thicknesses l and comparing the resulting values of the ratio $I(l)/l$ with those computed from (22.18).* Thus, in principle, we can find all the factors in (22.18) which depend on the properties of the material medium. Then the scattering coefficient $\kappa = I_e(0)\kappa_0$ can be found; this parameter characterizes the true intensity of the Raman lines of the material.

Actual measurements following this procedure [476] revealed a certain divergence between the theoretical curve and the experimental data for thin cuvettes. Figure 83 plots the results of measurements for one powder fraction of stilbene; the cuvette was placed directly at the spectrometer slit. The divergence is readily attributable to the breakdown of the assumption of diffuse exciting radiation, which is particularly felt for thin cuvettes.

Further measurements were carried out with the cuvette mounted at a certain distance from the slit; the scattered radiation was focused by a condenser lens onto the slit. The experiment also showed that the curve of Raman scattering intensity vs. the cuvette thickness is sensitive to the ratio α of the illuminated cuvette surface to the total surface. A good arrangement between theory and experiment concerning the dependence of the Raman scattering intensity on Ll is observed for α between

---

* In order to determine R, we require measurements for two values of l only. Measurements for other l are essential in order to determine the fit of Eq. (22.18) with the experiment.

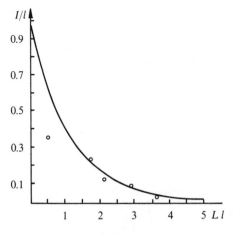

Figure 83

The ratio I/l vs. Ll for Raman scattering. The solid curve is theoretical, the dots mark the experimental data (stilbene, fraction No. 4, DFS-12 spectrometer).

0.4 and 0.6. The line intensities in stilbene were measured in [476] for a number of fractions and cuvette thicknesses satisfying this α. For known I, L, and l, the parameter R was found for various fractions (Table 52).

Figure 84 compares the results of calculations using (22.18) with the experimental findings. The agreement is quite adequate.

The results show that Eq. (22.18) can be applied to determine the true intensity of Raman lines under approximate experimental conditions.

Measurements of absolute Raman scattering intensities and their comparison for various disperse media are likely to yield valuable results. This aspect is considered in [477].

A number of recent reports deal with measurements of the absolute coefficient or cross section (see §2) of Raman scattering in liquids [12, 16, 291, 478–480]. The

Table 52

PARAMETERS OF VARIOUS FRACTIONS OF
A DISPERSE MEDIUM

Fraction number	Grain size, mm	L	R
1	From 0.1 to 0.2	1.18	0.30
2	From 0.2 to 0.3	1.15	0.25
3	From 0.3 to 0.4	0.99	0.20
4	From 0.4 to 0.5	0.72	0.10

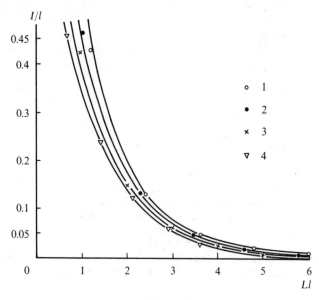

Figure 84

Experimental and theoretical plots of I/l vs. Ll. Solid curves — calculated for the appropriate R and L from the table, dots — experimental data; 1, 2, 3, 4 are the fraction numbers.

greatest methodological difficulty in these measurements is how to allow for the difference in the apertures of the exciting and the scattered light. In all the above sources, the measurements were carried out so that the directions of incidence and scattering made an angle of from 90° to 20° to each other. Under these conditions, additional measurements and corrections are required to allow for the aperture difference. The simplest approach in this respect is to measure the scattered radiation in the direction of incidence. No measurements of Raman scattering cross sections have been carried out in this geometry, however, apparently because of the strong background of exciting light.

The Raman scattering cross sections of stilbene powders and single crystals were measured in [477] by photographic and photoelectric methods. According to (22.18), the Raman scattering cross section of this material per molecule inside a certain solid angle is

$$\sigma = \frac{I}{I_e(0) \, lf \, (R, \, Ll) \, N},\tag{22.20}$$

where N is the number of molecules in unit scattering volume.

Stilbene powders consisting of two fractions were used in [477]; first fraction with grain size from 0.1 to 0.2 mm, second fraction with grain size from 0.4 to 0.5 mm. The powder was packed in plane cuvettes 2 and 4 mm thick, 12 mm in diameter.

A mercury discharge lamp (4358 Å line) was used as the exciting source. The integrated intensity of the stilbene Raman line $\Delta v = 1593\ \mathrm{cm}^{-1}$ was measured together with the integrated intensity of the exciting line. The exciting line was attenuated by a certain factor using neutral light filters. The absolute Raman scattering coefficient of the stilbene powder for a certain solid angle was determined using (22.20). Measurements of the Raman scattering cross section in a stilbene single crystal were carried out by the same method. Cylindrical stilbene crystals were used, 15 mm in diameter and from 5 to 50 mm long. The attenuation of the exciting line in these crystals was seen to follow (22.19). Experiments carried out with two crystals 15 mm in diameter and 20 and 50 mm long gave $R = 0.008$, i.e., a figure which can hardly affect the value of the function $f(R, Ll)$ (a legitimate result for single crystals). The parameter R in the single crystal can therefore be taken as zero in all subsequent calculations. Eq. (22.20) thus takes the following simplified form for single crystals:

$$\sigma = \frac{I}{I_e(0)e^{-Ll}lN}.\tag{22.21}$$

For $L = 0$ this relation clearly gives the Raman scattering cross section of transparent liquids. The experimental setup for measurements of the RS cross section in powders and crystals is shown in Figure 85.

Two different condenser lenses with focal distances of 60 and 120 mm were used. The measured RS cross section was found to be independent of the condenser focal distances for exit apertures of 6° and less. The solid angle $\Delta\Omega_{\mathrm{av}}$ in which Raman

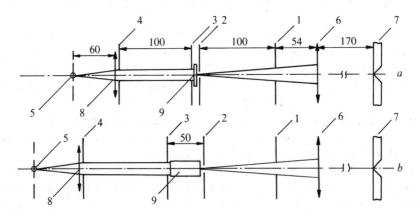

Figure 85

Experimental setup for measurements of the absolute Raman scattering coefficient σ of powders (*a*) and single crystals (*b*).

1, 2, 3, 4) stops,   5) lamp,   6) condenser,   7) spectrometer slit,   8) lens ($f = 60$ mm), 9) cuvette with powder or crystal.

scattering occurs in a transparent medium is readily found by integration over the volume of the crystal (or the liquid). It is assumed that the molecules lying at a certain distance r from the center of the crystal emit in the same solid angle as the molecules lying at the center of the crystal. Simple calculations yield

$$\Delta\Omega_{av} = \frac{S}{ab}, \tag{22.22}$$

where S is the illuminated condenser area, a is the distance from the frontal surface of the crystal to the condenser, b is the distance from the rear surface of the crystal to the condenser. More exact calculations yield virtually the same result.

This procedure was applied to determine the RS cross section of powdered stilbene and of a stilbene crystal for various solid angles. The results are listed in Table 53. These results were obtained assuming a spherical diagram for the 1593 cm^{-1} line of stilbene; the results can be readily converted to other shapes of the polar scattering diagram. The relative error in the RS cross section is $\pm$ 20%. The agreement in the results obtained under different conditions shows that this method is definitely suitable for measuring the RS cross sections in powders and crystals.

The RS cross section of powdered benzene was also measured. Powdered frozen benzene with grain size from 0.3 to 0.04 mm was packed in circular quartz cuvettes 12 mm in diameter and 1, 2, 3, 4, and 5 mm thick. The intensity of the benzene 992 cm^{-1} line was measured for excitation with a low-pressure mercury lamp (4358 Å line) with an interference filter at 101, 172, and 252° K. The RS cross section of this line was virtually independent of temperature. Table 53 therefore gives average data.

To compare the Raman lines in solids and liquids, we also measured the RS cross sections in liquid benzene at room temperature and in liquid stilbene at + 150°C (excitation with the mercury 4358 Å line). The benzene RS cross section was measured in a glass tube 1050 mm long and 28 mm in diameter, illuminated by a parallel beam. The exit aperture did not exceed 5°. The measurements of the benzene RS cross sections were carried out for various effective cuvette diameters, defined by an appropriate stop. The RS cross sections of liquid stilbene were measured in metal tubes 12 mm in diameter with quartz windows.

The results of measurements, corrected for the scattering diagram of the benzene 992 cm^{-1} line, are also listed in Table 53. The results for stilbene were obtained assuming a spherical scattering diagram for the 1593 cm^{-1} line. The difference in the RS cross sections of the respective liquid and crystal is quite significant.

The data for liquid benzene fit the previous figure $\sigma \cdot 10^{28} = 1.9$ cm^2, obtained in [12, 480].

Table 53 also lists the data for $NaClO_3$ crystals, obtained with excitation by the mercury 4358 Å line, and for GaP and CdS crystals obtained with excitation by the

Table 53

RAMAN SCATTERING CROSS SECTIONS OF SOME CRYSTALS AND LIQUIDS

Compound	State of aggregation*	Characteristics of scattering object**	$\Delta\Omega_{av} \cdot 10^3$ sterad	$\sigma \cdot 10^{28}$ cm^2
Stilbene				
$\Delta v = 1593$ cm^{-1}	P	Fraction 1	33.4	469
	P	Fraction 2	33.3	464
	S	$d = 15$	25	460
	S	$d = 11$	25	458
	L	$d = 12, l = 104$	47	27
	L	$d = 12, l = 23$	20	25
Benzene				
$\Delta v = 992$ cm^{-1}	P	—	7.9	55
	L	$d = 26, l = 1050$	14	2.1
	L	$d = 18, l = 1050$	4.2	2.0
NaClO$_3$				
$\Delta v = 936$ cm^{-1}	P	$T = 101$	—	7.7
	P	$T = 293$	—	7.2
	P	$T = 483$	—	7.9
GaP				
$\Delta v = 402$ cm^{-1}	P	$T = 103$	—	200
	P	$T = 293$	—	390
	P	$T = 723$	—	980
	S	$T = 293$	—	300
CdS				
$\Delta v = 207$ cm^{-1}	P	$T = 293$	—	0.7

* P — powder, S — single crystal, L — liquid.

** d is the diameter in mm, l is the length in mm, T is the temperature in °K.

6328 Å line of a He–Ne laser. The strong temperature dependence of the RS cross section in GaP is attributed to the shift of the electronic absorption band of this crystal with changes in temperature [477].

CHAPTER IV

Stimulated Raman Scattering

23. LINE INTENSITIES IN STIMULATED RAMAN SCATTERING AND THE DEPENDENCE ON EXCITATION CONDITIONS

1. First experimental results

Stimulated Raman scattering (SRS) was first discovered by Woodbury and Ng [481] in 1962 in their work with high-power pulsed radiation from a ruby laser. The luminescence time of the ruby laser in their experiments was reduced by using an optical switch in the form of a nitrobenzene Kerr cell, and they observed side frequencies in the laser emissions. These frequencies were characteristic of the Raman spectrum of nitrobenzene, though of anomalously high intensity. A number of later reports dealt with various aspects of SRS (see reviews [482, 483]). Some aspects of this effect which reveal a number of characteristic features of both the ordinary Raman scattering and the laser emission emerged from these studies.

It is significant that the main factor influencing the excitation of stimulated Raman spectra is the power of the exciting radiation, and not its energy. Sufficient power levels are generated by "giant pulse" lasers, also known as Q-switched lasers.

We know from the general laser theory that the lasing intensity is mainly determined by the ratio of the actual upper level population to the minimum population corresponding to the threshold of the laser emission. The lasing threshold is determined by the losses in the resonator. However, very large population inversions (above the threshold value) cannot be achieved under normal conditions, since as soon as the upper level population reaches the threshold value, laser emission begins, the population rapidly falls below the threshold value, and the emission stops. If the pumping pulse is sufficiently powerful and long, a number of relatively weak laser pulses are observed. The increase of pumping power mainly increases the *number* of pulses, so that the laser energy is increased without achieving any increase in laser power. It thus follows that in order to increase the population inversion, the threshold should be raised, which can be achieved by increasing the resonator losses. This is not quite sufficient, however. In order to attain maximum laser power, we require a special device which will markedly reduce the losses as soon as the population inversion reaches the maximum. The currently used devices fall into three principal groups, electrooptical, optico-mechanical, and optical.

In the electrooptical method, the system includes a Kerr cell placed between crossed polaroids which act as a switch. When high voltage is applied to the cell, it rotates the plane of polarization of the incident light through a certain angle and the beam passes unimpeded through the polaroids. This setup, however, requires complex high-voltage equipment. Moreover, it is inconvenient for use with SRS, since the cell material generally gives parasitic lines in the Raman spectrum.

A typical example of an optico-mechanical switch is the rotary mirror (or a total internal reflection prism). This setup requires very high rotation speeds, but it is nevertheless simpler than the Kerr-cell switch.

Optical switches are becoming progressively more popular. If a sufficiently powerful beam hits an absorbing medium, all the molecules are excited and the material becomes transparent. It retains its transparency as long as the molecules remain in excited states. Cryptocyanine and KS-19 glass can be used for these switches. Power levels reaching the order of magnitude of 1 gigawatt have been attained in this way.

SRS is essentially dependent on the position of the active medium relative to the resonator. In the first studies of SRS the scattering material was placed in the resonator cavity. Figure 86 shows a diagram of the setup developed by Eckhardt et al. [484]. A cylindrical ruby laser measuring 76×9.5 mm with a polished surface was used. The ruby was pumped with a spiral flash lamp (not shown in the figure) in axial geometry. Mirrors with multilayer dielectric coatings were used in the resonator. A quartz Wollastone prism was used as the polaroid. A Kerr cell with KH_2PO_4

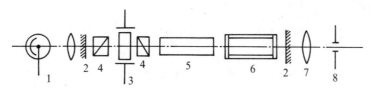

Figure 86

Experimental setup

1) photomultiplier,   2) multilayer dielectric mirrors,   3) Kerr cell,   4) polarizers,   5) ruby rod,
6) cell with scattering liquid,   7) condenser lens,   8) entrance slit.

replacing the original nitrobenzene acted as a switch. The KH_2PO_4 crystal is convenient in that it has no characteristic Raman lines of its own. The scattering cell was from 2.5 to 10 cm long. The emergent light was collected at both ends of the instrument. At one end, a photomultiplier recorded the ruby radiation (6943 Å), and at the other end, a spectral instrument was provided, isolating the scattering line. The ruby laser pulse had a peak power of 0.2–2 MW with a duration of 20–70 nsec, which corresponded to energy of 0.05–0.2 J.

The advantage of these ruby laser systems is that the 6943 Å exciting line is particularly strong in the resonator; moreover, the same resonator is used to pump the ruby and to induce the emission of the liquid.

The same experimental procedure was applied in [484] and later in [485] to study a number of liquids (benzene, toluene, pyridine, cyclohexane, nitrobenzene, etc.). The spectrum of each compound showed one or two Stokes lines and their harmonics. These lines correspond to the strongest symmetrical lines in the ordinary Raman spectra. The second and the third harmonics coincide with the corresponding overtones; unlike the overtones, the harmonic frequencies are exact integral multiples of the fundamental frequencies (Table 54).

The authors pointed to three facts which, in their opinion, reveal the existence of lasing at the displaced frequencies: 1) the beam emerging from the cell is highly parallel, like the ruby laser beam; 2) the scattering lines become narrower as the pumping energy is raised (0.6 cm^{-1}, as compared to several cm^{-1} in ordinary Raman

Table 54

SRS IN SOME LIQUIDS

Compound	$\Delta \nu_{SRS}$, cm^{-1}	$\Delta \nu$, cm^{-1}	Compound	$\Delta \nu_{SRS}$, cm^{-1}	$\Delta \nu$, cm^{-1}
Benzene	990 ± 2	992	1-Bromonaphthalene	1368 ± 4	1363
	$2 \times (990 \pm 2)$			—	3060
	3064 ± 4	3064			
			Pyridine	992 ± 2	991
Nitrobenzene	—	1004		$2 \times (992 \pm 5)$	
	1344 ± 2	1345		—	3054
	$2 \times (1346 \pm 2)$				
	$3 \times (1340 \pm 5)$		Cyclohexane	—	801
				2852 ± 1	2853
Toluene	—	785			
	1004 ± 4	1002	Deuterobenzene	944 ± 1	945
				$2 \times (944 \pm 1)$	
				—	2292

Note. $\Delta \nu_{SRS}$ is the shift of the SRS line relative to the ruby laser line, $\Delta \nu$ are the frequencies of the strongest Raman scattering lines.

scattering); 3) both the ruby laser output power and the test cell length, i.e., the optical path of the beam in the active medium, have certain threshold values.* When the threshold value is exceeded, the output power at the displaced frequency rapidly increases, reaching 0.01–0.1 of the total laser power, i.e., 10–100 kW.

A strong line suppression effect was noted in [485]: in case of two or more Raman-active media, the stimulated Raman scattering in the weaker lines is suppressed by the emission in the stronger lines. The authors attributed this suppression effect to the decrease in the power of the exciting laser line owing to partial degradation of its energy through Raman scattering.

Since the excitation of SRS spectra is associated with very high laser thresholds, this effect could be originally observed only in Q-switched systems. Recently, SRS was observed with an ordinary ruby laser, although its power was approximately two orders of magnitude below the power of the Q-switched laser [486]. The SRS threshold corresponded to a 360 J pump with pumping flashes about 500 μsec long. Long-duration pumping thus permitted attaining the threshold of SRS.

In the second type of SRS instruments, the scattering cell is placed outside the resonator cavity. In this geometry, the exciting pulse power should be much higher than in systems with the cell placed inside the cavity. This shortcoming, however, is more than offset by the fact that the system is adapted for wide-angle observations of scattered radiation, this being a highly important feature [487, 488].

Stoicheff [488] used a setup shown diagrammatically in Figure 87. The Q-switching was ensured by a rotating internal reflection prism. The rotation speed was 400 rev/sec. The pumping flashes were synchronized with the prism rotation. The energy emitted in the 6943 Å line varied from 0.1 to 0.8 J. The pulse duration was about 20 nsec. To ensure maximum power density, the laser emission was focused inside the scattering cell with a special lens ($f = 25$ cm). The cell length was varied from 2 to 70 mm. The laser beam cross section in the cell did not exceed 0.1 cm². The corresponding power density is estimated at 100 MW/cm².

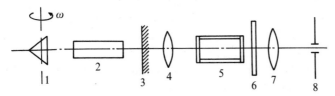

Figure 87

Experimental setup:

1) total reflection prism,   2) ruby rod,   3) multilayer dielectric mirror,   4) lens,   5) cell with scattering liquid,   6) filter,   7) condenser lens,   8) entrance slit.

---

* The concept of a threshold in this context is explained below, in §23.4.

Using this setup, Terhune [487] recorded both Stokes and anti-Stokes Raman scattering. The anti-Stokes radiation was observed to emerge from the cell at a certain angle to the axis, along the surface of a cone coaxial with the direction of incidence of the exciting radiation. Each harmonic is characterized by its own conical angle, and a color-sensitive film placed at a certain distance from the cell therefore shows concentric rings of different colors. The intensity of anti-Stokes lines in stimulated Raman spectra was found to be comparable to the intensity of the Stokes lines. The anti-Stokes lines are missing in the spectra taken with the cell mounted inside the resonator because the anti-Stokes radiation is emitted at a certain angle to the resonator axis, whereas the resonator is tuned to radiation directed along its axis.

Strong anti-Stokes radiation of liquid hydrogen, oxygen, and nitrogen was observed in [488]. None of these substances display any anti-Stokes radiation in ordinary Raman scattering, apparently because of the excessively low temperatures involved.

Further development of the experimental techniques led to observations of SRS in gases [489]. Somewhat later, six harmonics were observed in the anti-Stokes part of the spectrum of hydrogen compressed to 100 atm [490]. Stimulated radiation with wavelengths around 2500 Å was thus obtained.

Stimulated Raman scattering of diamond, calcite, and sulfur single crystals was observed in [491]. A type IIA diamond crystal was used, shaped into a disk about 9 mm in diameter and 2.95 mm thick, cut at right angles to the [111] axis. The spectrum showed Stokes frequencies at 1325 and 2661 cm^{-1} and an anti-Stokes frequency at 1335 cm^{-1}. The spectrum of calcite showed lines at 1075 cm^{-1} and 2171 cm^{-1}, and the spectrum of sulfur showed lines at 216, 472, and 946 cm^{-1}.

SRS spectra of some powders were obtained in [492]. The discovery of SRS in disperse media is highly significant for disclosing the exact mechanism of the phenomenon.

Given a sufficiently high exciting power, we can thus apparently induce SRS in any transparent material in any state of aggregation.

The report of Akhmanov et al. [493] is of considerable interest as it proposes a new excitation source. The second harmonic of a neodymium-activated glass laser ($\lambda \sim 0.53\,\mu$) was used as the exciting line. The SRS thresholds of a number of materials were compared for excitation with ruby and glass lasers. The second-harmonic excitation lowers the threshold, and, in the authors' opinion, this effect cannot be entirely attributed to the increase in the Raman scattering intensity corresponding to the factor v^4.

2. Semiclassical theory of stimulated Raman scattering

The principal features of SRS can be interpreted on the basis of semiclassical analysis. A general method was proposed by Townes [494, 495].

Consider a molecule of polarizability α in an electric field E. The field E imparts an electric moment $\mu = \alpha E$, and a potential energy $U = -\frac{1}{2}\alpha E^2$ to the molecule.

Let x be the vibration coordinate which describes some vibrational process in the molecule. Assuming that a driving force

$$F = -\frac{\partial U}{\partial x} = \frac{1}{2}\frac{\partial \alpha}{\partial x}E^2 \tag{23.1}$$

acts on the molecule, we obtain for the internal molecular vibrations

$$m\ddot{x} + R_0\dot{x} + fx = F_0 \cos \omega t \tag{23.2}$$

(a harmonic driving force is assumed). The solution of this equation for a frequency ω close to the resonance frequency $\omega_r = \sqrt{f/m}$ is

$$x = \frac{F_0}{R_0\omega} \sin \omega t \tag{23.3}$$

(R_0 is the phenomenological damping constant, f is the quasielastic constant of the molecule corresponding to a normal mode of frequency ω_r).

Suppose that the electric field E is a superposition of a number of plane waves with frequencies differing by some constant ω or (in a more general case) by a multiple of ω. In the simplest case of two such waves,

$$E = E_0 e^{i(\omega_0 t - k_0 r)} + E' e^{i(\omega' t - k' r + \phi)}, \tag{23.4}$$

where $\omega_0 - \omega' = \omega$. Then

$$E^2 = E_0^2 + E'^2 + 2E_0 E' \cos\left[(\omega_0 - \omega')t - (k_0 - k')r - \phi'\right]. \tag{23.5}$$

The constant terms can be dropped, and we find

$$F_0 = \frac{d\alpha}{dx}E_0 E'. \tag{23.6}$$

Therefore,

$$x = \frac{E_0 E'\, d\alpha/dx}{R_0(\omega_0 - \omega')} \sin\left[(\omega_0 - \omega')t - (k_0 - k')r - \phi'\right]. \tag{23.7}$$

The molecular vibrations lead to an oscillation of the dipole moment

$$\mu = x\frac{d\alpha}{dx}E = \frac{E_0 E'\,(d\alpha/dx)^2}{R_0(\omega_0 - \omega')} \sin\left[(\omega_0 - \omega')t - (k_0 - k')r - \phi'\right]E. \tag{23.8}$$

The rate of energy exchange between the dipole moment and the field component of frequency ω' is expressed by the equality

$$p' = -\left\langle \frac{d\mu}{dt} E' \right\rangle , \qquad (23.9)$$

where the time average is taken. We thus obtain for the power pumped into the component E' by the initial field E_0

$$p' = \frac{1}{2R_0} \left(\frac{d\alpha}{dx}\right)^2 \frac{\omega'}{\omega_0 - \omega'} (E_0 E')^2 . \qquad (23.10)$$

For the Stokes component, $\omega' = \omega_0 - \omega_r$, $p' > 0$, and the radiation corresponding to the wave E' is amplified. For anti-Stokes radiation $\omega' = \omega_0 + \omega_r$, and this wave loses energy ($p' < 0$).

To explain the generation of anti-Stokes lines, consider the case when the field E has three components of different frequencies:

$$E = E_0 \exp \{i(\omega_0 t - k_0 r)\} + E_{-1} \exp \{i[(\omega_0 - \omega_r) t - k_{-1} r + \phi_{-1}]\} +$$

$$+ E_1 \exp \{i[(\omega_0 + \omega_r) t - k_1 r + \phi_1]\} . \qquad (23.11)$$

The same method as before can be applied to determine the molecular vibrations and the oscillating dipole moment. The result gives for the power amplification of the Stokes component

$$p_{-1} = \frac{1}{2R_0} \left(\frac{d\alpha}{dx}\right)^2 \frac{\omega_0 - \omega_r}{\omega_r} \times$$

$$\times \{(E_0 E_{-1})^2 + (E_0 E_1)(E_0 E_{-1}) \cos [(2k_0 - k_1 - k_{-1}) r + \phi_1 + \phi_{-1}]\} . \qquad (23.12)$$

The power amplification of the anti-Stokes component is

$$p_1 = \frac{1}{2R_0} \left(\frac{d\alpha}{dx}\right)^2 \frac{\omega_0 + \omega_r}{\omega_r} \times$$

$$\times \{-(E_0 E_1)^2 - (E_0 E_1)(E_0 E_{-1}) \cos [(2k_0 - k_1 - k_{-1}) r + \phi_1 + \phi_{-1}]\} . \qquad (23.13)$$

Thus, if $|E_{-1}| > |E_1|$, the component E_1 is amplified whenever

$$2k_0 = k_1 + k_{-1}, \qquad \cos (\phi_1 + \phi_2) < 0 . \qquad (23.14)$$

Here k_0, k_{-1}, and k_1 are, respectively, the wave vectors of the initial, the Stokes, and the anti-Stokes waves. If $\phi_1 + \phi_{-1} = \pi$, the amplification of the anti-Stokes line reaches its maximum. The amplification of the Stokes line somewhat diminishes in the corresponding direction because of the negative sign of the cosine.

Qualitatively, the generation of Stokes and anti-Stokes lines in Raman scattering can be interpreted proceeding from the concepts of modulation of the incident light wave by the coherent vibrations of the molecules. Indeed, numerical estimates show that a ruby laser pulse of about $100\ MW/cm^2$ power density may stretch and contract the intermolecular bonds by as much as 10^{-4} of the equilibrium value. This gives rise to elastic waves in the scattering volume, with frequencies equal to the molecular vibration frequency ω_r. In any constant-phase plane of such a wave, all the molecules vibrate synchronously and in phase, and this evidently results in periodic expansion and compression of the macroscopic specimen. The relative changes in the dielectric constant reach about 10^{-4}. These spatial changes of the dielectric constant act as a phase grid which scatters light waves. Since the dielectric constant is time-dependent, the light wave is modulated and satellites of frequencies $\omega_0 \pm m\omega_r$ (where $m = 1, 2, 3, \ldots$) are formed. It is readily seen that this modulation mechanism is in principle the same as the mechanism of light scattering by hypersonic waves of thermal origin. We thus return to the original ideas of Mandelshtam (see §1), on which his interpretation of Raman scattering was based. Note that hypersonic waves are generated at a much slower rate than the molecular vibrations. The rise time of elastic waves is approximately 10^{-9} sec.

Emission of Stokes lines does not impose any special constraints on the wave vectors, and Stokes radiation is therefore emitted in all directions. On the other hand, Eq. (23.14) shows that anti-Stokes radiation is emitted only in directions which span a cone of angle θ_1 relative to the initial beam direction. For small θ_1, direct calculations yield

$$\theta_1^2 = -\frac{1}{n}\frac{\omega_0 - \omega_r}{\omega_0 + \omega_r}\left[\Delta n_1 - \Delta n_{-1} + \frac{\omega_r}{\omega_0}(\Delta n_1 + \Delta n_{-1})\right]. \qquad (23.15)$$

Here n is the refractive index of the medium at the frequency ω_0, Δn_1 and Δn_{-1} are the differences between the refractive indices at the frequencies $\omega_0 \pm \omega_r$ and ω_0. For normal dispersion, all these quantities are positive. Since $\omega_r/\omega_0 \ll 1$, we find

$$\theta_1^2 \approx -\frac{1}{n}\frac{\omega_0 - \omega_r}{\omega_0 + \omega_r}(\Delta n_1 - \Delta n_{-1}). \qquad (23.16)$$

The angle θ_1 is thus determined by the steepness of the dispersion curve of the scattering material. Numerical estimates show that these angles are of the order of a few degrees.

It is significant that anti-Stokes radiation may be generated without raising the specimen to a higher threshold, provided that Stokes radiation is already emitted in the particular direction. Moreover, Stokes radiation of frequency $\omega_0 - \omega_r$ may give rise to a field E_{-2} of frequency $\omega_0 - 2\omega_r$. The radiation power at this frequency is made up of two components. One of these components is proportional to $E_{-1}^2 E_{-2}^2$; this conclusion emerges from calculations analogous to the above. The field of this frequency may also be produced as a result of the modulation of the field E_{-1} by dielectric constant fluctuations caused by the fields E_0 and E_{-1}. The generated power is then proportional to $E_0 |E_{-1}|^2 E_{-2}$. Since $|E_{-2}| < |E_0|$, this part of the radiation at the frequency $\omega_0 - 2\omega_r$ may reach the highest value as soon as the wave vector directions satisfy the additional conditions (see [494, 495]). Higher Stokes harmonics of frequencies $\omega_0 - m\omega_r$ are similarly obtained.

Note that the first mechanism producing the harmonic $\omega_0 - 2\omega_r$ becomes operative only after a certain threshold is reached, whereas the second mechanism has no threshold. The first mechanism is therefore probably effective when liquids are studied in a resonator, since the condition for the wave vectors is not observed. The second mechanism may prevail when the liquid is studied outside the resonator, as the condition for the wave vectors is satisfied and no additional threshold is imposed.

The anti-Stokes harmonic of frequency $\omega_0 + 2\omega_r$ is generated without any threshold restrictions when the frequency $\omega_0 + \omega_r$ is modulated by vibrations of frequency ω_r. Radiation at this frequency is emitted in a direction defined by the equality

$$k_0 - k_{-1} = k_2 - k_1 . \tag{23.17}$$

The angle between k_0 and k_2 is approximately $2\theta_1$. Other anti-Stokes harmonics of frequencies $\omega_0 + m\omega_r$ are generated in a similar way in cones coaxial with the direction of the primary beam.

The principal features of SRS are thus fully explained by the semiclassical theory.

3. Quantum theory of stimulated Raman scattering

The elementary theory of SRS follows directly from the quantum-mechanical expression (5.53) for the transition probability corresponding to the scattering of a frequency-charged photon. According to this expression, the probability of Raman scattering consists of two terms: a term proportional to the number n of exciting photons of frequency ω, and a term proportional to the product nn', where n' is the number of scattered photons of frequency ω' propagating in the direction of the primary beam:

$$W_R = k_1 nn' + k_2 n .$$

Consider a simplified model of SRS (see [483, 496]). Let a light pulse propagate along the axis of a cylindrical cell of finite length. The material inside the cell is characterized by the absorption coefficients α and α' for the exciting and the scattered radiation, respectively. In this case, the change in the number of exciting and scattered photons n and n' observed when the pulse traverses a layer of thickness dx is described by the equations

$$\frac{dn}{dx} = -\alpha n - k_2 n - k_1 nn',$$ (23.18a)

$$\frac{dn'}{dx} = -\alpha' n' + k_2 n + k_1 nn'.$$ (23.18b)

The first term in Eqs. (23.18a) and (23.18b) describes radiation losses in the medium (absorption, scattering, etc.), the second term corresponds to ordinary Raman scattering, and the third term is responsible for the stimulated Raman scattering.

We will solve this set of equations assuming small absorption, which is the case most frequently encountered in practice. We will further assume that $\alpha = \alpha'$ and the number of photons n_0' of frequency ω' at the entrance to the cell ($x = 0$) is zero. These conditions are generally satisfied in practice. From (23.18a) and (23.18b) we then have

$$n + n' = n_0 e^{-\alpha x},$$ (23.19)

where n_0 is the number of photons of frequency ω entering the cell. Substituting $n' = v(x)e^{-\alpha x}$ and inserting (23.19) in (23.18b), we obtain

$$\frac{dv}{dx} = v[q \cdot (n_0 - v) - k_2] + k_2 n_0,$$ (23.20)

where $q = k_1 e^{-\alpha x}$. For relatively small αx (i.e., the absorption along the length l of the cell is small), $q \approx k_1$ and $v(x) = n'$. Integrating (23.20), we obtain

$$\ln\left[\frac{(k_2/k_1) + n'}{n_0 - n'}\right] = (k_1 n_0 + k_2)x + C.$$ (23.21)

Seeing that at the boundary $n'(0) = 0$ and writing $k_2/k_1 = b$, we find

$$\ln\left(1 + \frac{n'}{b}\right) - \ln\left(1 - \frac{n'}{n_0}\right) = k_1 x(n_0 + b),$$ (23.22)

whence

$$n' = \frac{b[e^{k_1 x(n_0 + b)} - 1]}{1 + (b/n_0)\, e^{k_1 x(n_0 + b)}}.$$ (23.23)

At the exit from the cell, i.e., at $x = l$, we have, writing $k_1 l = a$,

$$n' = \frac{b[e^{a(n_0 + b)} - 1]}{n + (b/n_0)\, e^{a(n_0 + b)}}.$$ (23.24)

The constants a and b can be readily calculated if the probability of Raman scattering is expressed from (5.53b), which corresponds to the case of perfect correlation between the properties of SRS and those of the exciting radiation (see §5). To simplify the mathematics, we will assume that the exciting radiation is of constant intensity inside a narrow cone of solid angle Ω, dropping to zero outside that cone. Factoring out from the integrand in (5.53b) the slowly varying factor $|S_{k1}|^2$, dropping the polarization factor, and using the normalization condition (4.61), we find

$$W_R(\omega', \Omega')\,d\omega'\,d\Omega' =$$

$$= \frac{(2\pi)^2\,\omega\omega'n}{\hbar^2}\,|\,S_{k1}\,|^2 \left[\frac{n'_\infty\rho(a)\rho(\Omega')}{(q_k - q_1)^2} + \frac{F_k(\infty)\omega'^2}{(2\pi c)^3}\right]d\omega'\,d\Omega'. \qquad (23.25)$$

In actual experiments, one usually measures the integrated intensity, and the detector collects the entire radiation flux propagating within a cone of solid angle Ω'. Eq. (23.25) therefore should be integrated over all the frequencies ω' and over the angle Ω'. Using (4.60) and assuming that $F_k(\infty)$ is a dispersion function with a half-width $q_k - q_1$ (see (4.94)), we obtain after this integration.

$$W_R = \frac{(2\pi)^2\,\omega\omega'n}{\hbar^2(q_k - q_1)^2}\,|\,S_{k1}\,|^2 \left[n'_\infty + \frac{\pi(q_k - q_1)\Omega'\omega'^2}{(2\pi c)^3}\right]. \qquad (23.26)$$

Let N_i be the number of scattering particles in unit volume, c_i the volume concentration of the scattering substance, n and n'_∞ the number of exciting and scattered photons in unit volume in vacuum, $\bar{n}$ and $\bar{n}'$ the refractive indices of the medium for the exciting and the scattered light, respectively. For the radiation density increment inside a layer of thickness $dx' = dx/\bar{n}$ we then have

$$dn'_\infty = \frac{\omega\omega'c_iN_0\,|\,S_{k1}\,|^2\,n}{\hbar^2\delta^2c^2}\left[n'_\infty + \frac{\omega'^2\,\delta c\Omega'}{4\pi(c/\bar{n}')^3}\right]dx'. \qquad (23.27)$$

Here N_0 is the total number of molecules in unit volume, Ω' is the solid angle inside the scattering medium, δ is the line width in cm^{-1} ($q_k - q_1 = 2\pi c\delta$). Comparing (23.27) with (23.18), we find

$$k_1 = \frac{\omega\omega'c_iN_0\,|\,S_{k1}\,|^2}{\hbar^2\delta^2c^2}, \qquad k_2 = \frac{\omega\omega'^3c_iN_0\,|\,S_{k1}\,|^2\,\Omega'\bar{n}'^3}{4\pi\hbar^2\delta c^4}. \qquad (23.28)$$

The exciting and the scattered radiation are generally characterized by the total power I_e or I', respectively. Here,

$$I_e = \hbar\omega nS'c/\bar{n}, \qquad I' = \hbar\omega'n'_\infty S'_1c/\bar{n}', \qquad (23.29)$$

where S' is the cross section of the channel propagating the radiation in the scattering medium ($S' = S/\bar{n}^2$, $S'_1 = S/\bar{n}'^2$, where S is the channel cross section in vacuum).

Using (23.29), we rewrite Eq. (23.27) in the form

$$dn'_\infty = \frac{\omega' c_i N_0 |S_{k1}|^2 I_e \bar{n}^2}{\hbar^3 \delta^2 c^3} \left[n'_\infty + \frac{\omega'^2 \delta \Omega \bar{n}'^3}{4\pi c^2 \bar{n}^2} \right] \frac{dx}{S(x)}, \qquad (23.27a)$$

where Ω is the solid angle confining the exciting radiation in vacuum. We introduce the absolute cross section σ of the ordinary Raman scattering, which is defined by the relation (see §22)

$$I' = \sigma c_i N_0 \Omega l I_e. \qquad (23.30)$$

Thus,

$$\sigma = \frac{\omega'^4 |S_{k1}|^2}{4\pi \hbar^2 \delta c^4}, \qquad (23.31)$$

i.e., this is the RS cross section per unit line width (see (2.16), (2.47), (6.8)). Inserting (23.31) in (23.27a), we find

$$dn'_\infty = \frac{4\pi \sigma c c_i N_0 \bar{n}^2 I_e}{\hbar \omega'^3 \delta} \left[n'_\infty + \frac{\omega'^2 \delta \Omega \bar{n}'^3}{4\pi c^2 \bar{n}^2} \right] \frac{dx}{S(x)}. \qquad (23.27b)$$

If the exciting radiation is directed into the scattering medium without focusing lenses and self-focusing effects are ignorable, $S(x)$ may be regarded as constant. Integrating (23.27b) and using (23.29), we then find, making use of the relation $n + n'_\infty = n_0$ $(I_0 = \hbar \omega n_0 Sc/\bar{n}^3)$,

$$I' = \frac{(\omega'/\omega)(\bar{n}/\bar{n}')^3 \, b \left[e^{a(I_0+b)} - 1 \right]}{1 + (b/I_0) e^{a(I_0+b)}}. \qquad (23.32)$$

Here

$$a = \frac{4\pi \sigma c c_i N_0 \bar{n}^2 l}{\hbar \omega'^3 \delta S}, \qquad b = \frac{\hbar \omega \omega'^2 \delta \Omega S (\bar{n}'/\bar{n})^3}{4\pi c \bar{n}^2}. \qquad (23.33)$$

Eq. (23.27b) is also readily integrated in the case of exciting radiation focused on the scattering cell. In this case, however, the main contribution from SRS is only confined within a small region near the focus. If this region is in the form of a cylinder of effective length Δl and effective cross section ΔS, we may use Eq. (23.32).

In many cases, SRS is investigated near the detection "threshold" of the Raman line; this detection "threshold" is fixed by the experimental conditions and is attained for a certain exciting intensity $I_e = \pi$. For the threshold value $I' = I'(\pi)$ we have from (23.32) (assuming for simplicity $\bar{n}' = \bar{n}$)

$$\ln \left[1 + \frac{I'(\pi)\omega}{\omega' b} \right] - \ln \left[1 - \frac{I'(\pi)\omega}{\omega' \pi} \right] = a(\pi + b). \qquad (23.34)$$

Near the threshold and slightly above the threshold, we may take $I'(\pi)/\pi \ll 1$, $I'/I_e \ll 1$, and thus ignore the second term in the left-hand side of Eq. (23.34). This gives

$$\ln\left[1 + \frac{I'\omega}{\omega'b}\right] - \ln\left[1 + \frac{I'(\pi)\omega}{\omega'b}\right] = a(I_e - \pi). \qquad (23.35)$$

This equation is convenient for comparison with experimental findings, since it contains the difference $I_e - \pi$, which is directly measured in all experiments.

From expression (23.33) for the constant b we conclude that the left-hand side of (23.34) is independent of the parameters l and c_i (we again assume that the second term on the left in (23.34) is negligible). Therefore, comparing two scattering media which differ in these parameters, we find from (23.34)

$$a_1(\pi_1 + b) = a(\pi + b). \qquad (23.36)$$

Hence

$$\frac{\pi}{\pi_1} = \frac{a_1}{a}\left[1 + \frac{b}{\pi_1}\left(1 - \frac{a}{a_1}\right)\right]. \qquad (23.37)$$

Let the threshold π_1 of the first material be used as standard. Then the ratio $r = b/\pi_1$ is constant under the given experimental conditions. Comparing two media with different values of the parameter z ($z = l$ or c_i), we find

$$\frac{\pi}{\pi_1} = \frac{1 + r(1 - z/z_1)}{(z/z_1)}. \qquad (23.38)$$

In particular, for $r \ll 1$, we have

$$\frac{\pi_1}{\pi} = \frac{z}{z_1}. \qquad (23.39)$$

In the previously cited studies [483, 496], SRS was excited by a Q-switched ruby laser. The laser emission was focused by a lens with $f = 250$ mm into the scattering cell. Particular attention was paid throughout the measurements to strict standardization of the experimental conditions. The setup therefore had been specifically designed without mirrors and other easily damaged components.

To determine the threshold, the laser beam was attenuated by a stack of glass plates mounted in front of the scattering cell. By changing the number of glass plates, the intensity of the incident radiation was varied (albeit discontinuously), and the "threshold" was defined as the minimum intensity at which a single flash was just enough to produce Raman scattering. This method had the advantage of great simplicity, and yet it ensured sufficiently accurate measurement results (with an error of about 10%).

SRS spectra were photographed using a diffraction-grating spectrograph with

13 Å/mm dispersion. Several series of experiments were carried out for each material.

The parameters of the ordinary Raman lines (the integrated intensity I_∞, the line width δ, the depolarization ρ) were measured on a photoelectric spectrometer with 5 Å/mm dispersion using the mercury 4358 Å line as the source of exciting radiation.

The intensity was measured by photographic photometry. The gray scale was calibrated with a stepped attenuator. The light source was provided by a laser flash, to avoid the undesirable Schwartzschild effect. The spectrograms were processed and measured by the usual methods, with all the possible precautions. The measure-able intensity range was extended with the aid of neutral filters, whose transmittance had been measured under identical conditions. Note that the transmittance of light filters for the flash radiation was found to be substantially higher than for ordinary radiation of the same wavelength. The intensity of the exciting light was measured with a stack of light plates, as in threshold measurements.

Using the same experimental setup, the authors observed SRS spectra of 12 compounds of various classes (benzene, bromobenzene, chlorobenzene, toluene, pyridine, orthoxylene, styrene, pentadiene-1,3, 2-methylbutadiene-1,3, carbon di-sulfide, carbon tetrachloride, nitrobenzene).

Special attention was focused on quantitative measurements of the excitation thresholds and line intensities in SRS. The first Stokes component was mainly studied; the data that follow refer in their entirety to this component.

To establish the relationship between the intensity of the exciting radiation and the SRS intensity, we measured the line intensities as a function of the exciting intensity above the threshold. The data for carbon disulfide, benzene, and toluene are shown in Figures 88 and 89. The straight lines in these figures plot the theoretical

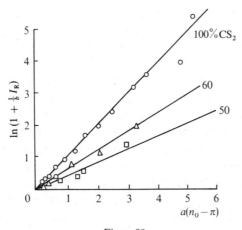

Figure 88

SRS intensity vs. the exciting intensity above the threshold for CS_2 and CS_2–benzene mixtures.

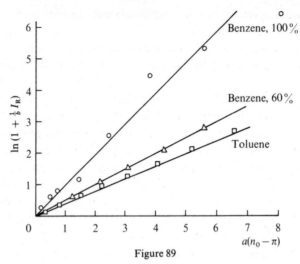

Figure 89

SRS intensity vs. the exciting intensity above the threshold for benzene, toluene, and benzene–CS_2 mixtures.

line intensities, according to Eq. (23.35). The constants a and b in this equation were determined as follows. The experimental points for carbon disulfide or benzene were applied to plot $\ln [1 + I'\omega/\omega'b]$ vs. $I_e - \pi$ (I' was measured in relative units, depending on film speed at the frequencies corresponding to the particular spectral line, and $I_e - \pi$ was measured on another relative scale). By varying the constant b, the plot could be reduced to a straight line. For the corresponding value of b, the constant a was found from the requirement that the straight line should have a slope angle of $45°$.

The same value of the constant b was retained for the intensity of the line in a mixture or in the spectrum of another compound with a close Raman line; the constant a was again found from the slope of the experimental line. The resulting values of the constant a are listed in Table 55. Note that the conditions of measurements were such that only the relative values of this parameter could be compared.

From Figures 88 and 89 we conclude that the approximate relation (23.35) provides an adequate description of the observed Raman scattering intensity as a function of the exciting light intensity above the threshold. For toluene, the experimental results are fairly consistent with the intensity ratio of the toluene and benzene lines in ordinary Raman scattering.

Eq. (23.34) was used to plot the Raman scattering intensity vs. the intensity of the exciting light. The curves (Figure 90) provide a qualitative picture of the phenomenon for various values of the exciting light intensity above the threshold.

Interesting findings regarding the SRS intensity as a function of the exciting light intensity were obtained by Bret and Mayer [497]. Proceeding from Placzek's general

Table 55

INTENSITY OF SRS LINES IN VARIOUS COMPOUNDS

Compound	Δv, cm^{-1}	c_i	a/a_0	I/I_{benz}
Carbon disulfide	656	1.0	1.0	—
		0.6	0.6	—
		0.5	0.41	—
Benzene	992	1.0	1.0	1.0
		0.6	0.5	—
Toluene	1004	1.0	0.40	0.42

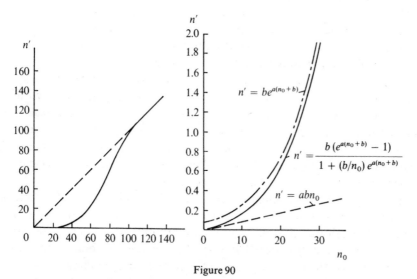

Figure 90

SRS intensity vs. the intensity of exciting radiation from Eq. (23.24) for $a = 0.1$, $b = 0.1$. The figure on the right shows the initial section of the curve on an enlarged scale.

expression for the transition probabilities in Raman scattering, they derived a relation of the SRS intensity to the exciting light intensity and the n_0/n_0' ratio, where n_0' is the number of photons of frequency ω' at the cell entrance. Dropping the term corresponding to ordinary Raman scattering in Placzek's expression, we may write

$$\frac{dn'}{dx} = knn',$$
(23.40)

whence, using the boundary conditions, we find

$$n_i' = n_0' e^{knol}.$$ (23.41)

Assuming n_0 to be independent of l, we obtain from (23.41) for the gain G

$$G = \frac{\int n_0'(t) e^{kno(t)l} dt}{\int n_i'(t) dt}.$$ (23.42)

Eq. (23.42) contains integrals over time. This is a consequence of the fact that the widths of the SRS exciting pulses differ by a factor of 2–3. The integration is carried out graphically.

Two different types of experiments were carried out in [497]. In experiments of the first type, G was measured as a function of n_0 at the cell entrance; n_0' was kept constant. RG Schott filters mounted before the cell adjusted the exciting light intensity. The plot of ln G vs. a quantity proportional to n_0 is distinctly linear, in accordance with the previous theoretical reasoning.

In experiments of the second type, ln G was measured as a function of the ratio $g = n_0'/n_0$ at the cell entrance for constant n_0; neodymium glass mounted in front of the cell served to this end. The experimental results reveal a decrease in ln O with increasing g. The authors unfortunately did not go into a theoretical interpretation of the effect. Incidental polarization measurements have shown that the gain is zero when the polarization vectors of the fields n_0 and n_0' at the cell entrance are orthogonal. This result confirms the coherence of SRS.

Wang [498] measured the intensity of the first Stokes line of benzene in a wide range of exciting power values. The measurements were carried out in a parallel beam; the cell length varied from 3.7 to 90 cm. Distinct "saturation" is observed in the top part of the curves (Figure 91). It would be of interest to compare these experimental data with the theoretical equation (23.32). The corresponding curves are also shown in Figure 91. The general trend of the theoretical curves follows the experimental data, although saturation is seen to appear at much higher exciting power values. This divergence is clearly attributed to the pumping of energy from the first Stokes line into the higher harmonics and back into the exciting line, a factor ignored in the theory developed in §23.3 (for a treatment of this effect, see §24). Experimental data of [498] give the following values of the constants (for $l = 1$ cm): $a \approx 0.1$ MW^{-1} · · cm, $b \approx 10^{-11}$ MW · cm^{-2}.

The constants a and b can be computed theoretically using Eq. (23.33) for $\lambda_e = 6942.6$ Å, $\lambda = 7456$ Å, $N_0 = 6.75 \cdot 10^{21}$, $\delta = 1.8$ cm^{-1}, $\bar{n} = \bar{n}' = 1.50$. The cross section σ for excitation with the unpolarized light of the mercury 4358 Å line is equal to $2 \cdot 10^{-28}$ (see §22). The measurements were carried out at right angles to

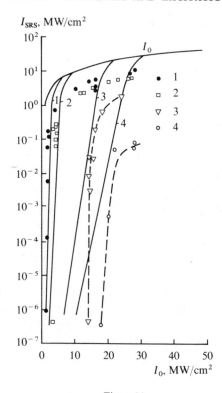

Figure 91

The intensity I_{SRS} of the first Stokes component of benzene SRS vs. the intensity of the exciting radiation for various cell lengths. The solid curves were obtained from Eq. (23.32) for $a \approx 0.1$ MW$^{-1} \cdot$cm,

$$b \approx 10^{-11} \text{ MW} \cdot \text{cm}^{-2}.$$

1) $l = 90$ cm,   2) $l = 45$ cm,   3) $l = 15$ cm,   4) $l = 10$ cm. The dots correspond to Wang's experimental data [498].

the line of incidence. SRS is observed using polarized laser radiation; the observations are made in the direction of incident light. Comparison of (3.19) and (2.59) shows that, in the second case, the absolute cross section is approximately double its value in the first case. Further, seeing that σ is a function of frequency (see Figure 15 and Eq. (23.31)) we used for the cross section $\sigma = 0.3 \cdot 10^{-28}$. From the data of [498], we have $\Omega \approx 10^{-6}$ sterad, $S \approx 1$ cm^2.

Inserting these numerical values in (23.33), we find (for $l = 1$ cm) $a = 0.05$ MW$^{-1} \cdot$ $\cdot$ cm, $b = 0.4 \cdot 10^{-11}$ MW $\cdot$ cm^{-2}. These values of the constants adequately fit the previous results, obtained directly from the experimental curves.

The dependence of SRS intensity on the concentration of scattering molecules was investigated in [496, 499]. The results of measurements (Figures 88 and 89) show that, for constant concentration, the SRS intensities are exponential functions of the exciting light intensity above the threshold value. The dependence of the line intensities on concentration in mixtures somewhat departs from the theoretical curves. This may be attributed to a certain reduction of scattering intensity in mixtures owing to molecular interactions. Similar intensity changes were often observed in ordinary Raman scattering.

An entirely different dependence of line intensity on concentration was observed in [500], where the line intensities of benzene and nitrobenzene mixtures were measured. The authors came to the conclusion that the molecular interaction makes a highly significant contribution to SRS in mixtures. According to their data, the benzene SRS lines were observed in benzene–heptane mixtures up to concentrations of 75% of heptane. The intensity of the first Stokes line of benzene remained constant with changing concentration (to first approximation) up to heptane contents of 50% (Figure 92). Further increase of the heptane concentration led to a marked drop in the intensity of the benzene line. It is significant that the SRS lines of heptane were not observed altogether.

An entirely different picture was observed for the benzene–nitrobenzene mixture. Here, the intensity of the benzene (or nitrobenzene) SRS line slightly decreased with the decrease in concentration. At concentrations around 50%, the intensity dropped sharply by several orders of magnitude. At these concentrations, the only lines observed were the benzene line ν_1, the nitrobenzene line ν_2, and combination lines of the form $\nu = \nu_0 \pm (k_1\nu_1 + k_2\nu_2)$, where $k = \pm 1, \pm 2, \ldots$ For benzene (nitro-

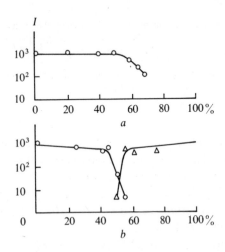

Figure 92

The relative intensity of SRS lines vs. concentration [500]:

a benzene–heptane mixture, b benzene–nitrobenzene mixture. The horizontal axis gives the concentration of nitrobenzene and heptane. O benzene, △ nitrobenzene.

benzene) concentrations of 40%, the benzene (nitrobenzene) SRS lines disappeared.

The dependence of SRS intensity on concentration obtained in [500] is substantially different from the theoretical function. The authors attribute this divergence between theory and experiment to the effect of molecular interactions. In justification of this assumption, they cite the results of [494] which indicate the possibility of a certain increase in the SRS line intensities of benzene in mixtures containing polarized molecules. In our opinion, however, this explanation is not very convincing. More comprehensive and rigorous analysis of the experimental conditions is apparently needed in this case.

4. Measurements of the threshold of stimulated Raman scattering

The existence of a certain excitation threshold for SRS is a natural result emerging from the general theory of lasers, where the lasing threshold constitutes one of the fundamental characteristics of the process. The first experiments discussed in the previous subsection seemed to confirm the existence of a SRS threshold. SRS lines appear on photographs only when a certain "threshold" exciting power is exceeded. The "threshold" is fixed with fairly high accuracy, about 10% of the measured value. Nevertheless, the concept of a SRS "threshold" finally proved to be physically unsound.

The unusual character of the SRS threshold already emerges from the basic fact that different spectrum recording techniques give different values of the threshold. For example, by changing over from one grade of photographic plates to another, we obtained markedly different thresholds, although the excitation conditions naturally remain the same. Moreover, it was found that a change in the number of laser flashes used to excite SRS may substantially lower the observed SRS threshold. The concept of the SRS threshold is thus only applicable to rigidly fixed experimental conditions, which include some specified technique of spectrum recording. It is generally assumed that the threshold is reached after exposure to a single exciting laser flash, and it is in this sense that we will use this concept (unless otherwise specified). The excitation threshold characterizes in this case a certain standard intensity of the SRS line which under the particular experimental conditions is sufficient to produce a measurable blackening of the photographic emulsion.

The high certainty of the threshold value obtained from experimental measurements is associated with the nonlinear trend of the function specifying the SRS intensity vs. the intensity of the exciting light. This nonlinear (approximately exponential) trend is generally retained "below the threshold". As an example, Figure 93 plots the SRS intensity vs. the exciting intensity just below the "threshold" (for a single laser flash), according to [501]; the number of flashes reached a few tens.

Despite the merely apparent character of the SRS threshold, detailed studies of this parameter are of considerable interest, since it is easily measured with high

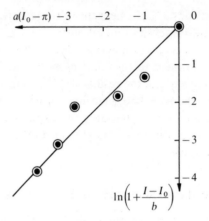

$$a(I_0 - \pi)$$

$$\ln\left(1 + \frac{I - I_0}{b}\right)$$

Figure 93

The intensity of SRS vs. the exciting intensity for nitrobenzene ($\Delta v = 1365 \text{ cm}^{-1}$) below the "threshold".

accuracy. The relation of the threshold to line characteristics, concentration, etc., can be treated within the framework of the elementary theory presented in the previous subsections.

Systematic studies of the SRS thresholds of a number of materials were carried out in [499, 502]. The results are summarized in Table 56. The threshold of benzene was assumed as 1.0. The table also gives the line parameters in ordinary Raman spectra. We see that the SRS threshold is mainly determined by the intensity of the lines in ordinary Raman scattering, whereas the depolarization is apparently of minor importance. To a crude approximation, the reciprocal threshold is determined by the line intensity per unit line width, which fits Eqs. (23.33) and (23.39) if the

Table 56

THE DEPENDENCE OF THE SRS THRESHOLD ON THE PARAMETERS OF RAMAN LINES

Compound	Δv, cm^{-1}	δ, cm^{-1}	ρ	σ	$\dfrac{\sigma}{\delta}$	$\dfrac{1}{\pi_{exp}}$	$\dfrac{1}{\pi_{calc}}$
Benzene	992	1.8	0.06	1	1	1	1.0
Toluene	1004	1.6	0.07	0.38	0.42	0.40	0.42
Pentadiene-1,3	1655	15	0.31	1.6	0.2	0.5	0.25
2-Methylbutadiene-1,3	1638	7	0.21	1.3	0.3	0.5	0.40
Carbon disulfide	656	1	0.25	1.6	3	1.4	3.0
Styrene	998	2	—	0.7	0.6	0.5	0.67
	1602	3	—	0.9	0.6	—	0.61
	1634	3	—	1.6	0.9	0.9	1.1

dependence of the constant b on the properties of the scattering material and the particular line can be ignored. A more rigorous relation which allows for this dependence of the constant b is readily derived from (23.34). For $b \ll \pi$, we have

$$\frac{\pi_1}{\pi} = \frac{a/a_1}{1 + (1/a_1\pi_1) \ln (\omega_1' b_1/\omega' b)}. \tag{23.43}$$

Here a, b, π, ω' correspond to the line being studied, $a_1, b_1, \pi_1, \omega_1'$ correspond to a comparison line (in the present case, the benzene 992 cm^{-1} line). The thresholds calculated from (23.43) for $a_1\pi_1 = 12$ are listed in the last column of Table 56. For this value of the product $a_1\pi_1$, we have (in benzene) $I_1'(\pi)\omega/\omega_1' b_1 = 2 \cdot 10^5$. In these experiments, the threshold power is $\pi_1 \approx 0.5 \text{ MW}$, so that $a_1 \approx 24 \text{ MW}^{-1} \cdot \text{cm}$. Since a focused beam of exciting radiation was used with $\Omega \approx 10^{-2}$ sterad, we find, taking $\Delta S = 10^{-5} \text{ cm}^2$ and using (23.33), that $b = 10^{-12} \text{ MW} \cdot \text{cm}^{-2}$ and $\Delta l = = 5 \cdot 10^{-3} \text{ cm}$. We thus have $I_1'(\pi) = 2 \cdot 10^{-7} \text{ MW}$, which approximately coincides with the threshold value $I'(\pi)$ from [498] (see Figure 91). These numerical estimates will prove useful at a later stage.

Measurements of the excitation threshold as a function of concentration were carried out in [496, 499]. CS_2–benzene mixtures with concentrations of 80, 60, 50, and 40% were studied, and also pure CS_2 and pure benzene. The excitation thresholds of the 656 cm^{-1} line are plotted in Figure 94 (left curve). This line can be excited with CS_2 concentration in the mixture ranging from 100 to 50% (by volume). At CS_2 concentrations of 40%, the excitation of the benzene 992 cm^{-1} line began to be observed (Figure 94, right curve). The solid lines in Figure 94 are the theoretical

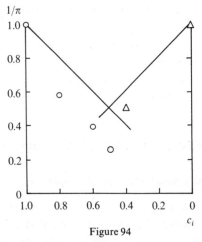

Figure 94

SRS excitation threshold vs. the concentration of scattering molecules for benzene–carbon disulfide mixtures. Left curve, the CS_2 656 cm^{-1} line; right curve, the benzene 992 cm^{-1} line; c_i is the volume concentration of CS_2 in the mixture.

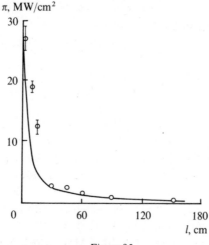

Figure 95

SRS threshold of benzene vs. cell length l. The curve was calculated from the equality $\pi = \pi_0 l_0 / l$ (π_0 is the threshold for cell length $l_0 = 150$ cm). Dots represent experimental data [498].

curves corresponding to (23.39). The slight divergence between the experimental and the theoretical results for the threshold vs. concentration can be attributed to changes in the conditions of self-focusing, which is a highly significant factor in this case (see §25.4), as well as to molecular interactions.

Zubov and Zubova studied the dependence of the benzene excitation threshold on cell length [503]. No focusing lenses were used, and the laser beam therefore remained parallel inside the cell. The dependence of threshold on cell length was observed to follow Eq. (23.39).

Wang [498] studied the dependence of threshold on cell length l in a wider range of l values. Wang's data for benzene are marked by dots in Figure 95. The solid line is the theoretical curve corresponding to Eq. (23.39). We see that the experimental and calculated data show a good fit.

24. INTENSITY DISTRIBUTION AND LINE WIDTHS IN SRS SPECTRA

1. Some features of intensity distribution in SRS spectra

SRS spectra generally show only some of the frequencies of the entire Raman spectrum of the substance. If the SRS spectrum is excited by a single laser flash, one of the frequencies generally appears, together with its Stokes and anti-Stokes harmonics. Originally, this was regarded as an inevitability in SRS spectra, since the excitation of one of the frequencies leads to a significant attenuation of the incident radiation power, which is pumped into Raman scattering power, the remaining power being insufficient for the excitation of other frequencies. Calculations show that about 80 % of the exciting radiation power are indeed pumped into SRS. Nevertheless, styrene simultaneously emits two lines with the frequencies $v_1 = 999 \text{ cm}^{-1}$ and $v_2 = 1626 \text{ cm}^{-1}$ [499], and in [504] combination frequencies of the form $N_1 v_1 \pm N_2 v_2$ were observed in the styrene spectrum, in addition to these fundamentals and their harmonics. Both components and combination frequencies are also observed in mixtures at high power levels (see §23.3).

The most significant feature of SRS spectra is the anomalously high intensity of the anti-Stokes lines and of the Stokes and anti-Stokes harmonics. The intensity ratio for these harmonics clearly depends on the experimental conditions. According to [505], in the benzene SRS spectrum the first Stokes line contains 85 % of the scattered radiation, the second Stokes line 9.8 %, and the third 0.1 %; the first anti-Stokes line contains 0.8 % of the scattered radiation, the second line 0.7 %, and the third 0.002 %.

Sharp lines in SRS spectra are often accompanied by continuous spectral regions of varying intensity, which may be regarded as fairly wide bands. In certain cases, the lines appear to split into several components (see §24.5).

2. Reversal of Raman scattering

The general theory (see Chapter I) shows that the pumping of energy from one spectral region into another is a reversible process in Raman scattering. Indeed, the probability of a transition involving absorption of a quantum $\hbar\omega$ and emission of a quantum $\hbar\omega'$ is, according to (5.53),

$$W_R = K \left[nn' + \frac{n\omega'^2}{(2\pi c)^3} \right],$$ (24.1)

where n is the number of exciting photons, n' is the number of photons with the changed frequency ω'. The factor K is the same for $\omega \rightarrow \omega'$ and $\omega' \rightarrow \omega$ processes, and the probability of the reverse process, i.e., absorption of a quantum $\hbar\omega'$ and emission of a quantum $\hbar\omega$, is expressed by the same formula in which ω will have to be replaced by ω' and n by n', and vice versa.

If continuous-spectrum radiation is directed at the system, a certain redistribution of energy will occur, but on the whole the spectrum will remain continuous. If a certain frequency (ω_0, say) is missing from the continuous spectrum, the process will occur in one direction only: energy will be pumped from frequencies $\omega = \omega_0 \pm \omega_r$ into the frequency ω_0. An "absorption" band will develop at ω'.

An experiment of this kind was first carried out by Landsberg and Barashanskaya [506]. The light from a continuous-spectrum source (a 1000 watt incandescent lamp) was passed through a cell containing a solution of praseodymium and neodymium salts, which give a sharp absorption band. The emergent light was then aimed at a quartz crystal. The radiation scattered by the quartz showed a spurious absorption band, as well as the true one. Its frequency shift relative to the "main" absorption band was equal to the quartz characteristic frequency ($\omega_r = 465$ cm^{-1}). Later, Kastler [507] applied this effect to explain some features of astrophysical spectra. To the best of our knowledge, nobody so far has reproduced the Landsberg and Barashanskaya experiment, although Stoicheff tried to make some progress in this direction [508].

The term nn' in (24.1) is not absolutely essential for interpreting the origin of the reverse Raman scattering. This term, however, leads to another important effect which is only characteristic of stimulated Raman scattering. This effect was studied by Jones and Stoicheff [508]. The radiation of an ordinary Q-switched laser was passed through two cells placed one after the other; the beam was focused into the second cell. When both cells contained the same liquid (benzene), self-reversal of the first benzene anti-Stokes line was observed. Even more remarkable results were obtained in experiments with different liquids in the two cells. Note that under certain excitation conditions, the anti-Stokes lines may be quite wide (up to 100 cm^{-1}) [509]. The second cell thus may receive radiation comprising a strong monochromatic line ω_0 and a quasicontinuous background $\omega' = \omega_0 + \omega_r \pm \Delta\omega$. In this case, the background radiation emerging from the second cell shows a sharp ($\delta \approx 2$ cm^{-1}) absorption band displaced relative to the "exciting" line ω_0 by the precise amount equal to the characteristic vibration frequency of the liquid filling the second cell. The first cell was filled with toluene, and the second with benzene or nitromethane. A single flash sufficed for observations of the benzene "absorption" band, whereas no fewer than ten flashes were required to develop the nitromethane "absorption" band. This is not surprising, since the nitromethane line is shifted almost by 85 cm^{-1} relative to the toluene line; the corresponding shift in the toluene–benzene system is 11 cm^{-1}.

The observed effect can be interpreted as follows. The $\omega_0 \rightarrow \omega'$ and $\omega' \rightarrow \omega_0$ transitions ($\omega' = \omega_0 + \omega_r$) occur simultaneously, and for sufficiently strong "exciting" radiation ω_0 their probabilities are comparable. However, the intensity of a transition is proportional to a first approximation to the number of particles occupying the initial state. The initial state of the $\omega' \rightarrow \omega_0$ transition is the ground state, whereas the initial state of the $\omega_0 \rightarrow \omega'$ transition is the first excited level. Under normal conditions, virtually all the molecules are in the ground state, so that the $\omega' \rightarrow \omega_0$ transition is much stronger than the $\omega_0 \rightarrow \omega'$ transition. A paradoxical effect is thus observed, whereby energy is pumped from the relatively weak radiation component ω' into the more powerful radiation of frequency ω_0. It is readily seen that this effect is possible when the product nn' in (24.1) is sufficiently high while n is only moderately large. When the number of "exciting" photons n is high, a considerable contribution will be associated with the induced transition $\omega_0 \rightarrow \omega_0 - \omega_r$ raising molecules to the excited levels and thereby enhancing the intensity of the $\omega_0 \rightarrow \omega'$ transition. This was indeed observed in experiments. An increase in the laser output power eventually suppressed the absorption, and a SRS line of the liquid in the second cell appeared at the frequency corresponding to the absorption band. The above reasoning is also applicable to the interpretation of the "reversal" of the SRS Stokes lines [509].

3. Quantum theory of intensity distribution in SRS spectra [510]

The semiclassical theory of SRS presented in §23 gives some basic ideas concerning the generation of harmonics and anti-Stokes lines. This theory, however, does not provide any information regarding the quantitative distribution of intensity in SRS spectra. The more rigorous quantum theory is still unfortunately far from being complete. Moreover, the basic mechanism of the phenomenon has not been established yet. We will therefore consider two probable mechanisms of SRS, and develop a nonlinear-optics approach to the theory of SRS.

Successive excitation of harmonics

The primary event of Stokes scattering produces an excited molecule and a photon of degraded frequency $\hbar\omega_{-1}$. Stokes interaction of the photon $\hbar\omega_{-1}$ with an unexcited molecule gives a photon $\hbar\omega_{-2}$, where $\omega_{-2} = \omega - 2(\omega - \omega_{-1})$, i.e., the first harmonic is generated. These processes are repeated generating Stokes harmonics of progressively higher order. The interaction of an exciting photon $\hbar\omega$ with an excited molecule produces an anti-Stokes photon $\hbar\omega_1$, and the molecule drops back to the ground state. The interaction of an anti-Stokes photon $\hbar\omega_1$ with an excited molecule produces an anti-Stokes harmonic of frequency $\hbar\omega_2$, where $\omega_2 = \omega + 2(\omega - \omega_{-1})$, etc. The two competing processes are the scattering of anti-Stokes photons by unexcited molecules producing lower-frequency photons, and the scattering of Stokes photons by excited molecules producing higher-frequency photons.

   We will now draw up the system of differential equations describing the successive process of excitation of Stokes and anti-Stokes harmonics, with allowance for the two competing processes in the anti-Stokes region (in the Stokes region, these processes are negligible at moderate power levels). Let $n, n_{-1}, n_{-2}, n_{-3}, \ldots$ be the number of photons of the exciting light and of the Stokes harmonics with the frequencies ω, $\omega_{-1}, \omega_{-2}, \omega_{-3}, \ldots$, respectively; similarly, let $n_1, n_2 \ldots$ be the number of photons with anti-Stokes frequencies $\omega_1, \omega_2, \ldots$ Let N be the number of unexcited molecules in unit volume, N^* the number of molecules in an excited state corresponding to the vibrational frequency $\omega_i = \omega - \omega_{-1}$. We assume that N^* in general depends on the number of incident photons n, i.e., it is a nonequilibrium quantity.

   As in §23.3, we will consider the exciting light flux propagating along the axis of the tube with the scattering material. For the change in the number of photons in a layer of thickness dx perpendicular to the tube axis, we may write

$$\frac{dn_{-3}}{dx} = -\alpha n_{-3} + N p_{-3} n_{-2} + N \kappa_{-3} n_{-2} n_{-3}, \tag{24.2a}$$

$$\frac{dn_{-2}}{dx} = -\alpha n_{-2} + N p_{-2} n_{-1} + N \kappa_{-2} n_{-1} n_{-2} - N p_{-3} n_{-2} - N \kappa_{-3} n_{-2} n_{-3}, \tag{24.2b}$$

$$\frac{dn_{-1}}{dx} = -\alpha n_{-1} + N p_{-1} n + N \kappa_{-1} n n_{-1} - N p_{-2} n_{-1} - N \kappa_{-2} n_{-1} n_{-2}, \tag{24.2c}$$

$$\frac{dn}{dx} = -\alpha n + N p_{-1} n + N \kappa_{-1} n n_{-1} - N^* p_1 n -$$

$$- N^* \kappa_1 n n_1 + N p n_1 + N \kappa n n_1, \tag{24.2d}$$

$$\frac{dn_1}{dx} = -\alpha n_1 + N^* p_1 n + N^* \kappa_1 n n_1 - N^* p_2 n_1 - N^* \kappa_2 n_1 n_2 -$$

$$- N p n_1 - N \kappa n n_1 + N p_1 n_2 + N \kappa_1 n_1 n_2, \tag{24.2e}$$

$$\frac{dn_2}{dx} = -\alpha n_2 + N^* p_2 n_1 + N^* \kappa_2 n_1 n_2 - N p_1 n_2 - N \kappa_1 n_1 n_2. \tag{24.2f}$$

We will now consider higher-order harmonics. The coefficients κ_i, p_i are per molecule: $k_{1i} = N_i \kappa_i$; $k_{2i} = N_i p_i b_i = p_i / \kappa_i$, where N_i is the number of scattering molecules of a given species in unit volume, i is the harmonic index.

Taking $n_{-3} \ll n_{-2}$, $n_{-2} \ll n_{-1}$, $n_{-1} \ll n$, $n_2 \ll n_1$, $n' \ll n_{-1}$, $N^* \ll N$, we may consider each harmonic individually, ignoring all the higher harmonics. Therefore, for $n_{-1} = n'$ we may assume its value from (23.23). We will also ignore the first terms in (24.2a)–(24.2f): they describe small absorption. Under these simplifying assumptions, Eq. (24.2b) takes the form

$$\frac{dn_{-2}}{N(p_{-2} + \kappa_{-2} n_{-2})} = n_{-1} dx, \tag{24.3}$$

and similarly

$$\frac{dn_{-3}}{N(p_{-3} + \kappa_{-3} n_{-3})} = n_{-2} dx, \tag{24.4}$$

etc. It is readily seen that the first Stokes component acts as an exciting line for the second Stokes component, etc.

For $n_{-1}(x)$ we will insert an approximate expression which is valid when the argument of the exponential function is not too large:

$$n_{-1}(x) = b[e^{k_1 (n_0 + b) x} - 1].$$
(24.5)

Thus

$$\ln\left(1 + \frac{n_{-2}}{b_{-2}}\right) = N\kappa_{-2}\left[\frac{b}{k_1(n_0 + b)}(e^{k_1 (n_0 + b) x} - 1) - x\right].$$
(24.6)

This readily gives $n_{-2}(x)$. Inserting this result for $n_{-2}(x)$ in (24.4), we find

$$n_{-3}(x) = b_{-3}\{e^{N\kappa - 3[F(x) - F(0)]} - 1\},$$
(24.7)

where

$$F(x) = \int n_{-2}(x)dx.$$
(24.8)

Continuing this successive process, we can find the number of photons for Stokes harmonics of any order.

For the first anti-Stokes component, we find from (24.2e), ignoring terms proportional to n_2,

$$\frac{dn_1}{dx} = -(\alpha + N^*p_2 + Np)n_1 + N^*p_1 n + (N^*\kappa_1 - N\kappa)nn_1.$$
(24.9)

Note that the factor $N^*\kappa_1$ corresponds to the scattering of a photon of frequency ω, and the factor $N\kappa$ to the scattering of a photon of frequency ω_1. The frequencies and the angular distributions are different for these two cases. Therefore, although $N \gg N^*$, there may be frequencies and angles for which

$$N^*\kappa_1(\omega, \Omega) - N\kappa(\omega_1, \Omega_1) > 0.$$
(24.10)

For these frequencies and angles, amplification occurs at the frequency ω_1 (additional restrictions are imposed by the Second Law of Thermodynamics). The "reversal" of Raman scattering has been discussed earlier in the beginning of this section. The characteristic angular distribution of the anti-Stokes radiation is treated in the next section.

Suppose that (24.10) is satisfied. Then Eq. (24.9) has the same form as Eq. (23.18b) if we write

$$\alpha_1 = \alpha + N^*p_2 + Np, \quad k_{2a} = N^*p_1,$$
(24.11)
$$k_{1a} = N^*\kappa_1(\omega, \Omega) - N\kappa(\omega_1, \Omega_1).$$

The "losses" in this case are made up of the true absorption losses and the losses associated with the ordinary Raman scattering. Ignoring these losses, we find

$$\frac{dn_1}{k_{2a} + k_{1a}n_1} = n(x)dx. \tag{24.12}$$

As x increases, the number of exciting photons $n(x)$ diminishes owing to the generation of Stokes and anti-Stokes photons corresponding to harmonics of various orders. However, only the first Stokes component is of prevalent importance (most of the exciting photons are converted to this frequency), whereas the other harmonics give minor corrections. Therefore, to first approximation, we may use Eq. (23.19) for $n(x)$, so that together with (24.5), we find

$$n(x) = n_0e^{-\alpha x} - b\left[e^{k_1(n_0+b)x} - 1\right]. \tag{24.13}$$

Inserting (24.13) in (24.12), we can integrate the resulting equation. A certain difficulty is associated with the fact that the number of excited molecules N^* increases as a result of Stokes scattering and therefore $N^* = f(x)$. To simplify the mathematics, we will henceforth assume that $f(x)$ remains fairly constant along the entire scattering cell. Thus,

$$N^* = f(\bar{x}) = \text{const.} \tag{24.14}$$

Integration of (24.12) then gives

$$n_1 = \frac{k_{2a}}{k_{1a}}\left[e^{k_{1a}(\phi(x)-\phi(0))} - 1\right], \tag{24.15}$$

where

$$\phi(x) - \phi(0) = \frac{n_0}{\alpha}\left[1 - e^{-\alpha x}\right] - b\left[\frac{1}{k_1(n_0+b)}(e^{k_1(n_0+b)x} - 1) - x\right]. \tag{24.16}$$

To a first approximation.

$$\phi(x) - \phi(0) = n_0x \tag{24.17}$$

and hence

$$n_1 = \frac{k_{2a}}{k_{1a}}\left[e^{k_{1a}n_0x} - 1\right]. \tag{24.18}$$

This expression differs from the corresponding expression for the first Stokes component (24.5) only in the actual values of the parameters. Note, however, that according to (24.11), k_{1a} is a function of the number of excited molecules N^*. For the high laser power levels used in SRS, N^* may not be equal to the equilibrium value, increasing with n_0. Also n_1 will increase faster than n_{-1} with increasing n_0. If, on the other hand, N^* corresponds to its equilibrium values, i.e., it is independent of n_0, we conclude that the ratio n_1/n_{-1} should decrease with increasing n_0 because the parameters of the function $n_1(n_0)$ are smaller than the corresponding parameters of the function $n_{-1}(n_0)$.

For the second anti-Stokes harmonic we find from (24.2f), again ignoring the losses,

$$\frac{dn_2}{N^*p_2 + [N^*\kappa_2(\omega_1, \Omega_1) - N\kappa_1(\omega_2, \Omega_2)]n_2} = n_1 dx. \qquad (24.19)$$

Inserting for n_1 its expression from (24.18), we find n_2 by integration. Repeating the same procedure, we successively find n_3, etc.

Four-photon excitation of SRS

According to Terhune's four-photon SRS mechanism [487], two quanta of exciting radiation are observed and Stokes and anti-Stokes quanta are emitted. The theory of four-photon SRS was developed by a number of authors, and the principal results were derived in [511, 512]. The state of a molecule does not change in the four-photon process. The process also satisfies the synchronism condition (see §23.2), $2k = k_{-1} + k_1$, where k, k_{-1}, k_1 are the wave vectors of the exciting radiation, the Stokes component, and the anti-Stokes component, respectively.

In accordance with the general theory (see §4), the four-photon process leaving the molecule in its initial state may proceed only through the intermediacy of two independent, but simultaneous processes of Stokes and anti-Stokes scattering. The probability of this four-photon process W_{4ph} is equal to the product of the probabilities of Stokes and anti-Stokes scattering:

$$W_{4ph} = W_{st} \cdot W_{ast}. \qquad (24.20)$$

Inserting for W_{st} and W_{ast} their expressions from (5.53) and using the notation of §23.3, we find

$$W_{4ph} = n^2(k_1 n_{-1} + k_2)(k_1' n_1 + k_2'). \qquad (24.21)$$

The coefficients k_1 and k_2 correspond to the Stokes component, k_1' and k_2' to the anti-Stokes component. Changing over from the probability of the four-photon process to the number of photons emitted by a material layer of thickness dx (using the same procedure as in §23.3), we find

$$k_1' = \frac{4\pi\omega\sigma_1 c^2}{\omega_1^3 \delta}, \qquad k_2' = \frac{\sigma_1 \omega \bar{n}_1^3 \Omega'}{\omega_1}, \qquad \sigma_1 = \sigma(\omega_1). \qquad (24.22)$$

For k_1, k_2, Eqs. (23.28) remain in force.

Further calculations will be carried out under two alternative assumptions.

a) The increase in the number of Stokes photons n_{-1} emitted at the angle corresponding to the synchronism condition in the four-photon process is small compared to that in the main process. Thus from (24.12), considering the general model of the phenomenon and using (23.18b), we find

$$\frac{dn_1}{k_1' n_1 + k_2'} = n^2(x)\left[k_1 n_{-1}(x) + k_2\right] dx = n\, dn_{-1}. \tag{24.23}$$

Writing $b' = k_2'/k_1'$ and assuming that the process occurs mainly in the end portion of the working volume of the active medium, when approximately $n(x) = n(l)$ (l is the length of the active medium), we find

$$n_1 = b'\left(e^{k_1 n(l) n_{-1}} - 1\right). \tag{24.24}$$

b) If the Stokes radiation emitted at the angle corresponding to the synchronism condition is mainly excited by the four-photon mechanism, we may take $n_1 = n_{-1}$. Eq. (24.23) is thus replaced with

$$\frac{dn_1}{(n_1 + b)(n_1 + b')} = k_1 k_1' n^2(x) dx. \tag{24.25}$$

Integration over $n = n_0$ readily gives

$$n_1 = \frac{bb' k_1 k_1' n_0^2 x}{1 - bk_1 k_1' n_0^2 x}. \tag{24.26}$$

Let us now consider four-photon processes which raise the molecule to an excited vibrational state. To return to the model of Raman scattering described in §4, we assume that the intermediate state L is the excited vibrational state of the molecule. The transitions from the initial state 1 to the intermediate state L and from L to the final state k each involve two photons. We have to consider several different alternatives in this case.

1. In the initial state, the molecule is unexcited and interacts with two quanta of exciting radiation. The energy of this initial state is

$$E_1 = \varepsilon_1 + 2\Phi. \tag{24.27}$$

In the intermediate state L, the molecule is in an excited vibrational state ε_k, having absorbed one quantum Φ and emitted an anti-Stokes quantum $\Phi_1 = \hbar\omega_1$. The energy of the intermediate state is thus

$$E_L = \varepsilon_k + \Phi + \Phi_1, \tag{24.28}$$

$$E_L' - E_1' = \varepsilon_k - \varepsilon_1 + \Phi_1 - \Phi = \hbar\left[2\omega_i + i(q_1 - q_k)\right].$$

In the final state, the molecule occupies the same energy level ε_k, having absorbed the second quantum Φ and emitted a quantum of the second Stokes harmonic

$\Phi_{-2} = \hbar\omega_{-2}$. The energy of the final state is thus

$$E_k = \varepsilon_k + \Phi_1 + \Phi_{-2},$$

(24.29)

$$E'_k - E'_1 = \varepsilon_k - \varepsilon_1 + \Phi_1 + \Phi_{-2} - 2\Phi = \hbar[x + i(q_1 - q_k)].$$

For the probability of this process, using (4.41), we find

$$W_R^l = \frac{|H'_{1L}|^2 |H'_{Lk}|^2 |f_{k1}|^2}{|E'_1 - E'_L|^2 |E'_k - E'_1|^2}.$$

(24.30)

The matrix element H'_{1L} can be calculated as a "compound" matrix element of the $1 \to L$ transition with the participation of excited electronic states l of the molecule. Using (4.91), we find

$$|H'_{1L}|^2 = \left| \sum_l \frac{H'_{1l} H'_{lk}}{\omega_l^e - \omega_e + i(q_1 - q_l)} + \frac{H'_{1l'} H'_{l'k}}{\omega_l^e + \omega_k + i(q_1 - q_l)} \right|^2.$$

(24.31)

The second matrix element H'_{Lk} coincides with the matrix element H'_1 expressed by (5.42), where $n_\mu = n_e$, $n_\lambda = n_{-2}$. In SRS the polarizations of the exciting and the scattered radiation are identical, i.e., $(e_\lambda e_\mu) = 1$, and we thus have

$$|H'_{Lk}|^2 = \frac{e^4 (2\pi h)^2 n}{\mu^2 \omega \omega_{-2}} \left[n_{-2} + \frac{\omega_{-2}^2}{(2\pi c)^3} \right].$$

(24.32)

Using (5.53), (5.54), we find

$$W_R^l = \frac{(2\pi)^2 e^4 n^2 [k'_1 n_1 + k'_2] [n_{-2} + \omega_{-2}^2/(2\pi c)^3]}{\mu^2 [4\omega_i^2 + (q_k - q_1)^2] \omega \omega_{-2}}.$$

(24.33)

Using (24.33), we find along the same lines as in the previous cases

$$\frac{dn_1}{k'_1 n_1 + k'_2} = An^2(x) [n_{-2} + b^*_{-2}] dx,$$

(24.34)

where

$$A = \frac{3\pi\sigma_T c^4 c_i N_0}{2\omega\omega_{-2} [4\omega_i^2 + (q_k - q_1)^2]}, \qquad b^*_{-2} = \frac{\omega_{-2}^2}{(2\pi c)^3},$$

(24.35)

$\sigma_T = (8\pi/3) (e^2/\mu c^2)^2 = 6.65 \cdot 10^{-25}$ cm^2 is the Thompson scattering cross section.
    Assuming that $n_{-2}(x)$ is independent of the process being considered (alternative a), we find

$$n_1 = b' \left\{ \exp\left[k'_1 A \int_0^x n^2(x) (n_{-2} + b^*_{-2}) dx \right] - 1 \right\},$$

(24.36)

where $n_{-2}(x)$ is expressed by (24.6). If, on the other hand, $n_{-2} = n_1$ (alternative b), we find, as in (24.26),

$$n_1 = \frac{b'b^*_{-2}Ak'_1 n_0^2 x}{1 - b^*_{-2}Ak'_1 n_0^2 x}. \tag{24.37}$$

II. Now suppose that the intermediate state L is an excited vibrational state attained by the molecule when it absorbs two photons of the exciting radiation. Then

$$E_L = \varepsilon_k, \tag{24.38}$$

$$E'_L - E'_1 = \varepsilon_k - \varepsilon_1 - 2\Phi = \hbar[\omega_i - 2\omega + i(q_1 - q_k)]. \tag{24.39}$$

On jumping from the intermediate state L to the final state, the molecule remains excited vibrationally, and emits two quanta Φ_1 and Φ_{-2}. This process is described by Eq. (5.43). We again arrive at an expression of the form (24.34), although with different numerical coefficients. Since in this case

$$\frac{1}{\hbar^2}|E'_L - E'_1|^2 = (2\omega - \omega_i)^2 + (q_k - q_1)^2 \gg 4\omega_i^2 + (q_k - q_1)^2,$$

the probability of Raman scattering according to process II is less than the probability W_R^1, and we will not consider this process or its analogs in any further detail.

Let us now compare the different processes of excitation of SRS harmonics described above. The process of successive excitation is apparently the main factor for Stokes harmonics of second and higher order. Indeed, using the estimates of the experimental benzene threshold (see §23), we obtain from (24.5) and (24.6) for the threshold of the second Stokes harmonic $(a\pi)_{-2} \approx 3a_1\pi_1$. This value adequately fits the experimental data. Amplification of the first anti-Stokes component in successive excitation is possible, as we have seen above, only for those frequencies and angles when the "reverse" process is forbidden. Ignoring the reverse process, we obtain Eq. (24.18) for the intensity of the first anti-Stokes component, which differs from Eq. (24.5) for the first Stokes component in the first approximation only in the exact value of the concentration of the scattering molecules. If we assign the equilibrium value to the concentration c_i^* of molecules in the excited vibrational state, i.e., $c_i^* = 0.008$ (for the benzene 992 cm^{-1} line), we obtain for the threshold of the first anti-Stokes component $(a\pi)^a_{suc} = 120a_1\pi_1$. The concentration c_i^* increases in SRS, but it can hardly be expected to change appreciably. The process in question (proceeding without the synchronism conditions) may thus be effective only at high exciting power levels.

Let us now consider four-photon excitation processes of SRS. In the presence of an appropriate Stokes component, for a process which does not change the vibrational state of the molecule, we have from (24.24), using (23.29) and (24.22),

$$\frac{I_1}{b'} = \exp\left[\frac{1.13 \cdot 10^{-9} I_e I_{-1}}{S'^2}\right] - 1, \qquad (24.24a)$$

where $b' = \hbar\omega_1^3 \, \delta S\Omega / 4\pi c$. This equality differs from (23.32) mainly in the value of the exponential argument. If for Stokes scattering near the threshold we take $I_1/b' \approx 2 \cdot 10^5$ (see §23.4), we find for this exponential argument $1.13 \cdot 10^{-9} I_e I_{-1}/S'^2 = = 12$.

Assuming a channel cross section of $10^{-5} \, \text{cm}^2$, we can satisfy this relation, according to (23.32), by taking an exciting power of $I_e \approx 1.5 \, \text{MW}$. The threshold of this process is thus only slightly higher than the threshold of the Stokes SRS. Note that there is a pronounced dependence between the intensity of the anti-Stokes component generated in this process and the channel cross-section area. Because of this dependence, the process mainly takes place inside the region where the exciting radiation is focused.

The characteristic feature of this excitation mechanism is that it has a virtually unattainable threshold when considered as an independent process. Indeed, using (24.26), we find for the threshold power in this case $I_e(\pi) = 10^{15} \, \text{MW}$.

The above estimates show that the four-photon process with the synchronism condition satisfied should make a considerable contribution to the excitation of the higher harmonics. The possible processes include, e.g., $2k_1 = k + k_2$, $2k_{-1} = = k + k_{-2}$, $k + k_{-1} = k_1 + k_{-2}$, etc.

To assess the four-photon SRS processes which involve a change in the vibrational state of the molecule (i.e., when the synchronism condition is not satisfied), we will first compare the values of the parameters k_1 and A entering Eqs. (24.23) and (24.34), respectively. Using (23.28) and (24.35), we find for the benzene $992 \, \text{cm}^{-1}$ line

$$k_1 = 2 \cdot 10^{-16}, \qquad A = 2 \cdot 10^{-20}.$$

Eqs. (24.23) and (24.34) are both of the same type, with n_{-1} and n_{-2} interchanged. To obtain an approximate estimate, we thus replace (24.24a) with the equality

$$\frac{I_1}{b'} = \exp\left[\frac{1.13 \cdot 10^{-13} I_e I_{-2}}{S'^2}\right] - 1. \qquad (24.24b)$$

For $I_e = 10 \, \text{MW}$, $I_{-2} \approx 1 \, \text{MW}$, the threshold is reached only for $S' \approx 10^{-7} \, \text{cm}^2$. Light-transferring filaments of this cross section possibly form as a result of self-focusing and self-channeling processes. There is thus a possibility that the four-photon process will make a considerable contribution at high exciting power levels.

4. SRS as a nonlinear-optics effect

The linear relationship between the polarization vector P and the electric field strength E,

$$P = \kappa E, \tag{24.40}$$

is an approximation. At high field strengths, optical effects are described by a more complex equation of the form

$$P = \kappa E + P^{\text{non}}, \tag{24.41}$$

where P^{non} describes the departure from linear behavior. For the Fourier component of polarization corresponding to the frequency ω_p we have

$$P_i^{\text{non}}(\omega_p) = \chi_{ijk}(\omega_p, \omega_q, \omega_r)\, E_j(\omega_q) E_k(\omega_r) +$$

$$+ \chi_{ijkl}(\omega_p, \omega_q, \omega_r, \omega_s)\, E_j(\omega_q) E_k(\omega_r) E_l(\omega_s) + \dots \tag{24.42}$$

Nonlinear susceptibilities of various orders χ_{ijk}, χ_{ijkl}, etc., formally describe the nonlinear properties of the medium.

Nonlinear effects arising at high radiation intensities are the subject of the rapidly developing science of nonlinear optics. SRS has been treated from the viewpoint of nonlinear optics by a number of authors [513–521]. We will confine our discussion to the results summarized by Bloembergen [514].

As a first step toward the nonlinear-optical treatment, let us consider the simple case of an anharmonic oscillator [514]. The equation of motion of this oscillator in an electrical field with Fourier components $\pm \omega_1$ and $\pm \omega_2$ is

$$\ddot{x} + \Gamma \dot{x} + \omega_0^2 x + vx^2 = \frac{2e}{m} \operatorname{Re}\left[E_1 e^{i(k_1 z - \omega_1 t)} + E_2 e^{i(k_2 z - \omega_2 t)} \right]. \tag{24.43}$$

The solution of this equation in the linear approximation is

$$x(\omega_1) = \frac{eE_1}{mD(\omega_1)} e^{i(k_1 z - \omega_1 t)}, \tag{24.44}$$

where $D(\omega) = \omega_0^2 - \omega^2 - i\Gamma\omega$. In the nonlinear approximation of the lowest order the solution acquires terms with second-harmonic frequencies $2\omega_1$, $2\omega_2$ and also sum and difference terms $\omega_1 + \omega_2$ and $\omega_1 - \omega_2$, corresponding to beating of two light waves. For the second harmonic and the difference frequency we have, respectively,

$$x(2\omega_1) = -\frac{e^2 E_1^2 v}{m^2 D^2(\omega_1) D(2\omega_1)} e^{i(2k_1 z - 2\omega_1 t)}, \tag{24.45}$$

$$x(\omega_1 - \omega_2) = -\frac{e^2 v E_1 E_2^*}{m^2 D(\omega_1) D^*(\omega_2) D(\omega_1 - \omega_2)} e^{i[(k_1 - k_2) z - (\omega_1 - \omega_2) t]}. \tag{24.46}$$

Eq. (24.45) leads to expressions for the nonlinear polarization and the nonlinear susceptibility responsible for the generation of the second harmonic:

$$P_x^{non}(2\omega) = N_0 ex(2\omega) = \chi_{xxx}(2\omega, \omega, \omega) E_x^2(\omega), \tag{24.47}$$

$$\chi_{xxx}(2\omega, \omega, \omega) = -\frac{N_0 e^3 v}{m^2 D^2(\omega) D(2\omega)}, \tag{24.48}$$

where N_0 is the mean electron density. An analogous expression is readily obtained from (24.46) for the susceptibility at the difference frequency.

If the difference $\omega_1 - \omega_2$ is close to the resonance frequency ω_0, the Fourier component (24.46) is the only one that need be considered in the calculation of non-linear effects of the next higher order. The term vx^2 in Eq. (24.43) is responsible for the appearance of additional components with frequencies $2\omega_1 - \omega_2, \omega_1 - 2\omega_2$ in this case. Thus, for example,

$$[\chi^{non}(\omega_2)]^* = \chi^{non}(-\omega_2) = \frac{e^3 v^2 E_2^* |E_1|^2}{m^3 [D^*(\omega_2)]^2 |D(\omega_1)|^2 D(\omega_1 - \omega_2)}, \tag{24.49}$$

which gives

$$\chi_{xxxx}(\omega_2) = \frac{N_0 e^4 v^2}{m^3 D^2(\omega_2) |D(\omega_1)|^2 D^*(\omega_1 - \omega_2)}. \tag{24.50}$$

In resonance $\omega_1 - \omega_2 = \omega_0$; if, moreover, $\omega_1 \gg \omega_0$, the function $D^*(\omega_1 - \omega_2)$ is purely imaginary, whereas the other factors in the denominator of (24.50) are real. Therefore,

$$\chi_{xxxx}(\omega_2) = -\frac{iN_0 e^4 v^2}{m^3 \omega_0 \Gamma(\omega_1^2 - \omega_0^2)^2(\omega_2^2 - \omega_0^2)^2}. \tag{24.51}$$

Similarly, we find that

$$\chi_{xxxx}(\omega_1) = \chi_{xxxx}^*(\omega_2), \tag{24.52}$$

and also

$$\chi_{xxxx}(2\omega_1 - \omega_2) = \frac{N_0 e^4 v^2}{m^3 D^2(\omega_1) D^*(\omega_2) D(2\omega_1 - \omega_2) D(\omega_1 - \omega_2)}. \tag{24.53}$$

According to (24.51), the imaginary part of χ_{xxxx} is negative in resonance. The absorption is therefore negative at the lower frequency ω_2 and positive at the higher frequency ω_1. For sufficiently large $|E(\omega_1)|^2$, the negative absorption may exceed all the losses at the frequency ω_2, and the field $E_2(\omega_2)$ will grow exponentially in space. The rate of this growth is determined by $|E(\omega_1)|^2$. Under certain conditions, laser generation may be observed at the frequency ω_2. This effect corresponds to SRS, whereby a quantum $\hbar\omega_1$ is absorbed, a quantum $\hbar\omega_2$ is emitted (Stokes radiation), and the energy of the system increases by the amount $\hbar\omega_0 = \hbar(\omega_1 - \omega_2)$. If there is radiation at the frequency ω_1 and at the Stokes frequency ω_2, nonlinear polarization is observed at the anti-Stokes frequency $2\omega_1 - \omega_2 = \omega_1 + \omega_0$. The corresponding Fourier component is determined by Eq. (24.53). Polarization components of frequencies $\omega_1 \pm n\omega_0$ also appear.

The above expressions for χ^{non} are proportional to the cube of the field amplitudes, i.e., they correspond to the second term in the expansion of polarizability (24.42). Analogous expressions derived in §23.2 from the elementary analysis and in §23.3 from Placzek's quantum-mechanical formula are proportional to the square of the field amplitudes, i.e., they correspond to the first term in the expansion (24.42).

Let us now consider wave generation in a nonlinear medium under the action of harmonic fields. Let the nonlinear medium propagate waves of frequencies ω_i, wave vectors k_i, and polarization vectors e_i ($i = 1, 2, \ldots$). These waves set up a non-linear polarization $P^{non. s}$ in the medium, with the combination frequency $\omega_s = \sum_i l_i \omega_i$.

This nonlinear polarization enters as an additional term in Maxwell's equations and thus in the wave equation also. The additional term acts as a nonlinear source radiating a wave of frequency ω_s. The superscript "non.s" corresponds to this "nonlinear source".

In what follows, we assume that the boundary of the nonlinear medium coincides with the plane $z = 0$, and the incident waves are plane waves.

Let us now apply the general considerations described above to the particular case of SRS. Let ω be the laser frequency, ω_v the vibrational frequency, $\omega \pm l\omega_v$ the combination frequencies. In a complete treatment of SRS, we have to deal with a system of equations for coupled waves at all frequencies, which, in general, may propagate in various directions. This approach, unfortunately, results in a highly complex problem, and we therefore should introduce a number of simplifying assumptions. First, waves of frequency ω_v are omitted from analysis; this is justified in view of the strong absorption of the optical phonons by the medium. Second, the laser field E_L is assumed to be known. This approximation corresponds to conditions which always prevail in the initial stage of the scattering process, when the strong laser beam hits the plane boundary ($z = 0$) of the nonlinear medium.

We will only consider Stokes and anti-Stokes waves with frequencies ω_{-1} and ω_1 and amplitudes E_{-1} and E_1^*, respectively. Further suppose that all waves are equally polarized, so that scalar expressions may be assumed for the susceptibility. In this approximation, the generation of coupled Stokes and anti-Stokes waves is described by the set of equations (see [514])

$$\nabla^2 E_{-1} - \frac{\varepsilon_{-1}}{c^2} \frac{\partial^2 E_{-1}}{\partial t^2} = \frac{4\pi}{c^2} \frac{\partial^2}{\partial t^2} P_{-1}^{non}, \tag{24.54}$$

$$\nabla^2 E_1^* - \frac{\varepsilon_1^*}{c^2} \frac{\partial^2 E_1^*}{\partial t^2} = \frac{4\pi}{c^2} \frac{\partial^2}{\partial t^2} P_1^{non}. \tag{24.55}$$

For nonlinear polarization, we have from [514]

$$P^{non}_{-1} = (\chi_{-1} + \chi_0) |E_L|^2 E_{-1} + [(\chi_{-1}\chi_1^*)^{1/2} + \chi_0] E_L^2 E_1^*, \qquad (24.56)$$

$$P^{non}_1 = (\chi_1 + \chi_0) |E_L|^2 E_1 + [(\chi_{-1}^*\chi_1)^{1/2} + \chi_0] E_L^2 E_{-1}^*. \qquad (24.57)$$

Here χ_{-1} and χ_1 are, respectively, the Stokes and the anti-Stokes nonlinear susceptibilities, which may be complex numbers in general; χ_0 is the real nonresonance component of susceptibility. The frequency dependence of the real and the imaginary part of the susceptibility $\chi_{-1} = \chi'_{-1} + i\chi''_{-1}$ is shown in Figure 96. We readily see that in terms of the dependence on the field amplitude, Eqs. (24.56) and (24.57) are equivalent to Eq. (24.49), previously obtained for an anharmonic oscillator.

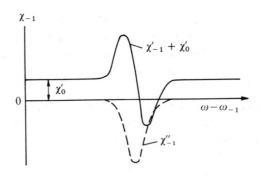

Figure 96

Dispersion of complex susceptibility [514].

The exciting wave can be written in the form

$$E_L = 2 \, \text{Re} \, [E_L e^{i(k_L r - \omega t)}]. \qquad (24.58)$$

The Stokes and the anti-Stokes wave will be sought in the form of plane waves with constant-amplitude planes parallel to the interface between the linear and the nonlinear medium. The solutions of Eqs. (24.54) and (24.55) are therefore written in the form

$$E_{-1}(r, t) = E_{-1} e^{i(k_{-1} r - \omega_{-1} t)}, \qquad (24.59)$$

$$E_1^*(r, t) = E_1^* e^{-i(2k_L - k_{-1}) r} e^{i(2\omega - \omega_{-1}) t}. \qquad (24.60)$$

Inserting these solutions in the wave equations, we obtain two algebraic equations. The determinant of the system should vanish. For each set of values of $(k_x)_{-1}$, $(k_y)_{-1}$, and ω_{-1}, this gives a fourth-degree equation in the unknown $(k_z)_{-1}$. The negative imaginary part of the root $(k_z)_{-1}$ corresponds to amplification.

Calculations carried out under certain additional simplifying assumptions ([514]) lead to the following intensity ratio of the anti-Stokes to Stokes components:

$$\frac{|E_1|^2}{|E_{-1}|^2} = \left(\frac{2\pi\omega^2_{-1}}{c^2 (k_z^m)_{-1}}\right) \frac{|\chi_{-1} + \chi_0|^2}{(\Delta k)^2} |E_L|^4 . \tag{24.61}$$

Here $(k_z^m)_{-1}$ is the tangential component of the wave vector without a pumping field, Δk is the matching of the wave vectors of the Stokes and anti-Stokes waves in the direction of the z axis, which characterizes the departure from the synchronism conditions.

5. Width and shape of SRS lines

The question of width and shape of SRS lines can be readily studied in the two limiting cases considered in § 5. In the case of complete correlation in the properties of scattered and exciting radiation,* the SRS lines "repeat" the width and the shape of the exciting line, growing narrower as I_e increases. In the absence of this correlation, the SRS line width can be found as follows.

According to the general expression (5.53), the intensity distribution within the contour of a Raman line is determined by the factor $F_k(\infty)$ (4.94). If the width of the exciting line is substantially less than $q_k - q_1$, as is usually the case in SRS, $F_k(\infty)$ is an ordinary dispersion function

$$F_k(\infty) = \frac{1}{(\Delta\omega)^2 + (q_k - q_1)^2}, \tag{24.62}$$

where $\Delta\omega = a = \omega_k + \omega_i - \omega_e$. Isolating the factor $F_k(\infty) = f(\Delta\omega)$, we rewrite Eq. (23.24) for the intensity of the first Stokes line in SRS spectra in the form

$$n' = \frac{b[e^{aof(\Delta\omega)(n_0 + b)} - 1]}{1 + (b/n_0) e^{aof(\Delta\omega)(n_0 + b)}}. \tag{24.63}$$

This expression describes the intensity distribution within the contour of the first Stokes line.

In the typical SRS range, we may take for n' the approximate expression

$$n'(\Delta\omega) = be^{aof(\Delta\omega)n_0}. \tag{24.64}$$

According to this expression, the SRS line contour changes as the intensity of the exciting radiation (proportional to n_0) is increased; near the line peak, because of the exponential dependence of $n'(\Delta\omega)$ on n_0, the growth is faster than at the line wings.

---

* Note that the frequency correlation function introduced on p. 56 follows from the ordinary expression for the probability of Raman scattering, which allows for energy conservation in the process.

As a result, the line loses its dispersion contour: the wing intensity is too small compared to the line peak. The line width also diminishes with increasing n_0. The half-width 2δ of the distribution (24.64) can be readily found from the condition

$$n'(\delta) = \tfrac{1}{2} n'(0).$$

We thus find (see [501])

$$\delta = (q_k - q_1) \sqrt{\frac{\ln 2}{a_0 f(0) n_0 - \ln 2}} \approx (q_k - q_1) \sqrt{\frac{\ln 2}{a_0 f(0) n_0}} = (q_k - q_1) \sqrt{\frac{\ln 2}{a n_0}}.$$

$$(24.65)$$

The line width is seen to be inversely proportional to $\sqrt{n_0}$.

6. Experimental studies of the intensity distribution in SRS spectra

Observations of the intensity distribution in SRS spectra under various excitation conditions help to elucidate the contribution from the various excitation mechanisms considered above. However, detailed studies are still very few.

The relative intensity of the first and second Stokes lines and of the first anti-Stokes line in the CS_2 spectrum at temperatures between $+ 20°C$ and $- 100°C$ was studied in [522]. On cooling, the line intensity in ordinary Raman spectra of CS_2 generally increases [292]. The SRS intensity therefore also increases with the decrease in temperature, and a marked redistribution of intensity is observed between the different lines. Figure 97 illustrates the intensity distribution in the CS_2 spectrum at various temperatures.

A considerable increase in the relative intensity of the second Stokes component qualitatively fits the theory of §24.3. On the whole, SRS is complicated by "saturation" and self-focusing effects (see §25.4).

The intensity of different SRS components as a function of the excitation energy was studied in [523]. The measurements were made photographically in CS_2 (the 656 cm^{-1} line) and calorimetrically in liquid nitrogen (2330 cm^{-1} line) (see also [524]). The SRS components in liquid nitrogen were isolated with light filters. The results of liquid-nitrogen measurements are shown in Figure 98. We see that at low excitation energies W_0, the intensity I of the SRS components approximately follows an exponential curve, and the exponential index (proportional to the slope of the linear section of the curves in Figure 98) decreases with the increase in the order of the harmonic. As W_0 increases, the rate of energy growth of the SRS components slows down. For large W_0, the curves corresponding to low-order harmonics show "saturation" (the horizontal section of the curves). It is also remarkable that the energy $W(l)$ of the exciting radiation transmitted through the specimen remains virtually constant despite considerable changes in the incident energy W_0 entering the specimen.

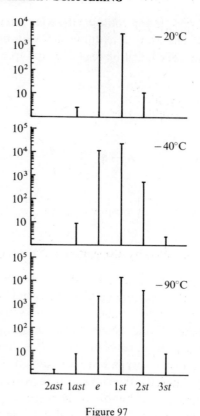

Figure 97

Intensity distribution in the SRS spectrum of carbon disulfide.

We see from Figure 98 that as the pumping energy is increased, the energy of components of progressively higher order shows a substantial increase. It is noteworthy that the second-order Stokes component increases so fast that it soon exceeds in intensity both the first Stokes component and the exciting radiation transmitted through the specimen. The second Stokes component accounts for 32% of the incident exciting energy, which is 47% of the incident number of photons.

If the energy of the SRS components is not exceedingly high, the theory of successive excitation of the Stokes components leads to an exponential dependence of the energy of the n-th component on the energy of the $(n-1)$-th component. This conclusion is consistent with the experimental data for the second Stokes component in liquid nitrogen, plotted in Figure 99 (curve 2). Note, however, that the slope of curve 2 is slightly greater than the slope of curve 1, which describes the dependence of the energy of the first Stokes component on the energy of the exciting radiation. It therefore seems that scattered radiation associated with other scattering mecha-

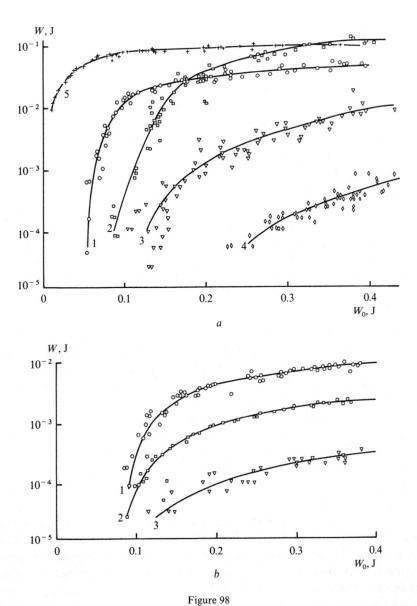

Figure 98

The energy of SRS components W in liquid nitrogen vs. the energy of exciting radiation W_0:

a curves 1, 2, 3, 4 correspond to the first, second, third, and fourth Stokes components of SRS, curve 5 gives the exciting radiation leaving the specimen; *b* curves 1, 2, 3 correspond to the first, second and third anti-Stokes components of SRS.

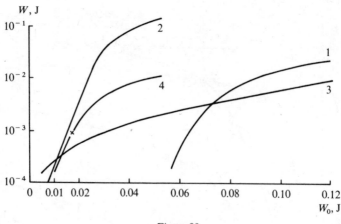

Figure 99

The energy of the first Stokes component vs. the exciting energy (1); the energy of the second Stokes component vs. the energy of the first Stokes component (2); the energy of the third Stokes component vs. the energy of the second Stokes component (3); the energy of the first anti-Stokes component vs. the energy of the first Stokes component (4).

nisms also makes a certain contribution to the second Stokes component. This conclusion is borne out by the reduction of the threshold with the increase in the order of the harmonic (curves 1, 2, 3). Thus although the successive excitation mechanism plays an important role in the generation of the Stokes components, it is evidently reinforced by other mechanisms also.

Analysis of Eqs. (24.2) describing the successive excitation of SRS components has been carried out for the case of low component energies. An approximate solution of the equations for the case when the exciting radiation, the first Stokes component, and the second Stokes component all have comparable energies reveals rapid pumping of energy into components of progressively higher order. This result is consistent with the experimental findings. A somewhat unexpected result is the stabilization of this pumping process, which is responsible for the almost horizontal section in the curves of Figure 98. The solution of Eqs. (24.2) seems to indicate a decrease in the intensity of the exciting radiation transmitted through the specimen and in the intensity of the first Stokes component following an increase in the intensity of the incident radiation. This can be attributed to the existence of reverse processes pumping the energy from higher to lower components and thus competing with the successive excitation mechanism.

Data relating to the correlation in the intensities of the first anti-Stokes and the first Stokes component are of particular importance for elucidating the actual SRS mechanism. The data are plotted in Figure 99 (curve 4) for liquid nitrogen and in Figure 100 for CS_2.

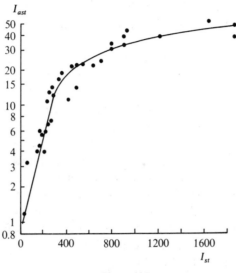

Figure 100

The intensity of the first anti-Stokes component of SRS vs. the intensity of the first Stokes component for carbon disulfide. The intensities are given in relative units.

The scattered radiation was recorded in angles of 20–25°, i.e., the results of measurements gave an intensity integrated over a range of angles. We see from Figures 99 and 100 that the intensity of the first anti-Stokes component over the initial section is an exponential function of the intensity of the first Stokes component. This exponential dependence is in good agreement with Eq. (24.24) if we remember that the intensity of the exciting radiation which emerges from the cell is hardly dependent on the incident light intensity.

The results of [525], in which stimulated and ordinary (spontaneous) Raman spectra were observed simultaneously, are of considerable interest to disclosing the relationship between SRS and spontaneous scattering. Scattering was excited by a parallel beam from a ruby laser without Q-switching. The length of the scattering cell was 100 cm. Benzene, toluene, and nitrobenzene were studied. At energies of 1J and higher, the spectra of these liquids showed a number of characteristic lines (the benzene spectrum showed lines at 607, 992, 1178, and 1586 cm^{-1}) and on the whole the SRS spectrum was not unlike the ordinary Raman spectrum. As the exciting energy was increased, the spectra revealed a marked amplification of one of the lines which further developed a second harmonic. This is a typical feature of SRS. The intensity of the remaining lines was not affected.

Simultaneous observation of SRS and spontaneous Raman scattering can be regarded as an argument in favor of independent excitation of the various vibrational frequencies. It seems that the spontaneous Raman spectrum is always accompanied by SRS, although the energy of the stimulated lines is generally below the "threshold" value for the particular experimental conditions and the lines therefore remain undetectable.

As the exciting power is increased, SRS gains in importance. The exponential growth of the intensity of SRS lines with the increase in the excitation intensity creates an impression of a "sudden" or "jump-like" switch-on of the SRS. A continuous transition from linear to exponential dependence of Raman line intensities on the intensity of the exciting radiation was actually observed in acetone [526].

The actual SRS is considerably complicated by the appearance of various extraneous optical and mechanical processes, including self-focusing and self-channeling of light, which are triggered by the exceedingly high power levels in the medium. As a result, the simple model of SRS described above is not quite applicable. The most significant feature is the "jump-like" transition from spontaneous Raman scattering to stimulated Raman scattering in some substances and mixtures (see, e.g., [526]). These sudden jumps are apparently observed in those cases when the self-focusing threshold is below the SRS threshold.

The "competition" between the excitation of various vibrational frequencies (see §24.1) is apparently significant only at high exciting powers, when a considerable part of this radiation is converted into SRS. It should be remembered that in a typical SRS region the intensity of SRS lines very rapidly increases with the increase in the intensity of the exciting radiation (see, e.g., Figure 91). Of two lines in the spontaneous Raman spectrum showing a small difference in intensity, one may fall below the threshold, while the intensity of the second line may nevertheless exceed the threshold. As the exciting power is increased, the first line may still remain below the threshold, while the intensity of the second line will become so high that the pumping of energy into SRS at the corresponding frequency is very significant. Thus, in general, simultaneous observation of two vibrational frequencies requires special, highly favorable conditions.

A case of "competition" is reported in [527] for SRS in pyridine. The pyridine Raman spectrum shows two lines of close intensities, those at 990 and 1030 cm^{-1}. The threshold for the second line in SRS is a factor of 3.5 higher than the threshold for the first line. When some neodymium nitrate is added to pyridine (the absorption of the 990 cm^{-1} line in this salt is stronger than the absorption of the 1030 cm^{-1} line), the threshold of the 1030 cm^{-1} line is lowered and the threshold ratio becomes 1.3.

Narrow lines in SRS spectra are generally accompanied by a fairly strong "background" which forms wide bands. This intensity distribution, which may be referred to as the "coarse structure" of the lines, was studied in [501] for SRS spectra of carbon disulfide.

The appearance of wide continuous bands, according to Shimoda's calculations [528], may be attributed to the multimode structure of the exciting radiation. Bloembergen et al. [529] proved this in direct experiment. In their experiments, the ruby laser radiation had two components with a frequency splitting $\Delta\omega = 1.6\,\mathrm{cm}^{-1}$. The first Stokes component in this case showed up to 50 side bands with the same frequency spacing. The side lines often remained unresolved, leading to quasi-continuous line broadening in the form of a background. The broadening in benz-aldehyde at 85°C was 5 times the broadening at − 25°C. The background is about 50 Å wide at 85°C. The decrease of band width at lower temperatures is attributed by the authors to the increase of viscosity and the corresponding increase in the orientation time of molecules, after which self-focusing becomes operative.

The study of SRS spectra in the region of the first Stokes frequency [530] revealed a characteristic splitting of the lines into several components. This effect is particularly prominent for exciting powers which are only slightly above the threshold value. The splitting is very irregular: the number of components varies from 1–2 to 5–6, and the spacing between the extreme components ranges from 1–2 to 10–12 cm⁻¹. As the exciting power is increased, the number of components and the spacing both decrease. For exciting radiation power exceeding the threshold value by a factor of 2–4, a single sharp line remains.

Specimen spectra are shown in Figure 101.

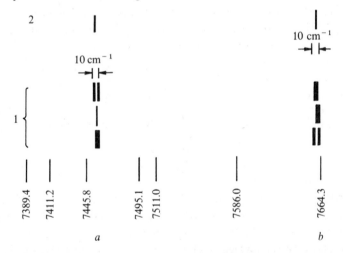

Figure 101

The splitting of SRS lines in benzene (*a*) and nitrobenzene (*b*). Photograph 1 taken near the excitation threshold (three specimen spectra are given because of the inherent instability of the process). No splitting is observed when the threshold is exceeded by a factor of 2–4 (photograph 2).

The origin of the complex line structure is not clear at this stage. It is apparently associated with characteristic processes which take place in the interaction of the material medium with high-power radiation. This effect may also be possibly due to the multimodal structure of the exciting radiation.

25. ANGULAR CHARACTERISTICS OF SRS

1. The angular distribution of SRS

The most remarkable effect observed in experimental work with SRS is probably the highly unusual angular distribution of the radiation at anti-Stokes frequencies (see §23.1). Whereas the distribution of the first Stokes frequency has a sharp peak in the direction of propagation of the exciting radiation, the maximum intensity of the anti-Stokes radiation makes a certain angle with the primary direction, the exact value of the angle being characteristic of the particular scattering medium and the order of the harmonic. This property of SRS was first interpreted by Townes and co-workers [494, 495] proceeding from the semiclassical theory of §23.2.

More general relations reflecting momentum conservation are written in the form

$$k_0 + k_{n-1} = k_{-1} + k_n, \tag{25.1}$$

$$k_0 + k_{-1} = k_{n-1} + k_{-n}, \tag{25.2}$$

where k_j are the wave vectors of light waves of frequencies $\omega_j = \omega_0 \pm j\omega_v$ ($j = 1, 2, 3, \ldots$, the minus sign corresponds to Stokes frequencies). The case $n = 1$ is illustrated in Figure 102. For small θ, we have from the figure

$$\theta_1^2 = \frac{(k_{-1} + k_1 - 2k_0)(k_{-1} - k_1 + 2k_0)}{2k_0 k_1}.$$

We may generally set $2k_0 \approx k_1 + k_{-1}$. The formula thus takes the simpler form

$$\theta_1^2 = \frac{2k_{-1}(k_1 + k_{-1} - 2k_0)}{k_1(k_1 + k_{-1})}.$$

Chiao and Stoicheff [531] confirmed the validity of Eqs. (25.1) and (25.2) for crystals. These authors worked with calcite, whose refractive index is accurately known in a wide spectrum of frequencies. Calcite crystals 5–10 cm long were used as specimens; the orientation of the crystals was such that the incident beam traversed the specimen as an ordinary ray. A Q-switched ruby laser was used as the exciting source. The laser power reached 10 MW with pulse duration of 30 nsec. Under these conditions,

Figure 102

Momentum conservation in SRS.

the symmetrical vibration of the CO_3^{2-} ion at 1085.6 cm^{-1} was excited. Five harmonics of this fundamental frequency were obtained. A range of filters was used to isolate various wavelengths. A typical photograph of the angular distribution is shown in Figure 103.

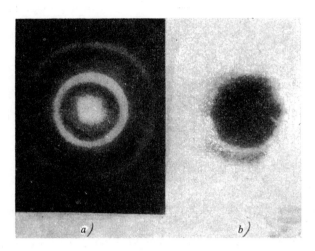

Figure 103

Angular distribution of SRS in calcite [531]:

a anti-Stokes components, *b* Stokes components (negative). Laser beam incident at right angles to the crystal surface.

A simple, and yet reliable method was used to measure the angles. The scattered radiation was photographed on a plate which intercepted the beam emerging from the crystal. If the exciting beam was perpendicular to the entrance and the exit faces of the crystal, the anti-Stokes components produced dark concentric rings on the photographic plate. Stokes radiation produced a dark central spot with bright rings on it, corresponding to the absorption of the first Stokes frequency (Table 57). By altering the distance from the photographic plate to the crystal and measuring the diameters of the rings, one can calculate the angles of divergence of the various wavelengths and also the exact position of the cone "apex". These measurements have shown that, if the exciting beam is focused inside the crystal, the cone apex falls at the focus of the focusing lens. If, on the other hand, the radiation is focused outside the crystal, the cone apex lies right near the exit surface of the crystal.

A symmetrical picture is observed only when the exciting radiation beam is perpendicular to both the entrance and the exit plane of the crystal. A slight tilt of the crystal leads to a nonuniform distribution of intensity along the ring circumference. Ring sections corresponding to maximum intensity of anti-Stokes radiation fall on one side of the center, and the sections corresponding to Stokes components

Table 57

EXPERIMENTAL AND THEORETICAL VALUES OF SRS EMISSION AND
ABSORPTION ANGLES IN CALCITE

Frequency	Emission angles, 10^{-2} rad		Absorption angles for the first Stokes component, 10^{-2} rad	
	experiment	theory	experiment	theory
$\omega_0 - 2\omega_v$	5.2 ± 0.1*	5.57	1.8 ± 0.1*	2.22
$\omega_0 + \omega_v$	2.50 ± 0.03	2.49	2.90 ± 0.03	2.90
$\omega_0 + 2\omega_v$	5.03 ± 0.08	4.91	3.26 ± 0.06	3.21
$\omega_0 + 3\omega_v$	7.64 ± 0.2	7.29	3.50 ± 0.06	3.55
$\omega_0 + 4\omega_v$	10.2 ± 0.4	9.61	3.77 ± 0.06	3.86

* Values obtained for $f = 20$ cm. All the other results extrapolated to $f \to \infty$.

of higher than first order and to the absorption of the first Stokes component lie diametrically opposite from the center.

Studies of the dependence of the SRS angular distribution on various factors have shown that the angles are mainly determined by the scattering medium. The angles are independent of the length of the scattering specimen and hardly depend on temperature (about 3% for $\Delta T = 100°$C). They are fairly sensitive, however, to the focal distance of the focusing lens. Chiao and Stoicheff attribute this effect to the fact that the wave vector k_0 in the focus of a lens is somewhat smaller than the wave vector of a plane wave. At the same time, the angles are highly sensitive to any changes in k_0. Lenses with various focal distances were correspondingly used in measurements (8, 20, 30, 50, and 127 cm). The results were then extrapolated to $f \to \infty$ (plane wave).

The theoretical calculation was based on the relation

$$\theta_n = \beta_n \pm (\beta_n^2 + \delta_n - \gamma_n)^{1/2}, \qquad (25.3)$$

where

$$\beta_n = \frac{k_{n-1}\theta_{n-1}}{k_{-1} + k_n}, \qquad \delta_n = \frac{2k_{-1}(k_n + k_{-1} - k_0 - k_{n-1})}{k_n(k_{-1} + k_n)},$$

$$\gamma_n = \frac{(k_{n-1} - k_{-1})\beta_n\theta_{n-1}}{k_n}.$$

The angles describing the direction of absorption of the first Stokes component were calculated from the formula

$$(\theta_{-1})_n = \frac{k_{n-1}\theta_{n-1} - k_n\theta_n}{k_{-1}}. \qquad (25.4)$$

The results of measurements and calculations using (25.3) and (25.4) are listed in Table 57 above.

Detailed studies of the angular distribution of the intensity of the first Stokes component of SRS have shown that the wing of this distribution has no maxima in the direction corresponding to the synchronism condition. It is therefore concluded [531, 532] that SRS cannot follow the four-photon scheme $2k_0 = k_1 + k_{-1}$, which should lead to additional Stokes radiation at the synchronism angle. This remark is valid, however, only for a four-photon process when considered independently. In actual fact, the four-photon process is significant when the intensity of the Stokes component is controlled by other mechanisms, and not by the four-photon mechanism itself (see §24.3). The experimental results, therefore, do not contradict the four-photon scheme.

Calculations based on the synchronism relations and analogous conditions give a poorer fit with the experimental findings for the angular distribution of SRS in liquids. Hellwarth et al. [533] obtained significant variance between theory and experiment for nitrobenzene. Note that Chiao and Stoicheff used calcite in their studies because its dispersion was known in a wide range of frequencies. Since no comparable data were available for nitrobenzene, separate measurements of the refractive index of nitrobenzene at the relevant wavelengths had to be made [533]. The calculations gave the following angles:

$$\theta_1 = 2.5° \pm 0.2°, \quad \theta_{-2} = 12.4° \pm 1°, \quad \theta_{-3} = 16° \quad \text{or} \quad 12° \pm 1°$$

(according to different calculation procedures). The experimental results were significantly different:

$$\theta_1 = 3.1° \pm 0.1°, \quad \theta_{-2} = 3.9 \pm 0.1°, \quad \theta_{-3} = 3.8° \pm 0.1°.$$

Further studies of the angular distribution of SRS in liquids have shown that the effect is considerably more complicated than originally assumed. Garmire [534] established two classes of high-order SRS in liquids. Class I gives an angular distribution which obeys the synchronism conditions (25.1), (25.2). According to [534], radiation of this class had not been observed in previous experiments because the Stokes radiation at the corresponding angles is of negligible intensity. Class II radiation is generally sufficiently strong; it is emitted along the generators of cones whose angles differ by 30% and more from the angles calculated from the synchronism conditions. The rings in the case of class II radiation may be diffuse and are sometimes split into several components.

SRS was excited by a parallel beam from a 10 MW giant-pulse ruby laser. The intensity of Stokes radiation near the synchronism direction was enhanced by setting the axis of the scattering cell at an angle θ to the direction of the laser beam. The cell was 10 cm long, and the end-windows of the cell were strictly parallel. Part of the Stokes radiation at an angle θ was reflected back from the glass–air interface, and the radiation intensity in the given direction increased correspondingly by a factor of 10^4.

The origin of class II radiation in [534] is associated with the splitting of the laser beam in the liquid into very thin filaments (see below).

The attempts to design a SRS resonator not coupled with the master laser resonator are of special interest for the study of the angular distribution of SRS. The angle between the SRS resonator axis and the master laser axis in [535] was about 2.5°. Generation at the first Stokes frequency of benzene was observed under these conditions. In [536], the resonator axis was perpendicular to the master laser axis. With maximum master laser power (about 5 MW), the radiation power at the first Stokes frequency of nitrobenzene was 150 kW and 10 kW in the forward direction and in the transverse direction, respectively. The second Stokes harmonic was also observed in the transverse direction, but its intensity reached about 1 % of the intensity of the first Stokes component in the same direction.

SRS at large angles to the primary beam is of considerable interest for understanding the general features of the angular distribution of SRS. Direct experiments of Stoicheff [488], Maker and Terhune [537] and others show that the first-order Stokes radiation is concentrated in the forward direction in a very narrow cone. Observations of Stokes radiation at a certain direction to the primary beam show that a small fraction of this radiation is distributed more or less uniformly in all directions. The origin of this isotropic Stokes component will be considered in §25.3.

Polarization data regarding SRS lines [537] are of considerable interest. The measurements were carried out in gaseous hydrogen with a focused beam. The state of polarization of the SRS lines coincided within the margin of experimental error with the plane of polarization of the laser beam. If the laser beam was elliptically polarized, the SRS polarization also showed elliptical polarization, with the same eccentricity.

2. Asymmetry of the stimulated Raman scattering

It follows from the general theory (see §3) that the angular diagram of Raman scattering should be symmetrical relative to the "forward" and "back" directions of the exciting beam. Experimental data on the whole do not contradict this conclusion. The asymmetry of the scattering diagram observed by some authors is not too large, and may be treated as a certain "anomaly."

The situation is radically different for stimulated Raman scattering. The first studies of Stoicheff [509] and Maker and Terhune [537] have shown that the forward scattered power is much higher than the power of the back-scattered flux.

Forward and back-scattered intensities in SRS were measured in [522, 538] by a more rigorous experimental procedure than in [509, 537]. Because of the instability of SRS, a special technique was developed, with simultaneous recording of the forward and back-scattered fluxes. A schematic diagram of the setup is shown in Figure 104.

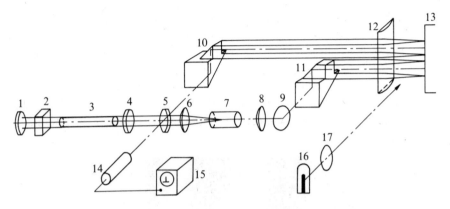

Figure 104

Experimental setup for measuring the scattering asymmetry:

1, 4) plane mirrors of the ruby laser; 2) cell with cryptocyanine; 3) ruby; 5, 9) glass plates; 6, 8) lenses; 7) cell; 10, 11) rotary prisms; 12) cylindrical lens; 13) spectrograph; 14) photodiode; 15) oscillograph; 16) ribbon lamp; 17) lens.

Liquid nitrogen, carbon disulfide, and calcite were studied. Forward and back-scattered SRS were observed for a number of Stokes and anti-Stokes components. The measured forward-to-back-scattered intensity ratios are listed in Table 58.

We see from the table that the intensity of the forward scattering is generally much higher than the intensity of back-scattered light. It is significant that a change in the intensity of the exciting light does not affect the value of I_f/I_b.

The observed back-scattering may be a consequence of secondary phenomena, e.g., Mandelshtam–Brillouin scattering, so that the actual asymmetry of the scattering diagram is even higher.

The structure of a small-aperture SRS beam (less than 3°) was studied in [522].

Table 58

ASYMMETRY OF SRS

Compound		I_b/I_f				
	t, °C	2 ast	1 ast	exc.	1 st	2 st
Carbon disulfide $\Delta v = 656$ cm^{-1}	20	—	6	—	9	100
Calcite $\Delta v = 1085$ cm^{-1}	20	3	10	21	5	4
	−100	3	21	25	5	4
	−196	3	80	75	5	4
Liquid nitrogen (in a spherical vessel) $\Delta v = 2330$ cm^{-1}	−196	—	55	22	27	—

SRS was measured in carbon disulfide at 656 cm^{-1} in the direction of the exciting beam* and in the opposite direction. The same experimental procedure was used as before, but without a collecting cylindrical lens. The photographic plate in the forward direction showed the Stokes component in the form of a diffuse spot, whereas in the back direction this component was observed in the form of several spots or a central spot surrounded by a diffuse ring (Figure 105). The radius of the ring on the photographic plate was 2 mm. The opening angle of the corresponding cone is found to be

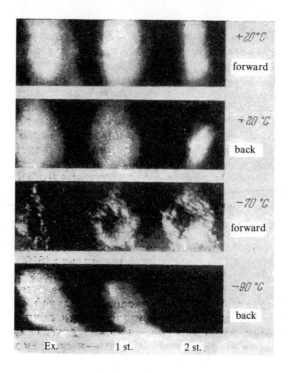

Figure 105

Structure of the SRS light beam in CS$_2$.

close to 1°. This angular range had not been studied before, since generally the scattered flux had been viewed in the forward direction and recorded without preliminary spectral decomposition (the individual components were isolated with interference filters). The ruby laser beam in this case was fairly wide, covering the entire angular range. When the temperature was lowered to − 80°C, the complex structure of the back-scattered beam vanished: the entire flux was collected to a single point on the axis of the system [522].

---

* The studies described in §25.1 measured the angular distribution of SRS at angles greater than about 3°.

3. Possible interpretation of the angular distribution of SRS

The theory of SRS is far from being satisfactory in all that concerns the angular distribution and the spectral properties.

Let us first consider the first Stokes component of SRS. The angular distribution of this component of the scattered flux is characterized by a sharply pronounced forward directivity. When the ruby laser beam is focused inside the cell, virtually the entire scattered flux of the first Stokes frequency is concentrated inside a geometrical cone emerging from the focus with a given entrance aperture. This angular distribution of intensity is generally attributed (see, e.g., [514]) to the considerable difference in the length of the optical path l along the laser beam and transversally to it.* Since the intensity of the SRS lines is an exponential function of l, this factor naturally must be taken into consideration. However, simple geometrical analysis leads to the conclusion that the optical path difference cannot produce the highly directional scattering observed in experiments [510].

In the previous subsection we have stressed that the forward scattering markedly prevails over back-scattering. Because of the exponential dependence of the SRS intensity on the intensity of ordinary Raman lines and other factors, a marked "forward–back" asymmetry could have arisen, generally speaking, following a very slight preferred forward directivity (compared to the back direction). This non-equivalence of the two directions is possibly inherent in the spontaneous Raman scattering (see §3) or may arise as the waves propagate through the nonlinear medium (see [514]). If this were so, however, an increase in the exciting power, the cell length, etc., should have led to an increase in the ratio I_f/I_b, which is apparently not so in practice.

The above peculiar features of the angular distribution of SRS are readily understood if we assume a correlation between the properties of the SRS radiation and the exciting radiation (see §5 and §23.3). According to (5.35b), the angular distribution of the SRS component is described by the same function $\rho(\Omega')$ which determines the angular distribution of the exciting radiation $\rho(\Omega)$. The angular distribution of the SRS thus "repeats" the angular distribution of the exciting radiation. If the exciting radiation is concentrated in a narrow range of angles $\Omega \leq \Omega_0$, SRS is also confined within a narrow cone. This radiation is naturally directed forward only.

These conclusions are fully borne out by recent experimental data of [539], where the angular distribution of SRS in CS_2 was studied. The scattered radiation was passed through a spectrograph (an unconventional procedure in SRS measurements), so that the various components were fully separated.

The exciting radiation was focused inside a scattering cell by a lens L_1. Another

---

* Note that the primary source of radiation at the first Stokes frequency is the ordinary Raman scattering, whose angular distribution in the relevant range of angles is almost uniform (see §2).

lens L_2 was mounted so that its frontal focus coincided with the focus of L_1, and the rear focal plane coincided with the plane of the spectrograph slit (which was moved farther away at a later stage). The intensity distribution recorded by the photographic plate in this geometry clearly corresponds to the angular distribution of SRS. By changing the focal distance of the lens L_1, and using stops of various aperture, one can adjust the angular distribution of the exciting radiation entering the cell.

The angular distribution of the exciting radiation and of the SRS Stokes components is shown in Figure 106. We see that the first Stokes component "repeats" to a certain approximation the angular distribution of the exciting line.

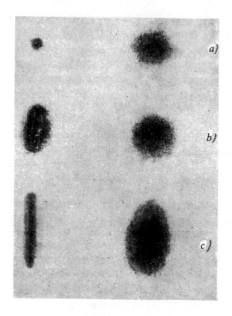

Figure 106

Angular distribution of the first Stokes component of SRS in CS_2 for various angular distributions of the exciting radiation:

a circular stop $d = 13.8$ mrad, *b* rectangular stop 6.9×27.6 mrad^2, *c* rectangular stop 3.4×58.6 mrad^2.

A similar pattern was observed for the first Stokes components of benzene, acetone, and calcite, and also for the second Stokes component of carbon disulfide.

Thus in case of successive excitation, the second Stokes component of SRS "repeats" the first component, which acts as an exciting line for the second component.

For exciting power levels of 1–10 MW, the ordinary Raman scattering is quite strong (see §24.5). Moreover, part of the radiation at all frequencies is scattered owing to the optical inhomogeneity of the medium. This explains the origin of the isotropic first Stokes component, observed in any direction relative to the primary beam. This isotropic radiation can be amplified by enclosing the system in a resonator (see § 25.1).

Successive excitation of SRS does not account for the presence of anti-Stokes rings and for second- and higher-order harmonics of Stokes radiation and absorption rings. The scattered radiation propagating in these directions is apparently produced by four-photon processes considered in § 24. We recall that these processes satisfy the synchronism conditions (25.1), (25.2). The phenomenon on the whole is rendered more complex by various secondary effects which arise when high-power radiation interacts with the material medium (see next subsection).

4. Self-focusing and its effect on SRS

One of the most interesting effects of modern nonlinear optics is the self-focusing of a strong light beam which causes its splitting into a number of thin light-transferring filaments. This effect is associated with the dependence of the refractive index on the light intensity:

$$n = n_0 + n_2 E^2 + \ldots \tag{25.5}$$

For power densities of from 100 to 1000 MW/cm^2, some liquids, e.g., CS$_2$ have $n_2 \sim 10^{-12}$ CGSE, and the nonlinear corrections to the refractive index become quite significant.

In a medium with a refractive index described by Eq. (25.5), the refractive index on the beam is greater than that at the beam periphery, and the beam is therefore pinched toward the axis. As a result, the focus of a lens in a nonlinear medium is displaced (the focal distance as it were becomes shorter). The extent of the focal region also diminishes. Under certain conditions, waveguide propagation of light is observed (self-channeling of the light beam). These effects are treated in [514, 516, 540–543].

The dependence of the refractive index on light intensity may be associated with nonlinear polarization and also with electrostriction which arises owing to a mechanical interaction between the field and the medium.

In liquids with highly anisotropic molecules, self-focusing may be caused by the tendency of the molecules to orient themselves in a strong electrical field so that the axis of maximum polarizability points along the field vector. A high-intensity light beam thus renders the medium birefringent. Kelley [544] considered this effect in some detail. It follows from this result that the threshold power P for self-focusing is inversely proportional to the Kerr constant B of the substance:

$$P = \beta/B, \tag{25.6}$$

where β is a constant dependent on the experimental conditions.

Self-focusing and the splitting of the laser beam into thin filaments of high-intensity light naturally alter the excitation conditions of SRS. The interrelationship of the two effects has been considered in [522, 529, 539–548].

The data of [522] show that in CS_2 at temperatures below $-50°C$, when self-focusing is always observed, the intensity of the exciting line transmitted through a 25 mm layer of the liquid drops to almost $\frac{1}{5}$ of the original intensity due to conversion of luminous energy into SRS (Figure 107). If the self-focusing and the self-channeling

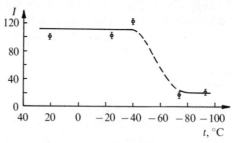

Figure 107

Intensity of the exciting radiation vs. temperature for a CS_2 cell.

conditions change, the energy distribution in the SRS spectrum is also markedly affected (see Figure 97). The dependence of the intensity of the first Stokes component on the intensity of the exciting line (with allowance for the temperature dependence of the scattering coefficient) will also reveal an abrupt change following a change in self-focusing conditions (Figure 108). Note that the angular distribution of the back-scattered SRS flux reveals characteristic changes when the self-channeling conditions are reached. We see from Figure 105 that the back-scattered beam is first split into separate filaments, which then merge into a single central light-transferring channel.

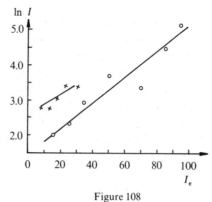

Figure 108

Intensity of the first Stokes line of CS_2 vs. the intensity of the exciting line.

○ first self-channeling region,   × second self-channeling region.

Without going into a detailed discussion of the results obtained in this rapidly developing branch of nonlinear optics, we will only note that self-focusing greatly complicates the observed features of SRS. Thus the complex angular intensity distribution of the anti-Stokes components in SRS, resulting in the formation of rings of first and second class, is associated according to Shimoda's semiclassical theory [549] with light scattering in filament regions which form in the medium under the action of high-power laser radiation.

Interaction of SRS with other nonlinear effects, which unfortunately fall outside the scope of this book, also has a substantial influence on radiation properties.

Further references on SRS will be found in Schrötter's review [550].

BIBLIOGRAPHY

1. LANDSBERG, G. S., *Izbrannye trudy (Selected Works)*, pp. 101–110, Izdatel'stvo AN SSSR. 1958; MANDELSTAM, L.I., *Polnoe sobranie trudov (Complete Works)*, Vol. 1, pp. 293, 305, Izdatel'stvo AN SSSR. 1947.
2. RAMAN, C. V. and K. S. KRISHNAN, *Nature*, **121**, 501. 1928.
3. LOMMEL, E., *Pogg. Ann.* **143**, 26. 1871; *Wiedem. Ann.* **3**, 251. 1878.
4. SMEKAL, A., *Naturwissenschaften*, **11**, 873. 1923.
5. MURNAGAN, F. D., *The Theory of Group Representations*. Baltimore, Johns Hopkins Press. 1938.
6. LANDAU, L. D. AND E. M. LIFSHITS, *Teoriya polya (Field Theory)*, Fizmatgiz. 1960.
7. PLACZEK, G., *Rayleigh-Streuung und Raman-Effekt*. Leipzig. 1934.
8. LANDAU, L. D. AND E. M. LIFSHITS, *Electrodinamika sploshnykh sred (Electrodynamics of Continuous Media)*, Gostekhizdat. 1957.
9. HANLE, W., *Ann. Physik*, **11**, 885. 1931; 15, 345. 1932.
10. PLACZEK, G., *Leipziger Vorträge*, p. 71. 1931.
11. POKROWSKI, G. I. and E. A. GORDON, *Ann. Physik*, **4**, 488. 1930.
12. KONDILENKO, I. I., P. A. KOROTKOV, and V. L. STRIZHEVSKII, *Optika i Spektroskopiya*, **8**, 471. 1960; **11**, 169. 1962.
13. KONDILENKO, I. I. and P. A. KOROTKOV, *Optika i Spektroskopiya*, **17**, 451. 1964.
14. SOKOLOVSKAYA, A. I. and P. D. SIMOV, *Optika i Spektroskopiya*, **15**, 622. 1963.
15. KOROTKOV, P. A., *Candidate's dissertation*, KHARKOV. 1965.
16. DAMEN, T. C., R. C. LEITE, and P. S. PORTO, *Phys. Rev. Lett.*, **14**, 9. 1965.
17. DIRAC, P., *The Principles of Quantum Mechanics*. Oxford, Clarendon Press. 1958.
18. STEPANOV, V. V., *Kurs differentsial'nykh uravnenii (A Course in Differential Equations)*. Gostekhizdat. 1953.
19. PONTRYAGIN, L. S., *Obyknovennye differentsial'nye uravneniya (Ordinary Differential Equations)*, "Nauka". 1965.
20. LANDAU, L. D. and E. M. LIFSHITS, *Kvantovaya mekhanika (Quantum Mechanics)*. Fizmatgiz. 1963.
21. WEISSKOPF, V., *Phys. Z.*, **34**, 1. 1933; *Ann. Physik*, **9**, 23. 1931; *Z. Phys.*, **85**, 451. 1933.
22. WEISSKOPF, V. and E. WIGNER, *Z. phys.*, **63**, 54; **65**, 18. 1930.
23. HEITLER, W., *The Quantum Theory of Radiation*. Oxford, Clarendon Press. 1936.
24. SUSHCHINSKII, M. M. and V. A. ZUBOV, *Optika i Spektroskopiya*, **13**, 766. 1962.
25. LANDAU, L. D. and E. M. LIFSHITS, *Mekhanika (Mechanics)*. Fizmatgiz. 1958.
26. SUSHCHINSKII, M. M., *ZhETF*, **20**, 304. 1950.

27. ORNSTEIN, L. S. and J. REKVELD, *Z. Phys.*, **61**, 593. 1930.
28. REKVELD, J., *Z. Phys.*, **68**, 543. 1931.
29. SIRKAR, S. C., *Indian J. Phys.*, **6**, 133. 1931.
30. WERTH, S. M., *Phys. Rev.*, **39**, 299. 1932.
31. SHORYGIN, P. P., *Doklady AN SSSR*, **87**, 201. 1952.
32. SCHORYGIN, P., L. KUZINA, and L. OSITJANSKAJA, *Microchim. Acta*, Nos. 2–3, 630. 1955.
33. FINKEL'SHTEIN, A. I. and P. P. SHORYGIN, *ZhFKh*, **26**, 1272. 1952.
34. KHALILOV, A. KH. and P. P. SHORYGIN, *Doklady AN SSSR*, **81**, 1031. 1951.
35. SHORYGIN, P. P. and L. Z. OSITYANSKAYA, *Doklady AN SSSR*, **98**, 51. 1954.
36. SHORYGIN, P. P. and L. L. KRUSHINSKII, *Materialy X vsesoyuznogo soveshchaniya po spektroskopii (Proceedings of the 10th All-Union Conference on Spectroscopy)*, Vol. 1, p. 215, Izdatel'stvo L'vovskogo Universiteta. 1957.
37. SCHORYGIN, P. and L. KRUSCHINSKI, *Z. Phys.*, **150**, 332. 1958.
38. KONDILENKO, I. I. and I. L. BABICH, *Materialy X vsesoyuznogo soveshchaniya po spektroskopii (Proceedings of the 10th All-Union Conference on Spectroscopy)*, Vol. 1, p. 218, Izdatel'stvo L'vovskogo Universiteta. 1957.
39. KONDILENKO, I. I. and P. A. KOROTKOV, *Ukrains'kii fizichnii zhurnal*, **3**, 765. 1958.
40. KONDILENKO, I. I., P. A. KOROTKOV, and V. L. STRIZHEVSKII, *Optika i spektroskopiya*, **9**, 26. 1960.
41. BEHRINGER, J., *Z. Elektrochem.*, **62**, 544. 1958; *Theorie der molecularen Lichstreuung*, Manuscript, München. 1967; SZYMANSKI, H. A., *Raman Spectroscopy, Theory and Practice*, p. 168. New York. 1967.
42. BEHRINGER, J. and J. BRANDMÜLLER, *Ann. Physik*, **7**, 234. 1959.
43. HOFMANN, W. and H. MOSER, *Z. Elektrochem.*, **64**, 310. 1960; BUYKEN, H., K. KLAUSS, and H. MOSER, *Ber. Bunsengesellschaft phys. Chem.*, **71**, 578. 1967.
44. BRANDMÜLLER, J. and H. MOSER, *Einführung in die Ramanspektroskopie*. Darmstadt, Steinkopff Verlag. 1962.
45. KONDILENKO, I. I., V. E. POGORELOV and V. L. STRIZHEVSKII, *Optika i Spektroskopiya* **13**, 649. 1962; *FTT*, **6**, 533. 1964.
46. TSENTER, M. YA. and YA. S. BOBOVICH, *Optika i Spektroskopiya*, **16**, 417. 1964.
47. KONDILENKO, I. I. and V. E. POGORELOV, *Optika i Spektroskopiya*, **19**, 41. 1965.
48. ZUBOV, V. A., *Fizicheskie problemy spektroskopii (Physical Problems in Spectroscopy)*, **1**, 381. 1962.
49. ZUBOV, V. A., *Optika i Spektroskopiya*, **13**, 861. 1962.
50. ZUBOV, V. A., *Optika i Spektroskopiya*, **14**, 576. 1963.
51. ZUBOV, V. A., *Trudy FIAN*, **30**, 3. 1964.
52. ZUBOV, V. A., Z. M. MULDAKHMETOV, and M. M. SUSHCHINSKII, In: *Optika i Spektroskopiya*, Collection No. 2, *Molecular Spectroscopy*, p. 324, Izdatel'stvo AN SSSR. 1963.
53. IVANOVA, T. M., *Dissertation*. Gosudarstvennyi Pedagogicheskii Institut, Moscow. 1964.
54. SHORYGIN, P. P. and T. M. IVANOVA, *Doklady AN SSSR*, **150**, 533. 1963.
55. SHORYGIN, P. P. and L. L. KRUSHINSKII, *Optika i Spektroskopiya*, **11**, 24. 1961; *Doklady AN SSSR*, **133**, 337. 1960.
56. DAVYDOV, A. S., *Kvantovaya mekhanika (Quantum Mechanics)*. Fizmatgiz. 1963.
57. GRADSHTEIN, I. S. and I. M. RYZHIK, *Tablitsy integralov, summ, ryadov i proizvedenii (Tables of Integrals, Sums, Series and Products)*. Fizmatgiz. 1963.

58. PIVOVAROV, V. M. and YA. S. BOBOVICH, *Optika i Spektroskopiya*, **6**, 249. 1959; SOKOLOVSKAYA, A. I., *Optika i Spektroskopiya*, **9**, 5, 582. 1960.

59. KONINGSTEIN, J. A. and O. S. MORTENSEN, preprint. 1967.

60. HERZBERG, G., *Molecular Spectra and Molecular Structure.* 1: *Spectra of Diatomic Molecules.* Princeton, N. J., Van Nostrand. 1950.

61. PLACZEK, G. and E. TELLER, *Z. Phys.*, **81**, 209. 1933.

62. CALLOMON, J. H. and B. P. STOICHEFF, *Canadian J. Phys.*, **35**, 373. 1957.

63. STOICHEFF, B. P., *High-Resolution Raman Spectroscopy.* In: THOMPSON, H. W., ed., *Advances in Spectroscopy,* **1**, 91. 1959. London, Interscience Publishers, Inc.

64. RASETTI, F., *Phys. Rev.,* **34**, 367, 1929; *Proc. Nat. Acad. Sci. U.S.*, **15**, 234, 515. 1929; *Z. Phys.*, **61**, 598. 1930.

65. DICKINSON, R. G., R. T. DILLON and F. RASETTI, *Phys. Rev.*, **34**, 582. 1929.

66. HERZBERG, G. and B. P. STOICHEFF, *Nature*, **175**, 79. 1955.

67. STOICHEFF, B. P., *Canadian J. Phys.*, **32**, 339. 1954.

68. LANGSETH, A. and B. P. STOICHEFF, *Canadian J. Phys.*, **34**, 350. 1956.

69. HANSEN, G. E. and D. M. DENNISON, *J. Chem. Phys.*, **20**, 313. 1952.

70. TRAMBARULO, R. and W. GORDY, *J. Chem. Phys.*, **18**, 1613. 1950.

71. WESTENBERG, A. A. and E. B. WILSON, *J. Amer. Chem. Soc.*, **72**, 109. 1950.

72. TATEVSKII, V. M., *Khimicheskoe stroenie uglevodorodov i zakonomernosti v ikh fiziko-khimicheskikh svoistvakh (Chemical Structure of Hydrocarbons and Regular Features in Their Physicochemical Properties).* Izdatel'stvo MGU. 1953.

73. SUSHCHINSKII, M. M., *UFN*, **65**, 441. 1958.

74. TYULIN, V. I., YU. N. PANCHENKO, YU. A. PENTIN, and V. M. TATEVSKII, *Optika i Spektroskopiya*, **16**, 992. 1964; COLE, A. R. H., C. M. MOHAY, and G. A. OSBORNE, *Spectr. Acta*, **A 23**, 909. 1967.

75. AMALDI, E. and G. PLACZEK, *Z. Phys.*, **81**, 259. 1933.

76. MIKHAILOV, G. V., *ZhETF*, **37**, 1570. 1959; **36**, 1368. 1959; *Trudy FIAN*, **9**, 316. 1958.

77. SOBEL'MAN, I. I., *UFN*, **54**, 551. 1954; *Trudy FIAN*, **9**, 316. 1958.

78. FERMI, E., *Molecules, Crystals and Quantum Statistics.* Translated by M. FERRO-LUZZI from the 1934 Italian edition, *Molecule e Cristalli.* New York, W. Benjamin. 1966.

79. ANDRYCHUK, D., *Canadian J. Phys.*, **29**, 151. 1951.

80. VOL'KENSHTEIN, M. V., M. A. EL'YASHEVICH, and B. I. STEPANOV, *Kolebaniya molekul (Molecular Vibrations)*, Vols. 1 and 2. Gostekhizdat. 1949.

81. EL'YASHEVICH, M. A., *Atomnaya i molekulyarnaya spektroskopiya (Atomic and Molecular Spectroscopy).* Fizmatgiz. 1962.

82. WILSON, E. B., J. C. DECIUS, and P. C. CROSS, *Molecular Vibrations. The Theory of Infrared and Raman Spectra.* New York, McGraw-Hill. 1955.

83. HERZBERG, G., *Molecular Spectra and Molecular Structure.* 2. *Infrared and Raman Spectra of Polyatomic Molecules.* Princeton, N.J., Van Nostrand. 1945.

84. SHMIDT, O. YU., *Abstraktnaya teoriya grupp (Abstract Group Theory).* GTTI. 1933.

85. KUROSH, A. G., *Teoriya grupp (Group Theory).* Gostekhizdat. 1953.

86. LYUBARSKII, G. YA., *Teoriya grupp i ee primenenie v fizike (Group Theory and Its Application in Physics).* Fizmatgiz. 1958.

87. BHAGAVANTAM, S. and T. VENKATARAYUDU, *Theory of Groups and Its Application to Physical Problems.* Waltair, India, Andhra Univ. 1948.

88. KOHLRAUSCH, K. W. F., *Raman Spectra*. 1950.

89. BELLAMY, L., *The Infrared Spectra of Complex Molecules*. London, Methuen. 1959.

90. YOST, D. M., D. DeVAULT, T. F. ANDERSON, and E. N. LASSETTRE, *J. Chem. Phys.*, **2**, 624. 1934.

91. GAGE, D. M. and E. F. BARKER, *J. Chem. Phys.*, **7**, 455. 1939.

92. EL'YASHEVICH, M. A., *Doklady AN SSSR*, **28**, 605, 1940; *ZhFKh*, **14**, 1381. 1940; **15**, 847. 1941; *ZhETF*, **13**, 65. 1943.

93. EL'YASHEVICH, M. A. and B. I. STEPANOV, *Doklady AN SSSR*, **32**, 48. 1941; *ZhFKh*, **17**, 145. 1943.

94. STEPANOV, B. I., *ZhFKh*, **15**, 865. 1941.

95. STEPANOV, B. I., *Izvestiya AN SSSR*, phys. ser., **11**, 357. 1947.

96. WILSON, E., *J. Chem. Phys.*, **7**, 1047. 1939; **9**, 76. 1941.

97. WILSON, E. and B. I. CRAWFORD, *J. Chem. Phys.*, **9**, 329. 1941.

98. CRAWFORD, B. and S. BRINKLEY, *J. Chem. Phys.*, **9**, 69. 1941.

99. PODLOVCHENKO, R. I. and M. M. SUSHCHINSKII, *Optika i Spektroskopiya*, **2**, 49. 1957; *Materialy X vsesoyuznogo soveshchaniya po spektroskopii*, No. 3 (8), p. 99, Izdatel'stvo L'vovskogo Universiteta. 1957.

100. SUSHCHINSKII, M. M., *Trudy FIAN*, **12**, 54. 1960.

101. MAYANTS, L. A., *Teoriya i raschet kolebanii molekul (Theory and Calculation of Molecular Vibration)*. Izdatel'stvo AN SSSR. 1960.

102. GANTMAKHER, F. R., *Teoriya matrits (Matrix Theory)*. Gostekhizdat. 1953.

103. *Tables of Interatomic Distances and Configurations in Molecules and Ions*, Supplement 1956–1959. Spec. publ., No. 18.

104. REDLICH, O., *Z. Phys. Chem.*, **B28**, 371. 1935.

105. SVERDLOV, L. M., *Doklady AN SSSR*, **78**, 1115. 1951.

106. BECKETT, C. W., K. S. PITZER, and R. SPITZER, *J. Amer. Chem. Soc.*, **69**, 2488. 1947.

107. ROSENTHAL, J. E. and G. M. MURPHY, *Rev. Mod. Phys.*, **8**, 317. 1936.

108. DUCULOT, C., *Acad. roy. Belgique, Classe des sciences, memoires*, **30**, No. 4, 1. 1957.

109. TISZA, L., *Z. Phys.*, **82**, 48. 1933.

110. KOMPANEETS, A. S., *ZhETF*, **10**, 1175. 1940.

111. VOL'KENSHTEIN, M. V., *Doklady AN SSSR*, **30**, 784. 1941; *ZhETF*, **11**, 642. 1941.

112. VOL'KENSHTEIN, M. V. and M. A. EL'YASHEVICH, *J. Phys.*, **9**, 101. 1944; *ZhETF*, **15**, 124. 1946.

113. KOVNER, M. A. and B. N. SNEGIREV, *Optika i Spektroskopiya*, **5**, 239. 1958; **9**, 170. 1960; **8**, 880. 1960.

114. SNEGIREV, B. N., *Optika i Spektroskopiya*, **15**, 816. 1963.

115. SVERDLOV, L. M., *Optika i Spektroskopiya*, **11**, 774. 1961.

116. PROKOF'EVA, N. I. and L. M. SVERDLOV, *Optika i Spektroskopiya*, **13**, 324. 1962; **15**, 315. 1963.

117. BORISOV, M. G., P. A. BAZHULIN and L. M. SVERDLOV, In: *Optika i Spektroskopiya, Collection No. 2, Molecular Spectroscopy*, p. 308, Izdatel'stvo AN SSSR. 1963.

118. PROKOF'EVA, N. I., L. M. SVERDLOV, and M. M. SUSHCHINSKII, *Optika i Spektroskopiya*, **15**, 464. 1963; **17**, 374. 1964.

119. FERIGLE, S. M. and A. WEBER, *Canadian J. Phys.*, **32**, 799. 1954.

120. VOL'KENSHTEIN, M. V., *ZhETF*, **18**, 138. 1948.

121. LANDSBERG, G. S., P. A. BAZHULIN, and M. M. SUSHCHINSKII, *Osnovnye parametry spektrov kombinatsionnogo rasseyaniya uglevodorodov (Principal Parameters of Raman Spectra of Hydrocarbons)*. Izdatel'stvo AN SSSR. 1956.

122. REITZ, A. W., *Z. Phys. Chem.*, **B33**, 179, 368. 1936; **B38**, 275, 381. 1937.

123. MAYANTS, L. S., *Trudy FIAN*, **5**, 63. 1950.

124. SUSHCHINSKII, M. M., *Izvestiya AN SSSR*, phys. ser., **17**, 608. 1953.

125. JONES, R. N. and C. SANDORFY, *Use of Infrared and Raman Spectra to Study Molecular Structure*. In: WEST, W., ed. *Chemical Applications of Spectroscopy*. New York, Interscience. 2nd ed. 1968.

126. EL'YASHEVICH, M. A., *Dissertation*, FIAN. 1944.

127. STEPANOV, B. I., *ZhFKh*, **14**, 474. 1940; **15**, 78. 1941.

128. SHULL, E. R., OAKWOOD, T. S., and D. H. RANK, *J. Chem. Phys.*, **21**, 2024. 1954.

129. FENSKE, M. R., W. G. BRAUN, R. WIEGAND, DOROTHY QUIGGLE, R. H. MCCORMICK, and D. H. RANK, *Anal. Chem.*, **19**, 700. 1947; BRAUN, W. G., D. F. SPOONER, and M. R. FENSKE, *Anal. Chem.*, **22**, 1074. 1950.

130. KUZNETSOVA, T. I. and M. M. SUSHCHINSKII, *Optika i Spektroskopiya*, **10**, 41. 1961.

131. EVANS, J. C. AND H. J. BERNSTEIN, *Canadian J. Chem.*, **34**, 1037. 1956.

132. TRESHCHOVA, E. G., V. M. TATEVSKII, T. I. TANTSYREVA, A. A. FAINZIL'BERG, and R. YA. LEVINA, *ZhFKh*, **25**, 1239. 1951.

133. PODLOVCHENKO, R. I., L. M. SVERDLOV, and M. M. SUSHCHINSKII, *Optika i Spektroskopiya*, **6**, 146. 1959.

134. ZELINSKII, N. D., *Izbrannye trudy (Selected Works)*, Vol. 2, Izdatel'stvo AN SSSR. 1941.

135. PLATE, A. F., *Kataliticheskaya aromatizatsiya parafinovykh uglevodorodov (Catalytic Aromatization of Paraffin Hydrocarbons)*, Izdatel'stvo AN SSSR. 1948.

136. SVERDLOV, L. M. and N. I. PROKOF'EVA, *Optika i Spektroskopiya*, **7**, 588. 1959; **13**, 324. 1962.

137. KUZNETSOVA, T. I. and M. M. SUSHCHINSKII, In: *Optika i Spektroskopiya*, Collection No. 2, *Molecular Spectroscopy*, p. 144, Izdatel'stvo AN SSSR. 1963.

138. ZHIZHIN, G. N., KH. E. STERIN, V. T. ALEKSANYAN, and A. L. LIBERMAN, *Zhurnal Strukturnoi Khimii*, **6**, 684. 1965.

139. ZHIZHIN, G. N., *Dissertation*, FIAN. 1965.

140. RATHJENS, G. W., N. K. FREEMAN, W. G. GWINN, and K. S. PITZER, *J. Amer. Chem. Soc.*, **75**, 5634. 1953.

141. GODCHOT, M., *C.R.*, **194**, 1547. 1937.

142. ALEKSANYAN, V. T., KH. E. STERIN, M. YU. LUKINA, L. G. SAL'NIKOVA, I. L. SAFONOVA, and B. A. KAZANSKII, *Uchenye Zapiski L'vovskogo Universiteta*, **3 (8)**, 64. 1957; *Optika i Spektroskopiya*, **7**, 178. 1959.

143. SHEPPARD, N. and D. M. SIMPSON, *Quart. Rev.*, **6**, 1, 1952.

144. GOUBEAU, J., *Die Raman-Spektren von Olefinen*, In: *Angew. Chemie*, Beiheft No. 56. 1948.

145. REA, D. G., *Analyt. Chem.*, **32**, 1638. 1960.

146. STEPANOV, B. I., *ZhFKh*, **15**, 78. 1941.

147. GRUZDEV, P. F., *ZhFKh*, **28**, 507. 1954.

148. SVERDLOV, L. M. and O. N. VINOKHODOV, *Doklady AN SSSR*, **100**, 45. 1955.

149. SVERDLOV, L. M. and N. M. PAKHOMOVA, *Doklady AN SSSR*, **91**, 51. 1953; *ZhETF*, **26**, 64. 1954.

150. SVERDLOV, L. M., *Optika i Spektroskopiya*, **1**, 752. 1956.
151. SVERDLOV, L. M., *Doklady AN SSSR*, **106**, 80. 1956.
152. SVERDLOV, L. M., *Uchenye Zapiski L'vovskogo Universiteta*, **3(8)**, 278. 1957.
153. SVERDLOV, L. M., *Doklady AN SSSR*, **112**, 706. 1957.
154. KAZANSKII, B. A., M. YU. LUKINA, A. I. MALYSHEV, V. T. ALEKSANYAN, and KH. E. STERIN, *Izvestiya AN SSSR*, chem. sci., No. 1, 36. 1956.
155. BAZHULIN, P. A. and KH. E. STERIN, *Izvestiya AN SSSR*, phys. ser., **11**, 456. 1947.
156. TRESHCHOVA, E. G., P. A. AKISHIN, and V. M. TATEVSKII, *Zhurnal Analiticheskoi Khimii*, **3**, 75. 1948; AKISHIN, P. A. and V. M. TATEVSKII, *Doklady AN SSSR*, **76**, 527. 1951.
157. SHORYGIN, P. P., *Izvestiya AN SSSR*, phys. ser., **12**, 576. 1948.
158. MARKOVA, S. V., P. A. BAZHULIN, and M. M. SUSHCHINSKII, *Optika i Spektroskopiya*, **1**, 41. 1956.
159. OTTING, W., *Der Ramaneffekt und seine analytische Anwendung*. Berlin. 1952.
160. MALYSHEV, V. I., *UFN*, **63**, 323. 1957.
161. BATUEV, M. I., V. A. PONOMARENKO, A. D. MATVEEVA, and A. D. PETROV, *Doklady AN SSSR*, **95**, 805. 1954; *Izvestiya AN SSSR*, chem. sci., No. 9, 1070; No. 10, 1243. 1956.
162. ARBUZOV, A. E., M. I. BATUEV, and V. S. VINOGRADOVA, *Doklady AN SSSR*, **54**, 603. 1946.
163. POPOV, E. M., M. I. KABACHNIK, and L. S. MAYANTS, *Uspekhi Khimii*, **30**, 846. 1961.
164. MIZUSHIMA, S. I., *Raman Effect*. In: *Handbuch der Physik*, **26**, Berlin. 1958.
165. *Catalog of selected Raman Spectral Data* (Project 44). Nat. Bureau of Standards, Washington. 1949.
166. AKISHIN, P. A. and V. M. TATEVSKII, *Doklady AN SSSR*, **89**, 287. 1953.
167. PIAUX, L. and M. GAUDEMAR, *Bull. Soc. chim. France*, **6**, 786. 1957.
168. KOVALEV, I. F., *Optika i Spektroskopiya*, **8**, 315. 1960.
169. LANDSBERG, G. S., B. A. KAZANSKII, P. A. BAZHULIN, T. F. BULANOVA, A. L. LIBERMAN, E. A. MIKHAILOVA, A. F. PLATE, KH. E. STERIN, M. M. SUSHCHINSKII, G. A. TARASOVA, and S. A. UKHOLIN, *Opredelenie individual'nogo uglevodorodnogo sostava benzinov pyramoi gonki kombinirovannym metodom (Determination of the Individual Hydrocarbon Composition of Direct Distillation Benzines by a Combined Method)*. Izdatel'stvo AN SSSR. 1959.
170. HORROCKS, W. D. and E. A. COTTON, *Spectrochim. Acta*, **17**, 134. 1961.
171. SHORYGIN, P. P., *Dissertation*. Fiziko-Khimicheskii Institut im L. Ya. Karpova. 1949.
172. TATEVSKII, V. M., E. G. TRESHCHOVA, V. R. SKVARCHENKO, and R. YA. LEVINA, *ZhFKh*, **23**, 657. 1949; TRESHCHOVA, E. G., V. M. TATEVSKII, R. YA. LEVINA, A. A. FAINZIL'BERG, and E. A. VIKTOROVA, *ZhFKh*, **26**, 1266. 1952.
173. SHORYGIN, P. P., *Izvestiya AN SSSR*, phys. ser., **12**, 576. 1948.
174. KHALILOV, A. KH. and P. P. SHORYGIN, *Doklady AN SSSR*, **78**, 27, 1177. 1951.
175. HARRAND, M. and H. MARTIN, *Bull. Soc. chim. France*, **10**, 1383. 1956.
176. FINKEL'SHTEIN, A. I., *Dissertation*. Fiziko-Khimicheskii Institut im. L. Ya. Karpova. 1950.
177. SUSHCHINSKII, M. M. and V. I. TYULIN, *Doklady AN SSSR*, **35**, 505. 1954.
178. ZUBOV, V. A., *Thesis*. MGU. 1955.
179. YAKOVLEV, T. V., *Thesis*. Institut Vysokomolekulyarnykh Soedinenii AN SSSR. 1953.
180. BOBOVICH, YA. S. and V. V. PEREKALIN, *Zhurnal Strukturnoi Khimii*, **1**, 313. 1960.

181. BOBOVICH, YA. S. and YA. A. EIDUS, *Optika i Spektroskopiya*, **16**, 424. 1964.
182. BOBOVICH, YA. S., E. S. LIPINA, and V. V. PEREKALIN, *Zhurnal Strukturnoi Khimii*, **5**, 546. 1964.
183. EIDUS, YA. A., *Dissertation*. Gosudarstvennyi Pedagogicheskii Institut im. V. I. Lenina, Moscow. 1965.
184. BOBOVICH, YA. S., *Optika i Spektroskopiya*, **19**, 279, 886. 1965; 20, 252. 1966.
185. HAMMETT, L. P., *Physical Organic Chemistry*, London. 1940.
186. JAFFE, H. H., *Chem. Rev.*, **53**, 191. 1953.
187. PETROV, A. D., YU. P. EGOROV, V. F. MIRONOV, G. I. NIKISHIN, and A. A. BUGORKOVA, *Izvestiya AN SSSR*, chem. sci., No. 1, 50. 1956.
188. PETROV, A. A., V. A. KOLESOVA, and YU. I. PORFIR'EVA, *ZhOKh*, **27**, 2081. 1957.
189. EGOROV, YU. P. and E. A. CHERNYSHEV, *Trudy L'vovskogo Universiteta*, **3(8)**, 390. 1957.
190. SHORYGIN, P. P. and Z. S. EGOROVA, *Doklady AN SSSR*, **118**, 763. 1958.
191. MIRONOV, V. F., YU. P. EGOROV, and A. D. PETROV, *Izvestiya AN SSSR*, chem. sci., **8**, 1400. 1959.
192. YÜ WAO-SHAN, V. N. NIKITIN, and M. V. VOL'KENSHTEIN, *ZhFKh*, **36**, 681. 1962.
193. JESSON, J. P. and H. W. THOMPSON, *Proc. Roy. Soc. (London)*, **A268**, 68. 1962.
194. FACER, G. H. and H. W. THOMPSON, *Proc. Roy. Soc. (London)*, **A268**, 79. 1962.
195. BOBOVICH, YA. S. and N. M. BELYAEVSKAYA, *Optika i Spektroskopiya*, **19**, 198. 1965; BOBOVICH, YA. S., *Optika i Spektroskopiya*, **20**, 68. 1966.
196. KOHLRAUSCH, K. W. F., *Z. phys. Chem.*, **B18**, 61. 1932.
197. VOL'KENSHTEIN, M. V., *Konfiguratsionnaya statistika polimernykh tsepei (Conformation Statistics of Polymer Chains)*, IZDATEL'STVO AN SSSR. 1959.
198. BIRSHTEIN, T. M. and O. B. PTITSYN, *Konformatsii makromolekul (Conformations of Macromolecules)*. "Nauka". 1964.
199. EDGELL, W. D. and G. J. GLOCKLER, *J. Chem. Phys.*, **9**, 375. 1941.
200. MIZUSHIMA, S., Y. MORINO, and M. TAKEDA, *J. Chem. Phys.*, **9**, 826. 1941.
201. MIZUSHIMA, S., *Structure of Molecules and Internal Rotation*. New York. Academic Press. 1954.
202. SHEPPARD, N., *Uspekhi Spektroskopii*, **1**, 354. 1963.
203. SOSINSKII, M. L., *Dissertation*, MFTI. 1956.
204. SHEPPARD, N. and G. J. SZASZ, *J. Chem. Phys.*, **17**, 86. 1949.
205. PODLOVCHENKO, R. I. and M. M. SUSHCHINSKII, *Optika i Spektroskopiya*, **2**, 49. 1957.
206. PODLOVCHENKO, R. I., L. M. SVERDLOV, and M. M. SUSHCHINSKII, *Optika i Spektroskopiya*, **6**, 146. 1959.
207. HARRIS, G. M. and F. E. HARRIS, *J. Chem. Phys.*, **31**, 1450. 1959.
208. KARPLUS, M., *J. Chem. Phys.*, **33**, 316. 1960.
209. CLINTON, W. L., *J. Chem. Phys.*, **33**, 632. 1960.
210. LASSETRE, E. and L. DEAN, *J. Chem. Phys.*, **17**, 317. 1949.
211. OOSTERHOFF, L. J., *Disc. Faraday Soc.*, **10**, 79. 1951.
212. AU CHIN-TANG, *J. Chin. Chem. Soc.*, **18**, 2. 1951.
213. MASON, E. A. and M. M. KREEVOY, *J. Amer. Chem. Soc.*, **77**, 5808. 1955.
214. BORISOV, N. P. and M. V. VOL'KENSHTEIN, *Zhurnal Strukturnoi Khimii*, **2**, 469. 1961.
215. VAN DRANEN, J., *J. Chem. Phys.*, **20**, 1982. 1952.
216. ASTON, J. G., S. ISSEROW, G. J. SZASZ, and R. M. KENNEDY, *J. Chem. Phys.*, **12**, 336. 1944.

217. MAGNASCO, V., *Nuovo cimento*, **24**, 425. 1962.
218. PENTIN, YU. A. and V. M. TATEVSKII, *Vestnik MGU*, No. 3, 631. 1955.
219. BERNSTEIN, H. J., *J. Chem. Phys.*, **17**, 262. 1949.
220. ZIRNIT, U. A., *Trudy FIAN*, **39**, 55. 1967.
221. ZIRNIT, U. A. and M. M. SUSHCHINSKII, *Optika i Spektroskopiya*, **15**, 190. 1963.
222. VOL'KENSHTEIN, M. V., *Uspekhi Khimii*, **13**, 234. 1944.
223. GODNEV, I. N., *Vychislenie termodinamicheskikh funktsii po molekulyarnym dannym (Calculation of Thermodynamic Functions from Molecular Data)*. GOSTEKHIZDAT. 1956.
224. FATELEY, W. G. and F. A. MILLER, *Spectrochim. Acta*, **19**, 611. 1963.
225. HERSCHBACH, D. R., *J. Chem. Phys.*, **31**, 91. 1952.
226. CRAWFORD, B. L., *J. Chem. Phys.*, **8**, 273. 1940.
227. ZIRNIT, U. A. and M. M. SUSHCHINSKII, *Optika i Spektroskopiya*, **16**, 902. 1964.
228. FATELEY, W. G. and F. A. MILLER, *Spectrochim. Acta*, **18**, 977. 1962.
229. ZIRNIT, U. A. and M. M. SUSHCHINSKII, In: *Optika i Spektroskopiya*, Collection No. 2, *Molecular Spectroscopy*, p. 153. Izdatel'stvo AN SSSR. 1963.
230. SCOTT, O. W. and G. WADDINGTON, *J. Amer. Chem. Soc.*, **75**, 2006. 1963.
231. KILPATRICK, J. E. and K. S. PITZER, *J. Amer. Chem. Soc.*, **68**, 1066. 1956.
232. MAGNASCO, V., *Nuovo cimento*, **24**, 425. 1962.
233. LANDSBERG, G. S. and V. I. MALYSHEV, *Doklady AN SSSR*, **3**, 365. 1936.
234. ANANTHAKRISHNAN, R., *Proc. Indian Acad. Sci.*, **2**, 452. 1935.
235. WELSH, H. L., M. F. CRAWFORD, and G. D. SCOTT, *J. Chem. Phys.*, **16**, 97. 1948.
236. MOSZYNSKA, B., *Bull. Acad. polon. sci.*, **7**, 455. 1959.
237. VENKATESWARLU, K. and G. THYAGARAJAN, *Z. Phys.*, **156**, 569. 1959.
238. BOGDANOV, V. D. and M. M. SUSHCHINSKII, *Izv. AN SSSR*, phys. ser., **22**, 1067. 1958.
239. NABERUKHIN, YU. I and M. M. SUSHCHINSKII, *Optika i Spektroskopiya*, **9**, 576. 1960.
240. MULDAKHMETOV, Z. M. and M. M. SUSHCHINSKII, *Optika i Spektroskopiya*, **2**, 320. 1963.
241. MULDAKHMETOV, Z. M. and M. M. SUSHCHINSKII, *Optika i Spektroskopiya*, **14**, 819. 1963.
242. SUSHCHINSKII, M. M. and Z. M. MULDAKHMETOV, *Optika i Spektroskopiya*, **16**, 234. 1964; **17**, 45. 1964.
243. MULDAKHMETOV, Z. M., *Trudy FIAN*, **39**, 7. 1967.
244. HEMPTINNE, M. de and C. MANNENBACK, *Proc. Indian Acad. Sci.*, **9**, 286. 1939.
245. JONES, L. H. and U. GOLDBLATT, *J. Mol. Spectr.*, **2**, 103. 1958.
246. JONES, L. H. and R. S. MCDOWELL, *J. Mol. Spectr.*, **3**, 632. 1959.
247. MILLS, I. M., *Spectrochim. Acta*, **16**, 35. 1960.
248. SADULLAEV, B. L. and M. M. SUSHCHINSKII, *Optika i Spektroskopiya*, **23**, 46. 1967.
249. VOL'KENSHTEIN, M. V., *UFN*, **29**, 54. 1946.
250. FERMI, E., *Z. Phys.*, **71**, 250. 1931.
251. DENNISON, D. M., *Rev. Mod. Phys.*, **12**, 175. 1940.
252. LANGSETH, A. and J. R. NIELSEN, *Phys. Rev.*, **46**, 1057. 1934.
253. ALIEV, M. R. and V. T. ALEKSANYAN, *Doklady AN SSSR*, **169**, 1329. 1966.
254. FELDMAN, T., G. G. SHEPHERD, and H. L. WELSH, *Canad. J. Phys.*, **34**, 1425. 1956; FELDMAN, T., J. ROMANKO, and H. L. WELSH, *Canad. J. Phys.*, **33**, 138. 1955.
255. ALLEN, H. C. AND P. C. CROSS, *Molecular Vib-Rotors*. New York–London. 1963.
256. STERIN, KH. E., *Trudy FIAN*, **9**, 13. 1958; *Izvestiya AN SSSR*, phys. ser. **11**, 345. 1947; **14**, 411. 1950; *Doklady AN SSSR*, **62**, 219. 1948.

257. KOVNER, M. A. and A. V. CHAPLIK, *Optika i Spektroskopiya*, **13**, 56. 1962.
258. SOBEL'MAN, I. I., *Vvedenie v teoriyu atomnykh spektrov (Introduction to the Theory of Atomic Spectra)*. Fizmatgiz. 1963; *Shirina spektral'nykh linii (Width of Spectral Lines)*, In: *Fizicheskii entsiklopedicheskii slovar'*, Vol. 5. 1966.
259. VOL'KENSHTEIN, M. V., *Stroenie i fizicheskie svoistva molekul (Structure and Physical Properties of Molecules)*, Izdatel'stvo AN SSSR. 1955.
260. SHORYGIN, P. P., *Zhurnal Fizicheskoi Khimii*, **23**, 873. 1949.
261. SECHKAREV, A. V. and N. I. DVOROVENKO, *Izvestiya Vuzov*, physics, No. 1, 13. 1965; No. 1, 5. 1965.
262. SECHKAREV, A. V., E. G. BRUTAN, and N. I. DVOROVENKO, *Trudy Komissii po Spektroskopii AN SSSR*, **1**, 293. 1964.
263. SECHKAREV, A. V., *Optika i Spektroskopiya*, **19**, 721. 1965.
264. SECHKAREV, A. V., *Doctorate thesis*. Kemerovskii Gornyi Institut. 1965; *Thesis*. Sibirskoe Otdelenie AN SSSR, Novosibirsk. 1965.
265. MAY, A. D., J. C. STRYLAND, and H. L. WELSH, *J. Chem. Phys.*, **30**, 1099. 1959.
266. NEPORENT, B. S. and N. G. BAKHSHIEV, *Optika i Spektroskopiya*, **5**, 634. 1957; **8**, 777. 1960.
267. GIRIN, O. P. and N. G. BAKHSHIEV, *UFN*, **79**, 235. 1963.
268. VOL'KENSHTEIN, M. V., *UFN*, **18**, 153. 1937.
269. FRANKEL, J. *Kinetic Theory of Liquids*. New York, Dover Publications Inc. 1955. [English translation.]
270. VOL'KENSHTEIN, M. V., *Mezhmolekulyarnoe vzaimodeistvie (Molecular Interaction)*. In: *Fizicheskii entsiklopedicheskii slovar'*, Vol. 3. 1963.
271. HIRSCHFELDER, T. O., C. F. CURTIS, and R. B. BIRD, *Molecular Theory of Gases and Liquids*. N.Y., Wiley. 1954.
272. KIRKWOOD, J., *J. Chem. Phys.*, **4**, 592. 1936; **7**, 911. 1939; **8**, 205. 1940.
273. RAKOV, A. V., *Trudy FIAN*, **27**, 111. 1964.
274. REZAEV, N. I., *Materialy X vsesoyuznogo soveshchaniya po spektroskopii (Proceedings of the 10th All-Union Conference on Spectroscopy)*, Vol. 1, p. 230, Izdatel'stvo L'vovskogo Universiteta. 1957.
275. REZAEV, N. I., *Vestnik MGU*, No. 2, 145. 1957.
276. BAZHULIN, P. A. and A. I. SOKOLOVSKAYA, *Issledovaniya po eksperimental'noi i teoreticheskoi fizike (Studies in Experimental and Theoretical Physics)*. G. S. Landsberg Memorial Collection, p. 56, Izdatel'stvo AN SSSR. 1959.
277. REZAEV, N. I., *Optika i Spektroskopiya*, **5**, 12. 1958.
278. RAKOV, A. V., *Optika i Spektroskopiya*, **7**, 202. 1959.
279. SOBEL'MAN, I. I., *Izvestiya AN SSSR*, phys. ser., **17**, 554. 1953.
280. LANDAU, L. D. and E. M. LIFSHITS, *Statisticheskaya fizika (Statistical Physics)*. "Nauka". 1964.
281. VALIEV, K. A., *ZhETF*, **40**, 1832. 1961.
282. VALIEV, K. A., *Optika i Spektroskopiya*, **11**, 465. 1961.
283. VALIEV, K. A. and L. D. ESKIN, *Optika i Spektroskopiya*, **12**, 758. 1962.
284. VALIEV, K. A., *Optika i Spektroskopiya*, **13**, 505. 1962.
285. ZUBOV, N. V., N. V. SHALOMEEVA, V. S. GORELIK, and M. M. SUSHCHINSKII, *Preprint FIAN*, No. 188. 1968.

286. KONDILENKO, I. I., *Doctorate thesis*, Kiev University. 1964.
287. KONDILENKO, I. I. and I. L. BABICH, *Ukrains'kii Fizichnii Zhurnal*, **5**, 532. 1960.
288. BOBOVICH, YA. S. and V. M. PIVOVAROV, *Doklady AN SSSR*, **97**, 801. 1954.
289. SOKOLOVSKAYA, A. I. and P. A. BAZHULIN, *Izvestiya AN SSSR*, phys. ser., **22**, 1068. 1958.
290. SOKOLOVSKAYA, A. I. and P. A. BAZHULIN, *Optika i Spektroskopiya*, **8**, 394. 1960.
291. SOKOLOVSKAYA, A. I., *Optika i Spektroskopiya*, **9**, 582. 1960.
292. SOKOLOVSKAYA, A. I., *Trudy FIAN*, **27**, 63. 1964.
293. REA, D., *J. Opt. Soc. Amer.*, **49**, 50. 1959.
294. SUSHCHINSKII, M. M., *Doklady AN SSSR*, **33**, 21. 1941.
295. SUSHCHINSKII, M. M., *Trudy FIAN*, **5**, 185. 1950.
296. RANK, D. H., R. W. SCOTT, and M. R. FENSKE, *Ind. Eng. Chem., Anal. Ed.*, **14**, 816. 1942.
297. MICHEL, G., *Spectr. Acta*, **5**, 218. 1952; **12**, 400. 1958; *Bull. Soc. Chim. Belg.*, **72**, 125. 1963.
298. MICHEL, G. and R. GUEIBE, *Bull. Soc. Chim. Belg.*, **70**, 323. 1961.
299. MARINO, J., I. MIYAGEWA, A. WADA, and K. YOSHIDA, *J. Chem. Soc. Japan, Pure Chem. Sec.*, **75**, No. 10. 1954.
300. SYRKIN, YA. K., M. V. VOL'KENSHTEIN, and A. R. GANTMAKHER, *ZhFKh*, **14**, 1569. 1940.
301. BOROD'KO, YU. G. and YA. K. SYRKIN, *Optika i Spektroskopiya*, **9**, 677. 1960; *Doklady AN SSSR*, **131**, 868. 1960.
302. REA, D., *J. Molecular Spectr.*, **4**, 507. 1960.
303. PIVOVAROV, V. M. and YA. S. BOBOVICH, *Optika i Spektroskopiya*, **3**, 134. 1957.
304. BOBOVICH, YA. S. and T. P. TULUB, *ZhETF*, **30**, 189. 1956.
305. PIVOVAROV, V. M. and L. D. KISLOVSKII, *Optika i Spektroskopiya*, **5**, 251. 1958.
306. MIERZECKI, R., *Acta phys. polonica*, **19**, No. 1. 1960.
307. EVANS, J. C. and H. J. BERNSTEIN, *Canad. J. Chem.*, **34**, 1127. 1958.
308. BABICH, I. L., I. I. KONDILENKO and V. L. STRIZHEVSKII, *Ukrains'kii Fizicheskii Zhurnal*, **7**, 742. 1962.
309. SOKOLOV, N. D., *UFN*, **57**, 205. 1955.
310. BRIEGLEB, G., *Zwischenmolekulare Kräfte und Molekülstruktur*. Berlin. 1937.
311. LANDSBERG, G. S. and S. A. UKHOLIN, *Doklady AN SSSR*, **16**, 399. 1937.
312. UKHOLIN, S. A., *Doklady AN SSSR*, **16**, 403, 1937.
313. LANDSBERG, G. S. and V. I. MALYSHEV, *Doklady AN SSSR*, **18**, 549. 1938.
314. MALYSHEV, V. I., *Doklady AN SSSR*, **20**, 549. 1938; **24**, 676. 1939.
315. MALYSHEV, V. I., *Izvestiya AN SSSR*, phys. ser., **5**, 13. 1941.
316. LANDSBERG, G. S., V. I. MALYSHEV, and V. E. SOLOV'EV, *Doklady AN SSSR*, **24**, 873. 1939.
317. MALYSHEV, V. I. and M. V. SHISHKINA, *ZhETF*, **20**, 297. 1950.
318. SHUBIN, A. A., *Izvestiya AN SSSR*, phys. ser., **9**, 198. 1945; *Trudy FIAN*, **9**, 125. 1958.
319. PIMENTEL, G. C. and A. L. MCCLELLAN, *The Hydrogen Bond*. San Francisco–London, Freeman. 1960.
320. PROSS, A. W. and F. VAN ZEGGEREN, *Spectrochim. Acta*, **16**, 563. 1960.
321. HALFORD, J. O., *J. Chem. Phys.*, **14**, 395. 1946.
322. ZIRNIT, U. A. and M. M. SUSHCHINSKII, *Optika i Spektroskopiya*, **16**, 903. 1964.
323. STANEVICH, A. E., In: *Optika i Spektroskopiya*, Collection No. 2, *Molecular Spectroscopy*, p. 205. 1963.

324. MIYAZAWA, T. and K. S. PITZER, *J. Amer. Chem. Soc.*, **81**, 74. 1959.
325. KRISHNAMURTI, P., *Indian J. Phys.*, **6**, 401. 1931.
326. BAYARD, P., *Bull. Soc. Roy. Sci. Liege*, No. 12, 179. 1943.
327. CHIORBOLY, P., *Ann. chim.*, **47**, 443. 1957.
328. PLATTEM, S., S. VALLADAS-DUBOIS, and H. VOLKINGER, *C.R.*, **228**, 182. 1949.
329. KASTHA, G., *Indian J. Phys.*, **30**, 519. 1956.
330. GLATZER, G. and G. MELCHER, *Internat. Tag. Europ. Molekülspektroskopiker,* Bologna. 1953.
331. REZAEV, N. I. and A. N. VASIL'EVA, *Vestnik MGU*, ser. III, **21**, 15. 1960.
332. MIERZECKI, R., *Acta phys. polonica*, **19**, 41. 1960.
333. MIERZECKI, R., *Current Sci.*, **25**, 200. 1956.
334. MIERZECKI, R., *Bull. Acad. Polon. Sci.*, Cl. III, **3**, 259, 263. 1955.
335. LAKSHMANAN, B. R., *J. Indian Inst. Sci.* **A36**, 218. 1954.
336. SCHWAB, G. M. and G. GLATZER, *Z. Elektrochem.*, **61**, 1028. 1957.
337. BATUEV, M. I., *Doklady AN SSSR*, **53**, 507. 1946.
338. SIMOVA, P., *Izvest. Bulgar. Akad. Nauk*, phys. math. tech. sci., phys. ser., **2**, 107. 1951.
339. IZMAILOV, N. A. and L. M. KUTSINA, *Izvestiya AN SSSR*, phys. ser., **17**, 740. 1953.
340. MATHIEU, J. P., *Spectres de vibration et symétrie des molécules et des cristaux.* Paris, 1945.
341. KITTEL, C., *Introduction to Solid State Physics.* New York, J. Wiley. 2nd ed. 1959.
342. ZIMAN, J., *Principles of the Theory of Solids.* Cambridge Univ. Press. 1964.
343. SHUBNIKOV, A., *Opticheskaya kristallografiya (Optical Crystallography)*, Izdatel'stvo AN SSSR. 1950.
344. BELOV, N. V., *Strukturnaya kristallografiya (Structural Crystallography).* Izdatel'stvo AN SSSR. 1950.
345. BORN, M. and HUANG, KUN, *Dynamical Theory of Crystal Lattices.* Oxford Univ. Press. 1954.
346. KOVALEV, O. V., *Nepivodimye predstavleniya prostranstvennykh grupp (Irreducible Representations of Space Groups).* Kiev, Izdatel'stvo AN UkrSSR. 1961.
347. FADEEV, D. K., *Tablitsy osnovnykh unitarnykh predstavlenii fedorovskikh grupp (Tables of the Main Unitary Representations of Fedorov Groups).* Izdatel'stvo AN SSSR. 1961.
348. LOMONT, J. S., *Application of Finite Groups.* New York. 1959.
349. BORN, M. and T. KARMAN, *Phys. Z.*, **13**, 297. 1912.
350. BORN, M. and M. GOEPPERT-MAYER, *Theory of the Solid State.* 1937.
351. MARADUDIN, A., E. W. MONTROLL, and J. WEISS, *Theory of Lattice Dynamics in the Harmonic Approximation.* In: *Progress in Solid State Physics*, 1965.
352. BHAGAVANTAM, S., *Proc. Indian Acad. Sci.*, **A37**, 350. 1953.
353. LAST, J. T., *Phys. Rev.*, **105**, 1740. 1957.
354. POULET, H., *J. Phys.*, **26**, 684. 1965.
355. GORELIK, V. S., *Kristallografiya*, **13**, 696. 1968; GORELIK, V. S. and M. M. SUSHCHINSKII, *UFN*, **96**, No. 2. 1969.
356. HAMERMESH, M., *Group Theory and Its Application to Physical Problems.* Reading, Mass. Addison-Wesley Press. 1962.
357. RAMAN, C. V., *Proc. Indian Acad. Sci.*, **A14**, 459. 1941; **A18**, 237. 1943; **A26**, 339, 356, 370, 383, 391, 396. 1947; **A34**, 61, 141. 1951; **A44**, 99. 1956.
358. KRISHNAN, R. S. and R. S. KATIYAR, *J. Phys.*, **26**, 630. 1965.

359. KRISHNAN, R. S. and N. KRISHNAMURTY, *J. Phys.*, **26**, 633. 1965.

360. RAMANATHAN, K. G., *Proc. Indian Acad. Sci.*, **A28**, 454. 1948.

361. KRISHNAN, R. S. and N. KRISHNAMURTY, *J. Phys.*, **26**, 600. 1965.

362. COCHRAN, W. and R. A. COWLEY, *J. Phys. and Chem. Solids*, **23**, 447. 1962.

363. MERTEN, L., *Z. Naturforsch*, **A15**, 47. 1960.

364. LOUDON, R., *Proc. Phys. Soc. (London)*, **82**, 393. 1963.

365. POULET, H., *Ann. phys.*, **10**, 908. 1955.

366. TAMM, I. E., *Z. phys.*, **60**, 345. 1930.

367. OVANDER, L. N., *UFN*, **86**, 3. 1965; *FTT*, **3**, 2394. 1961; *FTT*, **5**, 872. 1963.

368. BIRMAN, G. L. and A. K. GANGULY, *Phys. Rev. Lett.*, **17**, 647. 1966.

369. STRIZHEVSKII, V. L., *FTT*, **3**, 2932. 1961; **4**, 1492. 1962; **5**, 1511. 1963.

370. THEIMER, O and A. C. SAXMAN, *J. Phys.*, **26**, 697. 1955.

371. SOBEL'MAN, I. I., *Issledovaniya po eksperimental'noi i teoreticheskoi fizike (Studies in Experimental and Theoretical Physics)*. G. S. Landsberg Memorial Collection, p. 192. Izdatel'stvo AN SSSR. 1959.

372. LOUDON, R., *J. Phys.*, **26**, 677. 1965.

373. LOUDON, R., *Adv. Phys.*, **13**, 423. 1964.

374. SAKSENA, B. D., *Proc. Indian Acad. Sci.*, **A11**, 229. 1940; **A12**, 93. 1940.

375. CHANDRASEKHARAN, V., *Z. Phys.*, **175**, 63. 1963.

376. NARAYANAN, P. S. and K. VEDAM, *Z. Phys.*, **158**, 158. 1961.

377. PERRY, C. H. and D. B. HALL, *Phys. Rev. Lett.*, **15**, 700. 1965.

378. GORELIK, V. S., I. S. ZHELUDEV, and M. M. SUSHCHINSKII, *Kristallografiya,* **11**, 604, 1966.

379. LOUDON, R., *Proc. Phys. Soc.*, **84**, 379. 1964.

380. CABANNES, J., *C.R.*, **188**, 1041. 1929.

381. NISI, H., *Proc. Imp. Acad. Tokyo*, **5**, 127. 1929.

382. RASETTI, F., *Nature*, **127**, 626. 1931; *Nuovo cimento*, **9**, 72. 1932; KRISHNAN, R. S., *Proc. Indian Acad. Sci.*, **A22**, 182. 1945.

383. FLEURY, P. A. and G. M. WORLOCK, *Phys. Rev. Lett.*, **18**, 665. 1967.

384. KRISHNAMURTI, D., *Proc. Indian Acad. Sci.*, **A46**, 183. 1957.

385. STEKHANOV, A. I., *Optika i Spektroskopiya*, **3**, 143. 1958.

386. CHANDRASEKHARAN, V., *Proc. Indian Acad. Sci.*, **A28**, 409. 1948.

387. KRISHNAMURTI, D., *Proc. Indian Acad. Sci.*, **A47**, 276. 1958.

388. ZUBOV, V. G. and L. P. OSIPOVA, *Kristallografiya*, **6**, 418. 1961.

389. KISELEV, D. F. and L. P. OSIPOVA, *Kristallografiya*, **11**, 279, 401. 1966.

390. KISELEV, D. F., *Kristallografiya*, **11**, 886. 1966.

391. KRISHNAN, R. S., *Proc. Indian Acad. Sci.*, **A22**, 329. 1945; *Nature*, **155**, 452. 1945.

392. KLEINMAN, D. A. and W. G. SPITZER, *Phys. Rev.*, **121**, 1324. 1961; 125, 16. 1961.

393. NABERUKHIN, YU. I., *Optika i Spektroskopiya*, **13**, 498. 1962.

394. MENZIES, A. C., *Rep. Progr. Phys.*, **16**, 89. 1953.

395. MITRA, S. S., *Solid State Phys.*, **13**, 1. 1962.

396. GROSS, E. F. and M. F. VUKS, *Nature*, **135**, 100, 431. 1935; *J. phys. et radium*, **7**, 113. 1936.

397. GROSS, E. and E. KOMAROV, *Acta Physicochimica URSS*, **6**, 637. 1937; VUKS, M., *loc. cit.*, **6**, 11. 1937; GROSS, E. F. and A. I. RASKIN, *Izvestiya AN SSSR*, phys. ser., **4**, 29. 1940.

398. ANSEL'MAN, A. I. and N. N. PORFIR'EVA, *ZhETF*, **19**, 438. 1949.

399. PROFIR'EVA, N. N., *ZhETF*, **19**, 692. 1949; **22**, 590. 1952.

400. RASKIN, A. I., A. V. SECHKAREV, and F. I. SKRIPOV, *Doklady AN SSSR*, **66**, 837. 1949; SKRIPOV, F. I., *Doklady AN SSSR*, **66**, 1075. 1949.

401. GROSS, E. F. and A. I. RASKIN, *Doklady AN SSSR*, **24**, 125. 1939; RASKIN, A. I., *Izvestiya AN SSSR*, phys. ser., **11**, 367. 1947.

402. GROSS, E. F. and A. V. KORSHUNOV, *Izvestiya AN SSSR*, phys. ser., **4**, 32. 1940.

403. GROSS, E. F., A. V. KORSHUNOV, and V. A. SEL'KIN, *ZhETF*, **20**, 292. 1950; **22**, 579. 1952.

404. VUKS, M. F., *ZhETF*, **7**, 270. 1937; **16**, 410. 1946.

405. KORSHUNOV, A. V. and V. E. VOLKOV, *Fizicheskie problemy spektroskopii (Physical Problems of Spectroscopy)*, Vol. 1, p. 398, Izdatel'stvo AN SSSR. 1962.

406. PORFIR'EVA, N. N., *ZhETF*, **33**, 47. 1957.

407. BHAGAVANTAM, S., *Proc. Indian Acad. Sci.*, **13A**, 543. 1941.

408. SKRIPOV, F. I., *Dissertation*, LENINGRAD. 1952.

409. BOBOVICH, YA. S. and T. P. TULUB, *Optika i Spektroskopiya*, **6**, 566. 1959; **9**, 747. 1960; RAKHIMOV, A. A., *Dissertation*, FIAN, Moscow. 1966; STEKHANOV, A. I. and E. V. CHISLER, *FTT*, **3**, 3514. 1961.

410. SHUR, M. S., *FTT*, **9**, 57. 1966; **8**, 1290. 1966; **8**, 2504. 1966.

411. FRÜHLING, A., *Recherches sur le spectre Raman de quelques monocristaux aromatiques*. Thèses a la faculté des sciences de l'Université de Paris, Serie A, No. 2308. 1950.

412. BUZHULIN, P. A. and A. A. RAKHIMOV, *FTT*, **7**, 94. 1965.

413. KORSHUNOV, A. V., *Trudy Sibirskogo Lesotekhnicheskogo Instituta*, **18**, 27. 1958; KORSHUNOV, A. V. and A. F. BONDAREV, *Optika i Spektroskopiya*, **15**, 182. 1963; KORSHUNOV, A. V., A. F. BONDAREV, and E. K. TUSTANOVSKAYA, *Spektroskopiya, metody i primeneniya (Spectroscopy, Methods and Application)*. "Nauka". 1964.

414. BAZHULIN, P. A., A. V. RAKOV, and A. A. RAKHIMOV, *Optika i Spektroskopiya*, **16**, 1027. 1964; BAZHULIN, P. A. and A. A. RAKHIMOV, *FTT*, **7**, 2088. 1965.

415. BONDAREV, A. F., *Izvestiya Sibirskogo Otdeleniya AN SSSR*, chem. ser., **7**, 74. 1963.

416. IVANOV, E. N., K. A. VALIEV, and M. M. BIL'DANOV, In: *Optika i Spektroskopiya*, Collection No. 3, *Molecular Spectroscopy*, p. 319, "Nauka". 1967.

417. RAKHIMOV, A. A. and L. A. SHELEPIN, *Trudy 2-i konferentsii po zhidkomu sostoganiyu (Proceedings of the 2nd Conference on the Liquid State)*, p. 80, Samarkand. 1968.

418. DAVYDOV, A. S., *Teoriya pogloshcheniya sveta v molekulyarnykh kristallakh (Theory of Light Absorption in Molecular Crystals)*, Kiev, Izdatel'stvo AN UkrSSR. 1951; *UFN*, **82**, 393. 1964.

419. DOWS, D. A., *Phys. and Chem. Organ. Solid State*, **1**, 658. 1963.

420. FAILKOVSKAY, O. V., *Optika i Spektroskopiya*, **17**, 397. 1964.

421. ITO, M., *Spectrochim. Acta*, **21**, 2063. 1965.

422. LANDSBERG, G. S. and L. I. MANDEL'SHTAM, *Z. Phys.*, **58**, 250. 1929.

423. GINZBURG, V. L., *Doklady AN SSSR*, **105**, 240. 1935; *FTT*, **2**, 2031. 1960; *UFN*, **77**, 621. 1962. GINZBURG, V. L. and A. P. LEVANYUK, *ZhETF*, **39**, 132. 1960.

424. JONA, F. and G. SHIRANE, *Ferroelectric Crystals*. New York, Pergamon Press. 1961.

425. COCHRAN, W., *Adv. Phys.*, **9**, 387. 1960; **10**, 401. 1961.

426. YAKOVLEV, I. A. and T. S. VELICHKINA, *UFN*, **63**, 411. 1957.

427. BALLANTYNE, J. M., *Phys. Rev.*, **136**, A429. 1964.

428. MURZIN, V. N. and A. I. DEMESHINA, *Optika i Spektroskopiya*, **13**, 826. 1962; *FTT*, **6**, 182. 1964.

429. BAZHULIN, P. A. and I. M. AREF'EV, *FTT*, **7**, 409. 1965.
430. ARBATSKAYA, A. N., I. S. ZHELUDEV, U. A. ZIRNIT, and M. M. SUSHCHINSKII, *Kristallografiya*, **10**, 335. 1965.
431. KRISHNAN, R. S. and P. S. NARAYANAN, *Crystallography and Crystal Perfection.* London–New York. 1963.
432. CHISLER, E. V., *FTT*, **7**, 2258. 1965.
433. GORELIK, V. S., I. V. GAVRILOVA, I. S. ZHELUDEV, G. V. PEREGUDOV, V. S. RYAZANOV, and M. M. SUSHCHINSKII, *ZhETF Letters*, **5**, 214. 1967.
434. VAKS, V. G., V. M. GALITSKII, and A. I. LARKIN, *Preprint IAE*-1141. 1966.
435. HENRY, C. H. and J. J. HOPFIELD, *Phys. Rev. Lett.*, **15**, 964. 1965.
436. PORTO, S. P. S., B. TELL, and T. S. DAMEN, *Phys. Rev. Lett.*, **16**, 450. 1966.
437. COUTURE-MATHIEU, L. and J. P. MATHIEU, *C.R.*, **231**, 838. 1952; *J. Phys.* **13**, 271. 1952; WELL, A. and J. P. MATHIEU, *C.R.*, **238**, 2510. 1954.
438. TRAMER, A., *C.R.*, **249**, 2531. 1959.
439. CORRE, Y., *C.R.*, **257**, 3352. 1964.
440. COUTURE, L. and J. P. MATHIEU, *Ann. phys.*, **3**, 521. 1948; MATHIEU, J. P., *J. chim. phys.*, **46**, 58. 1949.
441. BORN, M. and M. BRADBURN, *Proc. Roy. Soc.*, **A188**, 161. 1947.
442. SMITH, H. M., *Phil. Trans.*, **A241**, 105. 1948.
443. VAN HOVE, L., *Phys. Rev.*, **89**, 1189. 1953.
444. LOUDON, R. and F. A. JOHNSON, *Proc. Roy. Soc.*, **A281**. 1964.
445. PHILIPS, J. C., *Phys. Rev.*, **104**, 1263. 1956.
446. FERMI, E. and F. RASETTI, *Z. Phys.*, **71**, 689. 1931.
447. KRISHNAN, R. S., *Proc. Indian Acad. Sci.*, **A18**, 298. 1943; *Proc. Roy. Soc.*, **A187**, 188. 1946; *Nature*, **159**, 266. 1947.
448. GROSS, E. and A. STEKHANOV, *Izvestiya AN SSSR*, phys. ser., **11**, 364. 1947.
449. GROSS, E. F., P. P. PAVINSKII, and A. I. STEKHANOV, *UFN*, **43**, 536. 1951.
450. WELSH, H. L., M. F. CRAWFORD, and W. J. STAPLE, *Nature*, **164**, 737. 1949.
451. STEKHANOV, A. I. and A. P. KOROL'KOV, *FTT*, **11**, 3156. 1962.
452. KRISHNAN, R. S. and N. KRISHNAMURTHY, *J. Phys.*, **26**, 630. 1965.
453. LAX, M. and J. J. HOPFIELD, *Phys. Rev.*, **124**, 115. 1961.
454. BIRMAN, J. L., *Phys. Rev.*, **127**, 1093. 1962; **131**, 1489. 1963.
455. LOUDON, R., *Phys. Rev.*, **A137**, 1784. 1965.
456. RUSSEL, J. P., *J. Phys.*, **26**, 620. 1965.
457. MENZIES, A. C., *Nature*, **124**, 511. 1929.
458. TABOURY, M. F., *J. Bull. Soc. Chem.*, **5**, 205. 1943.
459. LANDSBERG, G.S. and F.S. BARYSHANSKAYA, *Izv. AN SSSR*, phys. ser., **10**, 509. 1946.
460. GUBER, W. and K. H. RIGGERT, *Z. Naturforsch*, **6a**, 464. 1951.
461. BRANDMÜLLER, J., *Z. angew. Phys.*, **5**, 95. 1953.
462. SIMON, A., H. KRIEGSMANN, and E. STEGER, *Z. phys. Chem.*, **205**, 181. 1956.
463. LUTHER, H., D. MOOTZ, and F. RADWITZ, *J. prakt. Chem.*, **5**, 242. 1958.
464. BERGMANN, G. and G. THIMM, *Naturwissenschaften*, **45**, 359. 1958.
465. SCHRADER, B., F. NERDEL, and G. KRESZE, *Z. phys. Chem.*, **12**, 132. 1957.
466. SCHRADER, B., F. NERDEL, and G. KRESZE, *Z. analyt. Chem.*, **170**, 43. 1959.
467. BOBOVICH, YA. S. and V. M. PIVOVAROV, *ZhETF*, **29**, 696. 1955.

468. DANIL'TSEVA, G. E., V. A. ZUBOV, M. M. SUSHCHINSKII, and I. K., SHUVALOV, *ZhETF*, **44**, 2193. 1963.

469. L'VOVA, A. S., V. A. ZUBOV, M. M. SUSHINSKII, and V. A. CHIRKOV, *Optika i Spektroskopiya*, **23**, 168. 1967.

470. BRANDMÜLLER, J., H. HACKER, and H. W. SCHRÖTTER, *Chemische Berichte*, **99**, 765. 1966; BRANDMÜLLER, J., K. BURCHARDI, H. HACKER, and H. W. SCHRÖTTER, *Z. angew. Phys.*, **23**, 112. 1967; BRANDMÜLLER, J., *Naturwissenschaften*, **54**, 293. 1967.

471. MOSER, H. and D. STIELLER, *Z. angew. Phys.*, **12**, 280. 1960.

472. GERSHUN, A. A., *Trudy GOI*, **4**, 38. 1928.

473. IVANOV, A. P., *ZhETF*, **26**, 275. 1954.

474. SHUVALOV, I. K., *Thesis*, MFTI. 1962; DANIL'TSEVA, G. E., V. A. ZUBOV, M. M. SUSHCHINSKII, and I. K. SHUVALOV, *Trudy Komissii po Spektroskopii AN SSSR (Proceedings of the Committee on Spectroscopy of the Academy of Sciences of the USSR)*, **1**, 696. 1965.

475. SCHUSTER, A., *Astrophys. J.*, **21**, 1. 1905.

476. RYAZANOV, V. S. and M. M. SUSHCHINSKII, *Optika i Spektroskopiya*, **23**, 580. 1967.

477. RYAZANOV, V. S. and M. M. SUSHCHINSKII, *ZhETF*, **54**, 1099. 1968.

478. BRANDMÜLLER, J. and H. W. SCHRÖTTER, *Z. Phys.*, **149**, 131. 1957.

479. SCHRÖTTER, H. W. and H. J. BERNSTEIN, *J. Mol. Spectr.*, **7**, 464. 1961; **12**, 1. 1964.

480. KONDILENKO, I. I. and P. A. KOROTKOV, *Optika i Spektroskopiya*, **17**, 1051, 1057. 1964.

481. WOODBURY, E. J. and W. K. NG, *Proc. IRE*, **50**, 2367. 1962.

482. ZUBOV, V. A., M. M. SUSHCHINSKII, and I. K. SHUVALOV, *UFN*, **83**, 197. 1964.

483. ZUBOV, V. A., M. M. SUSHCHINSKII, and I. K. SHUVALOV, *UFN*, **89**, 49. 1966.

484. ECKHARDT, G., R. W. HELLWARTH, F. G. McCLUNG, S. E. SCHWARZ, D. WEINER, and E. J. WOODBURY, *Phys. Rev. Lett.*, **9**, 455. 1962; *Electronic Design*, **11**, 28. 1963.

485. GELLER, M., D. P. BORTFELD, and W. R. SOOY, *Appl. Phys. Letts*, **3**, 36. 1963.

486. GELLER, M., D. P. BORTFELD, W. R. SOOY, and E. J. WOODBURY, *Proc. IEEE*, **51**, 1236. 1963.

487. TERHUNE, R. W., *Bull. Amer. Phys. Soc.*, **8**, 359. 1963; SHAVLOVA, A., *UFN*, **81**, 745. 1963.

488. STOICHEFF, B. P., *International School of Physics "Enrico Fermi,"* XXXI Course, August 19–31, 1963.

489. MINCK, R. W., R. W. TERHUNE, and W. G. RADO, *Appl. Phys. Letts*, **3** (10), 181. 1963.

490. DUMARTIN, S., B. OKSENGORN, and B. VODAR, *C.R.*, **259**, 4589. 1964.

491. ECKHARDT, G., D. P. BORTFELD, and M. GELLER, *Appl. Phys. Letts*, **3**, 137. 1963.

492. ZUBOV, V. A., G. V. PEREGUDOV, V. A. CHIRKOV, I. K. SHUVALOV, and M. M. SUSHCHINSKII, *ZhETF Letters*, **5**, 188. 1967; ZUBOV, V. A., A. V. KRAISKII, and M. M. SUSHCHINSKII, *Preprint FIAN*, No. 129. 1968; SCHROTTER, H. W., *Naturwissenschaften*, **54**, 513. 1967.

493. AKHMANOV, S. A., A. I. KOVRIGIN, A. K. ROMANYUK, N. K. KUL'KOVA, and R. V. KHOKHLOV, *ZhETF*, **48**, 1202. 1965.

494. GARMIRE, E., F. PANDARESE, and C. H. TOWNES, *Phys. Rev. Letts*, **11**, 160. 1963.

495. TOWNES, C. H., *International School of Physics "Enrico Fermi"*, XXXI Course, August 19–31, 1963.

496. ZUBOV, V. A., M. M. SUSHCHINSKII, and I. K. SHUVALOV, *Zhurnal Prikladnoi Spektroskopii*, **3**, 336. 1965.

497. BRET, G. and G. MAYER, *C.R.*, **258**, 3265. 1964.

498. WANG, C. C., *J. Appl. Phys.*, **37**, 1943. 1966.

499. ZUBOV, V. A., M. M. SUSHCHINSKII, and I. K. SHUVALOV, *ZhETF*, **47**, 784. 1964; **48**, 378. 1965.

500. KAISER, W., M. MAIER, and J. A. GEORDMAIN, *Appl. Phys. Letts*, **6**, 25. 1965.

501. ZUBOVA, N. V., N. P. KUZ'MINA, V. A. ZUBOV, M. M. SUSHCHINSKII, and I. K. SHUVALOV, *ZhETF*, **51**, 101. 1966.

502. BEREZIN, V. I., V. A. ZUBOV, M. L. KATS, M. A. KOVNER, N. K. SIDOROV, L. S. STAL'-MAKHOVA, M. M. SUSHCHINSKII, YU. P. TURBIN, and I. K. SHUVALOV, *Zhurnal Prikladnoi Spektroskopii*, **4**, 351. 1966.

503. ZUBOVA, N. V. and V. A. ZUBOV, *Optika i Spektroskopiya*, **22**, 838. 1967.

504. BORTFELD, D. P., M. GELLER, and G. ECKHARDT, *J. Chem. Phys.*, **40**, 1170. 1964.

505. BREWER, R. G., *Phys. Letts*, **11**, 294. 1964.

506. LANDSBERG, G. S. and F. S. BARYSHANSKAYA, *Naturwissenschaften*, **8**, 183. 1930; LANDSBERG, G. S., *Selected Works*, p. 112. Izdatel'stvo AN SSSR. 1959.

507. KASTLER, A., *J. Chem. Phys.*, **46**, 72. 1949.

508. JONES, W. I. and B. P. STOICHEFF, *Phys. Rev. Letts*, **13**, 657. 1964.

509. DUMARTIN, S., B. OKSENGORN, and B. VODAR, *C.R.*, **261**, 3767, 4031. 1965.

510. SUSHCHINSKII, M. M., *Preprint FIAN*, No. 151. 1967.

511. BUCKINGHAM, A. D., *J. Chem. Phys.*, **43**, 25. 1965.

512. NISHIKAWA, K. and F. TAKANO, *J. Phys. Soc. Japan*, **22**, 1446. 1967.

513. AKHMANOV, S. A. and R. V. KHOKHLOV, *Problemy nelineinoi optiki (Problems of Nonlinear Optics)*. Izdatel'stvo VINITI. 1964.

514. BLOEMBERGEN, N., *Nonlinear Optics*. New York, Benjamin. 1965.

515. BLOEMBERGEN, N. and Y. R. SHEN, *Phys. Rev.*, **137**, No. 6A, 1787. 1965.

516. AKHMANOV, S. A. and R. V. KHOKHLOV, Introductory Article to Russian translation of [514], Moscow. 1966.

517. FAIN, V. M. and YA. I. KHANIN, *Kvantovaya radiofizika (Quantum Radiophysics)*, "Sovetskoe Radio". 1965.

518. LUGOVOI, V. N., *ZhETF*, **48**, 1216. 1965; **51**, 931. 1966.

519. LUGOVOI, V. N., *Preprint FIAN*, A-60. 1965; A-95. 1965.

520. STEPANOV, B. T. and P. A. APANASEVICH, *Zhurnal Prikladnoi Spektroskopii*, **1**, 202. 1964; **2**, 37. 1965.

521. PLATONENKO, V. T. and R. V. KHOKHLOV, *ZhETF*, **46**, 555. 1964; **46**, 695. 1964.

522. SOKOLOVSKAYA, A. I., A. D. KUDRYAVTSEVA, T. P. ZHBANOVA, and M. M. SUSHCHINSKII, *ZhETF*, **53**, 429. 1967.

523. ZUBOV, V. A., A. V. KRAISKII, K. A. PROKHOROV, M. M. SUSHCHINSKII, and I. K. SHUVALOV, *Preprint FIAN*, No. 17. 1968; *ZhETF*, **55**, 443. 1968.

524. RAGUL'SKII, V. V. and F. S. FAIZULLOV, *ZhETF Letters*, **6**, 887. 1967.

525. ZUBOV, V. A., N. P. KUZ'MINA, and M. M. SUSHCHINSKII, *Optika i Spektroskopiya*, **24**, 618. 1968.

526. BRET, G., *Appl. Phys. Letts*, **8**, 151. 1966.

527. MOVSESYAN, M. E. and ZH. O. NINOYAN, *Optika i Spektroskopiya*, **24**, 241. 1968.

528. SHIMODA, K., *Japan. J. Appl. Phys.*, **5**, 615. 1966.

529. BLOEMBERGEN, N., P. LALLEMAND, and A. PINE, *IEEE J. Quantum Electr.*, **2**, 246. 1966.

530. ZUBOVA, N. V., M. M. SUSHCHINSKII, and V. A. ZUBOV, *ZhETF Letters*, **2**, 63. 1965.

531. CHIAO, R. and B. P. STOICHEFF, *Phys. Rev. Letts*, **12**, 290. 1964; *Bull. Amer. Phys. Soc.*, **9**, 490. 1964.

532. ZEIGER, H. J., P. E. TANNENWALD, S. KERN, and R. HARENDEEN, *Phys. Rev. Letts*, **11**, 419. 1963.

533. HELLWARTH, R. W., F. I. McCLUNG, W. G. WAGNER, and D. WEINER, *Bull. Amer. Phys. Soc.*, **9**, 490. 1964.

534. GARMIRE, E., *Phys. Letts*, **17**, 251. 1965.

535. TAKUMA, H. and D. A. JENNINGS, *Bull. Amer. Phys. Soc.*, **9**, 499. 1964; *Appl. Phys. Letts*, **4**, 185. 1964.

536. DENNIS, J. H. and P. E. TANNENWALD, *Appl. Phys. Letts*, **5**, 58. 1964.

537. MAKER, P. D. and R. W. TERHUNE, *Phys. Rev.*, **137**, 3A, 801. 1965.

538. SOKOLOVSKAYA, A. I., G. L. BREKHOVSKIKH, A. D. KUDRYAVTSEV, and M. M. SUSH-CHINSKII, *Preprint FIAN*, No. 2. 1969.

539. ARBATSKAYA, A. N. and M. M. SUSHCHINSKII, *Preprint FIAN*, No. 13. 1969.

540. CHIAO, R., E. GARMIRE, and C. TOWNES, *Phys. Rev. Letts*, **13**, 479. 1964; **16**, 347. 1966.

541. ASKAR'YAN, G. A., *ZhETF*, **42**, 1567. 1962.

542. TALANOV, V. M., *Izvestiya Vuzov*, radiophysics, **7**, 564. 1962.

543. PIEKARA, A., *IEEE J. Quantum Electronics*, **2**, 249. 1966.

544. KELLEY, P. L., *Phys. Rev. Letts*, **15**, 1005. 1966.

545. MAIER, M. and W. KAISER, *IEEE J. Quantum Electronics*, **2**, 296. 1966.

546. LALLEMAND, P. AND N. BLOEMBERGEN, *Phys. Rev. Letts*, **15**, 1010. 1965.

547. SHEN, Y. R. and Y. I. SHAHAM, *Phys. Rev. Letts*, **15**, 1008. 1965.

548. WANG, C. C., *Phys. Rev. Letts*, **16**, 344. 1966.

549. SHIMODA, K., *Japan J. Appl. Phys.*, **5**, 86. 1966.

550. SCHRÖTTER, H. W., *Naturwissenschaften*, **54**, 657. 1967.

SUBJECT INDEX

441